Cult Flicks
and
Trash Pics

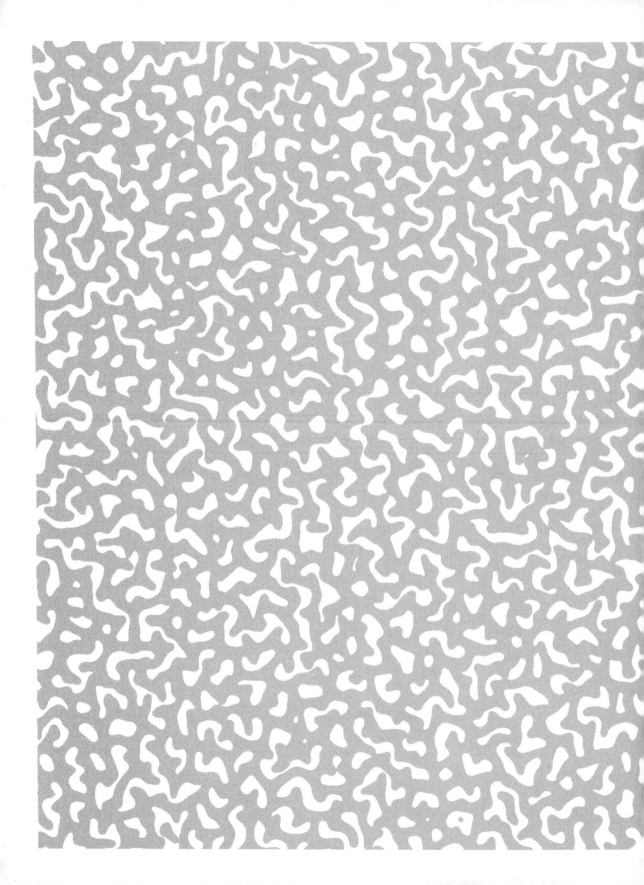

VideoHound's Complete Guide to

Cult Flicks
and
Trash Pics

VISIBLE
INK
PRESS

Detroit · New York · Washington, D.C. · Toronto

VideoHound's Complete Guide to Cult Flicks and Trash Pics

Published by Visible Ink Press™, a division of Gale Research Inc.
835 Penobscot Bldg.
Detroit, MI 48226-4094

Visible Ink Press and *VideoHound* are trademarks of
Gale Research Inc.

Most Visible Ink products are available at special quantity discounts when purchased in bulk by corporations, organizations, or groups. Customized printings, special imprints, messages, and excerpts can be produced to meet your needs. For more information, contact Special Market Manager, Gale Research Inc., 835 Penobscot Bldg., Detroit, MI 48226.

ISBN 0-7876-0616-2

CREDITS

DIRECTOR . . . . Carol Schwartz

PRODUCERS . . . . Martin Connors, Julia Furtaw, and Terri Schell

CAST OF CHARACTERS . . . . Brian Thomas, Donald Leibenson, Mike Mayo, Charles Cassady,
Carol Schwartz, James Buffington, Paul Gaita, Bill White,
Jason Hirsch, Brad Morgan, Jim Craddock, Michelle Banks, and
Amanda Moran

ART DIRECTION . . . . Mary Krzewinski and Cindy Baldwin

ENGINEERING . . . . Don Dillaman

PRODUCTION . . . . Mary Beth Trimper, Dorothy Maki, Evi Seoud, and Shanna Heilveil

POST-PRODUCTION . . . . General Graphics Services

SPIN DOCTORS . . . . Susan Stefani, Lauri Taylor, and Jenny Sweetland

PHOTOGRAPHS . . . . The Kobal Collection

PHOTO EDITING . . . . Barb Yarrow, Randy Bassett, Pam Hayes, Christine Tomassini,
Devra M. Sladics, and Jim Craddock

CAPTIONS . . . . Susan Stefani and Jane Hoehner

TECHNICAL ADVISORS . . . . Jim Olenski (Thomas Video), Brian Thomas, Mike Mayo,
Donald Leibenson, Charles Cassady, Dave Yount (*Video Eyeball
Magazine*), and Alan Smithee

CHUCK CUNNINGHAM STAND-INS . . . . Geoff and Lisa Collins, Steve and Tina Lane, and
Marty Smith

STUNT HOUND . . . . Kramer

RESEARCH . . . . Thomas Video, Clawson, MI
(the official vid store of *Cult Flicks and Trash Pics*)

In Memory of Al Adamson (1929-1995)

Thanks to: Sara Bernstein, Ian Goodhall, Amy Hall, Mike Huellmantel, Karen Hill, Joyce
Jakubiak, Sandy Jaszczak, Amanda Moran, Brad Morgan, Theresa MacFarlane, Kathleen Maki,
Tara Sheets, and Linda Thurn for their patient accommodation.

And more thanks to: Dan Bono, Nancy Ziemski, Carolyn Fischer, Meghan O'Meara, Al Bodgan,
Gary Adler, David Michaels, Raz, our friends in cyberspace, and the gang at Thomas Video.

Still more thanks to: Martin Connors, Julia Furtaw, and Terri Schell for their blind
faith and unending support.

Special thanks to: Brian "John" Thomas, Jim "Aren't you tired of watching movies?" Olenski, Mike "I'm not watching that movie again!" Mayo, Charles "Why are you asking me that?" Cassady, Donald "You're putting that in the book?!" Leibenson, Susan "My name's not going in this, is it?" Stefani, Jane "You're scaring me!" Hoehner, Mary "It's a little sleazy, isn't it?" Krzewinski, and Don "Aren't we having fun yet?" Dillaman for their very special last-minute support.

Published on location in Detroit, MI.

The canine character portrayed in this book considers himself to be purely fictitious; any
resemblance to an actual dog, living or dead, is merely an hallucination.

A Cunning Canine Production
Visible Ink Press © MXMXCVI

This book has been rated

by the Editor

Contents

VideoHound's Complete Guide to

Cult Flicks and Trash Pics

Pan in on a Golden Retriever sitting at a typewriter in a cluttered studio, strewn with Taco Bell remains, half-empty and sticky Jolt Cola bottles, and burning cigarette butts (which he obsessively lights and holds but never actually inhales). The dog is adorned strangely, in dark sunglasses, a pencil-thin moustache, and an angora sweater. His eyes are a bit dazed, and he is given to darting them about suspiciously as he runs his paws through his greased-back hair.

HOUND: Good eeeeeeven-ing. I've been asked to tell you about our latest VideoHound gem, *VideoHound's Complete Guide to Cult Flicks and Trash Pics.* For this book, we've culled what we term the "Mongrel Video"--the masterpieces, the misfits, and the misunderstood. We wanted to give special attention to cult movies, trash film, underground flicks, alternative cinema, and camp outings--movies so bad they're good, as well as movies so bad we don't want you to think they might have some camp value, and movies so good the truly cool people watch them over and over again. The Hound felt these movies deserved special treatment, so these pics were re-evaluated and spotlighted with you in mind--the "alternative" film connoisseur.

He suddenly whirls toward the window, but the giant tentacles that had begun to ooze across the glass retreat just in time. Shrugging, he looks back to the camera.

HOUND: This has truly been the beast that took over my life. I'm no longer invited to parties, I think probably because people react strangely to my choice of cocktail conversation ("Can you think of any movies that contain necrophilia?" "What's your favorite castration flick?" "Did you ever stop to think that *Eraserhead* is really just an allegory for the human condition as influenced by the cold war?"). Friends can never get a hold of me anyway, because the good people at my vid store have tired of taking my calls. And I almost lost my coveted job over the dispute involving the cost-benefit analysis of including scratch-n-sniff reviews, 3-D picture stills, and souvenir bones in every book (I still think it could've worked).

The Hound's typewriter suddenly metamorphizes into a giant dung beetle. Unfazed, he reaches for a can of Raid and, effectively paralyzing the insect, he continues to speak.

HOUND: Two questions are prone to setting me over the edge (and off to the hardware department at Sears for weaponry): "Why didn't you include [insert your favorite cult/trash title here]?" and "Don't you think you need a new hobby?" With regard to the first question, my publisher initially limited me to 1000 reviews, but I kept slipping them in until s/he recognized my handwritten scrawl on the list o' videos and took my crayon away from me. Since then, I've had to content myself with adding them to my hopeful roll call for *Cult Flicks and Trash Pics 2* (please feel free to share with me your own cryptic scrawlings).

At this point the Hound flashes a placard to the camera, which reads "Help Me! I'm being held captive by my VCR!" The camera spins wildly away from his visage, blanks briefly, and returns to see him grudgingly holding a new placard that reads "Write Me! VideoHound's Cult Flicks and Trash Pics, Visible Ink Press, 835 Penobscot Bldg., Detroit, MI 48226."

HOUND: With regard to the second question...mongrel video isn't a hobby, it's a way of life.

At this point, a giant lobster bursts through the door, lunging at the Hound in a suggestive manner. After a brief struggle in which the Hound successfully eradicates the lobster by hitting the rewind button on his oversized remote control, he composes himself, readjusts his crooked 'stache, and continues.

HOUND: I've patterned the reviews after my wildly successful *VideoHound's Golden Movie Retriever* format. Entries contain movie title, plot synopsis and critical review, my rating (WOOF! to four bones), year released, MPAA rating, whether the film is B&W or in color, length in minutes, cast, director, writer, awards, format, price, and a distributor code in case you can't find the flick in your local video haunt. Thrown in there as well, for selected videos, are song titles from the movie (only if it has music), alternate titles for the film, the country it was produced in (if other than the U.S. of A.), voiceover credits, and composers and lyricists (again, only interesting if there are music and lyrics). Please see the "Instructions for Use" for a sample entry and instructions for understanding it.

The Hound leans back in his chair and begins to pick brown leaves from a strange and unusual plant.

HOUND: I must comment on the rating system used in *Cult Flicks and Trash Pics*. One of the incentives for compiling this collection of mongrel video was that the Hound knows a great many people (a scary crowd, that they are) that actually seek out the **WOOF!**s for their preferred entertainment. To accommodate these people, movies were often re-rated in the context of the genre (such as it is) we've defined herein--videos were given bones for both their artistic merit AND demerit. These flicks were rated on overall entertainment value; therefore, in addition to existing four-bone winners (such as *The Cabinet of Dr. Caligari*, *Harold and Maude*, and *Psycho*), many formerly lower-rated videos (even **WOOF!**s) have joined the ranks of the four-bone hall of fame (see *Plan 9 from Outer Space*, *Pink Flamingos*, and *Reefer Madness*). If you are a fan of mongrel video, you can trust a **WOOF!** in this book to be a complete and total waste of time, lacking in any camp value whatsoever.

He continues plucking leaves.

HOUND: I've carried over some of your favorite aspects of *VideoHound's Golden Movie Retriever* as well. In *Cult Flicks and Trash Pics* you'll find an Alternate Title Index (particularly since the movies in this book are often the movies that hide-- as they sometimes should--under various aliases), a cast index, a director index, and a distributor guide. Of course, the Hound has provided his patented Category Index, adding such genre-specific classifications as "Mondo Movies," "Roadshow Movies" "Where's My Johnson?," "The Loving Dead," "Monkee Business," "The Legend of Ed Gein," and my favorite, "Vincent Price Pines Away at His Dead Wife's Portrait." As if that weren't enough, I've also provided a section entitled "Cult Connections," an exhaustive (and exhausting) list of 'zines, fan clubs, World Wide Web home pages, online newsgroups, and books to peruse when your VCR finally gives its last rattle of death and leaves you without any other mongrel entertainment. Ouch!

He yelps and yanks his paw from the plant, and then peers at it closely. Spotting a drop of blood on his paw, he picks up the coffee tin housing the plant and drops it in the wastebasket. He brushes off his paws and continues.

HOUND: To top it off, we've added a wealth of material on the directors and actors we most admire, amusing prattle on such topics as movies that never were (and sequels that never materialized), photos, and our favorite lines from our favorite flicks.

The Hound's editor enters at this point, showing off his 300-pound body in a tight pink evening gown, sporting prosthetic female anatomy and a half-shaved head, and smelling faintly of dog doo-doo. Spotting the camera, the editor mugs for it, displaying slightly brown-tinged teeth, then sashays from the office. The Hound sighs.

HOUND: So here's that number again--

He scrambles to grab the "approved" placard.

HOUND: *VideoHound's Cult Flicks and Trash Pics*, Visible Ink Press, 835 Penobscot Bldg., Motown, Michigan, four-eight-two-two-six. Or contact me via cyberspace at my new Web Site, www.videohound.com. Tell me what you think of *Cult Flicks and Trash Pics*, and pass on your suggestions for its sequel, tentatively titled *Escape from the Bride of the Reanimated Amazing Colossal Cult Flicks and Trash Pics in 3-D.* What movies should we cover? What people should we spotlight? What resources (including that photocopied rag you produce in your own cluttered basement) should we include? And most importantly, what subjects did we neglect to categorize? I depend on you to do a lot of my work, and so far, you haven't let me down.

The Hound jumps out of his chair as, suddenly, a foil-covered saucer crashes through the ceiling. A silver-toned humanoid emerges, bearing a book entitled To Serve VideoHound. The Hound screams in terror, and dashes out of camera range.

The End...or is it?

Instructions for Use

1. Make yourself comfortable on the couch with remote control within reach.

2. Begin reading the book at any page; if you are confused, refer to the hints below.

Alphabetization

Titles are arranged on a word-by-word basis, including articles and prepositions. Leading articles (A, An, The) are ignored in English-language titles; the equivalent foreign articles are not ignored (because so many people—not you, of course—don't recognize them as articles); thus, *The Abominable Dr. Phibes* appears in the As, but *La Cage aux Folles* appears in the Ls. If you're still with us, some other points to keep in mind:

- Acronyms appear alphabetically as if regular words. For example, *C.H.U.D.* is alphabetized as "CHUD," *A*P*E* as "APE."

- Common abbreviations in titles file as if they were spelled out, so *Dr. Terror's House of Horrors* will be alphabetized as "Doctor Ter-ror's House of Horrors" and *The St. Valentine's Day Massacre* as "Saint Valentine's Day Massacre."

- Movie titles with numbers (such as *2001: A Space Odyssey*) are alphabetized as if the number was spelled out—so Kubrick's classic would appear in the Ts as if it were "Two Thousand and One: A Space Odyssey."

Indexes

Alternate Titles Index

Can't find the movie you're looking for and can't believe we didn't include it? Many many movies have been retitled through the years (sometimes many many times each); this handy-dandy index will point you in the right direction. Alternate titles are also noted within the reviews themselves.

Cast Index

Despite the first name/last name appearance, cast names are alpha-betized by last name; movie titles that appear in this book, with year of release, are listed alphabetically under each cast member's name.

Also included are cameo appearances, so you might see a hammy director show up here and there.

Director Index

Same as above but for directors. Get it?

Category Index

Over 300 classifications ranging from the general ("Action-Adventure") to the ultra specific ("Vincent Price Pines Away at His Dead Wife's Portrait") allow the user to identify titles by type, genre, theme, motif, and other whimsical ways, including cross references to keep you looped in the index indefinitely. The preceding "Category List" defines the terms, in case you need help understanding our sometimes bizarre thought processes or idiosyncratic naming conventions (we still don't get very specific about the category "Where's My Johnson?" however; it's too painful).

Distributor Guide

Each video review ends in a cryptic code, which is your key to where to purchase your own personal copy of your favorite cult flick. The "Distributor List" tells you what distributor each code represents, and the subsequent "Distributor Guide" provides you with addresses, phone numbers, and fax numbers of these benevolent sources. A caution: a small number of distributors adhere to a nomadic lifestyle that includes frequent address changes. A tiny minority on the list in any given year will also go out of business. Studio distributors typically do not sell to the general public; they generally act as wholesalers, selling only to retail outlets. Up to three distributors are listed in order to give you more choice. Those video reviews that contain the code "OM" for a distributor are trying to tell you that the flick is on moratorium (distributed at one time, though not currently); those few instances when the distributor is not known, the code "NO" appears in the review. For new theatrical releases that had not yet made it to video as of the printing of this book, the code "NYR" (not yet released) will appear.

Sample Review

Each review contains up to 18 tidbits of information, as enumerated on the next page. Please realize that we faked a bit of info in this review, because we couldn't find one single movie that coincidentally contained every single element that might appear in a review. If anyone out there finds that singular entry, please let us know. And then get a real hobby.

➊ The Rocky Horror Picture Show

➋ Anyone out there who purchased this book NOT see this movie? Campy, vampy, and anything but subtle, the mother of all cult hits arrived on home video after 15 years of midnight screenings. On tape, of course, the audience participation element is lost. (Or at least lessened; what you and your friends want to do in the privacy of your own place is none of the Hound's business.) So, what about the movie itself? It's not bad. The story isn't too important in this kinky musical send-up of old horror movies. The rock score is loud and energetic; the lyrics surprisingly witty. Sarandon and Bostwick are fine as the innocent heroine and hero, but the film belongs to Tim Curry's Dr. Frank-N-Furter. He redefines outrageous excess as the mad scientist who favors mascara, high heels, and fishnet hose. Curry wrings every drop of mad humor from the role—and there's a lot to wring. In the process, he shows how a talented stage actor can overpower a screen production, either film or video. Followed by the disappointing *Shock Treatm* ➌ ♫ The Time Warp; Science Fiction Double Feature; Wedding Song; Sweet Transvestite; The Sword of Damocles; Charles Atlas Song; Whatever Happened to Saturday Night; Touch-a Touch-a Touch Me; Eddie's Teddy. ➍ **AKA:** Rocky Horror.

➎ 🦴 🦴 🦴 ▷

➏ 1975 ➐ (R) ➑ 105m/ ➒ C ➓ *CA* ⓫ Tim Curry, Susan Sarandon, Barry Bostwick, Meat Loaf, Little Nell, Richard O'Brien; ⓬ *D:* Jim Shar- ⓭ *W:* Jim Sharman, Richard O'Brien; ⓮ *M:* Richard O'Brien. ⓯ Gale's Film Fest 76: Best Picture. ⓰ **VHS, LV** ⓱ $19.98 ⓲ *FOX, FCT, PMS*

1. Title (see also #4 below, and the "Alternate Titles Index")

2. Description/review (we call 'em as we see 'em)

3. Song Titles

4. Alternate titles (we faked it here)

5. One- to four-bone rating (or Woof!), four bones being the ultimate praise

6. Year released

7. MPAA rating

8. Length in minutes

9. Black and white (B) or Color (C)

10. Country in which the flick was produced (we faked it here, too)

11. Cast, including cameos and voiceovers (V)

12. Director(s)

13. Writer(s)

14. Music (composer/lyricist)

15. Awards (again, fake!)

16. Format, including VHS, Beta, and Laservideo/disk (LV)

17. Price (at highest retail level)

18. Distributor code (see also "Distributor Guide")

Abbott & Costello Go to Mars

Poor parody of sci-fi films finds the frantic duo aboard a rocket ship accidentally heading off into outer space. They don't land on Mars, but Venus, which is populated by lots of pretty women and no men. This after a detour to New Orleans during the Mardi Gras, which the boys mistake for Mars. There's really no story line here, just a collection of skits strung together by a weak device. Compounding the problem is the lack of any inventiveness in the humor. All you get for your rental are some tired, old when-the-Earth-was-young jokes and very poor slapstick. Fans of 50s' cheesecake may wish to fast forward to the last half hour. Aside from that, this is strictly for A&C diehards and little kids. ♫

1953 77m/B Bud Abbott, Lou Costello, Mari Blanchard, Robert Paige, Martha Hyer, Horace McMahon, Jack Kruschen, Anita Ekberg; **D:** Charles Lamont; **W:** John Grant, D.D. Beauchamp. **VHS $14.98** *MCA*

Abbott & Costello Meet Dr. Jekyll and Mr. Hyde

Abbott and Costello take on evil Dr. Jekyll, who, as Mr. Hyde, is terrorizing London. A lame attempt at recapturing the success of *Abbott and Costello Meet Frankenstein,* this is clearly the weakest of the *A&C Meet a Monster* series. Bud and Lou play American cops on the London police force who constantly foul up. Thrown off the force in disgrace, they vow to catch the serial killer who has been terrorizing the city. While there is some funny stuff here the problem with the film is the villain. He is far too serious in tone and execution, providing an off-kilter counterpoint to Bud and Lou's antics. Additionally, traditional supernatural monsters such as Dracula and The Mummy, not being the product of misguided science, hold a fonder place in our hearts than Dr. Jekyll. The archetype for A&C to play off against was simply all wrong. Another movie to watch when the weather turns nasty. ♫♫

1952 77m/B Bud Abbott, Lou Costello, Boris Karloff, Craig Stevens, Helen Westcott, Reginald Denny; **D:** Charles Lamont. **VHS, Beta $14.95** *MCA*

Abbott & Costello Meet Frankenstein

Big-budget A&C classic is one of their best efforts and was rewarded handsomely at the box office—saving Universal from bankruptcy yet again (the first time was with *Buck Privates* (1941)), while also saving the stalled movie career of the comedy duo. Two unsuspecting baggage clerks deliver a crate containing the last but not quite dead remains of Dracula and Dr. Frankenstein's monster to a wax museum. The fiends are revived, wreaking havoc with the clerks. A tremendously entertaining comedy, sometimes almost as scary as it is funny. Chaney makes a special appearance to warn the boys that trouble looms. Lugosi resumed his classic screen portrayal of Dracula over the objections of studio heads, who wanted John Carradine for the part. Last film to use the Universal Frankenstein creature pioneered by Karloff in 1931. Although credited to Strange, many scenes of the monster were played by stuntman Eddie Parker. **AKA:** Abbott and Costello Meet the Ghosts. ♫♫♫♫

1948 83m/B Bud Abbott, Lou Costello, Lon Chaney Jr., Bela Lugosi, Glenn Strange, Lenore Aubert, Jane Randolph; **D:** Charles T. Barton; **V:** Vincent Price. **VHS, Beta, LV $14.95** *MCA*

"Ah, you young people, making the most out of life...while it lasts."
--Dracula (Bela Lugosi) to Lou Costello in *Abbott & Costello Meet Frankenstein.*

Bela Lugosi tells Lou Costello to "pick two" in *Abbott & Costello Meet Frankenstein.*

Abbott & Costello Meet the Invisible Man

Abbott and Costello play newly graduated detectives who take on the murder case of a boxer (Franz) accused of killing his manager. Using a serum that makes people invisible, the boxer helps Costello in a prizefight that will frame the real killers, who killed the manager because the boxer refused to throw a fight. Great special effects and hilarious gags make this one of the best from the crazy duo. 🦴🦴🦴

1951 82m/B Bud Abbott, Lou Costello, Nancy Guild, Adele Jergens, Sheldon Leonard, William Frawley, Gavin Muir, Arthur Franz; **D:** Charles Lamont. **VHS** $14.98 *MCA*

Abbott & Costello Meet the Killer, Boris Karloff

An entertaining little Abbott and Costello murder mystery. Bud and Lou play hotel employees who get caught in the middle when a guest checks out via foul play (as opposed to the front desk). The boys, fearing their own erro- neous implication, set out to catch the killer. Number one on their suspect list is good ol' Boris. The plot, while nothing overly inventive, provides Lou and Bud with ample opportunity for their usual antics. Karloff, here playing a psychic, looms menacingly through most of his scenes. But did he do it or is he just a very effective red herring? It's a mystery, so you'll just have to watch it to find out. While not one of A&C's best films, it's far from their worst. Worth watching for both fans of the duo and general viewers. Karloff, given little to do, does it well and his legions will want to take it in also. 🦴🦴🦴

1949 84m/B Bud Abbott, Lou Costello, Boris Karloff, Lenore Aubert, Gar Moore, Donna Martell, Alan Mowbray, James Flavin, Roland Winters; **D:** Charles T. Barton. **VHS, Beta, LV $14.98** *MCA*

Abbott & Costello Meet the Mummy

Okay, fast-paced comedy from the duo has them stranded in Egypt with a valuable medallion which leads to secret treasure, an evil cult, and a zipper-suited mummy who guards the tomb. Funny climax manages to have three bandaged look alikes scrambling around; it's almost up to the monster chase in *Abbott & Costello Meet Frankenstein.* The last of the films the twosome made for Universal, this one's worth a look just for the opening cabaret sequence featuring a violent, then-popular dance form known as "apache dancing," which, fortunately for humanity, has gone the way of the lambada. 🦴🦴▷

1955 90m/B Bud Abbott, Lou Costello, Marie Windsor, Michael Ansara, Dan Seymour, Kurt Katch, Richard Deacon, Mel Welles, Edwin Parker; **D:** Charles Lamont; **W:** John Grant. **VHS $14.98** *MCA, FCT*

The Abductors

Caffaro's super-agent takes on international white slavery, a worthy target for any exploitation effort. While the novelty is a tough and intelligent on-screen heroine, sufficient sleaze and violence bring it all down to the proper level of swampland video. Sequel to the never-to-be-forgotten *Ginger.* 🦴

1972 (R) 90m/C Cheri Caffaro, William Grannell, Richard Smedley, Patrick Wright, Jennifer Brooks; **D:** Don Schain. **VHS, Beta $39.95** *MON*

The Abominable Dr. Phibes

After being disfigured (and believed dead) in a freak car accident, a twisted genius decides that the members of a surgical team let his wife die and shall each perish by a different Biblical plague. Highly stylish, the murders all have a ceremonial feel to them. Though set in the 1920s, Phibes' equipment seems a bit ahead of its time—and where did he get a Frank Sinatra record? High camp balances gore with plenty of good humor, with the veteran cast of British character actors in top form. Munro appears only in photographs as the deceased wife, Victoria Regina (which was also the name of the hit play that made Price a star). ♫♫♫
1971 (PG) 90m/C *GB* Vincent Price, Joseph Cotten, Hugh Griffith, Terry-Thomas, Virginia North, Susan Travers, Alex Scott, Caroline Munro; **D:** Robert Fuest. **VHS, Beta, LV $14.98** *VES, LIV, ORI*

Absolution

Two English boys trapped in a Catholic boarding school conspire to drive a tyrannical priest over the edge of sanity. As a result, bad things (including murder) occur. Burton is interesting in sadistic character study. Not released in the U.S. until 1988 following Burton's death, maybe due to something written in the will. ♫♫
1981 (R) 105m/C *GB* Richard Burton, Dominic Guard, Dai Bradley, Andrew Keir, Billy Connolly, Willoughby Gray; **D:** Anthony Page. **VHS, Beta, LV $9.95** *SIM, TWE, FCT*

The Adventures of Baron Munchausen

From the director of *Time Bandits, Brazil,* and *The Fisher King* comes an ambitious, imaginative, chaotic, and under-appreciated marvel based on the tall (and often confused) tales of the Baron. Munchausen encounters the King of the Moon, Venus, and other odd and fascinating characters during what might be described as an circular narrative in which flashbacks dovetail into the present and place and time are never quite what they seems. Wonderful special effects and visually stunning sets occasionally dwarf the actors and prove what Gilliam can do with a big budget. ♫♫♫♪

1989 (PG) 126m/C John Neville, Eric Idle, Sarah Polley, Valentina Cortese, Oliver Reed, Uma Thurman, Sting, Jonathan Pryce, Bill Paterson, Peter Jeffrey, Alison Steadman, Charles McKeown, Dennis Winston, Jack Purvis; **Cameos:** Robin Williams; **D:** Terry Gilliam; **W:** Terry Gilliam; **M:** Michael Kamen. Nominations: Academy Awards '89: Best Costume Design, Best Makeup. **VHS, Beta, LV, 8mm $19.95** *COL, CRC*

The Adventures of Buckaroo Banzai Across the Eighth Dimension

The title character (Weller) is your basic Japanese-American neurosurgeon-rock star-adventurer-particle physics expert. His jet car, which looks suspiciously like a Ford pick-up with a thyroid condition, is souped up with the Oscillation Overthruster which overthrusts him right into the eighth dimension, where the Lectroids live. (The Red and Black Lectroids hate each other and have something to do with Orson Welles' *War of the Worlds* radio broadcast.) The wild plot doesn't make much sense, but then it never tries to. Curiously, the film's deadpan humor, filled with throwaway jokes, cuts against the grain of the furious pace. A talented cast seems to have understood exactly what director Richter was aiming for. Fans who are on the same whimsical wavelength have made this one a cult hit. Those who value logic and coherence in storytelling will find rough sledding. **AKA:** Buckaroo Banzai. ♫♫♫
1984 (PG) 100m/C Peter Weller, Ellen Barkin, Jeff Goldblum, Christopher Lloyd, John Lithgow, Lewis Smith, Rosalind Cash, Robert Ito, Pepe Serna, Vincent Schiavelli, Dan Hedaya, Yakov Smirnoff, Jamie Lee Curtis; **D:** W.D. Richter; **M:** Michael Boddicker. **VHS, Beta, LV $9.99** *VES, LIV*

The Adventures of Priscilla, Queen of the Desert

Two drag queens and a transsexual traverse the Australian Outback in a pink bus (nicknamed Priscilla) on their way to a gig in a small resort town. Along the way they encounter, and perform for, the usual assortment of local characters. Scenes depicting homophobic natives play out as expected. Finest moments occur on the bus or onstage (with an homage to ABBA). Strong performances, especially by Stamp as the widowed

> **"Love means never having to say you're ugly."**
> --Vincent Price in *The Abominable Dr. Phibes.*

> **"I've got a galaxy to run. I don't have time for flatulence and orgasms."**
> --the King of the Moon (Robin Williams) in *The Adventures of Baron Munchausen.*

Bernadette, rise above the cliches in what is basically a road movie in women's clothing. 🎵🎵🎵

1993 (R) 102m/C *AU* Terence Stamp, Hugo Weaving, Guy Pearce, Bill Hunter; **D:** Stephan Elliott; **W:** Stephan Elliott. Academy Awards '95: Best Costume Design; Australian Film Institute '94: Best Costume Design; Nominations: Australian Film Institute '94: Best Actor (Stamp), Best Actor (Weaving), Best Cinematography, Best Director (Elliott), Best Film, Best Screenplay; Golden Globe Awards '95: Best Actor—Musical/Comedy (Stamp), Best Film—Musical/Comedy. **VHS, LV** *PGV*

Africa, Blood & Guts

A documentary that captures the racial, ethnic, political, and social upheavals that rocked Africa during the 1960s. Originally planned as a documentary contrasting old and new views of the continent, everything changed with the start of a bloody revolution where everybody seemed to be killing everybody else. Much gory and violent footage, including real torture, murder, mass execution, piles of corpses and severed hands, and the slaughter of human and animal alike. The original version, nearly an hour longer, is more well rounded, explaining the political situation that caused the revolution. From the makers of *Mondo Cane,* who were lucky to get out of Africa with their lives. Not for the squeamish—for once you can't comfort yourself by repeating, "It's only a movie." **AKA:** Africa Addio. 🎵🎵▷

1967 83m/C D: Gualtiero Jacopetti, Franco Prosperi. **VHS, Beta** *VDC*

After Hours

An absurd, edgy black comedy that's filled with novel twists and turns and often more disturbing than funny. An isolated uptown New York yuppie (Dunne) takes a late night stroll downtown and meets a sexy woman in an all-night coffee shop. From there he wanders through a series of threatening and surreal misadventures, leading to his pursuit by a vigilante mob stirred by ice cream dealer O'Hara. Something like *Blue Velvet* with more

Catholicism and farce. Or similar to *Something Wild* without the high school reunion. Great cameos from the large supporting cast, including Cheech and Chong as burglers. A dark view of a small hell-hole in the Big Apple. 🦴🦴🦴▷

1985 (R) 97m/C Griffin Dunne, Rosanna Arquette, John Heard, Teri Garr, Catherine O'Hara, Verna Bloom, Linda Fiorentino, Dick Miller, Bronson Pinchot; ***Cameos:*** Richard "Cheech" Marin, Thomas Chong; ***D:*** Martin Scorsese; ***M:*** Howard Shore. Cannes Film Festival '86: Best Director (Scorsese); Independent Spirit Awards '86: Best Director (Scorsese), Best Film. **VHS, Beta, LV $19.98** *WAR*

Aguirre, the Wrath of God

Herzog at his best, combining brilliant poetic images and an intense narrative dealing with power, irony, and death. Spanish conquistadors in 1590 search for the mythical city of gold in Peru. Instead, they descend into the hell of the jungle. Kinski is fabulous as Aguirre, succumbing to insanity while leading a continually diminishing crew in this compelling, extraordinary drama shot in the jungles of South America. Both English- and German-language versions available. 🦴🦴🦴▷

1972 94m/C GE Klaus Kinski, Ruy Guerra, Del Negro, Helena Rojo, Cecilia Rivera, Peter Berling, Danny Ades; ***D:*** Werner Herzog; ***W:*** Werner Herzog. **VHS $59.95** *NYF, APD, INJ*

Airplane!

Classic lampoon of disaster flicks is stupid but funny and launched a bevy wanna-be spoofs. A former pilot who's lost both his girl (she's the attendant) and his nerve takes over the controls of a jet when the crew is hit with food poisoning. The passengers become increasingly crazed and ground support more surreal as our hero struggles to land the plane. Clever, fast-paced, and very funny parody mangles every Hollywood cliche within reach. The gags are so furiously paced that when one bombs it's hardly noticeable. Launched Nielsen's second career as a comic actor. And it ain't over till it's over: don't miss the amusing final credits. Followed by *Airplane 2: The Sequel*. 🦴🦴🦴▷

1980 (PG) 88m/C Robert Hays, Julie Hagerty, Lloyd Bridges, Peter Graves, Robert Stack, Leslie Nielsen, Stephen Stucker, Ethel Merman; ***Cameos:*** Kareem Ab-

dul-Jabbar, Barbara Billingsley; ***D:*** Jerry Zucker, Jim Abrahams, David Zucker; ***W:*** Jerry Zucker, Jim Abrahams, David Zucker; ***M:*** Elmer Bernstein. **VHS, Beta, LV, 8mm $14.95** *PAR*

Airplane 2: The Sequel

Not a Zucker, Abrahams and Zucker effort, and sorely missing their slapstick and script finesse. The first passenger space shuttle has taken off for the moon and there's a mad bomber on board. Given the number of stars mugging, it's more of a loveboat in space than a fitting sequel to *Airplane*. Nonetheless, some funny laughs and gags. 🦴🦴

1982 (PG) 84m/C Robert Hays, Julie Hagerty, Lloyd Bridges, Raymond Burr, Peter Graves, William Shatner, Sonny Bono, Chuck Connors, Chad Everett, Stephen Stucker, Rip Torn, Ken Finkleman, Sandahl Bergman; ***D:*** Ken Finkleman; ***M:*** Elmer Bernstein. **VHS, Beta, LV $14.95** *PAR*

The Alchemist

See humans transformed into murderous zombies! A bewitched man seeks revenge upon the evil magician who placed a curse on him, causing him to live like an animal. Painfully routine, with a few chills along the way. Amonte is an alias for Charles Band. Filmed in 1981 and released four years later. **WOOF!**

1981 (R) 86m/C Robert Ginty, Lucinda Dooling, John Sanderford, Viola Kate Stimpson, Bob Glaudini; ***D:*** James Amonte; ***M:*** Richard Band. **VHS, Beta $79.98** *VES, LIV*

Alice Sweet Alice

Little Alice (Sheppard) is a naughty girl, but did she really stab her goody-two-shoes sister (Shields) to death, then burn the body inside an oak chest in church during First Communion service? That's the question that keeps you guessing until the very end of this shocking, suspenseful horror thriller, full of bizarre images and sudden violence. Rereleased and retitled to cash in on Shield's presence in the cast. Filmed in Lou Costello's home town of Paterson, New Jersey. Sole later made the intriguing *Tanya's Island*. ***AKA:*** Holy Terror; Communion. 🦴🦴🦴

1976 (R) 112m/C Brooke Shields, Linda Miller, Paula Sheppard; ***D:*** Alfred Sole. **VHS, Beta $29.95** *REP, MRV, BTV*

A

"**H**ave you ever seen a grown man naked, Tommy?"

--Captain Oveur (Peter Graves) in *Airplane!*

Lloyd Bridges
repeats himself
in *Airplane!*

Alice's Restaurant

Based on the popular and funny 20-minute Arlo Guthrie song "Alice's Restaurant Massacre" about a Flower Child during the Last Big War who gets hassled for littering, man. Step back in time and study the issues of the hippie era, including avoiding the draft, dropping out of college, and dealing with the local pigs. Sort of a modern movie in the cinematic ambling genre, in that nothing really happens. 🦴🦴▷

1969 (PG) 111m/C Arlo Guthrie, James Broderick, Pat Quinn, Geoff Outlaw; **D:** Arthur Penn. Nominations: Academy Awards '69: Best Director (Penn). **VHS, Beta $19.95** *MVD, MGM*

Alien

Terse direction, stunning sets and special effects, and a well-seasoned cast save this from being another "Slimy monster from Outerspace" story. Instead it's a grisly rollercoaster of suspense and fear (and a huge box office hit). Intergalactic freighter's crew is invaded by an unstoppable carnivorous alien intent on picking off the crew one by one. While the cast mostly bitches and banters while awaiting the horror of their imminent departure, Weaver is exceptional as Ripley, a self-reliant survivor who goes toe to toe with the Big Ugly. Futuristic, in the belly of the beast visual design creates a vivid sense of claustrophobic doom enhanced further by the ominous score. Oscar-winning special effects include the classic baby alien busting out of the crew guy's chest routine, a rib-splitting ten on the gore meter. Successfully followed by *Aliens* and *Alien 3.* 🦴🦴🦴▷

1979 (R) 116m/C Tom Skerritt, Sigourney Weaver, Veronica Cartwright, Yaphet Kotto, Harry Dean Stanton, Ian Holm, John Hurt; **D:** Ridley Scott; **W:** Dan O'Bannon; **M:** Jerry Goldsmith. Academy Awards '79: Best Visual Effects; Nominations: Academy Awards '79: Best Art Direction/Set Decoration. **VHS, Beta, LV $19.98** *FOX*

Alien Contamination

Tale of two astronauts who return to Earth from an expedition on Mars carrying some deadly bacterial eggs. Controlled by a Martian intent on conquering the world, the eggs infect people and cause them to explode. A sloppy, squishy attempt to cash in on the success of *Alien,* this one nevertheless earns extra points for its generous buckets of yucky slime. Fan turned director Cozzi is also the auteur behind *Starcrash* (1979) and *Hercules* (1983). **AKA:** Contamination. 🦴🦴

1981 (R) 90m/C *IT* Ian McCulloch, Louise Monroe, Martin Mase, Samuel Rauch, Lisa Hahn; **D:** Lewis (Luigi Cozzi) Coates; **W:** Lewis (Luigi Cozzi) Coates. **VHS, Beta** *NO*

Alien Dead

Meteorite lands on obnoxious teens, turning them into flesh-eating ghouls. Would you believe flying ace Eddie Rickenbacker is involved? Florida-lensed junk owns its place in history as the first commercially released feature from Fred Olen Ray, shot for only $12,000. Guest star Buster Crabbe—one-time Flash Gordon—looks like he'd rather be somewhere else in this, his last screen appearance. Occasionally amusing dialogue: "She's deader than Mother's Day in an orphanage." **AKA:** It Fell From the Sky. 🦴🎵

1985 (R) 87m/C Buster Crabbe, Linda Lewis, Ray Roberts; **D:** Fred Olen Ray; **W:** Fred Olen Ray. **VHS, Beta $19.95** *ACA, GHV*

The Alien Factor

Another low-budget crazed critter from outer space dispatch, this one featuring multiple aliens, one of whom is good, who have the misfortune of crash landing near Baltimore. The grotesque extraterrestrials jolt a small town out of its sleepy state by wreaking havoc (except for the good one, of course). Decent special effects for a low-budget cheapie, the cast also doubled as the crew. The main focus shifts to the intellectual problem of trying to separate the good alien from his identical evil cronies. Executed with a genuine affection for the genre, this is a fine film for fans of both regional and amateur film making. Worth a view, even if you're not. 🦴🦴🎵

1978 (PG) 82m/C Don Leifert, Tom Griffith, Mary Mertens, Dick Dyszel; **D:** Donald M. Dohler. **VHS, Beta $59.95** *NO*

Alien from L.A.

Why would any red-blooded male break up with supermodel queen Kathy Ireland, you ask? One look at this exceedingly bad tale of a valley girl stumbling into the Lost Continent of Atlantis will show you why. Or rather, one listen will do it. When Ireland opens her mouth in the first scene, you are suddenly glad that the *Sports Illustrated* swimsuit issue hasn't gone interactive yet. Her voice soars into a range that only dogs can hear, making it easy to understand why her on-screen boyfriend dumps her in the opening scene. Looking about as dorky as a beautiful person can, Kathy then embarks on a journey to find her father, a professor who is off on some kind of archeological expedition. This journey takes her to Atlantis, which oddly enough is right near Los Angeles. Once there, she meets all kinds of strange and wacky villains, finds true

Sports Illustrated swimsuit model Kathy Ireland (with William Moses) demonstrates why she's not a spokesmodel in Alien from L.A. Ouch! That voice!

THE HOUND SALUTES: AL ADAMSON

What a difference a decade makes. Al Adamson and Ed Wood both made zero-budget films frequently starring aging horror film stars and cast with a not-too-talented regular stock company about juvenile delinquents, monsters, and twisted sex. Adamson's films were made with far less style, vision, and craft than Wood's films, which were at the very least nicely photographed. But while Wood's films quietly sank into the box office toilet, Adamson's made a fortune. What's the deal here?

The deal is marketing. While Wood's films tried vainly to compete with more competently made studio B-pictures in neighborhood movie houses, Adamson's fare was gobbled up by drive-in crowds hungry for the cheap thrills available in the more permissive '60s. And Adamson knew how to provide the shocks, even when sometimes it was only shock at how abysmally cheap the production turned out to be. His production company, Independent International, gave the pictures a hard sell with high energy trailers and garish poster art (often by comics artist Gray Morrow). Adamson pictures were often reworked and rereleased under many different titles, sometimes simultaneously. He added footage to his early feature *Psycho A Go-Go!* and released it as *Fiend With the Electronic Brain*, then did the same thing again later and released it as *Blood of Ghastly Horror*.

Sometimes he indulged in the common exploitation technique of buying a foreign feature and adding new footage to it for stateside release. One such patch-up job was *Horror of the Blood Monsters*, in which he took extensive footage from a black & white Filipino fantasy movie about warring tribes of mutant cave people, tinted it different colors, and cut in new footage featuring vampires and space travel. The tinted footage was advertised as a new process called "Spectrum X," and the whole mess was sold over and over again under many titles.

Adamson originally wanted to be a dancer and actor, until his father Victor Adamson, a New Zealand cowboy star who came to Hollywood in the early '20s and made dozens of Westerns under the

continued...

love, defeats the bad guys, etc., etc., etc. And through it all, all you can think about is THAT VOICE. Weakly plotted, acted, and filmed. Like, really. 🦴

1987 (PG) 88m/C Kathy Ireland, Thom Mathews, Don Michael Paul, Linda Kerridge, William R. Moses; *D:* Albert Pyun; *W:* Albert Pyun. **VHS, Beta, LV $79.95** *MED*

Alien Massacre

One of the worst films of all time—which makes it required viewing! Five short horror stories about zombies and vampires, hosted by the cordial but stiff Carradine, who also stars as a warlock in the first story, "The Witches Clock." In the second, Scotland Yard detectives (who are curiously without British accents) hunt the "King Vampire" killer. In "The Monster Raid," the corpse of a mad scientist metes out revenge to his killers, including his widow ('30s leading lady Hudson, who still looks good). In "Spark of Life," Chaney is a mid-1800s mad scientist (with a telephone!) bringing the dead back to murderous life. In "Count Alucard," Evans is the vampire Count who tries to get a bite, but his intended victim Harker is not what he seems. The flick goes by many names, and stinks in all of them. The stock company cast shows up under different guises in each story, as do the cheap sets. The script could have come directly from a 1950s horror comic-book. From fearless young showman Hewitt, who brought you *Journey to the Center of Time, Horrors of the Red Planet,* and the spook show featurette *Monsters Crash the Pajama Party. AKA:* Dr. Terror's Gallery of Horrors; Return from the Past; The Blood Suckers; Gallery of Horror. 🦴🦴🦴🦴

1967 90m/C Lon Chaney Jr., John Carradine, Rochelle Hudson, Roger Gentry, Mitch Evans; *D:* David L. Hewitt. **VHS, Beta $19.95** *ACA, MRV*

Aliens

The bitch is back, some 50 years later. Popular sequel to *Alien* amounts to nonstop, ravaging combat in space. Contact with a colony on another planet has mysteriously stopped. Fresh from deep space sleep, Ripley and a slew of pulsar-equipped Marines return to confront the mother alien at her nest, which is also inhabited by a whole bunch of the nasty critters spewing for a fight. Something's gotta give, and the Oscar-winning special effects are especially inventive (and messy) in the alien demise department. Dimension (acting biz talk) is given to our hero Ripley, as she discovers maternal instincts lurking within her space suit while looking after a young girl, the lone survivor of the colony. Tension-filled gore blaster. Rarely does one line from a movie perfectly capture its atmosphere, but when Private Hudson (Bill Paxton) screams, "We're on an express elevator to Hell—going down!" you've been warned about what to expect in this dark actionfest. Followed by *Aliens 3*. 🦴🦴🦴🦴

1986 **(R)** 138m/**C** Sigourney Weaver, Michael Biehn, Lance Henriksen, Bill Paxton, Paul Reiser, Carrie Henn, Jenette Goldstein; *D:* James Cameron; *W:* Walter Hill; *M:* James Horner. Academy Awards '86: Best Sound Effects Editing, Best Visual Effects; Nominations: Academy Awards '86: Best Actress (Weaver), Best Art Direction/Set Decoration, Best Film Editing, Best Sound, Best Original Score. **VHS, Beta, LV** **$19.98** *FOX*

All the Lovin' Kinfolk

Low-budget late-'60s drive-in fare from veteran Hayes is everything that fans of the genre expect. Country cousins graduate from high school and find that life is different in the city. The humor ranges from stereotyped Hillbilly jokes to rowdy bawdiness. Some of the sex scenes—particularly those involving semi-professional actors—have an embarrassed quality. Cult favorite Uschi Digart makes a brief but energetic uncredited appearance. *AKA:* Kin Folk; Kinfolk; The Closest of Kin. 🦴🦴🦴

1989 **(R)** 80m/**C** Mady Maguire, Jay Scott, Anne Ryan, John Denis, Donna Young; *D:* John Hayes. **VHS** *NO*

All You Need Is Cash

"The Rutles" star in this parody of The Beatles' legend, from the early days of the "Pre-Fab Four" in Liverpool to their worldwide success. A marvelous pseudo-documentary, originally shown on NBC-TV and with various SNL alumni (including Weis), that captures the development of the Beatles and '60s rock with devastating effect. Served as the inspiration for *This Is Spinal Tap*. *AKA:* The Rutles. 🦴🦴🦴

1978 70m/**C** Eric Idle, Neil Innes, Ricky Fataar, Dan Aykroyd, Gilda Radner, John Belushi, George Harrison, Paul Simon, Mick Jagger, John Halsey; *D:* Eric Idle, Gary Weis. **VHS, Beta, LV** **$14.95** *MVD, MLT*

Allegro Non Troppo

An energetic and bold collection of animated skits set to classical music in this Italian version of Disney's *Fantasia*. Watch for the evolution of life set to Ravel's Bolero, or better yet, watch the whole darn movie. Features Nichetti (often referred to as the Italian Woody Allen, particularly by people in Italy) in the non-animated segments, who went on to write, direct, and star (he may have sold concessions in the lobby as well) in *The Icicle Thief*. 🦴🦴🦴

1976 **(PG)** 75m/**C** IT Maurizio Nichetti; *D:* Bruno Bozzetto. **VHS, LV** **$29.95** *BMG, IME, INJ*

Alligator

Dumped down a toilet 12 long years ago, lonely alligator Ramon resides in the city sewers, quietly eating and sleeping. In addition to feasting on the occasional stray human, Ramon devours the animal remains of a chemical plant's experiment involving growth hormones and eventually begins to swell at an enormous rate. Nothing seems to satisfy Ramon's ever-widening appetite: not all the people or all the buildings in the whole town, but he keeps trying, much to the regret of the guilt-ridden cop and lovely scientist who get to know each other while trying to nab the gator. Mediocre special effects are only a distraction in this witty eco-monster take. 🦴🦴🦴

1980 **(R)** 94m/**C** Robert Forster, Lewis Teague, Jack Carter, Henry Silva, Robin Riker, Dean Jagger; *D:* Lewis Teague; *W:* John Sayles, Frank Ray Perilli. **VHS, Beta** **$14.98** *LIV*

Alone in the T-Shirt Zone

Our hero is a bumbling T-shirt printer who couldn't get a slogan right for love or money. Trying to find love, fame, and fortune while pissing off the boss and his clients just doesn't work, and his nothing plans to create a best-selling slogan are all destined to fail. Billed as a comedy (and it certainly couldn't have been intended as anything else), this is decidedly unfunny stuff. Only a few bombed

A

"We're on the express elevator to hell...going down!"
--Private Hudson (Bill Paxton) in *Aliens*.

name Denver Dixon, introduced young Al to
directing during the filming of *Halfway to Hell*
in 1955. Adamson directed (and sometimes
produced and acted in) several features in the
mid-'60s, but few were released at the time due
to trouble with backers and distributors. His
career didn't really take off until he joined up
with writer/producer Sam Sherman (who had
interviewed Dixon for his *Screen Thrills
Illustrated* magazine) to form Independent
International. For their first feature, Sam gave
Al the title *Satan's Sadists*, expecting a horror
picture. Instead, Adamson made a biker movie,
cheaper and rougher than any that had been made.
They took off after that, making more biker,
horror, and action films, and even a few kiddy
features.

Several of Adamson's features were shot at the
ranch of another friend of his father, George
Spahn, which was also the home of what turned
out to be the Manson family. During the filming
of *Lash of Lust*, Adamson had to throw Manson off
the set for being a nuisance. After the
massacre, Adamson returned to the ranch to film
Angels' Wild Women, which pitted bikers vs. a
Manson-type gang. Another Spahn Ranch picture
was *The Female Bunch* (sort of a Western *Faster
Pussycat! Kill! Kill!*), in which Lon Chaney
played a drunken old ranch hand. His cancer-
battered voice sounds terrible, but Adamson
liked working with him so much he cast him as a
mute in his next picture, to be called *Satan's
Blood Freaks*. In what would be his last movie,
Chaney plays another of his patented moron
roles, which he'd played so many times since *Of
Mice and Men* only this time, Lennie is called
Groton, and he runs around decapitating people
with an ax! Then, in a secret lab under Venice
Beach amusement pier, J. Carroll Naish puts 'em
back together. The picture didn't work until
they added a lot more scenes featuring some
famous monsters, took out a bunch of biker
stuff, and retitled it *Dracula vs. Frankenstein*--
and it went on to make a small fortune.

Other regular members of Adamson's stock company
over the years included former Disney child star
Russ Tamblyn (*tom thumb*, *War of the Gargantuas*),
the ever-available John Carradine, Hollywood's

continued...

T-shirt slogans offer a brief chuckle. Heck, it's
a T-shirt movie; shouldn't there at least be
some gratuitous breasts? One would think so,
but not the guys who made this. Rent it only
under extreme duress. ♪

1986 81m/C Michael Barrack, Taylor Gilbert, Bill
Barron. **VHS, Beta $19.95** *NWV*

Altered States

Obsessed with the task of discovering the inner man, Hurt's ambitious researcher ignores
his family while consuming hallucinogenic
drugs and floating in an immersion tank. He
gets too deep inside, slipping way back
through the evolutionary order and becoming
a menace in the process. Confusing script
based upon Chayefsky's (alias Sidney Aaron)
confusing novel is supported by great special
effects and the usual self-indulgent and
provocative Russell direction. Chayefsky
eventually washed his hands of the project after artistic differences with the producers.
Others who departed from the film include
initial director William Penn and special effects genius John Dykstra (relieved ably by
Bran Ferren). Hurt's a solemn hoot in his first
starring role. ♪ ♪ ♪

1980 (R) 103m/C William Hurt, Blair Brown, Bob
Balaban, Charles Haid, Dori Brenner, Drew Barrymore; **D:** Ken Russell; **W:** Paddy Chayefsky. Nominations: Academy Awards '80: Best Art Direction/Set
Decoration, Best Original Score. **VHS, Beta, LV
$14.95** *WAR*

The Amazing Colossal Man

A standard '50s sci-fi film about atomic radiation, as Gordon once again demonstrates
why his initials are B.I.G. by reversing the
theme of *The Incredible Shrinking Man*.
Colonel Manning is exposed to massive doses
of plutonium when he gets too close to an A-
bomb test while trying to rescue people from
a crashed plane. The former good-guy grows
to seventy feet, escapes from the top secret
army base where he was being studied, and
starts taking out his anger on a helpless Las
Vegas. Can anything stop his murderous rampages? Some of the f/x are pretty good, but a
lot of them are laughably bad, with Gordon
trying to get by with double exposures instead
of matte shots. Inspired the origin of the in-

credible Hulk comics character. Followed by *War of the Colossal Beast*. 🦴🦴🦴

1957 79m/B Glenn Langan, Cathy Downs, William Hudson, James Seay, Russ Bender, Lyn Osborn; **D:** Bert I. Gordon. **VHS $9.95** *COL, FUS*

The Amazing Transparent Man

A mad scientist is forced to make a crook invisible in order to steal the radioactive materials he needs. A snaky crime boss has them both under his thumb. The crook decides to rob banks instead. Shot at the Texas State Fair in Dallas for that elusive futuristic look. For Ulmer fans only—don't expect another *Detour*. Aside from some exterior shots that emphasize the barren Texas plains, the direction is merely pedestrian, with little of Ulmer's usual visual magic. The invisibility transformation effects are great looking—instead of merely fading away, portions of the actor are wiped gradually. Made simultaneously with *Beyond the Time Barrier*. Chapman was also

in *Charlie Chan at the Wax Museum* (1940), *Spy Smasher Returns* (1942), and *Flight to Mars* (1952). 🦴🦴

1960 58m/B Douglas Kennedy, Marguerite Chapman, James Griffith, Ivan Triesault; **D:** Edgar G. Ulmer. **VHS $16.95** *NOS, SNC*

The Amazing Transplant

When a loser finds out that his studly playboy friend is dying, he is granted a most unusual request. The "love enhancing" transplant does wonders for him, much to the pleasure of his sexual partners. However, he finds himself in a pickle when the "something extra" he's acquired proves to be too much for him to handle, turning him into a crazed killer rapist. Before long, a police dick is hot on his trail. An incredibly strange film, shot in Wishman's trademark style. Ultra-cheap, with the camera focusing on whoever's not talking, or on people's feet, or on inanimate objects—anything to help disguise the post-dubbing of all dialogue. Quite possibly inspired by the old Robert Wiene film *Hands of Orlac* (1925, and remade at least

A

"The purpose of our suffering is only more suffering."
--William Hurt in *Altered States*.

The third bed was just right!: *Amazing Colossal Man*.

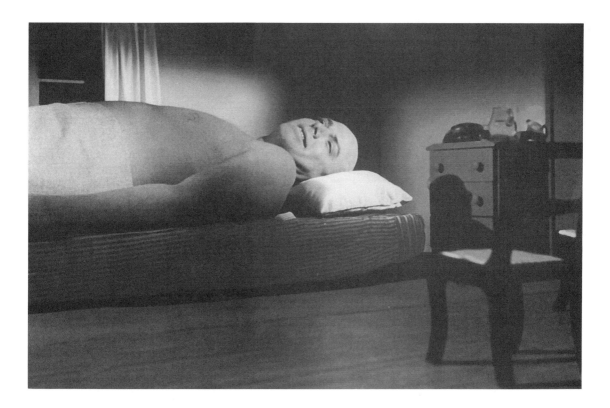

Story continued...

busiest dwarf Angelo Rossito, performance artist/art film director Brother Theodore (who narrated some of I.I.'s wildest trailers, as well as the feature *Horror of the Blood Monsters*), and familiar character players Paula Raymond (*Beast from 20,000 Fathoms*), Robert Dix (*Deadwood 76*), Kent Taylor (*The Crawling Hand*), Lawrence Tierney's brother Scott Brady (*Castle of Evil*), John "Bud" Cardos (director of *The Dark*, *Kingdom of the Spiders*, etc.), Greydon Clark (director of *Satan's Cheerleaders*, etc.), stockbroker/actor Zandor Vorkov, Vicki Volante, Kent Osborne (director of *Cain's Way*), Gary Kent, Bambi Allen, and big John Bloom. Adamson was also one of the many Z-film directors to employ future award-winning cinematographers Vilmos Zsigmund and Laszlo Kovacs.

While casting for *Satan's Sadists*, Adamson went into a local restaurant and met Regina Carrol, who was filling in as a waitress. Carrol had been a professional actress/dancer since the age of five, and had been in A-movies with Elvis Presley and Jimmy Stewart. Adamson immediately cast her as Gina, "The Freak Out Girl," and used her in many of his subsequent films. The two were married in 1972. In between performances in Adamson epics, Carrol had a Las Vegas night club act and hosted her own TV talk show.

Adamson took a 10 year break from movies to manage some properties he'd acquired, but returned in 1994 to start work on a pair of UFO mondo pictures, with more features in the works. However, the fate of these projects is unknown, due to the director's recent bizarre death. In a scenario that could have come directly from one of his films, Adamson's body was found buried under his own house on August 7, 1995. Alledgedly, the murder was committed by Adamson's contractor/houseguest, who was remodeling the house. Al Adamson led a life that was truly stranger than fiction.

three times), in which a pianist lost hands are replaced with those of a killer. 🦴🦴🦴

1970 90m/C Juan Fernandez, Linda Southern; ***D:*** Doris Wishman. **VHS, Beta $24.95** *TPV*

Amazon Women on the Moon

A plotless, irreverent media spoof, depicting the programming of a slipshod television station as it crams weird commercials and shorts around a comical '50s' science fiction film. Inconsistent, occasionally funny anthology hangs together very loosely. Produced by Landis, with the usual amount of in-joke cameos and allusions to his other works of art. 🦴🦴

1987 (R) 85m/C Rosanna Arquette, Steve Guttenberg, Steve Allen, B.B. King, Michelle Pfeiffer, Arsenio Hall, Andrew Dice Clay, Howard Hesseman, Lou Jacobi, Carrie Fisher, Griffin Dunne, Sybil Danning, Henny Youngman, Monique Gabrielle, Paul Bartel, Kelly Preston; ***D:*** John Landis, Joe Dante, Carl Gottlieb, Peter Horton, Robert Weiss; ***M:*** Ira Newborn. **VHS, Beta, LV $14.98** *MCA*

The Ambulance

A New York cartoonist (Roberts) meets Turner on the street, and she immediately has some sort of attack, and is carried off in an ambulance. Roberts tries to find her, but finds she never arrived at any hospital. His probings uncover a plot to sell the bodies of dying diabetics. The slim plot turns into a surprisingly good no-money feature in the hands of low-budget king Cohen, whose script includes his trademark fully fleshed out characters and funny, realistic dialogue. Roberts is at his most likeable, and Jones, Gallagher, and Buttons are all wonderful in their supporting roles. Includes an appearance by Marvel Comics' Stan Lee (along with other Marvel employees) as himself—the portrayal of a cartoonist's life in this film is more far more accurate than most, except for the fact that we rarely see him working. 🦴🦴🦴

1990 (R) 95m/C Eric Roberts, James Earl Jones, Megan Gallagher, Richard Bright, Janine Turner, Eric (Hans Gudegast) Braeden, Red Buttons, Laurene Landon, Jill Gatsby, Nicholas Chinlund; ***D:*** Larry Cohen; ***W:*** Larry Cohen. **VHS, LV $19.95** *COL, EPC*

The American Friend

Tribute to the American gangster film helped introduce Wenders to American moviegoers.

Young Hamburg picture framer thinks he has a terminal disease and is set up by American expatriate Hopper to become a hired assassin in West Germany. The lure is a promise of quick money that the supposedly dying man can then leave his wife and child. After the first assasination, the two bond. Hopper is the typical Wenders protagonist, a strange man in a strange land looking for a connection. Great, creepy thriller adapted from Patricia Highsmith's novel *Ripley's Game*. Fuller and Ray (better known as directors) appear briefly as gangsters. 🦴🦴🦴▷

1977 127m/C *FR GE* Bruno Ganz, Dennis Hopper, Elisabeth Kreuzer, Gerard Blain, Jean Eustache, Samuel Fuller, Nicholas Ray, Wim Wenders; *D:* Wim Wenders; *W:* Wim Wenders. National Board of Review Awards '77: 5 Best Foreign Films of the Year; Nominations: Cannes Film Festival '77: Best Film. **VHS, Beta, LV $29.95** *FCT, GLV, INJ*

American Gothic

Ma and Pa (Yvonne DeCarlo, TV's "Lily Munster," and Rod Steiger) are a down-home couple who are given to phrases such as "Get your forty winks" and "Are you two people hitched?" Okay, that's not so weird, but their three middle-aged moronic offspring, Fanny, Teddy, and Wood, still act and dress like preadolescent children. Three stranded couples cross paths with this sickening clan with the usual fatal results. If you can push aside your pity for the career lows of DeCarlo and Steiger (Steiger speaks his lines in a slow twang that personifies boredom), you may enjoy this little flick for its outright silliness and twist end. *AKA:* Hide and Shriek. 🦴🦴▷

1988 (R) 89m/C Rod Steiger, Yvonne De Carlo, Michael J. Pollard, Sarah Torgov, Fiona Hutchinson; *D:* John Hough. **VHS, Beta, LV $89.95** *VMK*

American Tickler

A thigh-slappin' (or is it head-whacking?) series of satirical pastiches in the grand style of *Kentucky Fried Movie*, only more sophomoric. A tasteless collection of yearning to be funny sketches about American institutions. *AKA:* Draws. 🦴

1976 (R) 77m/C W.P. Dremak, Joan Sumner, Marlow Ferguson, Jeff Alin; *D:* Chuck Vincent. **VHS, Beta $59.95** *GEM*

An American Werewolf in London

Strange, darkly humorous version of the classic man-into-wolf horror tale became a cult hit, but never clicked with most American critics. Two American college students (Naughton and Dunne) backpacking through England are viciously attacked by a werewolf one foggy night. Dunne is killed, but keeps appearing (in progressively decomposed form) before the seriously wounded Naughton, warning him of impending werewolfdom when the moon is full; Dunne advises suicide. Seat-jumping horror and gore, highlighted by intensive metamorphosis sequences orchestrated by Rick Baker, are offset by wry humor, though the shifts in tone don't always work. Great moon songs permeate the soundtrack, including CCR's "Bad Moon Rising" and Van Morrison's "Moondance." 🦴🦴🦴▷

1981 (R) 97m/C David Naughton, Griffin Dunne, Jenny Agutter, Frank Oz, Brian Glover, David Schofield; *D:* John Landis; *W:* John Landis; *M:* Elmer Bernstein. Academy Awards '81: Best Makeup. **VHS, Beta, LV $14.98** *LIV, VES*

The Amityville Horror

Sometimes a house is not a home. Ineffective chiller that became a box-office biggie, based on a supposedly real-life occurrence in Amityville, Long Island. The Lutz family moves into the house of their dreams only to find it full of nightmares. Once the scene of a grisly mass murder, the house takes on a devilish attitude, plunging the family into supernatural terror. Pipes and walls ooze icky stuff, flies manifest in the strangest places, and doors mysteriously slam while exorcist Steiger staggers from room to room in scene-chewing prayer. Based on the Jay Anson book and followed by a number of sequels. 🦴🦴▷

1979 (R) 117m/C James Brolin, Margot Kidder, Rod Steiger, Don Stroud, Murray Hamilton, Helen Shaver, Amy Wright; *D:* Stuart Rosenberg; *W:* Sandor Stern. Nominations: Academy Awards '79: Best Original Score. **VHS, Beta, LV** *WAR, OM*

Amityville 2: The Possession

More of a prequel than a sequel to *The Amityville Horror* (1979). Relates the story of the

"**Have you ever talked to a corpse? It's boring!**"
—a dead Griffin Dunne whines to David Naughton in *An American Werewolf in London*.

house's early years as a haven for demonic forces intent on driving a father to beat the kids, a mother to prayer, and a brother to lust after his sister (before he murders them all). Young etc. portray an obnoxious family that you're actually glad to see wasted by the possessed son. A stupid, clumsy attempt to cash in on the success of the first film, which was also stupid and clumsy but could at least claim novelty in the bad housing development genre. Followed by *Amityville III: The Demon* in 1983. 🦴

1982 **(R)** 110m/C James Olson, Burt Young, Andrew Prine, Moses Gunn, Rutanya Alda; *D:* Damiano Damiani; *M:* Howard Blake. **VHS, Beta, LV $9.98** *SUE*

Amityville 3: The Demon

America's worst real-estate value dupes another funky buyer. The infamous Amityville house is once again restless with terror and gore, though supported with even less plot than the usual smidgin. Cynical reporter Roberts moves in while trying to get to the bottom of the story by way of the basement. Courtesy of 3-D technology, monsters sprang at theater patrons but the video version is strictly two-dimensional, forcing the viewer to press his or her face directly onto the television screen in order to derive similar effect. *AKA:* Amityville 3-D. 🦴 🦴

1983 **(R)** 98m/C Tony Roberts, Tess Harper, Robert Joy, Candy Clark, John Beal, Leora Dana, John Harkins, Lori Loughlin, Meg Ryan; *D:* Richard Fleischer; *W:* David Ambrose; *M:* Howard Blake. **VHS, Beta, LV $79.98** *VES, LIV*

Amsterdamned

A skin-diving serial killer emerges from the canals of Amsterdam to splash and slash in this arty Dutch crime thriller. Director Peter Maas' earlier picture, *The Lift*, was more highly regarded by some, probably because it was released in a subtitled, high-tone version, while this movie got the cheapjack dubbing treatment which turns it into gouda. The underwater stalking sequence which opens the picture can hold its own with the Italian masters. Unfortunately, things soon get bogged down in detective proceedings. Star Monique Van De Ven can be seen to better advantage in Paul Verhoven's first two films, *Turkish Delight* an *Keetje Tipple*. 🦴 🦴 🦴

1988 **(R)** 114m/C *NL* Monique Van De Ven, Huub Stapel; *D:* Dick Maas. **VHS, Beta, LV $89.98** *VES, LIV*

The Amy Fisher Story

Amy Fisher wishes she looked this good. Perhaps if she did, she could be acting in made-for-television movies like Barrymore instead of providing fodder for them. The ABC account draws from a variety of sources to dramatize the relationship between Amy and her married, ahem, friend, and Amy's subsequent attack on his wife. Although it tries not to take sides, it does include some pretty hot sex scenes which could be why this docudrama garnered the highest ratings of the three network productions released on TV. See also: *Casualties of Love: The 'Long Island Lolita' Story* and *Lethal Lolita—Amy Fisher: My Story.* 🦴 🦴

1993 96m/C Drew Barrymore, Anthony John Denison, Harley Jane Kozak, Tom Mason, Laurie Paton, Ken Pogue, Linda Darlow; *D:* Andy Tennant; *W:* Janet Brownell. **VHS $89.98** *ABC*

And Now for Something Completely Different

This compilation film introduced America to Monty Python's Flying Circus, British comedy's answer to the Beatles. An excellent introduction to the legendary troupe's iconoclastic humor, this representative sampling of the best sketches and naughty bits from the legendary BBC series includes "Dead Parrot," "Nudge-Nudge," "The World's Deadliest Joke," "Upperclass Twit of the Year," and, of course, "The Lumberjack Song." The original Monty Python TV shows are also available on videocassette. 🦴 🦴 🦴

1972 **(PG)** 89m/C *GB* John Cleese, Michael Palin, Eric Idle, Graham Chapman, Terry Gilliam, Terry Jones; *D:* Ian McNaughton; *W:* John Cleese, Michael Palin, Graham Chapman, Terry Gilliam, Terry Jones. **VHS, Beta, LV $19.95** *COL, TVC*

Android

When an android who has been assisting a quirky scientist in space learns that he is about

to be permanently retired, he starts to take matters into his own synthetic hands. Combines science fiction, suspense, and cloned romance. A must for Kinski fans. The android is the last of his kind—the others having been destroyed when their programming broke down, turning them into killer machines. Alone on a space station with scientist Kinski (who is trying to develop a higher-grade android), they are soon joined by three refugees from a damaged space cruiser. The three are secretly escaped prisoners and highly dangerous. Max, the android, falls in love with the girl of the group and soon his desire to protect her begins to supersede his programming. Noting this, Kinski soon plans Max's deactivation. Well executed, but throughout it is obvious where this one is heading. A few twists are wisely saved for the final reel, so it's not quite as predictable as it seems. The effects are on the lame side, with the space scenes strictly from hunger. Watch this for the story, not with any expectations of high-energy glitter. 🦴🦴▷

1982 (PG) 80m/C Klaus Kinski, Don Opper, Brie Howard; **D:** Aaron Lipstadt. **VHS, Beta, LV $69.95** MED

Andy Warhol's Bad

In the John Waters' school of "crime is beauty," a Queens housewife struggles to make appointments for both her home electrolysis clinic and her all-female murder-for-hire operation, which specializes in children and pets (who are thrown out of windows and knived, respectively). Her life is further complicated by a boarder (King) who's awaiting the go-ahead for his own assignment, an autistic child unwanted by his mother. One of Warhol's more professional-appearing films, and very funny if your tastes run to the tasteless. 🦴🦴🦴

1977 (R) 100m/C Perry King, Carroll Baker, Susan Tyrrell, Stefania Cassini; **D:** Jed Johnson. **VHS, Beta, LV $59.95** SUE, MLB

Andy Warhol's Dracula

Sex and camp humor, as well as a large dose of blood, highlight Warhol's treatment of the tale. As Dracula can only subsist on the blood of pure, untouched maidens ("were-gins"), gardener Dallesandro rises to the occasion in order to make as many women as he can ineligible for Drac's purposes. Very reminiscent of Warhol's *Frankenstein,* but with a bit more spoofery. Look for Roman Polanski in a cameo peek as a pub patron. **AKA:** Blood for Dracula; Young Dracula. 🦴🦴🦴

1974 (R) 106m/C *IT FR* Udo Kier, Arno Juergling, Maxine McKendry, Joe Dallesandro, Vittorio De Sica; **Cameos:** Roman Polanski; **D:** Paul Morrissey; **W:** Paul Morrissey. **VHS, Beta $79.95** *TRI, GEM, INJ*

Andy Warhol's Frankenstein

A most outrageous parody of Frankenstein, featuring plenty of gore, sex, and bad taste in general. Baron von Frankenstein (Udo Kier) derives sexual satisfaction from his corpses (he delivers a particularly thought-provoking philosophy on life as he lustfully fondles a gall bladder); his wife seeks her pleasure from the monster himself (Joe Dallesandro). Originally made in 3-D, this is one of Warhol's campiest outings. **AKA:** Flesh for Frankenstein. 🦴🦴▷

1974 (R) 95m/C *GE FR IT* Udo Kier, Dalia di Lazzaro, Monique Van Vooren, Joe Dallesandro; **D:** Paul Morrissey; **W:** Paul Morrissey. **VHS, Beta $79.95** *TRI, MLB*

Angel Heart

Exotic, controversial look at murder, voodoo cults, and sex in 1955 New Orleans. Bonet defiantly sheds her image as a young innocent (no more *Cosby Show* for you, young lady). Rourke is slimy as marginal NYC private eye Angel, hired by the devilish De Niro to track a missing big band singer who violated a "contract." His investigation leads him to the bizarre world of the occult in New Orleans, where the blood drips to a different beat. Visually stimulating, with a provocative sex scene between Bonet and Rourke, captured in both R-rated and unrated versions. Adapted by Parker from *Falling Angel* by William Hjortsberg. 🦴🦴▷

1987 (R) 112m/C Mickey Rourke, Robert De Niro, Lisa Bonet, Charlotte Rampling, Michael Higgins, Charles Gordone, Kathleen Wilhoite, Stocker Fountelieu, Brownie McGhee; **D:** Alan Parker; **W:** Alan Parker; **M:** Trevor Jones. **VHS, Beta, LV $14.95** *LIV, FCT*

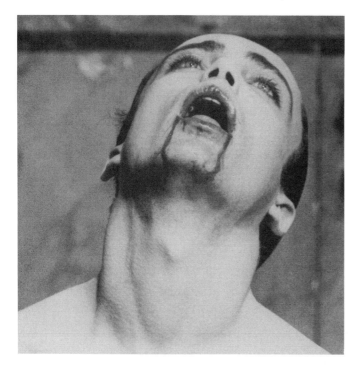

Animal Crackers

The second and possibly the funniest of the thirteen Marx Brothers films, *Animal Crackers* is a screen classic. Groucho is a guest at the house of wealthy matron Margaret Dumont and he, along with Zeppo, Chico, and Harpo, destroy the tranquility of the estate. Complete with the Harry Ruby music score—including Groucho's "Hooray for Captain Spaulding" with more quotable lines than any other Marx Brothers film: "One morning I shot an elephant in my pajamas. How he got into my pajamas, I'll never know." Based on a play by George S. Kaufman. ♫♫♫♪

1930 (G) 98m/B Groucho Marx, Chico Marx, Harpo Marx, Zeppo Marx, Lillian Roth, Margaret Dumont, Louis Sorin, Hal Thompson, Richard Greig; **D:** Victor Heerman; **W:** Morrie Ryskind. **VHS, Beta, LV $14.98** *MCA, FCT*

Annie Hall

Acclaimed coming-of-cinematic-age film for Allen is based in part on his own life. His love affair with Hall/Keaton is chronicled as an episodic, wistful comedy commenting on family, love, loneliness, communicating, maturity, driving, city life, careers, and various other topics. Abounds with classic scenes, including future star Goldblum and his mantra at a cocktail party; Allen and the lobster pot; and Allen, Keaton, a bathroom, a tennis racket, and a spider. The film operates on many levels, as does Keaton's wardrobe, which started a major fashion trend. Don't blink or you'll miss several future stars in bit parts. Expertly shot by Gordon Willis. ♫♫♫♫

1977 (PG) 94m/C Woody Allen, Diane Keaton, Tony Roberts, Paul Simon, Shelley Duvall, Carol Kane, Colleen Dewhurst, Christopher Walken, Janet Margolin, John Glover, Jeff Goldblum, Sigourney Weaver, Marshall McLuhan, Beverly D'Angelo, Shelley Hack; **D:** Woody Allen; **W:** Woody Allen, Marshall Brickman. Academy Awards '77: Best Actress (Keaton), Best Director (Allen), Best Original Screenplay, Best Picture; British Academy Awards '77: Best Actress (Keaton), Best Director (Allen), Best Film; Directors Guild of America Awards '77: Best Director (Allen); Golden Globe Awards '78: Best Actress—Musical/Comedy (Keaton); National Board of Review Awards '77: 10 Best Films of the Year, Best Actress (Keaton); National Society of Film Critics Awards '77: Best Actress (Keaton), Best Film; Nominations: Academy Awards '77: Best Actor (Allen). **VHS, Beta, LV $14.95** *MGM, FOX, CRC*

Udo Kier imitates Annie Lennox, with make-up by Tammy Faye Baker in *Andy Warhol's Dracula.*

Angels Hard as They Come

Jonathan Demme was Roger Corman's publicist when Corman directed him to write a motorcycle movie. The script was intended to be a biker version of Akira Kurosawa's *Rashoman,* until Corman got through revising it. Now, it is at best a curious footnote in the Oscar-winning director's career. Also of interest for Gary Busey's screen debut and as one of Scott Glenn's first films. ♫♫

1971 (R) 86m/C Gary Busey, Scott Glenn, James Iglehart, Gary Littlejohn, Sharon Peckinpah; **D:** Joe Viola; **W:** Jonathan Demme. **VHS, Beta $24.98** *SUE*

The Angry Red Planet

An unintentionally amusing sci-fi adventure about astronauts on Mars fighting off aliens and giant, ship-swallowing amoebas. Filmed using bizarre "Cinemagic" process, which turns almost everything pink. Wild effects have earned the film cult status. ♫♫♫

1959 83m/C Gerald Mohr, Les Tremayne, Jack Kruschen; **D:** Ib Melchior. **VHS, Beta $19.95** *NO*

Ants

A mad bug parable for the planet-obsessed 90s. Insecticide-infected ants turn militant and check into a local hotel to vent their chemically induced foul mood on the unsuspecting clientele. The guest register includes a gaggle of celebrities who probably wish they'd signed on the Love Boat instead. Made for television (an ant farm would probably be just too horrible on the big screen). *AKA:* Panic at Lakewood Manor; It Happened at Lakewood Manor. 🦴🦴📺

1977 100m/C Suzanne Somers, Robert Foxworth, Myrna Loy, Lynda Day George, Gerald Gordon, Bernie Casey, Barry Van Dyke, Karen Lamm, Anita Gillette, Moosie Drier, Steve Franken, Brian Dennehy, Bruce French, Stacy Keach, Rene Enriquez, James Storm; **D:** Robert Scheerer. **VHS, Beta** *LIV*

Apartment Zero

Haunting exercise in originality is a surprise from the first scene to the last. It's about the relationship between an eccentric, film-obsessed theatre owner (Firth) and a handsome, manipulative American (Bochner) who becomes his roommate in Buenos Aires, 1988. Does the newcomer have anything to do with a series of murders? Are death squads at work? Or is something else going on? Nothing is certain until the personalities of the two men have been revealed. The real story that's being told is the gradual striping away of the layers of disguise that both men wear. The performances are first rate. Film fans will catch references, both blatant and oblique, to *Blood Simple, Psycho, Rear Window,* and others. Despite the subject matter, there is no overt violence or sexual scenes; everything is suggestion and nuance. Watch carefully to catch everything that's going on, and this one is well worth watching carefully. In fact, it's worth watching carefully twice. 🦴🦴🦴📺

1988 (R) 124m/C *GB* Hart Bochner, Colin Firth, Fabrizio Bentivoglio, Liz Smith; **D:** Martin Donovan; **W:** Martin Donovan, David Koepp. **VHS, Beta, LV** **$14.95** *ACA, FCT, IME*

A*P*E*

D*O*G! A*P*E* is thirty-six feet tall and ten tons of animal fury who destroys anything that comes between him and the actress he loves. The plot doesn't go anywhere—in fact it refuses to leave! A U.S.-Korean co-production, this is a cheap rip-off of the Kong remake, which also throws in a rubber shark at the beginning. The title may have been the distributor's attempt to sell this turkey as a M*A*S*H-flavored send-up. As part of the unsuccessful '70s 3-D revival, occasionally something flies at the camera. The appealing DeVarona plays a movie star who comes to Korea to make some crummy movie, followed by Arrants as her reporter boyfriend. The producers thank the U.S. Army for their cooperation, yet all the officers are portrayed as buffoons. The second worst looking ape costume in movie history, behind *The Mighty Gorga,* and the guy inside has no idea how an ape behaves. Effects are not just cheap, but also poorly planned and executed. As DeVarona whimpers at the end: "Why?! Why?!" From the director of *I Dismember Mama* (1972). 🦴

1976 (PG) 87m/C Rod Arrants, Joanna DeVarona, Alex Nicol; **D:** Paul Leder. **VHS, Beta $19.95** *NWV*

Apocalypse Now

Coppola's $40 million epic vision of the Vietnam War was inspired by Joseph Conrad's novella "Heart of Darkness," and continues to be the subject of debate. Disillusioned Army captain Sheen travels upriver into Cambodia to assassinate overweight renegade colonel Brando. His trip is punctuated by surrealistic battles and a terrifying descent into a land where human rationality seems to have slipped away. Considered by some to be the definitive picture of war in its overall depiction of chaos and primal bloodletting; by others, over-wrought and unrealistic. May not translate as well to the small screen, yet worth seeing if for nothing more than Duvall's ten minutes of scenery chewing as a battle-obsessed major ("I love the smell of napalm in the morning!"), a study in manic machismo. Stunning photography by Vittorio Storaro, awe-inspiring battle scenes, and effective soundtrack montage. Both Sheen and Coppola suffered emotional breakdowns during the prolonged filming, and that's a very young Fishburne in his major film debut. Available in widescreen format on laserdisc and in a remastered version in letterbox on VHS with a

remixed soundtrack that features Dolby Surround stereo. In 1991 a documentary detailing the making of the film, *Hearts of Darkness: A Filmmaker's Apocalypse,* was released. 🦴🦴🦴🦴

1979 (R) 153m/C Marlon Brando, Martin Sheen, Robert Duvall, Frederic Forrest, Sam Bottoms, Scott Glenn, Albert Hall, Laurence "Larry" Fishburne, Harrison Ford, G.D. Spradlin, Dennis Hopper, Colleen Camp, Tom Mason; **D:** Francis Ford Coppola; **W:** Francis Ford Coppola, John Milius; **M:** Carmine Coppola. Academy Awards '79: Best Cinematography, Best Sound; British Academy Awards '79: Best Director (Coppola), Best Supporting Actor (Duvall); Golden Globe Awards '80: Best Director (Coppola), Best Supporting Actor (Duvall), Best Score; National Board of Review Awards '79: 10 Best Films of the Year; National Society of Film Critics Awards '79: Best Supporting Actor (Forrest); Nominations: Academy Awards '79: Best Adapted Screenplay, Best Art Direction/Set Decoration, Best Director (Coppola), Best Film Editing, Best Picture, Best Supporting Actor (Duvall). **VHS, Beta, LV, CD-I $29.95** *PAR*

The Applegates

Ecologically correct Amazonian beetles are more than a little miffed about the slash-and-burn tactics in their home and decide to es-

tablish a kinder, gentler habitat. Bug Begley and his brood transform themselves into average Americans, but then don't want to leave their decadent life: even insects aren't immune to the lure of sex, drugs, and cable shopping networks. Imaginative, often quite funny one-joke flick should've been shorter. Fits quite well as a double feature with Lehmann's earlier *Heathers.* **AKA:** Meet the Applegates. 🦴🦴◁

1989 (R) 90m/C Ed Begley Jr., Stockard Channing, Dabney Coleman, Cami Cooper, Bobby Jacoby, Glenn Shadix, Susan Barnes, Adam Biesk, Savannah Smith Boucher; **D:** Michael Lehmann; **W:** Michael Lehmann, Redbeard Simmons. **VHS, Beta, LV $89.98** *MED, FOX, VTR*

April Fool's Day

Rich girl Foreman invites eight college friends to spend the April Fool's weekend with her at her family's isolated island mansion. Everyone is subjected to an endless series of practical jokes when things apparently turn deadly and several of the kids begin disappearing. Lame spoof of *Friday the 13th* and other teenagers-in-peril slasher films. 🦴

1986 (R) 90m/C Deborah Foreman, Jay Baker, Pat Barlow, Lloyd Berry, Deborah Goodrich, Ken Olandt, Griffin O'Neal, Tom Heaton, Mike Nomad, Leah K. Pinsent, Clayton Rohner, Amy Steel, Thomas F. Wilson; **D:** Fred Walton; **W:** Danilo Bach; **M:** Charles Bernstein. **VHS, Beta, LV $19.95** *PAR*

Armistead Maupin's Tales of the City

When Mary Ann Singleton decides to stay put on the West Coast while on vacation, we are given a bird's eye view of '70s San Francisco. Based on Armistead Maupin's *Tales of the City* series (six novels based on his *San Francisco Chronicle* serial), this flick offers a counterculture soap opera involving the swinging scene and gay culture as experienced by the residents of 28 Barbary Lane, including the Ohio-white-bred Mary Ann, free-wheeling Mona, gay romantic Mouse, womanizer Brian, the elusive Norman, and the landlady, Mrs. Madrigal, who has a secret past we never do discover in Volume 1 (reason enough to rent the second volume). Other reasons to rent volume 2 include cameos by Karen Black (playing her jaded self at a fat farm) and Paul

Bartel (who is planning to make a mint on a gay nursing home). Graced with authentic '70s kitsch, music, pop culture, and language; relive Jim Jones, the Tylenol scare, and Green Goddess dressing. This three-volume video series was originally made for British TV. **AKA:** Tales of the City. 🦴🦴🦴

1993 360m/C *GB* Olympia Dukakis, Donald Moffat, Chloe Webb, Laura Linney, Marcus D'Amico, William Campbell, Thomas Gibson, Paul Gross, Barbara Garrick, Nina Foch, Edie Adams, Robert Downey, Meagen Fay, Lou Liberatore, Country Joe McDonald, Mary Kay Place, Parker Posey, Kevin Sessums; *Cameos:* Paul Bartel, Karen Black, McLean Stevenson; *D:* Alastair Reid; *W:* Richard Kramer; *M:* John Keane. **VHS $59.95** *PGV*

Army of Darkness

Campbell returns for a third *Evil Dead* round as the square-jawed, none-too-bright hero, Ash, in this comic book extravaganza. As a grocery store clerk who regales his coworkers with the story of his experiences in the Evil Deads, he finds himself hurled back to the 14th-century through the powers of another evil book. There he romances a babe, fights an army of skeletons, and generally causes all those Dark Age knights a lot of grief, as he tries to get back to his own time. Raimi's technical exuberance is apparent and, as usual, the horror is graphic but even more tongue-in-cheek. Like *Evil Dead 2*, this entry in the series is reworked to stand on its own. Foreign videos contain the original ending, which is quite different. Fonda is seen briefly as the girl he left behind. **AKA:** Evil Dead 3. 🦴🦴🦴

1992 (R) 77m/C Bruce Campbell, Embeth Davidtz, Marcus Gilbert, Ian Abercrombie, Richard Grove, Michael Earl Reid, Tim Quill, Patricia Tallman, Theodore (Ted) Raimi, Ivan Raimi; *Cameos:* Bridget Fonda; *D:* Sam Raimi; *W:* Ivan Raimi, Sam Raimi; *M:* Danny Elfman, Joseph Lo Duca. **VHS, Beta, LV $19.98** *MCA, FCT*

Arnold

Outrageous featherweight black comedy involving a woman who marries a cadaver to gain his large inheritance. Lots of bizarre and creative deaths in this horror spoof, including acid-laced face cream and a shrinking suit; quoth the local policeman, "If they keep dying this way, we'll have to bury them piggyback!" Unusual wedding scene is a must-see.

Cast does a fine job with saucy, offbeat material, particularly Stevens, who has a touch for this kind of hard-to-define material. Recommended for her fans. 🦴🦴🦴

1973 (PG) 96m/C Stella Stevens, Roddy McDowall, Elsa Lanchester, Victor Buono, Bernard Fox, Farley Granger, Shani Wallis; *D:* Georg Fenady; *M:* George Duning. **VHS, Beta** *LIV*

The Arousers

From the *Psycho* file comes former Hollywood heartthrob Tab Hunter as a California gym teacher who kills his comely young bed partners when impotence rears its ugly head. What really arouses him is prostitutes who dress up as his deceased mother. It takes all kinds. Director Curtis Hanson later hit Hollywood pay dirt with *The Hand That Rocks the Cradle* and the Meryl Streep whitewater thriller, *The River Wild*. Hunter enjoyed a career resurgence of sorts in 1981 as John Waters' leading man (not counting Divine) in *Polyester*. **AKA:** Sweet Kill; A Kiss from Eddie. 🦴🦴🦴

1970 (R) 85m/C Tab Hunter, Nadyne Turney, Roberta Collins, Isabel Jewell, John Aprea, Angel Fox; *D:* Curtis Hanson. **VHS, Beta $24.98** *SUE*

The Asphyx

Nineteenth century doctor Stephens is studying death when he discovers The Asphyx, an aura that surrounds a person just before they die. Stephens delves deeper into his research and finds the keys to immortality. However, his irresponsibility in unleashing the obscure supernatural power on the world brings a swarm of unforeseen and irreversible troubles. High-class sci fi. **AKA:** Spirit of the Dead. 🦴🦴🦴

1972 (PG) 98m/C *GB* Robert Stephens, Robert Powell, Jane Lapotaire, Alex Scott, Ralph Arliss, Fiona Walker, John Lawrence; *D:* Peter Newbrook. **VHS, Beta $19.95** *MED*

Assassin of Youth

Girl is introduced to marijuana and soon becomes involved in "the thrills of wild parties," and the horrors of the "killer weed." Camp diversion. 🦴🦴

1935 70m/B Luana Walters, Arthur Gardner; *D:* Elmer Clifton. **VHS, Beta $16.95** *SNC, NOS, DVT*

"**T**rapped
in time.
Surrounded
by evil.
Low on gas."
--*Army of Darkness.*

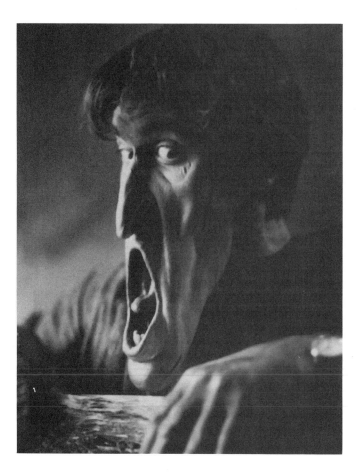

Bruce Campbell does a mean Lyle Lovett impression in *Army of Darkness*.

1988 85m/C Patti Astor, Christina Whitaker, Elizabeth Kaitan, Griffin O'Neal, Nick Cassavetes, Eddie Deezen; **D:** Patti Astor. **VHS**

Assault on Precinct 13

Urban horror invades LA when a sleepy police station is suddenly under siege from a violent youth gang. Paranoia abounds as the police are attacked from all sides and can see no way out. Carpenter's musical score adds much to the setting of this unique police exploitation story that somehow stands as Carpenter's adaptation of Howard Hawks' *Rio Bravo*. Semi-acclaimed and very gripping. 🦴🦴🦴

1976 91m/C Austin Stoker, Darwin Joston, Martin West, Tony Burton, Nancy Loomis, Kim Richards, Henry Brandon; **D:** John Carpenter; **W:** John Carpenter; **M:** John Carpenter. **VHS, Beta, LV $54.95** *MED*

The Astounding She-Monster

How can you not love a movie with a title like this? A bad script and snail-paced plot are a good start. A geologist (Clarke, *The Hideous Sun Demon* himself), wanting only to be left alone with his rocks, survives a brush with the kidnappers of a wealthy heiress only to happen upon an alien spacecraft that's crashed nearby. At the helm is a very tall, high-heeled sexy fem-alien (centerfold model Kilpatrick) in an obligatory skintight space outfit. "Excellent!", our rock jock thinks, but it seems she kills with the slightest touch. The crooks are led by Duncan, who must have felt right at home after his pictures with Ed Wood. Partially remade by Fred Olen Ray in 1989 as *Alienator*. **AKA:** Mysterious Invader. 🦴🦴

1958 60m/B Robert Clarke, Kenne Duncan, Marilyn Harvey, Jeanne Tatum, Shirley Kilpatrick, Ewing Miles Brown; **D:** Ronnie Ashcroft. **VHS $19.98** *SNC, MRV, CNM*

The Astro-Zombies

A contender as one of the worst movies of all time. Carradine plays a mad scientist creating photocell powered zombies who eat people's guts. Cult favorite Satana (*Faster Pussycat! Kill! Kill!*) stars as a dragon lady spy who wants Carradine's secrets, but wants to wear a series of ultrasexy outfits even more. This

Assault of the Killer Bimbos

The title sounds like a cult film. The box art, featuring three dive-bombing bimbettes certainly looks cultish. The movie itself, while innocent enough and well meaning, fails to hit the low notes that would give it true cult status. A show girl gets framed for the murder of her boss and takes off for the border with a couple girlfriends. On the way they get pursued by the expected dumb cops and meet up with horny, clean-cut hunks. Of course, in Mexico they meet up with the villain and extract comedic vengeance. Watchable mainly due to the likable female leads and pleasant, lightly camp execution, it will prove too tame for many viewers. Even the rare breast shot seems thrown in mainly to get the coveted "R" rating. Perhaps what we have here is a cult film for those who hate cult films. 🦴🦴

being the mid-'60s, all the moronic spy action takes precedence over the scenes of the heroic investigating scientist that would have dominated a decade before. The zombies all wear cool skull-like helmets. One of the eccentric Mikels' stupidest features, which means it's a heck of a lot of fun. One of the last appearances for familiar face Corey (*Sorry, Wrong Number, Rear Window*) who plays a CIA chief. Co-written and co-produced by Rogers of *M*A*S*H* fame. Next stop for Mikels: *The Girl in Gold Boots.* 🗡🗡🗡

1967 83m/C Tura Satana, Wendell Corey, John Carradine, Tom Pace, Joan Patrick, Rafael Campos; **D:** Ted V. Mikels; **W:** Ted V. Mikels, Wayne Rogers. **VHS, Beta $49.95** *NO*

At the Circus

Marx Brothers invade the circus to save it from bankruptcy and cause their usual comic insanity, though they've done it better before. Beginning of the end for the Marxes, a step down in quality from their classic work, though frequently darn funny. 🎵 Lydia the Tattooed Lady; Step Up and Take a Bow; Two Blind Loves; Blue Moon. **AKA:** The Marx Brothers at the Circus. 🗡🗡▷

1939 87m/B Groucho Marx, Chico Marx, Harpo Marx, Margaret Dumont, Kenny L. Baker, Florence Rice, Eve Arden, Nat Pendleton, Fritz Feld; **D:** Edward Buzzell. **VHS, Beta, LV $19.95** *MGM*

Atlas

To end a long siege, and to win the hand of princess Candia (Morris), the mighty Atlas (Forest) takes on the champion of his enemy Proximedes (Wolff). At the height of the Italian Hercules/Maciste craze, Corman went to Greece to show the Europeans how to make 'em even cheaper. The same fifty clumsy extras (including Griffith, Corman, and his buddy Dick Miller), bearing cardboard and tinfoil helmets, play both "armies." The large amount of post-dubbed dialogue makes it all sound more European. The first union film shot in Greece, due to Corman's efforts to keep his crew working. The script adds wit, style, and even some political commentary to the sword & sandal shenanigans, while avoiding all the more expensive cliches. Morris gets a great line: "So that's Atlas...I wonder who's holding up the Earth..." 🗡🗡▷

1960 84m/C Michael Forest, Frank Wolff, Barboura Morris, Walter Maslow; **D:** Roger Corman; **W:** Charles B. Griffith. **VHS $19.95** *DVT, SNC, HEG*

Atom Age Vampire

Mad scientist doing research on Japanese nuclear bomb victims falls in love with a woman disfigured in an auto crash. To remove her scars, he treats her with a formula derived from the glands of freshly killed women. A low-rent Italian version of *Eyes Without a Face (Horror Chamber of Dr. Faustus)* with a Jekyll/Hyde type monster thrown in, but entertaining in a mischievous, boy-is-this-a-stupid-film sort of way. Can this be the same Magnoli that directed *Purple Rain*? 🗡🗡

1961 71m/B *IT* Alberto Lupo, Susanne Loret, Sergio Fantoni; **D:** Albert Magnoli. **VHS, Beta $16.95** *SNC, NOS, VYY*

The Atomic Brain

An old woman hires a doctor to transplant her brain into the body of a beautiful young girl. Of the three who are abducted, two become homicidal zombies and the third starts to act catty when she's given a feline brain. Oh, and did we mention the hairy monster chained to a tether in the back yard? A serious contender to *Plan 9 From Outer Space*'s (unworthy) title of Worst Film Ever Made, this is a treasure trove of tripe: drunk, horny mad doctors; wheelchair-bound old biddies living in dilapidated gothic mansions; forbidden experiments with atomic power; mutations run amuck; and trampy Euro-dames (with atrocious fake accents). Add screamingly inept dialogue (by FOUR screenwriters!), a droning narrator, and feel your own brainpan go nuclear. A must-see for bad-brain movie devotees; makes a cerebral double bill with *The Brain That Wouldn't Die*. Director Mascelli provided camera work for Ray Dennis Steckler's *The Incredibly Strange Creatures Who Stopped Living and Became Mixed-Up Zombies* the following year as well as authoring a highly regarded book on cinematography. Co-producer/writer Jack Pollexfen is an old hand in the bad movie biz, having helmed the Lon Chaney, Jr., electric-psycho flick *The Indestructible Man*. **AKA:** Monstrosity. 🗡🗡🗡

1964 72m/B Frank Gerstle, Erika Peters, Judy Bamber, Marjorie Eaton, Frank Fowler, Margie Fisco; **D:**

A

THE HOUND SALUTES: CHARLES BAND

Band is a second generation filmmaker who's a throwback to the producer/showmen of Hollywood's "golden age." His field, though, is video originals, not theatrical releases. Over the past few years, he has created Full Moon Productions, essentially a studio within a studio at Paramount, specializing in fantasy and science fiction. In an interview he said that he hopes "Full Moon will become to fantasy what Disney is to family entertainment."

Band was, literally, born into the business. His father, Albert Band, worked with John Huston on *Red Badge of Courage*, and was the assistant director of *Asphalt Jungle*. In the 1950s, he made the well-regarded *I Bury the Living* with Richard Boone and *Face of Fire* with James Whitmore. From there, the Band family moved to Italy where Albert made sword and sandal movies with Steve Reeves. One of Full Moon's best efforts, *Meridian: Kiss of the Beast* was actually filmed on the family estate in Italy. These days, Albert and Charles have been co-directing Full Moon films.

The younger Band has to share directing duties because he is involved in every phase of Full Moon. "The ideas and concepts, the stories and critters, the marketing campaigns--that's a big part of the fun for me; seeing that vision come to life. We're trying to build up this Full Moon universe of characters and creatures. I liken the whole thing to the comic books of the '90s; crossover characters and team-ups, as Marvel Comics did in the '60s."

He also promotes the films to videostore owners with a traveling road show that features upcoming releases and the series' most popular characters.

Like all filmmakers, Band has had his share of successes and failures, but overall, Full Moon has become a recognized name in the field, and it's even branched out. Its Torchlight series is for more sexually oriented s-f (*Test Tube Teens from the Year 2000*), and under the Moonbeam label, it has been producing some remarkably successful fantasies for children.

continued...

Joseph Mascelli; *W:* Jack Pollexfen. **VHS $19.98** *NOS, SNC*

The Atomic Cafe

A chillingly humorous compilation of newsreels and government films of the 1940s and 1950s that show America's preoccupation with the A-Bomb. Some sequences are in black and white. Includes the infamous training film "Duck and Cover," which tells us what to do in the event of an actual bombing, as explained by a cartoon turtle. 🦴🦴🦴
1982 92m/C D: Kevin Rafferty. **VHS, Beta** *NO*

Attack of the 50 Foot Woman

A beautiful, abused housewife has a frightening encounter with a giant alien, causing her to grow to an enormous height. Then she goes looking for hubby. Perhaps the all-time classic '50s sci fi, a truly fun movie highlighted by the sexy, 50-foot Hayes in a giant bikini. Has intriguing psychological depth and social commentary done in a suitably cheezy manner. Also available with *House on Haunted Hill* on laser disc. 🦴🦴🦴🦴
1958 72m/B Allison Hayes, William Hudson, Roy Gordon; **D:** Nathan Hertz. **VHS, Beta, LV $14.98** *FOX, FCT*

Attack of the Giant Leeches

No lawyer jokes please. Cheapo Corman-produced fare about giant leeches in a murky swamp who suddenly decide to make human flesh their new food supply. Perturbed store keeper plays along by forcing his wife and lover into the murk. Leeches frolic. VeSota (*Daughter of Horror, The Undead*) is great as the cuckolded proprietor of the swampland's general store who's pushed a bit too far. Vickers (*Girls Town, Attack of the 50 Foot Woman*) is at her bad girl sexiest—it's a wonder that she hasn't left the swamp behind forever and run off to Hollywood. All this southern-fried melodrama is almost enough to make you forget about the monsters. Sometimes tedious, sometimes chilling, always low-budget and slimy. Especially disarming are the scenes in the underwater caves, as victims are kept at death's edge for periodic snacking by the loathsome leeches. Although the special effects aren't top notch, this might be a fine choice for a late night scare/laugh. Director Kowalski is often overshadowed by Corman, but he does a fine job here, and with the earlier *Night of the Blood Beast*. Twin billed with *A Bucket of Blood*. **AKA:** The Giant Leeches. 🎵🎵 👣

1959 62m/B Ken Clark, Yvette Vickers, Gene Roth, Bruno Ve Sota; *D:* Bernard L. Kowalski. **VHS $14.95** *VYY, SNC, NOS*

Attack of the Killer Refrigerator

Chiller featuring a group of sleazy college students having a wild party. In the process, they abuse a hapless refrigerator. Fed up, the vengeful appliance goes on a rampage of murder and destruction. Certain to make you view kitchen appliances in a new light. Planned sequels in the newfound kitchen-utility horror genre include *Refrigerator II: Brutally Defrosted* and *Bloody, Bloody Coffee Maker*. **WOOF!**

1990 ?m/C VHS *BFA*

Attack of the Killer Tomatoes

Candidate for worst film ever made, deliberate category. Horror spoof that defined "low budget" stars several thousand ordinary tomatoes that suddenly turn savage and begin attacking people. No sci-fi cliche remains untouched in this playfully silly parody. The action starts with a shot at *Jaws* as swimming tomatoes take on a hapless, bikini-clad swimmer. From there they stalk housewives ala slasher flicks and build up into a monstrous army bent on taking the country by force. This leads into a 50s' style confrontation between the U.S. army and the tomatoes that's not to be missed. The best line comes from a human who, disguised as a tomato, has infiltrated the tomato forces. As he and his new found veggie buddies sit around the campfire chumming it up, he commits the ultimate faux pas. "Anybody have some ketchup?" proves highly politically incorrect. Only a small band of cracked up, er, crack secret agents suspect the truth: that a single evil mastermind is controlling the tomatoes. Can they find and stop

him in time? (They must. After all, there are three sequels.) Winner of a "Golden Turkey" award, *Killer T's* also boasts an unforgettable title song along with a few lesser numbers. Disney re-released *Killer Tomatoes* as a special "Director's Cut" (can you stand it?) in 1995. 🎵🎵🎵 👣

1977 (PG) 87m/C George Wilson, Jack Riley; *D:* John DeBello. **VHS, Beta $19.95** *MED*

Attack of the Mushroom People

Secluded island is the site where castaways eating mysterious mushrooms have been turning into oversized, killer 'shrooms themselves. Trouble is, the only witness to this madness has gone insane. Will anyone believe him before it's too late? Despite the sensationalistic American title, this is a weirdly at-

"BAN THE B.L.T!"
Attack of the Killer Tomatoes.

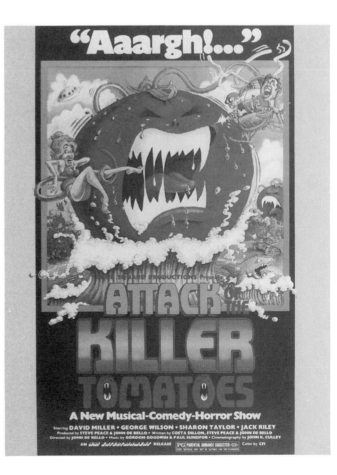

All of the Band films are notable for first rate production values, capable (if little known) casts, scripts that remain solidly within their genre and a dash (or more) of humor.

Admittedly, Band's films aren't going to make anyone forget *Close Encounters of the Third Kind*. They're not meant to. Instead, they're well-made, low-budget entertainment carefully aimed at fans of specific genres. As such, they deliver what they promise to the target audience.

mospheric horror film from the director of *Godzilla*. Art direction is excellent, as mold and fungus seem to be spreading from the corners of every frame. It's really creepy when those that have succumbed to hunger and begin to be transformed urge the others to "Come join us—it's delicious!" Marred by a ridiculous song performed by one of the boatniks before arriving at the island, the only lyrics for which are "La la la!" *AKA:* Matango; Fungus of Terror; Curse of the Mushroom People. 🦴🦴🦴

1963 70m/B *JP* Akira Kubo, Kenji Sahara, Yoshio Tsuchiya, Hiroshi Koizumi; *D:* Inoshiro Honda. **VHS** $20.00 *SMW*

Attack of the 60-Foot Centerfold

J. J. North, no stranger to Howard Stern listeners, gets her BIG break as Angel Grace, a model who desperately wants to be Centerfold of the Year. To enhance her already considerable endowments, she ingests an experimental formula that transforms her into a blonde behemoth. Another direct-to-video winner from Fred Olen Ray, director of *Bad Girls From Mars,* and *Hollywood Chainsaw Hookers.* Expect the best special effects a low budget can buy, hopeless acting, dumbfounding dialogue ("Help me, I'm huge"), movie in-jokes ("The doctor can't see you

now," a nurse says to the Invisible Man), incredibly gratuitous nudity and nostalgic cameos by Russ Tamblyn (*High School Confidential* and TV's *Twin Peaks*), Tommy Kirk (former Disney kid), and Stanley Livingston (Chip from TV's *My Three Sons*). 🦴🦴

1995 (R) 83m/C J.J. North, Tammy Parks, John Lazar; *Cameos:* Russ Tamblyn, Tommy Kirk, Stanley Livingston; *D:* Fred Olen Ray. **VHS** *NHO*

Attack of the Swamp Creature

A deranged scientist transforms himself into a giant walking catfish in order to wreak vengeance on colleagues who scoffed at this research. He also manages to abduct a few women on the side to create a race of genetically superior catfish-people for the usual world domination plans. Thoroughly unhinged Florida-lensed schlocker sports one of cinema's most jaw-droppingly ridiculous monsters ("Nothing at all like the catfish...but it's beautiful!") who is unwisely given maximum screen time to putter around his lab, draw pictures of intended victims, and visit Marineland with an atomizer, spritzing his fishy comrades with his mutation serum. Thriller Video's version has false credits and loses the doctor's loving pre-credits tribute to camouflaged marine life in favor of abundant hostess Elvira, whose interruptions into the movie are unwelcome and aren't as funny as the film itself. A more complete print runs on late-night TV under the title *Blood Waters of Dr. Z. AKA:* Blood Waters of Dr. Z; Zaat; The Legend of the Zaat Monster; Hydra. 🦴🦴🦴

1975 96m/C Frank Crowell, David Robertson; *D:* Arnold Stevens. **VHS, Beta $29.95** *LIV*

Auntie Lee's Meat Pies

Auntie Lee's meat pie business is booming thanks to her five beautiful nieces. They make their living with the old bump and grind: first they bump a guy off then they grind him up. Guys, you see, are the secret ingredient in the meat pies Auntie sells to support the family. While the talented Miss Black pursues her role with the appropriate maniacal quality, the rest of the cast is a bit dull, with the exception of Bowery Boy Huntz Hall. Four

Playboy Playmates make for some rather easy viewing nonetheless. Supposedly bizarre killings come off as too planned and other elements of intended humor, such as Morita's phoney Southern accent, never quite hit. Still, this film, billed as "A Cannibal Comedy With Taste," is quirky enough to watch. If you hated *The Karate Kid,* here's your chance to see Morita get his. Playmate Terry Weigel gained infamy as the first Playmate to do porno flicks. 𝄞𝄞 ▷

1992 (R) 100m/C Karen Black, Noriyuki "Pat" Morita, Pat Paulsen, Huntz Hall, Michael Berryman, David Parry, Stephen Quadros; *D:* Joseph F. Robertson. **VHS, LV $79.95** *COL*

Avenging Disco Godfather

Moore is a funky rappin' disco deejay who fights drug pushers on the side. When a teenage friend dies of an overdose, Moore goes after the gang that made him a junkie. At one point, he gets captured and has a dose forced on him, leading to a hokey, bargain-basement psychedelic trip sequence. Rudy indulges in parodies of *The Godfather* and martial arts movies. A feast of outrageously ugly mid-'70s fashions, but a step down from the Dolemite pictures. Title changes chart the rerelease pattern, trying to tap into whatever's hot at the time. *AKA:* Avenging Godfather; Disco Godfather. 𝄞𝄞

1976 (R) 99m/C Rudy Ray Moore, Lady Reed, Carol Speed, Jimmy Lynch; *D:* Rudy Ray Moore. **VHS, Beta $29.95** *XVC*

The Awful Dr. Orlof

Set in a bygone era, Dr. Orlof (Vernon) is a retired prison physician who needs unblemished skin to remedy the horrible disfigurement of his daughter Melissa (Lorys), ravaged by fire. He abducts promising young women candidates with the help of his blind zombie henchman Morpho (Valle), who simply cannot be trusted with a scalpel. After several surgical mishaps, they kidnap the perfect specimen, a woman who bears an uncanny resemblance to Melissa. Unfortunately, she is engaged to suspicious police Inspector Tanner (San Martin). French version with English subtitles that includes more explicit gore is also available. 𝄞𝄞 ▷

1962 86m/B Howard Vernon, Diana Lorys, Frank Wolff, Riccardo Valle, Conrado San Martin; *D:* Jess (Jesus) Franco; *M:* Jose Pagan, Antonio Ramirez Angel. **VHS $23.00** *SMW, VSM, TPV*

The Baby

Bizarre story of a social worker who resorts to swinging an ax to cut the apron strings of "baby," a retarded man-child, from his overprotective and insane (bad combination) mother and sisters. Low-budget production looks and feels like a low-budget production, but any movie featuring a grown man wandering about in diapers can't be all bad. 𝄞𝄞

1972 (PG) 85m/C Anjanette Comer, Ruth Roman, Marianna Hill, Suzanne Zenor, David Manzy, Michael Pataki; *D:* Ted Post. **VHS, Beta** *NO*

Back to the Beach

No way this should have worked, but it does! Old wave meets new wave in this affectionate spoof of the *Beach Party* series. Frankie Avalon and Annette Funicello (still fetching in polka dots) have a great time goofing on their screen images. They're married now. He's a stressed-out car salesman still riding on his "Big Kahuna" rep. She obliviously makes mountains of peanut butter sandwiches. With their punk rocker son (scene stealer Damien Slade), they makes waves when they pay a surprise visit to their daughter (Lori Loughlin) in Malibu. This is everything you'd want in a *Beach Party* movie. Bad girl Connie Francis tries to steal Frankie and makes wisecracks about Annette's breasts, Annette sings "Jamaica Ska," there's a pajama party, sizzling surf music by Dick Dale, and nostalgic guest stars, including Bob Denver and Alan Hale from *Gilligan's Island, Get Smart*'s Don Adams and Cleaver family members Barbara Billingsley, Tony Dow, and Jerry Mathers. Pee-Wee Herman inexplicably shows up to sing "Surfin' Bird." ♫ Absolute Perfection; California Sun; Catch a Ride; Jamaica Sky; Papa-Oom-Mow-Mow; Sign of Love; Sun, Sun, Sun, Sun, Sun; Surfin' Bird; Wooly Bully. 𝄞𝄞𝄞

1987 (PG) 92m/C Frankie Avalon, Annette Funicello, Connie Stevens, Jerry Mathers, Bob Denver, Barbara Billingsley, Tony Dow, Paul (Pee Wee Herman) Reubens, Edd Byrnes, Dick Dale, Don Adams, Lori Loughlin; *D:* Lyndall Hobbs; *M:* Stephen Dorff. **VHS, Beta, LV $19.95** *PAR*

THE HOUND SALUTES: PAUL BARTEL
Bartel, Bangles, Bright Shiny Beads

How can one identify a potential cult movie before seeing it? Simple. Administer what is scientifically known as a PH test-standing for "Paul's here." If Paul Bartel has something to do with a flick, it's definitely strange.

After studying film at UCLA and in Italy, the actor/director/writer/producer made his mark with *The Secret Cinema*, a now-famous $5,000 black-and-white short subject about a woman who discovers her whole life is being surreptitiously filmed and screened for the enjoyment of voyeuristic New Yorkers. Bartel's 1972 feature debut *Private Parts* also emphasized themes of paranoia and voyeurism, along with kinkiness and satirical decadence that tend to surface repeatedly throughout Bartel's career, whether he's behind the cameras (*Eating Raoul, Lust in the Dust*) or acting for other filmmakers, in the likes of *Amazon Women of the Moon* or *Desire and Hell at the Sunset Motel*. Portly, bearded, and cultured, Bartel has the demeanor of a somewhat seedy liberal-arts professor-- which is exactly how he's cast in *Rock 'n' Roll High School* and *Killer Party*.

Some of Bartel's most successful work has been in collaboration with laser-eyed cult actress/writer/painter Mary Woronov (also in both *Rock 'n' Roll High School* movies). In the dark-comedy classic *Eating Raoul* (1982) they starred as Paul and Mary Bland, an ambitious California couple of would-be restaurateurs who go from the sex business to murder with the same blase attitude. Paul and Mary Bland reappeared briefly in Roger Corman's *Chopping Mall*, and Bartel later adapted *Eating Raoul* as a stage musical.

Home-video fans can't help but encounter Bartel and Woronov in their many cameos together and separately. And for those who want a look at vintage Bartel, the original *Secret Cinema* has been released on video, as has Bartel's own lavish remake done in 1986 for Steven Spielberg's *Amazing Stories* TV show.

Bad Channels

Radio goes awry when female listeners of station KDUL are shrunk and put into specimen jars by a visiting alien, who plans to take the women back to his planet. Opposing the thing from beyond is a way-out disc jockey trapped in the radio station our visitor is using as a Holiday Inn. Hokey as it sounds, there is some entertainment value here. In the end one of the girls is left in her diminutive state, setting up a semi-sequel, *Dollman Vs. The Demonic Toys,* featuring little aliens and demons from several other Band productions. Mildly amusing comedy from the Full Moon factory features ex-MTV VJ Quinn and score by Blue Oyster Cult. Also available with Spanish subtitles. ♫♫

1992 (R) 88m/C Paul Hipp, Martha Quinn, Aaron Lustig, Ian Patrick Williams, Charlie Spradling; **D:** Ted Nicolaou; **W:** Jackson Barr. **VHS, Beta** *PAR*

Bad Girls from Mars

"B" movie sleaze-o-rama in which everyone is murdered, either before, after, or during sex, just like in real life. When the director of the film within this film hires an actress who is, shall we say, popular, to be the heroine of his latest sci-fier, the fun, slim as it is, begins. ♫♫

1990 (R) 86m/C Edy Williams, Brinke Stevens, Jay Richardson, Oliver Darrow; **D:** Fred Olen Ray; **W:** Sherman Scott, Mark Thomas McGee. **VHS $89.95** *VMK*

Bad Girls Go to Hell

From the sultana of sleaze, Wishman, comes this story of a ditsy-but-sexy housewife who accidentally commits murder; what follows is a plethora of perversion involving hirsute men and gender-bending women who are hell-bent on showing her how hot it is where bad girls go. **WOOF!**

1965 98m/B D: Doris Wishman; **W:** Doris Wishman. **VHS $19.98** *VTR*

The Bad Lieutenant

Social chaos and degeneration characterize story as well as nameless loner lieutenant Keitel, who is as corrupt as they come. Assigned to a case involving a raped nun, he's con-

fronted by his own lagging Catholic beliefs and the need for saving grace. From cult filmmaker Ferrara (*Ms. 45*) and filled with violence, drugs, and grotesque sexual situations. Tense, over-the-top, urban drama is not intended for seekers of the subtle. Rent it with *Reservoir Dogs* and prepare yourself for a long tense evening of top-rated Keitel and screen-splitting violence. "R" rated version is also available at 91 minutes. 🎜🎜🎜

1992 (NC-17) 98m/C Harvey Keitel, Brian McElroy, Frankie Acciario, Peggy Gormley, Stella Keitel, Victor Argo, Paul Calderone, Leonard Thomas, Frankie Thorn; *D:* Abel Ferrara; *W:* Zoe Tamerlaine Lund, Abel Ferrara; *M:* Joe Delia. Independent Spirit Awards '93: Best Actor (Keitel). **VHS, LV $19.98** *LIV, FCT*

The Bad Seed

When syrupy sweet little Rhoda (McCormack) loses a school prize to another student, she throws a tantrum, and later her rival turns up dead. The sneaky gardener (Jones) seems to know something, but dies in a suspicious fire before he can tell. Mom (Kelly) must face the fact that her little daughter may have inherited her mental problems. Maxwell Anderson's stage play is softened slightly for Hollywood, but still caused a sensation. Warners' efforts to head off controversy included changing the ending and including a hilariously silly curtain call, in which McCormack receives a sound spanking for committing heinous murders. The cast, many from the Broadway version, turn in some fine performances. Nicely directed by LeRoy, a former actor and silent comedy gag writer who eventually directed many screen classics, including *Little Caesar, Little Women* (1949), *Mr. Roberts,* and *FBI Story.* Little Patty grew up to appear in *Maryjane, The Mini-Skirt Mob,* and *Bug.* Remade for TV in 1985. 🎜🎜🎜

1956 129m/B Patty McCormack, Nancy Kelly, Eileen Heckart, Henry Jones, Evelyn Varden, Paul Fix; *D:* Mervyn LeRoy; *M:* Alex North. Golden Globe Awards '57: Best Supporting Actress (Heckart); Nominations: Academy Awards '56: Best Actress (Kelly), Best Black and White Cinematography, Best Supporting Actress (Heckart, McCormack). **VHS, Beta $59.95** *WAR*

The Bad Seed

Television remake of the 1956 Mervyn LeRoy movie with the same name. Story about a

sadistic little child who kills for her own evil purposes. Despite the fine cast, acting is not up to par with previous version. Neither is direction, cinematography, or anything else for that matter, although decent TV movies are a very rarely made. Do yourself a favor and watch the original instead. Wendkos started out directing Jayne Mansfield in *The Burglar* (1956), but is probably best known as a television director, and for the *Gidget* movies he made in the 1960s. 🎜🎜

1985 100m/C Blair Brown, Lynn Redgrave, David Carradine, Richard Kiley, David Ogden Stiers, Carrie Wells; *D:* Paul Wendkos. **VHS $59.95** *NO*

Bad Taste

A definite pleaser for the person who enjoys watching starving aliens devour the average, everyday human being. Alien fast-food manufacturers come to earth in hopes of harvesting all of humankind. The earth's fate lies in the hands of the government investigative team who must stop these rampaging creatures before the whole human race is gobbled up. Terrific make-up jobs on the aliens add the final touch to this gory, yet humorous cult horror flick. Amazingly, actor/director Jackson financed this, his first feature, as well as his next two, with grant money from the New Zealand government designated for indigenous film production—probably the only government grant to the arts ever given to a project that turned a profit. Jackson followed this with the wicked adult puppet film *Meet the Feebles.* 🎜🎜🎜

1988 90m/C *NZ* Peter Jackson, Pete O'Herne, Mike Minett, Terry Potter, Craig Smith, Doug Wren, Dean Lawrie; *D:* Peter Jackson. **VHS, LV $19.95** *FCT*

Badlands

Based loosely on the Charlie Starkweather murders of the 1950s, this impressive debut by director Malick recounts a slow-thinking, unhinged misfit's killing spree across the midwestern plains, accompanied by a starry-eyed 15-year-old schoolgirl. Sheen and Spacek are a disturbingly numb, apathetic, and icy duo. Oates, as always, makes the most of a key supporting role. The film defies conventions by leaving loose ends—what happens to the

> "**They got a little blue chair for little boys and a little pink chair for little girls.**"
> --Henry Jones warning the Bad Seed (Patty McCormack) about the wages of murder in *The Bad Seed.*

> "**I'll give you a dollar if you eat this collie.**"
> --Martin Sheen in *Badlands.*

Space nymphet Jane Fonda and Ted Turner look-alike John Phillip Law express their emotional range in *Barbarella*.

The Banker

Imagine what would happen if Jack the Ripper had a Sharper Image catalogue and an American Express Gold Card. He'd go out and buy all sorts of neat grown-up toys, like a crossbow with a laser sight, and use them to murder prostitutes. That's exactly what's going on in this one. The title character (Regehr) is a wealthy financier whose real passions are primitive religions and Snow White and the Seven Dwarfs. The rest of the cast are familiar B-movie stereotypes: veteran streetwise cop, rookie partner, TV newswoman. These three walking cliches threaten to sink the story in predictability, but the script is too smart for that. It becomes crazier and funnier as it goes along. Regehr manages to make a completely unbelievable character seem real, frightening, and funny, all at the same time. At key points, director Webb suggests more than he shows—the graphic violence takes place off-screen—making this one a potent guilty pleasure. Webb went on to make the Steven Seagal hit *Under Siege.* 🦴🦴🦴▷

1989 (R) 90m/C Robert Forster, Jeff Conaway, Leif Garrett, Duncan Regehr, Shanna Reed, Deborah Richter, Richard Roundtree, Teri Weigel, E.J. Peaker; **D:** William Webb. **VHS, Beta, LV** *NO*

young couple in the outbuilding?—and refusing either to glamorize or demonize its subjects. After following this one with the even more dazzling *Days of Heaven* in 1978, Malick virtually vanished from the entertainment business. 🦴🦴🦴▷

1974 (PG) 94m/C Martin Sheen, Sissy Spacek, Warren Oates; **D:** Terence Malick; **W:** Terence Malick. **VHS, Beta, LV $39.98** *WAR*

Bambi Meets Godzilla

A spoof on endless film credits, after which follows the classic clash between these two cinematic titans. A visual "one line" joke, this animated treasure must be seen to be appreciated. Available on the same tape as the wacky *Hardware Wars.* 🦴🦴🦴▷

1969 2m/B D: Marv Newland. **VHS, Beta $9.95** *PYR*

Barbarella

The popular French comic strip by Jean-Claude Forest comes to life in this wildly campy space opera. Fonda (Mrs. Vadim at the time) stars as the sexy bimbo sent by Earth's president in search of evil genius Duran Duran (O'Shea), who has invented a new positronic ray weapon and is hiding out in a decadent city that has returned to a barbaric state of "neurotic irresponsibility." In order to complete her mission, she must face biting dolls, leather robots, a blind angel (Law), the wicked Black Queen (Pallenberg), a clumsy revolutionary (Hemmings), and a living labyrinth, all while appearing in (and out of) eight eccentric, sexy outfits (designed by Jaques Fonteray). An attention-getting opening features Fonda in her famous zero-G strip tease. Since the acting and f/x are no better than the old *Flash Gordon* serials, and the script is so silly, the stagebound production design takes the spotlight. The sets, by art director Mario Garbuglia, are nearly the whole show, walking the line between futuristic stylishness and cheesy '60s prefab. Sure to be a delight to some, but tiresome to others—if you like this, you should check out other '60s Eurotrash sci-fi, such as *Wild, Wild Planet, Mission Stardust,* and *Danger: Diabolik* (also with Law). **AKA:** Barbarella, Queen of the Galaxy. ♫ ♫ ▷

1968 (PG) 98m/C Jane Fonda, John Phillip Law, David Hemmings, Marcel Marceau, Anita Pallenberg, Milo O'Shea; **D:** Roger Vadim; **W:** Terry Southern; **M:** Charles Fox. **VHS, Beta, LV $19.98** *FUS, PAR*

Barn of the Naked Dead

Perennial drive-in maniac Prine (*Grizzly, Simon, King of the Witches*) plays a circus-obsessed sicko who tortures waylaid showgirls in the eponymous shed while his radioactive monster dad runs amuck in the Nevada desert. Tawdry, scareless picture tries vainly for feminist subtext ("We're not the animals—you are!") but hard to see in light of endless whipping and mistreatment of women (who don't get naked, FYI). Mutant papa is dumb 50's style fun though. Rudolph's first film, directed/produced under the pseudonym Gerald Cormier (his later films could've used a few radioactive monsters too). **AKA:** Terror Circus; Nightmare Circus. ♫ ▷

1973 86m/C Andrew Prine, Manuella Thiess, Sherry Alberoni, Gylian Roland, Al Cormier, Jennifer Ashley; **D:** Alan Rudolph. **VHS** *NO*

Based on an Untrue Story

Campy spoof of popular "true story" television docudramas in which powerful Satin Chau (Fairchild), a perfume mogul, loses her sense of smell. Satin leaves her mentor Varda (Cannon) to discovery herself but finds that only her two separated-at-birth sisters, Velour (Lake) and Corduroy (Jackson), hold the secrets to the past. It's hard to spoof a genre that's become a cliche but this television movie does its best. ♫ ♫ ▷

1993 90m/C Morgan Fairchild, Dyan Cannon, Victoria Jackson, Ricki Lake, Harvey Korman, Robert Goulet, Dan Hedaya; **D:** Jim Drake. **VHS** *FXV*

Basket Case

A gory and amusing horror film about a pair of Siamese twins—one normal, the other gruesomely deformed. The pair were surgically separated at birth, and the evil disfigured twin was tossed in the garbage. Fraternal ties being what they are, the normal brother (Kevin Van Hentenryck) retrieved his twin—essentially a head atop shoulders—and totes him around in a basket (he ain't heavy). Together they begin twisted and deadly revenge, with the brother-in-a-basket in charge. Very entertaining, if you like this sort of thing (and the Hound does). Followed by two sequels, and if you still haven't had enough, watch director Henenlotter's *Brain Damage* for a cameo by Van Hentenryck. ♫ ♫ ♫

1982 89m/C Kevin Van Hentenryck, Terri Susan Smith, Beverly Bonner; **D:** Frank Henenlotter. **VHS, Beta, LV $19.95** *MED*

Basket Case 2

The original *Basket Case,* a horror comedy about a "normal" young man and his hideously deformed Siamese "twin," is one of the most bizarre exercises in excess ever committed to film or videotape. With its grimy, grainy look, relatively restrained special effects, and bizarre sense of humor, it became a solid cult hit. The disappointing sequel is a comparatively expensive production, but in this case, more is definitely less. Most of the action takes place on clean well-lighted sets with a glossy "Hollywood" look. The plot ignores key aspects of the first film. Until the conclusion, when writer/director Henenlotter does manage to twist some kinks into the action, the plot ambles along without focus or the raw craziness that drove the original. ♫ ▷

1990 (R) 90m/C Kevin Van Hentenryck, Annie Ross, Kathryn Meisle, Heather Rattray, Jason Evers, Ted Sorel, Matt Mitler; **D:** Frank Henenlotter; **W:** Frank Henenlotter; **M:** Joe Renzetti. **VHS, Beta, LV $9.99** *STE, IME, SGE*

Basket Case 3: The Progeny

In this sequel to the cult horror hits *Basket Case* and *Basket Case 2*, Belial is back and this time he's about to discover the perils of parenthood as the mutant Mrs. Belial delivers a litter of bouncing mini-monsters. Everything is fine until the police kidnap the little creatures and chaos breaks out as Belial goes on a shocking rampage in his newly created me-

Battle Beyond the Stars

A real find. *Star Wars* meets *The Seven Samurai* in one of Roger Corman's most ambitious productions. Richard Thomas is a long way from Walton mountain as he zooms about the galaxy recruiting warriors and space fighters to defend his peaceful planet from attack. John Sayles's script is loaded with in-jokes (the planet is named Akir in honor of *Seven Samurai* director Akira Kurosawa). Cast members George Peppard and Robert Vaughn (who starred in the *Samurai* remake, *The Magnificent Seven* and got his start in Corman's *Teenage Caveman*) play it loose, and just get a load of B-movie queen Sybil Danning's gravity-defying space suit. Action-meister Jim Cameron, who would go on to direct *The Terminator* films, *Aliens*, *The Abyss* and *True Lies*, served as art director. 🦴🦴🦴

1980 (PG) 105m/C Richard Thomas, Robert Vaughn, George Peppard, Sybil Danning, Sam Jaffe, John Saxon, Darlanne Fluegel; *D:* Jimmy T. Murakami; *W:* John Sayles; *M:* James Horner. **VHS, Beta, LV $19.98** *VES, LIV*

chanical body. Weird special effects make this a cult favorite for fans of the truly outrageous. 🦴🦴🦴

1992 (R) 90m/C Annie Ross, Kevin Van Hentenryck, Gil Roper, Tina Louise Hilbert, Dan Biggers, Jim O'-Doherty; *D:* Frank Henenlotter; *W:* Robert Martin, Frank Henenlotter; *M:* Joe Renzetti. **VHS $19.98** *MCA, SGE*

Batman

Holy television camp, Batman! Will the caped crusader win the Bat-tle against the combined forces of the Joker, the Riddler, the Penguin, and Catwoman? Will Batman and Robin save the United World Security Council from dehydration? Will the Bat genius ever figure out that Russian journalist Miss Kitka and Catwoman are one and the same? Biff! Thwack! Socko! Not to be confused with the Michael Keaton version of the Dark Knight, this is the pot-bellied Adam West Batman, teeming with Bat satire and made especially for the big screen. 🦴🦴🦴

1966 104m/C Burt Ward, Adam West, Burgess Meredith, Cesar Romero, Frank Gorshin, Lee Meriwether; *D:* Leslie Martinson. **VHS, Beta, LV $19.98** *FOX*

Battle Beyond the Sun

Former Russian movie *Niebo Zowiet* is Americanized. Everyone is trying to send a mission to Mars. Roger Corman was the producer; Francis Ford Coppola used the pseudonym "Thomas Colchart." 🦴🦴

1963 75m/C Edd Perry, Arla Powell, Bruce Hunter, Andy Stewart; *D:* Francis Ford Coppola; *M:* Les Baxter. **VHS $16.95** *NOS, SNC*

Battle for the Planet of the Apes

North America, 2670 A.D., brings us an old orangutan telling young chimps the story of ape history in this final chapter in the five-movie simian saga. His tale begins with Cornelius and Zera descending "upon Earth from Earth's own future to bring a savior, Caesar." The plot for this movie, told primarily in flashback, involves a tribe of human atomic bomb mutations who are out to make life miserable for the peaceful ape tribe. Some hard-to-follow time transformations (the old orangutan speaks of "changing lanes" in timelines) makes it difficult to put the whole series in perspective (if anyone besides the Hound was trying). 🦴🦴

1973 (G) 96m/C Roddy McDowall, Lew Ayres, John Huston, Paul Williams, Claude Akins, Severn Darden, Natalie Trundy; **D:** J. Lee Thompson. **VHS, Beta** $19.98 *FOX*

Battle of the Bombs

Collection of excerpts from the worst films of all time, including Arch Hall's *Eegah!* and *Wild Guitar.* Plus *Wild Women of Wongo, The Creeping Terror, The House of Mutant Women,* and the Ed Wood-scripted *Orgy of the Dead.* Some of these titles are worth seeing in their entirety, but this cassette makes a fun sampler, and concludes with a complete short subject, a laughable tent-show cautionary cheapie about "poor Sheila," an innocent who seeks stardom in Hollywood (impersonated by about three or four bare rooms and a field) and learns to regret it. That one alone makes this worth a rental. 🦴🦴

1985 60m/C VHS, Beta $39.95 *RHI*

Beach Blanket Bingo

The gang goes sky-diving and Frankie falls for Linda Evans in the fourth—and one of the best—in the *Beach Party* series. The guest star quotient is high, with Don Rickles as "Big Drop," Paul Lynde as "Bullets," who manages singer Evans, and Buster Keaton. Harvey Lembeck reprises his classic role as imbecilic motorcycle leader Eric Von Zipper, whose gang kidnaps Evans. Lest anyone believe that these films paint an accurate portrait of teenage life in the '60s, one of the subplots involves Jody McCrea (as the aptly named Bonehead) falling in love with a mermaid. Followed by *How to Stuff a Wild Bikini.* 🎵 Beach Blanket Bingo; The Cycle Set; Fly Boy; The Good Times; I Am My Ideal; I Think You Think; It Only Hurts When I Cry; New Love; You'll Never Change Him. 🦴🦴🦴

1965 96m/C Frankie Avalon, Annette Funicello, Linda Evans, Don Rickles, Buster Keaton, Paul Lynde, Harvey Lembeck, Deborah Walley, John Ashley, Jody McCrea, Marta Kristen, Timothy Carey, Earl Wilson, Bobbi Shaw; **D:** William Asher; **W:** Sher Townsend, Leo Townsend; **M:** Les Baxter. **VHS, Beta, LV** *NO*

The Beach Girls and the Monster

Here's one on the cutting edge of genre bending: while it meticulously maintains the philosophical depth and production values of '60s beach bimbo fare, it manages to graft successfully with the heinous critter from the sea genre to produce a hybrid horror with acres o'flesh. 🦴

1965 70m/B Jon Hall, Sue Casey, Walker Edmiston; **D:** Jon Hall; **M:** Frank Sinatra Jr. **VHS $19.98** *SNC*

Beach Party

The success of *Gidget* and *Where the Boys Are* inspired B-movie studio American-International to shift from bikers to beachniks. Meet Frankie, Dee Dee, Deadhead, and the rest of the gang who spend their time "surfin' all day and swingin' all night." Harvey Lembeck does his Brando bit as not-so-wild-one Eric Von Zipper, a moronic motorcycle gang leader, whom he portrayed in seven of the Beach movies. Robert Cummings stars as an anthropologist studying the sex lives of

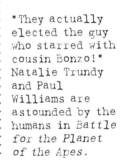

"They actually elected the guy who starred with cousin Bonzo!" Natalie Trundy and Paul Williams are astounded by the humans in *Battle for the Planet of the Apes.*

teenagers. With Morey Amsterdam (Buddy on *The Dick Van Dyke Show*), Beach Boy Brian Wilson as—what else—a surfer, and Vincent Price in a cameo. The music is by the big kahuna of the surf guitar, Dick Dale, who got big play on the *Pulp Fiction* soundtrack. One of the bikers is Peter "Columbo" Falk. The very definition of summer camp. *Muscle Beach Party* was next. ♪♪ Beach Party; Don't Stop Now; Promise Me Anything; Secret Surfin' Spot; Surfin' and a-Swingin'; Treat Him Nicely. 🐾🐾🐾

1963 101m/C Frankie Avalon, Annette Funicello, Harvey Lembeck, Robert Cummings, Dorothy Malone, Morey Amsterdam, Jody McCrea, John Ashley, Candy Johnson, Dolores Wells, Yvette Vickers, Eva Six, Brian Wilson, Peter Falk; *Cameos:* Vincent Price; *D:* William Asher; *W:* Lou Rusoff; *M:* Les Baxter. **VHS, Beta** *NO*

Beaks: The Movie

Two TV reporters try to figure out why birds of prey worldwide are suddenly attacking humans. At least the distributors knew they had a turkey on their hand with this blood-drenched bit of guano that rips off Hitchcock's *The Birds*; they promoted the videocassette release as an *Airplane!*-style comedy, even though the feature itself is meant to be serious. *AKA:* Birds of Prey. **WOOF!**

1987 (R) 86m/C Christopher Atkins, Michelle Johnson; *D:* Rene Cardona Jr. **VHS, Beta $14.95** *LIV*

The Beast from 20,000 Fathoms

Atomic testing defrosts a giant dinosaur in the Arctic; the hungry monster (the fictional "Rhedosaurus") proceeds onwards to its former breeding grounds, now New York City. Oft-imitated and highly successful saurian-on-the-loose formula (which debuted back in 1925 with *The Lost World*) is still fun, brought to life by Ray Harryhausen special effects. Based loosely on the Ray Bradbury story "The Foghorn." Once art director for Renoir, this was Lourie's first film as director, and he brings to it a great deal of noirish grit—the scenes in which the beast attacks a diving bell being especially atmospheric. He would come to specialize in monster epics, helming *The Colossus of New York, The Giant Behe-*

moth, and *Gorgo,* before returning to art direction. 🐾🐾🐾🐾

1953 80m/B Paul Christian, Paula Raymond, Cecil Kellaway, Kenneth Tobey, Donald Woods, Lee Van Cleef, Steve Brodie, Mary Hill; *D:* Eugene Lourie. **VHS, Beta, LV $19.95** *WAR, FCT, MLB*

The Beast of Yucca Flats

A really cheap, quasi-nuclear protest film. A Russian scientist is chased by communist agents into a nuclear testing area and is caught in an atomic blast. As a result, he turns into a club-wielding monster. Droning voice over narration is used in lieu of dialogue as that process proved too expensive. Tor doesn't have much to do besides wander around; his fellow Wood crony Conrad Brooks shows up as a Federal agent. Characters spend lots and lots of time climbing up and down hills. Director/writer/actor Francis was in lots of B westerns in the '40s and '50s. He later made *The Skydivers* and *Red Zone Cuba,* before ending up doing bit parts in movies for Russ Meyer and Ray Dennis Steckler. 🐾

1961 53m/B Tor Johnson, Douglas Mellor, Larry Aten, Conrad Brooks, Barbara Francis; *D:* Coleman Francis; *W:* Coleman Francis. **VHS $12.95** *SNC, CNM, MLB*

The Beast that Killed Women

Colonists at a sunny Florida nudist camp have their beach party interrupted by an escaped gorilla that sneaks into the camp every night to kill women and push guys into the pool. Director Mahon (*Rocket Attack USA*), in his first color effort, stretches these panicky moments into an hour of fleshy fun and games, with long stretches of dialogue between heavily accented topless women. Mostly told in flashback to provide convenient narration. One of the worst ape costumes in movie history. 🐾

1965 60m/C *D:* Barry Mahon; *W:* Barry Mahon. **VHS $24.95** *SMW, TPV*

The Beast Within

Young woman has the misfortune of being raped by an unseen creature in a Mississippi swamp. Seventeen years later, her son conceived from that hellish union begins to act quite strange, developing a penchant for shedding his skin before turning into an insect-like critter with a cannibalistic appetite. First film to use the air "bladder" type of prosthetic make-up popularized in later, and generally better, horror films. Contains some choice cuts in photo editing: the juxtaposition of hamburger and human "dead meat" is witty. Based on Edward Levy's 1981 novel. ♫ ♫ ▷

1982 (R) 98m/C Ronny Cox, Bibi Besch, L.Q. Jones, Paul Clemens, Don Gordon; *D:* Philippe Mora; *W:* Tom Holland; *M:* Les Baxter. **VHS, Beta $14.95** *MGM*

Beastmaster

The sentence is handed down to evil cult priest Rip Torn: "You are banished. No one will remember your name." It is more likely that the award-winning star of HBO's *The Larry Sanders Show* wishes that no one will remember this sword, sorcery, and sandals epic. Marc Singer stars as our blonde hero, who could teach Tarzan and Doctor Doolittle a thing or two about talking to the animals. Perhaps it's because his surrogate mother was a cow (don't ask). Tanya Roberts co-stars as a feisty slave girl, with John *Good Times* Amos as the mohawked Seth, who takes the Beastmaster under his wing, so to speak. There are also two ferrets for comic relief. Not without its campy charms. Believe it or not, this is one of cable TV's most dependable programs. Director Don Coscarelli is better known for *Phantasm*. ♫ ♫

1982 (PG) 119m/C Marc Singer, Tanya Roberts, Rip Torn, John Amos, Josh Milrad, Billy Jacoby; *D:* Don A. Coscarelli. **VHS, Beta, LV $19.98** *MGM*

Beat Girl

An architect's rebellious teenage daughter sinks to the bottom and gets involved with murder along the way. Starlet Noelle Adam never did become the British Bardot, but composer John Barry went on to write the James Bond theme. Christopher Lee and Oliver Reed give this modest JD picture a boost, and were it not for the "angry young men" who were already re-invigorating the cinema of delinquency, it may have had a chance. *AKA:* Wild For Kicks. ♫ ♫

1960 85m/B *GB* David Farrar, Noelle Adam, Christopher Lee, Gillian Hills, Shirley Anne Field, Oliver Reed; *D:* Edmond T. Greville; *M:* John Barry. **VHS $29.95** *SNC, FCT, HEG*

Beat the Devil

"Fatgut is my best friend. I will not betray him cheaply." Enroute by boat to Africa, Humphrey Bogart, wife Gina Lollobrigida, and a motley crew of "thoroughly bad guys" race to gain control over land that may contain a fortune in uranium. Their downfall is hastened by Jennifer Jones, a pathological liar, and her seemingly dimwitted husband. Mere plot synopsis does not begin to do justice to this quirky gem written by Truman Capote and directed by John Huston. Peter Lorre costars as a blonde German named O'Hara, but who should steal the show but a hookah-puffing Arab police officer who yearns to meet Rita Hayworth (practically swooning, he asked Bogie, "You are certain that you are a friend of the peerless Rita?"). It's a spoof, its defenders claim, but one played with an absolutely straight face. Audiences at first didn't get the joke, but over the years, *Beat the Devil* has gotten the last laugh by attracting a devoted cult following. As our Arab friend states upon gazing at this extraordinary cast of characters, "One look is not enough." ♫ ♫ ♫

1953 89m/C Humphrey Bogart, Gina Lollobrigida, Peter Lorre, Robert Morley, Jennifer Jones; *D:* John Huston. **VHS, Beta, LV $9.95** *MRV, NOS, COL*

The Beautiful, the Bloody and the Bare

Sordid screamer in the Herschell Gordon Lewis tradition. Set in New York City in the '60s, a depraved photographer named Pete is obsessed with the color red, which sends him into a blood frenzy. Inevitably, he starts killing the nude models who pose for him. With the nudie-cutie cycle drawing to a close, filmmakers trying to spice things up began to add all manner of weirdness to their naked lady epics, including comedy, drama, gore, science fiction, and in rare cases even plot. Johnson would later direct the bad girl classic *Teenage Gang Debs*. ♫ ▷

1969 ?m/C Adela Rogers St. John, Marlene Denes, Debra Page; *D:* Sande N. Johnson. **VHS $24.99** *MOV*

Bedazzled

Don't let Dudley Moore's failed sitcoms or such bombs as *Blame It on the Bellboy* put

B

MOVIES THAT NEVER WERE

You can search high and low, but you won't find any of the following titles on video-no, not even bootlegged from Japanese laser imports. That's because they don't exist. These are fictitious films, a spurious cinema dreamt up within the plot confines of real movies. Too bad; some of them sound pretty good. And others, well...

See You Next Wednesday. John Landis in-joke that is referred to in most of his movies (first appearing in *Schlock*); taken from a line of dialogue in *2001: A Space Odyssey.*

My Burning Bush. The title of the trash playing at Francine Fishpaw's (Divine) husband's porn theatre in *Polyester,* one of the many banes of her troubled existence in this John Waters' melodramatic spoof.

That's Armageddon and **A Fist Full of Yen.** Two of the many send-ups in *Kentucky Fried Movie.*

Dr. Tongue's 3-D House of Stewardesses. A midnight movie gem hosted by Count Floyd (Joe Flaherty) on TV's *SCTV.*

Disaster '76. From *Drive-In* (1976), a cheesy comedy about rowdy doings during a typical night at a Texas drive-in. Glimpsed throughout is this goofy pastiche of popular '70s pics; a crippled airliner crashes into a towering inferno during an earthquake and flood, pitting survivors against a great white shark. Final line: "Someday they'll rebuild Rio."

The Stand-Up. An intense portrait of an alcoholic night-club comic, this is an obsessive project of driven, dissolute director/choreographer Roy Scheider in Bob Fosse's bitterly autobiographical *All That Jazz* (1979). An undisguised takeoff on Fosse's own *Lenny.*

Night Wind. Blake Edward's vengeful Hollywood satire *S.O.B.* (1981) concerns this wholesome family musical that flops. Crazed director Richard Mulligan proceeds to reshoot *Night Wind* as erotic sex-travaganza, complete with a topless Julie Andrews. Inspired by—though not resembling—Edward's own ill-fated *Darling Lili.*

Mutants of 2051 A.D. Bob & Doug McKenzie's homemade postnuke cheapie gets an abortive premiere at the start of *Strange Brew* (1983). "Fleshy headed mutant, are you friend or foe?" "No way, eh. Radiation has made me an enemy of humanity!"

continued...

you off this classic British comedy. Moore and his better half, Peter Cook, wrote and star in this stylish, mod take-off of Faust. Moore is a hapless, lovelorn short-order cook who sells his soul for seven wishes. Cook is the Devil, who thwarts Moore's increasingly desperate bids to impress waitress Eleanor Bron. At one point, Moore becomes an animated fly on the wall. Don't ask how, but he winds up as a member of an order of trampoline-jumping nuns! Posing as a disdainful pop star, Cook sings the title song (with the memorable lyric, "You fill me with inertia"). Raquel Welch was born to play Lilian Lust, "the babe with the bust." Eleanor Bron co-starred with the Beatles in *Help.* 🎵🎵🎵🎵
1968 (PG) 107m/C *GB* Dudley Moore, Peter Cook, Eleanor Bron, Michael Bates, Raquel Welch; *D:* Stanley Donen; *W:* Dudley Moore, Peter Cook; *M:* Dudley Moore. **VHS, Beta, LV** *FOX*

Bedlam

Creeper set in the famed St. Mary of Bethlehem asylum in 18th-century London. After rebuffing the advances of her benefactor, the powerful Lord Mortimer (House), an actress (Anna Lee) is wrongfully committed, where she is at the mercy of the evil Master Sims (Karloff). Her only hope is to gain help from a gentle Quaker (Fraser) whom she'd ridiculed, and from the insane social structure of her frightening fellow inmates. Fine horror film and historical drama co-written by producer Lewton, with a good cast including Robert Clarke, Skelton Knaggs, and Elizabeth Russell in small roles. Chills flow during the asylum scenes. A series of Hogarth sketches served as inspiration. 🎵🎵🎵
1945 79m/B Jason Robards Sr., Ian Wolfe, Glenn Vernon, Boris Karloff, Anna Lee, Billy House, Richard Fraser, Robert Clarke, Elizabeth Russell, Skelton Knaggs; *D:* Mark Robson. **VHS, Beta, LV $19.95** *TTC, MED, FCT*

Bedtime for Bonzo

Environment versus heredity: the dilemma that was at the heart of some of the Three Stooges' best shorts is revived here with professor Ronald Reagan adopting simian Bonzo to prove "that even a monkey brought up in the right surroundings can learn the meaning of decency and honesty." He's engaged to Lucille Barkley, the dean's haughty daughter, but he falls in love with sweet Diana Lynn, Bonzo's nanny. Reagan's theories are put to the test when Bonzo steals some jewelry. Directed by Fred De Cordova, best known as Johnny Carson's *Tonight Show* producer. He also directed *Here Come the Nelsons, Frankie and Johnny* starring Elvis Presley, and *I'll Take Sweden* starring Bob Hope. Veteran character actor Jesse White, the skeptical cop investigating the jewel heist, was TV commercials' original Maytag repairman. Reagan made better films (*King's Row, The Killers*), but once he announced his presidential ambitions, this is the one that came back to haunt him. Followed by *Bonzo Goes to College.* ♫♫ ▷

1951 83m/B Ronald Reagan, Diana Lynn, Walter Slezak, Lucille Barkley, Jesse White, Bonzo the Chimp; **D:** Fred de Cordova. **VHS, Beta** $14.95 *MCA, FCT*

Beginning of the End

Produced the same year as *The Deadly Mantis*, Gordon's effort adds to 1957's harvest of bugs on a rampage "B"-graders. Giant, radia-tion-spawned grasshoppers attack Chicago, causing Graves to come to the rescue. Easily the best giant grasshopper movie ever made. You'll never forget the sound of all those giant legs rubbing together. Graves (*It Conquered the World*), Ankrum (*Earth Vs. the Flying Saucers*), and even Castle (*Target Earth*) were all veterans of cheap sci-fi battles for world domination. The ad campaign stressed the fact that they used "real live" grasshoppers in the movie, as opposed to that "phony" stop-motion stuff. Gordon would move on to more oversized bugs with *The Spider*, followed by other BIG productions. ♫♫ ▷

1957 73m/B Peggy Castle, Peter Graves, Morris Ankrum, Richard Benedict, James Seay; **D:** Bert I. Gordon. **VHS** *NO*

Bela Lugosi Meets a Brooklyn Gorilla

Lewis & Martin impersonators Mitchell & Petrillo (who were subsequently sued by the real team) get lost on a tropical island, where

Mant. "Half man, half ant, all terror!" This witheringly on-target recreation of atomic-monster flicks of the '50s and '60s is the centerpiece of Joe Dante's nostalgic comedy *Matinee* (1993). Dante has been urged to complete *Mant* and release it as a feature all by itself.

The Shook-Up Shopping Cart. *Matinee* also shows this insipid Disney-style comedy about a wheeled supermarket conveyance with a mind of its own. Joe Dante's way of showing the kind of family flick that drove crowds of kids to stuff like *Mant* instead.

Burnt Sienna Sunset. In Dan Bell's *The Shot* (1995) jobless actors steal the only complete print of this blockbuster war melodrama, prompting chases around Los Angeles by assorted misfits (including Sam Raimi's brother Ted as an officious cop).

Rambro. African-American *Rambo* spoof that is reviewed on the "Sneakin' into the Movies" segment (itself spoofing "At the Movies") in Robert Townsend's *Hollywood Shuffle.*

they meet mad scientist Lugosi. The title ape turns out to be crooner Mitchell. The duo isn't bad, but the comedy material is weak, and Lugosi can't do much to help. Another odd title on the Lugosi filmography, it's okay as light entertainment. Petrillo started out playing Lewis' son on the *Colgate Comedy Hour* at 16, went on to record unfunny prank phone call records in the '60s, and opened a Pittsburgh comedy club. Mitchell continued his singing career until his death in 1981. Both performers continued to appear in films separately through the '70s, notably: Petrillo starred in Doris Wishman's *Keyholes Are for Peeping,* and appeared in *The Brain that Wouldn't Die*; Mitchell directed, wrote, and starred in *The Executioner* (1974). **AKA:** The Boys from Brooklyn. 🦴🦴

1952 74m/B Bela Lugosi, Duke Mitchell, Sammy Petrillo; **D:** William Beaudine. **VHS, Beta $19.95** *NOS, SNC, AOV*

The Bellboy

Jerry Lewis haters (and you know who you are), this is not quite the film to make a convert out of you. But give credit where it is due; Jerry's first outing as a hyphenate (writer-director-star) is a much more successful evocation of silent comedy clowning than Mel Brooks's *Silent Movie.* Jerry is a hapless bellboy at Miami's ritzy Fountainbleau Hotel. Among the most memorable sight gags concerns a Volkswagen and the guest who wants Jerry to bring him what's in the trunk. Milton Berle cameos. In the tradition of his idol Charlie Chaplin, Jerry is silent throughout, but he does give himself the last word. 🦴🦴🦴

1960 72m/B Jerry Lewis, Alex Gerry, Bob Clayton, Sonny Sands; **Cameos:** Milton Berle, Walter Winchell; **D:** Jerry Lewis; **W:** Jerry Lewis. **VHS, Beta, LV $59.95** *LIV*

The Bellboy and the Playgirls

Early Coppola effort adds new 3-D film footage to Fritz Umgelter's 1958 German movie. Horny bellboy peeps into hotel rooms, trying to catch a glimpse of skin, not knowing that most of the time he's spying on another movie. Might've been funny if he'd opened the door to find two old guys with a projector and screen set up. Stars Playboy playmate (42-22-37) June "The Body" Wilkinson (*Private Lives of Adam and Eve*), with other centerfolds of the time. Not anybody's proudest moment, this nudie has received more widespread video distribution than so many others due to Coppola's name. Thankfully, he was hired by Corman after this mess. **AKA:** The Playgirls and the Bellboy; Mit Eva Fing Die Sunde An. 🦴

1962 93m/C June Wilkinson; **D:** Francis Ford Coppola; **W:** Francis Ford Coppola. **VHS** *NO*

Beneath the Planet of the Apes

In the first sequel, another Earth astronaut (James Franciscus) passes through the same warp and follows the same paths as Taylor (what are the chances of that?), through Ape City and to the ruins of bomb-blasted New York's subway system, where warhead-worshipping human mutants are found. The strain of sequelling shows instantly, but curiously the saga gets better (and more creative) with the next two chapters: *Escape from...* and *Conquest for...* 🦴🦴

1970 **(G)** 108m/C James Franciscus, Kim Hunter, Maurice Evans, Charlton Heston, James Gregory, Natalie Trundy, Jeff Corey, Linda Harrison, Victor Buono; **D:** Ted Post. **VHS, Beta, LV $19.98** *FOX, FUS*

Beneath the Valley of the Ultra-Vixens

The plot of this mad sex comedy defies description. It's set in "Small Town U.S.A." and involves most of the elements Meyer is famous (or infamous) for: insatiable, overdeveloped women; bumbling men; religion; Martin Borman; fantasy. The dialogue often lapses into Burma Shave doggerel with an on-screen narrator who tells us that heroine Lola Langusta (Natividad) is a "pulverizing crucible of fulfillment." The auteur calls this one "quintessential" Russ Meyer and he's right. 🦴🦴🦴▷

1979 90m/C Francesca "Kitten" Natividad, Ann Marie, Ken Kerr, Stuart Lancaster; **D:** Russ Meyer. **VHS $89.95** *RMF*

A Better Tomorrow

Though this action film isn't as polished as John Woo's *Hard Boiled* or *The Killer,* the themes and the strong directorial vision he brings to his work are evident throughout. In the opening scene, the music is a tip-off to what Woo is about. It could have come straight from a spaghetti western and Woo tells this crime story with the same kind of exaggeration. The wildly complex plot is about counterfeiting, betrayal, murder, and brothers on opposite sides of the law. The violence isn't as crisply choreographed as it is in Woo's more recent films. Some of the humor slips into slapstick and that doesn't help the overall tone. Neither does the atrocious dubbing. But fans who overlook those flaws will see another terrific performance by Chow Yun-Fat as the wise-cracking best friend. This guy is simply one of the best actors in the business. **AKA:** Yingxiong Bense. 🦴🦴▷

1986 95m/C CH Chow Yung Fat, Leslie Cheung, Ti Lung; **D:** John Woo. **VHS $39.95** *FCT, REP*

Beverly Hills Bodysnatchers

A mad scientist and a greedy mortician plot to get rich off a formula for bringing the dead back to life. The two butthead teens they hired

as assistants foul up the plans when a deceased Mafia godfather (Tayback) only gets a partial dose and terrorizes Beverly Hills in zombified form. Unfunny farce, in need of a quick burial. **WOOF!**

1989 **(R)** 85m/C Vic Tayback, Frank Gorshin, Brooke Bundy, Seth Jaffe, Art Metrano; **D:** Jon Mostow. **VHS, LV $39.95** *IME*

Beverly Hills Vamp

An LA madam and her pulchritudinous prostitutes are really female vampires who menace a lustful pack of eager college boys. To the rescue comes uber-nerd classmate Deezen. Director/producer Fred Olen Ray claims this mixture of bad gags and extensive nudity is a social statement about safe sex. Does that mean you should wrap a condom around your VCR, or abstain? 🦴

1988 **(R)** 88m/C Britt Ekland, Eddie Deezen, Debra Lamb; **D:** Fred Olen Ray. **VHS, Beta $79.95** *VMK*

Beyond the Valley of the Dolls

Sleazy, spirited non-sequel to *Valley of the Dolls.* Meyer (*Faster, Pussycat! Kill! Kill!*) di-

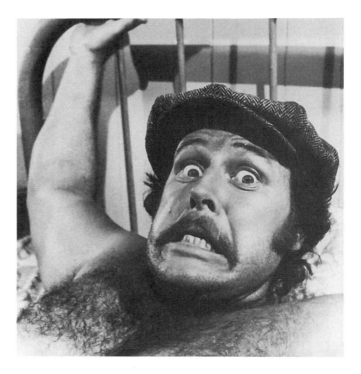

He's in for a huge surprise in *Beneath the Valley of the Ultra-Vixens.*

1974 **(R) 83m/C** Angie Dickinson, William Shatner, Tom Skerritt, Susan Sennett, Robbie Lee, Sally Kirkland, Noble Willingham, Royal Dano, Dick Miller; **D:** Steve Carver; **W:** William W. Norton Sr. **VHS, Beta $39.98** *NO*

Big Bad Mama 2

Belated Depression-era sequel to the 1974 Roger Corman gangster film, where the pistol-packin' matriarch battles a crooked politician with the help of her two daughters. So what if the title character was dead at the end of the first movie? Picky, picky, picky! Director Wynorski has gone on to become a mainstay on the video scene, grinding out B-movies at an astonishing rate in several genres. 🦴🦴

1987 **(R) 85m/C** Angie Dickinson, Robert Culp, Danielle Brisebois, Julie McCullough; **D:** Jim Wynorski; **W:** Jim Wynorski, R.J. Robertson. **VHS, Beta $14.95** *MGM*

The Big Bird Cage

Prison spoof sequel to *The Big Doll House* was one of the first Philippine babes-behind-bars prison flicks and is still one of the best. Check out the early '70s fashions—bell bottoms, hip huggers, and hot pants. The humor is broad and ribald with Rocco, the gay guard suffering a fate worse than death...actually a couple of fates worse than death. Bizarre moments are sprinkled throughout, none stranger than the scene where one skinny inmate slathers her body with chicken fat and runs naked through a river filled with floating coconuts. **AKA:** Women's Penitentiary 2. 🦴🦴🦴

1972 **(R) 93m/C** Pam Grier, Sid Haig, Anitra Ford, Candice Roman, Teda Bracci, Carol Speed, Karen McKevic; **D:** Jack Hill. **VHS, Beta $39.98** *WAR*

rected this Hollywood parody ("BVD," as it came to be known) about an all-girl rock combo and their search for stardom. Labeled the first "exploitation horror camp musical"— how can you pass that up? Screenplay by film critic Ebert, from an original story by Ebert and Meyer. Mondo trasho. 🦴🦴🦴▷

1970 **(NC-17) 109m/C** Edy Williams, Dolly Reed; **D:** Russ Meyer; **W:** Roger Ebert. **VHS, Beta, LV $19.98** *FXV, BTV*

Big Bad Mama

Would-be *Bonnie and Clyde* is cheesy, sleazy, and full of cornball humor. Tough and sexy machine-gun toting mother (Dickinson) moves her two nubile daughters out of Texas during the Depression. To support themselves, they steal—mostly from piggish louts who deserve to be stolen from—with Miller in hot comic pursuit. At the same time, the liberated trio gets a head start on the sexual revolution, creating sharp testosterone increases among the local men. Dickinson's memorable nude scenes with Shatner and Skerritt doubtless have a lot to do with the film's enduring cult status. *Big Bad Mama 2* arrived some 13 years later. 🦴🦴🦴

The Big Bus

Long before *Airplane* took off, Fred Freeman and Lawrence Cohen, the co-writers of *Start the Revolution Without Me,* rolled out this disaster-movie parody set aboard a nuclear-powered bus that contains a swimming pool, piano bar, and a bowling alley. Some bumps along the way but a great cast keeps this one rolling. Joseph Bologna is Dan Torrance, a shunned bus driver accused of cannibalism. Stockard Channing is Kitty, the woman who believes in him. John Beck is co-driver Shoulders O'Brien, so named not for his girth, but because that's where he tends to steer. Jose Ferrer is Ironman, who has sabotaged the Big Bus's inaugural run. Murphy Dunne is the definitive hateful lounge singer. 🎵🎵♭

1976 (PG) 88m/C Joseph Bologna, Stockard Channing, Ned Beatty, Ruth Gordon, Larry Hagman, John Beck, Jose Ferrer, Lynn Redgrave, Sally Kellerman, Stuart Margolin, Richard Mulligan, Howard Hesseman, Richard B. Shull; **D:** James Frawley; **M:** David Shire. **VHS, Beta $49.95** *PAR*

The Big Crimewave

Microbudgeted oddity from Winnipeg, concocted by and starring Paizs as a Chaplinesque loner and movie buff who accidentally wrecked his camera and now concentrates on perfecting his own screenplay, a tacky gangster drama amusingly re-enacted over and over again in his mind as it evolves and devolves. In between, our hero—who never speaks—daydreams obsessively over the glories and pitfalls of his imaginary stardom as a Disney/Spielberg/Lucas/Charles Foster Kane amalgam, before taking a bus to Kansas City (Kansas City?) to become a screenwriter. A feast of friendly jabs at genre films and Hollywood wannabes, this has the production values of a home movie and tends to ramble just as much, yet is riotously on-target at times. Originally called *Crimewave*; to avoid confusion with Sam Raimi's *Crime Wave*, U.S. video distributors clumsily superimposed *The Big...* over Paizs's painstakingly handmade title card. 🎵🎵🎵

1986 80m/C *CA* John Paizs, Eva Covacs, Darrel Baran; **D:** John Paizs. **VHS, Beta** *HHE*

The Big Doll House

Filmed in the Philippines for $125,000, this down-and-dirty Roger Corman production made millions and revitalized the women-in-prison genre. In her bust-out role, blaxploitation queen Pam Grier is the most formidable of female prisoners serving hard time in a penal colony. The sadistic warden doles out unusual discipline (snakes are an effective deterrent) before the prisoners rebel in the explosive climax. Followed by *The Big Bird Cage*. In 1974, Jonathan Demme delivered *Caged Heat*, the standard by which recent women-in-prison

movies are judged. **AKA:** Women's Penitentiary 1; Women in Cages. 🎵🎵♭

1971 (R) 93m/C Judy Brown, Roberta Collins, Pam Grier, Brooke Mills, Pat Woodell, Sid Haig, Christianne Schmidtmer, Kathryn Loder; **D:** Jack Hill; **M:** Les Baxter. **VHS, Beta $24.98** *SUE, NLC*

Big Meat Eater

Ultra-cheap musical gore-comedy from Canada about toy-robot extraterrestrials planning to use radioactive discards from a village butcher's shop as UFO fuel. The beef vendor, a natty Harold Lloyd look alike, doesn't realize his massive, fez-wearing employee Abdullah (the late blues singer Big Miller) is a psycho killer whose latest victim, the lustful mayor, has been resurrected by the aliens as a zombie with a potato mixer for a hand. The challenge of describing this whacked-out parody led one critic to coin the term "zoned movies," for films to which normal standards of good, bad, and incompetence simply cannot be applied. That says it all. "Meat your fate!...Meat your fate!" 🎵🎵

1985 81m/C *CA* George Dawson, Big Miller, Andrew Gillies; **D:** Chris Windsor. **VHS, Beta $49.95** *MED*

Big Store

Late Marx Brothers vehicle has some big laughs without the rapid-fire hilarity that made them famous. Groucho, Chico, and Harpo work as department-store detectives and foil a kidnapping and hostile takeover attempt. Unfortunately, they don't foil some pointless musical numbers dropped in to kill time, though one such interlude gives Harpo an especially charming pantomime at the harp, accompanied by two non-identical mirror images of himself. Videocassette release includes the short subject "A Night at the Movies," with humorist Robert Benchley demonstrating what could go wrong for a filmgoer in the era before VCRs. 🎵🎵♭

1941 96m/B Groucho Marx, Harpo Marx, Chico Marx, Tony Martin, Margaret Dumont, Virginia Grey, Virginia O'Brien; **D:** Charles Riesner. **VHS, Beta $19.95** *MGM, CCB*

Billy Jack

"Go ahead and hate your neighbor/Go ahead and cheat a friend...." Sing along with Coven

"Didn't think she'd notice that I cut the cheese," thinks an embarrassed John Carradine in *Billy the Kid Vs. Dracula.*

Billy the Kid Vs. Dracula

The title says it all. Dracula travels to the Old West, anxious to put the bite on a pretty lady ranch owner. Her fiancee, the legendary out-law Billy the Kid, steps in to save his girl from becoming a vampire herself. By the mid-'60s, Carradine was about to enter the final stage of his career, in which he would agree to ap-pear in any film at any price, in order to help support the Shakespeare company which was his true passion. Made back-to-back and dou-ble billed with the even worse *Jesse James Meets Frankenstein's Daughter.* 🦴 ▷

1966 95m/C Chuck Courtney, John Carradine, Melinda Plowman, Walter Janovitz, Harry Carey Jr., Roy Barcroft, Virginia Christine, Bing Russell; **D:** William Beaudine. **VHS, Beta $19.95** *NOS, SUE, VYY*

The Bird with the Crystal Plumage

An American writer living in Rome witnesses a murder; he becomes involved in the mys-tery when he begins to suspect that all was not as it appeared at the murder scene. Par-tially based on the Frederic Browne novel *The Screaming Mimi,* this is the first of Argento's "giallo" murder mysteries, with an unseen killer in black stalking victims in one sus-penseful scene after another. The opening murder scene, with Musante trapped between glass doors and able to do little but watch (much like a film audience) is unforgettable, and Argento would return to this theme again, most forcibly in *Terror at the Opera* (1987). A fine score by composer Morricone. **AKA:** L'U-cello dalle Plume di Cristallo; The Phantom of Terror. 🦴🦴🦴

1970 (PG) 98m/C *IT* Tony Musante, Suzy Kendall, Eva Renzi; **D:** Dario Argento; **W:** Dario Argento; **M:** Ennio Morricone. **VHS, Beta, LV $19.95** *VCI, MRV*

The Birds

Hitchcock attempted to top the success of *Psy-cho* with this terrifying tale of Man versus Na-ture, in which Nature alights, one by one, on the trees of Bodega Bay to stage a bloody act of revenge upon the human world. Only Hitchcock can twist the harmless into the hor-rific while avoiding the ridiculous; this is per-

and "One Tin Soldier," the surprise Top-40 one-hit wonder from this surprise box office sensation. Tom Laughlin, the 1970s' answer to Steven Seagal, wrote, directed, and stars as Billy Jack, a half-breed ex-Green Beret who is the mystical protector of the interracial Freedom School, whose Native-American and hippy students are hassled by the big-oted townspeople. Billy preaches peace and love, but when he sees injustice he...just...goes...berserk! Delores Taylor (Laughlin's wife) costars as the teacher who tries to subdue Billy's more violent impulses. Happily for the audience, she fails. Among the students are members of the comedy troupe the Committee, including Howard Hesseman, better known as Dr. Johnny Fever on TV's *WKRP in Cincinnati*. Billy Jack made his first appearance in the biker film, *Born Losers*. Two disastrous sequels followed, *The Trial of Billy Jack* and *Billy Jack Goes to Washington*. When last seen, Laughlin was hawking homeopathic medicine and running for president. 🦴🦴🦴

1971 (PG) 112m/C Tom Laughlin, Delores Taylor, Clark Howat; **D:** Tom Laughlin; **W:** Tom Laughlin. **VHS, Beta, LV $14.95** *WAR*

haps his most brutal film, and one of the cinema's purest, horrifying portraits of apocalypse. Based on a short story by Daphne Du Maurier; screenplay by novelist Evan Hunter (aka Ed McBain). 🎵🎵🎵🎵

1963 120m/C Rod Taylor, Tippi Hedren, Jessica Tandy, Veronica Cartwright, Suzanne Pleshette; **D:** Alfred Hitchcock. **VHS, Beta, LV $19.95** *MCA*

Bizarre Bizarre

A mystery writer is accused of murder and disappears, only to return in disguise to try to clear his name. This is an early collaboration between director Marcel Carne and poet/screenwriter Jacques Prevert, the creators of the 1944 classic *Children of Paradise*, considered by many to be the greatest film ever made. This one isn't so good, concealing a barely coherent plot beneath an onslaught of lame comedy routines, elevated by the invocation of the holy name surrealism. Includes appearances by several popular French comedians of the time, none of whom have passed into the pantheon of American pop culture. **AKA:** Drole de Drama. 🎵▷

1939 90m/B *FR* Louis Jouvet, Michel Simon, Francoise Rosay; **D:** Marcel Carne. **VHS, Beta $24.95** *NOS, HHT, DVT*

The Black Cat

The first of the Boris and Bela pairings stands up well years after release. Polished and taut, with amazing sets and interesting acting, and many a weird twist in the plot. Set in a fantastic house built upon the ruins of a battlefield, an architect and devil worshipper play chess for the lives of innocents. Karloff is at his most deviously evil and perverse, while Lugosi is the sympathetic hero, consumed with revenge. Although a triumph for Ulmer, he was unable to follow up on it due to studio politics and he eventually drifted into cheap, but sometimes brilliant, Poverty Row pictures. John Carradine can be glimpsed among the devil worshipers. Also available with *The Raven* (1935) on laserdisc in time compressed form. **AKA:** House of Doom. 🎵🎵🎵🎵

1934 65m/B Boris Karloff, Bela Lugosi, David Manners, Jacqueline Wells, Lucille Lund, Henry Armetta; **D:** Edgar G. Ulmer. **VHS, LV $9.95** *MED, MLB, MCA*

Black Sabbath

An omnibus horror film with three parts, climaxing with Karloff as a Wurdalak, a vampire who must kill those he loves. Also available with *Black Sunday* on Laser Disc. **AKA:** I Tre Volti della Paura. 🎵🎵🎵

1964 99m/C *IT* Boris Karloff, Jacqueline Pierreux, Michele Mercier, Lidia Alfonsi, Susy Anderson, Mark Damon, Rika Dialina; **D:** Mario Bava; **M:** Les Baxter. **VHS, Beta $16.95** *SNC*

The Black Six

When a black high school student is caught dating a white girl, her racist brother and his racist biker gang beat him to death on a football field. Word reaches older brother Bubba, and he and five other black motorcycle riding Vietnam veterans (played by six black National Football League veterans) come to town to track down and punish the gang. A lot of jive talk and not much action. Wills plays their high school coach, who seems a bit demented. Familiar faces Mikel Angel and Fred Scott show up in small parts. Direction is even worse than the performances and the editing is sloppy. Cimber (Matteo Ottaviano) is best known for his awful soap opuses with Jayne Mansfield (*Single Room Furnished*) and Pia Zadora (*Butterfly*). 🎵

1974 (R) 91m/C Gene Washington, Carl Eller, Lem Barney, Mercury Morris, Joe "Mean Joe" Greene, Willie Lanier, Rosalind Miles, John Isenbarger, Ben Davidson, Maury Wills; **D:** Matt Cimber. **VHS, Beta $49.90** *UNI*

Black Sunday

Burned at the stake with an iron "mask of Satan" nailed to her face one hundred years previously, a witch (the stunning Steele) returns with her vampire servant to do the bidding of Satan, attempting to replace her look-alike descendant in the process. Only a pair of kindly doctors, stranded while traveling to a medical convention, stand in her way. A must see for horror fans; firsts for Steele as star and Bava as director—one of the creepiest, while at the same time most atmospherically beautiful films ever made. After serving as director of photography for mentor Riccardo Freda (and on many diverse Italian films) and helping him finish directing *Caltiki, the Immortal*

41

Cult Flicks and Trash Pics

Monster, this was an international hit (despite tampering by AIP for the U.S. version) for Bava. He would go on to direct the classics *Black Sabbath, Blood and Black Lace, Twitch of the Death Nerve,* and many other fantastic films. *AKA:* Mask of Satan. 🦴🦴🦴🦴

1960 83m/B *IT* Barbara Steele, John Richardson, Ivo Garrani, Andrea Checchi, Arturo Dominici; *D:* Mario Bava; *M:* Les Baxter. **VHS $19.98** *SNC, MRV, MOV*

Black Venus

A soft-core epic, starring the former Miss Bahamas, Josephine Jacqueline Jones, about the 18th-century French aristocracy. Laughably based upon the stories of Balzac. European film dubbed in English. **WOOF!**

1983 (R) 80m/C Josephine Jacqueline Jones, Emiliano Redondo; *D:* Claude Mulot. **VHS, Beta $79.95** *MGM*

Blackboard Jungle

Well-remembered urban drama about an idealistic teacher in a slum area who fights doggedly to connect with his unruly students. Bill Hailey's "Rock Around the Clock" over the opening credits was the first use of rock music in a mainstream feature film. Based on Evan Hunter novel. 🦴🦴🦴🦴

1955 101m/B Glenn Ford, Anne Francis, Louis Calhern, Sidney Poitier, Vic Morrow, Richard Kiley, Margaret Hayes, John Hoyt, Warner Anderson, Paul Mazursky, Jamie Farr; *D:* Richard Brooks; *W:* Richard Brooks. Nominations: Academy Awards '55: Best Art Direction/Set Decoration (B & W), Best Black and White Cinematography, Best Film Editing, Best Screenplay. **VHS, Beta $19.95** *MGM*

Blackenstein

Doctor into nouveau experimentation restores a Vietnam vet's arms and legs, but a jealous assistant gives our man a bogus injection, turning him into Blackenstein, a large African American with a chip on hulking shoulder (and a square afro to boot) who enjoys ripping off women's clothes before killing them and otherwise causing big trouble. Inevitable follow-up to *Blacula* lacks that film's inventive re-tooling of horror legend for blaxploitation genre, but very patient gore/sleaze hounds will dig flesh and blood displays. Ex-mob moll/stripper Liz Renay (*Desperate Liv-*

ing, The Thrill Killers) gets top billing, but real star is Kenneth Strickfaden's explosive lab equipment; he created effects for the original Universal *Frankenstein* as well as Mel Brooks' *Young Frankenstein. AKA:* Black Frankenstein. 🦴🦴🦴

1973 (R) 87m/C John Hart, Ivory Stone, Andrea King, Liz Renay, Joe DiSue; *D:* William A. Levey. **VHS, Beta $29.95** *MED*

Blacula

Eighteenth-century African prince Mamuwalde seeks the aid of Count Dracula in fighting the slave trade, but gets vampirized and locked in a coffin for his efforts. Two hundred years later, he's freed by a pair of campy antique dealers and stalks the streets of Los Angeles, trying to quench his insatiable desire for blood while pursuing a woman (Vonetta McGee) who resembles his long-dead wife. Successful melding of blaxploitation and horror benefits from stately performance by Shakespearean vet Marshall (later the King of Cartoons on *Pee Wee's Playhouse*). With Denise Nichols (of TV's *Room 222*), Thalmus Rasulala, and Elisha Cook, Jr. (as a hook-handed hospital orderly). Followed by an inferior sequel, *Scream, Blacula, Scream* with Pam Grier (directed by Bob Kelljan of *Return of Count Yorga* fame) and numerous pathetic imitators (*Blackenstein, Dr. Black and Mr. Hyde, Abby*). 🦴🦴🦴

1972 (PG) 92m/C William Marshall, Thalmus Rasulala, Denise Nicholas, Vonetta McGee; *D:* William Crain. **VHS, Beta, LV $9.98** *ORI*

Blade Runner

Los Angeles, the 21st century. World-weary cop tracks down a handful of renegade "replicants" (synthetically produced human slaves who, with only days left of life, search madly for some way to extend their prescribed lifetimes). Moody, beautifully photographed, dark thriller with sets from an architect's dream. Based on "Do Androids Dream of Electric Sheep" by Philip K. Dick. Laser edition features restored footage, information about special effects, and production sketches. Director's cut, released at 117 minutes, removes Ford's narration and the last scene of the film, which Scott considered too "up," and inserts several short scenes, including a dream sequence. 🦴🦴🦴🦴

1982 (R) 122m/C Harrison Ford, Rutger Hauer, Sean Young, Daryl Hannah, M. Emmet Walsh, Edward James Olmos, Joe Turkel, Brion James, Joanna Cassidy; **D:** Ridley Scott; **W:** Hampton Fancher, David Peoples; **M:** Vangelis. Nominations: Academy Awards '82: Best Art Direction/Set Decoration. **VHS, Beta, LV, 8mm $9.95** *COL, WAR, CRC*

Blades

Another video novelty from Troma, detailing the efforts of golf course personnel to try and stop a vicious, extra-large, unmanned power mower that lurks around the greens and grinds up duffers with regularity. Pic is an utterly straight-faced parody of *Jaws,* but acting and dialogue remain so matter-of-fact and sober that it doesn't feel like a spoof—just a rerun. Where are the jokes?! 🦴🦴

1989 (R) 101m/C Robert North, Jeremy Whelan, Victoria Scott, Jon McBride; **D:** Thomas R. Rondinella. **VHS, Beta, LV $79.98** *MED*

Blast-Off Girls

Scuzzball promoter Boojie Baker (Dan Conway) sets out to avenge himself for being blacklisted by the rock 'n' roll industry. He discovers a fresh group and renames them The Big Blast (played by the Faded Blue), but without corporate backing he can only pay them with groovy clothes and mini-skirted girls. Trouble ensues when they unexpectedly hit the charts and want real money. Trying to compete in the mid-'60s trend toward psychedelic rock & roll pictures, Lewis finds himself out of his depth. Pioneering the concept of blatant product placement, Colonel Harlan Sanders agrees to pay the band free chicken in exchange for playing at one of his restaurants (while in reality, he was paying Lewis for the commercial). Features some location shooting at Chicago night clubs. 🦴🦴

1967 83m/C Ray Sager, Dan Conway; **D:** Herschell Gordon Lewis. **VHS $19.99** *MOV, SMW*

Blazing Saddles

Wild, wacky spoof by Brooks of every cliche in the western film genre. Little is Black Bart, a convict offered a reprieve if he will become a sheriff and clean up a nasty frontier town; the previous recipients of this honor have all swiftly ended up in shallow graves. A crazy, silly film with a cast full of loveable loonies including comedy greats Wilder, Kahn, and Korman. Watch for the Count Basie Orchestra. A group writing effort, based on an original story by Bergman. Was the most-viewed movie in its first year of release on HBO cable. 🦴🦴🦴▷ **1974 (R) 90m/C** Cleavon Little, Harvey Korman, Madeline Kahn, Gene Wilder, Mel Brooks, John Hillerman, Alex Karras, Dom DeLuise, Liam Dunn; *D:* Mel Brooks, Alan Uger; *W:* Mel Brooks, Norman Steinberg, Andrew Bergman, Richard Pryor, Alan Uger; *M:* John Morris. Nominations: Academy Awards '74: Best Film Editing, Best Song ("Blazing Saddles"), Best Supporting Actress (Kahn). **VHS, Beta, LV $14.95** *WAR*

Blazing Stewardesses

The Hound salutes the distributor for truth in advertising, as they stamped this as one of the world's worst videos. Semi-plotless tale has busty low-I.Q. stewardesses (who remain clothed at all times) relaxing at a Palm Springs dude ranch under siege from hooded riders, aging gags from the Ritz Brothers (in polka dot bellbottoms and Hawaiian shirts!), and even a song from Yvonne De Carlo who plays the local madame. Off-beat flick has an undeniable curiosity value—note the flimsy airplane set, the likes of which have not been seen since *Plan 9 from Outer Space*—but it's not the guilty pleasure that the title implies. 🦴▷ **1975 (R) 95m/C** Yvonne De Carlo, Bob Livingston, Donald (Don "Red") Barry, Regina Carrol; *Cameos:* The Ritz Brothers; *D:* Al Adamson. **VHS** *NO*

The Blob

Sci-fi thriller about a small town's fight against a slimy jello invader from space. Slightly rebellious McQueen (in his first starring role) redeems himself when he saves the town with quick action. Low-budget, horror/teen-fantasy became a camp classic. Other titles considered for this flick included *The Glob, The Glob that Girdled the Globe, The Meteorite*

Monster, The Molten Meteorite, and The Night of the Creeping Dead. Followed by a worthless sequel in 1972, Son of Blob, and a worthwhile remake in 1988. Laserdisc contains an additional fifteen minutes of McQueen interviews and the trailers for both the original and the 1988 remake. ♫ ♫ ♫ ▷

1958 83m/C Steve McQueen, Aneta Corseaut, Olin Howland, Earl Rowe; **D:** Irvin S. Yeaworth Jr. **VHS, Beta, LV $19.95** COL, GEM, MLB

Blood and Black Lace

Beautiful models are being brutally killed and an inspector is assigned to the case, but not before more gruesome killings occur. With this film, Bava pioneered the "giallo"—a type of stylish murder mystery featuring a killer in black, and a minimal plot with the accent on terror rather than detection, then the subject of wildly popular, yellow covered paperback fiction in Italy. The story is violent and suspenseful, and Bava brings to it his trademark atmospheric cinematography, careful use of color, and perverse manipulation of characters. Just as the models are turned into mere objects to be decorated with designer clothing by the fashion industry, Bava shows us how they can become mere objects to be horribly murdered by the cinema industry—both used to manipulate the buying public. ♫ ♫ ♫

1964 90m/C IT FR GE Cameron Mitchell, Eva Bartok, Mary Arden; **D:** Mario Bava. **VHS, Beta $59.95** MED

Blood and Roses

A girl who is obsessed with her family's vampire background becomes possessed by a vampire and commits numerous murders. The photography is good, but the plot is hazy and only effective in certain parts. It also moves rather slowly with more talk than action. Perhaps just a tad racy for it's day, it really is only for those who must see every Vadim or vampire film ever made. Tough to recommend this and it's place in this book is really only deserved by it's reputation and one-time scarcity. Based on the book Carmilla by Sheridan LeFanu. Later remade as The Vampire Lovers and The Blood-Spattered Bride, both of which are more interesting and much trashier. **AKA:** Et Mourir de Plaisir. ♫

1961 74m/C Mel Ferrer, Elsa Martinelli, Annette Vadim, Marc Allegret; **D:** Roger Vadim; **W:** Roger Vadim. **VHS** PAR

Blood Beach

This modest little horror film almost seems embarrassed by the silliness of its own plot—a giant critter living under the Santa Monica beach and sucking the unwary into the sand. It's not nearly as campy or as sleazy as some horror fans might want, but the film isn't without interest and humor. Somehow it works. ♫ ♫ ▷

1981 (R) 92m/C David Huffman, Marianna Hill, John Saxon, Burt Young, Otis Young; **D:** Jeffrey Bloom. **VHS, Beta $54.95** MED

Blood Diner

The Tutman brothers dig up their madman uncle's brain and obey its instructions on how to resurrect the evil goddess Sheetar. Using their diner as a front, they kill shapely young girls for demonic rituals, and make creative use of the corpses in both the culinary and black arts. Goofball parody of the notorious 60s splatter flicks of Herschell Gordon Lewis (especially Blood Feast) is what you'd have to call an acquired taste. Some cartoonishly fun moments mix in with the requisite gore and nudity, and it's certainly more enjoyable than the nauseating originals. Compare/contrast with a later H. G. Lewis spoof Bloodsucking Pharoahs of Pittsburgh. ♫ ♫

1987 88m/C Rick Burks, Carl Crew; **D:** Jackie Kong. **VHS, Beta $19.98** VES, LIV

Blood Feast

With the nudie-cutie cycle winding down, director Lewis and producer Dave Friedman needed a new type of picture to sell. Since they couldn't raise the kind of budgets that Hollywood pictures have, they needed to do something that Hollywood wouldn't touch. The million dollar answer: explicit gore! Lets you have it right in the first scene, as a woman is attacked in the bath tub and gets her leg hacked off. A demented caterer/anthropologist/Egyptian high priest (Arnold, wearing fuzzy fake eyebrows) butchers hapless young women to splice them together in order to bring an Egyptian goddess back to life. While

45

THE HOUND SALUTES: MARIO BAVA

Born in 1914, Mario Bava was an influential Italian cinematographer and director who created horror films that were best-known for their special effects, stunning photography, and use of light and color. His early years in film were spent as a cinematographer until he stepped in and rescued the film *I Vampiri* after the original director walked off the set. In 1960, Bava released one of his most famous films, *La Maschera del Demonio* (released in the United States as *Black Sunday*), a vampiric tale of a princess revived by a drop of blood. The film launched the horror career of actress Barbara Steele and influenced any number of filmmakers who followed in Bava's footsteps. Bava, who had a firm belief in the supernatural, was not shy about including gore in his films, which often led to his films being banned or censored in England, Canada, Mexico, and the United States. His works often featured titles straight out of the B-movie catalog--*Kill Baby Kill*, *Blood and Black Lace*, and *Twitch of the Death Nerve* are a few of the best. Bava died in 1980.

detective Wood is on the killer's trail, his girlfriend (playmate Mason) is in the killer's classroom, and her mother is hiring him to cater a party. Heads are sliced open, throats cut, tongues torn out—isn't Egyptology fascinating? Enormously profitable, especially on the drive-in circuit. A no-budget classic, reportedly shot in four days in and around a Florida motel. Lewis was also responsible for the repetitive soundtrack, which is available on LP. *AKA:* Feast of Flesh. 🦴🦴🦴🦴

1963 70m/C Connie Mason, Thomas Wood, Malcolm Arnold; *D:* Herschell Gordon Lewis. **VHS, Beta $29.95** *VTR*

Blood Freak

An absolutely insane anti-drug, Christian splatter film. A Floridian Christian biker/bodybuilder (Hawkes) gets involved with two sisters, and the "bad" sister turns him on to weed. He gets a job on their father's turkey farm, where scientists use him as a guinea pig in a chemical experiment. The combination transforms him into a turkey monster, lusting for junkie blood! The turkey monster goes on a gory rampage, at one point cutting off a guy's leg. Narrated by a chain smoker who has a coughing fit. Don't miss it. You'll wonder whether it's the cast or you that's on drugs. Hawkes named his character Herschell, after his idol Herschell Gordon Lewis, director of *Blood Feast, 2000 Maniacs,* etc. Grinter also directed the equally strange *Flesh Feast.* 🦴🦴▷

1972 86m/C Steve Hawkes, Dana Culliver, Randy Grinter Jr., Tina Anderson, Heather Hughes; *D:* Steve Hawkes, Brad Grinter. **VHS, Beta** *NO*

Blood of Dracula

This was producer Herman Cohen's female version of his big hit *I Was a Teenage Werewolf.* A wicked headmistress of a girls boarding school uses hypnotism to bring out the bloodsucker in shy student Harrison. She transforms physically as well, becoming a weird-looking creature, and starts feeding on other students. Strock also directed *I Was A Teenage Frankenstein* (with which this was double billed), *The Magnetic Monster, Gog, The Crawling Hand,* and the instructive *How To Make a Monster.* Ultra-litigious Universal threatened to sue over the title. They don't make 1950s rock 'n 'roll girls' school vampire movies like this anymore. *AKA:* Blood is My Heritage. 🦴🦴

1957 71m/B Sandra Harrison, Louise Lewis, Gail Ganley, Jerry Blaine, Heather Ames, Malcolm Atterbury; *D:* Herbert L. Strock. **VHS $9.95** *COL, MLB*

Blood of Dracula's Castle

Couple inherits an allegedly deserted castle but upon moving in, discover the vampire infestation. Young women are kept chained in the dungeon for continual blood supply; also present are a hunchback and a werewolf. Awesome Adamson production is highlighted by the presence of the gorgeous Volante. Early cinematography effort by the renowned Laszlo Kovacs. *AKA:* Dracula's Castle. 🦴🦴

1969 84m/C John Carradine, Alexander D'Arcy, Paula Raymond, Ray Young, Vicki Volante, Robert Dix, John Cardos; *D:* Jean Hewitt, Al Adamson. **VHS, Beta $29.95** *NO*

Blood of Ghastly Horror

In 1965, Adamson made a film called *Psycho A Go-Go*, in which maniac Joe Corey (Morton) tries to recover the booty from a bungled jewel robbery. In 1968, he added new footage that revealed how Corey received a brain injury in Viet Nam, repaired with an electronic implant by Dr. Vanard (Carradine), which had the unfortunate side effect of turning him into a psycho killer. In 1971, Adamson was at it again—adding more new footage with Kirk (*Mars Needs Women, Catalina Caper*) as a too-intense cop on the trail of a monster created by Corey's mad doctor father (Taylor) to get revenge on Vanard's daughter (Carrol). Most of the previous film(s) was included as flashbacks, and released as this confusing, wildly complicated "sequel." Who knows when Adamson will strike next? Not to be missed, for those whose psyches can stand the strain. Unleashed to theatres in "Chill-o-rama," the video version is annoyingly cropped. *AKA:* The Fiend with the Atomic Brain; Psycho a Go Go!; The Love Maniac; The Man with the Synthetic Brain; The Fiend with the Electronic Brain. 🗡🗡▷

1972 87m/C John Carradine, Kent Taylor, Tommy Kirk, Regina Carrol, Roy Morton; **D:** Al Adamson. **VHS $14.95** *MOV*

Blood Orgy of the She-Devils

Exploitative gore nonsense about female demons, beautiful witches, and satanic worship. Some movies waste all their creative efforts on their titles and this is one of them. It does, however, epitomize everything many love about old drive-in fair: stupid plots, naked babes, and an evil, sexy villainess who get hers in the end. A perfect example of the genre that no trash fan should miss. Laughably bad, sexy junk sure to entertain the mildly demented. 🗡🗡🗡

1974 (PG) 73m/C Lila Zaborin, Tom Pace, Leslie McRae, Ray Myles. **VHS, Beta** *NO*

Blood Simple

A jealous husband hires a sleazy private eye to murder his adulterous wife and her lover. A dark, intricate, morbid morality tale that deviates imaginatively from the standard murder mystery thriller. First film scripted by the Cohen brothers. 🗡🗡🗡▷

1985 (R) 96m/C John Getz, M. Emmet Walsh, Dan Hedaya, Frances McDormand; **D:** Joel Coen; **W:** Ethan Coen, Joel Coen; **M:** Carter Burwell. Independent Spirit Awards '86: Best Actor (Walsh), Best Director (Coen). **VHS, Beta, LV $14.98** *MCA*

Bloodbath at the House of Death

Kenny Everett, a British TV comic with a reputation for Ernie Kovacs-type visual innovations, shows little evidence of same in this heavy-handed horror spoof about scientists investigating a murder-strewn haunted mansion. One of the researchers is gay, tee-hee. Price plays the leader of a local cult, and a depressing number of gags derive merely from hearing him and other actors swear. 🗡

1985 92m/C *GB* Kenny Everett, Pamela Stephenson, Vincent Price, Gareth Hunt; **D:** Ray Cameron. **VHS, Beta $59.95** *MED*

Bloodfist

Wilson's film debut has him starring in a *Bloodsport* clone. When his brother is killed in a Philippine Kumite tournament, Wilson heads for Manila to kick the you-know-what out of the killer. Only one problem: who did it? Enter the kindly (well, not really), old fighting master who trains Wilson and gets him into the Kumite ring. From there it's one bout after another ("Arena of Death" films are even cheaper to make in the Philippines) until the obvious happens. To the writer's credit, the killer isn't easy to spot until the final reel. Here action is the name of the game and on a purely visceral level the film delivers, though it will remain strictly viewing for the martial arts fan. As a side note, Corman reshot the same basic script for several other low-budget and less successful films. 🗡🗡🗡

1989 (R) 85m/C Don "The Dragon" Wilson, Rob Kaman, Billy Blanks, Kris Aguilar, Riley Bowman, Michael Shaner; **D:** Terence H. Winkless. **VHS, Beta $14.95** *MGM*

Bloodfist 2

Six of the world's toughest martial artists find themselves kidnapped and forced to do the bidding of the evil Su. The mysterious recluse

> "Mara, Queen of the Black Witches, and her wolf pack of voluptuous virgins invade Satan's tortured realm of the unknown..."
>
> —*Blood Orgy of the She-Devils.*

> "The truth is, he was alive when I buried him."
>
> —John Getz in *Blood Simple.*

stages a series of incredible fights between the experts and his own army of drugged warriors in an agreeable *Enter the Dragon* ripoff. In this one, the criminal mastermind has developed a drug to enhance the physical prowess of his own martial artists. As a demo for his skeptical clientele, his plan is to pit his men against the World Champions in the always-cheap-to-produce "Arena of Death." What he doesn't prepare for is the boy-next-door good looks of Don Wilson, who wins the baddy's daughter's heart. The story is familiar, the quality of production is good, and the martial arts sequences well choreographed. This belongs in the library of any martial arts fan. Followed by four more in-name-only sequels, all starring the always-busy Wilson. 🎵🎵◁

1990 (R) 85m/C Don "The Dragon" Wilson, Maurice Smith, James Warring, Timothy Baker, Richard Hill, Rina Reyes; **D:** Andy Blumenthal. **VHS, Beta** $14.95 *MGM*

Bloodlust

More teenagers fall prey to yet another mad scientist, who stores their dead bodies in glass tanks. Low-budget ripoff of *The Most Dangerous Game* and other such films. A must for Mike Brady (Robert Reed) fans though. 🎵

1959 89m/B Wilton Graff, June Kennedy, Robert Reed, Lilyan Chauvin; **D:** Ralph Brooke; **W:** Ralph Brooke. **VHS** $16.95 *SNC, NOS*

Bloodsucking Freaks

Virtually plotless Troma gagfest full of torture, cannibalistic dwarfs, and similar debaucheries, all played out on a Soho Grand Guignol stage (horror shows that allegedly contained real torture and death). Features "The Caged Sexoids," if that tells you anything (a cage of naked cannibal women tended by a dwarf). Not to mention the woman who has her brain sucked out through a straw. Filmed in "Ghoulovision" and originally rated X. **AKA:** The Incredible Torture Show. 🎵🎵◁

1975 (R) 89m/C Seamus O'Brian, Niles McMaster; **D:** Joel M. Reed. **VHS, Beta** $59.98 *VES*

Bloody Mama

Corman's violent, trashy story of the infamous Barker Gang of the '30s, led by the blood-

thirsty and sex-crazed Ma Barker (Winters, can't you just picture it?) and backed by her four perverted sons. De Niro is the space cadet sibling, Walden the homosexual ex-con, Stroud the sadistic mama lover, and Kimbrough the lady killer. They're joined by Walden's prison lover, Dern, who also has a thing for Ma Barker. Winters is a riot in this perverse stew of crime, violence, and, of course, sentimental blood bonding (the family that slays together, stays together). First of the Corman-produced (and sometimes directed) "Mama" movies, followed by *Big Bad Mama* and *Crazy Mama*. 🎵🎵🎵

1970 (R) 90m/C Shelley Winters, Robert De Niro, Don Stroud, Pat Hingle, Bruce Dern, Diane Varsi, Robert Walden, Clinton Kimbrough, Scatman Crothers; **D:** Roger Corman. **VHS, Beta, LV** $69.95 *VES, LIV*

Blow-Up

A young London photographer (Hemmings) takes pictures of a couple in the park and finds that he may have recorded evidence of a murder. Though somewhat dated by 1960s modishness, this is Antonioni's most accessible film, a sophisticated treatise on perception and the film-consumer-as-voyeur. It's a brilliantly assembled and wrought example of virtually silent storytelling. The sexual material, quite daring in its day, won't raise any eyebrows now. In fact, Vanessa Redgrave's extended topless sequence in which she keeps her arms crossed and her back often turned toward the camera is unintentionally funny. Though the story is still enigmatic and deliberately difficult to follow, it does make sense. Key images, particularly the scenes in the park, are hauntingly memorable. The film's influence can be seen in *A Clockwork Orange* and *Last Tango in Paris*. Brian DePalma's *Blow Out* is a half-hearted remake, of sorts. Cassette version crops the sides of the widescreen image, serving the story poorly in important scenes. 🎵🎵🎵◁

1966 111m/C *GB IT* David Hemmings, Vanessa Redgrave, Sarah Miles, Jane Birkin, Veruschka; **D:** Michelangelo Antonioni; **W:** Tonino Guerra, Michelangelo Antonioni; **M:** Herbie Hancock. Cannes Film Festival '67: Best Film; National Society of Film Critics Awards '66: Best Director (Antonioni), Best Film; Nominations: Academy Awards '66: Best Director (Antonioni), Best Story & Screenplay. **VHS, Beta, LV** $19.98 *MGM, FCT, INJ*

Blue Movies

A couple of jerks try their hand at making porn films with predictable results. 'Nuff said? **WOOF!**

1988 (R) 92m/C Larry Linville, Lucinda Crosby, Steve Levitt, Darien Mathias, Larry Poindexter; ***D:*** Paul Koval. **VHS, Beta $29.95** *ACA*

Blue Sunshine

Title refers to a deadly strain of homebrew L.S.D. sampled by Stanford students in 1967. Ten years later the former acidheads, suffering massive chromosomal damage, mutate into uncontrollable psychopathic baldies and kill anyone within reach. Potent premise about yuppies' sins catching up with them has brought this horror-thriller abundant critical praise, but it's a mediocre affair with some unfortunate unintentional humor. One drug-monster running amok on a dance floor is subdued by a blast of '70s disco music (and no, it's not "Le Freak"), and a clue is provided by a talking parrot. Lead actor King later went on to a profitable behind-the-scenes career as a producer/director of erotica like *Wild Orchid*. 🦴🦴

1978 (R) 94m/C Zalman King, Deborah Winters, Mark Goddard, Robert Walden, Charles Siebert, Ann Cooper, Ray Young, Alice Ghostley; ***D:*** Jeff Lieberman; ***W:*** Jeff Lieberman. **VHS, Beta $69.95** *VES*

Blue Velvet

Disturbing, unique exploration of the dark side of American suburbia, involving an innocent college youth who discovers a severed ear in an empty lot, and is thrust into a turmoil of depravity, murder, and sexual deviance. Brutal, grotesque, and unmistakably Lynch; an immaculately made, fiercely imagined film that is unlike any other. Mood is enhanced by the Badalamenti soundtrack. Graced by splashes of Lynchian humor, most notably the movie's lumber theme. Hopper is riveting as the chief sadistic nutcase and Twin Peaks' MacLachlan is a study in loss of innocence. Cinematography by Frederick Elmes. 🦴🦴🦴

1986 (R) 121m/C Kyle MacLachlan, Isabella Rossellini, Dennis Hopper, Laura Dern, Hope Lange, Jack Nance, Dean Stockwell, George Dickerson, Brad Dourif; ***D:*** David Lynch; ***W:*** David Lynch; ***M:*** Angelo Badalamenti. Independent Spirit Awards '87: Best Actress (Rossellini); Montreal World Film Festival '86: Best Supporting Actor (Hopper); National Society of Film Critics Awards '86: Best Director (Lynch), Best Film, Best Supporting Actor (Hopper); Nominations: Academy Awards '86: Best Director (Lynch). **VHS, Beta, LV $19.98** *WAR*

The Blues Brothers

As an excuse to run rampant in Chicago, Jake and Elwood Blues attempt to raise $5000 for their childhood orphanage by putting their old band back together. Good music and lots of cameos. Like most feature films based on *Saturday Night Live* skits, this one feels padded. It's all too long, too loud, and too silly but terrific production numbers from Cab Calloway and Aretha Franklin make up for a lot of flaws. Director Landis doesn't repeat his landmark comic success he achieved with *National Lampoon's Animal House,* but for those who love the nothing-exceeds-like-excess *Mad Mad Mad Mad World* school of comedy will have a grand time with all the car chases, crashes, etc. Carrie Fisher's "armed avenger" is a real scene-stealer. 🦴🦴🦴

"Yeah, we may be a little bloated, but we sure can dance!" Dan Aykroyd and John Belushi are *The Blues Brothers.*

THE HOUND SALUTES: LINDA BLAIR
The Blair Essentials

If any actress is due for receiving the line "What's a nice girl like you doing in a place like this?" it's Linda Blair. After her blockbuster childhood role as an adolescent possessed by a demon in *The Exorcist* (for which she received a 1974 Oscar nomination), Blair became one of the home video's most popular bar girls. Meaning she was behind bars most of the time.

It all started right after *The Exorcist*. Not even the relatively straightlaced world of network TV offered a safe haven for Linda; her 1974 TV movie *Born Innocent* cast her as a 14-year old runaway sentenced to a reform school for girls, where prime-time indignities suffered by the heroine include a now-notorious rape scene. In *Sweet Hostage*, a year later, Blair was held captive by a deranged Martin Sheen. Surprise! It was a quality TV-movie and literary adaptation, but one can only assume that casting agents looked no farther than the title. Throughout the '80s Linda was in a women's prison in the sleazoid *Chained Heat*, in an tropical women's prison in *Savage Island*, and in an East German women's prison in the lurid Cold-War exploitationer *Red Heat*. She was captive again in *Bail Out*, and harassed by punks and/or monsters in *Hell Night* and *Grotesque*.

In fairness, Linda Blair has been fighting back against her B-movie tormentors, in *Savage Streets*, *Nightforce*, and *Silent Assassins*, and has shown a sense of humor about herself more than once--most notably as a patient of exorcist Leslie Nielsen in the Certain-Occult-Thriller spoof *Repossessed*.

1980 (R) 133m/C John Belushi, Dan Aykroyd, James Brown, Cab Calloway, Ray Charles, Henry Gibson, Aretha Franklin, Carrie Fisher, John Candy; **Cameos:** Frank Oz, Steven Spielberg, Twiggy, Paul (Pee Wee Herman) Reubens, Steve Lawrence, John Lee Hooker; **D:** John Landis; **W:** Dan Aykroyd, John Landis; **M:** Ira Newborn. **VHS, Beta, LV $19.95** *MCA*

Body Heat

"You're not very bright. I like that in a man," vamps Kathleen Turner to lawyer William Hurt before she persuades him to kill her husband. Then things really go wrong. Hot love scenes supplement a twisting mystery with a surprise ending. Hurt and Turner (in her film debut) became stars under Kasdan's direction. (The three would reunite for *The Accidental Tourist*.) Rourke's arsonist, Danson's soft shoe, and the famous wind chime scene shouldn't be missed. This neo-noir recreated the femme fatale who would become so popular in such '90s hits as *Fatal Attraction* and *Basic Instinct* and hundreds of "erotic thriller" videos. Kasdan has gone on to make serious, meaningful films but nothing he's done to date is nearly as much fun. John Barry's smoky score is one of finest. ♫ ♫ ♫ ♫ ▷

1981 (R) 113m/C William Hurt, Kathleen Turner, Richard Crenna, Ted Danson, Mickey Rourke; **D:** Lawrence Kasdan; **W:** Lawrence Kasdan; **M:** John Barry. **VHS, Beta, LV $19.98** *WAR*

Body of Evidence

Madonna naked—big deal—in another *Basic Instinct* wannabe. Sex itself is the weapon the Material Girl is accused of using on her older and infirm hubby. Mantegna as the prosecutor; Dafoe as the lawyer who succumbs to his client's, ...er, charms, in S&M sex scenes involving hot wax and broken glass. Madonna's lack of performance is the least of the film's problems since everyone seems to have forgotten any acting talent they possess. Another box office flop in the series of Madonna vehicles, *Body* was the subject of a ratings flap (yawn) but this film shouldn't be seen by anybody. An unrated version is also available. **WOOF!**

1992 (R) 99m/C Madonna, Willem Dafoe, Joe Mantegna, Anne Archer, Michael Forest, Charles Hallahan, Mark Rolston, Richard Riehle, Julianne Moore, Frank Langella, Juergen Prochnow, Stan Shaw; **D:** Uli Edel; **W:** Brad Mirman; **M:** Graeme Revell. **VHS, Beta, LV $14.95** *MGM*

The Bone Yard

Child-sized mummified bodies brought to a fortress-like county morgue aren't murder victims after all, but demonic Chinese spirits in dormant form...though not for long. Revived, the hungry little terrors trap a police psychic and others in the bowels of the building. Genuinely offbeat spook show with unexpectedly good performances (and a most unusual heroine in extra-large-sized Rose), though it falters when some far sillier monsters show up in the finale. Still a noteworthy effort, awaiting cult discovery. The video distributor, confused by the content (and presence of comic actors Diller and Fell), released *The Boneyard* in two cassette boxes, one making it look like a Troma-style spoof, the other straight-up horror. 🦴🦴🦴

1990 (R) 98m/C Ed Nelson, Deborah Rose, Norman Fell, Jim Eustermann, Denise Young, Willie Stratford Jr., Phyllis Diller; **D:** James Cummins; **W:** James Cummins. **VHS, Beta $19.95** *PSM*

Bonnie & Clyde

Beatty and writer Robert Benton based their story on the violent careers of Bonnie Parker and Clyde Barrow, who roamed the Southwest robbing banks. In the Depression era—when any job, even an illegal one—was cherished, money, greed, and power created an unending cycle of violence and fury. The film itself though is less concerned with social justice than the sexual identities of the protagonists. On its initial release, the new gangster picture was highly controversial. In fact, it was panned by some important reviewers who later reassessed their first opinions. Its influence is undeniable, with a brilliantly constructed script and graphic depictions of bloodshed that helped to spur mainstream cinematic proliferation. Established Dunaway as a star; produced by Beatty in one of his best performances. Nominated for multiple Academy Awards; supporting actress Estelle Parsons and cinematographer Burnett Guffey took home statuettes. 🦴🦴🦴

1967 111m/C Warren Beatty, Faye Dunaway, Michael J. Pollard, Gene Hackman, Estelle Parsons, Denver Pyle, Gene Wilder, Dub Taylor; **D:** Arthur Penn; **W:** David Newman, Robert Benton. Academy Awards '67: Best Cinematography, Best Supporting Actress (Parsons); Nominations: Academy Awards '66: Best Actor (Beatty), Best Actor (Hackman, Pollard), Best Actress (Dunaway), Best Director (Penn), Best Picture, Best Story & Screenplay; Academy Awards '67: Best Costume Design. **VHS, Beta, LV $19.98** *WAR, BTV*

Born Innocent

As if *The Exorcist* weren't bad enough, Blair is back for more abuse-on-film, this time as a 14-year-old runaway from a dysfunctional family who lands in a reform school for girls. There, she must struggle to be as brutal as her peers in order to survive. Fairly tame by today's standards, but controversial at its made-for-TV premiere, chiefly due to a rape scene involving a broom handle. First trip up the river for Blair. 🦴🦴🦴

1974 92m/C Linda Blair, Joanna Miles, Kim Hunter, Richard Jaeckel; **D:** Donald Wrye. **VHS, Beta** *NO*

Born Losers

When a gang of motorcycle riding punks (more than one of which seems to be overcompensating for their repressed homosexuality) gang rape a quartet of young women; when those women are threatened with death if they testify; when the law punishes those that act in their own defense, and frees those that flagrantly threaten society—that's when a man has to stand tall and pass out a little home-

Hey guys, you'll never win that $1000 with a loser attitude like that! Elizabeth James and Tom Laughlin are *Born Losers*.

"It's bad enough having no immune system, but having to wear this giant cabbage on my head is too much!" muses John Travolta in *The Boy in the Plastic Bubble.*

"I...ain't much of a lover boy...there ain't much of a percentage in it."
—Clyde Barrow (Warren Beatty) in *Bonnie & Clyde.*

52

made justice. The original *Billy Jack* film in which Laughlin created what he considered a new kind of movie hero in the Native American martial arts expert and veteran Green Beret. Classic drive-in fare, with good characterization and fine use of camera and editing. Russell gets special guest credit as the hard-boiled mother of one of the girls, and Russ Meyer regular Stuart Lancaster is mostly wasted in a small role as the cowardly sheriff. An understated pacifist message wrapped in drive-in style thrills. The next entry in the series, *Billy Jack,* would not be quite so understated. 🦴🦴🦴

1967 (PG) 112m/C Tom Laughlin, Elizabeth James, Jeremy Slate, William Wellman Jr., Robert Tessier, Jane Russell; *D:* Tom Laughlin; *W:* Tom Laughlin. **VHS, Beta, LV $59.95** *VES, LIV*

Boxcar Bertha

Scorsese's vivid portrayal of the South during the 1930s' Depression is *Bonnie and Clyde* with an unapologetic political bias. Barbara Hershey is a free-wheeling, free-thinking woman who winds up in cahoots with anti-establishment train robber David Carradine. Based on the book *Sister of the Road* by Boxcar Bertha Thom-

son. Judged as a Scorsese picture, it may not deserve comparison to *Good Fellas, Raging Bull,* or even *Cape Fear,* but judged as a low-budget American International drive-in flick, it's cinematic sippin' whiskey. 🦴🦴🦴

1972 (R) 90m/C Barbara Hershey, David Carradine, John Carradine; *D:* Martin Scorsese. **VHS, Beta, LV $69.95** *VES, LIV*

Boxing Helena

Highly publicized as the film that cost Basinger almost $9 million in damages, the debut of director/writer Jennifer Lynch (daughter of David) explores the dark side of relationships between men and women. Sands is Dr. Nick Cavanaugh, a surgeon who becomes dangerously obsessed with the beautiful, yet unattainable Helena (Fenn). When she is hit by a car near his home, he performs emergency surgery and amputates her arms and legs, forcing her to be dependent on him. Metaphorically a situation, albeit an extreme one, that mirrors the power struggle in any sexual relationship. Problematic in some aspects, although equally fascinating as it is disturbing. 🦴🦴🦴

1993 (R) 107m/C Julian Sands, Sherilyn Fenn, Bill Paxton, Kurtwood Smith, Betsy Clark, Nicolette Scorsese, Art Garfunkel; *D:* Jennifer Lynch; *W:* Jennifer Lynch; *M:* Graeme Revell. **VHS, LV** *ORI*

A Boy and His Dog

In the post-holocaust world of 2024, a young man (Don Johnson) and his telepathic canine (McIntire supplies narration of the dog's thoughts) cohort search for food and sex. They happen upon a community that drafts Johnson to repopulate their largely impotent race; Johnson is at first ready, willing, and able, until he discovers the mechanical methods they mean to employ. Based on a short story by Harlan Ellison. The dog was played by the late Tiger of "The Brady Bunch." 🦴🦴🦴

1975 (R) 87m/C Don Johnson, Suzanne Benton, Jason Robards Jr., Charles McGraw, Alvy Moore; *D:* L.Q. Jones; *V:* Tim McIntire. **VHS, Beta, LV $9.99** *CCB, MED, MRV*

The Boy in the Plastic Bubble

John Travolta is a teenager born with immunity deficiencies just tryin' to stay alive in a specially controlled environment in this made-for-TV melodrama, featuring Robert "Mike Brady" Reed, to round out the full '70s picture. An early role for Travolta, made during the same year as *Carrie* and during the height of his sweathog fame. 🦴🦴▷

1976 100m/C John Travolta, Robert Reed, Glynnis O'Connor, Diana Hyland, Ralph Bellamy, Anne Ramsey; **D:** Randal Kleiser. **VHS, Beta $59.95** *PSM*

The Brady Bunch Movie

Grunge and CDs may be the norm in the '90s, but the Bradys still live in the 8-track world of the '70s, where Davy Jones rocks and every day is a sunshine day. Then greedy developer McKean schemes to cash in on Mike and Carol's financial woes. (Hawaii! The Grand Canyon! What were they thinking?) Great ensemble cast capably fills the white platform shoes of the originals—Cole sounds just like Mr. Brady, Cox hilariously channels Jan's tormented middle child angst, and Taylor's self-absorbed Marcia, Marcia, Marcia is dead-on, right down to the frosty pursed lips. Look for neat-o cameos from some original Bradys and most of the Monkees, and Brady in-jokes ("Where is Tiger, anyway?"). 🦴🦴🦴

1995 (PG-13) 88m/C Shelley Long, Gary Cole, Michael McKean, Jean Smart, Henriette Mantel, Christopher Daniel Barnes, Christine Taylor, Paul Sutera, Jennifer Elise Cox, Jesse Lee, Olivia Hack, David Graf, Jack Noseworthy, Shane Conrad, RuPaul; **Cameos:** Ann B. Davis, Florence Henderson, Davy Jones, Barry Williams, Christopher Knight, Michael Lookinland, Mickey Dolenz, Peter Tork; **D:** Betty Thomas; **W:** Bonnie Turner, Terry Turner, Laurice Elehwany, Rick Copp; **M:** Guy Moon. **VHS** *NYR*

Brain Damage

A tongue-in-bloody-cheek farce about a brain-sucking parasite. The parasite in question, Aylmer, addicts our dubious hero to the euphoria induced by the blue liquid the parasite injects into his brain, paving the way for the bloody mayhem that follows. Poor shadow of Henenlotter's far-superior *Basket Case*. In fact, it even includes an inside-joke cameo by Van Hentenryck, reprising his *Basket Case* character; look for him on the subway. 🦴🦴▷

1988 (R) 89m/C Rick Herbst, Gordon MacDonald, Jennifer Lowry; **Cameos:** Kevin Van Hentenryck; **D:** Frank Henenlotter. **VHS, Beta $14.95** *PAR*

Brain Dead

Low-budget but brilliantly assembled puzzle-film about a brain surgeon who agrees to perform experimental surgery on a psychotic to retrieve some corporately valuable data—his first mistake, which begins a seemingly endless cycle of nightmares and identity alterations. A mind-blowing sci-fi feast from ex-*Twilight Zone* writer Charles Beaumont. 🦴🦴🦴▷

1989 (R) 85m/C Bill Pullman, Bill Paxton, Bud Cort, Patricia Charbonneau, Nicholas Pryor, George Kennedy; **D:** Adam Simon. **VHS, Beta $14.95** *MGM*

The Brain from Planet Arous

Nuclear scientist Agar is inhabited and controlled by an evil alien brain named Gor. First Gor mashes Agar's fiancee (Steve Allen's sister-in-law, Meadows), and then he tries to do the same thing to the whole world! A good alien brain named Vol shows up to help and inhabits the body of the Meadows' dog to spy on Gor. Agar has never been better—using his mental powers to blow up planes and buildings, flash-fry his enemies—laughing mania-

THE HOUND SALUTES: JOE BOB BRIGGS

Anybody can die at any time!

"It was an attempt to revive a form of humorous newspaper fiction that was practiced in the late nineteenth century by writers like Ambrose Bierce and Mark Twain." John Bloom's explanation for his troublesome alter ego, Joe Bob Briggs, tasteless redneck critic whose "Joe Bob Goes to the Drive-in" column went out to newspapers nationwide. "I thought of it as a weekly stink bomb tossed into the boring gray matter of the American newspaper."

It was just before VCRs saturated households. Joe Bob championed B-movies and cult wannabes when the venues most closely identified with them were drive-ins. Joe Bob covered splatter, kung-fu, car-chase cheapies, low-budget barbarians, and horror dregs, playing Texan outdoor screens.

At one point Joe Bob's top three were *The Beast Within*, *I Dismember Mama*, and *Mad Monkey Kung Fu*. The highest compliment Joe Bob could pay a motion picture: "Anybody can die at any time!" In his reviews Joe Bob kept a count of violent acts, bimbos, and exposed breasts.

John Bloom, a seemingly normal, serious film reviewer, introduced Joe Bob in the *Dallas Times Herald* in 1982. The column was picked up by the Los Angeles Times syndicate and appeared in 57 newspapers across the country. And Bloom, like Twain and Bierce before him, let his imagination run wild. Joe Bob's column customarily strayed off the topic of movies and into his own white-trash version of Lake Woebegone: Briggs described his colorful lifestyle (four ex-wives, the pleasure of smoking Arkansas polio weed), politics (reactionary anticommunist--for there are no drive-ins in China), and circle of friends (like those who formed DAMM, Drunks Against MADD Mothers). Cinema took a back seat to Joe Bob's folksy commentaries on sex, religion, and his perennial enemies like the "National Organization of Bimbos."

In April 1985, Briggs/Bloom, ostensibly to review *The Last Dragon*, devoted most of his page

continued...

---

cally behind his weird alien eyes. High camp and lots of laughs. 🦴🦴🦴

1957 80m/B John Agar, Joyce Meadows, Robert Fuller, Henry Travis; **D:** Nathan Hertz Juran. **VHS, Beta, LV $19.95** *SNC, CNM, AOV*

Brain of Blood

The leader of a middle eastern country is dying, but a mad scientist (Taylor) promises to transplant his brain into a young body. When agents of a competing political group screw up his plans, he instead uses the body of a gigantic deformed idiot (Bloom), which upsets both monster and his new brain. There's also a dungeon under the lab (where little Angelo teases chained women), and lots of espionage nonsense featuring Williams and Carrol ("the Freak-out Girl"), and lots of dull discussion. Another monster messterpiece from the Adamson, director of *Dracula vs. Frankenstein*. Uses the soundtrack music from *Mad Doctor of Blood Island*. **AKA:** The Creature's Revenge. 🦴🦴

1971 107m/C Kent Taylor, John Bloom, Regina Carrol, Angelo Rossitto, Grant Williams, Reed Hadley, Vicki Volante, Zandor Vorkov; **D:** Al Adamson. **VHS, Beta** *NO*

The Brain That Wouldn't Die

Love is a many-splattered thing when a brilliant surgeon keeps the decapitated head of his fiancee alive after an auto accident while he searches for a suitably stacked body onto which to transplant the head. Absurd and satiric (head talks so much that Doc tapes her/its mouth shut) adding up to major entry in trash film genre; much of the gore was slashed for the video, however. **AKA:** The Head That Wouldn't Die. 🦴🦴

1963 92m/B Herb Evers, Virginia Leith, Adele Lamont; **D:** Joseph Green. **VHS, Beta $19.98** *SNC, MRV, FCT*

The Brainiac

In this cheaply made horror from Mexico, a sorcerer sentenced for black magic returns in the form of a nobleman to strike dark deeds upon the descendants of those who judged him. Full of mind-twisting weird images. He first arrives in the form of a large, very fake looking meteor, before turning into suave

Salazar (who also produced, but usually cast himself as the hero in his films). At times, he turns himself into a hideous monster that looks a bit like a paper mache Bela Lugosi mask, and feeds on his victims' brains and blood with a long forked tongue. In one outrageous scene, he dines on a silver platter full of brains. German Robles, famous for playing a vampire in a series of films, shows up in a supporting role. 🦴🦴

1961 75m/B *MX* Abel Salazar, Ariadne Welter, Mauricio Garces, Rosa Maria Gallardo. **VHS, Beta** $54.95 *SNC, MRV, HHT*

Brazil

The acclaimed nightmare comedy about an Everyman trying to survive in a surreal paper-choked bureaucratic society. There are copious references to *1984* and *The Trial,* fantastic merging of glorious fantasy and stark reality, and astounding visual design. Our story follows the life of a petty bureaucrat in a society where the lives of the people are dictated by the paperwork flow of an uncaring government. Early on he becomes enamored of a young rebel and begins to yearn for freedom. Soon his spirit soars, characterized in his fantasies by a winged man battling the evil forces surrounding him. As he aids the rebels, a combination of government snafus and investigations turn his life into a nightmare. And the winged man goes down in flames. This black comedy was directed by Monty Python alumnus Gilliam and ultimately proves a bit depressing in its final cut, which he had to fight to keep intact. Seems the studio thought the public would prefer a happy ending. Not a film for those who can't deal with frustration. 🦴🦴🦴🦴

1985 **(R)** 131m/C *GB* Jonathan Pryce, Robert De Niro, Michael Palin, Katherine Helmond, Kim Greist, Bob Hoskins, Ian Holm, Peter Vaughan, Ian Richardson; *D:* Terry Gilliam; *W:* Terry Gilliam, Tom Stoppard; *M:* Michael Kamen. Los Angeles Film Critics Association Awards '85: Best Film; Nominations: Academy Awards '85: Best Art Direction/Set Decoration, Best Original Screenplay. **VHS, Beta, LV** $19.95 *MCA, FCT*

The Breakfast Club

Of all the John Hughes teen angst movies, this one has perhaps aged better than others. It tells the tale of five students from different cliques at a Chicago suburban high school who are forced to spend a day together in detention. All the classic high school archetypes are represented—the nerd (Hall), the jock (Estevez), the burnout (Nelson), the princess (Ringwald), and the space cadet (Sheedy). Even with the stock characters, this is a rather well done teenage culture study that delves a little deeper than the standard adult view of adolescent stereotypes. Writer and director Hughes still had his touch with teenage films here and hadn't yet descended into the puerile (yet profitable) land of *Home Alone* and *Baby's Day Out,* which he wrote and produced. This is most often cited as the true coming-out party for the Brat Pack—the first film where so many of the hot, young actors and actresses appeared together and made themselves known to the general public. The acting, writing, and music (featuring Simple Minds and Wang Chung) make this a vastly superior movie to the next Brat Pack ensemble piece, *St. Elmo's Fire.* 🦴🦴🦴

1985 **(R)** 97m/C Ally Sheedy, Molly Ringwald, Judd Nelson, Emilio Estevez, Anthony Michael Hall, Paul Gleason, John Kapelos; *D:* John Hughes; *W:* John Hughes; *M:* Gary Chang, Keith Forsey. **VHS, Beta, LV** $19.95 *MCA, FCT*

Breathless

Godard's first feature catapulted him to the vanguard of French filmmakers. A carefree Parisian crook, who emulates Humphrey Bogart, falls in love with an American girl with tragic results. Wonderful scenes of Parisian life. Established Godard's Brechtian, experimental style. Belmondo's film debut. Mistitled "Breathless" for American release, the film's French title actually means "Out of Breath"; however, the fast-paced, erratic musical score will leave you breathless. In French with English subtitles. Remade with Richard Gere in 1983 with far less intensity. **AKA:** A Bout de Souffle. 🦴🦴🦴🦴

1959 90m/B *FR* Jean-Paul Belmondo, Jean Seberg, Daniel Boulanger, Jean-Pierre Melville, Liliane Robin; *D:* Jean-Luc Godard; *W:* Jean-Luc Godard. Berlin International Film Festival '60: Best Director (Godard). **VHS, Beta** $24.95 *NOS, MRV, CVC*

The Bride

Sting tries to flashdance the Bride of Frankenstein in this romantic melodrama that aims for

B

"Could you juice me again, the colors are starting to fade."
--Rick Herbst in *Brain Damage.*

"My mother's away for Christmas. She's spending it at the plastic surgeon's."
--Jonathan Pryce on Kathryn Helmond in *Brazil.*

Story continued...

to parodying the treacly all-star charity song "We are the World." Joe Bob's version: "We are the weird/We are the starvin'/We are the scum of the filthy earth/So let's start scarfin'..."

It was all a local race-baiting politician needed to spearhead the Joe Bob Briggs backlash. Despite a front-page apology by the paper, about 250 African-American protestors demanded that *Times Herald* editors bury Briggs. Bloom refused to go along and resigned instead. Since the *Los Angeles Times* and the *Times Herald* shared the same interim publisher, Bloom lost both his job and his syndicate. In a farewell column, Joe Bob compared his "assassination" to Lincoln's and Kennedy's. And he gave three stars to *Lust in the Dust*.

But Joe Bob was not gone for good. Another syndicate picked up the column, and Bloom went on the road as a stand-up comedy act, in character as Briggs, singing "We are the Weird" as a finale. He played *The Tonight Show*, *Late Night with David Letterman*, and guest-hosted a cable-TV schlock-movie slot. He stays in touch with fans via his own newsletter ("Just like drugs, the first one's free"), and has authored several Joe Bob books, including an autobiography, *A Guide to Western Civilization, or My Story*.

Still, one has to wonder if the Bloom is off Joe Bob Briggs, for reasons other than political-correctness. Most American drive-ins had shut down by the end of the 1980s, and those that survive try to cater to a "family" crowd, rather than a Joe Bob rabble. The VCR has become the medium for deliciously trashy exploitation and cult pics. Even Joe Bob had to acknowledge that when, a few years ago, he put out his own tape, a Joe-Bob-in-Concert videocassette.

the literary high-mindedness which Kenneth Branaugh eventually brought to the story. Jennifer Beals plays the undead object of desire as a liberated woman on the '80s, and Sting comes across like a sensitive schoolteacher on the verge of suspension for sexual harassment. Director Roddam goes about his humorless business with all the cinematic zeal of a *Vogue* photographer. He even drags in has-been model Verushka, who appeared in Antonioni's *Blow Up* twenty years before, for a pointless cameo. 🎵 📼

1985 (PG-13) 118m/C Sting, Jennifer Beals, Anthony Higgins, David Rappaport, Geraldine Page, Clancy Brown, Phil Daniels, Veruschka; ***D:*** Franc Roddam; ***M:*** Maurice Jarre. **VHS, Beta, LV $9.95** *FOX*

The Bride & the Beast

Newlywed to big-game hunter Fuller, blushing bride Austin is strangely drawn to Spanky, a gorilla kept in the basement. That night, Spanky escapes for some Spanky hanky-panky, but is shot to death by Fuller. A hypnosis session reveals that Austin may be a reincarnated gorilla, which would explain her fondness for angora sweaters. A ludicrous jungle tale, and probably the only Ed Wood script that would have been improved if Wood had directed it himself. As it is, Weiss loads on the stock footage with a shovel, without the hyperbolic narration by Criswell or Timothy Farrell that would make it tolerable. A subplot about an escaped killer tiger is used as an excuse for the insertion of long, dull chunks of the Sabu picture *Man-Eater of Kumaon*—the same scenes which were also used in Sabu's aptly named quasi-UFO movie *Jungle Hell,* making for quite an ordeal when both pictures played as double features. Adapted as a musical theatre production in 1995. ***AKA:*** Queen of the Gorillas. 🎵 📼

1958 78m/B Charlotte Austin, Lance Fuller, William Justine; ***D:*** Adrian Weiss; ***W:*** Edward D. Wood Jr.; ***M:*** Les Baxter. **VHS, Beta** *AOV*

The Bride of Frankenstein

The classic sequel to the classic original. When his wife is kidnapped by his old associate Dr. Pretorious (Thesiger, in a highly amusing role), Dr. Frankenstein (Clive) is forced to help build a mate for his monster.

More humor than the first, but also more pathos, including the monster's famous but short-lived friendship with a blind hermit, who teaches the monster to speak. Karloff's monster is once again touching and frightening at the same time. The unhappy, neurotic Clive disliked playing in horror films, which may have added to his tortured performances in them. Lanchester plays both the bride and Mary Shelley in the opening sequence. O'Connor contributes standout comedy relief. Features a spectacular score by Franz Waxman. 🎵🎵🎵🎵

1935 75m/B Boris Karloff, Elsa Lanchester, Ernest Thesiger, Colin Clive, Una O'Connor, Valerie Hobson, Dwight Frye, John Carradine, E.E. Clive, O.P. Heggie, Gavin Gordon, Douglas Walton; **D:** James Whale. Nominations: Academy Awards '35: Best Sound. **VHS, Beta, LV $14.95** *MCA, MLB*

Bride of Re-Animator

Herbert West is back, and this time he not only re-animates life but creates life—sexy female life—in this sequel to the immensely popular *Re-Animator*. High camp and blood curdling gore make this a standout in the sequel parade. Available in a R-rated version as well. 🎵🎵▷

1989 99m/C Bruce Abbott, Claude Earl Jones, Fabiana Udenio, Jeffrey Combs, Kathleen Kinmont, David Gale; **D:** Brian Yuzna; **M:** Richard Band. **VHS, Beta, LV $89.95** *LIV*

Bride of the Monster

Lugosi stars as a mad scientist trying to create a race of giant atomic supermen. Ed Wood's attempt at creating something like the classic Universal monster pictures ended up looking more like one of Lugosi's poverty row epics. Features appearances by many Wood trademarks, including weird dialogue, mismatched scenes, poor continuity, and angora. Johnson joins the Wood stock company with his portrayal of Lobo, one of Bela's former guinea pigs. King and McCoy got the romantic leads by investing in the production. Marco debuts his character "Kelton the Cop," which he reprised for *Plan 9 From Outer Space* and *Night of the Ghouls*. A must see. **AKA:** Bride of the Atom. 🎵🎵🎵🎵

1956 70m/B Bela Lugosi, Tor Johnson, Loretta King, Tony McCoy, Paul Marco, Dolores Fuller, Conrad Brooks, Harvey Dunne, Don Nagel; **D:** Edward D. Wood Jr. **VHS, Beta $19.95** *NOS, SNC, VYY*

The Brood

An emotionally disturbed woman (Eggar) falls under the influence of mad doctor (Reed). Through his unorthodox treatments, her rage is made manifest in the form of a brood of mutant children. The brood act her violent emotional states, taking retribution on those who threaten their mother. Director Cronenberg mixes the traditional mad scientist story with his trademark gross-out special effects, to create a disturbing combination of physical and psychological terror. Remember, mom always said not to make her angry. Look especially for the truly bizarre "birth" scene. Cronenberg's obsession with physical malformities continued with *Videodrome, The Fly, Dead Ringers*, and *Naked Lunch*. 🎵🎵🎵

1979 (R) 92m/C CA Samantha Eggar, Oliver Reed; **D:** David Cronenberg; **W:** David Cronenberg; **M:** Howard Shore. **VHS, Beta, LV $19.98** *SUE*

A Bucket of Blood

Venerable character actor Dick Miller's finest hour! He portrays Walter Paisley, a busboy at the Yellow Door coffeehouse where he is an object of ridicule. An aspiring artist, he is a wretched failure until he accidentally kills the landlady's cat, covers it with clay and passes it off as a sculpture, "Dead Cat." Suddenly, he is hailed as a genius. But what will he do for an encore? Narcotics cop Burt Convy is the "inspiration" for his next work, "Murdered Man." This absolutely essential Roger Corman classic is worthless as a horror film, but priceless as a hip black comedy that satirizes the beatnik coffeehouse scene. He filmed it in five days. His next film, *Little Shop of Horrors*, was filmed in two. Both were written by Charles Griffith. Julian Burton is great as a beat poet ("Either a rock is a rock or it's sculpture/Either a sound is a sound or it's music"). Corman graduates Joe Dante and Alan Arkush paid homage by casting Miller as Walter Paisley in *Hollywood Boulevard*. 🎵🎵🎵▷

1959 66m/B Dick Miller, Barboura Morris, Antony Carbone, Julian Burton, Ed Nelson, Bert Convy; **D:** Roger Corman; **W:** Charles B. Griffith. **VHS, Beta $19.95** *NOS, RHI, SNC*

"You should have been more careful."
--Sensitive he-man Jean-Paul Belmondo to Jean Seaberg on finding out he's going to be a father in *Breathless*.

~~~

"I've been cursed for delving into the mysteries of life."
--Dr. Frankenstein (Colin Clive) in *The Bride of Frankenstein*.

Can someone give
this movie a
hand? Ann
Magnuson in
Cabin Boy.

ate, and later to squelch, a slave revolt. This uncompromising movie is so shocking the first time around that it may require a second viewing to reassure oneself that it really happened. **AKA:** Quemimada!. ♫♫♫♫
1970 (PG) 112m/C *IT* Marlon Brando, Evarist Marquez, Renato Salvatori; **D:** Gillo Pontecorvo; **M:** Ennio Morricone. **VHS, Beta, LV $19.98** *MGM, CRC, FCT*

Bury Me an Angel

In one of the few biker movies done by a woman, party girl Dag witnesses her brother gunned down. She fixes up a motorcycle and takes off with two hippie boyfriends on a cross-country pursuit of the killer, in defiance of squares like the rural sheriff who bellows "What the cornbread hell is going on here anyway?" As in many such two-wheeler sagas, there's an honest attempt at serious message-sending, wherein Dag searches her soul over the morality of her revenge—aforementioned soul-searching usually preceded by Dag taking all her clothes off. *Grizzly Adams* star Dan Haggerty portrays a sensitive artist. ♫ ▷
1971 85m/C Dixie Peabody, Terry Mace, Clyde Ventura, Dan Haggerty, Stephen Whittaker, Gary Littlejohn; **D:** Barbara Peeters. **VHS, Beta, LV $19.95** *NWV, HHT*

Cabin Boy

So you think you're a big Chris Elliott fan, huh? You say you've followed this goofy comedian since his early days as The Guy Under the Seats on *Late Night with David Letterman,* that you even have every episode of his series *Get a Life* on tape? That your firm belief is that any film starring Elliott must be a funny movie that you'd see over and over? Well guess what—you're WRONG, WRONG, WRONG! You won't believe how wrong you are until you see this foul mess, in which obnoxious "fancy lad" Elliott mistakenly boards the wrong boat and becomes the new cabin boy for a ridiculous bunch of mean, smelly sailors. Fish out of water saga is so bad it's—well, bad, a blundering attempt at parody that's just plain stupid. Surprisingly produced by Tim Burton, this effort has just about zero redeeming value. Look for Chris' real life dad Bob as the lad's dad; good friend Letterman appears briefly as

Bug

The city of Riverside is threatened with destruction after a massive earth tremor unleashes a super-race of ten-inch mega-cockroaches that belch fire, eat raw meat, and are virtually impervious to Raid. Produced by gimmick-king William Castle, who wanted to install windshield wiper-like devices under theatre seats that would brush against the patrons' feet as the cockroaches crawled across the screen; unfortunately, the idea was squashed flat. ♫♫
1975 (PG) 100m/C Bradford Dillman, Joanna Miles, William Castle; **D:** Jeannot Szwarc; **M:** Charles Fox. **VHS, Beta $19.95** *PAR*

Burn!

Gillo Pontecorvo, director of the acclaimed pseudo-documentary *Battle of Algiers* and the rarely seen Oscar-nominated *Kapo,* made this remarkable indictment of imperialist manipulation of third world politics. Marlon Brando, in what he considers his finest role, plays a 19th century British ambassador who is sent to a Portuguese-run Caribbean island to cre-

nasty "Old Salt," but uses the alias Earl Hofert in the final credits. As usual, the acerbic Letterman gets the best line, "Man, oh, man do I hate them fancy lads." We know how you feel Dave. The only laughs this movie ever got came when Letterman made fun of his cameo while hosting the Oscars. **WOOF!**

1994 (PG-13) 80m/C Chris Elliott, Ann Magnuson, Ritch Brinkley, James Gammon, Brian Doyle-Murray, Russ Tamblyn, Brion James, Ricki Lake, Bob Elliott; *Cameos:* David Letterman; *D:* Adam Resnick; *W:* Adam Resnick; *M:* Steve Bartek. **VHS, LV** *TOU*

The Cabinet of Dr. Caligari

A pioneering German film in the most extreme expressionistic style about a hypnotist (Krauss) in a carnival whose star attraction is a somnambulist (Veidt) kept in a trance for years. In a time when filmmakers were striving for realism, Wiene's artistic vision created a sensation. Highly influential in its approach to lighting, composition, design, storyline, and acting. Aside from the films of Lon Chaney, Germany's UFA Studios dominated the world

of fantasy films following WWI. Other outstanding examples include Fritz Lang's *Metropolis, Siegfried,* and *Woman in the Moon,* as well as Paul Wegener's *The Golem* and *The Student of Prague,* and Wiene's *Hands of Orlac.* With the rise of Hitler, most of the German artists fled to Hollywood, where they would help shape the studio horror films of the '30s. Much imitated. Silent. 🦴🦴🦴🦴

1919 52m/B *GE* Conrad Veidt, Werner Krauss, Lil Dagover; *D:* Robert Wiene. **VHS, Beta, LV $11.95** *SNC, REP, MRV*

Caddyshack

Ask many thirtysomething males what their favorite comedy ever is, and you might be surprised at how many votes this film gets. In fact, it seems to be a badge of honor for any male who went to college in the 1980s to be able to quote damn near every scene from this flick, especially those involving Carl the greenskeeper (Bill Murray) and nouveau rich jerk Al Czervik (Rodney Dangerfield). The action takes place at Bushwood Country Club,

"I should have stayed home and played with myself...." Chevy Chase, Ted Knight, and Rodney Dangerfield in *Caddyshack.*

VIDEO GENRES
What You See and What You Get

The photographs and text on the average video box promise the moon and the stars. Even the cheesiest B-flick will claim to provide pulse-pounding thrills, matchless suspense, uncontrollable laughs, sizzling sex, etc., etc. The film itself seldom lives up to the overwrought advertising, but everyone understands that it's all part of the game and accepts the hype with a sense of humor. Still, what do the words and images really mean? Here's a thumbnail analysis of genre box art and copy:

Genre: Action Adventure

The box features: A guy with bulging muscles, no shirt (or tattered shirt), and a big weapon pointing upward at a significant phallic angle. Something exploding in the background. (Beautiful girl in background is a popular option.)

The film contains: Lots of explosions (old junker cars are a popular target); gunfights wherein multiple bad guys with greasy ponytails simulate being shot by automatic weapons. Multiple blood squibs explode on their torsos as they dance the funky chicken, almost always in slow motion.

Genre: Erotic thriller

The box features: Beautiful long-haired woman, naked or barely dressed (unrated or R-), her eyes closed in rapturous delight. Male may or may not be present behind her. The words "passion," "forbidden," "obsession," "instinct," "illicit," "midnight" or "private" are likely to appear in title.

The film contains: Story about infidelity and/or murder of jealous/ abusive/ violent/ inattentive/ ineffective husband. Simulated sex scenes in which female nudity features prominently but male nudity is coyly concealed.

Genre: Martial arts

The box features: A snarling guy with fists clenched and at least one foot raised to head level or above. Something blowing up in the background.

continued...

where caddy O'Keefe is bucking to win the club's college scholarship. Characters involved in various sophomoric set pieces include obnoxious club president Knight, a playboy who is too laid back to keep his score (Chase), and the aforementioned duo of Murray and Dangerfield. Occasional dry moments are followed by scenes of pure (and tasteless) anarchy, so watch with someone immature. I mean, the blonde bombshell character's name is "Lacey Underall" for crying out loud! Despite (and often because of) the maturity level, this movie has withstood the test of time and is still flat-out funny. Does for golf what *Major League* tried to do for baseball. 🦴🦴🦴🦴

1980 (R) 99m/C Chevy Chase, Rodney Dangerfield, Ted Knight, Michael O'Keefe, Bill Murray, Sarah Holcomb, Brian Doyle-Murray; **D:** Harold Ramis; **W:** Brian Doyle-Murray, Doug Kenney, Harold Ramis. **VHS, Beta, LV $19.98** *WAR*

Caged Heat

Low-budget babes-behind-bars film touted as the best sexploitation film of the day. Demme's directorial debut is a genre-altering installment in Roger Corman's formulaic cell-block Cinderella cycle. Recycled plot—innocent woman is put behind bars, where she loses some of her innocence—boasts an updated treatment. These babes may wear hot pants and gratuitously bare their midriffs, but they're not brainless bimbos. They're strong individuals who work together to liberate themselves. Reached cult status. Cult diva Steele returned to the big screen after six years to play the wheelchair-ridden prison warden, written specifically for her. **AKA:** Renegade Girls; Caged Females. 🦴🦴

1974 (R) 83m/C Juanita Brown, Erica Gavin, Roberta Collins, Barbara Steele, Ella Reid, Cheryl "Rainbeaux" Smith; **D:** Jonathan Demme; **W:** Jonathan Demme. **VHS, LV** *SUE, NWV*

Caligula

Infamous, expensive, extremely graphic, and sexually explicit adaptation of the life of the mad Roman emperor, Caligula. Scenes of decapitation, necrophilia, rape, bestiality, and sadomasochism abound. Biggest question is why Gielgud, O'Toole, and McDowell lent their talents to this monumentally abhorred film (not to mention Gore Vidal on the writing end, who didn't want the credit). Adult magazine publisher Bob Guccione coproduced and didn't particularly want to release it. Also available in a censored, "R" rated version. 🎵 🎬

1980 143m/C *IT* Malcolm McDowell, John Gielgud, Peter O'Toole, Helen Mirren; *D:* Tinto Brass; *W:* Gore Vidal. **VHS, Beta, LV $79.95** *VES, HHE*

Canadian Bacon

Feature film debut for Moore, who irritated many with *Roger & Me.* Title refers to the military code name for a campaign to whip up anti-Canadian hysteria and justify a U.S. invasion of its neighbor to the north. Evil political advisor Pollak convinces well-meaning but inept President Alda that it's just the thing to get the presidential popularity up and those defense industries humming. Ugly Americans abound, at expense of polite Canadians, eh? Bipartisan satire was filmed in Toronto, which is shown to good advantage. Candy in one of last roles is the superpatriotic sheriff of Niagara Falls, New York. 🎵🎵🎬

1994 (PG) m/C Alan Alda, Kevin Pollak, John Candy, Rhea Perlman, Rip Torn, Bill Nunn, Kevin J. O'Connor, Steven Wright, G.D. Spradlin; *Cameos:* Michael Moore; *D:* Michael Moore; *W:* Michael Moore; *M:* Elmer Bernstein. **VHS** *NYR*

Candy Stripe Nurses

Even hard-core Roger Corman fans might find his final installment in the nursing comedy pentad to be a lethargic exercise in gratuitous "sexual situations." Bet those uniforms don't meet hospital standards. The previous films in the series are: *The Student Nurses, Private Duty Nurses, Night Call Nurses,* and *The Young Nurses. AKA:* Sweet Candy. 🎵

1974 (R) 80m/C Candice Rialson, Robin Mattson, Maria Rojo, Kimberly Hyde, Dick Miller, Stanley Ralph Ross, Monte Landis, Tom Baker; *D:* Allan Holleb. **VHS, Beta $59.95** *SUE*

Cannibal Women in the Avocado Jungle of Death

This parody of the John Milius school of chest-thumping, macho adventure movie is a sleeper. Dr. Hunt (Tweed), "a respected, middle-of-the-road feminist" and ethno-historian,

treks off into the dangerous Avocado Jungle, just east of Los Angeles, to find out what happened to Dr. Kurtz (Barbeau) who disappeared there. Was she killed by the man-hating Piranha Women, or has she gone native and joined them? Playmate and video veteran Tweed effectively underplays the cool comedy with some refreshingly intelligent moments. Lawton, writer of *Pretty Woman* and *Under Siege,* directed under the alias "J.D. Athens." 🎵🎵🎵

1989 (PG-13) 90m/C Shannon Tweed, Adrienne Barbeau, Karen Mistal, Barry Primus, Bill Maher; *D:* J.F. Lawton; *W:* J.F. Lawton. **VHS, Beta, LV $79.95** *PAR*

Cannonball

Assorted ruthless people leave patches of rubber across the country competing for grand prize in less than legal auto race. Not top drawer New World but nonetheless a cult item. Inferior to Bartel's previous cult classic, *Death Race 2000.* Most interesting for plethora of cult cameos, including Scorsese, Dante, and grandmaster Corman. *AKA:* Carquake. 🎵🎵

1976 (PG) 93m/C David Carradine, Bill McKinney, Veronica Hamel, Gerrit Graham, Robert Carradine, Sylvester Stallone, Jonathan Kaplan; *Cameos:* Martin Scorsese, Roger Corman, Joe Dante; *D:* Paul Bartel; *M:* David A. Axelrod. **VHS, Beta** *NO*

Captain Kronos: Vampire Hunter

Captain Kronos fences thirsty foes in Hammer horror hybrid; a swashbuckling horror movie. Artsy, atmospheric and atypical, it's written and directed with tongue firmly in cheek by Clemens, who penned many an *Avengers* episode. The distinctive Hammer atmosphere is always fun. Her many fans will appreciate Munro's tastefully shadowed love scene. *AKA:* Kronos. 🎵🎵🎵

1974 (R) 91m/C *GB* Horst Janson, John Carson, Caroline Munro, Ian Hendry, Shane Briant, Wanda Ventham; *D:* Brian Clemens; *W:* Brian Clemens. **VHS, Beta $44.95** *PAR*

Careful

Butler-in-training Neale courts Neville in an alpine mountain village where silence is golden, or at least being quiet will lessen the

C

"**A sadistic she-devil leading a pair of perverts on a raging ride through hell!**"
--*Bury Me an Angel.*

"**Man oh man, do I hate them fancy lads!**"
--David Lettermen in *Cabin Boy,* referring to Chris Elliot.

The film contains: Several carefully choreographed fights with fists, feet, and a variety of hand-held weapons. Hundreds of extras will be kicked, chopped, hit, and dispatched by a virtuous young hero defending his school/province/teacher/employer.

Genre: Star vehicle you've never heard of

The box features: Photograph that is identifiably the star, but somehow doesn't quite look like him or her.

The film contains: Either an embarrassment made early in the star's career or a more recent feature deemed too off-beat and/or bad for theatrical release. As a rule of thumb: the bigger the star's name, the less likely the film will be enjoyable as serious entertainment. It does, however, have real potential as unintentional comedy or alternative classic.

> **"So he says to me, 'On your deathbed, you will have total consciousness'. So I got that going for me."**
>
> --Carl the Greenskeeper (Bill Murray) in *Caddyshack.*

chance of an avalanche. Dig a little deeper and you find incest, repression, and other nasty things. Highly individualistic black comedy parodies German Expressionism and Freudian psychology to the point of absurdity, dealing with snow, sex, sleep, spirits, and obsessive/compulsive personality disorders. Third film from Canadian cult director Maddin is awash in vivid primary colors when it suits the scene's mood and employs between-scenes titles in a homage to cinematic antiquity. 🎵🎵

1994 100m/C Kyle McCulloch, Gosia Dobrowolska, Jackie Burroughs, Sarah Neville, Brent Neale, Paul Cox, Victor Cowie, Michael O'Sullivan, Vince Rimmer, Katya Gardner; **D:** Guy Maddin; **W:** Guy Maddin, George Toles; **M:** John McCulloch. **VHS** *NYR*

Carnival of Souls

Some movies come back to haunt you. Industrial filmmaker Herk Hervey's first, and only, feature is the best film ever made in Lawrence, Kansas. It is also one of the eeriest and most influential horror films you have perhaps never heard of. A critically acclaimed 1989 theatrical revival on the art house circuit rescued this essential creepshow from late-night TV obscurity. Candace Hilligoss stars as Mary, a church organist who seemingly survives a car crash only to be haunted by unsettling visions of pasty-faced ghouls. George Romero's *Night of the Living Dead* owes this a debt of gratitude. Laserdisc version offers restored picture quality and a refined audio track, as well as introductory feature on the movie's background. 🎵🎵🎵

1962 80m/B Candace Hilligoss, Sidney Berger, Frances Feist, Stan Levitt, Art Ellison, Herk Harvey; **D:** Herk Harvey. **VHS, Beta, LV $19.99** *MRV, SNC, NOS*

Carnival Rock

Those expecting teenage hi-jinx on the midway will be very disappointed. Although this one has great rockin' tunes, they are unfortunately only there to interrupt some depressing melodrama. Stewart is the lovesick owner of a carnival pier night club who spends the whole picture mooning over singer Cabot, even after he loses everything to her fiancee (Hutton). Corman regulars Miller, VeSota, Haze, and Nelson are on hand, and Adrian (from *Bluebeard, Lady of Burlesque, Horror Island,* and many more) is always popping up in another harpy role. Aside from the music, the most satisfying moments are when Cabot catches Adrian with a terrific right cross, and later when Hutton tags Stewart. Performances include The Platters ("Remember When"), David Houston ("One and Only," "Teenage Frankie and Johnnie"), The Shadows ("The Creep"), The Blockbusters ("Carnival Rock"), Bob Luman ("This is the Night," "All Night Long"), and Cabot herself, who sings and dances to "Ou-Shoo-Bla-D" and "There's No Place Without You." Twin billed with *Teenage Thunder.* 🎵🎵

1957 80m/B Susan Cabot, Brian Hutton, David J. Stewart, Dick Miller, Iris Adrian, Jonathan Haze, Ed Nelson; **D:** Roger Corman. **VHS, Beta $9.95** *RHI, AOV, FCT*

The Carpetbaggers

"You dirty, filthy, perverted monster!" screams Carroll Baker. "You're the meanest, cruelest, most loathsome thing I've ever met!" That pretty much sums up George Peppard's character (or lack of it) in this so-bad-it's-good, can't-turn-it-off film of Harold Robbins' best-selling potboiler. This guy's incredible. He's ruthless, despicable...well, pretty much what Baker said. Any similarity between this millionaire tycoon and Howard Hughes is not necessarily a coincidence. Likewise for sexpot Carroll Baker and screen goddess Jean Harlow and Martha Hyer and Jane Russell. Long-suffering Elizabeth Ashley stands by her man though he treats her like dirt. Alan Ladd, in his last American film, costars as movie western hero Nevada Smith, a character spun off in his own movie that starred Steve McQueen. A must-see for those who can't resist taking out the trash. Rent it with *The Oscar*. 🎞🎞🎞

1964 (PG) 150m/C George Peppard, Carroll Baker, Alan Ladd, Elizabeth Ashley, Lew Ayres, Martha Hyer, Martin Balsam, Robert Cummings, Archie Moore, Audrey Totter; *D:* Edward Dmytryk; *W:* John Michael Hayes; *M:* Elmer Bernstein. National Board of Review Awards '64: Best Supporting Actor (Balsam). **VHS, Beta $14.95** *PAR*

Carrie

It's scary just how bad most films based on books by Stephen King are. This is a rare exception. Brian DePalma, the man who would be Hitchcock, enjoyed his first mainstream success with this influential, much-copied horror film about a tormented high school misfit. No wonder it connected with teenage audiences. Sissy Spacek stars as naive, repressed Carrie White, the target of cruel classmates who plot to humiliate her at the prom. Their bloody practical joke unleashes all of Carrie's pent-up rage and she makes full use of her telekinetic powers to exact her revenge. Piper Laurie, as Carrie's religious fanatic mother, was nominated for an Academy Award. William Katt co-stars as her dreamy prom date, with Nancy Allen (DePalma's leading lady on and off screen) as Carrie's chief nemesis. The film debuts of Betty Buckley, Amy Irving, and P. J. Soles (Riff Randle in *Rock and Roll High School*) and an early screen credit for John Travolta. 🎞🎞🎞

1976 (R) 98m/C Sissy Spacek, Piper Laurie, John Travolta, William Katt, Amy Irving, Nancy Allen, Edie McClurg, Betty Buckley, P.J. Soles; *D:* Brian DePalma; *M:* Pino Donaggio. National Society of Film Critics

Awards '76: Best Actress (Spacek); Nominations: Academy Awards '76: Best Actress (Spacek), Best Supporting Actress (Laurie). **VHS, Beta, LV $14.95** *MGM, FOX, CRC*

The Carrier

Smalltown Sleepy Rock is ideal family-raising turf until a plague mysteriously blights inhabitants, and townspeople are out to exterminate all potential carriers. The disease is transmitted by touch, so the population has taken to wrapping their bodies in plastic to avoid any potential contamination from others (sound familiar?). Silverman is a standout as the local spiritual leader; mob scenes are well orchestrated. Filmed on location in Manchester, Michigan. 🎞🎞

1987 (R) 99m/C Gregory Fortescue, Steve Dixon, Paul Silverman; *D:* Nathan J. White. **VHS, Beta** *NO*

Casablanca

Can you see George Raft as Rick? Jack Warner did, but producer Hal Wallis wanted Bogart. Considered by many to be the best film ever made and one of the most quoted movies of all time, it rocketed Bogart from gangster roles to romantic leads as he and Bergman (who never looked lovelier) sizzle on screen. Bogart runs a gin joint in Morocco during the Nazi occupation, and meets up with Bergman, an old flame, but romance and politics do not mix, especially in Nazi-occupied French Morocco. Greenstreet, Lorre, and Rains all create memorable characters, as does Wilson, the piano player to whom Bergman says the oft-misquoted, "Play it, Sam." Without a doubt, the best closing scene ever written; it was scripted on the fly during the end of shooting, and actually shot several ways. Written from an unproduced play. See it in the original black and white. Laserdisc edition features restored imaging and sound and commentary by film historian Ronald Haver about the production, the play it was based on, and the famed evolution of the screenplay on audio track two. 50th Anniversary Edition contains a restored and remastered print, the original 1942 theatrical trailer, a film documentary narrated by Lauren Bacall, and a booklet. 🎞🎞🎞🎞

C

"**T**hese women are serious about their taste in men."
--*Cannibal Women in the Avocado Jungle of Death.*

"**C**ats or death? What'll it be? Cats...or death!"
--*The Carrier.*

1942 (PG) 102m/B Humphrey Bogart, Ingrid Bergman, Paul Henreid, Claude Rains, Peter Lorre, Sydney Greenstreet, Conrad Veidt, S.Z. Sakall, Dooley Wilson, Marcel Dalio, John Qualen, Helmut Dantine; **D:** Michael Curtiz; **W:** Julius J. Epstein, Philip C. Epstein, Howard Koch; **M:** Max Steiner. Academy Awards '43: Best Director (Curtiz), Best Picture, Best Screenplay; National Board of Review Awards '45: 10 Best Films of the Year; Nominations: Academy Awards '43: Best Actor (Bogart), Best Black and White Cinematography, Best Film Editing, Best Supporting Actor (Rains), Best Original Score. **VHS, Beta, LV, 8mm $19.98** *MGM, FOX, TLF*

Castle of Blood

After betting Edgar Allen Poe that he can survive a stay overnight in a haunted castle, a writer (Riviere) is forced to deal with a number of creepy encounters—the foremost being the lovely Elizabeth Blackwood (Steele), a ghostly woman without a heartbeat. The ghosts of the castle are forced to forever repeat their bloody deaths. Cult favorite Steele enhances this atmospheric chiller. Prolific actor/director Margheriti has many fun exploitation features to his credit (*Horror Castle, Battle of the Worlds, Cannibal Apocalypse*), including the inferior color remake *Web of the Spider*. **AKA:** Castle of Terror; Coffin of Terror; Danza Macabra. 🦴🦴🦴

1964 85m/B IT FR Barbara Steele, George Riviere, Margrete Robsahm, Henry Kruger, Montgomery Glenn, Sylvia Sorente; **D:** Anthony (Antonio Margheriti) Dawson. **VHS $16.95** *SNC*

The Castle of Fu Manchu

The final chapter in a series starring Lee as the wicked doctor. This time, Lee has developed a gadget which will put the earth into a deep freeze, and at his mercy. To fine tune this contraption, he enlists the help of a gifted scientist by abducting him. However, the helper/hostage has a bad ticker, so Lee must abduct a heart surgeon to save his life, and thus, the freezer project. Most critics felt this was the weakest installment in the series. **AKA:** Assignment: Istanbul; Die Folterkammer des Dr. Fu Manchu. 🦴

1968 (PG) 92m/C GE SP IT GB Christopher Lee, Richard Greene, H. Marion Crawford, Tsai Chin, Gunther Stoll, Rosalba (Sara Bay) Neri, Maria Perschy; **D:** Jess (Jesus) Franco. **VHS $19.95** *MRV*

Casualties of Love: The "Long Island Lolita" Story

Told from the Buttafuoco's point of view, Amy Fisher was nothing but a wacko fatally attracted teenager who misunderstood Joey's harmless flirtations and deliberately went after his wife with a gun. The Buttafuocos received $300,000 from CBS to tell their side of the story which features Milano, who resembles Amy not in the least, as the lead. One of three competing network television versions of the sordid story. See also: *The Amy Fisher Story* and *Lethal Lolita—Amy Fisher: My Story.* 🦴🦴

1993 (PG-13) 94m/C Jack Scalia, Alyssa Milano, Phyllis Lyons, Jack Kehler, Michael Bowen, J.E. Freeman, Nicky Corello, Lawrence Tierney, Peter Van Norden, Anne DeSalvo; **D:** John Herzfeld; **W:** John Herzfeld. **VHS $59.95** *COL*

Cat People

In this atmospheric, intelligent, and effective shocker, a young dress designer is the victim of acurse that changes her into a deadly panther who must kill to survive, much to her new husband's distress. The first of a series of B-budget horror films assigned producer Val Lewton, this was a big hit for RKO when released (over $2 million at the box office) and is now regarded as a classic horror film. While using many conventions of the form, Lewton is credited with creating (or at least defining) at least two new ones with this film: "The Walk," in which a protagonist walks down a dark alley/hallway/path, while something may or may not be stalking in the shadows; and "The Bus," a false scare which often acts in combination with "The Walk," named for the loudly hissing blast from a bus' air brakes that startles Jane Randolph (and audiences for over 50 years). 🦴🦴🦴🦴

1942 73m/B Jane Randolph, Elizabeth Russell, Jack Holt, Alan Napier, Simone Simon, Kent Smith, Tom Conway; **D:** Jacques Tourneur. **VHS, Beta, LV $19.95** *MED, BTV, TTC*

Cat Women of the Moon

Scientists land on the moon and encounter an Amazon-like force of leotard-attired female chauvinists. Remade as *Missile to the Moon.*

Featuring the Hollywood Cover Girls as various cat women. Available in its original 3-D format, but Rhino's tape is so poorly transferred as to be unwatchable. The decent cast had seen better days. Tufts got his show biz start as an opera singer, then moved on to Broadway musicals. When a football injury kept him out of the service during World War II, he became a leading Hollywood star in films like *So Proudly We Hail!* and *Bring on the Girls,* but the low-key demeanor of his screen personae made it difficult for him to keep the spotlight once the war was over. A hard drinker, he was sued by showgirls in the '50s for biting them on the thighs. Tufts died of pneumonia in 1970. Jory had been in *State Fair* (1933), *Gone with the Wind,* and played Oberon in *A Midsummer Night's Dream* (1935). Former Miss Utah Windsor became a star playing bad girls, and was in *Abbott & Costello Meet the Mummy, Swamp Women, The Killing,* and *The Day Mars Invaded Earth.* Hilton was a top editor (*The Killers*) before becoming a B-movie director. **AKA:** Rocket to the Moon. 🎵🎵🎵

1953 65m/B Sonny Tufts, Victor Jory, Marie Windsor, Bill Phipps, Douglas Fowley, Carol Brewster, Suzanne Alexander, Susan Morrow; **D:** Arthur Hilton; **M:** Elmer Bernstein. **VHS, Beta $12.95** *RHI, SNC, MWP*

Catch-22

Actor/scriptwriter Buck Henry's ambitious adaptation of Joseph Heller's epic black comedy novel about a group of American fliers in the Mediterranean during WWII. Biting anti-war satire with Arkin in one of his best roles, as the everyman bombardier Yossarian, who tries to fake insanity to get out of flying any more dangerous missions. Except insanity is exactly what the military thrives on, as medals are awarded for publicity reasons, one officer murders local prostitutes with impunity, and the base black-marketeer arranges a holocaust on behalf of his Axis clients. Perhaps too literal to the book's masterfully chaotic structure, causing occasional problems in the "are you following along department?" Unforgettable moments in Goya-esque caricature include Gen. Dreedle (Welles) growling "The next man who moans will be shot..." 🎵🎵🎵

1970 (R) 121m/C Alan Arkin, Martin Balsam, Art Garfunkel, Jon Voight, Richard Benjamin, Buck Henry, Bob Newhart, Paula Prentiss, Martin Sheen, Charles Grodin, Anthony Perkins, Orson Welles, Jack Gilford; **D:** Mike Nichols; **W:** Buck Henry. **VHS, Beta, LV $14.95** *PAR*

Chain Gang Women

Lee Frost, a seasoned veteran of the drive-in circuit, obviously made this *Cool Hand Luke* knockoff on the cheap. (Look at the credits closely and you'll see some of the same names working on both sides of the camera in several capacities.) Two escaped convicts plunder, rob, and rape until a victim's husband comes looking for revenge. Violence and sexual content are fairly tame by current standards, and the split-screen work is dated. It's still fun for those who remember "ozoners" with fondness. 🎵🎵▷

1972 (R) 85m/C Robert Lott, Barbara Mills, Michael Stearns, Linda York; **D:** Lee Frost. **VHS** *NO*

Chained for Life

Daisy and Violet Hilton, real-life Siamese twins who had appeared in *Freaks* twenty years previous, star in this old-fashioned "freak" show. When a gigolo deserts one twin on their wedding night, the other twin shoots him dead. The twins go on trial and the judge asks the viewer to hand down the verdict—how to punish the guilty one but free the innocent? Sheldon Leonard plays the twins' trusty manager. Though slow in parts (and the twins' acting is awful), this is an exploitation roadshow oddity that's hard to resist. Step right up! 🎵🎵▷

1951 81m/B Daisy Hilton, Violet Hilton; **D:** Harry Fraser. **VHS, Beta $16.95** *SNC, NOS, RHI*

Chained Heat

Seamy tale of the vicious reality of life for women behind bars. Naive Blair is imprisoned again (after another bad jailhouse gig in *Born Innocent*) and has usual assortment of negative experiences with domineering prisoners, degenerative guards, and the creepy warden who maintains a prison bachelor pad equipped with hot tub. Needless to say, she grows up in a hurry. Trashifying, archetypal women-in-prison effort that aims to satisfy full range of low-quality audience demands. Sequel to 1982's *Concrete Jungle.* 🎵🎵

"Let me see if I've got this straight. In order to be grounded, I've got to be crazy and I must be crazy to keep flying. But if I ask to be grounded that means I'm not crazy any more and I have to keep flying."
--Captain Yossarian (Alan Arkin) sums up "The Catch" in *Catch-22.*

1983 (R) 97m/C Linda Blair, Stella Stevens, Sybil Danning, Tamara Dobson, Henry Silva, John Vernon, Nita Talbot, Louisa Moritz; **D:** Paul Nicholas. **VHS, Beta, LV $29.98** *VES*

Change of Habit

Elvis or God? This is the choice facing nun Mary Tyler Moore in this hopelessly dated '60s relic. Elvis strains to be hip as a ghetto doctor who does not know of nurse Moore's calling. Of marginal interest is the casting of Edward Asner as an Italian cop. Perhaps he and Moore would look back on this film and laugh when they were paired soon after for the classic TV series, *The Mary Tyler Moore Show.* Other than two concert films, this was Elvis's cinematic swan song. Very loosely based on a true story! ♫ Change of Habit; Let Us Pray; Rubberneckin'. 🦴🦴

1969 (G) 93m/C Elvis Presley, Mary Tyler Moore, Barbara McNair, Ed Asner, Ruth McDevitt, Regis Toomey; **D:** William A. Graham; **M:** Billy Goldenberg. **VHS, Beta $14.95** *MCA, GKK*

Cheech and Chong's Up in Smoke

A pair of free-spirited burn-outs team up for a tongue-in-cheek spoof of sex, drugs, and rock and roll. The first and probably the best of the dopey duo's cinematic adventures was a box-office bonanza when released and is still a cult favorite. Why? The team's sporadic energy is still there, and Keach makes a good straightman to their amiable shtick. And, of course, for the core audience, drug humor has an enduring appeal. But to anyone who's not on Cheech and Chong's particular wavelength, the sloppily made, slapdash farce is virtually unwatchable. 🦴🦴▷

1979 (R) 87m/C Richard "Cheech" Marin, Thomas Chong, Stacy Keach, Tom Skerritt, Edie Adams, Strother Martin, Cheryl "Rainbeaux" Smith; **D:** Lou Adler. **VHS, Beta, LV $14.95** *PAR*

Cheerleader Camp

The video box from Prism's release promises lots of sexy laughs in what was billed as a horror spoof. Whoever did the liner notes deserves a prize for creative writing. What we have here is another stupid teens in the woods slasher flick. Cheerleading squads from across the country come together at a summer clinic at a camp in the woods. There they are hunted down and killed (in some very gory fashions) by a mystery killer. All the squads escape but one, whose vehicle is disabled by our mystery fiend, who bears these specific girls a grudge. Awash with obvious red herrings, the killer will be readily apparent to the alert viewer. Worse than that, this piece of trash lacks any significant amounts of humor, sex, nudity, or suspense. The only questions the viewer will have are "How will she die?" and "How bloody will it be?" Solely for Betsy Russell fans and gore hounds. *AKA:* Bloody Pom Poms. **WOOF!**

1988 (R) 89m/C Betsy Russell, Leif Garrett, Lucinda Dickey, Lorie Griffin, George Flower, Teri Weigel, Rebecca Ferratti; **D:** John Quinn. **VHS, Beta $14.95** *PSM, PAR*

Child Bride

"Where lust was called just!" After little waif Jennie's paw is killed by scumball moonshiner Jake Bolby (Richmond), she's left vulnerable when he comes to ask for her hand in marriage. Schoolmarm Miss Carol (Durrell) lobbies to outlaw underage matrimony, despite being whipped by Klansmen. The roadshow classic that took a bold stand against the child marriages that were common practice among the our hillbilly country cousins back in them thar days—while at the same time showing a wide-eyed skinny dipping scene of little 12-year-old Mills (later little Ruth Joad in *The Grapes of Wrath*). Richmond was a familiar player in silent films (*Tol'able David*). Little Angelo plays an evil hillbilly dwarf. *AKA:* Child Brides. 🦴🦴▷

1939 52m/B Warner Richmond, Angelo Rossitto, Shirley Mills, Diana Durrell, Bob Bollinger; **D:** Harry Revier. **VHS, Beta $16.95** *SNC, NOS, TPV*

Children Shouldn't Play with Dead Things

A band of foolhardy hippie filmmakers on an island cemetary skimp on special effects by using witchcraft to revive the dead. The plan works. Soon the crew has an island full of hungry ghouls to contend with. Film strives for yucks, frequently succeeds. A late night fave, sporting some excellent dead rising from their

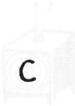

grave scenes as well as a selection of groovy fashions. Screenwriter/star Ormsby went on to write the remake of *Cat People*, while director Clark would eventually helm *Porky's*. **AKA:** Revenge of the Living Dead. 🦴🦴▷

1972 85m/C Alan Ormsby, Valerie Mamches, Jeff Gillen, Anya Ormsby, Paul Cronin, Jane Daly, Roy Engelman, Robert Philip, Bruce Solomon, Alecs Baird, Seth Sklarey; **D:** Bob (Benjamin) Clark; **W:** Alan Ormsby, Bob (Benjamin) Clark. **VHS, Beta $19.95** *VCI, MPI*

Chopper Chicks in Zombietown

Tough but sexy Chopper Chicks show up in that American vacation mecca, Zombietown, for a little rest and relaxation. Little do they know that a mad mortician has designs on turning our hot heroines into mindless zombie slaves. Can the buxom biker babes thwart the evil embalmer before it's too late, or will they abandon their Harleys to shuffle about in search of human flesh? From the Troma Team. 🦴🦴

1991 (R) 86m/C Jamie Rose, Catherine Carlen, Lycia Naff, Vicki Frederick, Kristina Loggia, Martha Quinn, Don Calfa; **D:** Dan Hoskins; **W:** Dan Hoskins. **VHS, LV $19.95** *COL, NLC*

Chopping Mall

It's teens vs. killer robots after an electrical storm isolates them in a mall. The robots, created by Robert Short, carry most of the action and they're pretty good. Imagine R2-D2 gone bad and you've got the idea. B-movie vet Wynorski keeps the pace quick and tosses in lots of movie jokes for fans, i.e. the kids arm themselves at Peckinpah's Sporting Goods. Updated imitation of the 1973 TV movie *Trapped*. **AKA:** Killbots. 🦴▷

1986 (R) 77m/C Paul Bartel, Mary Woronov, Barbara Crampton, John Terlesky, Dick Miller; **D:** Jim Wynorski; **W:** Jim Wynorski. **VHS, Beta $19.98** *LIV*

C.H.U.D.

Lowbrow sleeper about Cannibalistic Humanoid Underground Dwellers, a race of scaly, flesh-craving, sewer-dwelling uglies who go hunting for food on the streets of New York. Some freelance C.H.U.D. hunters don't swallow the government's story about the

creatures and discover that an acronym can conceal two meanings. The presence of real actors uplifts this cheesy monster mash, but only slightly. Comedic zombie-themed sequel, *C.H.U.D. 2: Bud the Chud*, also on video, is inexcusable. 🦴🦴

1984 (R) 90m/C John Heard, Daniel Stern, Christopher Curry, Kim Greist, John Goodman; **D:** Douglas Cheek; **W:** Shepard Abbott. **VHS, Beta, LV $9.99** *STE, MRV*

Cinema Shrapnel

A tour through the wonderful world of screen hype and bad movies, with scenes from terrible trailers, maudlin fundraising shorts, and glitzy movie premieres. 🦴🦴

1987 60m/C VHS, Beta *NO*

City on Fire

Ringo Lam's gangster classic has Chow Yun-Fat as undercover cop Ko Chow, a man with split loyalties. Infiltrating a gang of jewel thieves, he gains their confidence and is included in their next heist. In a blaze of

Don't look now, but your ankle bracelet is alive! *C.H.U.D.*

Cult Flicks and Trash Pics

THE HOUND SALUTES: MEL BROOKS

May the Schwartz Be with You!

Mel Brooks began his career as a television writer for comic Sid Caesar in the 1950s, working on a staff that included such luminaries as Woody Allen, Carl Reiner, and Neil Simon. Brooks and Reiner subsequently formed a popular comedy team, performing and recording a series of sketches called "The 2000 Year-Old Man" (Brooks was the Old Man). In 1963, Brooks won an Oscar for the animated short film *The Critic*, in which he caustically maligned surreal animation. In 1965, Brooks teamed with Buck Henry to create the popular TV spy parody *Get Smart!*

In his films, Brooks often worked with the same troop of talented actors and writers, including Gene Wilder, Marty Feldman, Dom DeLuise, and Madeline Kahn, creating a string of comic masterpieces. He combined a love of classic Hollywood musicals, Jewish culture, social satire, and Nazi ridicule to create a brand of humor all his own. In 1968, Brooks wrote and directed *The Producers*, for which he won his second Oscar (best original screenplay). In 1973 and 1974, he delivered the double comic whammy of *Blazing Saddles* and *Young Frankenstein*. His genius for parody continued with the Hitchcock send-up *High Anxiety* (1977), the Star Wars gagfest *Spaceballs* (1987), and *Robin Hood: Men In Tights* (1993). Although Brooks' work has often been derided for being low-brow, Brooks would probably consider this a compliment. He once said, "My movies rise below vulgarity." Brooks will do anything to get a laugh, and more often than not he succeeds. Brooks also owns the production company Brooksfilms, which has produced such highly praised films as *The Elephant Man* (1980) and *My Favorite Year* (1982).

gunfire, the job goes wrong, with Chow taking a slug in the gut for his "boss" Lee Fu (Danny Lee). Shooting their way out, the gang reconvenes at an unused warehouse for review and recriminations, and some more gunfire. Quentin Tarantino liked it so much, some say, that he 'borrowed' whole scenes,

lines of dialogue, and the plot for his auspicious debut, *Reservoir Dogs*. Lam copped Best Director honors at the 1987 Hong Kong Film Awards, with Chow Yun-Fat picking up the award for Best Actor. 🦴🦴🦴
1987 98m/C *HK* Chow Yun-Fat, Danny Lee; **D:** Ringo Lam. **VHS $39.95** *FCT*

Clambake

Noxious Elvis vehicle about a rich man's son who wants success on his own terms, so he trades places with a water-skiing teacher. Inane, even in comparison to other Elvis ventures. 🎵 Clambake; The Girl I Never Loved; Hey, Hey, Hey; Confidence; Who Needs Money?; A House That Has Everything. 🦴
1967 98m/C Elvis Presley, Shelley Fabares, Bill Bixby, James Gregory, Gary Merrill, Will Hutchins, Harold Peary; **D:** Arthur Nadel. **VHS, Beta $14.95** *MGM*

Class of 1984

Nice-guy teacher King faces teen turmoil in the classroom, as sly student psycho Van Patten leads his groupies on a reign of terror through school halls, and the law does nothing since he's "just a kid." Finally the gang-rape of King's wife makes the worm turn. The punch line adds the only punch to this shallow update of *The Blackboard Jungle*, but pic does win the Criswell prize for prophecy; it accurately foretold the use of metal detectors in urban high schools. Fox has an early appearance as an ill-fated teacher's pet, and McDowall is memorable as an instructor who cracks under the pressure. Followed by the more overtly sci-fi (and more violent) *Class of 1999* pics. 🦴🐾
1982 (R) 93m/C *CA* Perry King, Roddy McDowall, Timothy Van Patten, Michael J. Fox, Merrie Lynn Ross, Stefan Arngrim, Al Waxman; **D:** Mark L. Lester; **W:** Mark L. Lester, Tom Holland. **VHS, Beta, LV $29.98** *VES*

Class of Nuke 'Em High

Team Troma once again experiments with chemicals, with violent results. Jersey high school becomes a hotbed of mutants and maniacs after a nuclear spill occurs. The honor students degenerate into street punks, forever high on contaminated marijuana; good teens Chrissy and Warren succumb to their lusts; a baby monster in the basement of the school grows into one big mother and it all goes "Boom" in the final reel. Loaded with dumb jokes, excessively ridiculous violence, and a tad less sex than one of Troma's normal (er, more usual?) films, this one delivers everything the experienced Troma viewer has come to expect. Available in both "R" and unrated versions, with the latter preferred; don't even bother with the sliced-up version shown on USA's cable network. Followed by the abysmal *Class of Nuke 'Em High Part 2*. 🦴🦴🦴

1986 (R) 84m/C Janelle Brady, Gilbert Brenton; **D:** Richard W. Haines. **VHS, Beta $9.98** *MED*

Class of Nuke 'Em High, Part 2: Subhumanoid Meltdown

The Troma team brings us back into the world of the strange. In this adventure, the evil Nuka-mama Corporation holds secret experiments at their "college" and create sub-humanoids as slave labor, swelling unemployment and wrecking the economy. This does not fare too well with the rest of society, including our heroes Roger the reporter, Professor Holt, and the scantily clad sub-humanoid Victoria. Once again this seems to be a made-for-the-money sequel. All the jokes seem forced and nothing really ever clicks. Only noteworthy new item was the introduction of a giant squirrel who, by the way, out-acts the cast. Troma planned to keep him as a continuing character, but so far he's yet to resurface. 🦴

1991 (R) m/C Lisa Gaye, Brick Bronsky, Leesa Rowland; **D:** Eric Louzil. **VHS, Beta, LV $19.98** *VTR, MED, FXV*

Clerks

A witty lesson in life behind (and under) the counter, from foul-mouthed Generation Xers. The movie chronicles a (very bad) day in the life of twenty-two year-old Dante Hicks (O'Halloran), a bright but disaffected New Jersey convenience store clerk who spends most of his life trapped behind the counter, when all he really wants to do is play roller-hockey and reunite with his ex-girlfriend. The next-door video store is clerked by his best friend

Randal (Anderson), who derives equal delight from insulting customers, watching dirty movies, and debating absolutely anything (especially anything sexual). Along with Randal, Dante's purgatory is populated by other lost souls, including drug-dealing Jay, Silent Bob (played by writer/director Smith), and bizarre patrons seeking everything from the perfect carton of eggs to milk with the best possible expiration date (the Hound can relate). Nothing much actually happens, but this very low-budget ($26,000) production has a decidedly scuzzy charm. And you'll never ask to use the bathroom at a 7-11 again. 🦴🦴🦴🐾

1994 (R) 91m/B Brian O'Halloran, Jeff Anderson, Marilyn Ghigliotti, Lisa Spoonhauer, Jason Mewes; **Cameos:** Kevin Smith; **D:** Kevin Smith; **W:** Kevin Smith; **M:** Scott Angley. Sundance Film Festival '94: Filmmakers Trophy; Nominations: Independent Spirit Awards '95: Best First Feature, Debut Performance (Anderson), First Screenplay. **VHS, LV** *MAX*

A Clockwork Orange

In the Britain of the near future, a sadistic punk leads a gang on nightly rape and murder sprees, then is captured and becomes the subject of a grim experiment to eradicate his violent tendencies in this extraordinary adaptation of Anthony Burgess' controversial novel. The film is an exhilarating experience, with an outstanding performance by McDowell as the funny, fierce psychopath. Many memorable, disturbing sequences, including a rape conducted while assailant McDowell belts "Singing in the Rain." Truly outstanding, provocative work from master filmmaker Kubrick. 🦴🦴🦴🦴

1971 (R) 137m/C *GB* Malcolm McDowell, Patrick Magee, Adrienne Corri, Michael Bates, Warren Clarke, Aubrey Morris, James Marcus, Steven Berkoff, David Prowse; **D:** Stanley Kubrick; **W:** Stanley Kubrick. New York Film Critics Awards '71: Best Director (Kubrick), Best Film; Nominations: Academy Awards '71: Best Adapted Screenplay, Best Director (Kubrick), Best Film Editing, Best Picture. **VHS, Beta, LV $19.98** *WAR, FCT, FUS*

Clue

For proof that Hollywood is running out of ideas, witness this adaption of the popular Parker Brothers board game, finding a group of characters in a spooky mansion faced with the murder of the man who had been black-

THE HOUND SALUTES: TOD BROWNING

Filmmaker Tod Browning is best known to cult movie fans as the director of *Freaks*, a stark and often horrifying look at the lives of the inhabitants of a circus sideshow. Released in 1932, *Freaks* tells the tale of the code of honor that exists amongst the deformed and handicapped members of the troupe--a code that leads to murder when one of their members is double-crossed by one of the so-called "normal" people. By using real circus freaks in his movie, Browning created a vision that was so disturbing to most filmgoers, the film was immediately recalled upon its release and later marketed in a highly edited version. In Britain, the film was banned for more than 30 years. Particularly grotesque is the final night scene, when the freaks crawl, slither, and hop their way through the mud and rain to exact their revenge by killing their tormentor. What seemed to escape most viewers is that Browning actually presented the freaks with compassion and respect. In the film, they are the sympathetic characters, while the "normal" people are shown to be devious and conniving with no ethics or morals. This respect that Browning showed was undoubtedly a product of his teen years, when he worked in a traveling carnival and in various burlesque shows. Browning is also known as the man who made Bela Lugosi famous when he directed the horror star in *Dracula*, the 1931 version of Bram Stoker's vampire tale that is considered among the best in the genre.

1985 **(PG) 96m/C** Lesley Ann Warren, Tim Curry, Martin Mull, Madeline Kahn, Michael McKean, Christopher Lloyd, Eileen Brennan, Howard Hesseman, Lee Ving, Jane Wiedlin, Colleen Camp, Bill Henderson; **D:** Jonathan Lynn; **W:** Jonathan Lynn, John Landis; **M:** John Morris. **VHS, Beta, LV $19.95** *PAR*

Cobra Woman

Technicolor adventure fantasy about the jungle queen (Maria Montez) of a cobra-worshipping cult and her evil twin sister who wants the throne for herself. Although she only appeared in four pictures, Montez was idolized by the followers of "camp" in the '60s. This is her last, and best, film, owing to an outrageous script by Richard Brooks (his first, featuring such choice phrases as "a wild dream of her decaying brain"), and director Robert Siodmak, who enjoyed pushing his Germanic foolishness full-throttle into "high-art" jungle melodrama. 🦴🦴🦴🦴

1944 **70m/C** Maria Montez, Jon Hall, Sabu, Edgar Barrier, Lois Collier, Lon Chaney Jr.; **D:** Robert Siodmak; **W:** Richard Brooks. **VHS $12.95** *NO*

Cocaine Cowboys

Lame rockers support themselves between gigs by peddling drugs then find out they've run afoul of the mob. Palance is the only worthwhile aspect of this rambling venture produced at Andy Warhol's home. 🦴🦴

1979 **(R) 90m/C** Jack Palance, Andy Warhol, Tom Sullivan, Suzanna Love; **D:** Ulli Lommel. **VHS, Beta** *MED, OM*

Cocaine Fiends

"Strips the soul bare! Inflames the senses!" Sister is given a magical "headache powder," while brother gets turned on by some bad girls. Drug use leads siblings into a squalid life of addiction, crime, prostitution, and eventually suicide. Ostensibly straight morality tale functions better as loopy camp. Features memorable slang. Wacky scenes at the aptly named "Dead Rat Cafe" turned up later in the Willy Castello highlight-fest *Confessions of a Vice Baron* (1942). Remake of silent *The Pace That Kills* (1928). **AKA:** The Pace That Kills. 🦴🦴

mailing them en masse. All are suspects, and they must uncover the guilty party within an hour. The theatrical version played with three alternative endings (varied from theatre to theatre); the video version shows all three successively. A no-hoper. You can't deduce from evidence shown the murderer's identity. Think about it—with three different solutions waiting in line, none of the clues can point in any one direction, so who cares? Desperate cast seems to be subsisting on sugar, judging by their wild eyes, frantic scurrying back and forth, and rapid-fire delivery of Tom Stoppard-esque gag lines. Curry comes off the best. 🦴🦴

1936 74m/B Lois January, Noel Madison, Willy Castello; **D:** W.A. O'Connor. **VHS, Beta $16.95** *SNC, NOS, MED*

Cockfighter

One of Roger Corman's rare box office failures. Three title changes and re-editing couldn't save it. "To my knowledge, no one had ever made a picture about cockfighting," Corman wrote in his autobiography. "Now I know why. No one wants to see a picture about cockfighting." But miss this at your peril. Warren Oates will leave you speechless in this compelling character study based on Charles Willeford's novel about a cockfighter who takes a vow of silence until he wins the championship bout. Willeford also wrote *Miami Blues,* which was filmed in 1990 by another Corman graduate, George Armitage. Invaluable character actor Harry Dean Stanton co-stars as Oates's nemesis. Cinematographer Nestor Almenadro would later win an Academy Award for *Days of Heaven.* Editor Lewis Teague went on to direct the *Romancing the Stone* sequel, *The Jewel in the Nile.* **AKA:** Gamblin' Man; Born to Kill; Wild Drifters. 🦴🦴🦴

1974 (R) 84m/C Warren Oates, Harry Dean Stanton, Richard B. Shull, Troy Donahue, Millie Perkins; **D:** Monte Hellman; **M:** Michael Franks. **VHS, Beta $59.98** *SUE*

The Cocoanuts

In their sound film debut, the Marx Brothers create their trademark, indescribable mayhem. Stagy and technically crude due to the limits of sound film production, the comedy is nonetheless delightful, with zany, free-for-all exchanges and madcap antics. Includes famous "viaduct" routine. Based on the Broadway hit show set in a seaside hotel, the plot is about the Florida land boom and a female jewel thief, as if anyone cared. Incidental music is rare due to the fact that the producer thought it might confuse the audience, unless they could see the orchestra playing. This is very probably the earliest feature film shown regularly on television, and probably the most watched film made before 1930. Featured songs include "When My Dreams Come True" and "Monkey Doodle-doo." The brothers previously made a lost silent comedy called *Humor Risk* in 1920, and Harpo Marx had previously appeared in the rare *Too Many Kisses* (1925). Followed by the even better *Animal Crackers.* 🦴🦴🦴

1929 96m/B Groucho Marx, Chico Marx, Harpo Marx, Zeppo Marx, Margaret Dumont, Kay Francis, Oscar Shaw, Mary Eaton; **D:** Robert Florey, Joseph Santley; **W:** George S. Kaufman, Morrie Ryskind; **M:** Irving Berlin. **VHS, Beta, LV $14.98** *MCA*

Color Me Blood Red

In this partial rip-off of Corman's *Bucket of Blood,* an artist decides that the red in his paintings is best rendered with human blood. He even manages to continue his art career—when not busy stabbing and mutilating the unsuspecting citizenry. The third entry in what came to be known as the "blood trilogy" from Lewis and producer David F. Friedman, after *Blood Feast* and *2000 Maniacs.* This is less bloody and less interesting than the other two, and the satirical jabs at the art world go nowhere. Things only perk up when the artist acquires a new subject, in anticipation of the moment when model becomes medium. Those crazy artists! **AKA:** Model Massacre. 🦴🦴

1964 74m/C Don Joseph, Sandi Conder; **D:** Herschell Gordon Lewis. **VHS, Beta $29.95** *NO*

Combat Shock

Vietnam veteran Frank Dunlan returns home and can't cope with the stresses of modern life, including unemployment, marriage, flashbacks, a broken toilet, an *Eraserhead*-inspired baby deformed by his exposure to Agent Orange, and the lowlifes who have been taking over the streets. Desperate, all he can do is use some of his acquired combat skills to go after some scum who have been trying to kill him, but his success as a vigilante does nothing to help his problems at home. A relentlessly bleak picture, with occasional repellent gross-outs and depressingly ugly urban rot. You won't find a more depressing film outside an art house cinema. Shot on a shoestring on location in New Jersey—and it looks like it. **AKA:** American Nightmares. 🦴🦴

1984 (R) 85m/C Ricky Giovinazzo, Nick Nasta, Veronica Stork; **D:** Buddy Giovnazzo. **VHS, Beta $9.99** *PSM*

The Comedy of Terrors

Comedy in which some deranged undertakers take a hands-on approach to ensuring their continued employment. Much fun is supplied by the performances of Price, Lorre, Karloff, and Rathbone, all veterans of the horror genre. Regretfully, the writing isn't up to the their level, leaving the viewer strangely entertained and disappointed at the same time. Price, a down-and-out undertaker, is besieged by financial problems and takes to the street, with his aide, Lorre, to drum up business. Things never go as planned, perpetually leaving the duo as bad off as ever. Karloff, as Price's senile father-in-law, never gets quite enough to do, and Rathbone, of Sherlock Holmes fame, steals his scenes as Price's pressing landlord. Certainly a must-watch for the fans of any of it's stars; others may want to pass. Price, Lorre, and Karloff can also be found together in *The Raven*. 🦴🦴🦴

1964 84m/C Vincent Price, Peter Lorre, Boris Karloff, Basil Rathbone, Joe E. Brown, Joyce Jameson; **D:** Jacques Tourneur; **W:** Richard Matheson; **M:** Les Baxter. **VHS, LV $79.98** *MOV*

The Commies Are Coming, the Commies Are Coming

Cult classic will leave viewers red from laughing in disbelief. Webb produced and narrates this anti-communist movie about a complacent goofus (Duggan) who takes his freedom for granted—until he wakes up one day to find that the Russians have taken over the United States. Filmed in a docudrama style, it captures the paranoia of the times, but seems a bit shrill and campy today. Webb lurks around in the bushes like Rod Serling in *Twilight Zone*. Re-released in 1984, just before the Evil Empire collapsed. Waggner started out acting in silent films before becoming a prolific screenwriter and director, ending up directing episodes of *The Untouchables, Batman,* and many others. He's probably best known for his Universal monster movies of the '40s, including *The Wolf Man* and *Man Made Monster*. **AKA:** Red Nightmare. 🦴🦴▷

1957 60m/B Jack Webb, Andrew Duggan, Robert Conrad, Jack Kelly, Peter Brown; **D:** George Waggner. **VHS, Beta $39.95** *RHI*

Complex World

Regional cult hit set at the original Heartbreak Hotel, a real-life Providence night spot (that has since closed and reopened). During one riotous night the club is attacked by both CIA-backed terrorists and a biker gang (led by pro wrestling's Captain Lou Albano), while dead rock superstars telephone to warn the patrons of impending doom. It sounds like a mess, but it mostly isn't. Filmmaker Wolpaw orchestrates and escalates the chaos, weaving in performances by notable New England eccentrics like hostile folk singer Stanley Matis, bizarre band The Young Adults, and unorthodox street preacher Tilman Gandy, Jr. ("God told us to laugh at you!"). The finished film played cinemas for months and months in Providence and Boston, but nationwide release plans were abandoned, spawning a lawsuit against the distributor that has kept this a videocassette rarity. It's worth hunting up, as is the soundtrack. ♪ Let's Get Naked and Break Things; Do the Heimlich; So I Married a Tree; Why Feed All the Broads?. 🦴🦴🦴

1992 (R) 81m/C Dan Welch, Bob Owczarek, Jay Charbonneau, Tilman Gandy Jr., David P.B. Stephens, Captain Lou Albano, Stanley Matis; **D:** James Wolpaw; **W:** James Wolpaw. **VHS** *NO*

The Conqueror

Wayne in pointed helmet and goatee is convincingly miscast as Genghis Khan in this woeful tale of the warlord's early life and involvement with the kidnapped daughter of a powerful enemy. Rife with stilted, unintentionally funny dialogue, Oriental western was very expensive to make (with backing by Howard Hughes), and is now listed in the "Fifty Worst Films of All Time." No matter; it's surreal enough to enable viewer to approximate an out-of-body experience. Even those on the set suffered; filming took place near a nuclear test site in Utah and many members of the cast and crew eventually developed cancer. 🦴🦴

1956 111m/C John Wayne, Susan Hayward, William Conrad, Agnes Moorehead, Lee Van Cleef, Pedro Armendariz Sr., Thomas Gomez, John Hoyt; **D:** Dick Powell; **W:** Oscar Millard. **VHS, Beta $19.95** *MCA*

The Conqueror Worm

"And the angels, all pallid and wan, Uprising, unveiling, affirm That the play is the tragedy 'Man,' And its hero the Conqueror Worm." Price turns in an excellent performance portraying the sinister Matthew Hopkins, a real-life 17th century witchhunter. Ogilvy plays a young soldier seeking out Hopkins to avenge the rape of his fiancee (Dwyer). No "ham" in this low-budget, underrated thriller. Price seems to know that what he's doing is wrong, but believes his evil and corruption is serving a higher purpose. The last of three films from director Reeves, who died from an accidental(?) overdose in 1969. Price and Reeves clashed on the set, but all for the better it seems. AIP changed the title and tried to shoehorn it into their already loose Poe series. Also available with *Tomb of Ligeia* on laserdisc. *AKA:* Witchfinder General; Edgar Allan Poe's Conqueror Worm. 🦴🦴🦴▷

1968 95m/C *GB* Vincent Price, Ian Ogilvy, Hilary Dwyer, Rupert Davies, Robert Russell, Patrick Wymark, Wilfrid Brambell; ***D:*** Michael Reeves. **VHS $59.99** *HBO, FCT*

Conquest of the Planet of the Apes

The apes turn the tables on the human Earth population when they lead a revolt against their cruel masters in the distant year of 1991. Because of an outer-space virus brought back by astronauts in 1973, all dogs and cats were wiped out; humans than turned to the ape population for domestic pets, and for domestics. There is a faction of the population that protests the slavery of apes (and the jobs they take away from humans; they carry protests signs that says "Unfair to Waiters!" and "Hire Men not Beasts.") Chief ape in this entry is Caesar, son of Cornelius (Roddy McDowall) and Zera (Kim Hunter) of the original *Planet of the Apes.* (Caesar is also played by Roddy McDowall, which lends that realistic family resemblence touch). Ricardo Montalban reprises his role as the circus leader who saved Caesar's life. The 4th film in the series. Followed by *Battle for the Planet of the Apes.* 🦴🦴▷

1972 (PG) 87m/C Roddy McDowall, Don Murray, Ricardo Montalban, Natalie Trundy, Severn Darden, Hari Rhodes; ***D:*** J. Lee Thompson. **VHS, Beta, LV $19.98** *FOX*

Consuming Passions

A ribald, food-obsessed English comedy about a young idiot who rises within the hierarchy of a chocolate company via murder. You'll never guess what the secret ingredient in his wonderful chocolate is. Based on a play by Monty Python's Michael Palin and Terry Jones, the film is sometimes funny, more often gross, and takes a single joke far beyond its limit. 🦴▷

1988 (R) 95m/C *GB* Vanessa Redgrave, Jonathan Pryce, Tyler Butterworth, Freddie Jones, Prunella Scales, Sammi Davis, Thora Hird; ***D:*** Giles Foster; ***W:*** Michael Palin. **VHS, Beta, LV** *NO*

Contempt

Fritz Lang plays Fritz, the director of a new film version of *The Odyssey,* at odds with his producer's artistic vision. The producer, played by a volatile Jack Palance, is based on Joseph E. Levine, who, not coincidentally, produced this picture. The novel from which the film was derived, Alberto Moravia's *A Ghost at Noon,* gives Godard's film its center: the deteriorating relationship between the screenwriter and his wife, for whom he has compromised his artistic values in order to raise her standard of living. The real subject of the film, however, is the agony a film director must endure when surrounded by idiots. Note: Since several languages are spoken in this film, one of the characters is a translator. In the dubbed video version, in which English is the sole language spoken, the translator becomes unnecessary and she is given all-new dialogue to give her character a function. *AKA:* Le Mepris; Il Disprezzo. 🦴🦴🦴🦴

1964 102m/C *IT FR* Brigitte Bardot, Jack Palance, Fritz Lang, Georgia Moll, Michel Piccoli; ***D:*** Jean-Luc Godard; ***W:*** Jean-Luc Godard; ***M:*** Georges Delerue. **VHS, Beta, LV $19.95** *COL, INJ, SUE*

Cool World

Underground cartoonist Jack Deebs enters his own adult cartoon *Cool World,* lured by his sex-kitten character "Holli Would," who needs him to leave her animated world and become human. Holli's plan is opposed by

THE HOUND SALUTES: TIM BURTON
Tim After Tim

In hindsight, only Tim Burton could have filmed the bio of cult movie legend Ed Wood. Instead of making the infamous worst-filmmaker-of-all-time into a sideshow freak, Burton imbued Wood with a sense of purpose, self-worth, and innate likeability. It was a case of one Hollywood eccentric respecting another.

Unlike poor Ed Wood, Tim Burton was quickly able to win over mass-audiences and critics alike with his strange, highly personal visions. The Cal Arts graduate and onetime Disney animator became one of the most successful cult-moviemakers ever, featuring exaggerated production design, freakishly outcast heroes, and scary/funny villains. Even when his movies showcased existing characters, like Batman and Pee Wee Herman, nobody can forget that these are Tim Burton shows. For proof, just look at the sequels--the ones done without Burton.

Ironically, *Ed Wood* was Tim Burton's first box-office disappointment, even as it earned critical raves as his most mature, moving, and well-crafted work. Such compliments don't pull the *Batman* crowd in, unfortunately. On the bright side, that means for legions of viewers *Ed Wood* awaits rediscovery on home video. But it's not the only relative rarity in Burton's background...

Family Dog: The best-received (particularly by the Hound!) episode of Steven Spielberg's TV anthology series *Amazing Stories*, this inventive cartoon conveyed the viewpoint of a pointy-headed mutt in a suburban household. It can be found on the *Amazing Stories* videocassette series. (A weekly animated half-hour based on *Family Dog* did not long endure.)

Vincent: A 1982 stop-motion short done for Disney, this cheerful, black-and-white grotesquerie anticipates *The Nightmare Before Christmas*. It deals with a small boy who (like Burton) idolizes Vincent Price and patterns his life after the mad scientists and florid

continued...

the only other human to occupy Cool World, a slick detective whose main job is to prevent noids (humans) and doodles (cartoons) from having sex and destroying the balance between the two existences. A mixture of live-action and wild animation. Director Bakshi's creations are not intended for children but this is less explicit than usual, which may be one of the problems. Little humor and a flat script combined with uninteresting characters leave this film too uninvolving for most. Still, the animated sections, blended neatly with live action, provide a wild ride and fans of the art will want to take it in. Those into illegal substances may enjoy it most of all. 🦴🦴

1992 (PG-13) 101m/C Gabriel Byrne, Kim Basinger, Brad Pitt, Michele Abrams, Deidre O'Connell, Carrie Hamilton, Frank Sinatra Jr.; **D:** Ralph Bakshi. **VHS, Beta, LV $14.95** *PAR, PMS, WTA*

The Corpse Grinders

Here, kitty, kitty! Low-budget bad movie classic in which a cardboard corpse-grinding machine makes nasty cat food that makes cats nasty. Sets are cheap, gore effects silly, and cat attacks ridiculous—the kitties look only mildly confused when they're supposed to be maddened killers hungry for human flesh. Some attempt is made at black humor, especially during the Burke & Hare flavored trips to the graveyard for raw material, but most of the entertainment comes from the audaciously awful quality of the entire production. Mikels is also responsible for *The Astro Zombies, Doll Squad,* and many more trash classics. 🦴🦴🦴

1971 (R) 73m/C Sean Kenney, Monika Kelly, Sandford Mitchell; **D:** Ted V. Mikels; **W:** Ted V. Mikels. **VHS, Beta** *NO*

Crash of the Moons

Rocky Jones, Space Ranger, must save two worlds from colliding with each other. Movie was spliced together from episodes of the sci-fi TV show from the '50s, and it shows. Rocky must pursuade an evil queen that he trying to save, not conquer, her world when its orbit intersects with another, more friendly planet. Cheezy special effects that would embarrass Ed Wood, and inane dialogue delivered incompetently make for a great "talk back to the screen" evening. 🦴🦴

1959 90m/B Richard Crane, Sally Mansfield. **VHS $29.95** *DVT, RXM*

The Crazies

A poisoned water supply makes the residents of a small town go on a chaotic, murderous rampage. When the army is called in to quell the anarchy, a small war breaks out. Here, for the first time, director George Romero deals with the horrific aspects of martial law. The film will be of interest primarily to those fans interested in the military theme that became so prominent in his *Dead* trilogy. For others, it may seen slow and improbable. *AKA:* Code Name: Trixie. 🦴🦴

1973 (R) 103m/C Lane Carroll, W.G. McMillan, Harold W. Jones, Lloyd Hollar, Lynn Lowry; *D:* George A. Romero; *W:* George A. Romero. **Beta** *NO*

Crazy Mama

Three women go on a crime spree from California to Arkansas, picking up men and having a hoot. Crime and comedy in a campy romp. Set in the 1950s and loaded with period kitsch. 🦴🦴🦴

1975 (PG) 81m/C Cloris Leachman, Stuart Whitman, Ann Sothern, Jim Backus, Linda Purl; *D:* Jonathan Demme. **VHS, Beta $69.98** *SUE*

Creature from the Black Lagoon

An anthropological expedition in the Amazon stumbles upon the Gill-Man, a prehistoric humanoid fish monster who takes a fancy to fetching Adams, a coed majoring in "science," but the humans will have none of it. Originally filmed in 3-D, this was one of the first movies to sport top-of-the-line underwater photography and remains one of the most enjoyable monster movies ever made. Gershenson's score became a "Creature Features" standard. Based on a story by Maurice Zimm. Sequels: *Revenge of the Creature* and *The Creature Walks Among Us.* 🦴🦴🦴

1954 79m/B Richard Carlson, Julie Adams, Richard Denning, Antonio Moreno, Whit Bissell, Nestor Paiva, Ricou Browning; *D:* Jack Arnold; *W:* Arthur Ross; *M:* Joseph Gershenson, Henry Mancini. **VHS, Beta, LV $14.95** *MCA, GKK*

Creature from the Haunted Sea

Poverty-stricken but entertaining Roger Corman monster comedy set in Cuba shortly after the revolution and centering around an elaborate plan to loot the Treasury and put the blame on a strange sea monster. A sort of remake of Corman's *Naked Paradise,* shot in Puerto Rico in about a week, back-to-back with *The Last Woman on Earth* (also starring Carbone, Wain, and Jones-Moreland) and *Battle of Blood Island.* Wain is really Robert Towne, an Oscar winner for writing *Chinatown,* but the best performances come from Beach Dickerson as a swabbie who communicates with animal sounds, and the dancing Cuban generals. Dickerson also built the hilariously awkward monster from army helmets, an oilcloth, pipe cleaners, and ping pong balls (and it shows). Watch for Corman in shades as a pay phone customer. Jazzbo Fred Katz's honking score is also heard in *Little Shop of Horrors.* 🦴🦴🦴

1960 76m/B Antony Carbone, Betsy Jones-Moreland, Beach Dickerson, Edward Wain, Edmundo Rivera Alvarez, Robert Bean; *Cameos:* Roger Corman; *D:* Roger Corman, Monte Hellman; *W:* Charles B. Griffith; *M:* Fred Katz. **VHS, Beta $19.95** *NOS, MRV, SNC*

Creature of Destruction

A beautiful young woman is hypnotized and her soul "transmigrated" into a hideous sea creature. It's all the misguided doings of Dr. Basso (Les Tremayne from *The Angry Red Planet* and the voice of Johnny Quest's dad), who commands the monster to kill some necking teens and special guest star, singer Scotty McKay, undoubtedly for ripping off the *Batman* theme during a musical number. Buchanan's leaden TV remake of Edward L. Cahn's *The She-Creature* will hypnotize viewers with queasy camera work, embalmed acting, and a bleak, who-cares ending lifted wholly from Roger Corman's *It Conquered the World* (also remade by Buchanan as *Zontar, the Thing From Venus*)—all this and a quote from Montaigne. The ping-pong-eyeballed monster appears in two other Buchanan flicks, *It's Alive* (1968) and *Curse of the Swamp Creature.* 🦴🦴

villains Price portrayed. The real Vincent Price narrates the tale, which appears on the laserdisc edition of *The Nightmare Before Christmas* amidst other creative shorts by Burton and the feature's director Henry Selick.

Frankenweenie: Another black-and-white Disney short, was the 1984 piece that won Burton the assignment to direct *Pee Wee's Big Adventure.* It's a gentle parody of James Whale's original *Frankenstein*, about a misunderstood, stitched-together pet pooch, with big names like Shelley Duvall, Daniel Stern, and Paul Bartel in the cast. Yet Disney judged it too odd and offbeat for kiddie viewers--until a few years ago, when Burton's popularity finally brought about the film's wide release on cassette.

Success will do that--just look at the tapes of Ed Wood's actual outtakes now on the market.

1967 ?m/B Les Tremayne, Aron Kincaid, Pat Delaney, Neil Fletcher, Ann McAdams; **D:** Larry Buchanan. VHS *NO*

Creature of the Walking Dead

Scientist brings his grandfather back to blood-thirsty life with horrifying results for the cast and the audience. Made cheaply and quickly in Mexico in 1960, then released with added footage directed by Warren—the man who gave us *Man Beast, Teenage Zombies, Frankenstein Island,* and many other trash classics. The new footage has Victor and VeSota (both in Warren's *The Wild World of Batwoman* at the time) obviously padding out the running time. Warren used the same trick many times. Madison was also in Warren's own *Man Beast* ten years earlier (or was it five?). **AKA:** *La Marca del Muerto.*

1960 74m/B *MX* Rock Madison, Ann Wells, George Todd, Willard Gross, Bruno Ve Sota; **D:** Fernando Cortes, Jerry Warren. VHS $16.95 *NOS, MRV, SNC*

The Creature Walks Among Us

Sequel to *Revenge of the Creature* has the Gill-Man once again being captured by scientists for studying purposes. Through an accidental lab fire, the creature's gills are burned off and he undergoes surgery in an attempt to live out of water. Final entry in the Creature series has little magic of the original. Also shot in 3-D. Available on laserdisc as part of a special Encore Edition Double Feature with *Revenge of the Creature.*

1956 79m/B Jeff Morrow, Rex Reason, Leigh Snowden, Gregg Palmer; **D:** John Sherwood; **W:** Arthur Ross; **M:** Henry Mancini. VHS, LV $14.98 *MCA, FCT*

Creeping Terror

Gigantic alien carpet monster (look for the tennis shoes sticking out underneath) devours slow-moving teenagers. Partially narrated because some of the original soundtrack was lost, with lots of bad acting, a worse script, laughable sets, and a ridiculous monster. Beware of the thermometer scene. **AKA:** The Crawling Monster; Dangerous Charter.

1964 81m/B Vic Savage, Shannon O'Neal, William Thourlby, Louise Lawson, Robin James; **D:** Art J. Nelson. VHS, Beta $54.95 *NO*

Creepshow

Romero and novelist/scriptwriter Stephen King pay tribute to E.C. Comics, the pulp horror comic books of the 1950s that were hated by parents and teachers, and, on the plus side, often grisly, grotesque, and morbidly humorous. Film tells five terror tales, decidedly uneven in quality. A rotted corpse rises to punish greedy heirs, a voracious monster gives a meek professor means to dispose of his enemies, and a husband concocts watery doom for his wife and her lover. King himself acts in one segment as a dumb farmer in a close encounter with meteor-borne alien moss. Best vignette deals with a phobia-ridden millionaire recluse besieged by swarms of cursed cockroaches. The feature is less than the sum of its parts, with the novelist's dialogue especially flat, but Romero's direction cleverly mimics narrative style of comic strips. The filmmaker would later produce his own TV anthology *Tales From the Darkside.* The lesser *Creepshow 2* was helmed by *Creepshow* cinematographer Michael Gornick.

1982 (R) 120m/C Hal Holbrook, Adrienne Barbeau, Viveca Lindfors, E.G. Marshall, Stephen King, Leslie

Nielsen, Carrie Nye, Fritz Weaver, Ted Danson, Ed Harris; *D:* George A. Romero; *W:* Stephen King. **VHS, Beta, LV $19.98** *WAR*

Crimewave

Zany spoof told in flashback by a murder suspect as he's being hauled toward the electric chair in Hudsucker State Penitentiary; he describes how the real villains were a pair of psychotic hit men on a rampage through Detroit after bungling a job. Raimi's camera leaps all over the place in this giddy rhapsody to cartoonish cinematography, '30s-style production design, nutty F/X, and pop-eyed performances. Will definitely hold your attention, even as your brain screams that this is a lot of wildly self-indulgent slapstick without a single point to make. The "Hall of Protection" sequence is simply astonishing. The Coen brothers went on to more ambitious, yet stylistically similar work in *The Hudsucker Proxy* and *Miller's Crossing*. *AKA:* The XYZ Murders; Broken Hearts and Noses.

1985 (PG-13) 83m/C Louise Lasser, Paul Smith, Brion James, Bruce Campbell, Reed Birney, Sheree J. Wilson, Edward R. Pressman, Julius W. Harris; *D:* Sam Raimi; *W:* Ethan Coen, Joel Coen, Sam Raimi. **VHS, Beta $19.98** *NLC*

Cry-Baby

An homage and spoof of '50s teen-rock melodramas by the doyen of cinematic Bad Taste, involving a terminal bad-boy high schooler (Johnny Depp) who goes with a square blond and starts an inter-class rumble; kind of *The Outsiders* gone bad. Contains hokey musical numbers, throwaway gags, and plenty of knee-bending to Elvis. Weak storyline (but who cares?), which is offset by a bevy of celeb appearances, in true Waters fashion. Cameos playing the kids' parents are the best—picture these couplings: Andy Warhol-veteran Joe Dallesandro and Joey Heatherton; David Nelson and Patty Hearst; Troy Donahue and Waters' regular Mink Stole; and, for good measure, Willem Dafoe throw in as a hateful

Just a bunch of all-American kids lookin' for some good, clean fun. The Drapes: Kim McGuire, Darren E. Burrows, Johnny Depp, Ricki Lake, and Traci Lords in *Cry-Baby*.

guard. Not up the standards of the later Waterstuff, but still worth watching. ♫♫▷

1990 (PG-13) 85m/C Johnny Depp, Amy Locane, Susan Tyrrell, Polly Bergen, Ricki Lake, Iggy Pop, Traci Lords, Kim McGuire, Darren E. Burrows, Troy Donahue, Mink Stole, Joe Dallesandro, Joey Heatherton, Patty Hearst, Willem Dafoe, Susan Lowe, Mary Vivian Pearce, David Nelson; **D:** John Waters; **W:** John Waters; **M:** Patrick Williams. **VHS, Beta, LV $19.95** *MCA*

Cult People

Interviews and film clips featuring a host of filmmaking's favorite cult personalities, edited from David DelValle's public access cable TV show. Some more film clips would spice things up—some appear to have been cut out. Merely serves as an appetizer. For the most part, these are interesting people with a rich history, but if you're at all interested in the subject, these small bits from each interview make you wish you could see the whole thing—or that you hadn't wasted your time. However, it is fun to watch DelValle gain weight throughout the tape. Theme music is extremely lame. ♫▷

1989 60m/C Patrick Macnee, Cameron Mitchell, James Karen, Russ Meyer, Curtis Harrington, Waris Hussein, Michael Sarne. **VHS $19.95** *FCT*

The Curse of Frankenstein

Young Victor Frankenstein reenacts his father's experiments with creating life from the dead resulting in a terrifying, hideous creature. The first in Hammer's Frankenstein series and followed by "Revenge of Frankenstein." From the Shelley story. Make-up by Jack Pierce, who also created the famous make-up for Universal's Frankenstein monster. ♫♫♫

1957 83m/C GB Peter Cushing, Christopher Lee, Hazel Court, Robert Urquhart, Valerie Gaunt; **D:** Terence Fisher; **W:** Jimmy Sangster. **VHS, Beta $14.95** *WAR, MLB*

Curse of the Blue Lights

Young lovers investigate mysterious lights in the desert, find a gaggle of ghouls robbing graves to make a serum that will resurrect the dreaded Muldoon Man, a lizardly, giant-sized missing link. Missing link in this film was the script, though in fairness most of the dialogue

is indecipherable as amateur actors try to talk under oodles of makeup goo. Homemade horror from Pueblo, Colorado, with little to recommend it aside from passing camp appeal. Also available in an unedited version. ♫

1988 (R) 93m/C Brent Ritter; **D:** John H. Johnson. **VHS, Beta** *NO*

Curse of the Devil

Paul Naschy is a brutish little man who has developed a cult following through his appearances in a string of horror films, most of which he wrote. In this one, he is turned into a werewolf by annoyed gypsies whose ancestors were slain by his. The werewolf makeup is tacky, and the transformation accomplished by three or four simple dissolves. Director Carlos Aured never did break away from his association with Naschy, although he did manage to sell a script which became *Triumphs of a Man Called Horse,* the low point of the "Richard Harris and the Indians" series. **AKA:** El Retorno de la Walpurgis. ♫

1973 (R) 73m/C MX SP Paul Naschy, Maria Silva, Patty Shepard, Fay Falcon; **D:** Carlos Aured; **W:** Paul Naschy. **VHS $19.98** *SNC*

Curse of the Queerwolf

A man is bitten on the butt by gay werewolf(!) and transforms into the title character. When the moon is full, he finds himself turning a werewolf—and gay! Pirro takes advantage of the outrageously funny idea of turning homophobia into a horror movie. Filmed in Santa Barbara in 8mm, the film stock of choice for a large number of ultra-low budget filmmakers in the late '80s. Since their films go straight to home video, they bypass almost all lab costs—some of the resulting features look better than transfers made from worn 35mm prints. From the director of *A Polish Vampire in Burbank.* ♫♫

1987 90m/C Michael Palazzolo, Kent Butler, Taylor Whitney; **D:** Mark Pirro. **VHS $9.95** *HHE*

Cyborg

In a deathly, dirty, post-holocaust urban world, a kickboxing wanderer agrees to aid a cyborg female reach a distant scientific installation. Seems she's carrying the cure to the plague

"Meee-teor shit!"
--Jordy Verrill (Stephen King) in *Creepshow.*

"...girls in tight slacks-- hysterectomy pants, I call them..."
--Mrs. Vernon- Williams (Polly Bergen) describing the signs of decadent youth in *Cry-Baby.*

that has devastated mankind and must make it to the installation to restore world peace, civilization as we know it, and all that other good stuff. Standing in the way is a bunch of mutant deviates, responsible for the murder of the wanderer's true love. These guys like the status quo, and will stop at nothing to doom this mission. They are, of course, quite stupid and actually let the hero live when they could have offed him twice during the course of the film. Still, this is pretty good stuff for a Cannon production, suitable for lovers of both low-rent post-apocalypse S.F. and martial arts. This vehicle took Van Damme one step closer to superstardom. 🦴🦴🦴▷

1989 (R) 85m/C Jean-Claude Van Damme, Deborah Richter, Vincent Klyn, Dayle Haddon; *D:* Albert Pyun; *W:* Kitty Chalmers. **VHS, Beta, LV $14.95** *MGM D*

Daddy's Boys

A hillbilly family turns to crime during the Great Depression, but one son defies his Bible-thumping psychotic of a father and strikes out on his own with a lover, Bonnie-and-Clyde fashion. The wrathful patriarch tracks them down, and things look bleak until both sides come to a mutual accommodation. Bizarre elements include murder victims who freeze upright in place (rather than just falling down) when slain by gunfire, and a planned crucifixion. Dim curio was produced cheaply by Roger Corman mainly because he had some fancy sets left over from shooting *Big Bad Mama 2* and wanted to get maximum use out of them. Directing debut of *After Hours* scriptwriter Minion. 🦴▷

1987 (R) 90m/C Daryl Haney, Laura Burkett, Raymond J. Barry, Dan Shor; *D:* Joe Minion; *W:* Daryl Haney. **VHS, Beta, LV $69.95** *COL*

Dance, Girl, Dance

Interest in lesbian film director Dorothy Arzner is on the rise, and this is one of her best pictures. This potpourri of dance, drama, and comedy features bad girl Lucille Ball and good girl Maureen O'Hara as dancers in a WWII nightclub troupe. Arzner opens up their private lives with a sensitivity rare in Hollywood films of the period. Surprisingly free of the hokum that usually cheapens this type of thing. 🎵 Mother, What Do I Do Now?; Jitterbug Bite; Morning Star. 🦴🦴🦴

1940 88m/B Maureen O'Hara, Louis Hayward, Lucille Ball, Virginia Field, Ralph Bellamy, Maria Ouspenskaya, Mary Carlisle, Katherine Alexander, Edward Brophy; *D:* Dorothy Arzner. **VHS, Beta, LV $19.98** *TTC*

Dancing Lady

No, you're not seeing things. That is Clark Gable and Joan Crawford mixing it up with Moe, Larry and Curly, the Three Stooges. The Stooges are stage hands in this backstage musical starring Joanie Dearest as an aspiring hoofer trying to make it on Broadway. But first she has to pass the audition with the Stooges as accompanists. "Why, I'm the best musician in the country," Moe brags. "But how are you in the city?" Curly replies. MGM's answer to *42nd Street* also marked the screen debuts of Fred Astaire and Nelson Eddy. A curiosity to be sure, but corny and dated. Would you have it any other way? 🎵 Everything I Have Is Yours; Heigh-Ho! The Gang's All Here; Hold Your Man; That's the Rhythm of the Day; My Dancing Lady; Let's Go Bavarian; Hey Young Fella. 🦴🦴▷

1933 93m/B Clark Gable, Joan Crawford, Fred Astaire, Franchot Tone, Nelson Eddy, Ted Healy, Moe Howard, Shemp Howard, Larry Fine; *D:* Robert Z. Leonard. **VHS, Beta $19.98** *MGM, TTC, FCT*

Dark Star

John Carpenter's directorial debut is a low-budget, sci-fi satire which focuses on a group of scientists whose mission is to destroy unstable planets. During their journey, they battle their alien mascot (who closely resembles a walking beach ball), as well as a "sensitive" and intelligent bombing device which starts to question the meaning of its existence. Enjoyable early feature from John "Halloween" Carpenter and Dan "Aliens" O'Bannon. Fun, weird, and unpredictable. 🦴🦴🦴

1974 (G) 95m/C Dan O'Bannon, Brian Narelle; *D:* John Carpenter; *W:* Dan O'Bannon, John Carpenter; *M:* John Carpenter. **VHS, Beta, LV $19.95** *HHT, IME, VCI*

Daughter of Horror

A young woman finds herself involved with a porcine mobster who resembles her abusive father. Trouble is, Dad's dead, and daughter

D

dearest abetted his departure. Obscure venture into expressionism that was initially banned by the New York State Board of Censors. Shot on a low budget (how low was it? So low that McMahon narrated because shooting with sound was too expensive). The 55 minutes tend to lag, although the film should be intriguing to genre enthusiasts and to fans of things pseudo-Freudian. *AKA:* Dementia. 🎵🎵

1955 60m/B Adrienne Barrett, Bruno Ve Sota, Ben Roseman; *D:* John Parker; *W:* John Parker. **VHS** $19.98 *NOS, SNC, MRV*

Dawn of the Dead

Romero's gruesome sequel is in part a parody of his own *Night of the Living Dead,* and in part a sardonic satire on consumerism. The recently dead are still walking around and feeding on the living. Like Prince Prospero in Poe's *Masque of the Red Death,* the four heroes attempt to lock the horror out by barricading themselves in a safe place—a huge shopping mall, complete with Muzak. Though not as gut-wrenching as the original, it's still violent, gory, graphic, and shocking, yet not without humor. Questions the violence created by the living humans in their efforts to save themselves. 🎵🎵🎵

1978 126m/C David Emge, Ken Foree, Gaylen Ross; *D:* George A. Romero; *W:* George A. Romero. **VHS, Beta, LV** $14.98 *REP, FCT*

A Day at the Races

Entertaining, vintage Marx Brothers fare has Groucho, a sleazy veterinarian with a penchant for the ponies, finagling his way into the top spot of a financially strapped sanitarium. there he woos perpetual foil Margaret Dumont (or, more properly, her money), saves the hospital, unites young lovers, and engages in his favorite pastime: parimutuel wagering. He is, of course, ably assisted by brothers Chico and Harpo, employees of said sanitarium. Funny by almost anybody's standards, the best scene occurs when Chico meets up with Groucho at the track and offers to sell him "inside" information. The ensuing negotiations result in an uproarious exchange that epitomizes the term "classic." Another memorable moment involves Harpo charming a number of local

children ala "The Pied Piper." A few brief slow spots do exist, but are easily overlooked when viewed in the context of the total picture. Fine viewing for anyone and an excellent film to start with if you've never seen one of the Marx Brothers movies. 🎵🎵 A Message from the Man in the Moon; On Blue Venetian Waters; Tomorrow is Another Day; All God's Chillun Got Rhythm. 🎵🎵🎵🎵

1937 111m/B Groucho Marx, Harpo Marx, Chico Marx, Sig Rumann, Douglass Dumbrille, Margaret Dumont, Allan Jones, Maureen O'Sullivan; *D:* Sam Wood. **VHS, Beta, LV** $19.95 *MGM, CCB*

Day of the Triffids

The majority of Earth's population is blinded by a meteor shower, which also releases spores that grow into monstrous flesh-eating plants. The killer plants spread quickly across the world, feeding on the hapless masses. Bands of humans lucky enough to have been spared being blinded fight for survival against the hordes of alien vegetation, including one such band trying to cross Europe to the safety of the ocean. The best scene in the film has the heros trapped in a villa protected by an electrified fence. Surrounded by wave upon wave of hungry ferns, they must plot their escape before power runs out and the veggies from beyond break through. Straight-laced SF/horror cross that delivers on all levels and should be sought out by lovers of the genres. This well-done film is an adaptation of John Wyndham's classic novel. 🎵🎵🎵

1963 94m/C Howard Keel, Janet Scott, Nicole Maurey, Kieron Moore, Mervyn Johns; *D:* Steve Sekely; *W:* Philip Yordan. **VHS, Beta, LV** $29.95 *MED, MRV, PSM*

The Day the Earth Stood Still

One of the most beloved science fiction films of all time stars Michael Rennie as alien Klaatu, who arrives in Washington, D.C., to warn Earth's leaders that our planet faces obliteration should they not halt atomic testing. His invitation to live in peace with "the other planets" is met with fear and hysteria. To understand our "strange, unreasoning attitudes," he escapes military hospital confinement and takes a room in a boarding house to live

among us. Patricia Neal co-stars as the woman with whom he entrusts his secret identity. Based on the Harry Bates story, "Farewell to the Master." Look for Francis Bavier (beloved Aunt Bea from *The Andy Griffith Show*) as one of the boarders, and don't forget the three words that can save the planet: "Klaatu Barada Nikto." A literate script ("There are several thousand questions I'd like to ask you," professor Sam Jaffe greets Klaatu), Bernard Herrmann's otherworldly score and, of course, Gort, an impregnable, unstoppable robot that shoots a melting death ray out of its visor, make this must viewing. Ray Kellogg, who did the awe-inspiring special effects, went on to direct *The Killer Shrews.* Go figure. 🦴🦴🦴🦴

1951 92m/B Michael Rennie, Patricia Neal, Hugh Marlowe, Sam Jaffe, Frances Bavier, Lock Martin, Bobby Gray; **D:** Robert Wise; **M:** Bernard Herrmann. **VHS, Beta, LV $14.98** *FOX, FCT, MLB*

Day the World Ended

The first science fiction film of exploitation director Roger Corman. Five survivors of nuclear holocaust discover a desert ranch house fortress owned by a survivalist (Birch) and his daughter (Nelson). With relatively abundant supplies, they fatuously wallow in false misery until a disfigured visitor, wasting away from radiation, stumbles into their paradise. His mutation into an alien being confronts them with the horror that lurks outside. 🦴

1955 79m/B Paul Birch, Lori Nelson, Adele Jergens, Raymond Hatton, Paul Dubov, Richard Denning, Mike Connors; **D:** Roger Corman. **VHS $9.98** *COL*

Dazed and Confused

First there was *American Graffiti,* then came *Fast Times at Ridgemont High,* and finally, there was this, a fond reminiscence on what it meant to be young and in high school in 1970s America. *Dazed and Confused* is an ensemble piece that takes place in one 24-hour period—the last day of school in 1976. Primary storylines involve Randall "Pink" Floyd, star quarterback and king of the school as leader of the new senior class, and young Mitch, who has to endure the hazings and hormonal attacks that come with being an incoming freshman. As one might expect, the last day of school is one big party, and the movie chronicles everyone's attempts to have a little fun. For Pink and the rest of his senior friends, this means nothing more than cruising around with a beer and a buzz, trying to play the mating game while chasing the freshmen so they can be properly initiated. For Mitch and his friends, it means trying to avoid the seniors and stay alive while trying to act cool and become a part of the in-crowd at the same time. Multiple story lines weave together and come apart—don't come to this movie expecting a complicated plot-culminating in an all—night bash by the radio tower that seems to bring the whole school together. Will Pink give in and sign the coach's pledge not to drink and do drugs if he plays football? Will Mitch survive and experience his first taste of young love (lust?)? This is about as deep as the movie gets, but who says that's a bad thing? This movie is flat out fun to watch, especially for anyone who went to high school in the 1970s. As he did earlier with *Slackers,* director Richard Linklater does a great job with a largely unknown cast, capturing the spirit of a generation shaped by Watergate, the Vietnam War, feminism, and marijuana. Biggest standouts are Wiley Wiggins as Mitch and Rory Cochrane as the perpetually stoned-out Slater. Groovy soundtrack features Alice Cooper, Deep Purple, KISS, and Foghat. 🦴🦴🦴◗

1993 (R) 97m/C Jason London, Rory Cochrane, Sasha Jensen, Wiley Wiggins, Michelle Burke, Adam Goldberg, Anthony Rapp, Marissa Ribisi, Parker Posey; **D:** Richard Linklater; **W:** Richard Linklater. **VHS, LV $19.98** *MCA*

Deadly Daphne's Revenge

Underachievers and proud of it, the Troma team merely glued a campy title to an amateurish rape drama from years back and released it as something fresh. Don't be fooled. Meant with utmost sincerity, the plot has hitchhiker Cindy picked up by a quartet of boozy hunters and violated by one of them. A gung-ho prosecutor indicts all four of the men, leading to angst, suicide, revenge, and murder-for-hire. Who's Daphne? A barely glimpsed asylum escapee serving as deus ex machina to bring the cheapie to a close. *Disclosure* it sure ain't. Entertaining it ain't either. **WOOF!**

"Klaatu Barada Nikto."

--Michael Rennie (Klaatu) in *The Day the Earth Stood Still.*

Nice car, snappy dresser, but there's something not right about this guy.... Simone Griffeth and David Carradine in *Death Race 2000*.

1993 98m/C Laurie Tait Partridge, Anthony Holt, Richard Harding Gardner; **D:** Richard Harding Gardner. **VHS, LV $89.95** *AIP*

Deadly Weapons

Chesty Morgan, she of the 73-32-36 figure, takes on the mob using only her God-given talents. Yes, the title refers to the first number. To avenge the murder of her lover, Chesty goes after Mafia hit men and smothers them to death with her gargantuan bosom. One of Joe Bob Brigg's "Sleaziest Movies in the History of the World" series. So bizarre it's actually anti-erotic. 🎵 🎬

1970 (R) 90m/C Chesty Morgan, Harry Reems; **D:** Doris Wishman. **VHS** *NO*

The Death Curse of Tartu

Another aspiring cult classic—meaning a low-budget flick so bad it's funny, though your tolerance may be sorely tested by this Florida-lensed spectacle of student archaeologists in the Everglades whose impromptu rock 'n' roll dance party (must be seen to be believed) disturbs the burial ground of an Indian medicine man. Zombie-like Tartu comes to life with a deadly prescription, though not a very exciting one. 🎵 🎬

1966 84m/C Fred Pinero, Doug Hobart; **D:** William Grefe. **VHS, Beta** *NO*

Death Race 2000

Roger Corman's freewheeling $3,000 knock-off of *Rollerball* leaves its pretentious, big budget inspiration in the dust. A leather-suited David Carradine is the defending champion of the nationally televised Transcontinental Death Race, in which participants score points for running over pedestrians. His challengers include Sylvester Stallone as Machine Gun Joe Viterbo, Mary Woronov as Calamity Jane, and Roberta Collins, of *Big Doll House* and *Caged Heat*, as Mathilda the Hun. Director Paul Bartel and Woronov, the Tracy and Hepburn of B films, starred together in *Rock and Roll High School* and Bartel's delicious black comedy, *Eating Raoul*. Cinematographer Tak Fujimoto later collaborated with another Corman graduate, Jonathan Demme, on *Something Wild, Married to the Mob, Silence of the Lambs,* and the Oscar-winning *Philadelphia.* Screenwriter Charles Griffith belongs in the Cult Movie Hall of Fame (should they ever erect one) as the writer of Corman's *Little Shop of Horrors* and *Bucket of Blood.* A year later, Stallone would become a Hollywood contender with the Oscar-winning *Rocky.* 🦴🦴🦴

1975 (R) 80m/C David Carradine, Simone Griffeth, Sylvester Stallone, Mary Woronov, Roberta Collins; **D:** Paul Bartel; **W:** Charles B. Griffith, Robert Thom. **VHS, Beta $19.95** *VDM, MRV*

Death Sport

In this sequel to the cult hit *Death Race 2000,* a group of humans play a game of death in the year 3000. The object is to race cars and kill as many competitors as possible. Not as good as the original, but still watchable. 🦴🦴

1978 (R) 83m/C David Carradine, Claudia Jennings, Richard Lynch, William Smithers, Will Walker, David McLean, Jesse Vint; **D:** Henry Suso, Allan Arkush. **VHS, Beta** *WAR, OM*

December 7th: The Movie

Banned for 50 years by the U.S. Government, this planned Hollywood explanation to wartime audiences of the Pearl Harbor debacle offers such "offensive" images as blacks fighting heroically alongside whites, loyal Japanese-Americans, and Uncle Sam asleep on the morning of the attack. The Chief of Naval Operations confiscated the original film, claiming it demeaned the Navy. The battle scenes were so realistic they fooled even documentarians. This isn't the most incisive video on the event—just an unforgettable snapshot. 🦴🦴▷

1991 82m/B Walter Huston, Harry Davenport; **D:** John Ford. **VHS $19.95** *KIT, CPM, FUS*

Deep Red: Hatchet Murders

When a psychic senses the identity of a murderer, she becomes the next victim. Hemmings, her neighbor, witnesses the murder, and is compelled to investigate the crime. Whenever anyone involved in the investigation learns the truth, they are killed before they can tell. Echoing his role in *Blow Up* (as well as Argento's earlier *The Bird with the Crystal Plumage*), Hemmings is haunted by the idea that he'd seen something important at the crime scene that he can't recall. Like most of his work, Argento's direction is stylish, rhythmic and ingeniously inventive, with the most breathtakingly original stalk-and-slay sequences ever captured on film, while his plot suffers from too many odd coincidences. The score is hard-driving and memorable, propelling much of the action. The chopped-up, 100 minute pan & scan U.S. version loses about 15 minutes of footage, and much character development. **AKA:** The Hatchet Murders; Profundo Rosso; Dripping Deep Red. 🦴🦴🦴

1975 100m/C David Hemmings, Daria Nicolodi; **D:** Dario Argento; **W:** Dario Argento. **VHS, Beta $19.99** *QVD*

Deepstar Six

This unintentional comedy is completely non-frightening science fiction. When futuristic scientists try to set up an undersea research and missile lab, a suboceanic monster (who looks for all the world like an angry palm tree) objects. Those who thought director Sean Cunningham could do no worse than *Friday the 13th* have been proved wrong. The cast members who aren't eaten and/or killed in the first reel handle the material more skillfully than it deserves. 🦴▷

1989 (R) 97m/C Taurean Blacque, Nancy Everhard, Greg Evigan, Miguel Ferrer, Matt McCoy, Nia Peeples, Cindy Pickett, Marius Weyers; **D:** Sean S. Cunningham; **W:** Lewis Abernathy. **VHS, Beta, LV** *NO*

Dementia 13

This eerie thriller, set in a creepy castle, is about the members of an Irish family who are being offed by a murderer, one by one. After directing some nudie films, Coppola jumped at the opportunity to join Roger Corman's crew in Europe making *The Young Racers,* starring Campbell. Knowing that Corman would make a second feature while in a foreign location, Coppola won the directing job with his script of the memorable ax murder scene. Incredibly, while *Dementia 13* was shooting in Ireland, Corman was in Greece

THE HOUND SALUTES: THE LASTING LEGEND OF THE LOCAL HORROR FILM HOST

The Hound fondly recalls when he was just a pup spending his Saturday afternoons watching classic (and not-so-classic) horror films. These times were made extra-special by those beloved local horror film hosts. There were many throughout this great country who did their part to bring schlock to the masses. This is but a partial list, an homage to all these great talents, some gone now to that great fake cemetery set in the sky. Their likes may never be seen again.

Keeping decomposing Detroit, the Hound's hometown, on edge were **Sir Graves Ghastly, Count Scarey,** and **the Ghoul,** a hippie host in a wig on late night TV circa the '70s. Haunting monstrous mid-Michigan was **Christopher Coffin** and **Count Zapula,** a balding spook touting local business. Spooking looney Los Angeles were **Moona Lisa and Seymour,** who emerged from a behind a wall of slime. Creeping about terrifying Tampa Bay, there was **Dr. Paul Bearer,** host of Saturday's *Creature Feature* for more than 25 years. In icky Illinois, there was **Son of Svengoolie.** In frightening Philly, **Dr. Shock** administered his own brand of medication, and in scary Wilkes-Barre, **Uncle Ted's Monster Mania** still drives the locals mad. Insane Indianapolis had **Sammy Terry** and his spider. In bloody Baltimore, there was **the Ghost Host,** and in weird Washington, D.C., there was **Count Gore De Vol.** And last but not least, putrid Pittsburgh had **Chilly Billy Cardilly,** who, with haunted castle-mates Stefan, Terminal Stare, and Georgette the fudge-maker, hosted *Chiller Theater.* Chilly Billy also had a small part as a news reporter in *Night of the Living Dead.*

For more tribute to those who hosted our horror, see the film Fright Night (1985), where Roddy McDowall plays a TV horror host who stumbles into a real-life vampire hunt. See also our sidebar on "The Ghoul Tube" (p. 176) adoration of those hosts who made it national.

setting up a deal for another film to be shot there with Campbell, Magee, and Coppola, called *Operation Titian,* which was subsequently reworked and rereleased as *Portrait in Terror, Blood Bath,* and *Track of the Vampire.* **AKA:** The Haunted and the Hunted. 🦴🦴▷

1963 75m/B William Campbell, Luana Anders, Bart Patton, Patrick Magee; **D:** Francis Ford Coppola; **W:** Francis Ford Coppola. **VHS, Beta $19.95** *NOS, MRV, SNC*

Demons

A horror film in a Berlin theatre is so involving that its viewers become the demons they are seeing. The new monsters turn on the other audience members, spreading the demon curse like a virus. Virtually plotless, very explicit—the victims are transformed in a variety of horrible ways. Rock soundtrack by Accept, Go West, Motley Crue, and others. Revered in some circles, blasted in others. Produced by Italian horror master Dario Argento; director Bava is the son of the great Mario Bava (*Black Sunday, Blood and Black Lace*)—a chip off the old block. Followed by *Demons 2.* **AKA:** Demoni. 🦴🦴🦴

1986 (R) 89m/C *IT* Urbano Barberini, Natasha Hovey, Paolo Cozza, Karl Zinny, Fiore Argento, Fabiola Toledo, Nicoletta Elni; **D:** Lamberto Bava. **VHS, Beta, LV $19.95** *NWV*

Der Todesking (The Death King)

From the man who gave us *Nekromantik I & II* comes this story of a chain letter that brings suicide to seven unfortunates, on seven successive days of one week. Each suicide is separated by the image of a naked, progressively decomposing man's body. Tamer than the *Nekromantiks,* but with a Nazi torture scene (involving castration with hedge clippers) bring it up (er, down) to *Nekro's* level. In German with confusing English subtitles: one minute of dialogue is summarized by the subtitle: "I quit"; in another scene, the subtitles continue long after the talking stops. Maybe if the Hound spoke German he could make more sense of it. 🦴🦴▷

1989 80m/C *GE* Herman Kopp, Heinrich Ebber, Michael Krause, Eva M. Kurz, Angelika Hock, Nicholas Petche; **D:** Jorg Buttgereit. **VHS** *FLT*

Deranged

Of the numerous movies based on the canni-balistic exploits of Ed Gein (*Psycho, Texas Chainsaw Massacre,* etc.), this is the most ac-curate. A dead-on performance by Blossom as the lonely grave-robbing cannibal, and a twisted sense of humor help move things along nicely. The two directors, Gillen and Ormsby, previously worked together (as actors) on Bob Clark's classic *Children Shouldn't Play with Dead Things.* An added attraction is the early special effect work of gore wizard Tom Savini. Tapes contain a mock-tabloid style documen-tary about Gein. 🦴🦴🦴

1974 (R) 82m/C *CA* Roberts Blossom, Cosette Lee, Robert Warner, Marcia Diamond, Brian Sneagle; *D:* Jeff Gillen, Alan Ormsby. **VHS $18.00** *FRG, MRV*

Desire and Hell at Sunset Motel

Semi-satire of film noir set at a dingy motel in 1950s Anaheim. Fenn is the bombshell wife of a toy salesman in town for a sales meeting. She's soon fooling around with another guy and her husband hires a psychotic criminal to spy on her as the new lover plots to kill hubby. Then Fenn gets slipped a Mickey Finn, and when she wakes up... Incredible plot twists re-peatedly pull the rug out right from under the viewer up until the final scene, in Castle's di-rectorial debut, a campy, crafty little B-flick that deserves more attention. Bartel is in his element as the voyeuristic motel manager. And yes, this could be considered an "erotic thriller," yet stays within the confines of a PG-13 rating. Nice trick! 🦴🦴🦴

1992 (PG-13) 90m/C Sherilyn Fenn, Whip Hubley, David Hewlett, David Johansen, Paul Bartel; *D:* Alien Castle; *W:* Alien Castle. **VHS, Beta, LV $89.98** *FXV, VTR*

Desperate Living

When newly discharged (but questionably cured) mental patient Peggy Gravel (Mink Stole) returns home and, in a paranoid frenzy believes her husband is trying to attack her, she and maid Grizelda Brown (Jean Hill) ac-cidently kill Mr. Gravel—the hefty Hill sits on him and smothers him to death. The guilty pair seek asylum in Mortville, a ghetto populated with the dregs of humanity, including a pout-ing Liz Renay as Muffy St. Jacques, and her lesbian lover, Mole McHenry (Susan Lowe). Mortville is ruled by the evil Queen Carlotta (Edith Massey), who makes life miserable for all (with such decrees as "backwards day," where all must walk backward, wear their clothes backward, etc.), and especially for her daughter, Princess Coo-Coo. Bizarre fairy tale from hell with some really good low-budget, disgusting makeup. Outrageous early Waters; less "out there" than *Pink Flamingos* but more creative (even though it could use a "Divine" touch), which puts his newer stuff (*Hairspray, Cry-Baby, Serial Mom*) in perspective for those new to his work. 🦴🦴🦴

1977 90m/C Mink Stole, Jean Hill, Edith Massey, Liz Renay, Susan Lowe, Mary Vivian Pearce, Cookie Mueller, Ed Peranio, Pat Moran; *D:* John Waters; *W:* John Waters. **VHS, Beta $19.95** *COL, NLC*

Destroy All Monsters

In the future, the world's governments will fi-nally accept and the fact that we share the planet with gigantic mutant monsters. The technology is developed to isolate them all on a remote island, where they can be safely studied. When alien babes take control of Godzilla and his monstrous colleagues, it looks like all is lost for Earth. Ghidra is even recruited to watchdog the alien base at Mount Fuji. United Nations forces, including the crew of the space battle cruiser SY3, are kept hopping trying to meet the alien threat. Can the planet possibly survive this madness? Clas-sic Toho monster slugfest also features Mothra, Rodan, Minya (Son of Godzilla), Angilas, Spiga, and Manda, with cameos by a few oth-ers. If you're wondering why relative un-known Gorosaurus (from *King Kong Escapes*) is featured so prominently—the reason has to do with the condition of the monster suits, some of which were in bad shape and not vi-tal enough to the plot to be rebuilt. Old Angi-las (from *Godzilla Raids Again*) picked up some admirers with this film, as a result of his courage shown in the scrap with Ghidrah. This was Honda's second to last Godzilla pic-ture, and the last really good one for nearly two decades. Dubbing is better than usual. U.S. video TV version is cropped and slightly edited. *AKA:* Kaiju Soshingeki. 🦴🦴🦴🦴

> "Ooohhh, I like the feel of that cold nylon on my big butt!"
> —a lingerie-wearing sicko cop (Turkey Joe) in *Desperate Living.*

1968 (G) 88m/C *JP* Akira Kubo, Jun Tazaki, Yoshio Tsuchiya, Kyoko Ai, Yukiko Kobayashi, Kenji Sahara, Andrew Hughes; **D:** Inoshiro Honda. **VHS $18.00** *FRG*

Detour

Considered to be the creme de la creme of "B" movies, a largely unacknowledged but cult-followed noir downer. Well-designed, stylish, and compelling, if a bit contrived and sometimes annoyingly shrill. Shot in only six days with six indoor sets. Down-on-his-luck pianist Neal hitches cross-country to rejoin his fiancee. His first wrong turn involves the accidental death of the man who picked him up, then he's en route to Destiny with a capital "D" when he picks up fatal femme Savage, as vicious a vixen as ever ruined a good man. Told in flashback, it's also been called the most despairing of all "B"-pictures. As noir as they get. ♫♫♫

1946 67m/B Tom Neal, Ann Savage, Claudia Drake, Edmund MacDonald; **D:** Edgar G. Ulmer. **VHS, Beta, LV $19.95** *BAR, MRV, SNC*

Detour to Danger

Two young men set out on a fishing expedition and run into crooks and damsels in distress. Unintentionally hilarious "acting" by the no-name cast make this a grade-Z "B" movie. Of interest only because it was filmed in the three-color Kodachrome process used primarily in documentaries. ♫♫

1945 56m/C Britt Wood, John Day, Nancy Brinckman; **D:** Richard Talmadge. **VHS, Beta, 8mm $19.95** *VYY*

The Devils

In 1631 France, a priest is accused of commerce with the devil and sexual misconduct with nuns. Since he is also a political threat, the accusation is used to denounce and eventually execute him. Based on Aldous Huxley's *The Devils of Loudun,* the movie features masturbating nuns and other excesses—shocking scenes typical of film director Russell. Supposedly this was Russell's attempt to wake the public to their desensitization of modern horrors of war. Controversial and flamboyant. ♫♫♫

1971 (R) 109m/C *GB* Vanessa Redgrave, Oliver Reed, Dudley Sutton, Max Adrian, Gemma Jones, Murray Melvin; **D:** Ken Russell; **W:** Ken Russell. National Board of Review Awards '71: Best Director (Russell). **VHS, Beta $19.98** *WAR, INJ*

Devil's Rain

You have to be in awe of any devil-worshipping movie that has Anton Szandor Lavey, High Priest of the Church of Satan, as the technical advisor. William Shatner and Tom Skerrit are brothers who do battle with Satan's head minister, Corbis (Ernest Borgnine), who has hound the brothers' family for 300 years over a stolen black book. What drive-ins and late night television was invented for. The movie goes overboard a bit with the waxey goo into which the devil's disciples melt during the climax (it might compel you to find some crackers), but (maybe thanks to Mr. Lavey), the movie shows that evil is, well, scary. Spooky twist ending demonstrates timeless truth: evil never dies, it just changes its appearance. John Travolta has a bit part as Corbis' flunky. ♫♫

1975 (PG) 85m/C Ernest Borgnine, Ida Lupino, William Shatner, Eddie Albert, Keenan Wynn, John Travolta, Tom Skerritt; **D:** Robert Fuest. **VHS, Beta, LV $19.95** *NO*

The Diabolical Dr. Z

When old Dr. Zimmer (Escribano) dies of cardiac arrest after the medical council won't let him make the world a kinder gentler place with his personality-altering technique, his dutiful daughter Irma (Karr)—convinced the council brought on dad's demise—is out to change some personalities in a big way. She picks up a conveniently similar-looking hitchhiker and uses the girl to fake her own death, then kidnaps Nadia (Blain), who dances under the name Miss Death, and has been dating Irma's ex-beau Philip (Montes). Irma uses her surgical techniques to make a slave of Nadia, sending her out to seduce and slay the targets of her revenge. A top-notch thriller from Franco (who also plays a comedic police detective). Every scene is interestingly framed, beautifully photographed, and stylishly designed, and is accompanied by an offbeat discordant music score. The mad lab features a weird variety of frightening instruments (including robot arms specifically designed for lifting and holding human captives). But the showstopper is the entrance of the stunning Estella Blain, who writhes across a spider web in a barely there bodystocking. Franco regular Vernon is on hand as the number-one item on Irma's revenge shopping list. *AKA:* Miss Muerte; Dans les Griffes du Maniaque. ♫ ♫ ♫ ▷

1965 86m/B *SP FR* Mabel Karr, Fernando Montes, Estella Blain, Antonio J. Escribano, Howard Vernon; *Cameos:* Jess (Jesus) Franco; *D:* Jess (Jesus) Franco. **VHS $19.98** *SNC*

Diabolique

Numerous remakes, imitations, and having to watch it in high-school French class haven't tempered the terror of this suspense classic by Clouzot, a director considered the Gallic answer to Alfred Hitchcock (the Hound doesn't want to know the question). Based on a novel by Pierre Boileau and Thomas Narcejac, the plot details how the abused wife and street-wise mistress of a sadistic schoolmaster conspire together to kill him. After the nightmarish ordeal of the murder, they sink his corpse in a scum-covered pool—but subsequent, eerie events hint that their tormentor isn't really dead. Or, at least, he isn't finished with them yet. Circulates on different video labels; non-Francophones should beware contrasty prints in which the English subtitles are largely indecipherable. Zut alors! *AKA:* Les Diabolique. ♫ ♫ ♫ ▷

1955 107m/B *FR* Simone Signoret, Vera Clouzot, Paul Meurisse, Charles Vanel, Michel Serrault; *D:* Henri-Georges Clouzot. National Board of Review Awards '55: 5 Best Foreign Films of the Year; New York Film Critics Awards '55: Best Foreign Film. **VHS, Beta, LV, 8mm $24.95** *VYY, NOS, SNC*

Diner

Levinson's directorial debut is a bitter-sweet and often funny look at the experiences of five young Baltimore men just after Christmas, 1959. Particularly notable is his casting

"So then I gave her the jumbo popcorn...." Mickey Rourke recalls last night's date for Kevin Bacon, Daniel Stern, and Timothy Daly in *Diner*.

of "unknowns" who gave fine performances and have since become household names. The characters are fully believable. Everybody knows guys like these who spend the best hours of their lives at their favorite diner. They talk, make strange bets with each other, argue, smoke cigarettes, and generally just hang out. They consider their time with each other to be the important, enjoyable part of their existence. What they do with their wives and girlfriends comes second and somehow, isn't as real to them. Levinson' evocation of his native city is just as strong as the characters and it's almost as important to the story. The diner itself and the streets of Baltimore have the proper used, run-down look to them. If the protagonists don't grow or change very much, well, that's a valid point for a film to make. And this one has gotten better with age. 🦴🦴🦴

1982 (R) 110m/C Steve Guttenberg, Daniel Stern, Mickey Rourke, Kevin Bacon, Ellen Barkin, Timothy Daly, Paul Reiser, Michael Tucker; **D:** Barry Levinson. Nominations: Academy Awards '82: Best Original Screenplay. **VHS, Beta, LV $14.95** *MGM*

Dinosaur Island

Five military men survive a plane crash and discover an island where scantily clad (leather bikinis being the fashion choice) lascivious ladies and prehistoric monsters live. The men must find a cache of equipment left on the island during WWII, which is guarded by a big leftover prop from *Carnosaur*. Will the awesome power of testosterone overcome the fierce dinosaurs which stand between the men and their objects of desire? Locations include Bronson Canyon, Leo Carillo Beach, and David Carradine's ranch. Some shooting was done over a hill from where *The Flintstones* (1994) was filming. Mainly an enjoyably silly sex comedy, with some pretty good stop-motion dinosaurs, courtesy of Jim Danforth. Drew would turn in her cave bikini to play an actress in *Dinosaur Valley Girls*. Nice to see veteran Hagen (*The Mini-Skirt Mob, Night Creature,* tons of TV) starring again. 🦴🦴🦴

1993 (R) 85m/C Ross Hagen, Richard Gabai, Antonia Dorian, Peter Spellos, Tom Shell, Griffin Drew, Steve Barkett, Toni Naples; **D:** Jim Wynorski, Fred Olen Ray; **W:** Bob Sheridan, Christopher Wooden. **VHS** *NHO, HVL*

"**You know, when can we Do It? Where do we Do It? Are your parents going to be out so we can Do It?**"

—Daniel Stern in *Diner.*

Divine

Two Divine flicks: In the first, Divine plays a naughty girl who, not surprisingly, since this one is titled *The Diane Linkletter Story,* ends up a successful suicide. *The Neon Woman* is a rare live performance, with Divine a woman who owns a strip joint and has a slew of problems you won't read about in Dear Abbey. 🦴🦴🦴

1990 110m/C Divine. **VHS $29.99** *FCT*

D.O.A.

How's this for an attention-grabbing opening: A man stumbles into a police station to report a murder, his own! Edmond O'Brien stars as a CPA whose San Francisco vacation turns fatal when he discovers he has been poisoned and has only a few days to live. He becomes his own detective and traces his plight to a shipment of iridium that he notarized and that fell into criminal hands. While some anachronistic touches are good for a chuckle (note the soundtrack's wolf-whistle reaction to the sight of a beautiful woman), this is quintessential film noir, cynical and bleak, charting an innocent man's descent into a nightmarish world. populated by maniacal assassins. Remade in 1969 as *Color Me Dead,* and in 1988 as a vehicle for Dennis Quaid and Meg Ryan. Available in a toxic colorized version. 🦴🦴🦴

1949 83m/B Edmond O'Brien, Pamela Britton, Luther Adler, Neville Brand, Beverly Garland; **D:** Rudolph Mate; **M:** Dimitri Tiomkin. **VHS, Beta $16.95** *SNC, NOS, VYY*

Doctor Butcher M.D.

Body parts are being stolen from a New York hospital, and when the thefts are linked to a primitive cannibal cult, a team is sent to their island to investigate. This artlessly filmed gorefest combines the then-popular Italian cannibal movies and a Frankenstein-like mad doctor, with enthusiastically gruesome results. Plot makes no sense, and there's very little in the way of suspense, but the unending parade of bloody effects is not exactly dull. A touch of humor is added by O'Brien (a dead ringer for George Bush) as the mad Dr. Abrero, who cuts out "patient's" vocal chords when their screaming disturbs his concentration. A feast for gorehounds, all others beware. For some reason, the American distributor added an entirely unrelated and nonsensical title sequence with a cheap looking zombie (filmmaker William Frumkes, who shot the footage) crawling out of a grave, as well as replacing the score with annoying electronic music. *AKA:* Queen of the Cannibals; Zombie Holocaust; The Island of the Last Zombies. 🦴🦴▷

1980 (R) 81m/C *IT* Ian McCulloch, Alexandra Cole, Peter O'Neal, Donald O'Brien; *D:* Frank Martin. **VHS, Beta** *NO*

Dr. Cyclops

The famous early Technicolor fantasia about mad scientist Dr. Thorkel, a kind of Lex Luthor with cola-bottle eyeglasses, who takes over a radium-rich mine in the Amazon jungle and exploits its atomic powers to miniaturize living beings. When five visitors learn his secret, Thorkel subjects them all to his infernal invention, including the token pretty lady biologist. Yes, kids, he shrunk the honey! Scenes of tiny people trying to elude Thorkel and his hungry cat Satanis waver between whimsical camp and high adventure—and it's worth recalling that Schoedsack also did the definitive giant-beast tale *King Kong*. Outdated, but still appealing and fun. 🦴🦴🦴

1940 76m/C Albert Dekker, Janice Logan, Victor Kilian, Thomas Coley, Charles Halton; *D:* Ernest B. Schoedsack. **VHS, Beta, LV $14.98** *MCA, FCT, MLB*

Doctor Duck's Super Secret All-Purpose Sauce

Conglomeration of video, music, and comedy clips directed by the former Monkee done in the style of his popular *Elephant Parts.* 🦴🦴🦴

1985 90m/C Michael Nesmith, Whoopi Goldberg, Jimmy Buffett, Rosanne Cash, Jay Leno; *D:* Michael Nesmith. **VHS, Beta, LV $9.95** *MVD*

Dr. No

The world is introduced to British secret agent 007, James Bond, when it is discovered that a mad scientist is sabotaging rocket launchings from his hideout in Jamaica. The first 007 film is far less glitzy than any of its successors but boasts the sexiest "Bond girl" of them all in Andress, and promptly made stars of her and Connery. On laserdisc, the film is in widescreen transfer and includes movie bills, publicity photos, location pictures, and the British and American trailers. The sound effects and musical score can be separated from the dialogue. Audio interviews with the director, writer, and editor are included as part of the disc. 🦴🦴🦴

1962 (PG) 111m/C *GB* Sean Connery, Ursula Andress, Joseph Wiseman, Jack Lord, Zena Marshall, Eunice Gayson, Margaret LeWars, John Kitzmiller, Lois Maxwell, Bernard Lee, Anthony Dawson; *D:* Terence Young; *M:* John Barry. **VHS, Beta, LV $19.98** *MGM, CRC, TLF*

Dr. Strangelove, or: How I Learned to Stop Worrying and Love the Bomb

It's the end of the world as we know it in Stanley Kubrick's classic black comedy that is undimmed by the collapse of the "evil empire." Sterling Hayden stars as cigar-chomping General Jack Ripper, who is convinced of a Communist conspiracy to sap "our precious bodily fluids" and orders American bombers to attack Russia. George C. Scott is in his element as military hawk General Buck Turgidson, but it's Peter Sellers' show all the way. In a bravura triple role, he portrays the befuddled American president Merkin Muffley, British officer Mandrake, and the wheelchair-bound former Nazi Dr. Strangelove. Aboard the plane racing toward its target are James Earl Jones and Slim Pickens as gung-ho pilot Major Kong. Keenan Wynn is Colonel "Bat" Guano, who has a memorable Coke machine encounter with "prevert" Sellers. Not to be missed. Pickens riding down the bomb to oblivion is one of the movies' most indelible images. Kubrick wisely decided to delete a climactic pie fight. As Muffley admonishes at one point, "Gentleman, you can't fight in here. This is the war room." 🦴🦴🦴🦴

1964 93m/B *GB* Peter Sellers, George C. Scott, Sterling Hayden, Keenan Wynn, Slim Pickens, James Earl Jones, Peter Bull; *D:* Stanley Kubrick; *W:* Terry Southern, Peter George, Stanley Kubrick; *M:* Laurie Johnson. British Academy Awards '64: Best Film; New York Film Critics Awards '64: Best Director (Kubrick); Nominations: Academy Awards '64: Best Actor (Sellers), Best Adapted Screenplay, Best Director

D

"I could easily kill you now, but I'm determined to have your brain."
--Donald O'Brian in *Dr. Butcher, M.D.*

(Kubrick). Best Picture. **VHS, Beta, LV, 8mm $19.95** *COL, HMV*

Dr. Terror's House of Horrors

All aboard for one of the first and best horror anthology films. Five strangers on a train make the acquaintance of mysterious Peter Cushing, who breaks out a tarot deck to tell their fortunes. Death is in the cards: The first man is killed by a female werewolf; the second is strangled by a haunted vine; and the third, a jazz musician, is fatally punished for playing voodoo music he overheard at a secret ceremony. The last two stories are best. Donald Sutherland stars as a man who believes his wife is a vampire. Finally, art critic Christopher Lee is menaced by the severed hand of the artist he has run over. If you like *The Twilight Zone,* you'll follow this to the end of the line. *AKA:* The Blood Suckers. 🦴🦴▷

1965 92m/C *GB* Christopher Lee, Peter Cushing, Donald Sutherland; *D:* Freddie Francis. **VHS $14.95** *REP, MLB*

Dolemite

An hilariously foul-mouthed ex-con attempts to settle the score with some of his former partners, who have taken over his night club in his absence. He recruits a band of kung-fu savvy ladies of the night to help out. Strange combination of action and comedy. Popular night club and "party record" comedian Moore wears some outrageous outfits and performs some of his most famous rap routines, including the old chestnut "The Jungle King." Moore's latest role is in the upcoming CD-ROM game "Dueling Firemen." 🦴🦴🦴

1975 (R) 88m/C Rudy Ray Moore, Jerry Jones; *D:* D'Urville Martin. **VHS** *XVC*

Dolemite 2: Human Tornado

Nobody ever said Moore was for everybody's taste. But, hey, when blaxploitation movies were the rage, Rudy the stand-up comic was out there rapping through a series of trashy movies that, when viewed today, have survived the test of time. This one's just as vile, violent, and sexist as the day it was released. When Rudy is surprised in bed with a white

sheriff's wife, he flees and meets up with a madam and a house of kung-fu-skilled girls who are embroiled in a fight with a local mobster. And that sheriff is still on his trail. This sequel is a bit less coherent than the original, but more action packed. *AKA:* The Human Tornado. 🦴🦴🦴

1976 (R) 98m/C Rudy Ray Moore, Lady Reed. **VHS** *XVC*

The Doll Squad

A group of voluptuous special agents, including leader York (*Curse of the Swamp Creature*), Lisa Todd (*Woman Hunt*), and Satana (*Faster Pussycat! Kill! Kill!*), fight an ex-CIA agent out to rule the world with his big rocket, in this early entry in the popular "assemble the squad" sub-genre. Mikels says *Charlie's Angels* ripped him off, and he's got a point—one of them's named Sabrina and even the music sounds the same! Eisley's career in trash films has been all over the map, starting off with Corman (*The Wasp Woman*), peaking in Fuller's *Naked Kiss,* cruising into pictures for David Hewitt (*Mighty Gorga, Journey to the Center of Time*), Mikels, Fred DeCordova's *Frankie and Johnnie* (with Elvis), starring as Margheriti's *Lightning Bolt,* Al Adamson (*Dracula Vs. Frankenstein*), and even Fred Olen Ray (*Deep Space*). *AKA:* Hustler Squad. 🦴🦴▷

1973 (PG) 93m/C Michael Ansara, Francine York, Anthony Eisley, Tura Satana; *D:* Ted V. Mikels. **VHS, Beta $39.95** *GHV, MRV*

Don't Look in the Basement

Things get out of hand at an isolated asylum and a pretty young nurse is caught in the middle. It seems the staff is dead, the loonies are in charge, and they won't let her leave. A fun, tongue-in-cheek little horror film, strait-jacketed by a low budget. Used the familiar "It's only a movie..." ad campaign. Brownrigg also gave us *Keep My Grave Open* and *Poor White Trash 2.* More movie madness from Texas, which seems to be a breeding spot for cinema trash. The goofy end titles are worth sticking around for. 🦴🦴▷

1973 (R) 95m/C Rosie Holotik, Anne MacAdams, William Bill McGhee, Rhea MacAdams, Gene Ross, Betty Chandler, Camilla Carr, Robert Dracup, Jessie

Kirby, Hugh Feagin, Harryete Warren, Jessie Lee Fulton, Michael Harvey; **D:** S.F. Brownrigg. **VHS, Beta** $14.98 *MPI*

Don't Look Now

Psychic killer, qu'est-ce que c'est? Donald Sutherland and Julie Christie, grieving over the accidental drowning of their five-year-old daughter, find death in Venice, where he has come to help restore a church. Sutherland is haunted by fleeting glimpses of a diminutive figure in a red parka associated with his daughter. The mystery deepens when the couple becomes involved with two sisters, one a blind psychic, who brings encouraging news from beyond concerning their daughter, and a warning to Sutherland to leave Venice. Based on a short story by Daphne Du Maurier. This menacing thriller is best known for an innovative sex scene between Sutherland and Christie that Roeg intecut with post-coital glimpses of the lovers changing the bedsheets and dressing for dinner. ♪♪♪

1973 (R) 110m/C Donald Sutherland, Julie Christie, Hilary Mason; **D:** Nicolas Roeg; **W:** Chris Bryant, Allan Scott; **M:** Pino Donaggio. **VHS, Beta, LV** $49.95 *PAR*

Dracula

Lugosi, in his most famous role, plays a vampire who travels to London from his home in Transylvania in his search for human blood. From Bram Stoker's novel. Lugosi's performance has come under attack over the years, criticized as slow and theatrical, while also heaping abuse upon his thick accent and saying that he only knew his lines phonetically (despite the fact that he'd been in America many years). In fact, all of this is part of a deliberate performance—Dracula is a being not only foreign to the British, but also a foreigner to the 20th century—and indeed, an alien to the human race and the entire natural world. It's no wonder that audiences have always been so deeply impressed by Lugosi's powerful performance—amused yet disturbed by the oddity of his accent and mannerisms, and not knowing quite what to make of him. The result is a masterpiece which would make Lugosi's name immortal (while helping to later destroy his career), marred significantly by

Browning's stagy and unsure handling—the director seemed to have a bit of trouble adapting to the demands of talking pictures. A Spanish version, shot concurrently, shows how each scene could be done to better effect, but does not have Lugosi's powerful presence. Sequelled by *Dracula's Daughter*. ♪♪♪♪

1931 75m/B Bela Lugosi, David Manners, Dwight Frye, Helen Chandler, Edward Van Sloan; **D:** Tod Browning. **VHS, Beta, LV** $14.95 *MCA, TLF, HMV*

Dracula Vs. Frankenstein

Ever see a low-budget monster movie in which incredibly strange creatures cause havoc at a California amusement pier, and a maniac is on the loose killing innocent people, while the director's wife appears in bizarre musical numbers? Or how about one where a disfigured mad scientist plots revenge against the men who laughed at his theories and ruined his career? Or the one where Count Dracula seeks help in reviving the Frankenstein monster from the lone descendant of Baron Frankenstein? You may have seen all these films at least once—but did you ever see all of these plots in one film? That's what happens when Vegas entertainer Judith Fontain (Carrol, the Freak-Out Girl) goes looking for her missing sister among the hippies of LA's beaches, where the heads have been rolling lately. Adamson's attempted revival of the classic monster movie is as clumsy and patched together as his title creature. The aging veterans of classic horror (Naish, Chaney, Rossito) meet the young faces of '60s trash exploitation (Carrol, Tamblyn, Eisley, Greydon Clark). As Eisley's character puts it: "It's not usually this gory on the premises." Kenneth Strickfaden supplies his original *Frankenstein* electrical props to the mad lab. Last film for Naish. Features a cameo by genre maven Forrest J Ackerman. ***AKA:*** Blood of Frankenstein; They're Coming to Get You; Dracula Contra Frankenstein; The Revenge of Dracula. ♪♪♪♪

1971 (R) 90m/C *SP* J. Carrol Naish, Lon Chaney Jr., Regina Carrol, Russ Tamblyn, Jim Davis, Anthony Eisley, Zandor Vorkov, John Bloom, Angelo Rossitto; ***Cameos:*** Forrest J. Ackerman; **D:** Al Adamson. **VHS** *NO*

91

Drive-In Sleaze

A mass of grade-Z movie trailers, from the '30s to the '70s, including *The Girl from S.I.N.*, *Mundo Depravados*, and *The Reluctant Sadist*. 🦴🦴

1984 55m/C VHS, Beta $19.95 *NO*

Driver's Seat

Extremely bizarre film with a cult following that was adapted from the novel by Muriel Spark. Liz stars as a deranged woman trying to keep a rendezvous with her strange lover in Rome. In the meantime she wears tacky clothes and delivers stupid lines. *AKA:* Psychotic; Identikit. WOOF!

1973 (R) 101m/C *IT* Elizabeth Taylor, Ian Bannen, Mona Washbourne, Andy Warhol; *D:* Giuseppe Patroni Griffi. **VHS, Beta $24.98** *SUE*

Duck Soup

All true Marx-ists recognize this comedy classic as the Brothers's funniest. Groucho is Rufus T. Firefly, leader of Freedonia. "If you think this country's bad off now," he sings, "just wait 'till I get through with it." Harpo and Chico are spies. Dowager Margaret Dumont is around for Groucho to bounce insults off of ("Remember," he declares in the heat of battle, "We're fighting for this woman's honor, which is probably more than she ever did"). As for Zeppo...well, does it matter? No piano and harp solos. No sappy romance. Just the perfect recipe of verbal and visual anarchy. Contains the famed "mirror scene" between Groucho and Harpo. Ironically, this was a box office flop that ended the Marx's association with Paramount. In the 1970s, it was rediscovered and embraced by college students for its anti-authoritarian attitude and anti-war satire. As for the title, Groucho reportedly explained: "Take two turkeys, one goose, four cabbages, but no duck, and mix them together, After one taste, you'll duck soup for the rest of your life." 🦴🦴🦴🦴

1933 70m/B Groucho Marx, Chico Marx, Harpo Marx, Zeppo Marx, Louis Calhern, Margaret Dumont, Edgar Kennedy, Raquel Torres, Leonid Kinskey, Charles Middleton; *D:* Leo McCarey; *W:* Harry Ruby, Nat Perrin, Bert Kalmar, Arthur Sheekman; *M:* Harry Ruby, Bert Kalmar. **VHS, Beta, LV $14.98** *MCA, FCT*

Duel

Just when you thought it was safe to get back on the highway.... This made-for-TV movie put Steven Spielberg in the driver's seat. Dennis Weaver stars as a traveling salesman who is inexplicably menaced by a malevolent monster truck and its unseen driver. Just as tense as the highway confrontations (which must have been good practice for *Jaws*) is the scene in which Weaver suspects that his pursuer is among the diners at a crowded truck stop. But which one? Paranoia that exceeds the speed limit. This version contains additional footage added for the foreign theatrical release. 🦴🦴🦴

1971 (PG) 90m/C Dennis Weaver, Lucille Benson, Eddie Firestone, Cary Loftin; *D:* Steven Spielberg; *W:* Richard Matheson; *M:* Billy Goldenberg. **VHS, Beta $14.98** *MCA*

Dune

When this unwieldy sci-fi saga (based on Frank Herbert's epic novel) first opened they handed out glossaries to give viewers a fighting chance at comprehending the story: in the year 10,191 the royal Atreides family is maneuvered onto the desert world Arrakis, where enemies plan to annihilate them. But the planet's ecosystem produces a precious spice drug essential to space travel, and young Paul Atreides fits a native prophecy of a coming messiah...Oh, there's more, about five hours' worth in Lynch's legendary original cut, ruthlessly trimmed for release. As it is, characters come and go abruptly, clumsy voice overs replace vanished chunks of narrative, and F/X range from awesome to awful. Yet with its sprawling Moorish sets, Lynchian imagery and stiffly mannered performances, *Dune* maintains unearthly grandeur and inscrutability unlike any mere *Star Wars* wannabe. Hunting up longer, more complete versions has become a fan obsession; confusion caused by two-part TV edition (in which "Alan Smithee" gets directorial credit) sporting a comic-strip prologue and restored scenes that expand the role of then-unknown supporting actor Patrick Stewart. 🦴🦴

1984 (PG-13) 137m/C Kyle MacLachlan, Francesca Annis, Jose Ferrer, Sting, Max von Sydow, Juergen Prochnow, Linda Hunt, Freddie Jones, Dean Stockwell, Virginia Madsen, Brad Dourif, Kenneth McMillan, Silvana Mangano, Jack Nance, Sian Phillips, Paul

Smith, Richard Jordan, Everett McGill, Sean Young, Patrick Stewart; **D:** David Lynch; **W:** David Lynch; **M:** Brian Eno. Nominations: Academy Awards '84: Best Sound. **VHS, Beta, LV $24.95** *MCA, FCT*

The Dunwich Horror

Young warlock acquires a banned book of evil spells, starts trouble on the astral plane and here at home. Stockwell is hammy; Dee is her inimitable blonde self. Film is loosely based on an H. P. Lovecraft story with a strong influence of TV's *Dark Shadows,* but it can also be seen as a curious precursor to the fiction and films of Stephen King. The generational conflicts of the 1960s loom large. Yes, that's Talia Coppola (Shire) as the nurse. 🦴🦴🦴

1970 90m/C Sandra Dee, Dean Stockwell, Lloyd Bochner, Ed Begley Sr., Sam Jaffe, Joanna Moore, Talia Shire; **D:** Daniel Haller; **W:** Curtis Hanson; **M:** Les Baxter. **VHS, Beta $9.98** *SUE*

Earth Girls Are Easy

Valley girl Valerie (Geena Davis) is having a bad week: first she catches her fiancee with another woman, then she breaks a nail, then furry aliens land in her swimming pool. What more could go wrong? When the aliens are temporarily stranded, she decides to make amends by giving them a head-to-toe makeover with the help of her hairdresser, Julie "I Like 'Em Big and Stupid" Brown. Devoid of their excessive hairiness, the handsome trio of fun-loving extraterrestrials (Jeff Goldblum, Jim Carey, and Damon Wayans), and set out to experience the Southern California lifestyle, with the help of surfer dude cum pool cleaner Michael McKean. Stupid, stupid, story that actually works, thanks to a colorful and energetic cast. Sometimes hilarious sci-fi/musical, featuring bouncy shtick, Julie's Brown's music, and a gleeful dismantling of modern culture. 🦴🦴🦴

1989 (PG) 100m/C Geena Davis, Jeff Goldblum, Charles Rocket, Julie Brown, Jim Carrey, Damon Wayans, Michael McKean, Angelyne, Larry Linville, Rick Overton; **D:** Julien Temple; **W:** Julie Brown, Charlie Coffey, Terrance McNally; **M:** Nile Rodgers. **VHS, Beta, LV $14.98** *LIV, VES*

Easy Rider

Slim-budget, generation-defining movie. Two young men in late 1960s undertake a motor-cycle trek throughout the Southwest in search of the real essence of America. Along the way they encounter hippies, rednecks, prostitutes, drugs, Nicholson, and tragedy. One of the highest-grossing pictures of the decade, undoubtedly an influence on two generations of "youth-oriented dramas," which all tried unsuccessfully to duplicate the original accomplishment. Psychedelic scenes and a great role for Nicholson are added bonuses. Look for the graveyard dancing scene in New Orleans. Features one of the best '60s rock scores around, including "Mean Streets" and "The Wanderers." 🦴🦴🦴🦴

1969 (R) 94m/C Peter Fonda, Dennis Hopper, Jack Nicholson, Karen Black, Toni Basil, Robert Walker Jr.; **D:** Dennis Hopper; **W:** Terry Southern. Nominations: Academy Awards '69: Best Story & Screenplay, Best Supporting Actor (Nicholson). **VHS, Beta, LV, 8mm $19.95** *COL, CCB*

Eat My Dust

Opie as a hellraisin', joy ridin' good ol' boy? Strap yourself in this freewheeling star vehicle for Ron Howard, who tears up the road and his sheriff dad's small town when he and friend Christopher Norris steal Dave Madden's stock car. The motorized chase takes up more than half of the film's running time. The musical score by Dave Grisman, father of bluegrass-roots Dawg music, is a gas. Madden is best known as Reuben Kincaid, manager to *The Patridge Family.* Look for Ron Howard's mascot, little brother Clint, as well as father Rance. Written and directed by Charles Griffith, who scripted the Roger Corman cult classics *Little Shop of Horrors* and *Bucket of Blood.* Corman produced, and secured the services of Howard (then on the hit TV show *Happy Days*) by promising him the opportunity to direct a film of his own. That was *Grand Theft Auto.* Howard most recently returned the favor by giving Corman a cameo in *Apollo 13.* 🦴🦴

1976 (PG) 89m/C Ron Howard, Christopher Norris, Warren Kemmerling, Rance Howard, Clint Howard, Corbin Bernsen; **D:** Charles B. Griffith. **VHS, Beta $9.98** *SUE*

Eaten Alive

A Southern wacko rents rooms to unsuspecting Yankee tourists, who occasionally

E

> **"As if things weren't bad enough, now I've been abducted by aliens."**
> —Geena Davis in *Earth Girls Are Easy.*

Why? Because they can't drive their rods. Dennis Hopper and Peter Fonda in *Easy Rider*.

"It's amazing what you can do with a cheap piece of meat if you know how to treat it."

—Paul Bland (Paul Bartel) speaking of Raoul (Robert Beltran) in *Eating Raoul*.

provide a meal for his huge pet crocodile. Cast of veteran character actors are delightfully unrestrained, especially Brand (*Cool Hand Luke*) as the lunatic inn keeper. The plot is tissue thin, but things keep hopping throughout. Director Tobe Hooper had some trouble finding a worthy follow-up to *The Texas Chainsaw Massacre*. This isn't it, but it's very entertaining in its own way. Englund is more recognizable with razor fingernails as Freddy Krueger of the *Nightmare on Elm Street* films. *AKA:* Death Trap; Starlight Slaughter; Legend of the Bayou; Horror Hotel Massacre. 🎵🎵▷

1976 (R) 96m/C Neville Brand, Mel Ferrer, Carolyn Jones, Marilyn Burns, Stuart Whitman, Robert Englund; *D:* Tobe Hooper. **VHS, Beta $59.95** *PSM*

Eating Raoul

The Blands are a happily married couple who share many interests: good food and wine, entrepreneurial dreams, and an aversion to sex. The problem is, they're flat broke. So, when the tasty swinger from upstairs makes

a pass at Mary and Paul accidentally kills him, they discover he's got loads of money; Raoul (future *Voyager* Beltran) takes a cut in the deal by disposing of—or rather recycling—the body. This may just be the way to finance that restaurant they've been wanting to open—if they can only get enough "clients." Wonderful, offbeat, hilariously dark comedy which added greatly to the cult esteem of Bartel and his stellar cast. Once an animator at UPA, Bartel's short films *The Secret Cinema* and *Naughty Nurse* got the attention of producer Gene Corman, who convinced his brother Roger to give Bartel a job. He directed the cult faves *Private Parts* and *Death Race 2000* for the Corman's, but found no one but his parents willing to finance *Eating Raoul*, and no one willing to distribute it once finished—until it caused a sensation at Filmex. We still await the announced sequel, *Bland Ambition*. 🎵🎵🎵▷

1982 (R) 83m/C Mary Woronov, Paul Bartel, Buck Henry, Ed Begley Jr., Edie McClurg, Robert Beltran, John Paragon; *D:* Mary Woronov, Paul Bartel. **VHS, Beta $19.98** *FOX*

E

Ecco

Shockumentary originally titled *World By Night 3,* featuring members of (one would hope) fringe European communities where gruesome flesh-severing rituals are performed on body parts of various species including humans. Segments include oral castration of a reindeer by Finnish brides prior to their wedding vows, a chicken beheaded over a would-be English witch, and a German swordsmanship contest where the winner is the one who receives the most cuts to the face. Letterboxed. Dubbed. *AKA:* World By Night 3. 🦴

1963 98m/B *IT* **D:** Gianni Proia; **W:** R.W. Cresse. **VHS $23.00** *SMW, TPV*

Ed Wood

Leave it to Burton to bring to the screen the story of the least talented movie director of all time. Depp is convincing (and engaging) as Ed Wood, Jr., the cross-dressing, angora-sweater-wearing, low-budget auteur of such notoriously "bad" cult films as *Glen or Glenda?* and *Plan 9 From Outer Space.* Landau appears in an Oscar-worthy performance, that of drug-addicted horror star Bela Lugosi. Much of the movie is about Wood's relationship with Lugosi, whose career is over by the time Wood befriends him. Clearly a labor of love for Burton, this is a hilarious and touching tribute to a Hollywood maverick with grade-Z vision. 🦴🦴🦴🦴

1994 (R) 127m/B Johnny Depp, Sarah Jessica Parker, Martin Landau, Bill Murray, Jim Myers, Patricia Arquette, Jeffrey Jones, Lisa Marie, Vincent D'Onofrio; **D:** Tim Burton; **W:** Scott Alexander, Larry Karaszewski. Academy Awards '94: Best Makeup, Best Supporting Actor (Landau); Los Angeles Film Critics Association Awards '94: Best Cinematography, Best Supporting Actor (Landau), Best Original Score; New York Film Critics Awards '94: Best Cinematography, Best Supporting Actor (Landau); Screen Actors Guild Award '94: Best Supporting Actor (Landau); Nominations: Golden Globe Awards '95: Best Actor—Musical/Comedy (Depp), Best Film—Musical/Comedy. **VHS, LV** *TOU*

Johnny Depp looks forward to lunch in *Ed Wood.*

THE HOUND SALUTES: WILLIAM CASTLE
Written in Amazing Gimmick-O!

William Castle was a producer/director who marketed some fairly decent pictures with the kind of gimmicks usually associated with charlatans. He would often appear before a film's credits to warn the audience about the perils of what was to come, as when he offered a free insurance policy in case of death by fright during the viewing of *Macabre*. He would produce a blatant rip-off like the *Psycho*-derived *Homicidal*, then turn around and put together something as original as *The Tingler*, which featured, for the first time in a Hollywood film, the dramatization of an LSD trip. Theatres showing *The Tingler* were wired for "Percepto," which sent electric shocks through certain audience members. The movie is also memorable for a fantastic color sequence that is still intact on some hard-to-find video transfers from the original negative. For the pseudo-supernatural murder mystery *The House on Haunted Hill*, a skeleton was rigged to fly over the heads of the audience. "Illusion-O" was simply 3-D under a different name, but it allowed one to see the ghosts in *13 Ghosts*, and when there were no ghosts to be seen, one could simply remove the glasses, avoiding the headaches which accompanied many "straight" 3-D pictures. *Homicidal* offered a "Fright Break," and *Mr. Sardonicus* featured a "Punishment Poll," allowing the audiences to decide the villian's fate. He made one last half-hearted attempt at gimmickry in his 1975 *Bug*, in which he wanted to install windshield wiper-like devices to achieve the affect of bugs skittered across the viewers' feet, but this gem was not to come to pass.

Despite all these gimmicks, the films were good, solidly made chillers. His work with Vincent Price in *The Tingler* and *House on Haunted Hill* gave the actor two of his meatiest contemporary roles. Although by no means a cinematic stylist, Castle was not a "bad" filmmaker. He simply marketed the pictures a if he had no confidence in their ability to draw audiences by

continued...

Ed Wood: Look Back in Angora

This Rhino documentary, narrated by Gary Owens, is done in true Woodian style: interviews, movie clips, home movies, and irrelevant stock footage are pieced together to tell the Ed Wood story in several segments, including "Drift Wood," "Holly-Wood," and finally, "Dead Wood." Includes testimony by those closest to him, including his wife, Kathy Wood: "Nobody gave a darn about Eddie when he was alive, and even less when he died, and all of a sudden,...huhn." See the rather dashing young director with the cleft in his chin become a bloated long-haired middle-aged star of his own soft-core porn. Ideal complement to the Time Burton movie to round out the education of true Woodaphiles. 🦴🦴🦴

1994 50m/C Dolores Fuller; **D:** Ted Newsom; **W:** Ted Newsom. **VHS** *RHI*

Eegah!

"Large man or giant causing a disturbance!" crackles the police radio in this infamous Arch Hall epic set in Palm Springs. Eegah, a desert-dwelling caveman holdover (complete with Alley-Oop wooden club) falls hard for Roxy, a typical '60s teen queen with a Hall as her jealous, guitar-strumming boyfriend. Dig that rock 'n' roll soundtrack—preferably with a shovel. Towering Richard Kiel went on to better things with outsized roles like Jaws in the James Bond adventures, but any jaws you hear hitting the floor will be your own as *Eegah!* strides entertainingly from peak to peak of ineptitude. Videocassette is hosted (uncut) by Elvira. 🦴🦴🦴

1962 93m/C Marilyn Manning, Richard Kiel, Arch Hall Jr., William Waters; **D:** Ray Dennis Steckler. **VHS, Beta $9.95** *RHI, FCT*

El Topo

Bizarre Western finds Jodorowsky as a man out to avenge his wife's death, then trapped into more and more violent action. What starts out looking like another spaghetti western, soon turns into something quite different—the contestants in Jodorowsky's quest to become the number one duelists become more mystical and mysterious as he goes along. Eventually, he tries to save his own soul with a Christlike resurrection. Takes the traditional master gunfighter story to another, more allegorical level. Although the heavy-handed direction is at times pretentious and difficult to follow, it also serves its exploitation roots very well, delivering exciting action and spectacular weirdness. Cartoonist/filmmaker Jodorowsky gave the psycho killer genre the same treatment nearly 20 years later in *Santa Sangre*, this time with his son in the lead role. 🦴🦴🦴◗

1971 123m/C *MX* Alejandro Jodorowsky, Brontis Jodorowsky, Mara Lorenzio, David Silva, Paula Romo; **D:** Alejandro Jodorowsky; **W:** Alejandro Jodorowsky; **M:** Alejandro Jodorowsky. **VHS** *NO*

Elephant Parts

A video album by ex-Monkee Michael Nesmith, which contains several amusing comedy sketches and original music. 🦴🦴

1981 60m/C Michael Nesmith. **VHS, Beta, LV $14.95** *MVD, PBS*

Elvira, Mistress of the Dark

A manic comedy based on Peterson's infamous B-movie horror-hostess character. Filled with naughty-but-nice risque humor, primarily delivered by Petersen, this fluffy little comedy should appeal to "teenagers" of all ages. Bad movie hostess Elvira, whose dream is to have her own Vegas show, learns of an inheritance from a rich aunt. Quitting her job, she slinks east to claim her due. There she's beset by anal-retentive townsfolk who resent her vampy posturing and an evil uncle who covets a book of spells that's been in the family for years. Oh, yeah, and by bunches of teenage boys, all with their tongues hanging out. Delivered with spunk and verve, Peterson plays her part to the hilt as horror's favorite not-so-bad girl, surely pleasing her fans and winning new ones exposed to her for the first time. Many great gags abound, but the best is a visual during a flashback to Elvira an infant. In the end there's even a rather stunning tassel twirling sequence that's not to be missed. Good, not-quite-clean fun for all. 🦴🦴

1988 (PG-13) 96m/C Cassandra Peterson, Jeff Conaway, Susan Kellerman, Edie McClurg, Daniel

Greene, W. Morgan Shepherd; **D:** James Signorelli. **VHS, Beta, LV $9.99** *STE, NWV*

The Empire Strikes Back

Second film in the epic *Star Wars* trilogy finds young Luke Skywalker and the Rebel Alliance plotting new strategies as they prepare to battle the evil Darth Vader and the forces of the Dark Side. Luke learns the ways of a Jedi knight from master Yoda, while Han and Leia find time for romance and a few adventures of their own. Introduces the charismatic Lando Calrissian, vulgar and drooling Jabba the Hut, and a mind-numbing secret from Vadar. Offers the same superb special effects and hearty plot as set by 1977's excellent *Star Wars*. Followed by *Return of the Jedi* in 1983. Also available on laserdisc with "The Making of 'Star Wars'." 🦴🦴🦴🦴

"No, I can't put them on the phone!" *Elvira, Mistress of the Dark*.

Story continued...

conventional means. His work as a producer gave us such classics as *Rosemary's Baby* and the TV anthology series *Ghost Story/Circle of Fear*. The pre-gimmick westerns *Americano* and *Conquest of Conchise* are best forgotten, but B classics like Joan Crawford chiller *Strait Jacket* will be enjoyed long after the cardboard axes which were passed out to moviegoers in 1964 are returned to dust.

> **"His stream of consciousness dialogue was like a ransom note, pasted together from words randomly cut out of a Korean electronics manual."**
>
> --A postulation on Ed Wood's methods in *Ed Wood: Look Back in Angora.*

1980 (PG) 124m/C Mark Hamill, Carrie Fisher, Harrison Ford, Billy Dee Williams, Alec Guinness, David Prowse, Kenny Baker, Frank Oz, Anthony Daniels, Peter Mayhew, Clive Revill, Julian Glover, John Ratzenberger; **D:** Irvin Kershner; **W:** Leigh Brackett, Lawrence Kasdan; **M:** John Williams; **V:** James Earl Jones. Academy Awards '80: Best Sound, Best Visual Effects; People's Choice Awards '81: Best Film; Nominations: Academy Awards '80: Best Art Direction/Set Decoration, Best Original Score. **VHS, Beta, LV** **$19.98** *FOX, FCT, RDG*

Enter the Dragon

The American film that broke Bruce Lee worldwide combines Oriental conventions with 007 thrills. Spectacular fighting sequences including Karate, Judo, Tae Kwon Do, and Tai Chi Chuan are featured as Lee is recruited by the British to aid in bringing down the opium empire of the evil Han, ruler of an island empire located outside of the government's normal jurisdictions. As it turns out, Han is also a renegade Shaolin monk from Lee's temple and Lee's sister's suicide was caused by one of Han's aides. With all this motivation Lee agrees to enter the annual martial arts tournament held on Han's island. There he teams up with several Americans to bring down the Han man. The final battle scene received some criticism since John Saxon, rather than Lee, fights to the death with Han's right hand man, Bolo. The mirrored room duel between Lee and Han is a classic, however. More unbelievable are the dozens of drunks who assist in demolishing Han's army of blackbelts in the final reel. This was the film debut of Jim Kelly and the only English-speaking film of Hong Kong superstar Angela Mao. *AKA:* The Deadly Three. ♫♫♫♪

1973 (R) 98m/C Bruce Lee, John Saxon, Jim Kelly; **D:** Robert Clouse. **VHS, Beta, LV $19.98** *WAR*

Equinox

Threadbare but surprisingly influential 16mm feature in which young archaeologists uncover horrors in a state forest, the result of a scientist (famed author Fritz Lieber in a wordless cameo) experimenting with an ancient book of spells. Protagonists are threatened by low-budget but nicely realized visual effects, including winged beasts, simian giants, and Satan. Names behind the scenes of this amateur film have gone on to Hollywood prominence, like F/X artists Dennis Muren (who produced) and David Allen, and assistant-cameraman-turned actor Ed Begley, Jr. Sitcom fans will of course notice *WKRP in Cincinnati* regular Bonner amidst the performers. Despite obvious flaws, it is deemed a minor classic; impressive in its way but ragged enough to tell Hollywood aspirants "This is cool—but you can do better!" The Hound can well imagine Sam Raimi watching *Equinox* before embarking upon *Evil Dead*. Also on tape as *The Beast. AKA:* The Beast. ♫♫♪

1971 (PG) 80m/C Edward Connell, Barbara Hewitt, Frank Bonner, Robin Christopher, Jack Woods; **Cameos:** Fritz Leiber; **D:** Jack Woods. **VHS** *NO*

Eraserhead

David Lynch's first feature is the infamous B&W cult classic about Henry Spencer, a numb-brained everyman with a towering Stan Laurel hairdo, trapped in a decayed, ironic parody of the modern urban landscape. In between grotesque visions, Henry innocently impregnates his girlfriend Mary X, and is left to look after a pestilent mutant baby resembling an embryo sheep's head sticking out of a wad of bandages ("He's...premature"). Reportedly inspired by Lynch's troubled state of mind when he was a young, unwilling father stuck in a Philadelphia slum, this is surreal, bizarre, darkly absurd and textured in the manner of your worst nightmare. The film has an inner, completely unpredictable logic all its own that has kept fans arguing about the meaning even as Lynch went on to more, uh, mainstream work. Nance later appeared in Lynch's *Dune* and in *Twin Peaks* as Pete the Logger. That's Sissy Spacek's husband, producer Jack Fisk, as the scarfaced Man in the Planet (and there is a thanks to Spacek—among others—in the closing credits). And a first look at Lynch's daughter, Jennifer (*Boxing Helena*), as the little girl. 🦴🦴🦴

1978 90m/B Jack Nance, Charlotte Stewart, Allen Joseph, Jeanne Bates, Judith Anna Roberts, Laurel Near, V. Phipps-Willson, Jack Fisk, Jean Lange, Darwin Joston, Hal Landon Jr., Jennifer Lynch; **D:** David Lynch; **W:** David Lynch. **VHS, Beta, LV** *COL, OM*

Erik the Viking

At various times, this ambitious story of a sensitive, caring Viking (Robbins) tries to be an adventure, a mythic fantasy, a Monty Pythonesque comedy, and a movie with a message. Not surprisingly, it's about a quarter to a third successful, at best. With the exception of the fetching Imogen Stubbs (as the obligatory princess) everyone looks pale and unpleasant. The action scenes are underpowered and the special effects appear to have been limited by a low budget. Fans looking for another *Time Bandits* will be disappointed. Great cast of character actors is wasted. 🦴🦴

1989 (PG-13) 104m/C *GB* Tim Robbins, Terry Jones, Mickey Rooney, John Cleese, Imogen Stubbs, Anthony Sher, Gordon John Sinclair, Freddie Jones, Eartha Kitt; **D:** Terry Jones; **W:** Terry Jones. **VHS, Beta, LV $89.98** *ORI*

Escape from New York

The ultimate urban nightmare: a ruined, future Manhattan is an anarchic prison for America's worst felons. When convicts hold the President hostage, a disgraced war hero unwillingly attempts an impossible rescue mission. Cynical but largely unexceptional sci-fi action, putting a good cast through tight-lipped peril. 🦴🦴🦴

1981 (R) 99m/C Kurt Russell, Lee Van Cleef, Ernest Borgnine, Donald Pleasence, Isaac Hayes, Adrienne Barbeau, Harry Dean Stanton, Season Hubley; **D:** John Carpenter; **W:** John Carpenter, Nick Castle; **M:** John Carpenter. **VHS, Beta, LV $14.98** *SUE, NLC, FUS*

Escape from the Planet of the Apes

Reprising their roles as intelligent, English-speaking apes, Roddy McDowall and Kim Hunter flee their world before it's destroyed, and travel back in time to present-day America. In L.A. they become the subjects of a relentless search by the fearful population, much like humans Charlton Heston and James Franciscus were targeted for experimentation and destruction in simian society in the earlier *Planet of the Apes* and *Beneath the Planet of the Apes*. Features Ricardo Montalban as a circus leader who aids and abets Cornelius and Zera. This third entry is the second high point in the saga; there is a steady decline in the next two sequels, *Conquest of...* and *Battle for...* 🦴🦴🦴

So that's where erasers come from: Jack Nance in *Eraserhead*.

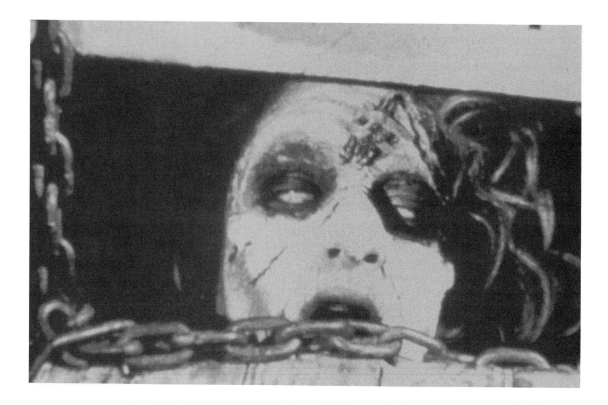

"Anybody home?"
The Evil Dead.

1971 **(G) 98m/C** Roddy McDowall, Kim Hunter, Sal Mineo, Ricardo Montalban, William Windom, Bradford Dillman, Natalie Trundy, Eric (Hans Gudegast) Braeden; **D:** Don Taylor; **M:** Jerry Goldsmith. **VHS, Beta, LV $19.98** *FOX, FUS*

Evil Clutch

A young couple vacationing in the Alps encounter several creepy locals when they find themselves in the midst of a haunted forest. The cinematography is extremely amateurish in this Italian gorefest and the English dubbing is atrocious. However, the special makeup effects are outstanding and the musical score adds a touch of class to this otherwise inept horror film. 🦴 ◿

1989 **(R) 88m/C** *IT* Coralina Cataldi Tassoni, Diego Riba, Elena Cantarone, Luciano Crovato, Stefano Molinari; **D:** Andreas Marfori; **W:** Andreas Marfori. **VHS, LV $79.95** *UND, RHI*

Evil Dead

The premise is a cliche—college students in a woodland cabin being bumped off by su-

pernatural monsters—but director Raimi, working with co-producer and star Campbell, turns this horror tale into a rude, gory comedy that's become a cult favorite. The stop motion and reverse action effects are handled with such inventive energy that they're not particularly offensive. Still, Raimi's horror work is strong stuff, recommended for fans only. The film was followed by two sequels—each stretching the limits of taste and humor farther—and lifted Raimi into the Hollywood mainstream. 🦴🦴🦴

1983 **(NC-17) 126m/C** Bruce Campbell, Ellen Sandweiss, Betsy Baker, Hal Delrich; **D:** Sam Raimi; **W:** Sam Raimi. **VHS, Beta, LV $14.99** *IME*

Evil Dead 2: Dead by Dawn

If the Three Stooges had ever made a *Friday the 13th* movie, it would have been something like this. Key elements: a cabin deep in the woods, an ancient Sumerian "Book of the Dead" that calls up murderous spirits, and a group of young people who don't last long. Director Raimi and star/co-producer Campbell let nothing stand in their way. The gory, nasty effects go far beyond any limits of reasonable taste, and they are matched by an equally berserk and outrageous sense of humor. This sequel/remake of the *Evil Dead* was followed by yet a third bloodfest, *Army of Darkness.* 🦴🦴🦴

1987 (R) 84m/C Bruce Campbell, Sarah Berry, Dan Hicks, Kassie Wesley, Theodore (Ted) Raimi, Denise Bixler, Richard Domeier; **Cameos:** Sam Raimi; **D:** Sam Raimi; **W:** Sam Raimi, Scott Spiegel; **M:** Joseph Lo Duca. **VHS, Beta, LV $14.98** *LIV, VES*

The Exorcist

Truly terrifying story of Linda Blair possessed by a malevolent spirit. Brilliantly directed by Friedkin, with underlying themes of the workings and nature of fate. Impeccable casting and unforgettable, thought-provoking performances. A rare film that remains startling and engrossing with every viewing, it spawned countless imitations and changed the way horror films were made. Based on the bestseller by Blatty, who also wrote the screenplay. Not for the squeamish. When first released, the film created mass hysteria in theaters, with people fainting and paramedics on the scene (but who can detect the reality from the marketing stunt?). 🦴🦴🦴🦴

1973 (R) 120m/C Ellen Burstyn, Linda Blair, Jason Miller, Max von Sydow, Jack MacGowran, Lee J. Cobb, Kitty Winn; **D:** William Friedkin; **W:** William Peter Blatty; **M:** Jack Nitzsche. Academy Awards '73: Best Adapted Screenplay, Best Sound; Golden Globe Awards '74: Best Director (Friedkin), Best Film—Drama, Best Screenplay, Best Supporting Actress (Blair); Nominations: Academy Awards '73: Best Actress (Burstyn), Best Art Direction/Set Decoration, Best Cinematography, Best Director (Friedkin), Best Film Editing, Best Picture, Best Supporting Actor (Miller), Best Supporting Actress (Blair). **VHS, Beta, LV $19.98** *WAR*

Exterminator

Vietnam vet hunts down the gang that assaulted his friend, and becomes the target of the police, the CIA, pimps, perverts, and just about everybody else in this bloody banal tale of murder and intrigue. The film is filled with groins being kicked and slow-motion bullets striking flesh. And since no one can be shot without flying about ten feet through the air, the overall effect soon becomes unintention-ally comic. Imagine *Taxi Driver* without the intelligence, insight, or power. Or don't imagine it. 🦴

1980 (R) 101m/C Christopher George, Samantha Eggar, Robert Ginty; **D:** James Glickenhaus. **VHS, Beta, LV $14.98** *SUE, NLC*

Faces of Death

Morbid, gruesome, "shockumentary" looks at death experiences around the world; uncensored film footage offers graphic coverage of autopsies, suicides, executions, and animal slaughter. Two more entries in the series follow. **WOOF!**

1974 88m/C VHS, Beta $19.98 *NO*

Fahrenheit 451

Chilling adaptation of the Ray Bradbury novel about a futuristic society that has banned all reading material and the firemen whose job it is to keep the fires at 451 degrees: the temperature at which paper burns. Werner is a fireman who begins to question the rightness of his actions when he meets the book-loving Christie—who also plays the dual role of Werner's TV-absorbed wife. Truffaut's first color and English-language film. 🦴🦴🦴

1966 112m/C FR Oskar Werner, Julie Christie, Cyril Cusack, Anton Diffring; **D:** Francois Truffaut. **VHS, Beta, LV $19.98** *MCA, MLB, INJ*

The Fall of the House of Usher

The moody Roger Corman/Vincent Price interpretation, the first of their eight Poe adaptations, depicting the collapse of the famous estate due to madness and revenge. Terrific sets by Daniel Haller (much of it bought in pieces from Universal) and solid direction by Corman, who cited his interest in psychology as the source of the picture's success. Price's inimitable presence as the doom-laden Usher is the center of attention, even when he's off-screen. The House's eerie surroundings were achieved by shooting footage of a burned forest, and Corman also shot the interior of a burning barn for the climax (footage which would end up in virtually all of the Poe films). **AKA:** House of Usher. 🦴🦴🦴

"**We've got chicken tonight. Strangest damn things-- they're man- made. Little damn things-- smaller than my fist. They're new!**"

--Mr. X (Allen Joseph) in *Eraserhead*, raving about some indeed damn strange poultry.

thing fresher? It's main claim to fame will always remain the fact that it is Hitchcock's final effort. Not really bad or good; hold off watching it until one of those boring, rainy days come along and you're in a curious mood. 🦴🦴🐾

1976 (PG) 120m/C Karen Black, Bruce Dern, Barbara Harris, William Devane, Ed Lauter, Katherine Helmond; *D:* Alfred Hitchcock; *W:* Ernest Lehman; *M:* John Williams. Edgar Allan Poe Awards '76: Best Screenplay; National Board of Review Awards '76: 10 Best Films of the Year. **VHS, Beta, LV $19.95** *MCA*

Fanny Hill: Memoirs of a Woman of Pleasure

Sexual exploits of an innocent in bawdy 18th-century London, as directed by notorious "Super Vixen" Meyer (though by Meyer standards, proceedings are fairly innocuous, if inept). Based on the novel. **WOOF!**

1964 105m/B Miriam Hopkins, Walter Giller, Alexander D'Arcy, Leticia Roman; *D:* Russ Meyer. **VHS, Beta** *NO*

Fantasia

Disney's most personal animation feature first bombed at the box office and irked purists who couldn't take the plotless, experimental mix of classical music and cartoons. It became a cult movie, embraced by more liberal generations of moviegoers, and, in some ways, can be seen as the prototype for MTV. The restored version is gorgeous, especially on disc where the sound and colors are lush. The hippos and crocodiles in "Dance of the Hours" are still one of the funniest things ever put on screen, and "Night on Bald Mountain" is just as frightening and powerful. A sequel, *Fantasia Continued,* is scheduled for 1998. 🎵 Toccata & Fugue in D; The Nutcracker Suite; The Sorcerer's Apprentice; The Rite of Spring; Pastoral Symphony; Dance of the Hours; Night on Bald Mountain; Ave Maria; The Cossack Dance. 🦴🦴🦴🦴

1940 116m/C VHS, LV $24.99 *DIS, FCT, RDG*

Fantastic Voyage

Still quite a trip in a 1960s, Raquel-Welch-in-a-skin-tight-diver's-suit kind of way. When a defecting Czechoslovakian scientist is shot, a

1960 85m/C Vincent Price, Myrna Fahey, Mark Damon; *D:* Roger Corman; *W:* Richard Matheson; *M:* Les Baxter. **VHS, Beta** *NO*

Family Plot

Alfred Hitchcock's last film focuses on the search for a missing heir undertaken by a phony psychic and her private-eye boyfriend, which evolves into a diamond theft. Attempted camp, lightweight mystery that stales with time and doesn't fit well into Hitchcock's genre. If, however, you're not a Hitchcock aficiando, this may be worth you're time. Both the direction and performances are adequate, the story brisk enough and executed with enough twists to maintain an aura of mystery. The main problems are a lack of laughs and a shortage of characters the viewer can truly cheer. The end result is a bit like drinking stale pop. You can do it, but why not open some-

medical team and a submarine are miniaturized and injected into his bloodstream to remove a blood clot in his brain. The crew includes Arthur Kennedy, Donald Pleasence, and chiseled Steven Boyd. One of them does want the operation to succeed. The special effects won an Academy Award—look out for those white corpuscles! Dennis Quaid took a similar voyage in Joe Dante's 1987 *Innerspace*. **AKA:** Microscopia; Strange Journey. 🦴🦴🦴

1966 100m/C Stephen Boyd, Edmond O'Brien, Raquel Welch, Arthur Kennedy, Donald Pleasence, Arthur O'Connell, William Redfield, James Brolin; *D:* Richard Fleischer. Academy Awards '66: Best Art Direction/Set Decoration (Color), Best Visual Effects; Nominations: Academy Awards '66: Best Color Cinematography, Best Film Editing. **VHS, Beta, LV $19.98** *FOX, CCB*

Far Out Man

When a flick bills itself as "A Tommy Chong Attempt," that's called truth in advertising. Even though it lasts for 84 minutes and has fictional characters and a loosely wrapped storyline about a middle-aged hippie's cross-country journey, this isn't really a film. It's a loose collection of skits, bits of business, animation and improvisation, all revolving around Chong's drug-based humor. For comparative purposes, *Cheech and Chong's Up in Smoke* looks like *Citizen Kane*. Even the comedian's most dedicated fans will have trouble with this lame "attempt." 🦴

1989 (R) 105m/C Thomas Chong, Rae Dawn Chong, C. Thomas Howell, Shelby Chong, Martin Mull, Paris Chong, Paul Bartel, Judd Nelson, Michael Winslow, Richard "Cheech" Marin; *D:* Thomas Chong. **VHS, Beta, LV $89.95** *COL*

Fast Times at Ridgemont High

American Graffiti this ain't. While *Fast Times* and *Graffiti* were both set in California, both based on real-life characters, and both set in high school, the teens of Ridgemont High are a little more into sex and drugs (rock and roll was big for both!) than their 1960s counterparts. Based on a novel and screenplay by Cameron Crowe, who posed as a student and enrolled in high school to gather his data, *Fast Times* does a pretty good job of making us laugh at the exploits of its largely goofball cast. And what a cast of young stars it is— Sean Penn, Phoebe Cates, Jennifer Jason-Leigh, Judge Reinhold, Forest Whitaker, and Eric Stoltz all went on to bigger and better things (although some didn't stay high-profile for very long). All the stock characters you would expect from any high school movie are here, with Penn as the stoned-out surfer the clear star of the show. Crowe and director Amy Heckerling do sneak in some serious topics—loss of virginity and abortion—but comedy is the key to this film. Ray Walston steals much of the comic thunder from the neophyte cast as Mr. Hand, the history teacher bent on making the best use of "our time." Watch for one of the bigger continuity gaffes you'll see in a mainstream movie—the big high school football game comes after Christmas. Heckerling returned to the high school halls in 1995 with the movie *Clueless*. One of the best of the high school coming-of-age genre. 🦴🦴🦴

1982 (R) 91m/C Sean Penn, Jennifer Jason Leigh, Judge Reinhold, Robert Romanus, Brian Backer, Phoebe Cates, Ray Walston, Scott Thomson, Vincent Schiavelli, Amanda Wyss, Forest Whitaker, Kelli Maroney, Eric Stoltz, Pamela Springsteen, James Russo, Martin Brest, Anthony Edwards; *D:* Amy Heckerling; *W:* Cameron Crowe. **VHS, Beta, LV $14.95** *MCA*

Faster Pussycat! Kill! Kill!

It doesn't get any better than this! Three sexy-but-tough go-go dancers—savage karate expert Varla (Satana), vicious Rosie (Haji), and girl-next-door gone bad Billie (Williams)—get their after-work kicks by hot-rodding in the California desert. They soon find themselves enveloped in murder, kidnapping, lust, and robbery after an impromptu desert race gets out of hand. They end up on a ranch owned by a hateful old man in a wheelchair (Lancaster) and his two grown sons, who may or may not be hiding a fortune. An exploitation masterpiece that takes the Bad Girl persona and raises it to operatic proportions. Easily the most watchable, fun, and funny production to spring from the mind of Russ Meyer. Those who haven't seen this cannot truly be called "cool." 🦴🦴🦴🦴

1966 83m/B Tura Satana, Haji, Lori Williams, Susan Bernard, Stuart Lancaster, Paul Trinka, Dennis Busch,

Ray Barlow, Mickey Foxx; **D:** Russ Meyer; **W:** Jack Moran, Russ Meyer. **VHS $79.95** *RMF, FCT, TPV*

Fat Guy Goes Nutzoid

Gotta love those Troma titles. A crude farce about an obese mental patient who escapes from the mental hospital and joins two teenagers on a wild trip to New York City. *AKA:* Zeisters. **WOOF!**

1986 85m/C Tibor Feldman, Peter Linari, John MacKay, Joan Allen; **D:** John Golden. **VHS, Beta $79.95** *PSM*

The Fearless Vampire Killers

Underrated, off-off-beat, and deliberately campy spoof of vampire films in which Tate is kidnapped by some fangy villains. Vampire trackers MacGowran and Polanski pursue the villains to the haunted castle and attempt the rescue. Only vampire movie with a Jewish bloodsucker ("Boy, have you got the wrong vampire," he proclaims to a maiden thrusting a crucifix at him). Inside the castle, Polanski is chased by the count's gay vampire son. Highlight is the vampire ball with a wonder-ful mirror scene. Many other amusing moments. *AKA:* Pardon Me, Your Teeth are in My Neck; Dance of the Vampires. ♫♫♫

1967 98m/C *GB* Jack MacGowran, Roman Polanski, Alfie Bass, Jessie Robbins, Sharon Tate, Ferdinand "Ferdy" Mayne, Iain Quarrier; **D:** Roman Polanski; **W:** Roman Polanski, Gerard Brach. **VHS, Beta, LV $19.98** *MGM*

Fellini Satyricon

Fellini's famous, garish, indulgent pastiche vision of ancient Rome, based on the novel *Satyricon* by Petronius, follows the adventures of two young men through the decadences of Nero's reign. Actually an exposition on the excesses of the 1960s, with the actors having little to do other than look good and react to any number of sexual situations. Crammed with excesses of every variety. In Italian with English subtitles. Also available on laserdisc with additional footage and letterboxing. *AKA:* Satyricon. ♫♫♫

1969 (R) 129m/C *IT* Martin Potter, Capucine, Hiram Keller, Salvo Randone, Max Born; **D:** Federico Fellini; **W:** Federico Fellini; **M:** Nino Rota. Nominations: Academy Awards '70: Best Director (Fellini). **VHS, Beta, LV $19.98** *MGM, FCT, INJ*

The Female Jungle

Below-average whocares whodunnit directed by Roger Corman stock-company actor Ve Sota. Police sergeant Tierney is caught between a rock and a hard place. The prime suspect in a murder case, Tierney discovers a series of clues that implicate his friend Carradine. Interesting only for the screen debut of the nympho-typecast Miss Jayne—of whom Bette Davis said "Dramatic art in her opinion is knowing how to fill a sweater." *AKA:* The Hangover. ♫

1956 56m/B Lawrence Tierney, John Carradine, Jayne Mansfield, Burt Kaiser, Kathleen Crowley, James Kodl, Rex Thorson, Jack Hill; **D:** Bruno Ve Sota. **VHS $9.95** *COL, FCT*

Female Trouble

Chronicles the "female trouble" experienced by Dawn Davenport (Divine) from her disappointing youth ("My parents'll be really sorry if I don't get them cha-cha heels!") to her decadent adult years, in which she aims to live her philosophy, "Crime is beauty." She is raped and impregnated (by herself, playing a dual role as a fat redneck with skid tracks in his underwear); she later phones the perpetrator to deliver the wittiest line: "Go f— yourself!" Dawns eventually find love and happiness (and glorifies it in her see-through wedding dress—white, of course), but her husband ultimately leaves her for Detroit "to find happiness within the auto industry." This gem features the return of the glorious Waters'-regular Edith Massey as Divine's aunt-in-law, resplendent in a black leather peekaboo catsuit (Edie suffers at Divine's hands in one of the worst displays of special effects on film). *Female Trouble* is an especially good complement for Waters' *Polyester,* another inspired pairing of Divine and Massey. 🦴🦴🦴▷

1974 (R) 95m/C Divine, David Lochary, Mary Vivian Pearce, Mink Stole, Edith Massey, Cookie Mueller, Susan Walsh, Susan Lowe, Ed Peranio, Pat Moran; **D:** John Waters; **W:** John Waters. **VHS, Beta** *NO*

Ferocious Female Freedom Fighters

This is the Troma version of Woody Allen's *What's Up, Tiger Lily?* Producer and writer Charles Kaufman took a low-budget Japanese martial arts movie, threw out the voice track, and added English dialogue (by the L.A. Connection comedy troupe) that has nothing to with the original story. In the middle of an involved fight scene, a character will say something like, "You know, as a rule, you should never refreeze seabass." The cast features an Oriental Elvis lookalike and a snake who has some very good lines. Funny for those who are already in the mood for something unusual. 🦴🦴▷

1988 90m/C Eva Arnaz, Barry Prima. **VHS, Beta, LV** *MED, IME*

Ferris Bueller's Day Off

It's almost graduation and if Ferris can get away with just one more sick day—it had better be a good one. He sweet talks his best friend (Ruck) into borrowing his dad's antique Ferrari and sneaks his girlfriend (Sara) out of school to spend a day in Chicago. Their escapades lead to fun, adventure, and almost getting caught (despite an attempt to set back the car's odometer by running the car in reverse gear). Broderick is charismatic as the notorious Bueller with Grey (*Dirty Dancing*) amusing as his tattle-tale sister doing everything she can to see him get caught. One nitpick: it would be impossible to get around Chicago to take in all those activities within a few hours. Early Sheen appearance as a juvenile delinquent who pesters Grey. Led to TV series, plus at least one copycat series. Features a fun cast of now-familiar faces. One of Hughes' more solid efforts. 🦴🦴🦴

1986 (PG-13) 103m/C Matthew Broderick, Mia Sara, Alan Ruck, Jeffrey Jones, Jennifer Grey, Cindy Pickett, Edie McClurg, Charlie Sheen, Del Close, Virginia Capers, Max Perlich, Louis Anderson; **D:** John Hughes; **W:** John Hughes; **M:** Ira Newborn. **VHS, Beta, LV, 8mm $14.95** *PAR, TLF*

The Fiendish Plot of Dr. Fu Manchu

A sad farewell from Sellers, who in his last film portrays Dr. Fu in his desperate quest for the necessary ingredients for his secret life-preserving formula. Sellers portrays both Dr. Fu and the Scotland Yard detective on his trail, but it's not enough to save this picture, flawed by poor script and lack of direction. 🦴

1980 (PG) 100m/C *GB* Peter Sellers, David Tomlinson, Sid Caesar, Helen Mirren; **D:** Piers Haggard. **VHS, Beta, LV $19.98** *WAR, FCT*

Film House Fever

A compilation of clips from sleazy, cult-type movies. Grindhouse vets will be disappointed by the overly familiar coming attractions and scenes—well-worn chestnuts like *Blood Feast* and *Two Thousand Maniacs* are trotted out for the umpteenth time—but there are some choice nuggets as well, including Herschell Gordon Lewis's *Living Venus* (with Harvey Korman) and *The Psychic,* Al Adamson's gory Western *Five Bloody Graves,* and the unbelievably threadbare *Bad Girls Do Cry.* Framing skits involving two couch-bound losers poking fun at footage won't pose a threat to TV's *Mystery Science Theater 3000,* but are notable for an early appearance by Steve (*Reservoir Dogs*) Buscemi. Okay starter it for aspiring trash hounds. 🦴🦴▷

"The world of the heterosexual is a sick and boring life."
--Ida (Edith Massey) counsels her nephew in *Female Trouble.*

"I WANT YOU TO HOLD IT BETWEEN YOUR KNEES."

"I'd like a plain omelet, no potatoes--tomatoes instead--a cup of coffee, and wheat toast."

"No substitutions."

"What do you mean? You don't have any tomatoes?"

"Only what's on the menu. You can have a number two, a plain omelet--it comes with cottage fries and rolls."

"Yeah, I know what it comes with, but it's not what I want."

"I'll come back when you've made up your mind."

"Wait a minute--I *have* made up my mind. I'd like a plain omelet, no potatoes on the plate, a cup of coffee, and a side order of wheat toast."

"I'm sorry. We don't have any side orders of toast. I can give you an English muffin or a coffee roll."

"What do you mean you don't make side orders of toast? You make sandwiches, don't you?"

"Would you like to talk to the manager?"

"You've got bread, and a toaster of some kind?"

"I don't make the rules."

"Okay, I'll make it as easy for you as I can. I'd like an omelet, plain, and a chicken salad sandwich on wheat toast--no mayonnaise, no butter, no lettuce. And a cup of coffee."

"A number two. Chick salad sand. Hold the butter, the lettuce, the mayonnaise. And a cup of coffee. Anything else?"

"Yeah. Now all you have to do is hold the chicken, bring me the toast, give me a check for the chicken salad sandwich, and you haven't broken any rules."

"You want me to hold the chicken, huh?"

"I want you to hold it between your knees."

--Jack Nicholson and Lorna Thayer in *Five Easy Pieces*.

1986 58m/C Jamie Lee Curtis, James Keach, Lon Chaney Jr., Harvey Korman. **VHS, Beta $59.98** *LIV, VES*

The First Nudie Musical

A harmless and fun film with a title that should win a "Truth in Advertising" award. When the young owner of a family run movie studio is forced into a corner by his creditors, he comes up with the title production as a means of staving off financial ruin. Unfortunately, one of the creditors has a son who wants to direct and forces an unwelcome compromise before agreeing to back the production. The son, of course, is a complete bumbler and the studio head must find a way to succeed despite this albatross. From here we're treated to the development of the entire production, from casting to the inevitable hit premiere. Very light weight and almost cutesy, *The First Nudie Musical* is filled with girls, gags, and an odd assortment of musical numbers ranging from the ordinary to the hilarious. The "Dance of the Dildos" is not to be missed. Look for Ron Howard in a small, but meaningless cameo. ♫ The First Nudie Musical; The Lights and the Smiles; Orgasm; Lesbian Butch Dyke; Dancing Dildos; Perversion; Honey, What Ya Doin' Tonight; Let 'Em Eat Cake; I Don't Have to Hide Anymore. 🎵🎵🎵

1975 (R) 93m/C Cindy Williams, Stephen Nathan, Diana Canova, Bruce Kimmel; **D:** Mark Haggard. **VHS, Beta $59.95** *MED, HHT*

A Fish Called Wanda

Absurd, high-speed farce about four criminals trying to retrieve $20 million they've stolen from a safety deposit box—and each other. Meanwhile, barrister Cleese falls for female thief Curtis. This one really is an "adult" comedy—sexy without being crude, with humor based on the characters, and a sharp intelligence that keeps the more outrageous foolishness in line. The darker side of the story may go too far at times but that's not a fatal flaw. Written by Monty Python alum Cleese and director Crichton, who understand that silence is sometimes funnier than speech, and that timing is everything. Wickedly funny, particularly Cleese who's unusually restrained. Crichton also made *The Lavender Hill Mob.*

Scheduled to be followed by a sort of sequel reuniting key cast members in 1996. 🦴🦴🦴

1988 (R) 98m/C John Cleese, Kevin Kline, Jamie Lee Curtis, Michael Palin, Tom Georgeson, Maria Aitken, Patricia Hayes, Geoffrey Palmer; **D:** Charles Crichton; **W:** John Cleese, Charles Crichton; **M:** John Du Prez. Academy Awards '88: Best Supporting Actor (Kline); British Academy Awards '88: Best Actor (Cleese), Best Supporting Actor (Palin); Nominations: Academy Awards '88: Best Director (Crichton), Best Original Screenplay. **VHS, Beta, LV $14.95** *MGM, BTV, FOX*

Fitzcarraldo

Title character is a turn-of-the-century European colonist determined to build an opera house in the middle of the Amazon jungles and have Enrico Caruso sing there. Key to realizing his ambitions is a business venture up-river, beyond impassible Amazon rapids. Fitzcarraldo's solution is a shortcut. Somehow, he must transport his steamboat over a mountain. Based on a true story, this is Herzog's most ambitious and accessible work, an ode to mad dreamers and schemers that works on all levels; as metaphor, exotic adventure, anthropological drama, and visionary spectacle. No special effects were used here—Herzog painstakingly staged everything you see, and indeed hauled a large boat up a mountainside, despite cost overruns, natural disasters, illness, and hostile natives. That behind-the-scenes ordeal is chronicled in the feature documentary *Burden of Dreams,* also on video, which includes early test footage with original stars Jason Robards and Mick Jagger (before Kinsky apprehensively signed on as lead). In German with English subtitles. 🦴🦴🦴🦴

1982 (PG) 157m/C *GE* Klaus Kinski, Claudia Cardinale, Jose Lewgoy, Miguel Angel Fuentes, Paul Hittscher; **D:** Werner Herzog; **W:** Werner Herzog; **M:** Popul Vuh. Cannes Film Festival '82: Best Director (Herzog); Nominations: Cannes Film Festival '82: Best Film. **VHS, Beta $69.95** *WAR, APD, INJ*

Five Easy Pieces

Nicholson's superb acting brings to life this character study of a talented musician who has given up a promising career and now works on the oil rigs. After twenty years he returns home to attempt one last communication with his dying father and perhaps, reconcile himself with his fear of failure and

desire for greatness. Black, Anspach, and Bush create especially memorable characters. Nicholson ordering toast via a chicken salad sandwich is a classic. 🦴🦴🦴🦴

1970 (R) 98m/C Jack Nicholson, Karen Black, Susan Anspach, Lois Smith, Billy Green Bush, Fannie Flagg, Ralph Waite, Sally Struthers, Helena Kallianiotes; **D:** Bob Rafelson; **W:** Adrien (Carole Eastman) Joyce, Bob Rafelson. Golden Globe Awards '71: Best Supporting Actress (Black); Nominations: Academy Awards '70: Best Actor (Nicholson), Best Picture, Best Story & Screenplay, Best Supporting Actress (Black). **VHS, Beta, LV, 8mm $14.95** *COL, WME*

The 5000 Fingers of Dr. T

Dr. Seuss (Ted Geisel) wrote the screenplay and designed this live-action story of a boy (Tommy Rettig, TV's Timmy from *Timmy and Lassie*) who tries to evade piano lessons and runs right into the castle of the evil Dr. Terwilliger (played masterfully by Hans Conreid, although a bit reminiscent of *Lost in Space*'s Dr. Smith), where hundreds of boys are held captive for piano lessons. Worse yet, they're forced to wear silly beanies with "happy fingers" waving on top. Luckily, the trusted family plumber is on hand to save the day through means of

Michael Palin really wishes that Kevin Kline had passed on the roasted garlic in *A Fish Called Wanda.*

107

Cult Flicks and Trash Pics

THE HOUND SALUTES: ROGER CORMAN

House of Roger

Almost since his start in Hollywood in 1954, Roger Corman, variously a writer, director, producer, and--on rare occasions--actor, has been identified with low-rent exploitation. At his peak, Corman personally cranked out nine pics a year, shooting some back-to-back to get twice the mileage out of sets, props, and hungry young actors. His original *Little Shop of Horrors*, for example, was shot for $28,000 with interior scenes completed in a mere two days, and was a quickie rewrite of his earlier *Bucket of Blood*, rushed before the cameras because Corman found some already built sets he could use. And then there were movie mutations like *Voyage to the Planet of Prehistoric Women* or *Ultra Warrior*, entire features patched together from stock-footage fragments of earlier Corman productions and/or obscure foreign films the maestro had purchased.

One the other hand, however, Corman's distribution companies, besides booking his stuff in flea-pits and drive-ins, brought American viewers some unqualified masterworks of world cinema--films by Fellini, Bergman, Kurosawa, Truffaut, and Herzog. You must ask yourself, though: how long would a Fellini or Herzog have lasted working in Corman's own down-and-dirty production outfits?

Don't be so quick to judge. Many of the struggling tyros who slaved under Corman did go on to greatness, and many credit Corman for teaching them filmmaking fundamentals. Let a few graduates of Roger Corman 101 stand and be counted...

Ford Coppola--Creator of the *Godfather* trilogy, *The Conversation*, *Bram Stoker's Dracula*, and *Apocalypse Now.* He was once Corman's $90-per-week assistant on such films as *The Haunted Palace*, *The Young Racers*, and *Battle Beyond the Sun.* Under Corman, Coppola directed his first feature, the ax-murder *Dementia 13*, for $22,000.

Martin Scorsese--Director of *Raging Bull*, *Goodfellas*, *Mean Streets*, *Taxi Driver*, *Cape Fear*, etc. Consistently voted America's finest

continued...

an atomic bomb. Seuss himself felt that *Dr. T* was "the worst experience in his life," but wonderful satire, horrible, horrible music, and mesmerizing Seussian sets make this a must-see for fans of the good doctor—and any one else with a sense of humor. 🦴🦴🦴

1953 88m/C Peter Lind Hayes, Mary Healy, Tommy Rettig, Hans Conried; **D:** Roy Rowland; **W:** Theodore "Dr. Seuss" Geisel, Allan Scott. Nominations: Academy Awards '53: Best Original Score. **VHS, Beta, LV $14.95** *COL, XVC, FCT*

Flaming Star

Elvis's bid to be taken seriously as an actor got a critical boost from this thoughtful western that tackles the issue of racial prejudice. Elvis stars as Pacer Burton, the half-breed son of a white settler and a Kiowa Indian. When his mother's tribe sounds the battle cry, he is forced to choose sides. Elvis sings only two songs, which may account for this film's lackluster showing at the box office. When this project was first developed, Marlon Brando and Frank Sinatra were slated to star. 🦴🦴🦴

1960 101m/C Elvis Presley, Dolores Del Rio, Barbara Eden, Steve Forrest, John McIntire, Richard Jaeckel, L.Q. Jones; **D:** Donald Siegel. **VHS, Beta $14.98** *FOX, MVD*

Flesh

An Andy Warhol-produced seedy urban farce about a day in the life of a bisexual street hustler who is trying to get enough money to pay for his girlfriend's abortion. A variety of drug-addicted, deformed, and sexually deviant people help him raise the cash, for favors, of course. This picture actually served as a how-to course in street survival for male hustlers in the late '60s. Fans of Joe Dallesandro will enjoy his extensive exposure (literally). This was director Paul Morrissey's first picture for Warhol, and was the first commercially successful underground film. Morrissey completed four more pictures for Warhol before breaking free and directing the atrocious Dudley Moore/Peter Cook spoof of *Hound of the Baskervilles*. Returning to his own territory on his own terms, he had a modest success with 1984's *Mixed Blood*. 🦴🦴🦴▷

1968 90m/C Joe Dallesandro, Geraldine Smith, Patti D'Arbanville; **D:** Paul Morrissey. **VHS, Beta $29.95** *TPV, PAR, FCT*

Flesh and Blood Show

Rehearsal turns into an execution ritual for a group of actors at a mysterious seaside theatre. Truth in titling: features blood, gore, and some sex. Shot in part in 3-D. *AKA:* Asylum of the Insane. 🦴

1973 (R) 93m/C *GB* Robin Askwith, Candace Glendenning, Tristan Rogers, Ray Brooks, Jenny Hanley, Luan Peters, Patrick Barr; *D:* Pete Walker. **VHS, Beta** $59.95 *NO*

The Flesh Eaters

A claustrophobic low-budget thriller about a film queen and her secretary who crash-land on an island inhabited by your basic escaped Nazi mad scientist (Kosleck, who made a regular job of playing Nazis). His latest experiment is with tiny flesh-eating sea creatures. The f/x are cheap, but remarkably well done (the swarming critters are achieved by simply scratching the film—simple but effectively weird looking), and there's a surprising amount of gore. Sleazy melodrama keeps things interesting between horrifying tragedies. Restored video release restores the more gruesome footage as well as Nazi experiment flashbacks which were cut from TV prints. Reportedly, Curtis died during production and his widow/co-producer had to scramble to finish shooting. 🦴🦴🦴

1964 87m/C Martin Kosleck, Rita Morley, Byron Sanders, Barbara Wilkin, Ray Tudor; *D:* Jack Curtis. **VHS, Beta** $39.95 *SNC*

Flesh Gordon

Soft-core spoof of the *Flash Gordon* series. Flesh takes it upon himself to save Earth from the evil Wang's sex ray; Wang, of course, being the leader of the planet Porno. Some special effects look like home movie material; others, notably the stop motion finale, are actually pretty good. Credit to Rick Baker who's gone on to more expensive and ambitious work. Look for cameo by real-life porn starlet Candy Samples. The original X-rated version has recently and belatedly appeared on tape. By current standards of graphic explicitness, it's pretty tame, but don't worry, the humor is still bawdy and rude. 🦴🦴🦴

1972 70m/C Jason Williams, Suzanne Fields, Joseph Hudgins, John Hoyt, Howard Zieff, Michael Ben-

veniste; *Cameos:* Candy Samples; *D:* Mike Light. **VHS, Beta, LV** $19.98 *MED, IME*

Flesh Gordon 2: Flesh Gordon Meets the Cosmic Cheerleaders

Emperor Wang (Hunt) threatens the Universe with his powerful Impotence ray. Flesh (Murdocco), along with Dale (Kelly) and Dr. Flexi Jerkoff (Travis), do battle. Director Ziehm delivers this one on a shoestring of less than $1 million and is not afraid to be offensive. The sex scenes are, however, watered down in an apparent attempt to gain a wider audience. Scatological jokes begin with flatulence and a sport called "codball," and then become seriously tasteless. Those who laugh should be thoroughly ashamed of themselves. 🦴🦴

1990 98m/C *CA* Vince Murdocco, Tony Travis, William Dennis Hunt, Robyn Kelly; *D:* Howard Ziehm. **VHS** *NHO*

The Flesh Merchant

An "expose" on the world of prostitution, good strictly for unintended laughs. Girl visits her sister in the big city, hoping for a modeling career, but is lured into a brothel by ruthless Hollywood vice lords. Gee, the money looks good... Connell also gave us the Amazon classic *Untamed Women* (1952). Produced by roadshow exploitation legend Dan Sonney, who gave us *Strip Tease Girl, A Virgin in Hollywood,* and *Can-Can Follies,* and later teamed up with Dave Friedman in the '60s for features like *Space Thing* and *Trader Hornee. AKA:* The Wild and the Wicked. 🦴▷

1955 90m/B Joy Reynolds, Mariko Perri, Lisa Rack, Guy Manford; *D:* W. Merle Connell. **VHS, Beta** $16.95 *SNC*

The Fly

The original sci-fi tale about a hapless scientist Hedison, experimenting with teleportation, who accidentally gets anatomically mixed with a housefly. Now, how to tell the wife? No matter how repellently fascinating the premise, an earnest, wordy script (by novelist James Clavell) and direction better suited

living filmmaker, his big break came as director of *Boxcar Bertha*, a more-or-less sequel to Corman's own *Bloody Mama* (which had featured a then-unknown Robert De Niro).

Peter Bogdanovich--Trendy director of *Paper Moon*, *The Last Picture Show*, and *Mask*. Assigned by Corman to reshape clips from a plodding Russian space epic *Planeta Burg* into *Voyage to the Planet of Prehistoric Women*. Also rewrote the immortal biker drama *The Wild Angels*. Corman financed his breathrough movie *Targets*.

Joe Dante--Director of the *Gremlins* films, *Matinee*, *Explorers*, and other fantasies. Cut trailers and co-scripted for Corman's sexploitation films of the 70s, and co-directed *Hollywood Boulevard* for producer Corman as part of a bet that the 35mm feature could be done for only $90,000.

Jonathan Demme--Director of *Silence of the Lambs* and *Philadelphia*. Under Corman he did the girls-in-prison trendsetter *Caged Heat* and produced two similarly themed predecessors *Angels Hard as They Come* and *The Hot Box*.

John Sayles--Novelist and art-house fave for *Passion Fish*, *The Secret of Roan Inish*, *Eight Men Out*, and *City of Hope*. But under producer Corman, an ace script doctor who put life into the screenplays of *Piranha* and *Battle Beyond the Stars*.

James Cameron--Blockbuster writer/director of the *Terminator* features, *True Lies*, *Aliens*, and *The Abyss*. Did F/X work for Corman's *Battle Beyond the Stars* and survived directorial debut *Piranha II: The Spawning*.

Jim Wynorski--Ummm...errr... Depends on your definition of greatness. One-time writer for *Castle of Frankenstein* magazine and a living encyclopedia of B-movie references and gags, this former Roger Corman publicist has become one of Corman's most prolific purveyors of direct-to-video product. With frequent collaborator R.J. Robertson, writer/director Wynorski has assaulted the senses with everything from straightfaced crime pics to camped-up horror sequels: *The Return of Swamp Thing*, *Beastmaster 2*, *Final Embrace*, *Chopping Mall*, *Big Bad Mama 2*, *House IV*, *Deathstalker 2*, and *Transylvania Twist*.

to domestic-crisis drama lend this a campy air even the actors couldn't ignore—rumor has it Price and Marshall had to stifle giggles while shooting the notorious "...help me...help meeeeeee!" climax. Required viewing nonetheless. Mediocre sequel *Return of the Fly* is also on video; the British-made *Curse of the Fly* (1965) is not. While this stays close to source material of George Langelaan's short story, David Cronenberg's 1986 remake took a boldly different approach. 🎬🎬🎬

1958 94m/C Vincent Price, David Hedison, Herbert Marshall, Patricia Owens; **D:** Kurt Neumann; **W:** James Clavell. **VHS, Beta, LV $14.98** *FOX*

Forbidden Planet

Hollywood's first big-budget science fiction movie lacks the slaphappy, youthful spirit of its more modest contemporaries. Instead, it has a script based on Shakespeare's *The Tempest* and a universal message—that the most dangerous monsters come from within each of us. The story concerns a rescue mission to colonists on the distant planet Altair-4, a young woman's coming of age, and her father's inappropriate reaction. By today's standards, the effects are flat, but Robby the Robot is still a scene-stealer. Perhaps because it's part of the mainstream, this one has always generated mixed reactions among cult and s-f fans. About as many dismiss it as love it. Laserdisc features formerly "cut" scenes, production and publicity photos, the original screen treatment, and special effects outtakes. 🎬🎬🎬🎬

1956 98m/C Walter Pidgeon, Anne Francis, Leslie Nielsen, Warren Stevens, Jack Kelly, Richard Anderson, Earl Holliman, George Wallace; **D:** Fred M. Wilcox. **VHS, Beta, LV $19.98** *MGM, CRC*

Forbidden World

Space scientists on a remote planet are stalked by their own creation, a hostile organism capable of changing its genetic structure as it grows and matures (though it merely looks like a giant rubber spider). Corman-produced quickie followup to *Galaxy of Terror* is a graphically violent ripoff of *Alien* that almost received an X rating for gore. One plus: the cramped, effectively claustrophobic set design. Remade unmemorably in 1990 as *Dead Space*. **AKA:** Mutant.

1982 (R) 82m/C Jesse Vint, Dawn Dunlap, June Chadwick, Linden Chiles; **D:** Allan Holzman; **W:** Jim Wynorski, R.J. Robertson. **VHS, Beta, LV $69.98** *SUE*

Forbidden Zone

A sixth-dimension kingdom is ruled by a midget, King Fausto, and inhabited by dancing frogs, bikini-clad (and less) tootsies, robot boxers, and degraded beings of all kinds. Trapped in this strange world, can there be any hope for a return to normalcy? Herve Villechaize (Tattoo of *Fantasy Island* fame) plays the demented, diminutive ruler who plots against the rest of his court. Perhaps, in the end, he proved wisest of all. For those interested in the truly bizarre, the strange visuals and story herein are must viewing. If you like your movies to have any sense of reality, look elsewhere. Original music by Oingo Boingo, and directed by founding member Danny Elfman, who later gained renown for scoring *Batman* and other megabucks flicks. 🦴🦴🦴

1980 (R) 75m/B Herve Villechaize, Susan Tyrrell, Viva; **D:** Richard Elfman; **W:** Matthew Bright, Richard Elfman; **M:** Danny Elfman. **VHS, Beta $39.95** *MED*

Frankenhooker

Jeffrey Franken is a nice guy; he didn't mean to mow his fiancee down in the front lawn. But sometimes bad things just happen to good people. Luckily Jeff thought to save her head and decides to pair it up with the body of some sexy streetwalkers. Voila! You have Frankenhooker: the girlfriend with more than a heart. The posters say it best, "A Terrifying Tale of Sluts and Bolts." Also available in an "R" rated version. 🦴

1990 (R) 90m/C James Lorinz, Patty Mullen, Charlotte J. Helmkamp, Louise Lasser; **D:** Frank Henenlotter. **VHS, LV** *SGE, FCT*

Frankenstein

The definitive expressionistic Gothic horror classic that set the mold, liberally adapted from the Mary Shelley novel about Dr. Henry Frankenstein, the scientist who robs graves to create a terrifying, yet strangely sympathetic monster. Great performance by Karloff as the creation, enhanced by Jack Pierce's original, grotesque makeup which made him a star. Several powerful scenes, excised from the original version, have been restored. Side two of the laser disc version contains the original theatrical trailer, plus a collection of photos and scenes replayed for study purposes. Spoofed—with great respect and affection—in Mel Brooks' *Young Frankenstein*. 🦴🦴🦴🦴

1931 71m/B Boris Karloff, Colin Clive, Mae Clarke, John Boles, Dwight Frye, Edward Van Sloan, Frederick Kerr, Lionel Belman; **D:** James Whale; **W:** Francis Edwards Faragoh, Garrett Fort, John Balderston, Robert Florey; **M:** David Broeckman. **VHS, Beta, LV $14.95** *MCA, TLF, HMV*

Frankenstein '80

Dr. Otto Frankenstein (former peplum star Mitchell from *Atlas in the Land of the Cyclops, Giant of Metropolis*, etc.) pieces together a sex-crazed monster (Papas) who goes on a killing spree. Richardson (*Black Sunday, One Million B.C., Torso*) plays the reporter on his trail. Though made at the height of the Eurogore boom, this is a bottom of the barrel Italian production with funky music and lots of blood, including some real surgical footage. Too slowly paced for the shocks to take effect. However, the monster is still more imposing than DeNiro's. The Hound wonders what a Freda or a Bava might have done with this. **AKA:** Mosaic. 🦴

1979 88m/C *IT GE* John Richardson, Gordon Mitchell, Leila Parker, Dada Galloti, Marisa Travers, Xiro Papas; **D:** Mario Mancini. **VHS, Beta $59.95** *NO*

Frankenstein General Hospital

A horror spoof wherein the twelfth grandson of the infamous scientist duplicates his experiments in the basement of a modern hospital. Not outrageous enough to go out of your way for, it does make a sincere effort to get a few laughs. Unfortunately, the writing just isn't there. While the cast tries with the few smidgens of material the writer provides, the effort is in vain and Frankie dies on the operating table. A few clever ideas, such as filming the dungeon scenes in black and white the rest in color, get a passing grade for effort, but never quite click. The producers should

"It's alive! It's alive!"
--Dr. Frankenstein (Colin Clive) in Frankenstein.

THE HOUND SALUTES: FRANKENSTEIN

On a rainy night in the June of 1816, from the mind of a teenage girl, modern literary horror and science fiction were born. The circumstances under which Mary Shelley's novel *Frankenstein* (as well as the first literary vampire tale and the classic ghost story) were created are not nearly as well known as her tale itself, but have been recounted often enough that they don't need to be retold here. Indeed, the story behind the story has been the basis of two movies itself, and portions of several others as well. Suffice it to say that all stories of science fiction and horror can be traced back to that night when young Mary had a very vivid nightmare in which a terrifying fiend was created by the hand of man.

As a result of her fiction, we now have horror and science fiction films as well. Fittingly, the first film to be called a "horror movie" was Universal's 1931 production of *Frankenstein*, from which all others have come. After all, the success of *Dracula*, released earlier that year, might have been a fluke--but *Frankenstein* proved that audiences would pay to be scared as much as they'd pay to laugh or cry.

It may be that Frankenstein was fated for the movies. Just as the Monster of the story was stitched together from pieces of the dead, Universal's producer Carl Laemmle stitched together their cinematic Monster from the genius of Jack Pierce's makeup, James Whale's direction, and Boris Karloff's performance. The results were so perfect that the image of the Frankenstein Monster as seen in this classic film has become ingrained into the fabric of our culture. And although the story has been the basis of works in all other mediums, Frankenstein lives in the movies better than anywhere else. With dozens of films based directly on characters from the novel, not to mention the hundreds with at least a tenuous connection to it, it may be the single most adapted work in all of cinema. No other name draws an audience so well. So well that the American distributor slapped the title *Frankenstein's Bloody Terror* on the Spanish film

continued...

have gone for the obvious and added a ton more skin to try and salvage it. A must-see only for Frankenstein and Kathy Shower fans, Considered by some the worst Frankenstein movie ever made. 🎵 ▷

1988 90m/C Mark Blankfield, Kathy Shower, Leslie Jordan, Irwin Keyes; *D:* Deborah Roberts. **VHS, Beta, LV** *NO*

Frankenstein Meets the Space Monster

A classic grade-Z epic about a human-looking NASA android who goes berserk after crash landing in Puerto Rico. Karen (*Poltergeist, Return of the Living Dead*) and Marshall (who went from *To Kill a Mockingbird* to this!) are sent to track it down, but run across weird-looking aliens intent on kidnapping poolside go-go girls for breeding purposes. They fix up their android buddy enough to try to stop the invaders, but the aliens counterattack with their watchdog space monster, Mull. It's cheap and stupid, and the makeup and costumes are wonderfully way-out. A must see. *AKA:* Mars Invades Puerto Rico; Frankenstein Meets the Spacemen. 🎵🎵🎵

1965 80m/B James Karen, Nancy Marshall, Marilyn Hanold; *D:* Robert Gaffney. **VHS, Beta $39.95** *PSM*

Frankenstein Unbound

Corman returns after nearly 20 years with a better than ever B movie. Hurt plays a nuclear physicist time traveler who goes back to the 1800s and runs into Lord Byron, Percy and Mary Shelley, and their neighbor Dr. Frankenstein and his monster. Great acting, fun special effects, intelligent and subtle message, with a little sex to keep things going. *AKA:* Roger Corman's Frankenstein Unbound. 🎵🎵🎵

1990 (R) 86m/C John Hurt, Raul Julia, Bridget Fonda, Jason Patric, Michael Hutchence, Catherine Rabett, Nick Brimble, Catherine Corman, Mickey Knox; *D:* Roger Corman; *W:* Roger Corman, F.X. Feeney; *M:* Carl Davis; *V:* Terri Treas. **VHS, Beta, LV $14.98** *FOX*

Frankenweenie

Black and white Leave-It-to-Beaveresque short that plays almost like one of the more light-hearted *Twilight Zone* episodes. Burton

graces the picture with cartoon-like images that foreshadow *The Nightmare Before Christmas*. Story is of budding young filmmaker Victor's dog Sparky (who stars in Victor's chef d'oeuvre outfit in dinosaur scales); the pup is hit by a car when he chases a ball out past their white picket fence. Victor conceives of a plan during a science lesson at school, and resurrects Sparky in the attic during an electrical storm. The neighborhood is in turmoil over the comical monster-dog, but rallies to save the day. This affectionate parody of the Frankenstein tale launched Burton's career. Paul Bartel, as the science teacher who sparks Victor's ingenuity, is a treat. 🦴🦴🦴🦴

1984 (PG) 27m/B Shelley Duvall, Daniel Stern, Barret Oliver, Paul Bartel, Joseph Maher, Jason Hervey; *D:* Tim Burton; *W:* Tim Burton; *M:* Michael Convertino, David Newman. **VHS, Beta $14.99** *TOU*

Freaked

Bizarre little black comedy throws everything at the screen, hoping some of the gross-out humor will prove amusing (and some does).

Greedy TV star Ricky Coogin (Winter) agrees to be the spokesman for E.E.S. Corporation, which markets a toxic green slime fertilizer to the third world. He's sent to South America to promote the product and is captured by the mad scientist proprietor (Quaid) of a mysterious sideshow, who douses him with the fertilizer. Before you know it he's an oozing half-man, half-beast, perfect to join other freaks as the latest attraction. Lots of yucky makeup. Reeves has an uncredited cameo as the Dog Boy. 🦴🦴🦴

1993 (PG-13) 80m/C Alex Winter, Randy Quaid, Megan Ward, Michael Stoyanov, Brooke Shields, William Sadler, Derek McGrath, Alex Zuckerman, Karyn Malchus; *Cameos:* Keanu Reeves; *D:* Alex Winter, Tom Stern; *W:* Alex Winter, Tim Burns, Tom Stern; *M:* Kevin Kiner; *V:* Bob(cat) Goldthwait. **VHS, LV** *FXV*

The Freakmaker

Exceedingly mad professor attempts to breed plants with humans in his lab and has the usual bizarre results. Experiments that fail go

We were *Freaked* too.

Story continued...

Mark of the Wolfman, despite the fact that it features a werewolf and some vampires, but not even a mention of Frankenstein!

What is the secret of this particular monster's success? For despite any theorizing about man's folly in pursuit of knowledge, it is "the Monster" itself that grabs our attention--be it in the form of a Golem or an Ogre or a Damned Thing from the Grave, there is something irresistibly fascinating and relentlessly horrifying about any large living mass that we know instinctively to be of Unnatural Origin. That is the basic principle defining the Monster, which Mary Shelley embodied so perfectly in a creature that even its own creator, who knew in infinite detail how the thing worked and had put all the intricate pieces together himself, could not help but be consumed with horror of it. And the movies don't just talk about the Monster--no matter how ridiculous the costume is, the movies show It to us. One thousand words times 24 frames per second equals a million delightful frights per reel. That's a formula that's been working for over 60 years.

> "Gooba, gobba, we accept you, one of us!"
>
> --*Freaks*.

1973 **(R)** 90m/C *GB* Donald Pleasence, Tom Baker, Brad Harris, Julie Ege, Michael Dunn, Jill Haworth; **D:** Jack Cardiff. **VHS, Beta $19.98** *VDC*

Freaks

The infamous, controversial, cult-horror classic about a band of circus freaks that exact revenge upon a beautiful aerialist and her strongman lover after enduring humiliation and attempted murder. Based on Ted Robbins story *Spurs*. It was meant to out-horror *Frankenstein,* but was so successful that it was repeatedly banned. Browning's film may be a shocker but it is never intended to be exploitative since the *Freaks* are the only compassionate, loyal, and loving people around. Browning's visuals are brilliant, but all the heavy accents of his performers (and subsequent poor sound quality of surviving prints) compound his difficulty getting his bearings in talkies. Disowned by MGM, it was saved from being a lost film by its sale to roadshow producer/director Dwain Esper (*Maniac, Reefer Madness*), who kept it on the road under various names and running times for decades after. Remade in 1967 as *She Freak.* **AKA:** Nature's Mistakes; Forbidden Love; The Monster Show. 🎵🎵🎵🎵

1932 66m/B Wallace Ford, Olga Baclanova, Leila Hyams, Roscoe Ates, Harry Earles, Violet Hilton, Daisy Hilton, Angelo Rossitto, Johnny Eck, Daisy Earles; **D:** Tod Browning. **VHS, Beta, LV $19.98** *MGM*

to Dunn, a dwarf who runs a freak show. Unexceptional geekshow steals shamelessly from *Freaks* and drew fire for mixing made-up monsters (a lizard woman and Venus-flytrap man) with real-life deformed people (including a frog boy, human skeleton, and the truly astounding Willie "Popeye" Ingram), as did *The Sentinel.* Pleasance and the sadly underappreciated Dunn distinguish material, with ex-Dr. Who Tom Baker, aging muscleman/executive producer Harris, and Hammer starlet Ege (*Creatures the World Forgot*). Credit sequence features exceptionally beautiful time-lapse photography and haunting synth-jazz score by Basil Kirchin. Director Cardiff was an Academy award-winning cinematographer (*Black Narcissus*) before branching into a low-budget directorial career. **AKA:** Mutations; The Mutation. 🎵🎵🎵

Friday the 13th

A true trailblazer, this flick was the first in the endless line of teenage slasher films that littered theatres in the early '80s. This much-imitated film is still one of the best of the genre. Camp Crystal Lake is set for a grand reopening after a strange history of unexplained deaths. Six counselors arrive to prepare, but end up having sex and getting killed by an array of sharp objects instead. Talk about dead-end jobs. Still, there really is a plot here, with many scares along the way, and a surprise ending. The Hound always hated summer camp, too. Special effects by gore-master Tom Savini. Followed by countless, pathetic sequels. 🎵🎵🎵

1980 **(R)** 95m/C Betsy Palmer, Adrienne King, Harry Crosby, Laurie Bartrarr, Mark Nelsor, Kevin Bacon; **D:** Sean S. Cunningham. **VHS, Beta, LV $14.95** *PAR*

Frigid Wife

Cheap exploitation flick about impotence and frigidity in a clinical setting, similar to *Test Tube Babies*. A wife can't relate to her husband sexually, so she goes to a shrink for help and he tries to straighten her out. From the first scene with the woman's mother, the problem becomes obvious. Incorporates footage from a much older feature, *A Modern Marriage*. More soap opera than anything else. *AKA:* A Modern Marriage. 🦴🦴🦴

1961 ?m/B Jeanne Neher, Sondra Fisher, Sid Noel, Bob Carr, Ken Elliott; **D:** Ben Parker. **VHS $16.95** SNC

Fritz the Cat

Ralph Bakshi's animated tale for adults about a cat's adventures as he gets into group sex, college radicalism, and other hazards of life in the '60s. Loosely based on the underground comics character by Robert Crumb. Originally X-rated. 🦴🦴🦴

1972 77m/C D: Ralph Bakshi. **VHS, Beta** WAR, OM

Frogs

Assorted folks gathered on a small island in Florida for the birthday celebration of wealthy patriarch Milland soon find that local reptiles, amphibians, insects, and other creepy-crawlers in the area are systematically attacking humans. Roger Corman's best entry in the horror genre of environmentally motivated animal-vengeance films. No big scares, but repeated closeups of hostile hissing snakes, lizards, turtles, and frogs evoke a foreboding sense of nature lethally turned against mankind. Cartoon closing scene is the only campy touch. 🦴🦴🦴

1972 (PG) 91m/C Ray Milland, Sam Elliott, Joan Van Ark, Adam Roarke, Judy Pace, Lynn Borden, Mae Mercer, David Gilliam, George Skaff; **D:** George McCowan; **M:** Les Baxter. **VHS, Beta** WAR, OM

From Russia with Love

Bond is back and on the loose in exotic Istanbul looking for a super-secret coding machine. He's involved with a beautiful Russian spy and has the SPECTRE organization after him, including villainess Rosa Klebb (she of the killer shoe). Lots of exciting escapes but not an over-reliance on the gadgetry of the later films. The second Bond feature, thought by many to be the best. The laserdisc edition includes interviews with director Terence Young and others on the creative staff. The musical score and special effects can be separated from the actors' dialogue. Also features publicity shots, American and British trailers, on-location photos, and movie posters. 🦴🦴🦴🦴

1963 (PG) 125m/C *GB* Sean Connery, Daniela Bianchi, Pedro Armendariz Sr., Lotte Lenya, Robert Shaw, Eunice Gayson, Walter Gotell, Lois Maxwell, Bernard Lee, Desmond Llewelyn, Nadja Regin, Alizia Gur, Martine Beswick, Leila; **D:** Terence Young; **M:** John Barry. **VHS, Beta, LV $19.98** *MGM, CRC, TLF*

Fugitive Girls

Classic sexploitation flick. Women in chains escape from prison and are chased across the country side. Four are hardened bad girls, one is wrongly convicted. Along the way they terrorize bikers, hippies, and just plain folk in their quest for undeserved freedom. With lots of make-believe violence and nudity, this is perfect for lovers of older drive-in fare. It ends with a nice little girl-girl brawl between little miss priss and the queen bitch, for those interested in cat fight cinema. Make some popcorn, take your portable VCR and TV out to your car, and relive those good ol' days. 🦴🦴🦴

1975 (R) 90m/C Jabee Amercombie, Renee Bond, Talie Cochrane, Donna Desmond, Margie Lanier, Edward D. Wood Jr.; **D:** A.C. Stephen. **VHS** NO

Futurekick

One of those movies that annoys you completely, then serves up a marvelously devious trick ending in its final moment. You don't know whether to applaud or throw things. In the slum-like New Los Angles of the next century, a murder victim's wife hangs around ubiquitous topless bars (the future's industrial base, apparently) in search of her husband's murderer. Available to help is a kickboxing cyborg bounty-hunter played by martial-arts champ Wilson. On second thought, throw things; much of this post-apocalyptic Roger Corman quickie is padded with footage lifted from previous post-apocalyptic Roger Corman quickies. 🦴🦴

"**M**ake his death a particularly unpleasant one."
--Number 1 of SPECTRE in *From Russia With Love.*

1991 (R) 80m/C Don "The Dragon" Wilson, Meg Foster, Christopher Penn, Eb Lottimer; **D:** Damian Klaus; **W:** Damian Klaus. **VHS** *NHO*

Galaxina

Despite not-bad special effects, the force is not with this lame *Star Wars* parody. Avery Schriber stars as Capt. Butt, which gives you a good indication of the level of humor. Dorothy Stratten, a Playboy Playmate of the Year, was murdered by her estranged husband the night the film premiered in Kansas City. She was the subject of two films, Bob Fosse's *Star 80* starring a surgically enhanced Mariel Hemingway, and the made-for-TV *Death of a Centerfold* starring Jamie Lee Curtis. 🦴

1980 (R) 95m/C Dorothy Stratten, Avery Schreiber, Stephen Macht; **D:** William Sachs. **VHS, Beta, LV $59.95** *MCA*

Galaxy of Terror

Astronauts sent to rescue a stranded spaceship find themselves with a new mission: find the hidden alien leader in a mysterious pyramid (which contains a gauntlet of weird death traps) before they all get killed by vicious aliens. Big first: Moran (Joanie on *Happy Days*) explodes. The entertaining cast also includes Sid Haig (*Spider Baby*). Inferior Corman-produced *Alien* imitation still manages to shock and displays generous gore and nudity, and the low budget f/x are well done. King (*Blue Sunshine*) later became a producer/director and churned out loads of well photographed erotic nonsense such, as *Wild Orchid*. Followed by *Forbidden World*. **AKA:** Mindwarp: An Infinity of Terror; Planet of Horrors. 🦴 🦴

1981 (R) 85m/C Erin Moran, Edward Albert, Ray Walston, Grace Zabriskie, Zalman King; **D:** B.D. Clark; **W:** Mark Siegler, B.D. Clark. **VHS, Beta, LV $9.98** *SUE*

Gamera, the Invincible

A crashing bomber plane releases a gigantic mutant turtle from the arctic ice. The flying, fire-breathing monster goes on the rampage in Japan, despite the delusions of little Kenny, who believes Gamera is "a friend to all children." In all, an enjoyable monster romp, with a rather unique and interesting conclusion. Daiei Studios created Gamera to compete with rival Toho's very successful Godzilla pictures. Like *Godzilla*, the American theatrical version of *Gamera* was altered to include added scenes featuring Anglo actors—in this case, Brian Donlevy and Albert Dekker as U.S. military men. This version has almost completely disappeared in favor of the current more straightforward video incarnation. After this initial outing, director Yuasa stepped down to concentrate on only the special effects. The giant turtle returned for seven silly sequels full of juvenile hijinks aimed at children (which also succeeded in dragging the Godzilla series down to the same level), before returning for a surprisingly good semi-remake in 1995. **AKA:** Gamera; Gammera; Daikaiju Gamera. 🦴 🦴 🦴

1966 86m/B *JP* Eiji Funakoshi, Harumi Kiritachi, Junichire Yamashiko, Yoshiro Uchida, Brian Donlevy, Albert Dekker, Diane Findlay, John Baragrey, Dick O'Neill; **D:** Noriaki Yuasa. **VHS, LV $9.99** *JFK, SNC*

Gas-s-s-s!

A gas main leak in an Alaskan defense plant kills everyone beyond thirtysomething and the post-apocalyptic pre-boomer survivors are left to muddle their way through the brume. Trouble is, AIP edited the heck out of the movie, much to Corman's chagrin, and the result is a truncated comedy; Corman was so displeased, in fact, he left to create New World studios. **AKA:** Gas-s-s-s. . . or, It May Become Necessary to Destroy the World in Order to Save It. 🦴 🦴 🦴

1970 (PG) 79m/C Robert Corff, Elaine Giftos, Pat Patterson, George Armitage, Alex Wilson, Ben Vereen, Cindy Williams, Bud Cort, Talia Shire; **D:** Roger Corman; **W:** George Armitage. **VHS, Beta** *NO*

Gates of Heaven

Errol Morris' documentary begins as a grotesque news item about the re-location of a pet cemetery, then becomes a character study of the owners of the pets who are interred there, and finally develops into a portrait of a family-run business. This cornucopia of oddballs ranges from an elderly paranoid given to front-porch philosophizing to a guitar-slinging reprobate trying his darndest to grow into a responsible cemetery worker. Although Morris has been criticized for the exploitation of people who are not quite all there, he goes beyond voyeuristic entertainment to create a strangely empathetic bond between spectator and freak. 🦴🦴🦴🦴

1978 85m/C D: Errol Morris. **VHS, Beta $19.98** *COL, FCT*

Gates of Hell

When a priest commits suicide in a graveyard, he unlocks one of the seven secret doorways to Hell, unleashing evil supernatural forces in a small New England town. Director Fulci was a dependable craftsman of a variety of different types of film in Italy, but he found international fame among horror fans when he it was discovered he possessed a special talent for delivering outrageously nausea-inducing horror epics, turning stomachs both on screen and in the audience, while also managing to maintain a level of eerie atmosphere. He's at it again here, as even seemingly unrelated subplots—as when a father discovers a guy fooling around with his teenage daughter and decides to drill some sense into his head—turn into gritty, blatantly gratuitous splatter. *AKA:* Paura Nella Citta Dei Morti Viventi; City of the Living Dead; The Fear; Twilight of the Dead; Fear in the City of the Living Dead. 🦴🦴🦴

1983 90m/C Christopher George, Janet Agren, Katherine MacColl, Robert Sampson; **D:** Lucio Fulci. **VHS, Beta** *IGP*

Geek Maggot Bingo

It's too bad director Zed waited until mid-"Bingo" to post a sign warning "Leave Now, It Isn't Going Get Any Better!" Conceived by the New York underground's don of the "Cinema of Transgression" to be an off-the-rack cult classic, this horror spoof is too long on in-jokes and short on substance to earn its number in the cult hall of fame. It does, however, boast Death as Scumbalina the vampire queen and Hell as a punk cowboy crooner (before alternative country hit the airwaves). TV horror-meister Zacherle narrates. *AKA:* The Freak From Suckweasel Mountain. 🦴

1983 70m/C Richard Hell, Donna Death, John Zacherle; **D:** Nick Zedd. **VHS $39.99** *MWF, MOV*

Get Crazy

If you like *Rock and Roll High School,* then graduate to this frantic comedy by the same director that unfolds over the chaotic course of a New Year's Eve concert. Any similarity between Malcolm McDowell and Mick Jagger and Lou Reed and Bob Dylan may not be coincidental. Former teen faves Fabian and Bobby Sherman are the bad guys who want to pull the plug. 🦴🦴🦴

1983 90m/C Malcolm McDowell, Allen (Goorwitz) Garfield, Daniel Stern, Gail Edwards, Ed Begley Jr., Lou Reed, Bill Henderson, Fabian, Bobby Sherman; **D:** Allan Arkush; **M:** Michael Boddicker. **VHS, Beta, LV $9.98** *SUE, NLC*

The Ghastly Ones

Three couples must stay in a haunted mansion to inherit an estate, but they're soon being violently killed off. East coast auteur Milligan curiously often chose to make his no-budget pictures as period pieces for no good reason, limiting himself unnecessarily. This may be a throwback to the old dark house mysteries of the early '30s, but there's no need to go back to gaslight days. And despite some creative use of cross cutting and hand-held camera, many scenes are much too dark to tell what's going on. Some lively dialogue and frequent gory murders get your interest, but several minutes of peering into a dark screen wears out ones patience. Milligan went on to more talk & mayhem wonders with *Gutter Trash, Bloodthirsty Butchers, The Rats are Coming! The Werewolves are Here!,* and many others. Remade as *Legacy of Blood.* 🦴🦴

1968 81m/C Don Williams, Maggie Rogers, Hal Belsoe, Veronica Redburn; **D:** Andy Milligan. **VHS, Beta** *NO*

Ghidrah the Three Headed Monster

Toho Studios quickly followed their excellent *Godzilla Vs. Mothra* with this even bigger monster rumble. A beautiful Asian princess (Wakabayashi, *You Only Live Twice*) is rescued from an assassination attempt by a UFO, and turns up later possessed by a Martian intelligence and spouting prophetic warnings.

Honest, the gila monster really is big: *The Giant Gila Monster.*

Sure enough, Godzilla and Rodan appear, and begin a playful (and highly destructive) tussle across the Japanese countryside. But the real danger arrives in the form of space monster Ghidrah, who materializes out of a meteorite. The twin fairies, in town for a TV appearance, recruit Mothra (who'd defeated Godzilla at their last meeting) to attempt to lead the battling Earth monsters against the invader. Nonstop fun for all ages, highlighted by the title creature: a gigantic, nightmarish, scaly horror that looks like a golden dragon out of Japanese legend. He'd be back the next year in *Godzilla Vs. Monster Zero.* The 1966 U.S. version was heavily re-edited, damaging continuity. *AKA:* Ghidorah Sandai Kaiju Chikyu Saidai No Kessan; Ghidora, The Three-Headed Monster; Ghidrah; The Greatest Battle on Earth; The Biggest Right on Earth; Monster of Monsters. ♫♫♫♪

1965 85m/C *JP* Akiko Wakabayashi, Yosuke Natsuki, Yuriko Hoshi, Hiroshi Koizumi, Takashi Shimura, Emi Ito, Yumi Ito, Kenji Sahara; *D:* Inoshiro Honda; *W:* Shinichi Sekizawa; *M:* Akira Ifukube. **VHS, Beta $19.95** *HHT, VCN, VHE*

The Ghost

An unfaithful wife (Steele) plots against her cruel husband. After his death, she's driven mad with fear by the ghost of her dead husband (or is he?) and their evil housekeeper. Plenty of twists and turns in this interesting thriller, all leading to a shock ending. Reinforced Steele's reputation as the queen of fright films in the early '60s. Former art critic Freda made the very first Italian horror film, the stylishly eerie *The Devil's Commandment* (1956), and continued to make fantastic films featuring gorgeous photography and set design thereafter. Semi-sequel to Freda's *The Horrible Dr. Hitchcock* (1962). *AKA:* Lo Spettro. ♫♫♫

1963 96m/C *IT* Barbara Steele, Peter Baldwin, Leonard Eliott, Harriet White; *D:* Riccardo (Robert Hampton) Freda. **VHS, Beta $14.95** *SNC*

The Giant Gila Monster

Through the magic of rear-projection film techniques, a giant lizard (yes, a gila monster) terrorizes the plucky teens of a small south-western town. You'd think from that descrip-tion that the cheesy special effects of the mon-ster would be the worst thing about this movie, but you'd be wrong—the acting is far worse! One young couple has a run in with the lizard while "talking" (nudge, nudge, wink, wink) out in the boondocks, and that good ol' 1950s moral is hard to miss—if you're going to be sexually promiscuous, you're go-ing to pay the price. All in all, the film pro-vides many unintentional laughs. 🦴🦴

1959 74m/B Don Sullivan, Lisa Simone, Shug Fisher, Jerry Cortwright, Beverly Thurman, Don Flourney, Pat Simmons; **D:** Ray Kellogg. **VHS $9.95** *NOS, RHI, SNC*

The Giant Spider Invasion

A meteorite carrying spider eggs crashes in rural Wisconsin, and soon the alien arachnids are popping out of geodes and growing to hu-mongous proportions. Notoriously bad spe-cial effects are the main attraction. The title critter may be the funniest ever to grace the screen, and it bears a striking resemblance—particularly around the eyes—to Kermit the Frog. Best moment is the unforgettable spider-in-the-blender scene. Veteran "B" cast is led by Steve Brodie, Alan Hale (the Skipper, whose first line is "Hi, little buddy!"), Barbara Hale (Della Street), and Bill Williams. They all seem to be having a grand time. 🦴🦴🐾

1975 (PG) 76m/C Steve Brodie, Barbara Hale, Leslie Parrish, Robert Easton, Alan Hale Jr., Dianne Lee Hart, Bill Williams, Christianne Schmidtmer; **D:** Bill Rebane. **VHS** *MOV*

Ginger

"Every man wanted her; no man could tame her...the best secret weapon ever to wear a dress!" Blonde bombshell Cheri Caffaro has a license to strip in this grind house relic in which a society girl is recruited by a private detective agency to go undercover (and boy, does she go undercover!) in a New Jersey drug, blackmail, and prostitution ring. Its pre-posterous plot and racial stereotypes were of out date even then, but the film did earn a mention in *Playboy*'s annual "Sex in the Cin-ema" roundup. Today's direct-to-video erotic thrillers offer much more graphic fast-forward

pleasures. Still, as *Variety* noted, "The girls are attractive...and nudity abounds." If you like that sort of thing. Believe it or not, there was a sequel, *The Abductors*, which was followed by *Girls Are for Loving*. 🦴

1972 90m/C Cheri Caffaro, William Grannell; **D:** Don Schain. **VHS, Beta $39.95** *MON*

The Girl Can't Help It

He was a former Warner Brothers animator. She was a voluptuous actress of cartoonish proportions. Director Frank Tashlin and Jayne Mansfield were made for each other. In her first film, Jayne stars as the seemingly no-tal-ent girlfriend to gangster Edmond O'Brien, who pressures press agent Tom Ewell to trans-form her into a singing star. A satirical rock and roll comedy that has not dated as well as its reputation might indicate. But the perfor-mances by such rock legends as Fats Domino ("Blue Monday"), Gene Vincent ("BeBop A Lula"), Eddie Cochran ("Twenty Flight Rock"), and Little Richard (the title tune) are timeless. In one surreal sequence, a drunken Ewell can-not escape the vision of old flame Julie Lon-don as she croons "Cry Me a River." Tashlin and Mansfield were paired again on the much-funnier *Will Success Spoil Rock Hunter*. 🦴🦴🐾

1956 99m/B Jayne Mansfield, Tom Ewell, Edmond O'Brien, Julie London, Ray Anthony; **D:** Frank Tash-lin. **VHS, Beta, LV $59.98** *FOX*

The Girl, the Body and the Pill

Herschell Gordon Lewis sexploitation flick has high school instructor getting fired for her sex education lectures, so she continues them in the privacy of her home. Meanwhile, stu-dents take up playing musical beds and learn about the pill. Takes on hot topics such as teen delinquency, sex education, abortion, and re-ligious fundamentalism, with less-than-scan-dalous results. Subplot involving prudish school board member (Bill Rogers) who's against sex ed having an affair with alcoholic single mom (Valedia Hill) is suitably overripe; he's forced to back down when mom gets pregnant after horny daughter switches her birth control pills with saccharine tablets!

"O.K., lady, I'll just take my PJs and go," says John Candy look-alike Edmond O'Brien to Jayne Mansfield in *The Girl Can't Help It.*

"The first motion picture about the great moral revolution"; according to Lewis, entire premise is built around a gag: what do you call a girl who doesn't use birth control? Mommy. Rogers starred in Lewis's *A Taste of Blood* and appeared in *Flesh-Feast, Shanty Tramp,* and other Florida-made Z-flicks. 🦴🦴

1967 ?m/C Bill Rogers, Nancy Lee Noble; **D:** Herschell Gordon Lewis. **VHS $19.99** *MOV*

Girls Are for Loving

Undercover agent Ginger, who wears a black belt with her pink nightie, faces real adventure when she battles it out with her counterpart, an equally seductive enemy agent. Film combines the blatant sexuality of a '70s softcore skin flick with the silliness of a '60s spy movie. The screwloose plot moves right along, but the fight scenes are slow and poorly choreographed. Her third and, to date, final adventure following *Ginger* (1970) and *The Abductors* (1971). 🦴🦴▷

1973 90m/C Cheri Caffaro, Timothy Brown; **D:** Don Schain. **VHS, Beta $39.95** *MON*

Girls! Girls! Girls!

When Elvis Presley received this script, he should have sent it back marked "Return to Sender," the only song of note that he sings in the film. Elvis is a tuna boat fisherman in Hawaii who moonlights as a nightclub singer to raise money to buy back his father's sailboat. Romantic distractions include sultry singer Stella and good girl Laurel Goodwin, who hides that she is wealthy. Also on the soundtrack are the title tune and the immortal "Song of the Shrimp." This was Elvis' 11th film in only six years! Director Norman Taurog, Elvis' favorite, did nine films with the King. He also directed *Boy's Town.* Original setting for the movie was intended to be New Orleans, and its title slated to be *Gumbo Ya-Ya.* 🎵 The Nearness of You; Never Let Me Go; Girls, Girls, Girls; Return to Sender; We're Coming in Loaded; A Boy Like Me, A Girl Like You; Song of the Shrimp; Earth Boy; The Walls Have Ears. 🦴🦴▷

1962 106m/C Elvis Presley, Stella Stevens, Laurel Goodwin, Jeremy Slate, Benson Fong, Robert Strauss,

Ginny Tiu, Guy Lee, Beulah Quo; **D:** Norman Taurog. **VHS, Beta $14.98** *FOX, MVD*

Glen or Glenda?

Legendary, appalling, quasi-docudrama about transvestism, with a sympathetic eye toward the maligned life-style choice. Wood himself pseudonymously plays Glen, an otherwise normal man ("not a homosexual," intones the narrator, about five or six times) who happens to enjoy women's clothes. We share his struggle to confess all to his girlfriend—he covets her angora sweater—and witness his disjointed dreams about a man in a devil suit and a fallen tree-trunk incident in Glen's living room. Plus the plight of Alan/Ann, an ex-Marine who undergoes a sex-change operation. In fact, Wood was supposed to make a poverty-row quickie wholly based on famous transsexual Christine Jorgenson, but the filmmaker let his own transvestite obsessions run away with the plot (plot?). And then there's guest-star Lugosi, as an omniscient commentator with a chemistry set, spouting incoherent prattle at the camera, usually to the backdrop of irrelevant stock footage. Required viewing to comprehend Tim Burton's biopic *Ed Wood* (and vice versa), Wood's directorial debut is one of the most compellingly bad films of this century, and not to be missed! Different versions circulate on video; technical quality varies widely, and some editions include graphic orgy footage spliced in later. **AKA:** He or She; I Changed My Sex; I Led Two Lives; The Transvestite. 🎵🎵🎵🎵
1953 70m/B Bela Lugosi, Edward D. Wood Jr., Lyle Talbot, Donald Woods, Dolores Fuller, Timothy Farrell; **D:** Edward D. Wood Jr. **VHS, Beta $19.95** *NOS, MRV, SNC*

Go West

The brothers Marx help in the making and unmaking of the Old West. More specifically, they help recover a land deed from bad guys. While there is nothing overly memorable here, the film is good for a few yucks and is still far funnier than a lot of the unfunny trash that passes for comedy in today's cinema. Even poor Marx Bothers material has enough to offer to make it good material for a rainy Sunday afternoon. 🎵🎵🎵

JUDGE YE NOT!

"In the making of this film, which deals with a strange and curious subject, no punches have been pulled--no easy way out has been taken. Many of the smaller parts are portrayed by persons who actually live, in real life, the characters they portray on the screen. This is a picture of stark realism--taking no sides--but giving you the facts--All the facts--as they are today. You are society...JUDGE YE NOT."

--introduction to *Glen or Glenda?*

1940 80m/B Groucho Marx, Chico Marx, Harpo Marx, John Carroll, Diana Lewis; **D:** Edward Buzzell. **VHS, Beta, LV $19.95** *MGM, CCB*

God Told Me To

The title is the only reason given when ordinary citizens suddenly commit mass murder. Is God ordaining angels of Death? This is the

The original Love Boat, fueled by a steamin' hunk of burnin' love: Elvis Presley in *Girls! Girls! Girls!*

THE HOUND SALUTES: GODZILLA

A South Pacific island was destroyed in an atomic bomb test in the late 1940s. A surviving descendant of the dinosaur age also survived the A-bomb by mutating into a gigantic creature sustained by nuclear energy. This creature came to be known as Godzilla.

Godzilla was actually born on a train. Producer Tomoyuki Tanaka's current project, an historical drama, was not going well, and he was returning to Tokyo to present a replacement project to his bosses at Toho Studios. Since the American film *The Beast from 20,000 Fathoms* was a hit at the box office, Tanaka envisioned an even bigger creature which would destroy Tokyo. Tanaka's special effects director, Eiji Tsuburaya, wanted the monster to be a giant octopus, but instead screenwriter Takeo Murata chose to make the beast a kind of mutant aquatic tyrannosaurus who could exhale radioactive flames. Christening the beast, they took the nickname of a portly Toho technician, Gojira (pronounced "Godzilla" to western ears, it translates as a combination of "gorilla" and "whale"). The chosen director Ishiro Honda, who would go on to direct nine Godzilla films and many other Toho sci-fi pictures, was a close friend and assistant director to the great Akira Kurosawa. Another important player was the distinguished classical composer Akira Ifukube, who lent his distinctive and expressive music to many of Toho's classics.

The finished film became not only a great epic of monster mayhem, but a reflection of the humiliation bred by Japan's aggression in WWII and subsequent defeat. Godzilla himself became an embodiment of the nightmare of atomic destruction, fresh from the horrors of Hiroshima and Nagasaki. In the end, the monster is destroyed through the mortal sacrifice of a pacifist scientist.

Toho spent over $1 million on the production, over ten times the budget of the average Japanese film of the time. The investment paid off immediately, as *Gojira* was a huge success at the box office. American rights were purchased

continued...

mystery facing a deeply religious New York homicide detective (LoBianco), who traces the crimes to a mysterious androgynous figure (Lynch), the product of a virgin birth. What is his own connection to this being? This cult-fave Larry Cohen epic, features his trademark NYC locations, vividly drawn characters, realistically handled situations and dialogue, and one hell of a weird premise. Andy Kaufman debuts as a killer cop at the St. Patrick's Day parade. *AKA:* Demon. 🎵🎵🎵♭

1976 (R) 89m/C Tony LoBianco, Deborah Raffin, Sylvia Sidney, Sandy Dennis, Andy Kaufman, Richard Lynch; *D:* Larry Cohen; *W:* Larry Cohen. VHS, Beta, LV $19.98 *NLC*

The Gods Must Be Crazy

An innocent and charming film. A peaceful Bushman travels into the civilized world to return a Coke bottle "to the gods." Along the way he meets a transplanted schoolteacher, an oafishly clumsy microbiologist and a gang of fanatical terrorists. A very popular film, disarmingly crammed with slapstick and broad humor of every sort. Followed by a weak sequel. 🎵🎵🎵♭

1984 (PG) 109m/C N!xau, Marius Weyers, Sandra Prinsloo, Louw Verwey, Jamie Uys, Michael Thys, Nic de Jager; *D:* Jamie Uys. VHS, Beta, LV $19.39 *FOX, FCT, TVC*

Godzilla, King of the Monsters

A prehistoric reptile emerges from the depths to terrorize Tokyo after he has been mutated by atomic testing. If one suspends disbelief enough to gloss over flaws in the less successful f/x, the monster makes an indelible impression of titanic, unyielding destructive force. Accurately reflecting the sense of helpless dread felt in Japan during the cold war, a message pleading for nuclear disarmament remained as a subtext throughout most of the Godzilla series. Burr's scenes are intercut in the American version, where he serves as a narrator telling the monster's tale in flashbacks. Once one has seen the original version, the inserted footage seems intrusive, but otherwise it blends in reasonably well. One of the first post-WWII Japanese films to break through commercially in the U.S. Followed by 21(!) sequels to date. *AKA:* Gojira. 🎵🎵🎵🎵

1956 80m/B *JP* Raymond Burr, Takashi Shimura, Akira Takarada, Akihiko Hirata; *D:* Inoshiro Honda, Terry Morse; *M:* Akira Ifukube. **VHS, Beta, LV** *PAR, VES*

Godzilla 1985

After 30 years, the Big G recovers from his apparent death from the effects of the oxygen destroyer in *Godzilla, King of the Monsters* and returns to destroy Tokyo all over again. Toho's revival of their biggest star features bigger, more spectacular f/x than before, the highlight being Godzilla's duel with the Defense Force's combat vehicle Super-X amid the crashing skyscrapers of downtown Tokyo. Disregarding the previous fourteen sequels (most of which were set in "the future" anyway), the plot marches along much like a '70s disaster film. Like it's predecessor, this one has inserted scenes for the reworked American edition with Burr reprising his role of journalist Steve Martin (who probably made a fortune writing books about Godzilla), while cutting about thirty minutes from the original. Burr maintains his composure, but the insert scenes are embarrassingly cheap and contain jarringly blatant product placements for Dr. Pepper. 🦴🦴🦴
1985 **(PG)** 91m/C *JP* Keiju Kobayashi, Ken Tanaka, Raymond Burr, Yasuka Sawaguchi; *D:* Kohji Hashimoto. **VHS, Beta, LV** $9.95 *NWV, STE*

Godzilla Vs. Biollante

Genetic scientist Surigama (Takahashi) uses cells from Godzilla's body to create hardy new crop strains, while also splicing the cells' DNA to that of his dead daughter, using that of her favorite rose as a catalyst. His experiments result in the gigantic plant/animal monster Biollante, a nightmare of creeping vines, snapping teeth, and corrosive sap. Meanwhile, Godzilla escapes from the volcano he was knocked into in *Godzilla 1985*, and attacks from the new Super-X2 and newly developed anti-nuclear bacteria fail to stop his rampage. Can Biollante help? Five years after their revival of the Godzilla series with *Godzilla 1995* (a direct sequel to *Godzilla* 1954, bypassing all previous "sequels"), Toho made a more definite commitment to their monster star with this poetic entry, marred by a confusing plotline and shallow characterization, but show-

ing imaginative visuals by upstart director Omori and Toho's new f/x wizard Koichi Kawakita. First appearance by psychic girl Miki Saegusa (Odaka), who became a series regular. The same team returned in 1991 for the even better *Godzilla Vs. King Ghidorah*, which awaits a U.S. release. Viewers received an unexpected bonus when HBO "accidently" transferred this to video in widescreen format. 🦴🦴🦴
1989 **(PG)** 104m/C *JP* Koji Takahashi, Yoshiko Tanaka, Megumi Odaka, Kunihiko Mitamura; *D:* Kazuki Ohmori; *W:* Kazuki Ohmori. **VHS, LV** $69.99 *NO*

Godzilla Vs. Megalon

While so many worthwhile films remain unavailable on home video, due to the assumption that it's in the public domain, *Godzilla vs. Megalon* proliferates across the land on countless cheap video labels and even onto CD-ROM. Overreacting to the tremendous popularity on Japanese TV of superhero programs like *Ultraman*, Toho sought to team their monster star with their own rubbery robot, Jet Jaguar, with ridiculous results. The underwater nation of Seatopia provides the menace, sending forth giant mutant roach Megalon to conquer the surface world, while hiring cyborg monster Gigan as backup. Most of the action conveniently takes place in open fields (and stock footage), far away from those expensive miniature buildings. After some skirmishes with Seatopian spies, the human heroes camp out on hillsides to watch the monster mayhem. A low mark in monster history. Adding insult to injury, NBC cut out half the footage and aired it in 1977 with campy segments hosted by John Belushi in a shoddy Godzilla costume. *AKA:* Gojira Tai Megaro. 🦴
1976 **(G)** 80m/C *JP* Katsuhiko Sasakai, Hiroyuki Kawase, Yutaka Hayashi, Robert Dunham; *D:* Jun Fukuda; *W:* Jun Fukuda, Shinichi Sekizawa; *M:* Richiro Manabe. **VHS, LV** $19.95 *NOS, MRV, NWV*

Godzilla Vs. Monster Zero

The denizens of mysterious Planet X have an offer for their new neighbors on Earth: King Ghidrah (whom the numerically minded X-ites have given the designation "0") is ravaging their world, and they want to bring Godzilla and Ro-

G

"Beware the big green dragon that sits on your doorstep... he eats little boys."
--Bela Lugosi in *Glen or Glenda?*, for no apparent reason.

123

Cult Flicks and Trash Pics

Story continued...

by producer Joseph E. Levine. Feeling that a
Japanese film might have trouble drawing an
audience less than ten years after WWII, Levine
integrated the film with new footage shot with
actor Raymond Burr, playing news service
reporter Steve Martin. Levine's version was also
a big success. Incidentally, the subtitled U.S.
version also had a successful run in Japan,
reportedly drawing howls of laughter in the
scenes in which Martin's translator appears to
be lying to him about what various characters
are saying.

With their monster star dead, Toho created a
second Godzilla and a new monster, Angilas, for
the sequel. The American version of this sequel,
known variously as *Gigantis the Fire Monster and
Godzilla Raids Again*, is a confusing mess, with
both monsters' names being sometimes used for
the other. This second Godzilla would go on to
star in 13 more sequels of widely varying
quality, finishing up in the '70s with a series
of cartoonish entries similar to the superhero
TV shows popular in Japan at the time. In the
mid-'80s, Toho produced a different sequel to
the original, *Godzilla 1985*, which theorizes
that the monster took 30 years to recover from
his apparent death, and ignores the entire
history of the second Godzilla. This sequel was
also a big hit and was also released to U.S.
theatres in an Americanized version with Raymond
Burr, to only moderate success. This has led to
a very successful revival of the series. The
latest four Godzilla films (with another due in
December 1995) have yet to be released in
America, despite plans for a big budget remake
by a U.S. studio.

While an ever more popular cultural icon in
Japan, Godzilla's reputation in America has
suffered quite a bit, mainly because the worst
films in the series are also the most
accessibleone of the worst, *Godzilla vs.
Megalon*, has become a staple of every two-bit
video label, due to the fact that it's somehow
come to be considered public domain (although
it's hard to see why a movie starring such a
heavily copyrighted character would be subject
to free use). Add to this the fact that while
most of the series was filmed in widescreen

continued...

dan there to drive him off, just as they kicked him off Earth. In return for the use of our monster exterminators, they offer a cure for all known diseases. Is the offer genuine, or are the X-ites, as astronaut Glenn (Adams) puts it: "Double-crossing finks!"? The answer comes when all three monsters are unleashed against the Earth. Despite the shaky logic of the plot, this direct sequel to *Ghidrah the Three-Headed Monster* remains one of the more entertaining entries in Toho's monster series. The addition of Adams as the hipster astronaut (at the suggestion of producer Henry Saperstein) provides as much amusement from his daddy-o dialogue and manner as it does the intended Anglo identification. Released in the U.S. in 1970 on a twin bill with *War of the Gargantuas*. **AKA:** Monster Zero; Battle of the Astros; Invasion of the Astro-Monsters; Invasion of the Astros; Invasion of Planet X; Kaiju Daisenso. 🦴🦴🦴▷
1968 (G) 93m/C JP Akira Takarada, Nick Adams, Kimi Mizuno, Jun Tazaki, Akira Kubo; **D:** Inoshiro Honda; **W:** Shinichi Sekizawa; **M:** Akira Ifukube. **VHS, Beta, LV $19.95** *PAR, FUS*

Godzilla Vs. Mothra

When the egg of giant monster Mothra is washed ashore by a storm, a greedy entrepreneur is quick to exploit it. Meanwhile, Godzilla reappears and goes on a rampage. Help is sought from the dying Mothra through her psychic link to the miniature twin princesses (played again by singers Yumi & Emi Ito), but she refuses until the egg is threatened. Excellent in all departments, this is a clear favorite among Godzilla fans. The contrast between the sci-fi based Godzilla and the more fantasy-oriented Mothra works wonderfully, with the lively script offering imaginative surprises at every turn. The characters are interesting and Godzilla, who seems to be really enjoying his reign of destruction, shows more personality than in previous appearances. Except for a sequence added at the request of American International, in which Godzilla is attacked by U.S. Navy missiles, the U.S. version is nearly the same as the original, and the dubbing was done decently. Unfortunately, half the image is lost in the cropped video release. **AKA:** Godzilla vs. the Thing; Godzilla vs. the Giant Moth; Godzilla Fights the Giant Moth; Mothra vs. Godzilla; Mosura Tai Goira. 🦴🦴🦴🦴

1964 88m/C JP Akira Takarada, Yuriko Hoshi, Hiroshi Koizumi; **D:** Inoshiro Honda. **VHS, Beta** **$19.95** PAR, FUS

Goldfinger

Ian Fleming's James Bond, Agent 007, attempts to prevent international gold smuggler Goldfinger and his pilot Pussy Galore from robbing Fort Knox. Features villainous assistant Oddjob and his deadly bowler hat. The third in the series is perhaps the most popular. Shirley Bassey sings the theme song. The laserdisc edition includes audio interviews with the director, the writer, the editor, and the production designer; music and sound effects/ dialogue separation; publicity stills, movie posters, trailers, and on-location photos. A treat for Bond fans. 🦴🦴🦴

1964 (PG) 117m/C GB Sean Connery, Honor Blackman, Gert Frobe, Shirley Eaton, Tania Mallet, Harold Sakata, Cec Linder, Bernard Lee, Lois Maxwell, Desmond Llewelyn, Nadja Regin; **D:** Guy Hamilton; **M:** John Barry. Academy Awards '64: Best Sound Effects Editing. **VHS, Beta, LV $19.98** MGM, CRC, TLF

The Gore-Gore Girls

Splatter horror director Lewis' final film follows a dapper detective's light-hearted search for a madman who's been mutilating and killing beautiful young bar dancers, much in the tradition of Italian thrillers like Blood and Black Lace. The violence is much more grim in this one; the mutilation of the corpses goes on for a long time, and the gritty, cheap photography adds to the realism. Lewis is the only director that has us spend more time with the victim after the murder than before. Henny Youngman drops in as himself in a strip club scene. Sick stuff that delivers the goods—not to be taken seriously. After this, Lewis continued his career as a direct mail advertising expert, amassing a huge fortune. 🦴🦴🐾

1972 84m/C Frank Kress, Amy Ferrell, Henny Youngman; **D:** Herschell Gordon Lewis. **VHS $19.99** MOV

Gore-Met Zombie Chef From Hell

The premise works for the Hound: an ancient demon opens a modern-day restaurant and slaughters one sleazy customer to feed the

next. And the title intrigued the Hound as well; he happily expected some slappy Troma schlock, but was disappointed to view a crude, humorless, graphic, and somehow depressingly gratuitious slash-and-gore piece— all of which could be good if it were funny or at least a little scary, but this one just doesn't seem to work. Best appreciated for its title, and that's about it. **WOOF!**

1987 90m/C Theo Depuay, Kelley Kunicki, C.W. Casey, Alan Marx, Michael O'Neill; **D:** Don Swan. **VHS, Beta** NO

Grand Theft Auto

TV star Ron Howard agreed to be in Eat My Dust in exchange for the chance to direct his first feature. A young couple elopes to Las Vegas in a gold Rolls Royce owned by the bride's father. The father, totally against the marriage and angered by the stolen Rolls, offers a reward for the safe return of the daughter and the car. A cross-country race and media event ensues, with everybody either out to get the reward for the young couple, or cheering them on. A promising start for the popular director, which did well at the drive-ins. 🦴🦴

1977 (PG) 84m/C Ron Howard, Nancy Morgan, Marion Ross, Barry Cahill, Clint Howard; **D:** Ron Howard; **W:** Ron Howard. **VHS, Beta $19.98** WAR

Grease

Film version of the hit Broadway musical about the trials and tribulations summer love must endure in order to survive the pressures of high school society. Nice girl Olivia Newton-John discovers that if she sings lame middle-of-the-road pop treacle and dresses like a tart, she will not lose her leather-jacketed summer boyfriend John Travolta, who must place status quo above personal desire. A cameo by Frankie Avalon singing "Beauty School Dropout" is fun, as well as music by the Sha-Na-Nas. Question: when the animated hot dog jumps into the bun at the climax of the concession stand advertisement, is the mockery intentional or simply a delusion induced by John Travolta's repressed libido? Followed by a weak sequel with none other than Michelle Pfeiffer as Olivia's successor. 🎵 Grease; Summer Nights; Hopelessly Devoted To You; You're the One That I Want; Sandy;

G

Story continued...

scope and stereo, they are almost exclusively seen in the U.S. in washed out, heavily edited, poorly dubbed, cropped, mono versions. And then, of course, there's simple racism.

But a growing cult of stateside fans is erupting around the big greenish-grey reptile who are crying out for quality video releases of the films in their original glory (with subtitles). Whether they see him as a campy rubber hero, a symbol of nuclear horror, a gigantic shadowy enigma, or a combination of all three, more and more people are becoming fascinated with the character. In the West, after 40 years, Godzilla is finally coming into his own.

Beauty School Dropout; Look at Me, I'm Sandra Dee; Greased Lightnin'; It's Raining on Prom Night. 🦴🦴🦴

1978 (PG) 110m/C John Travolta, Olivia Newton-John, Jeff Conaway, Stockard Channing, Eve Arden, Frankie Avalon, Sid Caesar; **D:** Randal Kleiser. People's Choice Awards '79: Best Film; Nominations: Academy Awards '78: Best Song ("Hopelessly Devoted to You"). **VHS, Beta, LV $14.95** *PAR, FCT*

Greetings

If all you know about Brian DePalma, the man who would be Hitchcock, is *Carrie, Dressed to Kill,* and *Scarface,* have we got a movie for you. His debut feature is a revelation, an exuberant underground romp through late-1960s New York City that plays like an X-rated episode of *The Monkees.* Robert DeNiro stars as a voyeuristic filmmaker. Gerritt Graham is obsessed with the Kennedy assassination. Jonathan Warden wants to avoid the draft. A bit dated, but infectious fun. DeNiro's character returned in a sequel of sorts, *Hi, Mom.* Also worth seeking out is DePalma's nonconformist comedy, *Get to Know Your Rabbit,* starring Tommy Smothers. 🦴🦴🦴

1968 (R) 88m/C Robert De Niro, Gerrit Graham, Allen (Goorwitz) Garfield; **D:** Brian DePalma; **W:** Brian DePalma. **VHS, Beta, LV $79.95** *VMK*

The Groove Tube

Twenty-five years of *Saturday Night Live* have long since dulled the edge off this series of satirical and scatological sketches that lampoon television. *Kentucky Fried Movie* holds up much better, but there are some classic bits among the misses (and isn't that what the fast-forward is for?). Still crazy after all these years: Kids show host Koko the Clown reading dirty books on the air; a VD awareness commercial, and producer-director Ken Shapiro as a blissed-out man in a pink pin-stripe suit dancing down the streets of New York. Look for Richard Belzer and, in his film debut, Chevy Chase. 🦴🦴▷

1972 (R) 75m/C Lane Sarasohn, Chevy Chase, Richard Belzer, Marcy Mendham, Bill Kemmill; **D:** Ken Shapiro. **VHS, Beta $19.95** *MED*

Grotesque

Blair comes in for more grueling abuse, as the plucky daughter in family massacred by overacting punks at a remote mountain lodge. After a while—a long while—the household's secret resident, a mutant hunchback son locked away from the world, breaks out and attacks the marauders, while plastic-surgeon uncle Tab Hunter knows some payback tricks of his own. It's a weak finish to a formula revenge plot, played too straight to be funny and too badly to be shocking, though there are obviously ambitions to be both. Filmed at Big Bear Lake, of all places. WOOF!

1987 (R) 79m/C Linda Blair, Tab Hunter, Guy Stockwell, Donna Wilkes, Nels Van Patten; **D:** Joe Tornatore. **VHS, Beta, LV $79.95** *MED*

Gruesome Twosome

"The most barbaric humor since the guillotine went out of style," said the pressbook for this outlandish horror comedy. Another guts/cannibalism/mutilation fun-fest by Lewis, about a boarding house landlady who's marketing wigs made from the hair of some very recently deceased college coeds. Her maniac son, kept locked in the cellar, takes care of the dirty work. Caught out of time and money, and short on running time, a long opening scene was improvised using mannequins and wigs as puppets. This was one of six features made by Lewis in 1967. 🦴🦴

1967 75m/C Elizabeth Davis, Chris Martell; **D:** Herschell Gordon Lewis. **VHS, Beta $39.98** *NO*

Gun Crazy

Annie Laurie Starr—Annie Oakley in a Wild West show—meets gun-lovin' Bart Tare, who says a gun makes him feel good inside, "like I'm somebody." Sparks fly, and the two get married and live happily ever after—until the money runs out and fatal femme Laurie's craving for excitement and violence starts to flare up. The two become lovebirds-on-the-lam. Now a cult fave, it's based on a MacKinlay Kantor story. Ex-stuntman Russell Harlan's photography is daring; the realism of the impressive robbery scenes is owed in part to the technical consultation of former train robber Al Jennings. And watch for a young Tamblyn as the 14-year-old Bart. *AKA:* Deadly is the Female. 🎵🎵🎵

1949 87m/B Peggy Cummins, John Dall, Berry Kroeger, Morris Carnovsky, Anabel Shaw, Nedrick Young, Trevor Bardette, Russ Tamblyn; *D:* Joseph H. Lewis. **VHS $19.98** *FOX, FCT*

The Gunslinger

When the town marshall is gunned down, his widow (Garland) takes over the job—struggling to keep law and order in a town overrun by outlaws while trying to catch her husband's killer. She's not afraid of any man, or even saloon owner Allison Hayes. Unique western has lots of action, Garland punching out bad guys in her tight jeans, and a surprise ending. One of two Westerns directed by Corman in the mid-'50s for American International, the other being *Apache Woman* (1955). 🎵🎵

1956 83m/C John Ireland, Beverly Garland, Allison Hayes, Jonathan Haze, Dick Miller, Bruno Ve Sota; *D:* Roger Corman; *W:* Charles B. Griffith. **VHS $19.95** *MLB, TIM, SNC*

Hairspray

Waters' first truly mainstream film, and one of his funniest. Details the struggle among teenagers in 1962 Baltimore for the top spot in a local TV dance show. Deals with racism and stereotypes, as well as typical "teen" problems (hair-do's and don'ts). Filled with near-tasteful social satire (although not without typical Waters touches that will please die-hard fans; the scene with Debbie Harry and a zit is more early Waterseque). Lake is lovable and appealing as Divine's daughter; Divine, in his last film, is convincing as an iron-

toting, muu-muu wearing mom. Look for Waters in a cameo and Divine as a man. Creative casting brings us Sonny Bono, Deborah Harry, Ric Ocasek of the Cars, and Pia Zadora in supporting roles. Great '60s music, which Waters refers to as "the only known remedy to today's Hit Parade of Hell." 🎵🎵🎵

1988 (PG) 94m/C Ricki Lake, Divine, Jerry Stiller, Colleen Fitzpatrick, Sonny Bono, Deborah Harry, Ruth Brown, Pia Zadora, Ric Ocasek, Michael St. Gerard, Leslie Ann Powers, Shawn Thompson, Clayton Prince, Mink Stole, Mary Vivian Pearce, Susan Lowe; *Cameos:* John Waters; *D:* John Waters; *W:* John Waters. **VHS, Beta, LV $14.95** *COL, FCT*

Halloween

John Carpenter's horror classic has been acclaimed "the most successful independent motion picture of all time." A deranged young man returns to his hometown with murderous intent after fifteen years in an asylum. Is he just a murder obsessed maniac, or possibly a vessel for absolute evil? Very, very scary—you feel this movie more than see it. Owes much of its success to Carpenter's eerie electronic soundtrack, which was influenced by that of *The Exorcist* and those of Italian director Dario Argento. Pleasence became a great cult favorite as a result of his role as the terrified yet obsessed psychiatrist Dr. Loomis. Followed by five sequels and scores of imitators. Carpenter went on to a hit-and-miss career, his best being *The Thing, Escape from New York, Big Trouble in Little China,* and the underappreciated *Memoirs of an Invisible Man.* 🎵🎵🎵🎵

1978 (R) 90m/C Jamie Lee Curtis, Donald Pleasence, P.J. Soles; *D:* John Carpenter; *W:* John Carpenter, Debra Hill; *M:* John Carpenter. **VHS, Beta, LV $19.98** *MED, VTR*

Happy Birthday to Me

Virginia (Melissa Sue Anderson) is a student at the elite Crawford Academy with some wild friends. She is troubled by her mom's death, and even more so when her psychiatrist reveals to her that she is a "very successful guinea pig" in an experiment regarding repressed memories. To top it off, she's plagued by ominous background music that generally never comes to fruition. Meanwhile, her friends are being murdered by someone they know (the classic dying line, "Oh, it's you!..."), in creative bloody ways that are the hallmark

> **"Your ratted hair is preventing yet another student's geometry education.... Whatever you call it, it's a hair-don't!"**
>
> —Tracy (Ricki Lake) Turnblad's teacher in *Hairspray.*

> **"I'm running for mayor...and I can't be in a freaky, weird movie right now."**
>
> —Sonny Bono in his biography, *And the Beat Goes On,* recalling his comments to John Waters regarding *Hairspray.*

127

Cult Flicks and Trash Pics

Kong cop who's out to shut down a gun-running operation. Two rival gangs are fighting for control of the business and an undercover cop is working for one of them. That's really all there is to the plot. Like Sam Peckinpah, Woo is more interested in elaborately choreographed action sequences, and the moral aftereffects of violence. Those two sides of the film come together in a long, impossible-to-describe finale involving dozens of characters in a hospital. Visually, this is one of Woo's most ambitious and inventive films. He uses freeze frames and various speeds of slow motion to punctuate key moments. Unfortunately, the dubbing on the tape version isn't as effective. The subtitled and letterboxed Criterion laserdisc is far superior. In either version, *Hard Boiled* is required viewing for action fans. *AKA:* Lashou Shentan. ♫♫♫♫

1992 126m/C *HK* Chow Yun-fat, Tony Leung, Philip Chan, Anthony Wong, Teresa Mo; **D:** John Woo; **W:** Barry Wong; **M:** Michael Gibbs. **VHS $92.98** *ORI, FCT*

Jimmy Cliff transforms a band of killers into a killer band in Roger Corman's *The Harder They Come.*

of trash horror (the one concession to originality is that they are at least not dying during sex). Is it Alfred, the misfit friend who not-so-secretly has a crush on Virginia? The resentful dean, Mrs. Patterson, who admonishes Virginia that "you and all your gang...you think that because you are rich you can sneer at people who have had to work hard...that you can do just as you please. Well, I'm afraid it doesn't work that way...." Fairly tame horror, but it's fun to see something more exciting than a covered wagon in the Big Woods for Anderson. For some real Anderson schlock, try and catch *Midnight Offerings*, a teenage witch tale that would put Sabrina to shame (the flick also boasts a brief appearance of Vanna White as a cheerleader). ♫♫

1981 (R) 108m/C *CA* Melissa Sue Anderson, Glenn Ford, Lawrence Dane, Sharon Acker, Frances Hyland, Tracy Bregman, Jack Blum, Matt Craven, Lenore Zann, David Eisner, Richard Rebrere, Lesleh Donaldson; **D:** J. Lee Thompson. **VHS, Beta, LV $69.95** *COL*

Hard-Boiled

This action masterpiece is one of John Woo's best. Chow Yun-Fat is Tequila, a tough Hong

A Hard Day's Night

Yesterday, all their troubles seemed so far away. But in the beginning, there was *Beatlemania,* captured in all its exhilaration by Richard Lester's "day-in-the-life" romp that hits the ground running and never slows down. John, Paul, George, and Ringo elude screaming fans, attend a press conference, and tape a television special. Wilfred Brambell, who portrays Paul's "very clean" grandfather, starred in the English TV series *Steptoe and Son,* which was Americanized as *Sanford and Son.* Patti Boyd, seen as a receptionist, became Mrs. George Harrison. Rock legend has it that she is "Layla." A companion video, *You Can't Do That: The Making of A Hard Day's Night,* is also available. It includes the premiere of "You Can't Do That," a performance deleted from the film, interviews. and behind-the-scenes footage. Phil Collins, who was one of those screaming teenagers, hosts. ♫♫ A Hard Day's Night; Tell Me Why; I Should Have Known Better; She Loves You; I'm Happy Just To Dance With You; If I Fell; And I Love Her; This Boy; Can't Buy Me Love. ♫♫♫♫

1964 90m/B *GB* John Lennon, Paul McCartney, George Harrison, Ringo Starr; **D:** Richard Lester.

Nominations: Academy Awards '64: Best Story & Screenplay, Best Original Score. **VHS, Beta, LV, CD-I $19.98** *MVD, MPI, CRC*

Hard Target

Woo's first American film is another version of *The Most Dangerous Game,* with wealthy hunters stalking combat veterans in New Orleans' French Quarter. It's a fitting vehicle for the Hong Kong director's full-bore style, though this isn't his best movie. Van Damme is fine in the lead; villains Vosloo and Henriksen are better. Henriksen's bizarre "Load me" moment—improvised on the set—is genuinely twisted. Throughout, the action is outlandish with inventive stunt work and one really neat mechanical rattlesnake. 🦴🦴🦴

1993 (R) 97m/C Jean-Claude Van Damme, Lance Henriksen, Yancy Butler, Arnold Vosloo, Wilford Brimley, Kasi Lemmons; **D:** John Woo; **W:** Chuck Pfarrer; **M:** Graeme Revell. Nominations: MTV Movie Awards '94: Most Desirable Male (Van Damme), Best Action Sequence. **VHS, LV $14.98** *MCA, BTV*

The Harder They Come

The movie that brought reggae music to America and was a perennial on the 1970s midnight movie circuit. Jimmy Cliff stars as Ivan, a country boy who arrives in the city to find his fame and fortune as a singer. Ripped off by a record producer, he instead makes a name for himself in the local ganja trade and becomes one of Kingston's Most Wanted after killing a policeman. That's when his record really climbs the charts, proving "You Can Get It If You Really Want." The film and a subsequent novel by Michael Thelwell were based on the exploits of Rhygin, a gunman and folk hero who lived in and around Kingston in the 1950s. The indispensable soundtrack features Cliff, Desmond Dekker, and Toots and the Maytels, and includes such reggae standards as "Sitting in Limbo," "Many Rivers to Cross," "Pressure Drop," and the title tune. 🦴🦴▷

1972 (R) 93m/C Jimmy Cliff, Janet Barkley, Carl Bradshaw; **D:** Perry Henzell. **VHS, Beta, LV $19.95** *CRC, FCT*

Hardware Wars and other Film Farces

Indie filmmaker/actor Ernie Fosselius created one of most successful short subjects ever with his 1977 parody of *Star Wars* starring a vacuum cleaner as R2D2, an "Oz"-style tin man as C3PO, and a general emphasis on common household appliances for Lucasfilm-scale starships and special effects. The homemade effort packs more laughs than *Spaceballs* into a fraction of the running time. This tape compilation also includes Fosselius' *Apocalypse Now* spoof centered on a deli; *Porklips Now*; the self-explanatory *Closet Cases of the Nerd Kind*; and Marv Newland's infamous cartoon snippet *Bambi Meets Godzilla.* 🦴🦴🦴▷

1978 51m/C D: Ernie Fosselius. **VHS, Beta** *PYR*

Harold and Maude

Cult classic pairs Bud Cort as a dead-pan disillusioned 20-year-old obsessed with suicide (his staged attempts are a highlight) and a loveable Ruth Gordon as a fun-loving 80-year-old eccentric. They meet at a funeral (a mutual hobby), and develop a taboo romantic relationship, in which they explore the tired theme of the meaning of life with a fresh perspective. The script was originally the 20-minute long graduate thesis of UCLA student

January-December romance: Bud Cort and Ruth Gordon in *Harold and Maude.*

129

Cult Flicks and Trash Pics

Higgins, who showed it to his landlady, wife of film producer Lewis. Features music by Cat Stevens. 🦴🦴🦴🦴

1971 **(PG) 92m/C** Ruth Gordon, Bud Cort, Cyril Cusack, Vivian Pickles, Charles Tyner, Ellen Geer, Eric Christmas, G. Wood, Gordon Devol; **D:** Hal Ashby; **W:** Colin Higgins; **M:** Cat Stevens. **VHS, Beta, LV, 8mm $14.95** *PAR*

The Haunted Palace

Price plays both a 17th-century warlock burned at the stake and a descendant who returns to the family dungeon and gets possessed by the mutant-breeding forebearer. The movie has its own identity crisis, with title and ambience from Poe but story from H.P. Lovecraft's "The Case of Charles Dexter Ward." Respectable but rootless chills, also available with the quasi-Lovecraft *Curse of the Crimson Altar* on laser disc. 🦴🦴 ▷

1963 **87m/C** Vincent Price, Debra Paget, Lon Chaney Jr., Frank Maxwell, Leo Gordon, Elisha Cook Jr., John Dierkes; **D:** Roger Corman. **VHS, Beta, LV $59.98** *HBO, MLB*

The Haunting

Four characters in search of...? A subtle, bloodless horror film about a weekend spent in a monstrously haunted mansion by a parapsychologist, the mansion's skeptic heir, and two mediums. A chilling adaptation of Shirley Jackson's *The Haunting of Hill House,* in which the psychology of the heroine is forever in question. The house itself is a perfect masterpiece of art direction. Another classic from director Wise. Knowing that the terror is invisible here, he explores the horror of inanimate objects, while the soundtrack roars and whispers. 🦴🦴🦴🦴

1963 **113m/B** Julie Harris, Claire Bloom, Russ Tamblyn, Richard Johnson; **D:** Robert Wise. **VHS, Beta, LV $19.98** *MGM, FCT*

He Knows You're Alone

Psycho guy jilted by his fiancee snaps, kills her, and vows to kill every woman engaged to be married in his small town. Among the stalked are Amy (O'Heaney), a bride to be, and her friends (including ex-boyfriend, Dan Scardino of *Squirm*). Standard slasher film with doses of gore and horror in moderate

amounts and relatively interesting characters. The real highlight is seeing Tom Hanks' screen debut (in a bit part). 🦴

1980 **(R) 94m/C** Don Scardino, Elizabeth Kemp, Tom Rolfing, Paul Gleason, Caitlin O'Heaney, Tom Hanks, Patsy Pease; **D:** Armand Mastroianni; **W:** Scott Parker. **VHS, Beta $59.95** *MGM*

Head

Infamously plotless musical comedy written by Jack Nicholson and starring the television pre-fab four of the '60s, the Monkees, in their only film appearance. A number of guest stars appear and a collection of old movie clips are also included. It's all an inspired send-up of the entertainment industry, with a cameo by Victor Mature as "the Big Victor" (as in RCA), a haughty laughing giant who tries to crush the boys underfoot. Some of the little-known songs rank with the group's best. The title was allegedly chosen so that a sequel could be advertised as "From the people who gave you *Head.*" 🎵 Circle Sky; Can You Dig It; Long Title: Do I Have To Do This All Over Again; Daddy's Song; As We Go Along; The Porpoise Song. 🦴🦴🦴

1968 **(G) 86m/C** Peter Tork, Mickey Dolenz, Davy Jones, Michael Nesmith, Frank Zappa, Annette Funicello, Teri Garr; **D:** Bob Rafelson; **W:** Jack Nicholson, Bob Rafelson. **VHS, Beta, LV $19.98** *RHI, COL, MVD*

Heat

Four years of superstardom begin to take their toll on Joe Dallesandro as evidenced by the tired state of affairs in this disappointing variation on the theme of Billy Wilder's *Sunset Boulevard.* The has-been movie star is played by Sylvia Miles, a casting coup for the Warhol gang, as she formerly appeared in the Troy Donahue camp classic, *Parrish,* and had a role in the prestigious *Midnight Cowboy.* Location news: most of the picture was shot at Los Angeles' infamous Tropicana Motel, where Tom Waits resided during the '70s, composing his early piano ballads there. 🦴🦴 ▷

1972 **102m/C** Joe Dallesandro, Sylvia Miles, Pat Ast; **D:** Paul Morrissey. **VHS, Beta $29.95** *TPV, PAR, FCT*

Heathers

Clique of stuck-up girls named Heather rule the high school social scene until the newest member (Winona Ryder's Veronica) decides that enough is enough. She and outlaw boyfriend J.D. embark (accidentally on her part, intentionally on his) on a murder spree disguised as a rash of teen suicides. Dense, take-no-prisoners black comedy with buckets of potent slang, satire, and unforgiving hostility. Humor this dark is rare; sharply observed and acted, though the ending is a bit of a cop out. Slater does his best Nicholson impression as the deeply disturbed J.D., whose twisted past and jaded outlook on life make him truly hate the hypocrisy and downright cruelty that occur everyday at every high school in America. Before her star turn on *Beverly Hills 90210* (where she symbolized everything this movie loves to hate), Shannon Doherty really had to stretch to play one of the bitchy Heathers. 🦴🦴🦴◁

1989 (R) 102m/C Winona Ryder, Christian Slater, Kim Walker, Shannen Doherty, Lisanne Falk, Penelope Milford, Glenn Shadix, Lance Fenton, Patrick Laborteaux, Jeremy Applegate; *D:* Michael Lehmann; *W:* Daniel Waters; *M:* David Newman. Edgar Allan Poe Awards '89: Best Screenplay; Independent Spirit Awards '90: Best First Feature. **VHS, Beta, LV $19.95** *STE, NWV, FCT*

Heavy Metal

This film features a series of animated S.F. and fantasy stories adapted from the magazine of the same title. Told with a variety of styles all encompass the theme of good versus evil (don't always bet on good). Best of the tales is Den, based on a character created by Richard Corbin. In a fluke happening a teenage boy finds his mind transferred across space and time to the body of a mighty warrior. The man-child Den is thrust into an ages old fight between religious cults, rescues barebreasted babes, and has a general, all around good time. Featuring a sound track compiled from the work of many top metal artists of the time, *Heavy Metal* was released on video for only a brief period. Copyright disputes, unresolved as of this writing, got it yanked from distribution. Used copies sell for as much as $300 in the secondary market, though boot

Heathers. "Not you, Heather... I'm talking to HEATHER."

copies are readily available at comic book shows and the like. ♫♫♫♫

1981 90m/C *CA* **V:** Roger Bumpass, John Candy, Jackie Burrows, Joe Flaherty, Dan Francks, Eugene Levy; **D:** Gerald Potterton. **VHS $9.98** *OM*

Hellhole

A young woman who witnesses her mother's murder is sent to a sanitarium where the doctors are perfecting chemical lobotomies. A very dumb but outlandish take on women in prison films. Is it a must for trash cinema lovers? Well, where else can you find perpetual airhead Judy Landers vs. long-time trash queen Mary Woronov? The casting alone makes it a must see. Amnesiac Landers must contend with mad scientist Woronov (who uses the inmates for her own evil experiments, not to mention as lesbian playthings) and the killer who wants to see her dead before her memory returns. All your favorite cliches raise their dear little heads, but they don't detract from the film. Rather, it's fun to see what this unlikely group does with them. Everybody meets a suitable ending, of course, leaving the trash cinema viewer feeling like he's visited an old friend. ♫♫♫

1985 (R) 93m/C Judy Landers, Ray Sharkey, Mary Woronov, Marjoe Gortner, Edy Williams, Terry Moore, Dyanne Thorne; **D:** Pierre De Moro. **VHS, Beta, LV $14.95** *COL*

Hell's Angels Forever

A revealing ride into the world of honor, violence, and undying passion for motorcycles on the road. Documentary was filmed with cooperation of the Angels. Features appearances by Willie Nelson, Jerry Garcia, Bo Diddley, Kevin Keating, and Johnny Paycheck. ♫♫♫

1983 (R) 93m/C Willie Nelson, Jerry Garcia, Johnny Paycheck, Bo Diddley; **D:** Richard Chase. **VHS, Beta $59.95** *MED*

Hell's Angels on Wheels

As gas station attendant/poet, Jack Nicholson is an uneasy rider when he is invited to join a group of Hell's Angels led by Adam Roarke, the kind of guy you want to have around when you're stomped by sailors, but a must to avoid if you hook up with his old lady during an orgy. In the year of the biker film, this was the big hit (even the Angels endorsed it). Producer Joe Solomon is most fondly remembered as the advance publicist for the infamous birth-of-a-baby exploitation classic, *Mom and Dad.* After the success of *Hells Angels on Wheels,* he produced *Angels From Hell* and *Run, Angel Run.* Director Richard Rush is anything but prolific. After the cult classic *The Stunt Man,* it would be 14 years before directing the erotic thriller, *Color of Night,* which gained notoriety as the film in which star Bruce showed his Willis. Cinematographer Laszlo Kovacs later lensed *Easy Rider, Five Easy Pieces, Whats Up, Doc, Paper Moon, Shampoo, New York, New York,* and *The Last Waltz.* ♫♫▷

1967 95m/C Jack Nicholson, Adam Roarke, Sabrina Scharf, Jana Taylor, John Garwood; **D:** Laszlo Kovacs, Richard Rush. **VHS, Beta $39.95** *VMK*

Help!

Ringo becomes the target of a cult that will do anything to get the sacred ring that is stuck on his finger. The Beatles's second film is a surreal departure from the pseudo-documentary style of *A Hard Day's Night.* Unrelentingly silly and wears thin after awhile, but the great music takes up the slack. Victor Spinetti, the TV director in *A Hard Day's Night,* returns as the mad doctor who wants to rule the world. Roy Kinnear, a Lester regular who died on the set of Lester's *Return of the Musketeers,* is his assistant. Eleanor Bron was the waitress for whom Dudley Moore was willing to sell his soul to the Devil in *Bedazzled.* The laserdisc version includes a wealth of Beatles memorabilia, rare footage behind the scenes and at the film's premiere, and extensive publicity material. ♫♫ Help!; You're Gonna Lose That Girl; You've Got To Hide Your Love Away; The Night Before; Another Girl; Ticket To Ride; I Need You. ♫♫♫

1965 (G) 90m/C John Lennon, Paul McCartney, Ringo Starr, George Harrison, Leo McKern, Eleanor Bron, Victor Spinetti, Roy Kinnear; **D:** Richard Lester; **W:** Charles Wood, Marc Behm. **VHS, Beta, LV $19.98** *MPI, MVD, CRC*

Helter Skelter

This TV mini-series chronicles the harrowing story of the murder of actress Sharon Tate and four others at the hands of Charles Manson and his psychotic "family." Based on the book by prosecutor Vincent Bugliosi, adapted by J.P. Miller. Features an outstanding performance by Railsback as Manson. 🎞🎞🎞

1976 194m/C Steve Railsback, Nancy Wolfe, George DiCenzo, Marilyn Burns; **D:** Tom Gries; **M:** Billy Goldenberg. **VHS, Beta $59.98** *FOX*

Henry: Portrait of a Serial Killer

One of the most disturbing and frightening horror films anyone has ever made. Henry (chillingly underplayed by Rooker) is an illiterate drifter who moves from job to job, and kills at random. Though Henry claims to have been abused as a child, that doesn't explain him. Neither does the sexual element that some of the murders contain. Killing is simply something he does without emotion or pleasure. McNaughton tells the story with a deliberately flat, documentary style: stark naturalistic lighting and acting, Midwest locations, grainy color, limited music. The film

was rated X for violence and subject matter, but has been released on tape without a rating. In terms of on-screen acts of violence, *Henry* contains only a tiny fraction of the lurid excesses of a *Friday the 13th* or *Elm Street.* flick. But *Henry* is a real nightmare and these suggested horrors—including an unexpected ending—are much more terrifying than graphic cinematic schlock. 🎞🎞🎞

1990 (X) 90m/C Michael Rooker, Tom Towles, Tracy Arnold; **D:** John McNaughton; **W:** Richard Fire, John McNaughton. **VHS, Beta, LV $79.98** *MPI*

Hercules Against the Moon Men

It's no holds barred for the mighty son of Zeus when evil moon men start killing off humans in a desperate bid to revive their dead queen. One of a series of truly awful 1960s films about the giant warrior, this one featured the oh-so-masculine Alan Steel in the title role. His acting is wooden, but it's his odd appearance throughout much of the film that

It's called moisturizer. Look into it! *Hercules Against the Moonmen.*

in two equally unfortunate films. Somewhere, Steve Reeves is smiling. **AKA:** Hercules: The Movie; Hercules Goes Bananas. ♪

1970 (G) 93m/C Arnold Schwarzenegger, Arnold Stang, Deborah Loomis, James Karen, Ernest Graves; **D:** Arthur Seidelman. **VHS, Beta $59.98** *MPI*

The Hidden

A seasoned cop (Nouri) and a benign alien posing as an FBI agent (MacLachlan) team up to track down and destroy a hyper-violent alien criminal who survives by inhabiting the bodies of humans, using their bodies to go on murderous rampages. Much acclaimed, high-velocity action film with state-of-the-art special effects. MacLachlan's otherworldly FBI agent found echoes later when he starred in *Twin Peaks.* Followed by *The Hidden 2* (1995). ♪ ♪ ♪ ◁

1987 (R) 98m/C Kyle MacLachlan, Michael Nouri, Clu Gulager, Ed O'Ross, Claudia Christian, Clarence Felder, Richard Brooks, William Boyett; **D:** Jack Sholder; **W:** Bob Hunt; **M:** Michael Convertino. **VHS, Beta, LV $19.95** *MED, CDV, VTR*

Hideous Sun Demon

A physicist exposed to radiation must stay out of sunlight or he will turn into a scaly, lizard-like creature. Although commonly lumped in with most other '50s monster pictures, this one can also be taken as an allegory for alcoholism. Star/director Clarke hides from the Sun all day, but stays out all night in saloons, eventually alienating his friends as the monster within him gradually takes control. The scene of the maddened Clarke eating a rat was excised from most TV prints, but has been restored on video. **AKA:** Blood On His Lips; Terror From the Sun; The Sun Demon. ♪ ♪ ◁

1959 75m/B Robert Clarke, Patricia Manning, Nan Peterson; **D:** Robert Clarke. **VHS, Beta $9.95** *NOS, MRV, RHI*

High School Confidential

Dig Jerry Lee Lewis pounding out the title tune on a piano perched on a flat-bed truck. Dig Russ Tamblyn as the new bad boy at Santo Bello high school who talks tough ("You got thirty-two teeth, you wanna try for none?"), cracks wise, asks teacher Jan Sterling for a date, and resists relentless passes from his

A pack of Trojans (Ron Carey, Mary-Margaret Humes, Gregory Hines, and Mel Brooks) make history in *History of the World: Part 1.*

makes him look like a life-sized marionette. This one is so boring, you'll actually be happy when a huge sandstorm blows into town and makes the last half-hour of the movie almost unintelligible. Not even that fun to make fun of (although those wacky folks at *Mystery Science Theater 3000* gave it their best shot), it's really just kind of painful to watch. **AKA:** Maciste la Regina di Samar. ♪

1964 88m/C *IT FR* Alan Steel, Jany Clair, Anna Maria Polani; **D:** Giacomo Gentilomo. **VHS, Beta $16.95** *SNC, MRV*

Hercules in New York

One wonders if Arnold Schwarzenegger ever thought he'd be back after this inauspicious film debut as a Herculean mass of muscle sent by dad Zeus to Manhattan, where he behaves like a geek out of water and eventually becomes a professional wrestling superstar. The only possible reason to see this is to get a chuckle over his badly dubbed non-accented voice. If that's enough to sustain you for 93 minutes, be our guest. Schwarzenegger's body building rival Lou Ferrigno (see the documentary *Pumping Iron*) later played Hercules

"aunt" Mamie Van Doren. Dig Jackie Coogan (Uncle Fester from TV's *Addams Family*) as local drug lord Mr. X. Dig pre-*Bonanza* Michael Landon as the school straight arrow. Dig jive-talking John Drew Barrymore (Drew's dad!) and his hipster rendition of how Columbus discovered America. Dig it all, man. If you don't, you're from squaresville. *AKA:* Young Hellions. 🎵🎵🎵🎵

1958 85m/B Russ Tamblyn, Jan Sterling, John Blythe Barrymore Jr., Mamie Van Doren, Diane Jergens, Jerry Lee Lewis, Ray Anthony, Jackie Coogan, Charles Chaplin Jr., Burt Douglas, Michael Landon, Jody Fair, Phillipa Fallon, Robin Raymond, James Todd, Lyle Talbot, William Wellman Jr.; *D:* Jack Arnold. **VHS, Beta $14.98** *REP*

Highlander

A strange tale about an immortal 16th-century Scottish warrior who has had to battle his evil and equally immortal enemy through the centuries. The feud comes to blows in modern-day Manhattan. Connery makes a memorable appearance as the good warrior's mentor, but the film's real energy comes from spectacular battle and death scenes and a plot that defies comprehension. After becoming a surprise cult favorite for its flashy visual style, the film spawned weak sequels (which more or less jettisoned the already loose logic of the original) and a television series. Based on a story by Gregory Widen. Australian director Mulcahy also made the off-beat horror film, *Razorback*. 🎵🎵🎵

1986 (R) 110m/C Christopher Lambert, Sean Connery, Clancy Brown, Roxanne Hart, Beatie Edney, Alan North, Sheila Gish, Jon Polito; *D:* Russell Mulcahy; *W:* Gregory Widen, Peter Bellwood, Larry Ferguson; *M:* Michael Kamen. **VHS, Beta, LV $14.98** *REP*

Hillbillies in a Haunted House

Two country and western singers (Husky and Lansing) and their manager (Bowman), en route to the Nashville jamboree, encounter a group of foreign spies "haunting" a house. Lots of other country stars, such as Merle Haggard and Sonny James, perform—some by "dropping by" the house, others via television! The aging horror stars may have just been picking up a check, but they genuinely seem to be en-

joying themselves clowning around for a change. Around this same time, Boris Karloff was appearing in *Ghost in the Invisible Bikini* and Vincent Price starred in *Dr. Goldfoot and the Girl Bombs,* while other established talents were cavorting through episodes of *Batman,* so Carradine, Rathbone, and Chaney need not hang their heads. Features one of Rathbone's last film performances. George Barrows (*Robot Monster*) appears in his gorilla costume. Sequel to *Las Vegas Hillbillies* (1966). 🎵🎵

1967 88m/C Ferlin Husky, Joi Lansing, Don Bowman, John Carradine, Lon Chaney Jr., Basil Rathbone; *D:* Jean Yarbrough. **VHS, Beta $29.95** *VCI, AOV*

The Hills Have Eyes

A middle-class family from Cleveland is stranded in the California desert and meets the locals—a brutal tribe of cave-dwelling, inbred hillbilly cannibals. The cunning mutants attack without mercy, until the pitiful survivors strike back with a ferocity they didn't know they had. Theme of how "civilized" folk can shed their inhibitions and turn savage to survive is a familiar one, but Craven's sober-minded direction and the disturbingly powerful performances give the graphic gore-fest an real impact (even if that heroic Rin Tin Tin family dog is a bit much). The villains were inspired by the true-life Sawney Beane clan of old Scotland, whose foul deeds also fueled the 1991 video release *Blood Clan.* While Craven went on to bigger productions, his 1984 for-the-money follow-up *The Hills Have Eyes II* is best left ignored. 🎵🎵🎵

1977 (R) 83m/C Susan Lanier, Robert Houston, Martin Speer, Dee Wallace Stone, Russ Grieve, John Steadman, James Whitworth, Michael Berryman; *D:* Wes Craven; *W:* Wes Craven. **VHS, Beta, LV $19.95** *NO*

History of the World: Part 1

Brooks begins his cinematic spoof at the Dawn of Man with a parody of *2001* and hits the high spots between primordial humanity and the French Revolution, with narration by Orson Welles. Along the way, he's at his gross, tasteless, rambunctious best (or worst, depending on your point of view). Those who thought he went too far with the campfire

"**If you flake around with the weed, you'll end up using the harder stuff.**"
—Russ Tamblyn in *High School Confidential.*

"**Oh Bob? Do I have any openings that this man might fit?**"
—Empress Nympho (Madeline Kahn) asking her manservant if the new muscle-bound slave (Gregory Heines) could be put to good use in *History of the World: Part 1.*

1993 **(R) Rm/C** Max Parrish, Adrienne Shelly, Andrea Naschak, Sean Young, Diane Ladd, Bela Lehoczky, Ania Suli; *Cameos:* Timothy Leary; *D:* Joel Hershman; *W:* Joel Hershman. **VHS $92.98** *LIV*

Hold That Ghost

Abbott and Costello inherit a spooky abandoned roadhouse where the illicit loot of its former owner, a "rubbed out" mobster, is supposedly hidden. A&C's follow up to their *Buck Privates* was shelved for several months, due to the phenomenal success of the service comedy and the duo was hustled into the much more similar picture *In the Navy.* Although the main reason to put A&C in a haunted house was so they could include their famous candle routine (also seen in *Abbott & Costello Meet Frankenstein*), screenwriters Robert Lees and Fred Rinaldo crafted a solid comedy script for the team (with the usual special material by regular writer John Grant). Shemp Howard shows up for a small but familiar part as a soda jerk. Despite Universal's trepidation at sending out Abbott & Costello sans uniforms, *Hold That Ghost* was another huge hit for the team. *AKA:* Oh, Charlie. ♪♪♪

1941 86m/B Bud Abbott, Lou Costello, Joan Davis, Richard Carlson, Mischa Auer, The Andrews Sisters; *D:* Arthur Lubin. **VHS, Beta $14.95** *MCA*

scene in *Blazing Saddles* will find a lot to be offended by here. A good deal of the humor is based on sex and digestive functions, and the rest of it attacks organized religion. Overall, there are about as many hits as misses. Even Brooks' fans will have to admit that this one doesn't measure up to his earlier work. ♪♪♪

1981 **(R)** 90m/C Mel Brooks, Dom DeLuise, Madeline Kahn, Harvey Korman, Cloris Leachman, Gregory Hines, Pamela Stephenson, Paul Mazursky, Beatrice Arthur, Fritz Feld, John Hurt, Jack Carter, John Hillerman, John Gavin, Barry Levinson, Ron Carey, Howard Morris, Sid Caesar, Jackie Mason; *D:* Mel Brooks; *W:* Mel Brooks. **VHS, Beta, LV $14.98** *FOX*

Hold Me, Thrill Me, Kiss Me

Marriages don't get off to a much rockier start than they do in this comedy. Before the wedding is over, Eli (Parrish) and Twinkle (Young) are fighting. Then he sort of shoots her and steals her Porsche and a sack of cash. On the lam in a tacky pink trailer park, he becomes hopelessly entangled with his neighbors Sable (Naschak), a voracious topless dancer, and Danny (Shelly), her virginal younger sister. Overall, give first-time director Hershman credit for originality and irreverence. And he got solid performances from a motley cast, particularly Andrea Naschak, a former porn star who makes a brassy debut on legitimate video. ♪♪♪

Hollywood After Dark

Future TV star McClanahan plays a young starlet trying to make it big in Hollywood. When a producer asks her to come over for dinner and script reading, her boyfriend (who works in a junkyard—please note the symbolism) suspects there's a casting couch on the premises. Rue only plummets lower, even taking a job as (gasp) a stripper. Pure exploitation schlock, with overwrought dramatic acting which is not for the squeamish, although direction is well done. Contains bits of body-doubled nudity. Not released theatrically until 1968. Autuer Hayes also did an earlier Rue feature, *The Rotten Apple,* and later made the oddball horror epic *Grave of the Vampire.* ♪♪

1965 ?m/C Rue McClanahan; *D:* John Patrick Hayes; *W:* John Patrick Hayes. **VHS $16.95** *SNC, TPV*

Hollywood Boulevard

Producer Jon Davison bet Roger Corman that he could produce a film for $90,000. The result was this valentine to their mentor, an affectionate spoof of low budget, on-the-run exploitation filmmaking. The cast is a drive-in aficionado's dream, with Paul Bartel as the director of an ill-fated film for Miracle Pictures ("If it's good, it's a Miracle"), Candice Rialson as an aspiring actress, Mary Woronov as the Queen of the B's, and Dick Miller as agent Walter Paisley (his character's name in *A Bucket of Blood*). Along with the sex and violence there are in-jokes galore as well as generous helpings of stock footage from Corman-produced films. Directors Alan Arkush and Joe Dante got their start with Corman editing coming attractions. Arkush went on to direct *Rock and Roll High School.* Dante achieved his biggest success with *Gremlins.* 🦴🦴🦴

1976 (R) 93m/C Candice Rialson, Mary Woronov, Rita George, Jonathan Kaplan, Jeffrey Kramer, Dick Miller, Paul Bartel; **D:** Joe Dante, Allan Arkush. **VHS, Beta $39.98** *WAR, OM*

Hollywood Chainsaw Hookers

A campy, sexy, very bloody parody about attractive prostitutes who dismember their unsuspecting customers. Our story begins when a seedy, down-and-out P.I. is hired to find a runaway teen. It doesn't take long to find her working in a low-rent strip bar. He then discovers that she's hooked up with the Ancient Egyptian Chainsaw Cult. This film should be taken as seriously as it sounds. Over-the-top scenes include the opening, in which Micelle Bauer, nude save for a shower cap, dismembers some guy named Joe with unabashed glee (and a chainsaw, of course) and the final climactic battle with two babes dueling it out with chainsaws. A well-deserved "R" rating for copious amounts amount of comic book gore and lots of skin. This film was instrumental in propelling Fred Olen Ray into the lofty heights of cult directordom. Oh, yes, another rare film where scream queen Quigley makes it to the final reel with skin intact. 🦴🦴🦴🦴

1988 (R) 90m/C Linnea Quigley, Gunnar Hansen, Jay Richardson, Michelle (McClellan) Bauer; **D:** Fred Olen Ray. **VHS, Beta** *NO*

Hollywood Party

Durante plays a film star, famous for his "Schnarzan" jungle pictures, who decides to throw a gigantic bash at his Hollywood mansion in an effort to purchase some prized lions sought by a rival jungle star. Any plot is incidental as it is mainly an excuse to have numerous stars of the day appear in brief comic bits or musical numbers. Mickey Mouse and the Big Bad Wolf of Disney fame also appear in color animated footage combined with live action. Numerous MGM directors worked on parts of the film but Dwan was given the task of trying to pull the various scenes together (he is uncredited on-screen). A big hilarious party of a movie, with outrageous musical numbers and lots of great comedy. 🎵 Hollywood Party; Hello; Reincarnation; I've Had My Moments; Feeling High; Hot Chocolate Soldiers. 🦴🦴🦴🦴

1934 72m/B Jimmy Durante, Stan Laurel, Oliver Hardy, Lupe Velez, Ted Healy, Moe Howard, Curly Howard, Larry Fine, Robert Young, Charles Butterworth, Polly Moran, George Givot, Tom Kennedy; **D:** Allan Dwan; **V:** Walt Disney, Billy Bletcher. **VHS $19.98** *MGM*

The Hollywood Strangler Meets the Skid Row Slasher

Voiced-over narration, canned music, and an unfathomable plot are but a few of this would-be fright fest's finer points. Uninhibited by any narrative connection, two terrors strike fear in the heart of Tinseltown. While a psycho photographer cruises L.A. taking pictures of models he subsequently strangles, a woman working in a bare-bums magazine store takes a stab (with a knife) at lowering the city's derelict population. There's a word for this sort of dribble, and it isn't versimilitude. Steckler used an alias (not surprisingly) for this one—Wolfgang Schmidt. **AKA:** The Model Killer. 🦴🦴

1979 (R) 72m/C Pierre Agostino, Carolyn Brandt, Forrest Duke, Chuck Alford; **D:** Ray Dennis Steckler. **VHS** *NO*

Honeymoon Killers

The lurid title promises cheap thrills, but prepare yourself. This unjustly neglected sleeper has not lost its disturbing power to shock.

Shirley Stoler and Tony LoBianco star as overweight nurse Martha Beck and immigrant Ray Hernandez. She meets him through a torrid lonelyhearts correspondence, but painfully discovers after he takes her money that he is a gigolo. Rather than turn him in to the police, she quits her job, places her mother in a nursing home and becomes his partner, posing as his sister. But with each of his conquests, she becomes increasingly jealous and unstable, leading to grisly murders. Incredibly, based on a true story. Though initially dumped by distributor American International Pictures, *The Honeymoon Killers* was championed by critics. Harrowing, but essential viewing. Stoler's only other film of consequence was Lina Wertmuller's *Seven Beauties,* in which she played a Nazi prison camp commandant. *AKA:* The Lonely Hearts Killers. 🦴🦴🦴

1970 (R) 103m/C Tony LoBianco, Shirley Stoler, Mary Jane Higby, Dortha Duckworth, Doris Roberts, Marilyn Chris, Kip McArdle, Mary Breen, Barbara Cason, Ann Harris, Guy Sorel; *D:* Leonard Kastle. **VHS, Beta, LV $69.98** *LIV, VES*

The Horrible Dr. Hichcock

A sicko doctor (Flemyng), who accidentally killed his first wife while engaged in sexual antics, remarries to bring the first missus back from the dead using his new wife's blood. Genuinely creepy, mainly due to shock maestro Freda's intelligent direction. Finely controlled performance by Flemyng (*Blue Lamp, Chance Meeting*) as the necrophile M.D. Steele's second Italian horror film, after *Black Sunday.* Sequelled by *The Ghost. AKA:* L'Orribile Segreto Del Dr. Hichcock. 🦴🦴🦴

1962 76m/C *IT* Robert Flemyng, Barbara Steele; *D:* Riccardo (Robert Hampton) Freda. **VHS $69.95** *SNC*

The Horror Chamber of Dr. Faustus

A wickedly intelligent, inventive piece of Grand Guignol about a mad doctor who kills young girls so he may graft their skin onto the face of his accidentally mutilated daughter. Franju's style is remarkable for its mixture of beautifully poetic and horrifying images. Plotline was to be plundered repeatedly, notably for *The Awful Dr. Orlof, Atom Age Vampire, Circus of Horrors,* and *Faceless.* He gained international fame (and turned international stomachs) in 1949 for his feature documentary *Blood of the Beasts,* which was simply a detailed tour of the meat production industry, and later directed a modern remake of the popular *Judex* crime serial. Valli was in Carol Reed's *The Third Man,* and later turned up in films by Bava (*Lisa and the Devil*) and Argento (*Suspiria, Inferno*). Available dubbed and in French with English subtitles. *AKA:* Eyes Without a Face; Les Yeux Sans Visage; Occhi Senza Volto. 🦴🦴🦴🐾

1959 84m/B *FR* Alida Valli, Pierre Brasseur, Edith Scob, Francois Guerin; *D:* Georges Franju; *M:* Maurice Jarre. **VHS, Beta, LV $29.95** *SNC, TPV*

Horror of Party Beach

To any rational person, the "first horror monster musical" is an affront to good taste. But then again, if you were rational, you wouldn't be reading this book. So hit the beaches and do the Zombie Stomp with the Del-Aires. Just watch out for some of the screen's cheapest-looking monsters from the deep, the products of radioactive waste. Towering newspaper headlines keep us posted ("Mass Murder at Slumber Party!") and a black maid named Eulabel saves the day! From an exploitation standpoint, the merging of the horror and *Beach Party* genres is brilliant. Originally released on a double-feature with *Curse of the Living Corpse,* which featured Roy (*Jaws*) Scheider in his film debut, and Candace Hilligoss, star of *Carnival of Souls.* 🎵🎵 Zombie Stomp. *AKA:* Invasion of the Zombies. 🦴🦴🦴

1964 71m/C John Scott, Alice Lyon, Allen Laurel; *D:* Del Tenney. **VHS, Beta $39.95** *PSM*

Horse Feathers

Whatever it is, Groucho's against it in this Grade-A Marx Brothers classic. Groucho stars as Professor Wagstaff, the new head of Huxley College. His first priority is finding new members for the losing football team. Whom he finds by mistake at the local speakeasy (remember—the password is "Swordfish") are iceman Chico and dogcatcher Harpo. All three (four if you count Zeppo as—of all things—Groucho's son!) take turns romancing comely college widow Thelma Todd and performing the ditty "Everyone Says I Love You." The riotous climactic football game against hated Darwin University would not be topped until *M*A*S*H* nearly 40 years later. ♪♪♪◊

1932 67m/B Groucho Marx, Chico Marx, Harpo Marx, Zeppo Marx, Thelma Todd, David Landau, Nat Pendleton; **D:** Norman Z. McLeod. **VHS, Beta, LV** $14.98 *MCA*

The Hospital

Cult fave is a savage, bitterly sarcastic look at chaos in a urban New York hospital. While a multicultural rabble of leftists march in protest outside, the miserable patients inside suffer from neglect and compound ineptitude by greedy doctors and incompetent nurses—and that's even before a serial killer begins haunting the corridors. Scott is the burnt-out, suicidal chief physician who shouts screenwriter Paddy Chayefsky's immortal soliloquy into the night: "We cure NOTHING! We heal NOTHING!" The top-flight cast and Hiller's direction keep the madness as tightly controlled and wound as a time bomb. Though very much a specimen of its post-Woodstock, pre-Watergate era, the dark farce demands to be enjoyed today as the perfect antidote to *E.R.* ♪♪♪◊

1971 (PG) 101m/C George C. Scott, Diana Rigg, Barnard Hughes, Stockard Channing, Nancy Marchand, Richard Dysart; **D:** Arthur Hiller; **W:** Paddy Chayefsky. Academy Awards '71: Best Story & Screenplay; Berlin International Film Festival '72: Silver Prize; Golden Globe Awards '72: Best Screenplay; Nominations: Academy Awards '71: Best Actor (Scott). **VHS, Beta** $19.98 *MGM, FOX*

The House of Usher

Some serious overacting by Reed (as Roderick) and Pleasance (as his balmy brother) almost elevate this Poe retread to "so bad it's good" status, and there are a few admirably grisly moments. But, without other camp virtues, it's merely dreary. Adapted by Michael J. Murray and filmed in South Africa. ♪

1988 (R) 92m/C Oliver Reed, Donald Pleasence, Romy Windsor; **D:** Alan Birkinshaw; **W:** Michael J. Murray; **M:** Gary Chang. **VHS, LV** $79.95 *COL*

House of Wax

A deranged sculptor (Price, who else?) builds a sinister wax museum which showcases cre-

ations that were once alive. A remake of the early horror flick *Mystery of the Wax Museum*, and one of the '50s' most popular 3-D films. This one still has the power to give the viewer the creeps, thanks to another chilling performance by Price. Look for a very young Charles Bronson, as well as Carolyn "Morticia Addams" Jones as a victim. ♪♪♪

1953 (PG) 88m/C Vincent Price, Frank Lovejoy, Carolyn Jones, Phyllis Kirk, Paul Cavanagh, Charles Bronson; **D:** Andre de Toth. **VHS, Beta, LV** $19.98 *WAR, MLB*

House of Whipcord

Sleazoid exploitation elements predominate in this British cheapie, but you've got to admit it makes a point about moral fanaticism. Beautiful young women are kidnapped and tortured by a two puritanical old ladies and their sadistic nephew Mark E. DeSade. The meanies bring any girl suspected of sexual activity up before a senile, sightless judge (blind justice, get it?) to be sentenced for their "wickedness." Performances by the older thespians are bloody good, despite the degrading milieu. ♪♪

1975 102m/C *GB* Barbara Markham, Patrick Barr, Ray Brooks, Penny Irving, Anne Michelle; **D:** Pete Walker. **VHS, Beta** $39.95 *MON, LIV*

House on Haunted Hill

Vincent Price plays a wealthy man who throws a haunted house party and offers ten thousand dollars to anyone who can survive the night there. His guests, who arrive in funeral hearses, include a psychiatrist, a gambler, and an ingenue who gets to do a lot of screaming. Vintage cheap horror from the master of the macabre Castle, complete with blood dripping from the ceiling, dead rats, doors slamming, lights flickering, screams, hands slinking around doorways, and best of all, "Emergo": when a skeleton (nee Vincent Price) emerges from a vat of acid and moves off screen, a plastic skeleton emerged from a hidden cabinet next to the theatre screen, traveling over the audience and into the balcony. Also available with *Attack of the 50-Foot Woman* on laserdisc. ♪♪♪◊

1958 75m/B Vincent Price, Carol Ohmart, Richard Long, Alan Marshal, Elisha Cook Jr.; **D:** William Castle. **VHS, Beta, LV** $14.98 *FOX, SNC, FCT*

"The ghosts are moving tonight, restless, hungry...I'll show you the only real haunted house in the world."
--Vincent Price in *The House on Haunted Hill.*

How to Get Ahead in Advertising

Cynical British satire about a manic advertising man so disgusted with trying to sell a pimple cream that he quits the business. Subsequently he grows a boil on his neck that talks and begins to take over his life. Acerbic, somewhat off-balance attack on British values in the 1980s, with an ambitious pimple embodying the ultimate in yuppie greed. Writer/director Robinson later admitted that the emphasis on the ad world was a mistake that obscured the anti-Thatcherist themes, but Grant's insane rantings and ravings are hilarious whatever the context. 🦴🦴🦴

1989 (R) 95m/C *GB* Richard E. Grant, Rachel Ward, Susan Wooldridge, Mick Ford, Richard Wilson, John Shrapnel, Jacqueline Tong; **D:** Bruce Robinson; **W:** Bruce Robinson; **M:** David Dundas, Rick Wentworth. **VHS, Beta, LV** *NO*

How to Make a Doll

H.G. Lewis' boneheaded sex farce about an extremely shy professor whose ineptness with women inspires him to invent android females to satisfy his sexual needs. He breaks his glasses and falls in love with Agnes, a homely grad student secretly in love with him. Highlight has computer turning a girl into a rabbit after he tell it he wants her to be his "dream bunny." 🦴🦴

1968 ?m/C Robert Wood, Jim Vance, Pamela Rhea; **D:** Herschell Gordon Lewis. **VHS $24.99** *MOV, TPV*

The Howling

Overshadowed by John Landis' *An American Werewolf in London*, but really much better. Dee Wallace (the mother in *E.T.*) stars as a traumatized newswoman who is sent to a California encounter group run by Patrick Macnee (John Steed in *The Avengers*). Little does she know that it is a coven of werewolves. Co-screenwriter John Sayles, director Joe Dante, and Rob Bottin's hair-raising transformation effects deliver the goods with a bite and a sly wink (one character can be seen reading a book by Thomas Wolfe, get it?). A feast of references for horror film buffs. The characters portrayed by Kevin McCarthy, John Carradine, and Slim Pickens were named after werewolf movie directors. That's King of the B's Roger Corman making a phone call, Sayles as a morgue attendant, and Dick Miller as occult book store owner Walter Paisley (the name of his character in *A Bucket of Blood*). Never mind the sequels of which there are—at last count—six, the latest being *The Howling: Full Moon Rising*. 🦴🦴🦴

1981 (R) 91m/C Dee Wallace Stone, Patrick Macnee, Dennis Dugan, Christopher Stone, Belinda Balaski, Kevin McCarthy, John Carradine, Slim Pickens, Elisabeth Brooks, Robert Picardo, Dick Miller; **Cameos:** John Sayles, Roger Corman; **D:** Joe Dante; **W:** John Sayles, Terence H. Winkless; **M:** Pino Donaggio. **VHS, Beta, LV $14.95** *COL, SUE*

Humanoids from the Deep

Mutant salmon monsters—possibly teen-age mutant salmon monsters—rise from the depths of the Pacific coast and decide to chomp on some bikinied babes. Violent and bloody, but what fan can resist such a wonderfully cheesy title? Film never strays from the standard-issue B-movie plot. The critters are obviously guys in rubber suits, but so what? You were expecting maybe Meryl Streep and Dustin Hoffman? **AKA:** Monster. 🦴🦴🦴

1980 (R) 81m/C Doug McClure, Ann Turkel, Vic Morrow, Cindy Weintraub, Anthony Penya, Denise Balik; **D:** Barbara Peeters; **W:** Frank Arnold; **M:** James Horner. **VHS, Beta** *WAR, OM*

The Hunger

A beautiful 2000-year-old vampire (Deneuve) needs help when she realizes that her current lover (Bowie) is aging fast. Enter a blood specialist (Sarandon) whose research involves geriatrics. Visually sumptuous modern horror tale, spun out at an appropriately languid pace, complete with soft-focus lesbian love scenes between Deneuve and Sarandon, and an understated mix of violence and sly humor. Bowie adds the right element of sexual mystery to the proceedings. This one paved the way for a generation of MTV-influenced escapist films emphasizing glossy style over story. A laserdisc edition features a letterboxed screen and original movie trailer. 🦴🦴🦴

1983 (R) 100m/C Catherine Deneuve, David Bowie, Susan Sarandon, Cliff DeYoung, Ann Magnuson, Dan

Hedaya, Willem Dafoe; **D:** Tony Scott; **W:** Michael Thomas. **VHS, Beta, LV $79.95** *MGM*

I Accuse My Parents

Juvenile delinquent tries to blame a murder and his involvement in a gang of thieves on his mom and dad's failure to raise him properly. Didn't the Menendez brothers try this defense? Follows the Hollywood tradition of casting 30 year olds as high school students. Gets a bit starchy and doesn't live up to the whiny opening accusation. I accuse the producer! Hughes, who had a lively career in B-movies, is probably best remembered as the female lead in *The Ox-Bow Incident* (1943). Miljan had a busy career in early talkies, was in the Lon Chaney classics *Phantom of the Opera* (1925) and *The Unholy Three* (1930), and survived to appear as the blind man in *The Ten Commandments* (1956). 🎵🎵

1945 70m/B Mary Beth Hughes, Robert Lowell, John Miljan; **D:** Sam Newfield. **VHS, Beta $16.95** *SNC, NOS, DVT*

I Am Curious (Yellow)

How Swede it is! Fifteen minutes should just about satisfy any curiosity you may have about this infamous Swedish import that upon its arrival in the States was seized and branded obscene. That was then, this is now. Lena Nyman's personal odyssey of political and sexual self-discovery is tedious, and despite some full frontal nudity, mostly tame stuff ("All you do is talk and ask questions," her latest boyfriend yells.) Nyman is not exactly, in her words, "the model type" with her "drooping breasts and fat belly," but the flesh is certainly willing (on the floor, on palace steps, in a tree). We are supposed to be shocked that she is on her 24th lover ("The first 19 were no fun," she states). That's less than Andie McDowell in *Four Weddings and a Funeral*. Filmed concurrently with *I Am Curious (Blue)*. In Swedish with English subtitles. 🎵🎵▷

1967 95m/B *SW* Lena Nyman, Peter Lindgren; **D:** Vilgot Sjoman. **VHS $59.95** *HTV*

An eternally young Catherine Deneuve checks John Stephen Hills' swollen gland in *The Hunger*.

and you'll see why *Mama* gives splatter/sex-ploitation films a bad name. *AKA:* Poor Albert and Little Annie. ♫

1974 (R) 81m/C Zooey Hall, Joanne Moore Jordan, Greg Mullavey, Marlene Tracy; *D:* Paul Leder. **VHS, Beta $24.95** *GEM*

I Drink Your Blood

Hippie Satanists looking for kicks spike an old man's drink with LSD. To get revenge, the old codger's grandson sells the nasty flower children meat pies injected with the blood of a rabid dog. The hippies then turn into canni-balistic maniacs, infecting anyone they bite, and heads roll. In this orgy of violence, a knife, a rifle, an ax, a dagger, a machete, an elec-tric knife, a shotgun, a wooden stake, a pitch-fork, teeth, a sword, a revolver, and a garden hose are all used as deadly weapons. From the man responsible for *I Spit on Your Grave* and *Stigma*; originally played on a double bill with *I Eat Your Skin*. ♫ ♫ ♪

1971 (R) 83m/C Bhasker, Jadine Wong, Ronda Fultz, Elizabeth Marner-Brooks, George Patterson, Riley Mills, Iris Brooks, John Damon; *D:* David E. Durston. **VHS $18.00** *FRG, TPV*

I Eat Your Skin

A swingin' playboy author investigates reports of voodoo ceremonies on uncharted Voodoo Island, and discovers a mad scientist creating gruesome hash-face zombies. Story would be right at home in old he-man adventure mag-azines, with a cool calypso/jazz soundtrack and wacky comedy relief. From Del Tenney, the man who brought you *Horror of Party Beach*. Blood and guts, retitled and rereleased on a gourmet double bill with *I Drink Your Blood*. *AKA:* Zombies; Voodoo Blood Bath; Zombie. ♫ ♫

1964 82m/B William Joyce, Heather Hewitt, Betty H. Lindon; *D:* Del Tenney. **VHS $9.95** *RHI, SNC, FCT*

I Married a Monster from Outer Space

The vintage thriller about a race of monster-like aliens from another planet who infiltrate earth. Despite its tabloid title, this is an effec-tive '50s sci-fi creeper. Two years after *Inva-sion of the Body Snatchers* and five years af-

"It's easy! Just pat your head and rub your tummy!" *I Married a Monster from Outer Space.*

I Dismember Mama

Read that title a few more times; it's by far the most entertaining thing about his flick. Albert (Zooey Hall), who's locked up in a minimum-security mental institution, believes that all women are whores—including his own Mama. Cheesed off when a perceptive, but ill-fated, hospital attendant calls Albert "a spoiled rotten, 30 million dollar rat," Albert offs him. (C'mon, Albert, he just delivered the line, he didn't write it!) He escapes the institution and immediately calls Mama. Cagey cops predict that move (like, who wouldn't?) and are stak-ing Mom's place when Albert arrives. Leder insults viewer intelligence for cheap thrills, which ain't all that thrilling. This one is no-tably lacking in blood and gore; just two off-screen murders and a window-suicide that comes more as a relief than a shock. Add a score that recalls *The Streets of San Francisco*,

ter *Invaders from Mars,* the angle of small town sci-fi paranoia was getting to be familiar territory, but Louis Vittes script gives the story a new twist. Tryon is kidnapped and replaced by an alien on the eve of his wedding, leading to a marriage of doubt and suspicion, as beautiful wife Talbott can't understand the change in her husband's personality. After a year of marriage, she finally discovers the truth, but keeps it hidden when no one believes her. Then it's Tryon's turn to be perplexed at the change in her. The sympathetic handling of the invaders, along with the well done creature costumes and f/x by technical pioneer John P. Fulton, serve to raise this one above the crowd. 🦴🦴🦴

1958 78m/B Tom Tryon, Gloria Talbott, Maxie "Slapsie" Rosenbloom, Mary Treen, Ty Hardin; ***D:*** Gene Fowler Jr. **VHS, Beta $49.95** *PAR, MLB*

I Married a Vampire

Perhaps the worst movie ever made (and that's not a recommendation). A young country girl comes to the big city where she is taken advantage of by friends, strangers, bosses, etc. As her life sinks further into misery, she falls in love with a mysterious man during a series of boring conversations. The man turns out to be a vampire and, being equally smitten with our heroine, extracts revenge upon those who have wronged her. This utterly worthless film leaves the viewer underwhelmed with the lack of sex, violence, and humor that pervade the entire production. Tax-loss cinema at it's worst. Buy it and you'll never need Sominex again. WOOF!

1987 85m/C Rachel Gordon, Brendan Hickey; ***D:*** Jay Raskin. **VHS, Beta $9.99** *PSM*

I Spit on Your Grave

One of the most notorious pieces of trash ever put to celluloid, this flick is disgusting even by exploitation standards. A woman attempting to write a novel at a secluded upstate New York lake cabin is brutally beaten and raped by four men. Despite being left for dead, she recovers, and exacts grisly revenge on each of her attackers. Covers every cliche in the book, from the town idiot who goes along with the plan to the woman's obvious revenge (think Lorena Bobbitt). Lots of violent terror and gory

death, totally irresponsibly portrayed. Truly one of the worst of the worst. Also available in a 102-minute version. ***AKA:*** Day of the Woman. WOOF!

1977 (R) 98m/C Camille Keaton, Eron Tabor, Richard Pace, Gunter Kleeman; ***D:*** Mier Zarchi; ***W:*** Mier Zarchi. **VHS, Beta, LV $39.95** *VES*

I Walked with a Zombie

The eeriest of the famous Val Lewton/Jacques Tourneur horror films. Dee, a young American nurse, comes to Haiti to care for the catatonic matriarch of a troubled family. Local legends bring themselves to bear when the nurse takes the ill woman to a local voodoo ceremony for "healing." Superb, startling images and atmosphere create a unique context for this serious *Jane Eyre*-like story. Like the other films in the Lewton horror series, the protagonists deal with earthier, more psychological terrors. Conway and Dee must deal with the overpowering guilt of their mutual attraction, while the zombie wife's illness sends chills down the spine. The giant, corpse-like Darby Jones and the lilting troubadour Sir Lancelot

It's better than sleeping with one: *I Walked with a Zombie.*

143

Cult Flicks and Trash Pics

TEN BEST GIMMICKS USED IN CULT/TRASH FILM
or, The William Castle Legacy

Presented here for his entertainment, the Hound shares his ten top favorite movie gimmicks, ranked from cool to the very coolest. William Castle, of course, dominates the list (watch the movie *Matinee*, for which Castle was the inspiration, to get the idea).

1. Souvenirs.
Theatre patrons for Castle's *Strait Jacket* were given toy bloody axes; the audiences for *Zotz!* received plastic Zotz coins. Lucky viewers of *Mad Doctor of Blood Island* received vials of green "blood." The Hound himself still treasures the vial of "Toxique" cologne he received at the premiere of *The Toxic Avenger, Part 3: The Last Temptation of Toxie*.

2. "Fright Insurance Policy"
The inimitable Castle offered the audience of *Macabre* the opportunity to take out insurance policies against dying of fright. To complete the effect, he had nurses stationed in the lobbies and ambulances waiting at the curbs.

3. Time Outs.
In the 1966 version of *Ten Little Indians* (the cool version featuring Fabian), right before the last murder, the action is frozen and a clock is superimposed on the screen to give viewers sixty seconds to guess who-dun-it; flash backs are shown of all the previous murders to help the audience puzzle out the plot. William Castle, of course, did his own version by offering viewers a *Fright Break* during the showing of *Homicidal*.

4. Alternate Endings.
The producers of the 1985 film *Clue*, based on the board game, distributed three different versions of the movie, each with a different ending and solution to the who-dun-it. The video version contains all three; movie goers could pick which ending those chose to see--an ingenious ploy by the producers to encourage the public to see the movie three times. Of course, Castle had already done it better. In his 1961 *Dr. Sardonicus*, viewers were invited to take

continued...

made enough of an impression that they each showed up in other films throughout the '40s in similar roles, notably *Zombies on Broadway* and *The Ghost Ship*. 🦴🦴🦴▷

1943 69m/B Frances Dee, Tom Conway, James Ellison, Christine Gordon, Edith Barrett, Darby Jones, Sir Lancelot; **D:** Jacques Tourneur. **VHS, Beta, LV $19.98** *MED, FCT, MLB*

I Wanna Be a Beauty Queen

Divine hosts the "Alternative Miss World" pageant featuring all sorts of, well, alternative contestants. Divine is always a treat, but it's only entertaining for the first half-hour or so. For Her fans only. 🦴▷

1985 81m/C Divine, Little Nell, Andrew Logan. **VHS, Beta $19.95** *AHV, FCT, HHE*

I Was a Teenage TV Terrorist

Two surly teens hold down dull, dead-end jobs at a seedy cable-TV operation. For kicks they turn to petty crime and robberies, finally staging a phony terrorist takeover on the air to hold the station for ransom. Performances and 16mm production values are defined by the pic's original title *Amateur Hour*. Yet with its uncompromisingly bitter tone and cruel conclusion, this Troma satire has a sharper edge than *The Toxic Avenger* or other shaggy spoofs from the notorious NY-based distributor. **AKA:** Amateur Hour. 🦴🦴

1987 85m/C Adam Nathan, Julie Hanlon; **D:** Stanford Singer; **W:** Kevin McDonough. **VHS, Beta $79.98** *LIV*

I Was a Teenage Werewolf

Rebel Without a Cause meets *The Curse of the Werewolf* in this drive-in rock 'n' roll horror. A troubled young man (pre-*Bonanza* Landon, in his first feature film appearance) suffers from teen angst and low production values, and falls victim to shrink Bissel. The good doctor turns out to be a bad hypnotist, and Landon's regression therapy takes him beyond childhood into his, gasp, primal past, where he sprouts a premature beard and knuckle hair. Misconstrued and full of terrible longings, the hairy highschooler is understood only by girlfriend Lime and misunderstood

hair-sprouting teen viewers. Directorial debut of Fowler. 🦴🦴🐾

1957 70m/B Michael Landon, Yvonne Lime, Whit Bissell, Tony Marshall, Dawn Richard, Barney Phillips, Ken Miller, Cindy Robbins, Michael Rougas, Robert Griffin, Joseph Mell, Malcolm Atterbury, Eddie Marr, Vladimir Sokoloff, Louise Lewis, S. John Launer, Guy Williams, Dorothy Crehan; **D:** Gene Fowler Jr.; **W:** Ralph Thornton. **VHS $9.95** *COL, FCT, MLB*

I Was a Zombie for the FBI

Aliens who look just like old-fashioned gangsters land near Pleasantville, USA, and make a deal with a couple of human criminals to rule the world. Their extraterrestrial super-science hypnotizes victims "clinically in what is known as a zomboid state," while just-the-facts-ma'am federal agents combat the un-American menace and their badly animated reptile monster. Black-and-white production by Memphis State University students is a dry, deadpan recreation of McCarthy-era sci-fi quickies, so close to the real thing that the mirth turns to tedium under an interminable running time. Still, some kind of achievement. 🦴🦴

1982 105m/B D: Maurice Penczner. **VHS, Beta** *NO*

Ilsa, Harem Keeper of the Oil Sheiks

The naughty Ilsa works for an Arab sheik in the slave trade. More graphic violence and nudity from the makers of *Ilsa, She-Wolf of the S.S.* Ilsa, who hasn't aged a bit since WWII, keeps the girls in line with her cruel tortures. Plot makes an appearance when rebels try to overthrow the cruel sheik, but the main attraction here is Thorne and her enormous talents. Some viewers may find this film excessively exploitative and sensational. 🦴🦴

1976 (R) 45m/C Dyanne Thorne, Michael Thayer. **VHS, LV $59.98** *CIC*

Ilsa, She-Wolf of the SS

The torture-loving Ilsa Koch (Thorne) runs a medical prison camp for her slobbering Nazi bosses. Plot is incidental to nudity, sadism and violence. Thorne stands out (literally) as the cruel commandant, torturing the female pris-

oners by day, bedding her pick of the males by night—and woe to the man who fails to satisfy her lusts. The acting is—well, incidental. Created a furor when released. This S&M Nazi women's prison is one of the first of a legion of imitators following the lead of Frost & Cresse's *Love Camp Seven* (1968). Followed by two official sequels. 🦴🦴

1974 (R) 45m/C Dyanne Thorne, Greg Knoph; **D:** Don Edmunds. **VHS, LV $59.98** *CIC*

Ilsa, the Tigress of Siberia

Everyone's favorite torturer has been working her wiles on political prisoners in Russia. Never knowing when enough is enough, she also turns her tender attentions on her guards in sadistic bunkhouse games of torture. Alas, all good things must come to an end and soon Ilsa finds herself on the run. The ultimate bad girl ends up in Canada, of all places, where she is spotted by a former victim who vows revenge. Who will meet their end in the icy wilderness? The weakest entry in the series, it's still loaded with sex, depravity, violence, amputations, and mutilations—everything a lover of Sadistic Cinema could ask for. Available in both "R" and unrated versions, with three companion films (one in title only) also reviewed herein. 🦴🦴

1979 85m/C Dyanne Thorne, Michel Morin, Tony Angelo, Terry Coady, Howard Mauer; **D:** Jean LaFleur. **VHS** *NO*

I'm Gonna Git You Sucka

Don't give Keenen Ivory Wayans's right-on parody of blaxploitation films the shaft. Wayans stars as Jack Spade, who returns home after a ten-year Army hitch to find that Mr. Big and his gold chains are corrupting the youth of "Any Ghetto, USA." He recruits a reluctant band of aging black heroes to help him stick it to the Man, but tougher than all of them is Spade's mama (Ja'net DuBois, neighbor Willona from TV's *Good Times*). Jim Brown (*Slaughter*), Isaac Hayes (*Truck Turner*), Bernie Casey (*Cleopatra Jones*), and Steve "Rambro" James (*American Ninja*) affectionately spoof their macho screen images in this *Airplane*-style gagfest. There are memorable cameos by Eve Plumb (*The Brady Bunch*), Clarence

Story continued...

part in a *Punishment Poll*; their vote dictated which alternate ending the theatre would show.

5. 3-D.

Best utilized in *House of Wax* starring Vincent Price, the archetype of the '50s 3-D flick. 3-D was also used in many Three Stooges shorts, for those people who want to see what it is really like to have Moe poke you in the eye. Spoofed wittily in *SCTV*'s Count Floyd midnight movie skits, where his favorite showings included *Dr. Tongue's 3-D House of Stewardesses* and *3-D House of Beef*. And the Hound must give a nod to *Friday the 13th, Part 3 in 3-D*, because the Hound himself, a veteran horror-movie goer, ducked when a eyeball seemed to fly into the audience.

6. "Illusion-O."

Yet another Castle gimmick, whereby the title characters in *13 Ghosts* could only be seen with 3-D type glasses that were distributed to the audience. When the glasses were removed, the ghosts disappeared.

7. "Emergo."

William Castle coined this word for *The House on Haunted Hill*. When Vincent Price's acid-eaten skeleton emerges (in 3-D) from a vat of acid and moves off screen, Castle rigged the theatres so that a skeleton would actually emerge (hence, "Emergo"...) from a box hidden next to the screen; the 3-D image would appear to actually materialize and fly over the audience's heads.

8. "Psycho-Rama"

Terror in the Haunted House was filmed with subliminal images and messages that flashed on the screen; the idea was so insidious and horrifying, it was banned by the government... but it's available to us now when we can pause on the screen and actually see the ridiculous oooh-scary pictures and messages that Rhino has superimposed.

9. "Percepto."

The best Castle device of all; for *The Tingler*, Castle wired the seats in the theatre so that when the characters on the screen were shocked in numbing fear, the audience got a jolt as well. See the movie *Matinee* for a dramatization of this electrifying invention.

continued...

Williams III (Link from *The Mod Squad*), Antonio Fargas (Huggy Bear in *Starsky and Hutch*), Damon Wayans, David Allen Grier, and Chris Rock. Not to mention "the director's sister" getting a nepotistic cameo as the world's worst lounge singer. At one point, a defensive John Vernon steps out of character as Mr. Big to justify his presence in an exploitation film. He cites Shelley Winters as a role model. 🎵🎵🎵

1988 (R) 89m/C Keenen Ivory Wayans, Bernie Casey, Steve James, Isaac Hayes, Jim Brown, Ja'net DuBois, Anne-Marie Johnson, Antonio Fargas, Eve Plumb, John Vernon, Clu Gulager, Kadeem Hardison, Damon Wayans, Gary Owens, Clarence Williams III, David Alan Grier, Kim Wayans, Robin Harris, Chris Rock, Dawnn Lewis, Jester Hairston; *Cameos:* Robert Townsend; *D:* Keenen Ivory Wayans; *W:* Keenen Ivory Wayans; *M:* David Michael Frank. **VHS, Beta, LV $19.95** *MGM*

I'm No Angel

"Beulah, peel me a grape." Well, you'd be hungry too if you spent your time eyeing playboy Grant as West does. She's a circus floozy who's prone to extorting money from her men (after hashing over their shortcomings with her seen-it-all-maid, the aforementioned Beulah). However, after wooing Grant, she sues for breach of promise. This leads to a comic courtroom scene with Grant bringing in all West's ex-lovers as witnesses. Grant's second film with West, following *She Done Him Wrong*. 🎵🎵🎵

1933 88m/B Mae West, Cary Grant, Gregory Ratoff, Edward Arnold, Ralf Harolde, Kent Taylor, Gertrude Michael, Russell Hopton, Dorothy Peterson, William B. Davidson, Gertrude Howard; *D:* Wesley Ruggles; *W:* Mae West. **VHS $14.98** *MCA, BTV*

Impulse

Perhaps the most embarrassing skeleton in Captain Kirk's closet. Shatner is at his eye-rolling hammiest as a murderously psychotic stud muffin and conman whose wardrobe combines the most outrageous elements of *Superfly* and a cheap Vegas lounge act. There's an Ed Wood ineptitude to the proceedings that gives the film a so-bad-it's-fun quality. Definitely a must-see for both Shatner's fans and his anti-fans. Should not be confused with the 1984 s-f film and the 1990 cop thriller of the same title. **AKA:** Want a Ride, Little Girl?; I Love to Kill. 🦴🦴

1974 (PG) 85m/C William Shatner, Ruth Roman, Harold Sakata, Kim Nicholas, Jennifer Bishop, James Dobbs; **D:** William Grefe. **VHS, Beta $79.95** *LIV, VES*

In the Cold of the Night

Another drowsy entry into the "to sleep perchance to have a nightmare" genre. A photographer with a vivid imagination dreams he murders a woman he doesn't know, and when said dream girl rides into his life on the back of a Harley, Mr. Foto's faced with an etiquette quandary: haven't they met before? Cast includes Hedren (Hitchcock's Marnie and Melanie Griffith's mother). 🦴

1989 (R) 112m/C Jeff Lester, Adrienne Sachs, Shannon Tweed, David Soul, John Beck, Tippi Hedren, Marc Singer; **D:** Nico Mastorakis. **VHS, LV $9.98** *REP*

The Incredible Two-Headed Transplant

Mildly deranged mad scientist Dern has a criminal head transplanted onto the shoulder of big John Bloom and the critter runs wild. One-time Ray Dennis Steckler editor Lanza (*The Glory Stompers*) grafts together classic exploitation elements (mad doctors, bikers, maniacs, freaks, Dern himself) to create his own incredible cinematic monster, which was ripped off by the better-known *The Thing With Two Heads* (with Rosey Grier and Ray Milland). Final AIP stop for woefully confused-looking Dern and debut for career creature Bloom (*Dracula vs. Frankenstein, Brain of Blood*). Albert Cole chews the scenery into submission as leering killer ("I'm running this monster!"). With Casey Kasem as Dern's concerned DJ pal (surprise!), TV horror host Seymour, and your chance to check out former Munster Pat Priest in a bubble bath, bikini, and ultimately, an animal cage. Bobbie Boyle warbles the theme song, "It's Incredible." John "Bud" Cardos (*Kingdom of the Spiders*) provides second unit direction. 🦴🦴🦴

1971 (PG) 88m/C Bruce Dern, Pat Priest, Casey Kasem, Albert Cole, John Bloom, Berry Kroeger; **D:** Anthony M. Lanza. **VHS** *NO*

Incredibly Strange Creatures Who Stopped Living and Became Mixed-Up Zombies

Cash Flagg stars as Jerry, a young bum out for kicks who runs afoul of a sideshow gypsy woman. Instead of her usual revenge tactic of turning people into hideously deformed (not to mention mixed-up) zombies for her basement dungeon, she hypnotizes him into becoming a crazed killer. The mayhem is frequently interrupted for bizarre, psychedelic dance numbers and nightmare sequences, which are as weird as anything created by Ken Russell or Ed Wood. Steckler frequently shows that he is a capable director, especially in the sequences showing the loneliness and confusion of his protagonist, but his films are also victims of his obsession with zero-budget, scriptless filmmaking. Cinematographers include the young Laszlo Kovacs and Vilmos Zsigmond, who went on to become Oscar winners. Steckler's then-wife Brandt turns in a sexy perf as the alcoholic dancer, while Atlas King (the Greek Fabian) plays the completely unintelligible roommate. This com-

Bernie Casey and Keenen Ivory Wayans in *I'm Gonna Git You Sucka.*

> "At first glance, everything looked the same. It wasn't. Something evil had taken possession of the town."
>
> --*Invasion of the Body Snatchers.*

pletely unpredictable and thoroughly entertaining feature is probably the best monster horror musical ever made. A must-see. ♪ Prison Wagon; The Mixed-Up Zombie Song; Shook Out of Shape. *AKA:* The Teenage Psycho Meets Bloody Mary; The Incredibly Strange Creatures. ♫♫♫♫

1963 90m/C Cash Flagg, Carolyn Brandt, Brett O'Hara, Atlas King, Sharon Walsh; *D:* Ray Dennis Steckler. VHS, Beta *NO*

Infra-Man

The Mighty Morphin Power Rangers TV show, with its cheesy monsters and hyper-kinetic fight sequences, owes a lot to this outrageous Hong Kong production. Ancient Princess Dragon Mom unleashes an incredible array of creatures (including Octopus Man and Beetle Man) on the Earth. She wreaks such apocalyptic havoc that a scientist is forced to tell the world's leaders, "This situation is so bad that it is the worst that ever has been." It's Infra-Man, a bionic superhero, to the rescue. Tremendous fun for all ages, with nonstop martial arts action and priceless corny English-dubbed dialogue ("Drop the Earthling to her doom"). It's "infratastic." *AKA:* The Super Inframan; The Infra Superman. ♫♫♫

1976 (PG) 92m/C *HK* Li Hsiu-hsien, Wang Hsieh, Yuan Man-tzu, Terry Liu, Tsen Shu-yi, Huang Chien-lung, Lu Sheng; *D:* Hua-Shan; *W:* Peter Fernandez. VHS, Beta $49.95 *PSM*

Invaders from Mars

Young boy cries "martian" in this sci-fi cheapy classic. He can't convince the townspeople of this invasion because they've already been possessed by the alien beings. His parents are zapped by the little green things first, making this perhaps an allegory for the missing Eisenhower/Stepford years. Includes previews of coming attractions from classic science fiction films. Remade in 1986 by Tobe Hooper. ♫♫▷

1953 78m/C Helena Carter, Arthur Franz, Jimmy Hunt, Leif Erickson; *D:* William Cameron Menzies. VHS, Beta $19.95 *MED, MLB*

Invasion of the Bee Girls

Beware beautiful women in dark sunglasses in this honey of a "B" film. Here's the buzz: William Smith stars as a federal agent investigating a series of mysterious deaths. Anitra Ford, of *The Big Bird Cage* fame, stars as the queen bee, who recruits unwitting women into her hive of seductresses. Their male victims die of sexual exhaustion. Cliff Osmond, a veteran of Billy Wilder films (*The Fortune Cookie, Kiss Me Stupid, The Front Page*) costars as the baffled sheriff. The murky audio sounds as if it were coming from a drive-in speaker, which ideally is the best way to experience this compellingly quirky and perversely comic thriller. An early screenplay by Nicholas Meyer, author of *The Seven Per Cent Solution*, and the director of *Time After Time, Star Trek: The Wrath of Khan,* and *Star Trek VI: The Undiscovered Country*. This was released the same year as *The Sting*. Probably a coincidence. *AKA:* Graveyard Tramps. ♫♫♫

1973 85m/C Victoria Vetri, William Smith, Anitra Ford, Cliff Osmond, Wright King, Ben Hammer; *D:* Denis Sanders; *W:* Nicholas Meyer; *M:* Charles Bernstein. VHS $69.98 *SUE*

Invasion of the Body Snatchers

The one and only post-McCarthy paranoid sci-fi epic, where a small California town is infiltrated by pods from outer space that replicate and replace humans. A chilling, genuinely frightening exercise in nightmare dislocation. Based upon a novel by Jack Finney. Remade in 1978. The laserdisc version contains commentary by Maurice Yacowar, the text of an interview with Siegel, and the original theatrical trailer. The film itself is presented in its original wide-screen format. 🦴🦴🦴🦴

1956 80m/B Kevin McCarthy, Dana Wynter, Carolyn Jones, King Donovan, Donald Siegel; **D:** Donald Siegel; **W:** Sam Peckinpah. **VHS, LV $14.98** *REP, CRC, MLB*

Invasion of the Space Preachers

Troma released (but didn't produce) this made-in-West-Virginia cheapie, set in an Appalachian town where the upstanding Reverend Lash is really a buglike alien planning to brainwash the world though hypnotic signals in his broadcast sermons. Out to silence the sham clergyman are two Ohio tourists, as-

sorted dopers, and a sexy space cop (played by Hahn, an area radio DJ). Done for $100,000, this aimless pic just hasn't got a prayer—unless you count "Klaatu barada nikto," lifted from *The Day the Earth Stood Still* in one of the few inspired moments. 🦴

1990 100m/C Jim Wolfe, Guy Nelson, Eliska Hahn, Gary Brown, Jesse Johnson, John Riggs; **D:** Daniel Boyd; **W:** Daniel Boyd. **VHS, Beta $79.95** *RHI*

The Invisible Maniac

A crazy voyeur perfects a serum for invisibility and promptly gets a job as a physics teacher in a high school, thus combining two genres of B-movies: dead teenager and horny teenager flicks. The not-so-special effects are predictable—tearaway blouses—and inexpensive. The cast is blandly attractive and the girls find themselves in the showers about every 15 minutes. For voyeurs who know how to use the fast-forward button. Get outta here, you maniac. 🦴🦴

"Think we could have that much fun if we put our heads together?" *The Incredible Two-Headed Transplant.*

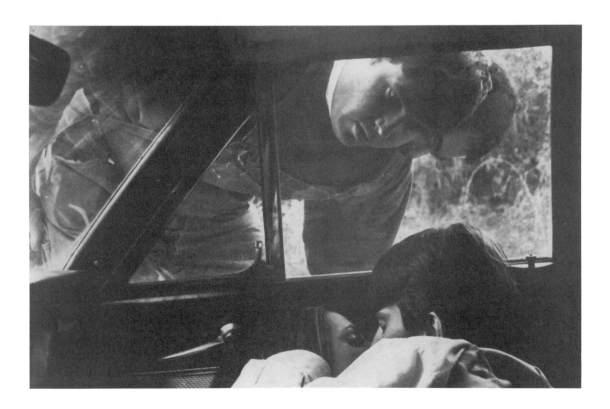

Hmmm...that bee-hive is definitely you! *The Invasion of the Bee Girls.*

"**The natives... they are restless tonight.**"

--Dr. Moreau (Charles Laughton) in the *Island of Lost Souls.*

1987 **(PG-13) 107m/C** Dustin Hoffman, Warren Beatty, Isabelle Adjani, Charles Grodin; **D:** Elaine May; **W:** Elaine May; **M:** Dave Grusin. **VHS, Beta, LV $14.95** *COL*

Island of Lost Souls

Horrifying adaptation of H.G. Wells *The Island of Dr. Moreau* was initially banned in parts of the U.S. because of its disturbing contents. Laughton is a mad scientist on a remote island obsessed with making men out of jungle animals. When a shipwreck survivor gets stranded on the island, little does he know that Laughton wants to mate him with Lota, the Panther Woman, to produce the first human-animal child. As unsettling today as it was in the '30s. Burke beat out more than 60,000 young women in a nationwide search to play the Panther Woman, winning the role because of her "feline" look. Remade as *The Island of Dr. Moreau.* 🦴🦴🦴🦴

1932 **71m/B** Charles Laughton, Bela Lugosi, Richard Arlen, Leila Hyams, Kathleen Burke, Stanley Fields, Robert F. (Bob) Kortman; **Cameos:** Alan Ladd, Randolph Scott, Buster Crabbe; **D:** Erle C. Kenton; **W:** Philip Wylie, Waldemar Young. **VHS $14.98** *MCA, FCT, BTV*

Isle of the Dead

A Greek general is quarantined with seemingly all manner of social vermin on a plague-infested island in the early 1900s. The fear is that vampires walk among them. Several characters begin to crack under the strains produced by the plague, the war, and rampant superstition. Catalepsy is added to the mix, bringing tensions to the breaking point. Characteristically spooky Val Lewton production with some original twists. Falls short of classic status due to uneven pacing, probably due to the fact that production was interrupted for some months. 🦴🦴🦴

1945 **72m/B** Boris Karloff, Ellen Drew, Marc Cramer, Jason Robards Jr.; **D:** Mark Robson. **VHS, Beta, LV $19.95** *TTC, MED, FCT*

It Came from Hollywood

Dan Aykroyd, John Candy, Cheech and Chong, and Gilda Radner introduce clips from some of the worst movies ever made. Unfortunately, this well-intentioned celebration of

1990 **(R) 87m/C** Noel Peters, Shannon Wilsey, Melissa Moore, Robert Ross, Rod Sweitzer, Eric Champnella, Kalei Shellabarger, Gail Lyon, Debra Lamb; **D:** Rif Coogan; **W:** Rif Coogan. **VHS $89.95** *REP*

Ishtar

The jury is still out on Elaine May's epic modern-day "Road" comedy starring Dustin Hoffman and Warren Beatty as Rogers and Clarke, two stupefyingly untalented singer-songwriters who become embroiled in Middle East intrigue. Pounced upon by critics for its (then) gargantuan, runaway budget, *Ishtar* has become synonymous with "bomb" (Kevin Costner's troubled production of *Waterworld* was dubbed "Fishtar" in pre-release stories). Hoffman and Beatty are no Hope and Crosby, but this is still worth a look for Charles Grodin, the modern master of the agitated slow burn, a scene-stealing camel, and the occasional pearls in May's script, such as Beatty reassuring a suicidal Hoffman, "You'd rather have nothing than settle for less," and Hoffman's desert encounter with circling vultures waiting for him and Beatty to collapse. "You mean they're here on spec?" he asks. 🦴🦴

"golden turkeys" is a real gobbler itself. The hosts are intrusive and unfunny, and considering some of the films they have foisted on the public, they are the last people who should make fun of other's cinematic flops (*Nothing But Trouble,* anyone?). This might be useful for novices who have never heard of director Ed Wood or such films as *High School Hellcats* and *Mars Needs Women.* Otherwise, skip it and use this book to seek out the originals. 🦴🦴

1982 (PG) 87m/C D: Malcolm Leo. **VHS, Beta, LV $59.95** *PAR*

It Came from Outer Space

Carlson spots a spaceship crash landing out in the Arizona desert, but can't get anyone to believe him. Alien Xenomorphs take on the form of local humans from the nearby town to repair their spacecraft. Good performances, well done f/x, and outstanding direction add up to a fine science fiction film. Based on the story by Ray Bradbury, who also wrote the script. One of the first uses of the soon-to-be familiar idea of aliens masquerading as human beings, along with *Invaders from Mars,* which was released the same month. Atmospheric and chilling, the second film directed by sci-fi specialist Arnold (*The Incredible Shrinking Man, The Creature from the Black Lagoon*). Originally filmed in 3-D. 🦴🦴🦴🦴

1953 81m/B Richard Carlson, Barbara Rush, Charles Drake, Russell Johnson, Morey Amsterdam; **D:** Jack Arnold; **W:** Ray Bradbury; **M:** Henry Mancini. **VHS $14.98** *MCA, MLB, GKK*

It Conquered the World

Vegetable critters from Venus follow a probe satellite back to Earth and drop in on scientist Van Cleef, who'd been their intergalactic pen pal (seems he thought a Venusian invasion would improve the neighborhood). Their travelling companions, little bat creatures, turn earth dwellers into murderous zombies, and it starts to look like the Venusians are trying to make earth their planetary exurbia. Early vintage zero-budget Corman, for schlock connoisseurs. Remade for television as *Zontar, the Thing from Venus.* 🦴🦴🦴

1956 68m/B Peter Graves, Beverly Garland, Lee Van Cleef, Sally Fraser, Charles B. Griffith, Russ Bender,

Jonathan Haze, Dick Miller, Karen Kadler, Paul Blaisdell; **D:** Roger Corman. **VHS $9.95** *COL, FCT, MLB*

It Takes a Thief

Mansfield's role in this British film noir is fairly small and she's actually not bad as a buxom gangstress who can outdrive and out think the crooks who work with her. The plot revolves around some hidden loot and various betrayals past and present. After an admirably snappy beginning, the film tends to lose some focus, but it's still fast-paced fun. Beware some prints (probably bootlegs) that have gaps at reel breaks, bad sound, grainy high-contrast black and white image, and the opening credits at the end! **AKA:** The Challenge. 🦴🦴🦴

1959 93m/B *GB* Jayne Mansfield, Anthony Quayle, Carl Mohner, Peter Reynolds, John Bennett; **D:** John Gilling. **VHS** *BBF*

"Is it the camel that stinks, or is it this movie?" Dustin Hoffman asks Warren Beatty in *Ishtar.*

It's a Gift

W.C. Fields is a grievously henpecked husband and father, running a New Jersey grocery store but determined to invest his family's finances

Boris Karloff appears a bit peevish in *Isle of the Dead*.

a Three Stooges short subject (and the Stooges do appear briefly, as firemen), about a random group of travelers who hear the confession of a dying criminal (Durante) giving vague directions to his buried cache of money. The crazed treasure-seekers wreck much of southern California and each other to get their hands on that loot. Ultimately exhausting film is undone by its overbearing, one-note script and a monster length (originally 192 minutes). But the parade of comic actors doing their utmost, abetted by mass quantities of faves in funny bit parts, yields some passing pleasure and have gained the movie a cult following. Laserdisc edition restores 20 minutes pruned from the general videocassette release, and includes interviews with cast members. 🦴🦴

1963 155m/C Spencer Tracy, Sid Caesar, Milton Berle, Ethel Merman, Jonathan Winters, Jimmy Durante, Buddy Hackett, Mickey Rooney, Phil Silvers, Dick Shawn, Edie Adams, Dorothy Provine, Buster Keaton, Terry-Thomas, Moe Howard, Larry Fine, Joe DeRita, Jim Backus, William Demarest, Peter Falk, Leo Gorcey, Edward Everett Horton, Joe E. Brown, Carl Reiner, ZaSu Pitts, Eddie Anderson, Jack Benny, Jerry Lewis; **D:** Stanley Kramer; **M:** Ernest Gold. Academy Awards '63: Best Sound Effects Editing; Nominations: Academy Awards '63: Best Color Cinematography, Best Song ("It's a Mad, Mad, Mad, Mad World"), Best Sound, Best Original Score. **VHS, Beta, LV** $29.98 *MGM, FOX, FCT*

It's a Wonderful Life

The movie that gave us that wonderful sitcom plot device: "What would the world be like if I'd never been born?" Corny but you still gotta love it. Look for Sheldon Leonard, who went on to produce a great deal of '60s television (including *The Dick Van Dyke Show*, *Gomer Pyle, USMC,* and *I Spy*), as the bartender at Martini's. For many years, the rights to this gem were up for grabs; TV stations could show it for free—which they did, over and over—turning it into a cult item by rote. Also available colorized; if you accidently rent or buy this version, just turn the color down until it's in its native black and white. The laserdisc version includes production and publicity stills, the theatrical trailer, and commentary by film professor Jeanine Basinger. Also available in a 160-minute Collector's Edition with original preview trailer, "The Making of 'It's a Wonderful Life,'" and a new digital transfer from the original negative. 🦴🦴🦴🦴

in an unseen California orange grove. A remake of the silent film *It's the Old Army Game,* the somewhat outdated film is essentially three long vaudeville sketches strung together, with fill-material culled from Fields' stage career. Some gags are as simple as the star trying to take a morning nap and tormented by one interruption after another, but in Fields' capable hands the material turns into a comedy classic. Blind, deaf old Mr. Muckle's path of devastation is not to be missed. 🦴🦴🦴

1934 71m/B W.C. Fields, Baby LeRoy, Kathleen Howard; **D:** Norman Z. McLeod. **VHS, Beta, LV** $14.95 *MCA, BAR*

It's a Mad, Mad, Mad, Mad World

Determined to forge the Ultimate Screen Comedy, the normally serious-minded producer/director Stanley Kramer helmed this overblown slapstick fracas, with an all-star cast backed by all-star cameos and some of the most impressive stuntwork put on film. But crushed under all that talent and production values is a wee little plot that would better fit

1946 125m/B James Stewart, Donna Reed, Henry Travers, Thomas Mitchell, Lionel Barrymore, Samuel S. Hinds, Frank Faylen, Gloria Grahame, H.B. Warner, Ellen Corby, Sheldon Leonard, Beulah Bondi, Ward Bond, Frank Albertson, Todd Karns, Mary Treen, Charles Halton; *D:* Frank Capra; *W:* Frances Goodrich, Albert Hackett, Jo Swerling; *M:* Dimitri Tiomkin. Golden Globe Awards '47: Best Director (Capra); Nominations: Academy Awards '46: Best Actor (Stewart), Best Director (Capra), Best Film Editing, Best Picture, Best Sound. **VHS, LV $9.95** *IGP, MRV, CNG*

It's Alive!

Not to be confused with Larry Cohen's mutant killer baby epic, this trance-inducing endurathon concerns a farmer feeding passerby to the area's cave-dwelling lizard man. You know you're in Buchanan country when the first five minutes of a film is static shot of dreary Texas scenery seen through a car windshield, with no music, no sound effects, nothing; when the narrator finally pipes in with "They say when it rains when the sun is still shining, the devil is kissing his wife," consider your fate sealed. Morose-looking Tommy Kirk (from *Mars Needs Women*) stars with regular Buchanan player Bill Thurman as the diabolical hayseed ("Wanna see my caged animals?") and the same damn ping-pong eyeball monster from *Creature of Destruction* and *Curse of the Swamp Creature*! Brave viewers are advised to fortify themselves with caffeine or other stimulants before attempting the scene where Thurman's housekeeper recounts her kidnapping and abuse, an endless flashback told in almost complete silence. Keep telling yourself: it's only a movie... 🦴🦴

1968 80m/C Tommy Kirk, Shirley Bonne, Bill Thurman; *D:* Larry Buchanan; *W:* Larry Buchanan. **VHS $15.95** *NOS, LOO*

It's Alive

Writer/director Larry Cohen delivers a bizarre tale of a mutant child born to a seemingly normal Los Angeles couple. The child escapes and goes on a murderous rampage. Deeper than most films of the genre, the movie raises questions still relevant today about unwanted pregnancies, the use of the Pill, our potentially toxic society, and how genetics and environmental factors may effect the unborn. The idea of terror brought on by children pervades late '60s and '70s horror. For other examples, see *Demon Seed, The Omen, Damien: Omen 2, The Exorcist, Rosemary's Baby,* and much later (and much worse) *The Unborn.* Special makeup effects by Academy Award winner Rick Baker (*An American Werewolf in London*) truly create a baby with a face only a mother could love. Great score by Bernard Herrmann and classic horror film ending make this a chilling and memorable film. Followed by two disappointing sequels. 🦴🦴🦴🦴

1974 (PG) 91m/C John P. Ryan, Sharon Farrell, Andrew Duggan, Guy Stockwell, James Dixon, Michael Ansara; *D:* Larry Cohen; *W:* Larry Cohen; *M:* Bernard Herrmann. **VHS, Beta $14.95** *WAR, FCT*

It's Alive 2: It Lives Again

In this lesser sequel to *It's Alive,* mutant babies continue to be born all over the country. The government creates a hit squad to eliminate them. The unfortunate father from the first film tries to warn the expecting couples beforehand and save the vicious, but misunderstood, tikes. The babies are kept hidden in a secluded villa, until the government tracks them down. Sensing danger, the babies turn to a killing spree to escape. Essentially a retread of the first film, with another couple drifting through the same story. Though some interesting issues remain, little new light is shed on them here. 🦴

1978 (R) 91m/C Frederic Forrest, Kathleen Lloyd, John P. Ryan, Andrew Duggan, John Marley, Eddie Constantine; *D:* Larry Cohen. **VHS, Beta $19.98** *WAR, FCT*

It's Alive 3: Island of the Alive

The second sequel to the tongue-in-cheek horror film, in which the infant mutant of the previous films has been left with other mutations to spawn on a desert island. Moriarty, leading a fine cast, is the disturbed papa, confused by his love for a monster son, who fights for the rights of what may well be the next level of human evolution. Typical Cohen mix of thoughtful truth and perversity, though little is left to say after the previous two episodes. Better to watch this than *Parenthood,* though. A small role goes to Isreal, director of *Tunnelvision* and *Bachelor Party.*

It's Not the Size That Counts

A chemical spill contaminates water everywhere and leads to universal male impotence. What a revolting development! But Lawson, the recipient of the world's first penis transplant, is still functioning normally. While girls line up, the richest man in the world (Price) plans a kidnapping. Lots of predictably bad jokes and bedroom farce antics follow, but the comic possibilities of impotence are never explored. Look for British stars Bernrad Lee, Julie Ege, and Judy Geeson in virtual cameos. Limp sequel to *Percy*. **AKA:** Percy's Progress. 🦴🦴▷

1974 90m/C Leigh Lawson, Elke Sommer, Denholm Elliott, Vincent Price; **D:** Ralph Thomas. **VHS $59.98** *SUE*

Jabberwocky

Monty Python animator Terry Gilliam takes a "wocky" on the wild side with his first film, an awesomely inventive medieval fantasy based on Lewis Carroll's timeless poem. Python peer Michael Palin stars as an innocent country bumpkin who, after a series of picaresque adventures, is enlisted to slay the dreaded beast that is ravaging the kingdom on Bruno the Questionable. *Monty Python and the Holy Grail* remains the last word on this sort of thing. Both films revel in slop, mud, and misery, but even by Python standards, this is bloody and scatalogical and not for the squeamish. Look for Terry Jones as a poacher. Python and Gilliam devotees wouldn't miss this. The faint of heart can proceed to Gilliams' more fanciful *Time Bandits, Brazil,* and *The Adventure of Baron Munchausen.* 🦴🦴▷

1977 (PG) 104m/C *GB* Michael Palin, Eric Idle, Max Wall, Deborah Fallender, Terry Jones, John Le Mesurier; **D:** Terry Gilliam; **W:** Terry Gilliam. **VHS, Beta, LV $19.95** *COL*

Jackson County Jail

"If you are who you say you are, you won't have any trouble." This bleak, nightmare vision of Bicentennial America compellingly combines the road film with the woman-in-

"Yes, Mr. Stern, we're all quite impressed. Now will you pull up your pants?" Michael Palin in *Jabberwocky.*

Made back-to-back with *A Return to Salem's Lot,* also with Moriarty. 🦴🦴

1987 (R) 94m/C Michael Moriarty, Karen Black, Laurene Landon, Gerrit Graham, James Dixon, Neal Israel, MacDonald Carey; **D:** Larry Cohen; **W:** Larry Cohen. **VHS, Beta $19.98** *WAR*

It's Dead—Let's Touch It!

A twisted satire about the fight between good and evil, as a pleasant little alien crash lands and is repeatedly abused by the motley assortment of degenerates he encounters. The Earthlings pay for their sins when the baby powder that the dead alien's carcass emits turns them into sickeningly nice pod-type people, culminating in an explosive ending. Slicker follow-up to Bogdan's *The Weasel That Dripped Blood.* 🦴🦴🦴

jeopardy genre. Disillusioned Yvette Mimieux quits her advertising job in Los Angeles and her unfaithful lover. Enroute to New York, she picks up hitchhikers who steal her car, stranding her in a small Arizona town where she is placed in jail and raped by a deputy. She kills her attacker and escapes with fatalistic truck hijacker Tommy Lee Jones ("I was born dead anyway," he shrugs before the climactic shootout in the midst of a parade). This was Jones' first starring role. Roger Corman was the executive producer of this surprise breakout hit that scored with audiences and critics. Familiar faces include Mary Woronov as a gun-toting hillbilly and Severn Darden, a veteran of Chicago's legendary improvisational comedy troupe, Second City, as the sheriff. Betty Thomas, another Second City alum, *Hill Street Blues* veteran, and the director of *The Brady Bunch Movie,* is a short-changing waitress. Robert Carradine is one of the hitchhikers. Director Miller remade this in 1978 for TV as *Outside Chance,* also starring Mimieux. 𝄞 𝄞 ♭

1976 (R) 84m/C Yvette Mimieux, Tommy Lee Jones, Robert Carradine, Severn Darden, Howard Hesseman, Mary Woronov; ***D:*** Michael Miller; ***W:*** Donald Stewart. **VHS, Beta $39.98** *WAR*

Jail Bait

After finishing *Glen or Glenda?,* Ed Wood was hired by Howco to produce, co-write, and direct this unusual crime drama. Don Gregor (Malone), son of a respected plastic surgeon, gets mixed up in a robbery with crook Vic Brady (Farrell, in one of many criminal roles). The jig is up when a secretary (Mona McKinnon in Ed's angora hat) walks in on the holdup, and Don ends up shooting the night watchman. When Don wants to turn himself in, Brady kills him, then coerces the plastic surgeon to change his face, leading to a payoff surprise ending. Since Bela Lugosi was ill at the time, silent film star Rawlinson filled in as the plastic surgeon, and died the next morning. Features a cast of Wood regulars and Ed himself can be heard as a radio announcer. First movie roles for future Hercules Reeves and erstwhile fashion model and TV weather girl Theodora Thurman. Talbot claims the company was chased off a location just as

James Cagney was about to do a walk-on. Uses the same piano/guitar score created by Hoyt Curtain for *Mesa of Lost Women,* but it's not half as annoying here. ***AKA:*** Hidden Face. 𝄞 𝄞

1954 80m/B Timothy Farrell, Clancy Malone, Lyle Talbot, Steve Reeves, Herbert Rawlinson, Dolores Fuller, Theodora Thurman, Conrad Brooks; ***D:*** Edward D. Wood Jr. **VHS, Beta $16.95** *SNC, AOV, LSV*

Jailbird Rock

We'd like to tell you that this isn't really a sweet-young-thing-in-prison musical, but it is. When Antin shoots her stepfather (he told her to turn that damn noise down?) she tries to bring down the Big House with song and dance. No kidding. 𝄞 ♭

1988 90m/C Ronald Lacey, Rhonda Aldrich, Robin Antin; ***D:*** Phillip Schuman. **VHS, Beta $79.95** *TWE*

Jailhouse Rock

This is one of a handful of Elvis Presley films that matter. Presley stars as Vince Everett, who kills a man in a bar fight and is convicted of manslaughter. Imprisoned, he shares a cell with Hunk Houghton (Mickey Shaughnessy), a country singer who shows him the ropes and how to play the guitar. When Vince is released, he becomes a music and movie sensation at the expense of those who helped him to the top of the charts. Light years from such fluff as *Girl Happy* and *Kissin' Cousins,* this is Elvis at his most raw and dangerous (he smashes a guitar over the table of a heckler and insults a roomful of jazz snobs jabbering about Dave Brubeck). Dean Jones has a nice bit as a disc jockey who initially plays Vince's record as background to a dog food commercial. Elvis sings "Treat Me Nice," "Baby, I Don't Care" and the multi-million selling title tune. The "Jailhouse Rock" production number is to Elvis what "Singin' in the Rain" was to Gene Kelly; his shining moment onscreen. ♫ Jailhouse Rock; Treat Me Nice; Baby, I Don't Care; Young and Beautiful; Don't Leave Me Now; I Wanna Be Free; One More Day. 𝄞 𝄞 𝄞

1957 (G) 96m/B Elvis Presley, Judy Tyler, Vaughn Taylor, Dean Jones, Mickey Shaughnessy, William Forrest, Glenn Strange; ***D:*** Richard Thorpe. **VHS, Beta, LV $14.95** *MGM*

and mayhem ensues. Will Jesse be forced to gun down his best friend? An insomnia cure for thousands of satisfied late show viewers. This wacky combination of western and horror genres was part of a double bill with *Billy the Kid Meets Dracula*. Last picture of the (approximately) 175 features directed by the ultra-prolific Beaudine, who got his start with comedy shorts in 1915, directed hits for Mary Pickford (*Sparrows*), poverty row horrors (*The Ape Man, Voodoo Man*), Bowery Boys comedies (*Spooks Run Wild, Ghosts on the Loose*), roadshow pictures (*Mom and Dad*), tons of TV episodes, and countless B-movie comedies, mysteries, musicals, and westerns. ♫♫▷

1965 95m/C John Lupton, Cal Bolder, Narda Onyx, Steve Geray, Estelita, Jim Davis, William "Bill" Fawcett, Nestor Paiva; ***D:*** William Beaudine. **VHS, Beta $19.98** *NOS, SUE*

Jesus of Montreal

A vagrant young actor (stage-trained Canadian star Bluteau) is hired by a Montreal priest to produce a fresh interpretation of an Easter passion play. Taking the good book at its word, he produces a contemporized literal telling that captivates audiences, inflames the men of the cloth, and wins the players' faith. Quebecois director Arcand (keep an eye out for him as the judge) tells a compelling, acerbically satirical and haunting story that never forces its Biblical parallels. In French with English subtitles. ***AKA:*** Jesus de Montreal. ♫♫♫▷

1989 (R) 119m/C *FR CA* Gilles Pelletier, Lothaire Bluteau, Catherine Wilkening, Robert Lepage, Johanne-Marie Tremblay, Remy Girard, Marie-Christine Barrault; ***D:*** Denys Arcand; ***W:*** Denys Arcand. Genie Awards '90: Best Actor (Girard), Best Director (Arcand), Best Film, Best Supporting Actor (Girard); Nominations: Academy Awards '89: Best Foreign Language Film. **VHS, LV $19.98** *ORI, FCT, INJ*

Jimmy, the Boy Wonder

Goremeister Lewis' attempt at a "family" film turns out just as weird as expected. A young boy goes on a magical trip to find out who stopped time and meets an absent-minded astronomer, the evil Mr. Fig, and then discovers what happens at world's end. ♫▷

1966 ?m/C D: Herschell Gordon Lewis. **VHS $19.99** *MOV, TPV*

"I told him not to ask me about my hair plugs, but did he listen? Noooo...." *Jesse James Meets Frankenstein's Daughter.*

Jason and the Argonauts

Mythological heroes Jason, Hercules, and the crew of the Argo set off on a quest to obtain the fabled Golden Fleece. The gods blessed this classic fantasy with a thrilling score by Bernard Herrmann and awesome special effects by Ray Harryhausen (*The Seventh Voyage of Sinbad, Mysterious Island*), who brings to life a giant bronze statue, a seven-headed hyrdra, and the peace de resistance, an army of sword-wielding skeletons. Even Neptune makes a big splash. ♫♫♫▷

1963 (G) 104m/C *GB* Todd Armstrong, Nancy Kovack, Gary Raymond, Laurence Naismith, Nigel Green, Michael Gwynn, Honor Blackman; ***D:*** Don Chaffey; ***W:*** Jan Read, Beverley Cross. **VHS, Beta, LV, 8mm $14.95** *COL, MLB, FUS*

Jesse James Meets Frankenstein's Daughter

The gunslinger (Lupton) and Frankenstein's granddaughter Maria (Onyx), meet up in the Old West. Maria puts the famous monster's brain into the body of Jesse's giant pal (Bolder)

Johnny Guitar

Women strap on six-guns in Nicholas Ray's unintentionally hilarious, gender-bending western. A guitar-playing loner wanders into a small town feud between lovelorn saloon owner Crawford and McCambridge, the town's resident lynchmob-leading harpy. This fascinating cult-favorite has had film theorists arguing for decades: is it a parody, a political McCarthy-era allegory, or Freudian exercise? The off-screen battles of the two female stars are equally legendary. Stick around for the end credits to hear Peggy Lee sing the title song. 𝄞𝄞𝄞𝄻

1953 116m/C Joan Crawford, Ernest Borgnine, Sterling Hayden, Mercedes McCambridge, Scott Brady, Ward Bond, Royal Dano, John Carradine; **D:** Nicholas Ray; **W:** Philip Yordan. **VHS, LV $14.98** *REP*

Just for the Hell of It

A quartet of teenage punks ruthlessly terrorize their suburban Miami 'hood while an innocent kid gets blamed. More exploitation from schlock king Lewis, who also wrote the theme song, "Destruction Inc" (pic's alternate title). Essentially the same cast as the director's *She Devils on Wheels,* filmed simultaneously. *AKA:* Destruction, Inc. 𝄞𝄞

1968 85m/C Rodney Bedell, Ray Sager, Nancy Lee Noble, Agi Gyenes, Steve White; **D:** Herschell Gordon Lewis. **VHS** *NO*

Kalifornia

Bandlands meets the '90s in a road trip with the hitchhikers from hell. Early Grayce (Brad Pitt) is your average slimeball who murders his landlord and hops a ride with his waifish girlfriend Adele (Juliette Lewis) from Kentucky to California with Brian (Duchovny), a yuppie writer interested in mass murderers, and his sultry photographer girlfriend Carrie (Michele Forbes). Pitt and Lewis were still an item when they made this. Pitt reportedly wanted to play against type, and as pretty boy gone homicidal, he succeeds. Extremely violent and disturbing. Also available in an unrated version. 𝄞𝄞𝄻

1993 (R) 117m/C Brad Pitt, Juliette Lewis, David Duchovny, Michele Forbes, Sierra Pecheur, Lois Hall, Gregory Mars Martin; **D:** Dominic Sena; **W:** Tim Metcalfe. **VHS, LV $19.95** *PGV, BTV*

Kenneth Anger, Vol. 1: Fireworks

Compilation of Anger's surrealistic works which merge images of cult figures with erotic fantasies. In "Fireworks," (1947) Anger stars as a man who discovers his growing need for perverse forms of sexual fulfillment. "Rabbit's Moon" (1950) combines an ancient Japanese legend with the interchangeable characters from the 16th Century Harlequin comedies dell'Arte. "Eaux D'Artifice" (1953) involves a strange adventure in the Tivoli Gardens of Denmark. 𝄞𝄞𝄻

1947 34m/C Kenneth Anger, Gordon Gray; **D:** Kenneth Anger. **VHS $29.99** *MFV, TPV*

"NO MORE WIRE HANGERS!" Joan Crawford in *Johnny Guitar.*

Kenneth Anger, Vol. 2: Inauguration of the Pleasure Dome

Mystic philosopher Aleister Crowley's writings are the basis for avant gardist Anger's Dionysian fantasy. A group of wizards transform into godlike entities and perform an

Brad Pitt and
Juliette Lewis
discuss recipes
from the *White
Trash Cookbook*
in *Kalifornia*.

erotic ceremony. Anais Nin plays a love goddess. 🦴🦴🦴

1954 38m/C Marjorie Cameron, Anais Nin; **D:** Kenneth Anger. **VHS $29.99** *MFV, TPV*

Kenneth Anger, Vol. 3: Lucifer Rising

Anger's shorts, "Kustom Kar," "Kommandos," "Puce Moment," and "Lucifer Rising" are full of machismo, sleaze and tinseltown tales. 🦴🦴🦴

1965 37m/C Bruce Byron, Johnny Sapienza; **D:** Kenneth Anger. **VHS $29.95** *TPV*

Kenneth Anger, Vol. 4: Invocation of My Demon Brother

Collection of surrealistic visions by explicit filmmaker Kenneth Anger. In "Lucifer Rising," Satan is reincarnated as a deity of light; "Invocation of My Demon Brother" features

tunes of Mick Jagger. Sex and violence aplenty. 🦴🦴🦴

1980 39m/C Leslie Huggins, Marianne Faithfull; **D:** Kenneth Anger; **M:** Mick Jagger, Bobby Beausoliel. **VHS $29.99** *MFV*

Kentucky Fried Movie

The first flight of the crew that gave us *Airplane, Police Squad,* and the *Naked Gun* films is a wild ride of faux coming attractions and movie and TV parodies. At once wildly funny (the extended Bruce Lee takeoff, *A Fistful of Yen*), sublimely silly (the educational film *Zinc Oxide*), and rousingly rude (the soft-core *Catholic High School Girls in Trouble*). Guest stars include "Incredible Hulk" Bill Bixby, Henry Gibson of *Laugh-In*, Tony Dow from *Leave It To Beaver*, one-time James Bond George Lazenby, and Donald Sutherland as "the clumsy waiter" in the disaster film spoof, *That's Armageddon*. Director John Landis hit it big with his next film, *National Lampoon's Animal House*. 🦴🦴🦴

1977 (R) 85m/C Bill Bixby, Jerry Zucker, Jim Abrahams, David Zucker, Donald Sutherland, Henry Gibson, George Lazenby; **D:** John Landis; **W:** Jerry Zucker, Jim Abrahams, David Zucker. **VHS, Beta, LV $59.95** *MED*

The Killer

A hitman with a conscience (Chow Yun-Fat), a blinded singer (Sally Yeh), a dedicated policeman (Danny Lee): they're caught up in the middle of a Hong Kong mob war in what many consider to be John Woo's best film to date. (It has earned legions of fans at film festivals and on video.) After an elegiac beginning in a candlelit Catholic church, the action shifts to a violent and inventive shoot-out. But this isn't an exercise in mindless cinematic mayhem. It's a story about friendship, loyalty, platonic love, and religious faith. With lots of automatic weapons and a hundred or so on-screen shootings. The tape version is available in both dubbed and subtitled editions; the Criterion laser disc is formatted in the original wide-screen image. It also contains commentary by Woo, and several extra features devoted to Hong Kong action movies and stars. ***AKA:*** Die Xue Shuang Xiong. 🦴🦴🦴🦴

1990 (R) 110m/C *HK* Chow Yun-fat, Sally Yeh, Danny Lee, Kenneth Tsang, Chu Kong; **D:** John Woo; **W:** John Woo. **VHS $89.95** *FXL, BTV, FCT*

Killer Klowns from Outer Space

Bozo-like aliens resembling demented clowns land on earth and set up circus tents to lure Earthlings in. Visually striking, campy but slick horror flick that'll make you think twice about your next visit to the big top. Mood is heightened by a cool title tune by the Dickies. Definite cult potential. 🦴🦴🦴

1988 (PG-13) 90m/C Grant Cramer, Suzanne Snyder, John Allen Nelson, Royal Dano, John Vernon, Peter Licassi, Michael Siegel; **D:** Stephen Chiodo; **W:** Charles Chiodo, Stephen Chiodo; **M:** John Massari. **VHS, Beta, LV $19.95** *MED, CDV*

K

Cooking up some hairball stew in *Kentucky Fried Movie.*

As if regular clowns aren't scary enough! *Killer Klowns from Outer Space.*

1986 (R) 91m/C Elaine Wilkes, Sherry Willis-Burch, Joanna Johnson, Paul Bartel, Martin Hewitt, Ralph Seymour; **D:** William Fruet. **VHS, Beta $79.98** *FOX*

The Killer Shrews

This certified "golden turkey" stars Baruch Lumet (father of famed director Sidney of *Serpico* and *Network* fame) as Dr. Craigis, who creates a serum that transforms tiny shrews into rabid beasts (actually dogs in make-up). Producer and co-star Ken Curtis is better known as Festus on the classic TV series, *Gunsmoke.* Ingrid Goude was Miss Universe of 1957. From the people who brought you *The Giant Gila Monster.* Director Ray Kellogg would later co-direct with John Wayne *The Green Berets,* the pro-Vietnam War epic in which the sun inexplicably sets in the East. 🦴🦴

1959 70m/B James Best, Ingrid Goude, Baruch Lumet, Ken Curtis; **D:** Ray Kellogg. **VHS $19.98** *SNC, MRV, HHT*

Killer Nerd

Harold Kunkle has had enough! Harassed by bullies, rejected by babes, he takes the law into his hands to exact his revenge. But his is no ordinary law, his is the law of the NERD! Radloff, an eccentric who logged appearances on MTV as the "genuine nerd from Cleveland" is no Pee Wee Herman but deserves better than this pee wee-league slasher spoof, shot for $10,000 by Ohioians with all the finesse of a convenience-store security camera. Obscure followup, *Bride of Killer Nerd,* also deserves your neglect. **WOOF!**

1991 90m/C Toby Radloff; **D:** Wayne A. Harold, Mark Steven Bosko. **VHS $59.95** *HHE*

Killer Party

Three coeds pledge a sorority and undergo a hazing in a haunted fraternity house. When the filmmakers run out of situations involving pranks and sex they bring in the standard mad slasher possessed by a ghost. Turn down any invitations to this tedious trash; not even the presence of Paul Bartel (*Eating Raoul, Lust in the Dust*) as a professor makes a difference. **WOOF!**

Killer Tomatoes Eat France

Professor Gangrene takes his tomato fetish to France, where the giant vegetables try to take over the streets. This fourth entry in the killer-vegetable (er, fruit) saga recaptures the zaniness of *Return of the Killer Tomatoes.* This time around infamous Professor Gangrene plans to use an ancient prophecy to install his henchman, Igor, on the throne of France. Never mind that France hasn't had a throne in almost two centuries. The play, so they say, is the thing. Only an American hitchhiker, a French peasant girl, and the ever-present Fuzzy Tomato stand in the dastardly one's way. The final Tomato flick assaults the viewer with a constant barrage of one liners and visual jokes that aren't not quite as rapid fire as a Zucker Brothers comedy, but it's clearly superior to most released-to-video comedies. Solid, playful laughs throughout. Viva la France! 🦴🦴🦴

1991 94m/C John Astin, Marc Price, Steve Lundquist; **D:** John DeBello. **VHS, LV $92.98** *FXV*

Killer Tomatoes Strike Back

The third *Killer Tomatoes* movie isn't in the league of *The Naked Gun* satires. In fact, it's the weakest of the four films in the *Tomato* trilogy. This time around tomato-mad scientist Astin harnesses the powers of trash-TV in a planned vegetable invasion. Standing in his way are a lone homicide cop and the requisite pretty girl. Perhaps due to a *Killer Tomatoes* cartoon series at the time, this isn't as saucy as its predecessors and is acceptable for family audiences. Enough of the jokes work to make it watchable, even if you're not a Tomato fan. However, it's tough to relate to the dick and his babe; even cheap little comedies need characters you can care about. At least we still have series regular Fuzzy Tomato to cheer for. 🐾🐾

1990 87m/C John Astin, Rick Rockwell, Crystal Carson, Steve Lundquist, John Witherspoon; **D:** John DeBello. **VHS $39.98** *FXV, IME*

The Killers

Like ruthless crime boss Ronald Reagan (yes—Ronald Reagan) slapping mistress Angie Dickinson, Don Siegel's remake of the 1946 film noir classic packs a wallop. Professional hit men Lee Marvin and Clu Gulager wonder why their latest victim (John Cassavettes) put up no resistance. Lee Marvin's kiss-off to the double-crossing Dickenson is a hard-boiled pulp classic. Originally produced for television, but was deemed too violent and released to theatres. Reagan's first film as a villain was his Hollywood swan song. Siegel would later direct *Dirty Harry*. Two years later, Reagan would be elected governor of California. **AKA:** Ernest Hemingway's the Killers. 🐾🐾🐾

1964 95m/C Lee Marvin, Angie Dickinson, John Cassavetes, Ronald Reagan, Clu Gulager, Claude Akins, Norman Fell; **D:** Donald Siegel; **M:** John Williams. **VHS, Beta $14.98** *MCA*

King Creole

This was Elvis's last film before being drafted into the army and his swan song as an actor to be taken seriously. Never again would he get as good a role (a singing busboy who runs afoul of gangsters), a director (Michael Curtiz of *Casablanca* fame), a script (co-written by Michael Gazzo, best-known as Pentangeli in *The Godfather, Part Two*), or supporting cast (Carolyn Jones, Vic Morrow, and grumpy old Walter Matthau as the hood who wants Elvis to sing in his club). The soundtrack is also fit for a King with such songs as "Trouble" and "Hard-Headed Woman." Based on Harold Robbins' novel, *A Stone for Danny Fisher*. 🎵 King Creole; Banana; New Orleans; Turtles, Berries and Gumbo; Crawfish; Don't Ask Me Why; As Long As I Have You; Trouble; Hard-Headed Woman. 🐾🐾🐾

1958 115m/B Elvis Presley, Carolyn Jones, Walter Matthau, Dean Jagger, Dolores Hart, Vic Morrow, Paul Stewart; **D:** Michael Curtiz. **VHS, Beta, LV $19.95** *MVD, FOX*

King Kong

The original beauty and the beast film classic tells the story of Kong, a giant ape captured in Africa and brought to New York as a sideshow attraction. Kong falls for Wray, escapes from his captors and rampages through the city, ending up on top of the newly built Empire State Building. Moody Steiner score adds color, and Willis O'Brien's stop-motion animation still holds up well. Remade numerous times with various theme derivations. Available in a colorized version (what a monstrosity). The laserdisc, produced from a superior negative, features extensive liner notes and running commentary by film historian Ronald Haver. 🐾🐾🐾🐾

1933 105m/B Fay Wray, Bruce Cabot, Robert Armstrong, Frank Reicher, Noble Johnson, Sam Hardy, James Flavin; **D:** Ernest B. Schoedsack; **M:** Max Steiner. **VHS, Beta, LV, 8mm $16.98** *TTC, MED, FUS*

King Kong Vs. Godzilla

The planet issues a collective shudder as the two mightiest monsters slug it out. In the Arctic Ocean, Godzilla frees himself from the iceberg prison he found himself in at the end of *Godzilla Raids Again*, destroys a nuclear sub for a snack, and heads for Japan to raise hell. Meanwhile, on tropical Farou Island, rare medicinal berries cause an ape to grow far beyond Kong size. The president of a Japanese drug company (Ichiro Arishima) has the beast captured, with plans to star him on the TV show he sponsors, but the monster escapes en route, and swims ashore to raise hell. Kong is subdued by the berry juice and transported to meet Godzilla, in the hope that the two menaces will finish each other off in a grand duel on Mt. Fuji. A co-production between Toho and vari-

K

"Oh, no, it wasn't the airplanes—it was beauty killed the beast."
—Robert Armstrong in *King Kong*.

A WWI Scottish soldier (Alan Bates) finds a battle-torn French town evacuated of all occupants except a colorful collection of escaped inmates from a nearby asylum, who have claimed the town as their own and assumed various roles in the community. When Bates makes a flip remark about being the "King of Hearts" (trying to match their surrealism line for line), they accept him as their unwilling leader; Bates must decide between his little insane community, or a world gone mad with war. Genvieve Bujold is cute as ballerina wannabe; look for Michel Serrault (*La Cage aux Folles*) as, not surprisingly, a would-be effeminate hairdresser. Light-hearted comedy with a serious message; definitely worthwhile. *AKA:* Le Roi de Coeur. ♫ ♫ ♫ ♫

1966 101m/C *FR GB* Alan Bates, Genevieve Bujold, Adolfo Celi, Francoise Christophe, Micheline Presle, Michel Serrault; **D:** Philippe de Broca; **M:** Georges Delerue. **VHS, Beta, LV** $19.95 *MGM, INJ, TVC*

Kiss Me Deadly

Aldrich's adaptation of Mickey Spillane's private eye tale takes pulp literature high concept. Meeker, as Mike Hammer, is a self-interested rough and tumble all American dick (detective, that is). When a woman to whom he happened to give a ride is found murdered, he follows the mystery straight into a nuclear conspiracy. Aldrich, with tongue deftly in cheek, styles a message through the medium; topsy-turvy camerawork and rat-a-tat-tat pacing tell volumes about Hammer, the world he orbits, and that special '50s kind of paranoia. Now a cult fave, it's considered to be the American grandaddy to French New Wave. Cinematography by Ernest Laszlo. ♫ ♫ ♫ ♪

1955 105m/B Ralph Meeker, Albert Dekker, Paul Stewart, Wesley Addy, Cloris Leachman, Strother Martin, Marjorie Bennett; **D:** Robert Aldrich. **VHS, Beta, LV** $19.98 *MGM, FCT*

KISS Meets the Phantom of the Park

The popular '70s costumed superhero rock band appears at an amusement park, much to the detriment of a mad scientist (Zerbe), who has been kidnapping people and turning them into animatronic slaves. Seeking revenge, he captures the quartet and replaces them with

Ace Frehley does Hamlet in KISS Meets the Phantom of the Park.

ous American parties, this was the first Godzilla film (or Kong film for that matter) to be shot in color and scope. The f/x are not as good as in sequels to follow, but acceptable—though the Kong costume is horrible. A persistent false rumor—that a different ending was seen in Japan with Kong defeated—makes no sense, as Godzilla is the villain in both versions. However, Universal drastically changed the original for U.S. release, adding senseless scenes while omitting vital footage, even going so far as to replace the score with stock library music. *AKA:* King Kong Tai Godzilla. ♫ ♫ ♫

1963 105m/C *JP* Michael Keith, Tadao Takashima, Mie Hama, Kenji Sahara; **D:** Inoshiro Honda. **VHS** $9.95 *GKK*

The King of Hearts

The lunatics have taken over more than the asylum in this charming little anti-war piece.

robot doubles. The crowd threatens to riot when the doubles play, but they actually don't sound much different. Veteran British fantasy director Hessler (*Golden Voyage of Sinbad*, *Scream and Scream Again*) does what he can with the cheap production values and silly script, but there's no mistaking that this is just a shoddy TV movie from animation studio Hanna-Barbera. Brion James has a supporting role as a security guard. Filmed mostly at Magic Mountain. Hoyt Curtain's score sounds just like his music for Scooby-Doo cartoons. ♫ Rock & Roll All Night; Beth; Shout It Out Loud. *AKA:* Attack of the Phantoms. 🦴🦴

1978 96m/C Gene Simmons, Paul Stanley, Peter Criss, Ace Frehley, Anthony Zerbe, Deborah Ryan, John Dennis Johnston; *D:* Gordon Hessler. **VHS, Beta $10.98** *MVD, WOV*

Kiss of the Spider Woman

In this acclaimed adaptation of Manuel Puig's novel, Valentin Arregui (Raul Julia) and Luis Molina (William Hurt) are cellmates in a Latin American prison. Valentin is a political prisoner and Molina is a homosexual jailed for a relationship with a young boy. Most of this dramaturgic movie takes place in their small cell, where Molina tell Valentin stories of romantic movies, all of which star the glamrous Leni Lamaison. Molina identifies with the heroine, but Valentin is outraged to discover that the movie Molina describes in most detail is a Nazi propaganda film. The two prisoners are divided by differences in what they find meaningful: although he has both a socialist girlfriend and a bourgeois lover (played by Sonia Braga, who is also Leni), Valentin lives first for his (failing) political cause; Molina, a window dresser who lives with his mother, spends all his energy searching in vain for a "real man." The movie focuses on the developing friendship between these two scarred men and how it irrevocably changes both their lives. Both actors deliver powerful performances; Hurt is particularly affecting as the wistful Molina. 🦴🦴🦴

1985 (R) 119m/C *BR* William Hurt, Raul Julia, Sonia Braga, Jose Lewgoy, Milton Goncalves, Nuno Leal Maia, Denise Dumont; *D:* Hector Babenco; *W:* Leonard Schrader; *M:* John Neschling, Wally Badarou. Academy Awards '85: Best Actor (Hurt); British Academy Awards '85: Best Actor (Hurt); Cannes Film Festival '85: Best Actor (Hurt); Independent Spirit Awards '86: Best Foreign Film; Nominations: Academy Awards '85: Best Adapted Screenplay, Best Director (Babenco), Best Picture. **VHS, Beta, LV, 8mm $19.95** *COL, BTV, NLC*

Koyaanisqatsi

A mesmerizing film that takes an intense look at modern life (the movie's title is the Hopi word for "life out of balance"). Without dialogue or narration, it brings traditional background elements, landscapes and cityscapes, up front to produce a unique view of the structure and mechanics of our daily lives, including such micro views as freeway traffic patterns and Twinkies moving through the line at a Hostess factory. Riveting and immensely powerful. A critically acclaimed and hypnotic score by Philip Glass, and Reggio's cinematography prove to be the perfect match to this brilliant film. Followed by *Powaqqatsi*. 🦴🦴🦴🦴

1983 87m/C *D:* Godfrey Reggio; *M:* Philip Glass. **VHS, Beta, LV $14.95** *MVD, FCT, MLB*

La Cage aux Folles

Adaption of the popular French play in which a gay nightclub owner (Ugo Tognazzi) and his neurotic cross-dressing lover (Michel Serrault) play it straight when Tognazzi's son from a long-ago liaison brings his fiancee and her conservative parents home for dinner. Charming music and lots of fun. So successful, it was followed by two inferior sequels, *La Cage aux Folles II* (1981) and *La Cage aux Folles III: The Wedding* (1986), and a Broadway musical. In French with English subtitles; a dubbed version is available, but Serrault's squawking just isn't the same in English. 🦴🦴🦴

1978 (R) 91m/C *FR* Ugo Tognazzi, Michel Serrault, Michel Galabru, Claire Maurier, Remy Laurent, Benny Luke, Carmen Scarpitta; *D:* Edouard Molinaro; *W:* Edouard Molinaro, Francis Veber, Jean Poiret; *M:* Ennio Morricone. Cesar Awards '79: Best Actor (Serrault); Golden Globe Awards '80: Best Foreign Film; Nominations: Academy Awards '79: Best Adapted Screenplay, Best Costume Design, Best Director (Molinaro). **VHS, Beta, LV $19.98** *MGM, FOX, CRC*

Lady Godiva Rides

Jordan plays the very American sounding Lady in a wild plot which has her escape the hang-

"I told them my father was a cultural attache... what'll they think when they find out he lives with a drag queen?"

--Remy Laurent in *La Cage aux Folles*.

FRANKENSTEIN MEETS GODZILLA?

The True Story in Cinema History

King Kong vs. Frankenstein

After his landmark success as the special effects genius behind *King Kong*, the career path of Willis O'Brien was far from smooth, with many disappointments. Aside from the Oscar he won for *Mighty Joe Young*, he spent most of his time as an effects man for hire. In his spare time, he busied himself trying to develop projects of his own, with little success. His *Valley of the Eagles* was cancelled, as was *Tarzan Meets Mighty Joe Young*. *The Beast of Hollow Mountain* was completed, but suffered from a low budget, and most of the f/x were the work of others. The remake of *The Lost World* was a fiasco without his stop-motion wizardry. *The Valley of Gwangi* was made after his death in 1962, and he wouldn't live to see his work in *It's a Mad, Mad, Mad, Mad World*.

Among the many story ideas he had was one for a second Kong sequel called *King Kong vs. Frankenstein*. In this fanciful tale, Kong survives his fall and is smuggled back to Skull Island (which must have resurfaced after sinking in *Son of Kong*). Meanwhile, the grandson of Dr. Frankenstein is following the family tradition, and has built a twenty foot monster he calls a Ginko using parts from different animals. Carl Denham brings both monsters to San Francisco to stage a boxing match between the two titans. Of course, they break free and do what monsters do: fight each other and destroy landmarks. They eventually end up toppling to their apparent deaths from the Golden Gate Bridge.

O'Brien's treatment was sold to producer John Beck (*Harvey*), who hired screenwriter George Worthing Yates to do a rewrite. Yates script made quite a few changes, including the new title *King Kong vs. Prometheus*, but for the most part left the story intact. In search of financing, Beck took the property to Toho Studios in Japan, seemingly the only place capable of making giant monster movies on a low budget (compared to the average American film). Toho jumped at the chance to pit the famous ape

continued...

man's noose after being convicted of murder aboard the phoniest looking sailing ship in cinema history, and becoming a wrasslin' dancehall girl in Tombstone, Arizona. For Stephen's first color feature since the classic *Orgy of the Dead*, he saved money on period costumes by not giving any to some of the women. Jordan's natural beauty and friendly personality made her the '60s Queen of Soft-core. She displays her bountiful talents in *Brand of Shame*, *Head Mistress*, *The Ramrodder*, *Her Odd Tastes*, *Marsha, the Erotic Housewife*, *The Muthers*, *Sweet Georgia*, *The Black Alleycats*, and dozens more. **AKA:** Lady Godiva Meets Tom Jones. 🦴🦴

1968 88m/C Marsha Jordan, Forman Shane; **D:** A.C. Stephen. **VHS $19.95** *VDM*

Lady in Red

Two Roger Corman apprentices, screenwriter John Sayles and former editor and second unit director Lewis Teague, breathed life into the then-dormant gangster genre by focusing not on John Dillinger, but on his girlfriend Polly Franklin. Pamela Sue Martin, TV's "Nancy Drew," stars as the farm girl who leaves her abusive home for Chicago, where she toughs out a woman's prison and later becomes a prostitute for legendary madam Anna Sage. It is not until Dillinger is gunned down outside the Biograph Theater that she learns her boyfriend was Public Enemy Number 1. Branded by the press as the infamous "Lady in Red," she embarks on a life of crime before heading for Hollywood. A game cast, with a restrained Robert Conrad as Dillinger, *One Flew Over the Cuckoo's Nest* Oscar-winner Louise Fletcher as Sage, and Christopher Lloyd and Dick Miller in bit parts. Martin would later join the *Dynasty* family as Fallon Carrington. Sayles and Teague later collaborated on *Alligator*. **AKA:** Guns, Sin and Bathtub Gin. 🦴🦴◁

1979 90m/C Pamela Sue Martin, Louise Fletcher, Robert Conrad, Christopher Lloyd, Dick Miller; **D:** Lewis Teague; **W:** John Sayles; **M:** James Horner. **VHS, Beta $69.98** *LIV, VES*

Last House on the Left

Two girls are kidnapped on the way to a rock concert by a gang of escaped convicts and ironically end up dead across the street from home. When the gang attempts to hole up at the first convenient house, the girls' quiet sub-urban parents exact bloody revenge. Tongue-in-cheek tone clashes with the repellent drawn-out rape and torture sequences, re-deemed quite a bit by the outrageously over the top second half and the tongue-in-cheek treatment given the inept criminals. Contro-versial and grim low-budget shocker; loosely based on Bergman's *The Virgin Spring.* The trailer popularized the line "Just keep repeat-ing: It's only a movie...it's only a movie...", used a decade before by H. G. Lewis for *Color Me Blood Red,* and may have been used much earlier. Craven went on to direct *The Hills Have Eyes* and *A Nightmare on Elm Street,* while producer Sean S. Cunningham created the *Friday the 13th* series. 🦴🦴🦴

1972 (R) 83m/C David Hess, Lucy Grantham, San-dra Cassel, Mark Sheffler, Fred J. Lincoln; **D:** Wes Craven. **VHS, Beta, LV $19.98** *LIV, VES, HHE*

The Last Season

To cover up a hunting mishap in the remote wilderness, the lead sportsman's master plan may be summed up as follows: shoot every-body. Cheapjack fight for survival ensues, in a feature-length thriller lensed on videotape. Entertainment highlight is merely that villain-ous thespian Cox bears a certain resemblance to fallen automaker John Z. DeLorean. WOOF!

1987 90m/C Christopher Gosch, Louise Dorsey, David Cox; **D:** Raja Zahr. **VHS** *NO*

Last Tango in Paris

Brando plays a middle-aged American who meets a French girl and tries to forget his wife's suicide with a short, extremely steamy affair. Bertolucci does everything he can to pump energy into the slowly moving story. Brando gives one of his best performances. Very con-troversial when made, still quite explicit and visually stunning. It's also talky, ponderous, and, once the novelty of the whole thing has worn off, it's much ado about very little. As Bertolucci would prove in *The Last Emperor* and *Little Buddha,* gripping narrative drive is not his forte. The X-rated version, at 130 min-utes, is also available. 🦴🦴▷

1973 (R) 126m/C *IT FR* Marlon Brando, Maria Schneider, Jean-Pierre Leaud; **D:** Bernardo Bertolucci; **W:** Bernardo Bertolucci. New York Film Critics Awards '73: Best Actor (Brando); National So-ciety of Film Critics Awards '73: Best Actor (Brando); Nominations: Academy Awards '73: Best Actor (Brando), Best Director (Bertolucci). **VHS, Beta, LV $29.98** *MGM, FOX*

The Last Temptation of Christ

Scorcese's controversial adaptation of the Nikos Kazantzakis novel, portraying Christ in his last year as an ordinary Israelite tormented by divine doubt, human desires and the voice of God. The controversy engulfing the film, as it was heavily protested and widely banned, tended to divert attention from what is an exceptional statement of religious and artistic vision. Excellent score by Peter Gabriel. 🦴🦴🦴▷

1988 (R) 164m/C Willem Dafoe, Harvey Keitel, Bar-bara Hershey, Harry Dean Stanton, Andre Gregory, David Bowie, Verna Bloom, Juliette Caton, John Lurie, Roberts Blossom, Irvin Kershner, Barry Miller, Tomas Arana, Nehemiah Persoff, Paul Herman; **D:** Martin Scorsese; **W:** Paul Schrader; **M:** Peter Gabriel. Nominations: Academy Awards '88: Best Director (Scorsese). **VHS, Beta, LV $19.95** *MCA*

The Last Wave

Richard Chamberlain, king of the TV minis-eries, acquits himself convincingly as an Aus-tralian lawyer who agrees to defend five Abo-rigines accused of manslaughter. Like his earlier *Picnic at Hanging Rock,* director Peter Weir creates a gripping sense of unease out of mystical, unexplainable events. Chamber-lain, unfamiliar with Aborigine beliefs, is haunted by apocalyptic visions. A psycholog-ical mystery that will leave you shaking in its wake. 🦴🦴🦴

1977 (PG) 109m/C *AU* Richard Chamberlain, Olivia Hamnett, David Gulpilil, Frederick Parslow; **D:** Pe-ter Weir; **W:** Peter Weir. **VHS, Beta** *FCT, RHI*

Laura

A corpse is a corpse, of course, of course, but for New York detective Dana Andrews, rav-ishing Gene Tierney is no ordinary murder vic-tim. The more he investigates her case, the more obsessed he becomes with her painted

L

"How do you like your hero? Over easy or sunny side up?"

--Paul (Marlon Brando) to Jeanne (Maria Schneider) in *Last Tango in Paris.*

Story continued...

against their own famous monster, and so *King Kong vs. Godzilla* was made, with a totally new script and a Kong costume that, for reasons that have never been explained, was woefully inadequate.

Frankenstein vs. Everybody

After the worldwide success of *King Kong vs. Godzilla*, Toho was anxious to make more monster rallies. The idea of a giant Frankenstein Monster, and the guaranteed box office that the name seems to generate, appealed to them. They planned to co-star the creature in a sequel to their hit giant moth picture called *Frankenstein vs. Mothra*, but again decided to substitute their proven champ, and the picture was made as *Mothra vs. Godzilla* (released in the U.S. as *Godzilla vs. the Thing*, and on video as *Godzilla vs. Mothra*). They also tried to make *Frankenstein vs. King Kong*, but perhaps RKO demanded too much money for Kong. They eventually made *King Kong Escapes* in 1967 as a co-production with animation studio Rankin-Bass, but failed to obtain Kong's services for the proposed sequel, which was turned into *Godzilla vs. the Sea Monster*.

The Frankenstein project continued to evolve. Since Toho's f/x genius Eiji Tsuburaya had a definite squid fixation (he had originally wanted Godzilla to be a giant squid), *Frankenstein vs. Devilfish* was announced, but footage of the big octopus proved to be unacceptable, and most of its scenes were cut out (none appear in the U.S. version, *Frankenstein Conquers the World*). Godzilla was called in to take the place of the rejected squid, but by this time the big G was busy fighting *Ghidrah, the Three-headed Monster*. The picture was finally completed with a completely new monster named Baragon, who turned out to be more cute than menacing, despite his carnivorous ways.

Frankenstein vs. Frankenstein

Toho's giant Frankenstein picture was enough of a success to warrant a sequel. The monster, who had grown from the mutated heart of the original Frankenstein Monster in the previous film, reaches his full height and grows a thick coat

continued...

portrait which hangs in her apartment. Imagine his surprise when Laura—still very much alive—returns from a vacation in the country. Classic film noir, with endlessly quotable dialogue. Clifton Webb, as an acerbic columnist and Laura's mentor, gets all the good lines. "In my case," he tells Andrews, "self-absorption is justified." Vincent Price is equally superb as a feckless admirer. Caught by Webb and Tierney with another woman, he proclaims his innocence. "In a moment of supreme disaster," Webb sneers, "he's trite." The height of director Otto Preminger's career (for the depth, see the hilariously overheated *Hurry Sundown*). Johnny Mercer's haunting theme song became a standard. The soundtrack is available on compact disc. 🦴🦴🦴🦴

1944 85m/B Gene Tierney, Dana Andrews, Clifton Webb, Lane Chandler, Vincent Price, Judith Anderson, Grant Mitchell, Dorothy Adams; **D:** Otto Preminger; **M:** David Raksin. Academy Awards '44: Best Black and White Cinematography; Nominations: Academy Awards '44: Best Director (Preminger), Best Interior Decoration, Best Screenplay, Best Supporting Actor (Webb). **VHS, Beta, LV $19.98** *FXV, PMS, BTV*

Leatherface: The Texas Chainsaw Massacre 3

Before Hannibal Lector gave cannibalism a certain sophistication, *The Texas Chainsaw Massacre* kept it simple. The saga of the butchering band of Texas yahoos continues in this third installment. Yet another group of wandering innocents (who undoubtedly haven't seen the first two films) fall prey to the flesh-wearing, chainsaw wielding behemoth Leatherface and his deranged clan. The sheer shock of the subject matter of the original made it frightening. The sequels lose this benefit and can not seem to make for it. Villains with more character (and more expression) than Leatherface have made other films more watchable. As one of the murdering lot says of his victims, "They just keep gettin' dumber." This would be equally applicable to the Chainsaw films. The inscription on Leatherface's saw reminds us, "The saw is family." And we all know how much we like having family over. 🦴

1989 (R) 81m/C Kate Hodge, William Butler, Ken Foree, Tom Hudson, R.A. Mihailoff; **D:** Jeff Burr; **W:** David J. Schow. **VHS, Beta, LV $19.95** *COL*

The Legend of the 7 Golden Vampires

You can almost hear some weasel pitching this one to the studio boys: "OK, first we start with an ancient Chinese legend, then we add some vampires, then we make the vampires martial arts masters, and finally we bring in well-known actor and veteran vampire hunter Peter Cushing to give us a little credibility. Piece of cake—we'll make millions on this one." WRONG! This joint venture between Hammer Films and the Shaw Brothers, a massive Hong Kong production company, is a feeble attempt to merge the popular martial arts and vampire genres. One of the great disasters in horror film history, this turkey put the final nail in Hammer's bankruptcy coffin. 🦴

1973 89m/C Peter Cushing, John Forbes-Robertson, Chan Shen. **VHS** *TTC*

The Legend of the Wolf Woman

A beautiful witch (Borel) uses black magic to assume the personality of the legendary wolf-woman, leaving a trail of gruesome killings across the countryside. Two hundred years later, her descendant Daniella inherits the curse, and the killing begins again. When she meets a man and falls in love, she's able to stave off the bloodlust—that is, until a gang of lowlifes break into their house. Genre fans will find this one surprisingly entertaining. The U.S. version is missing 15 minutes. *AKA:* Daughter of the Werewolf; Werewolf Woman; She-Wolf. 🦴🦴

1977 (R) 84m/C *IT* Anne Borel, Fred Stafford, Tino Carey, Elliot Zamuto, Ollie Reynolds, Andrea Scotti, Karen Carter; *D:* Raphael D. Silver. **VHS, Beta $19.95** *VIP*

Lemora, Lady Dracula

A pretty young church singer is drawn into the lair of the evil Lady Dracula, whose desires include her body as well as her blood. A perversely different kind of spook show—Lemora surrounds herself with a "family" of vampire children. Horror fans will enjoy some excellent atmosphere, particularly in a scene where the girl's church bus is attacked by zombie-like creatures. Very much like the fever dream a troubled child might have. Extra interest comes from the 1930s period setting, which is very unusual for a low-budget picture. Smith remains a '70s "B" movie favorite from her appearances in films such as *Caged Heat, Laserblast,* and *The Incredible Melting Man.* Perhaps a double feature with *Lady Frankenstein...? AKA:* The Lady Dracula; The Legendary Curse of Lemora. 🦴🦴🦴

1973 (PG) 80m/C Leslie Gilb, Cheryl "Rainbeaux" Smith, William Whitton, Steve Johnson, Monty Pyke, Maxine Ballantyne, Parker West, Richard Blackburn; *D:* Richard Blackburn. **VHS $18.00** *FRG*

Leningrad Cowboys Go America

An offbeat gem from start to "Finnish." Out on the frozen tundra, the world's worst polka band is advised to try their luck in America: "They'll buy anything there." When the band arrives in the New York, their optimistic promoter has big plans for them: Madison Square Garden! Yankee Stadium! Then he hears them, and promptly sends them packing to play a wedding in Mexico. Thus begins this deliriously deadpan cross-country, culture-clash odyssey through Memphis, New Orleans, Natchez, and Galveston. Despite the Cowboy's outrageous appearance (peaked, pointy pompadours and pointy shoes), this is stone-faced minimalist comedy, meaning it's so funny, you'll forget to laugh. Other Kaurismaki art house misfits include *Ariel* and *The Match Factory Girl.* Jim Jarmusch, director of *Stranger Than Paradise* and *Mystery Train,* and Kaurismaki's kindred spirit, cameos as a used car dealer. There's your coolness litmus test right there. In Finnish with English subtitles. 🦴🦴🦴

1989 (PG-13) 78m/C *FI* Jim Jarmusch, Matti Pellonpaa, Kari Vaananen, Nicky Tesco; *D:* Aki Kaurismaki; *W:* Aki Kaurismaki. **VHS, LV $79.98** *ORI, FCT, INJ*

Lenny Bruce Performance Film

Lenny Bruce was hailed as a comic genius by some, an obscene threat by others. Ultimately, the latter destroyed his career. This concert tape of Bruce's penultimate nightclub appear-

of brown hair. His living hand, which had been pulled off, floats out to sea and regenerates into an aquatic green-furred Frankenstein, who eventually clashes with his more friendly brother. The American producers thought the two monsters looked more like giant apes than Frankensteins, and changed everything to suit the title *War of the Gargantuas*.

And so winds the tangled trail of monster movie history. Will Godzilla ever meet up with the Frankenstein Monster? Will Mothra battle King Kong? Will Robert DeNiro reprise his Frankenstein Monster role and meet Gary Oldman's Dracula and Jack Nicholson's werewolf? Only time, and the ever twisted minds of movie producers, will tell.

ance at Basin Street West in San Francisco lets viewers decide. Poorly shot in black and white, with imperfect sound, this is still the only complete, unedited Lenny Bruce performance available, and for that reason it is worthwhile. Bruce covers his various arrests for obscenity charges, skewering the forces mounted against him, along with a range of other topics from religion to ethnic stereotypes. Though he comes across as bitter at this point in his career, glimpses of brilliance still show through. Though tame by today's standards, Bruce paved the way for such bold comics as Richard Pryor and Eddie Murphy. This film was to serve as evidence at his obscenity trial. Also included is Bruce's "Thank You Mask Man," a color cartoon parody of the Lone Ranger legend, with Bruce voicing all the characters. For a more complete biography, see *Lenny* (1974), starring Dustin Hoffman as Bruce. 🎻🎻🎻

1968 72m/B Lenny Bruce. **VHS, Beta $59.95** *VES, RHI, MVD*

Lethal Lolita–Amy Fisher: My Story

The only made-for-television Amy Fisher story out of three whose cast members even remotely resemble the real people—except of

course actress Parker is actually pretty. Minor details aside, this account is Amy's story, purchased by NBC for an undisclosed amount, portraying her as an incest victim who gets involved with an opportunistic married jerk who drags her into prostitution, leading her to take out her frustration on his wife. If this is true, the obvious question is "why?"...to which she answers, "He loves me. We have great sex. And he fixes my car." Oh. See also: *The Amy Fisher Story* and *Casualties of Love: The 'Long Island Lolita' Story*. **AKA:** Amy Fisher: My Story. 🎻🎻

1992 93m/C Noelle Parker, Ed Marinaro, Kathleen Lasky, Boyd Kestner, Mary Ann Pascal, Lawrence Dane, Kate Lynch; **D:** Bradford May. **VHS $89.98** *TTC*

Leviathan

A motley crew of ocean-floor miners are trapped when they are accidentally exposed to a failed Soviet experiment that turns humans into insatiable, regenerating fish-creatures. 🎻🎻

1989 (R) 98m/C Peter Weller, Ernie Hudson, Hector Elizondo, Amanda Pays, Richard Crenna, Daniel Stern, Lisa Eilbacher, Michael Carmine, Meg Foster; **D:** George P. Cosmatos; **W:** David Peoples, Jeb Stuart; **M:** Jerry Goldsmith. **VHS, Beta, LV $14.95** *MGM*

Linnea Quigley's Horror Workout

Horrifying aerobics with Linnea Quigley, one of horror's cleanest and most popular scream queens, featuring plenty of gory clips from her movies. The perky actress leads us through some healthy stretches while wearing some unhealthy leather and chains. Then she and her friends work out at a slumber party, despite the antics of a homicidal crasher. Later, the jogging blonde is pursued all the way home by a gang of zombies, so she leads them through an aerobics class. But leave it to Linnea to put the shower scene in first. Shot-on-video inanity not recommended for those with heart conditions. In case you haven't heard, Linnea is the dynamic star of *Assault of the Party Nerds, Creepozoids, Hollywood Chainsaw Hookers, Sorority Babes in the Slimeball Bowl-A-Rama, Return of the Living Dead,* and many other classics. 🎻🎻

1989 60m/C Linnea Quigley, Baby Jane Holzer, Amy Hunt, Kristine Seeley; **D:** Hal Kennedy; **W:** Hal Kennedy. **VHS** *NO*

Liquid Dreams

Stylish, low-budget, futuristic thriller that became a film-festival hit. Definitely not for all tastes, as the leading lady goes undercover as a dancer in a high-tech strip joint to solve her sister's murder. She finds the owners part of bizarre family-values conspiracy to change the nature of human sexuality via a brain-sucking ritual that provides the ultimate orgasm. Steamy erotica, ludicrous music-videos (putting a sordid spin on *The Wizard of Oz* of all things), provocative politics, Nancy Drew-level detection, and strong performances make for a strange brew indeed, and you don't want to know what the bad guy has in his pants! Memorable cameos by Paul Bartel and John Waters regular Mink Stole. Also available in a more explicit, unrated version. 🦴🦴▷

1992 (R) 92m/C Richard Steinmetz, Candice Daly, Barry Dennen, Juan Fernandez, Tracey Walter, Frankie Thorn; **Cameos:** Paul Bartel, Mink Stole; **D:** Mark Manos. **VHS, Beta $89.95** *ACA*

Liquid Sky

An androgynous bisexual model (Carlisle) living in Manhattan is the primary attraction for a tiny UFO, which lands atop her penthouse in search of the chemical nourishment that her sexual encounters provide. Low-budget, highly creative film, described as "Marxist/feminist science fiction" may not be for everyone, but the audience for which it was made has turned it into an enduring cult favorite. Despite the bizarre premise (or perhaps because of it) the film is remarkably successful in making its seedy punk world seem completely real and believable. Look for Carlisle also playing a gay male. The title refers to heroin. 🦴🦴🦴

1983 (R) 112m/C Anne Carlisle, Paula Sheppard, Bob Brady; **D:** Slava Tsukerman. **VHS, Beta, LV $59.95** *MED*

Little Shop of Horrors

"Feeed me, I'm starving!" The most famous words ever spoken by a man-eating plant are bellowed in this quintessential Roger Corman classic. Filmed in two days, this follow-up to *A Bucket of Blood* stars Jonathan Haze as schlimazel Seymour Krelboin, who becomes big man at Mushnik's skid row flower shop when he breeds a mysterious plant. The catch: This plant thrives on human blood and Seymour must somehow satisfy its increasingly voracious appetite. In a film about a man-eating plant, look for Corman regular Dick Miller as a man eating plants. Jack Nicholson secured this film's cult reputation with his Peter Lorre-esque bit as Wilbur Force, a masochistic dental patient. *Little Shop* blossomed into a hit off-Broadway musical by Howard Ashman and Alan Menken, who went on to write the Oscar-winning scores for Disney's *The Little Mermaid* and *Beauty and the Beast.* Muppetman Frank Oz made the movie of the musical starring Rick Moranis. Corman's original is available in a colorized version, but don't you dare. 🦴🦴🦴▷

1960 70m/B Jonathan Haze, Jackie Joseph, Mel Welles, Myrtle Vail, Leola Wendorff, Dick Miller, Tammy Windsor, Toby Michaels, Lynn Storey, Wally Campo, Jack Warford, Jack Nicholson; **D:** Roger Corman; **W:** Charles B. Griffith; **M:** Fred Katz. **VHS, Beta, LV $9.95** *CNG, MRV, NOS*

Lobster Man from Mars

When rich movie producer (Curtis) learns from his accountant that he must produce a flop or be taken to the cleaners by the IRS, he buys a homemade horror movie from a young filmmaker. The film is an ultra-low budget production featuring a kooky lobster man and a screaming damsel. It's hard to parody a bad movie without becoming a bad movie, but this one is o.k. If it isn't as laugh-out-loud funny, it has its moments, notably when a tough, metaphor-spouting private detective shows up. Old pros Curtis, Patrick MacNee, and Roddy McDowall give the low-budget production an air of class that it desperately needs. So does Deborah Foreman, the suitably plucky heroine. 🦴🦴

1989 (PG) 84m/C Tony Curtis, Deborah Foreman, Patrick Macnee, Roddy McDowall. **VHS, Beta, LV $14.95** *LIV*

The Lonely Lady

In the pantheon of movies that Hollywood makes about itself, this potboiler should prob-

L

"I guess there's no accounting for people's taste."

--Seymour (Jonathan Haze) Krellboin, referring to the man-eating plant in the original *Little Shop of Horrors.*

ably be ranked somewhere between *Mommie Dearest* and *Valley of the Dolls*. It's a big-budget stinker about the pitfalls and tribulations that young Jennilee (Zadora) encounters as she marries and sleeps her way to the top of the Tinseltown heap. Pia is a chipmunk-cheeked little cutie who's completely earnest and serious with atrocious material. Her endearing performance makes the film's badness a virtue. Big screen debut for Liotta. Adapted from the novel by Harold Robbins. 🦴🦴▷

1983 (R) 92m/C Pia Zadora, Lloyd Bochner, Bibi Besch, Joseph Cali, Ray Liotta; **D:** Peter Sasdy. **VHS, Beta, LV $59.95** *MCA*

Lords of the Deep

Producer Roger Corman puts in a cameo appearance (as a treacherous company boss, of all things) in this cheapie about underwater technicians trapped on the ocean floor with a menacing race of manta-like aliens. Low-budget, low-yield film was all wet when rushed out to capitalize in anticipation of undersea

sci-fi adventures like *The Abyss*. Cinematic small fry, you might say. 🦴▷

1989 (PG-13) 95m/C Bradford Dillman, Priscilla Barnes, Melody Ryane, Eb Lottimer, Daryl Haney; **C:** Roger Corman; **D:** Mary Ann Fisher; **W:** Daryl Haney, Howard R. Cohen. **VHS, Beta $14.95** *MGM*

Lost, Lonely, and Vicious

The ad copy says it all: "The white-hot story of what happens to boys and girls who come to Hollywood... seeking success and clawing their way to the top!" But the Hound will add that Clayton is a suicidal Hollywood actor who spends much of his time indulging his penchant for women and fast cars, figuring he may as well enjoy what little time he has left. Then he meets Wilson (*Invasion of the Animal People*), a drugstore clerk who moves him to reconsider his self-destructive ways. A thinly disguised fictional version of the James Dean legend. Schlocky drama wears out its welcome after a while—you may feel like slapping the whiny Clayton. 🦴🦴

1959 73m/B Ken Clayton, Barbara Wilson, Lilyan Chauvin, Richard Gilden, Carole Nugent, Sandra Giles, Allen Fife, Frank Stallworth, Johnny Erben, Clint Quigley, T. Earl Johnson; **D:** Frank Myers; **W:** Norman Graham. **VHS $23.00** *SMW, TPV*

Love Happy

Venerable critic James Agee once wrote that even the worst film the Marx Brothers could make "would be better worth seeing that most other things I can think of." *Love Happy* proves him wrong. For those who like Harpo best, the brothers' cinematic swan song is a mixed blessing. Though as a Marx Brothers film it is worse than even *The Big Store* and *A Night in Casablanca,* it is a showcase for Harpo's still-sublime clowning. The plot revolves around a fortune in missing diamonds hidden in a can of sardines unwittingly lifted by Harpo to help a struggling theatrical troupe. He is menaced by Ilona Massey, who resorts to torture to get Harpo to "talk." Groucho is private eye Sam Grunion, who helped Scotland Yard solve the famous uranium scandal ("I confessed," he states). The brothers share little screen time. Groucho even has his own sidekick, veteran character actor Eric Blore, a veteran of Fred Astaire and Ginger Rogers musicals. But Harpo goes out in a blaze of neon glory, a climactic rooftop chase that incorporates such advertising icons as the Mobilgas flying horse. A pre-*Perry Mason* Raymond Burr is one of Massey's goons. *Love Happy* is perhaps best remembered for an early screen appearance by Marilyn Monroe. She sashays into Groucho's office. "Is there anything I can do for you?" he leers, and then remarks to the audience, "What a ridiculous statement." 🎵🎵

1950 85m/B Groucho Marx, Harpo Marx, Chico Marx, Vera-Ellen, Ilona Massey, Marion Hutton, Raymond Burr, Marilyn Monroe; **D:** David Miller. **VHS, LV $19.98** *REP*

Love Me Tender

Elvis Presley, who worked briefly as a youth in Loewe's State movie theatre in Memphis, realized his dream of Hollywood stardom with this Civil War western originally titled *The Reno Brothers.* The title was changed after Elvis sang "Love Me Tender" on *The Ed Sullivan Show* and it rocketed up the charts. As farmboy Clint,

Elvis received third billing behind Richard Egan, his beloved brother thought killed in the war, and Debra Pagent, Egan's girl, but who marries Elvis in his absence. Elvis's first film was the last that was not designed as a starring vehicle for him. 🎵🎵📀

1956 89m/B Elvis Presley, Richard Egan, Debra Paget, Neville Brand, Mildred Dunnock, James Drury, Barry Coe; **D:** Robert D. Webb. **VHS, Beta $19.95** *MVD, FOX*

The Loved One

An outlandish, all-mocking dark comedy based on Evelyn Waugh's satirical novel about Hollywood and the funeral industry. Adrift in LA, rakish English youth Morse lands a job at a shady pet cemetery (the Happier Hunting Ground) while supervising his celebrity uncle's interment in Whispering Glades, a sprawling, gaudy memorial park where Liberace is a convivial salesman ("Would you like your eternal flame Standard Eternal or Perpetual Eternal?") and the nonliving can be commemorated in every way money can buy. Jonathan Winters is incredible in a dual role, one of them the venal "Blessed Reverend" and CEO of Whispering Glades who decides that death's got no future in it, and to stay profitable his necropolis must embark upon a new commercial venture: resurrection. And yes, that's young Paul Williams, later songwriter and *Phantom of the Paradise* star, as an adolescent whiz-kid who makes it possible. Moments of horrendous bad taste are worthy of John Waters—watch out for Mrs. Joyboy!—and a cast like this convenes once in a lifetime. 🎵🎵🎵📀

1965 118m/B Robert Morse, John Gielgud, Rod Steiger, Liberace, Anjanette Comer, Jonathan Winters, James Coburn, Dana Andrews, Milton Berle, Tab Hunter, Robert Morley, Lionel Stander, Margaret Leighton, Roddy McDowall, Bernie Kopell, Alan Napier, Paul Williams; **D:** Tony Richardson; **W:** Terry Southern, Christopher Isherwood; **M:** John Addison. **VHS, Beta, LV $19.95** *MGM*

The Loves of Hercules

The mythic mesomorph finds a mate with equiponderant chest measurements, and must save her from an evil queen. Somehow it eludes him that both queen and maiden are Miss Jayne in red and black wigs. Kudos for

Divine cunningly mixes prints with stripes and carries it off beautifully while Lainie Kazan looks on in *Lust in the Dust.*

the pavement, etc. Film wants to have it both ways as both a far-out F/X binge and an off-beat whimsey about the unlikeliest people finding love. It doesn't quite work, but is still worth checking out, especially for *Evil Dead* fans who want to try something different. ♫ The Reynolds Rap (You're Having a Nervous Meltdown). ♫ ♫ ♪

1992 (PG-13) 87m/C Theodore (Ted) Raimi, Deborah Foreman, Bruce Campbell, Brian McCree, Eddie Rosmaya, Michele Stacey; **D:** Josh Beck; **W:** Josh Beck; **M:** Joseph Lo Duca. **VHS, LV** *NO*

Lust in the Dust

When part of a treasure map is found on the derriere of none other than Divine, the hunt is on for the other half, and, of course, the other derriere. This comedy western travels to a sleepy town called Chile Verde (green chili for those who don't speak Spanish) and the utterly ridiculous turns comically corrupt. Deliciously distasteful fun with jokes involving midgets, flatulence, and, of course, sex. Features Divine and Lainie Kazan singing really bawdy love songs. Co-producer Hunter is the steely eyed gunfighter hero but he wisely lets his co-stars have all the best moments. By the way, the title was originally applied by Hollywood wags to David O. Selznick's 1946 *Duel in the Sun.* ♫ ♫ ♫

1985 (R) 85m/C Tab Hunter, Divine, Lainie Kazan, Geoffrey Lewis, Henry Silva, Cesar Romero, Gina Gallego, Courtney Gains, Woody Strode, Pedro Gonzalez-Gonzalez; **D:** Paul Bartel; **W:** Philip John Taylor; **M:** Peter Matz. **VHS, Beta, LV $14.95** *NWV, STE, HHE*

worst dubbing and special effects; a must see for connoisseurs of kitsch. *AKA:* Hercules and the Hydra. **WOOF!**

1960 94m/C *IT FR* Jayne Mansfield, Mickey Hargitay; **D:** Carlo L. Bragaglia. **VHS $19.98** *SNC, VDM*

Lunatics: A Love Story

Sam Raimi associates wrought this untypical comedy starring Sam's brother Ted as an ex-mental patient buffeted by grotesque hallucinations and afraid to leave his apartment. Misdialing a party-line, he reaches Foreman, just dumped by her boyfriend and no model of sanity herself. When stereotyped street punks harass his lady fair, our schizoid hero must summon up the courage to stagger to rescue, despite nonstop delusions of giant brain-eating spiders, huge fiery cracks opening up in

Luther the Geek

Little Luther's visit to the circus is dramatically changed when he sees the geek, a sideshow freak, biting off chicken's heads and drinking their blood. All grown up as a creepy yahoo with metal dentures, Luther terrorizes a mother and her sexy daughter at their remote Illinois homestead. Pointless, sadistic, stupid horror sleaze. The best geek movie remains the dead-serious *Nightmare Alley* (1947). **WOOF!**

1990 90m/C Edward Terry, Joan Roth, J. Jerome Clarke, Tom Mills; **D:** Carlton J. Albright. **VHS** *NO*

Machine Gun Kelly

Corman found Euro-appeal with this '30s style gangster bio. Bronson, who was just gaining a reputation as an action lead, stars as criminal Kelly, who's convinced by his moll to give up bank robbery for kidnapping. Amsterdam, the wisecracking writer from *The Dick Van Dyke Show*, is the fink who turns him in. 🦴 🦴 🦴

1958 80m/B Charles Bronson, Susan Cabot, Morey Amsterdam, Barboura Morris, Frank De Kova, Jack Lambert, Wally Campo; *D:* Roger Corman; *W:* Mike Werb. **VHS $9.95** *COL, FCT*

Mad Doctor of Blood Island

The second of the Philippine-made Blood Island Trilogy. In this sequel to *Brides of Blood,* former teen idol Ashley (*Frankensteins' Daughter, Beach Party*) returns to Blood Island and encounters an ugly chlorophyll monster created by Dr. Lorca (Ronald Remy), which survived for *Beast of Blood.* After Ashley's acting and recording career in the U.S. wound down, he came to the Philippines to star in the Blood Island pictures, then stayed to act in and produce a string of exploitation features. Costar Angelique Pettyjohn was a Playboy centerfold and acted in several features (*Biohazard, Repo Man*), as well as starring in porn under the name Heaven St. John. Audiences were given vials of "green blood" as a gimmick/souvenir/snack. *AKA:* Tomb of the Living Dead; Blood Doctor. 🦴 🦴 🦴

1969 110m/C John Ashley, Angelique Pettyjohn, Ronald Remy; *D:* Gerardo (Gerry) De Leon. **VHS, Beta** *NO*

Mad Love

A brilliant surgeon (Lorre) falls madly in love with an actress, but she rebuffs him. When her pianist husband's hands are cut off in a train accident, Lorre agrees to attach new hands, using those of a recently executed murderer. Lorre then kills the man's stepfather, and to drive him crazy uses psychological terror to make the pianist think he killed him. There's also an appearance by the supposedly executed murderer who shows up to reclaim his hands. A real chiller about obsessive love and psychological fear. The only downfall to this one is the unnecessary comic relief by Healy. Lorre's first American film. *AKA:* The Hands of Orlac. 🦴 🦴 🦴

1935 70m/B Peter Lorre, Colin Clive, Frances Drake, Ted Healy, Edward Brophy, Sara Haden, Henry Kolker; *D:* Karl Freund. **VHS $19.98** *MGM*

Mel Gibson is cheesed off to the "max" in *Mad Max*.

Mad Max

Wire-taut suspense on the stark highways of the future, when civilization has started to unravel and traffic cops called Interceptors are the only remaining source of authority. The best of them, Max, seeks personal revenge against the vicious Toecutter and his roving band of outlaw bikers. Dark humor, Dickensian characters, deft action (not deft enough,

173

THE HOUND SALUTES: PAM GRIER
The Mocha Mogul of Hollywood

In the early days of her career--now immortalized on videotape--Pam Grier quickly became one of the most bankable stars in the movie business. In 1977 *Newsweek* magazine called her "the most popular attraction in black B movies," and *Ms.* magazine dubbed her "the Mocha Mogul of Hollywood."

She got her start in Russ Meyer's camp masterpiece *Beyond the Valley of the Dolls* and went on to make a string of women-in-prison flicks for American International.

"They were my sounding board," she said in an interview later, "where I really learned filmmaking. I was working for Roger Corman...and making $500 a day. I was green; I was hungry. These were my first roles so I made them as close to Shakespeare as possible. That's how I approached it and it got me work. The characters stood out. I got recognized."

Before anyone else realized the market existed, she tapped into the nascent women's movement with *Coffy* (1973), one of the first films of its time to show an independent woman in a "demonstrative" role. She got the idea for the character of a nurse who fights neighborhood drug dealers from her uncle, a Denver vice cop who showed her how men and women detectives worked together. She worked out the script with Jack Hill, who had directed her earlier films, and *Coffy* became a hit.

She continued to work steadily in "blaxploitation" films until their time passed. Then she took time off to study her craft and won memorable feature roles as a strung-out killer whore in *Fort Apache, the Bronx* and the most beautiful woman in the world in *Something Wicked This Way Comes.*

Since then she's worked often on TV and in film, though she'll probably always be known for those early drive-in hits that continue to find fans on tape.

though—one stuntman was killed) and Miller's restless camera made this low-budget tale an international hit—and spawned its own sub-genre of countless, tacky post-nuke imitations. *Mad Max* itself builds to an action climax that just isn't there, so the Hound recommends watching the feature on a double-bill with the slam-bang sequel *The Road Warrior* (alias *Mad Max 2*). *Mad Max Beyond Thunderdome* followed in 1985. 🦴🦴🦴▷

1980 (R) 93m/C Mel Gibson, Joanne Samuel, Hugh Keays-Byrne, Steve Bisley, Tim Burns, Roger Ward; **D:** George Miller; **W:** George Miller. **VHS, Beta, LV** **$29.98** *LIV, VES*

The Magic Christian

This priceless British black comedy stars Peter Sellers as wealthy Sir Guy Grand, who impulsively adopts a vagrant (Ringo Starr) and sets out to teach him that people will do anything for money. Guest stars include Laurence Harvey, who is bribed to interrupt his performance of *Hamlet* with a striptease, Yul Brynner in drag singing "Mad About the Boy" to an understandably nervous Roman Polanski, Christopher Lee in his signature role as Dracula, and a whip-cracking Raquel Welch. It is a bit dated, but in the words of the Paul McCartney-penned hit performed by Badfinger, "If you want it, here it is, come and get it." Based on the novel by Terry Southern, who also wrote *Candy* and co-wrote the screenplay for *Dr. Strangelove*. A pre-Monty Python Graham Chapman and John Cleese co-wrote the screenplay and appear briefly. 🦴🦴▷

1969 (PG) 101m/C *GB* Peter Sellers, Ringo Starr, Isabel Jeans, Wilfrid Hyde-White, Graham Chapman, John Cleese, Peter Graves, John Lennon, Yoko Ono, Richard Attenborough, Leonard Frey, Laurence Harvey, Christopher Lee, Spike Milligan, Yul Brynner, Roman Polanski, Raquel Welch; **D:** Joseph McGrath; **W:** Terry Southern. **VHS, Beta, LV $59.98** *REP, MRV*

Magical Mystery Tour

On the road with an oddball assortment of people, the Beatles experience a number of strange incidents around the English countryside. Compared to contemporary rock videos, this slaphappy little fantasy looks pretty tame, almost primitive at times. And the truth is that it's not really comparable to the group's other film work. The music—remixed by longtime Beatles producer George Martin for the videodisc version—is the main attraction. These songs are some of the Fab Four's more baroque and complex. Originally made for British television. ♬ Magical Mystery Tour; Blue Jay Way; Your Mother Should Know; The Fool on the Hill. ♬♬♪

1967 55m/C *GB* John Lennon, George Harrison, Ringo Starr, Paul McCartney, Victor Spinetti. **VHS, Beta, LV $19.98** *MPI, MED, WFV*

Malcolm

This whimsical comedy from Down Under stars Colin Friels as Malcolm, who is kind of an Australian Gump with a genius for mechanical gadgets. His new neighbors, professional thieves, recruit the unwitting Malcolm to put his skills to criminal use. The devices, including a car that splits down the middle and armed mobile ashtrays, are astounding. A Best Picture winner in its native country. David Parker, husband to director Nadia Tass, designed the gadgets and wrote the screenplay that was inspired by his brother. ♬♬♪

1986 (PG-13) 86m/C *AU* Colin Friels, John Hargreaves, Lindy Davies, Chris Haywood, Charles Tingwell, Beverly Phillips, Judith Stratford; **D:** Nadia Tass; **W:** David Parker. Australian Film Institute '86: Best Actor (Friels), Best Film. **VHS, Beta, LV $79.98** *LIV, VES*

Man Bites Dog

A group of filmmakers follow the activities of a serial killer who has hired them to record his casual carnage. As the filming develops, the filmmakers become more deeply implicated in his crimes, until they become his henchmen. This satire on the celebrity of criminals is both hilarious and appalling. The pseudo-documentary realism of its cheap B&W photography brings the graphic violence unsettlingly close to home. In French with English subtitles. Also available in an unrated edited version. ♬♬♬♬

1991 (NC-17) 95m/B *BE* Benoit Poelvoorde, Remy Belvaux, Andre Bonzel; **D:** Benoit Poelvoorde, Remy Belvaux, Andre Bonzel; **W:** Benoit Poelvoorde, Remy Belvaux, Andre Bonzel, Vincent Tavier. **VHS $89.95** *FXL, FCT*

The Man Who Fell to Earth

Although much of the plot was stolen from Robert Heinlein's novel *Stranger in a Strange Land,* this is an entertaining and technically adept science fiction classic about a man from another planet (Bowie, in a bit of typecasting) who ventures to Earth in hopes of finding water to save his family and drought-stricken planet. Instead he becomes a successful inventor and businessman, along the way discovering the human vices of booze, sex, and television. Full of odd moments and eccentric performances. Also available in a restored version at 138 minutes, which is much better. Remade for television in 1987 and based on Walter Tevis' novel. ♬♬♬

1976 (R) 118m/C *GB* David Bowie, Candy Clark, Rip Torn, Buck Henry, Bernie Casey; **D:** Nicolas Roeg. **VHS, Beta, LV $19.95** *COL*

The Manchurian Candidate

Perhaps the best political thriller of the 1960s is still sharp and shocking today, and tons of fun to watch. Tells the story of an American Korean War vet who suspects that he and his platoon may have been brainwashed during the war, with his highly decorated, heroic friend programmed by commies to be an operational assassin. The film was years ahead of its time in the amount of visual information that's packed into the screen. (Notice the way images of Lincoln are repeated in the background.) The attitudes on sex and race are equally avant-garde. It's also a bitter satire on the naivete and machinations of the left and right. Excellent performances by an all-star cast, with Lansbury, Gregory, Silva, and Deigh particularly delicious as the villains. But Harvey is the real star, and his performance becomes more impressive with repeated viewings. He gives his Raymond Shaw character the emotional depth of a true tragic hero and easily overshadows co-star Sinatra. In many ways, this film was the high-water mark for everyone involved—the cast, director Frankenheimer, writer/producer George Axelrod, even novelist Condon. Though they've all done fine work since, none has approached this level. Based on the Richard Condon novel. Tape features a special interview with

M

"There are two kinds of people in the world: those who walk into a room and immediately turn the TV on, and those who immediately turn it off."
—Laurence Harvey in *The Manchurian Candidate.*

THE GHOUL TUBE
National Horror Hosts

Bane of parents, heroes to youngsters and insomniacs everywhere, the late-nite creature-feature TV host is an American institution. Long before *Mystery Science Theater 3000* turned schlock-movie hosting into an art, forerunners could be found ruling the weekend channels.

It might have been glamour ghoul **Vampira** (Maila Nurmi) on KABC-TV in Los Angeles, or it could have been any number of defrocked weathermen on low-power UHF stations throughout the midwest, but everyone has fond memories of the likes of Sinister Seymour, Sir Graves Ghastly, the Ghoul, Chilly Billy Cardille, Superhost, John Stanley, Frank and Drac, Ernie "Ghoulardi" Anderson, and many more.

Elena M. Watson recently authored an entire book devoted to the subject (*Television Horror Movie Hosts: 68 Vampires, Mad Scientists, and Other Denizens of Late-Night Airwaves Examined and Interviewed*, published by McFarland), and the feature *Fright Night* and its sequel are built around Roddy McDowell's terrific portrayal of a washed-up horror host battling bona fide bloodsuckers.

A few faves can be found on home video. **Elvira** (Cassandra Peterson), widely syndicated in the '80s and '90s, leads the cassette field, not only with her 1988 feature-film vehicle *Elvira, Mistress of the Dark*, but also a series of tapes in which she hosts/mocks dreck like *Eegah!* and Ed Wood's *Night of the Ghouls*. Purists take note: in contrast to the TV edits, these films are presented uncut, saving Elvira's wisecracks for the opening and closing.

John Zacherle, host of NYC's Shock Theater, has a tape called *Horrible Horror*, interspersing original coming-attraction trailers and clips from the likes of *Robot Monster* and *13 Ghosts* with his own comedy-relief sketches.

Attention must be paid to two prime-time faves-turned-horror-emcees. **John Astin**, the original Gomez from ABC-TV's *The Addams Family*, introduces a selection of horror excerpts in *Terror on Tape*. And wherever the Addams family

continued...

Sinatra and Frankenheimer in which Sinatra is deified. 🦴🦴🦴🦴

1962 126m/B Frank Sinatra, Laurence Harvey, Angela Lansbury, Janet Leigh, James Gregory, Leslie Parrish, John McGiver, Henry Silva, Khigh Deigh; **D:** John Frankenheimer; **W:** George Axelrod, John Frankenheimer; **M:** David Amram. Golden Globe Awards '63: Best Supporting Actress (Lansbury); National Board of Review Awards '62: Best Supporting Actress (Lansbury); Nominations: Academy Awards '62: Best Film Editing, Best Supporting Actress (Lansbury). **VHS, Beta, LV $19.98** *MGM*

Mandingo

The anti-*Roots*. Remember the dumbstruck audience watching "Springtime for Hitler" in Mel Brooks' *The Producers?* That will be your face during the 127 minutes of this putrid, fetid potboiler of love and slavery in the pre-Civil War South. For starters, there is one of the screen's most distinguished actors, James Mason, as the master of the Falconhurst plantation. The scene in which he rubs his feet on a supine black child to cure his rheumatism is a career low point. Then there is boxer Ken Norton, down for the count in his film debut, as a slave forced to have sex with Susan George, the white wife of Perry King, Mason's disabled heir, who has taken slave Brenda Sykes as his mistress. Look for Paul Benedict as an abusive slave owner. A curious role for George and Louise Jefferson's dimwitted neighbor. Based on Kyle Onstott's unaccountable bestseller. Followed in 1976 by *Drum,* which at least has Pam Grier and Warren Oates to recommend it. 🦴🦴

1975 (R) 127m/C James Mason, Susan George, Perry King, Richard Ward, Ken Norton, Ben Masters, Brenda Sykes, Paul Benedict, Ji Tu Cumbuka; **D:** Richard Fleischer; **M:** Maurice Jarre. **VHS, Beta, LV $59.95** *PAR*

Maniac

A mad scientist is murdered and impersonated by his much crazier assistant, who has designs on raising the dead and searches for victims on which to experiment. Bizarre "adults only" exploitation roadshow feature was considered very risque for its time, and includes eaten eyeballs, a cat fight with syringes, nudity, mad ranting and raving, and a rapist who thinks he's an orangutan. Jaw-dropping weirdness, a real pieces of showmanship history, and a must for genre aficionados. From the father of the modern exploitation film, Dwain Esper, maker of *Marihuana* and *Reefer Madness*. 🦴🦴🦴▷

1934 67m/B Bill Woods, Horace Carpenter, Ted Edwards, Thea Ramsey, Jennie Dark, Marcel Andre, Celia McGann; **D:** Dwain Esper. **VHS, Beta $14.95** *VDM, SNC, MRV*

Maniac

A psycho murderer slaughters and scalps his victims, adding the "trophies" to his collection. Carries a self-imposed equivalent "X" rating due to its highly graphic gore quotient, provided by makeup man Savini. A tour-de-force by Spinell (ad libbing most of his own dialogue), who takes the sweat & sleaze quotient of his serial killer character to an uncomfortable extreme, yet is oddly charming when wooing Munro. Although shot without a budget in 16mm, this looks as good most pictures from 1980, and was one of the first to use Dolby stereo. For extremely strong stomachs only. 🦴🦴🦴

1980 91m/C Joe Spinell, Caroline Munro, Gail Lawrence, Kelly Piper, Tom Savini; **D:** William Lustig; **W:** Joe Spinell, C.A. Rosenberg. **VHS, Beta $54.95** *MED*

Manos, the Hands of Fate

OK, so *Plan 9 from Outer Space* is bad, and *Attack of the Killer Tomatoes* is right up there in the Hall of Shame too, but THIS movie...well, you just have to see it to believe how bad it is. Lesser known than those movies, horrible acting, nonexistent direction, dim lighting, and laughable special effects nevertheless elevate this story of a family ensnared by a satanic cult a notch above your average bad horror film. Highlights include a Satan-like character who can't stop laughing; the dreaded "hounds of hell" (or are those mangy dogs with big ears glued on?); and Torgo the monstrous henchman, who you know is evil because he has giant kneecaps (a sure sign of the devil's work). Honestly, that's it—that's how you know Torgo is a monster. Notable as the one of the most often requested movies on Comedy Central's satiric *Mystery Science Theater 3000,* this one is good for a laugh. Hal P. Warren gets full blame for this horror show—he wrote and directed

it and stars as the patriarch of the trapped family. 🦴🦴🦴▷

1966 74m/C Tom Nayman, Diane Mahree, Hal P. Warren, John Reynolds; **D:** Hal P. Warren; **W:** Hal P. Warren. **VHS $19.98** *SNC*

The Manster

Womanizing, whiskey-swilling American journalist Dyneley (*House of Mystery*) receives a mysterious injection from a crazed scientist (Nakamura) and sprouts unsightly hair and an extra head. He loses his marbles (wouldn't you?) and starts killing people, and eventually he splits into two warring beings. A very unusual film which is loaded with weird Freudian images and unnerving atmosphere, and found its influence on a generations of horror films, including *War of the Gargantuas, Army of Darkness,* and *How to Get Ahead in Advertising.* Shot entirely on location in Japan; half the cast and crew are Japanese. Another masterpiece from the director who brought *The Monster From Green Hell.* **AKA:** The Manster—Half Man, Half Monster; The Split. 🦴🦴🦴

1959 72m/B *JP* Peter Dyneley, Jane Hylton, Satoshi Nakamura, Terri Zimmern; **D:** Kenneth Crane. **VHS $19.98** *SNC, MRV*

Mantis in Lace

A go-go dancer (lovely Stewart, who has an odd, hard-to-place accent) lures men back to her warehouse crash pad, then slaughters them while tripping on LSD. Once again, the world's dumbest detectives are assigned to the case. Cinematography by pre-*Easy Rider* Laszlo Kovacs. Watch it for the "hep" dialogue, cool theme song, and wild hallucination sequences. Russ Meyer regular Lancaster shows up as a psychologist who wants to analyze Stewart as much as sleep with her, only to become her latest victim. Barrington was a well known model and dancer, who also appeared in Rotsler's *Agony of Love, The Girl with the Hungry Eyes,* and many exploitation films. Some prints have more blood and nudity than others. **AKA:** Lila. 🦴🦴🦴

1968 (R) 68m/C Susan Stewart, Steve Vincent, M.K. Evans, Vic Lance, Pat Barrington, Janu Wine, Stuart Lancaster, John Carrol, Judith Crane, Cheryl Trepton; **D:** William Rotsler. **VHS $24.95** *TPV*

M

Story continued...

shows up their CBS rivals *The Munsters* are sure to follow; **Al "Grampa" Lewis** weighs in with the cassette series *Grampa's Monster Movies* and *Grampa's Sci-Fi Hits.*

In broadcast markets where the late-night creature-feature host has lasted long enough, the stations themselves just might issue a best-of compilation. For example, after thirty years on WJW-TV in Cleveland, **"Big Chuck" Schodowski** has been commemorated by a multi-volume cassette series spotlighting co-hosts **"Li'l John" Rinaldi, Bob "Houlihan" Wells,** and the Ernie Kovacs-style sketches they sandwiched in between commercial breaks. Though few kinescopes or tapes survive from the golden age of TV hosts, you might want to contact any station with a late-nite eminence to find out if any nostalgic collections are available.

Marihuana

An unintentionally hilarious, cautionary film about the exaggerated evils of pot smoking. A good girl, complete with portrait of Washington over the mantle, goes bad after she tries a dose of the devil's weed. Her friend goes swimming and drowns, she gets pregnant, her boyfriend joins the narcotics dealers and is killed in a police raid, and she only goes down deeper into a pool of crime—first dealing drugs, then kidnapping and murder. Contains the immortal line: "Slippery drinks for sliding girls!" Another rich slice of exploitation history from the man who brought you *Reefer Madness. AKA:* Marijuana: The Devil's Weed; Marijuana, Weed with Roots in Hell. ♫♫

1936 57m/B Harley Wood, Hugh McArthur, Pat Carlyle; ***D:*** Dwain Esper. **VHS, Beta $16.95** *SNC, VYY, HEG*

Marnie

Tippi Hedren (Melanie Griffith's mom) stars as Marnie, a cool blonde with an hysterical fear of men, thunderstorms, and the color red. She is also a thief, caught in the act of emptying the company safe by her employer Sean Connery. Rather than turn her in to the police, and determined to uncover the root of her neuroses, he blackmails her into marrying him. This was Connery's American film debut after thrilling the world as James Bond. Hitchcock discovered Hedren in a television commercial before casting her in *The Birds.* For this project, she was his blonde of second choice. He originally bought the rights to Winston Graham's novel for Grace Kelly, who had abandoned Hollywood to marry Prince Ranier of Monaco. *Marnie* was not a box office success. To the casual viewer, the obvious rear projection and humorless script are off-putting. *Marnie's* staunchest defenders rank it among Hitchcock's best. ♫♫♫

1964 130m/C Tippi Hedren, Sean Connery, Diane Baker, Bruce Dern; ***D:*** Alfred Hitchcock; ***W:*** Jay Presson Allen. **VHS, Beta, LV $19.95** *MCA*

Married Too Young

Between trips to the malt shop and the raceway, high school honeys Lloyd & Lund elope, keeping the marriage secret because of disapproval from the parental units. The folks find out when Lund leaves the marriage license lying around, and both the country club set and the white trash pair hit the ceiling. When the boy groom trades his med school plans for a monkey wrench in order to support the little missus, he finds much trouble with the hot rod heavies, who talk him into working on stolen cars for some fast cash. A more mainstream version of the old "parents are to blame" roadshow melodramas, complete with a stern Judge delivering a closing lectures. As the villain, "special guest star" Dexter is so oily you could fry eggs on him. Some of the odder-sounding dialogue is doubtless the work of Ed Wood, who had a hand in the script. Lloyd was also in *Girls Town, Mutiny in Outer Space,* and *Frankenstein's Daughter* (while Lund was across town acting in *Frankenstein 1970*). *AKA:* I Married Too Young. ♫♫◗

1962 76m/B Harold Lloyd Jr., Jana Lund, Anthony Dexter, Marianna Hill, Trudy Marshall, Brian O'Hara, Nita Loveless; ***D:*** George Moskov. **VHS $59.98** *HHT, SNC*

Mars Needs Women

When the Martian singles scene starts to drag, Martian playboys cross the solar system in search of fertile single Earth babes with healthy chromosomes to help them repopulate the planet. Seems Dr. Marjorie Bolen (Batgirl Craig), an expert in extraterrestrial reproduction who won a Pulitzer for her book *Space Genetics,* is at the top of their dance cards. Buchanan's goofiest picture is this farcical look at interplanetary dating practices that has a plot that's short on logic. When Fellow #1 from the red planet (Kirk) pops into Houston Control (none of that sparkly Trek-style transport for these dudes) to request volunteers for Martian mating, they get a knee-jerk refusal (why? plenty of Earth girls would jump at the chance). Although the Martians are portrayed to be non-threatening, they first attempt to get girls via teleportation (unsuccessfully, they say, but there's no explanation of what happened to the women), and later they capture the women, without even asking for permission. A note to squares: on Mars they "abandoned neckties 50 years ago as foolish vanity." 🦴🦴▷

1966 80m/C Tommy Kirk, Yvonne Craig; **D:** Larry Buchanan; **W:** Larry Buchanan. **VHS $19.98** *SNC*

Martin

Martin is a charming young man, though slightly mad. He freely admits his need to drink blood, while fantasizing about being a traditional movie vampire. Contemporary vampire has found a new abhorrent means of killing his victims—he subdues them, then draws the blood with a hypodermic. A neglected winner from director Romero (*Night of the Living Dead*), it contains some exciting and suspenseful sequences, while never losing its wry sense of humor. 🦴🦴🦴

1977 (R) 96m/C John Amplas, Lincoln Maazel; **D:** George A. Romero; **W:** George A. Romero. **VHS, Beta, LV** *NO*

The Marx Brothers in a Nutshell

A tribute to the Marx Brothers, narrated by Gene Kelly. Contains clips from *Duck Soup,* *Horse Feathers, Animal Crackers, Cocoanuts,* and *Room Service.* Also contains rare outakes and interviews with the brothers, plus guest appearances by Dick Cavett, Robert Klein, David Steinberg, and others. Indispensible for fans. 🦴🦴🦴▷

1990 100m/B Groucho Marx, Chico Marx, Harpo Marx, Zeppo Marx, Robert Klein, David Steinberg, George Fenneman, Dick Cavett. **VHS, LV $19.98** *FCT*

The Mask

Obscure gory horror film about a psychiatrist who is transformed into a killer via a mask, filmed mostly in 3-D. The video has special 3-D packaging and limited edition 3-D glasses, so you can still experience the terror at home. The best way to appreciate this loopy wonder is to see it with a large group. Then when the narrator orders, "Put the mask on now," and everyone dons glasses, it becomes a comedy. *AKA:* Eyes of Hell; The Spooky Movie Show. 🦴🦴▷

1961 85m/B *CA* Paul Stevens, Claudette Nevins, Bill Walker, Anne Collings, Martin Lavut; **D:** Julian Roffman. **VHS, Beta, LV $12.95** *RHI, MLB*

Masque of the Red Death

Roger Corman redoes Ingmar Bergman's *Seventh Seal* in one of his best and most lavish Edgar Allan Poe adaptations. Price attacks his role as the evil Prince Prospero with obvious delight, but he's still almost upstaged by Hazel Court at her loveliest. The script by s-f/horror veteran Charles Beaumont borrows freely from other Poe stories, most obviously "Hop-Frog," and the film is fleshed out with moderate doses of '60s sin, sex, and psychedelia. The result has aged well and is a pleasant surprise for fans who haven't seen it in decades. Photographed by Nicholas Roeg. Remade in 1989 with Corman as producer, and again in 1990 by others. 🦴🦴🦴▷

1965 88m/C *GB* Vincent Price, Hazel Court, Jane Asher, Patrick Magee; **D:** Roger Corman. **VHS, Beta $14.98** *ORI, LIV, MLB*

Masque of the Red Death

Roger Corman's second attempt at Edgar Allan Poe's horror tale pales compared to his

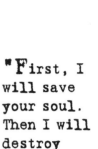

M

THE HOUND SALUTES: HAMMER FILMS

Throughout the 1960s and early 1970s, Hammer Films and vampires were synonymous to horror film fans. Founded in 1948 by Will Hammer and Sir John Carreras, the studio specialized in science fiction monster movies in its early years before making its first vampire movie, *The Horror of Dracula*, in 1958. Led by the creative team of director Terence Fisher, screenwriter/director Jimmy Sangster, and actors Peter Cushing and Christopher Lee, Hammer Films churned out dozens of vampire films of mostly B-grade quality. Hammer films are easily spotted because of their heavy doses of gore and sexuality. The studio routinely pushed the censorship envelope in Britain and the United States, offering lots of blood in full Technicolor and lots of cleavage on its numerous female vampires. Lee and Cushing often rose above mediocre material to turn in excellent performances as Dracula and vampire hunter Abraham van Helsing, respectively.

By the mid-'70s, the studio was in financial trouble, and its slide into bankruptcy was speeded up by the infamous film *The Legend of the Seven Golden Vampires*, a combination vampire/martial arts film that stands as one of the goofier horror movies ever released. The studio announced that it was back in business (working with Warner Brothers) in 1993, but several ambitious projects announced at that time have yet to see the light of day. Schlock horror buffs can only hope the studio escapes from its grave and grosses out another generation of vampire fans.

Vincent Price version made 25 years earlier. Under-aged cast adds youth appeal but subtracts credibility from the fable of a sadistic prince and his sycophants staging an orgiastic feast, trying to ignore the plague raging outside castle walls. Only late in the plot does veteran actor Macnee materialize to add a proper note of doom—quite a change from his jovial role as John Steed on TV's *The Avengers*. 🎬🎬

1989 (R) 90m/C Patrick Macnee, Jeffery Osterhage, Adrian Paul, Tracy Reiner, Maria Ford; **D:** Larry

Brand; **W:** Larry Brand, Daryl Haney. **VHS, Beta, LV** $14.95 *MGM, IME*

Massacre at Central High

A new student takes matters into his own hands when gang members harass fellow students at a local high school. Other than some silly dialogue, this low-budget production is above average. The violence is sometimes ridiculous, sometimes surprising and shocking. As one of the first teen action/revenge flicks, it has earned something of a cult following. One brief but effective love scene probably has something to do with that, too. So does a strong political element to the story. Co-star Stevens has gone on to produce, direct, and star in many low-budget films on video. 🎬🎬🎬

1976 (R) 85m/C Derrel Maury, Andrew Stevens, Kimberly Beck, Robert Carradine, Roy Underwood, Steve Bond; **D:** Renee Daalder; **W:** Renee Daalder. **VHS** $79.95 *MPI*

Master Blaster

You know a fad's not cool anymore when it's the main gimmick in a vacant-headed exploitation thriller. Here those tag-style camouflage survival games go through the wringer. During a championship match in the wilderness (conveniently attended by misfits and suspicious types from all over), some psycho starts using real bullets instead of harmless paintball guns. Graphically violent, graphically cliched. **WOOF!**

1985 (R) 94m/C Jeff Moldovan, Donna Rosae, Joe Hess, Peter Lunblad; **D:** Glenn Wilder. **VHS** $13.95 *MVD, PSM*

Matinee

"MANT: Half-man, Half-ant, All Terror!" screams from the movie marquee after Lawrence Woolsey, promoter extraordinare (and modeled after the king of gimmicks, William Castle), and Ruth Corday, his leading lady, roll into Key West circa 1962. Meanwhile, teen Gene Loomis listens to his health teacher push the benefits of red meat and his girlfriend question life, while worrying about his dad, stationed in Cuba. Builds sly parallels between real life and movie horror by juxtaposing Woolsey hyping his schlock, shown in "Atomo-Vision," against JFK solemnly announcing the Russian's approach. It's the next best thing to being there for those we are too young to have experienced a Castle gimmick first hand, in the theatre. Fun, nostalgic look at days gone by—and the matinees that died with them. 🦴🦴🦴

1992 (PG) 98m/C John Goodman, Cathy Moriarty, Simon Fenton, Omri Katz, Lisa Jakub, Kellie Martin, Jesse Lee, Lucinda Jenney, James Villemaire, Robert Picardo, Dick Miller, John Sayles, Mark McCracken, Jesse White, David Clennon, Luke Halpin; **D:** Joe Dante; **M:** Jerry Goldsmith. **VHS, Beta, LV $19.98** MCA, BTV

Mesa of Lost Women

Mad scientist creates brave new race of vicious women with long fingernails. A hijacked plane crash lands on his remote mesa. Sort of like Dr. Moreau goes to Mexico. So bad it's a wanna-B. Addams Family buffs will spot the Fester in Coogan, who was just starting his comeback. Gets extra bones for weirdness, but gets them taken away for the soundtrack: Hoyt Curtain's piano/guitar score is so horribly irritating that it was used in two more movies. This is Ron Ormand at a transition point between his Lash LaRue Westerns and dirt-cheap weird exploitation pictures. **AKA:** Lost Women; Lost Women of Zarpa. 🦴🦴

1952 70m/B Jackie Coogan, Richard Travis, Allan Nixon, Mary Hill, Robert Knapp, Tandra Quinn, Lyle Talbot, Katherine Victor, Angelo Rossitto, Herbert Tevos; **D:** Ron Ormond. **VHS $16.95** NOS, MRV, SNC

Metropolis

Now a classic meditation on futurist technology and mass mentality, this fantasy concerns mechanized society. In the awesome future city of Metropolis, the upper classes wallow in luxury, while the lower classes toil in the bowels of the city. The son of the ruler of Metropolis ventures into the lower city after glimpsing the beautiful Maria (Helm), but is shanghaied into the workers' army. Meanwhile, the influential Maria is captured by a mad scientist (Klein-Rogge) and replaced with an android double, who incites the workers to riot. Original set design and special effects made this an innovative and influential film

in its day. Is now considered one of the hippest and fascinating films of the sci-fi genre. Silent, with musical score. The 1984 re-release features some color tinting, reconstruction, and a digital score with songs by Pat Benatar, Bonnie Tyler, Giorgio Moroder, and Queen. 🦴🦴🦴🦴

1926 115m/B *GE* Brigitte Helm, Alfred Abel, Gustav Froehlich, Rudolf Klein-Rogge, Fritz Rasp; **D:** Fritz Lang. **VHS, Beta, LV $16.95** SNC, NOS, MRV

Microwave Massacre

Killer kitchen appliances strike again as late lounge comic Vernon murders nagging wife and 'waves her. Overcome by that Betty Crocker feeling, he goes on a microwave murdering/feeding spree of the local ladies. Lots of Roger Corman copying. 🦴

1983 (R) 80m/C Jackie Vernon, Loren Schein, Al Troupe; **D:** Wayne Berwick. **VHS $59.95** RHI, FCT

Mill of the Stone Women

While famous sculptor Professor Wahl (Preiss) is hard at work restoring the work created by his great grandfather 100 years ago—a mechanical pageant displaying statues of history's most infamous women, housed in a mill adjoining the castle (rather like a *House of Wax* on wheels)—art student Hans von Arnim (Brice) comes to write a monograph on the centennial. Wahl's demented daughter (the gorgeous Gabel), who has a rare disease that keeps her confined to the castle, falls for the student. When he gives her the brush off she has an attack and dies, only to turn up alive the next day. The girl's doctor gives him an hallucinogenic drug, which makes him have a nervous break down, convincing him that he'd imagined the whole episode. But when his fiancee disappears, he begins to suspect the truth. This starts out slowly, but suddenly comes on as strong as any Vincent Price film of that era, with a mad science lab, bringing the dead back to life, kidnapping, murder, arson, and illegal taxidermy techniques. Adapted from Peter Van Weigen's *Flemish Tales,* and dedicated to director Terence Fisher (*Horror of Dracula*). Ferroni was better known for his spaghetti westerns. A French-Italian production, filmed partially in Holland. **AKA:** Il Mulino Delle Donne di Pietra; Horror of the

"Mom's really swell. She even helps us hang up our clothes!" *Mommie Dearest.*

Stone Women; The Horrible Mill Women; Drops of Blood. 🦴🦴▷

1960 94m/C *FR IT* Pierre Brice, Scilla Gabel, Danny Carrel, Wolfgang Preiss, Herbert Boenne, Liana Orfei; **D:** Giorgio Ferroni. **VHS $16.95** *SNC*

Missile to the Moon

First expedition to the moon encounters not acres of dead rock but a race of gorgeous women in lingerie and high heels. Take one cheap, silly sci-fi groaner, then remove the name stars and the 3-D effects, and there you have it—a bad but entertaining remake of *Cat Women of the Moon,* featuring a bevy of beauty contest winners from New Hampshire to Yugoslavia. Cast is not quite as accomplished as the original's. Clarke (who took over Michael Landon's Teenage Werewolf role in *How to Make a Monster*) is pretty good, but he's no Sonny Tufts. Mitchell no doubt put this on her resume right next to *Queen of Outer Space.* Downs was also in *The Amazing Colossal Man* and *She Creature.* Stevens was the daughter of famed comedy director Sam Wood. Cook was in Arch Obeler's *Strange Holiday* and played Little Beaver in the "Red

Ryder" series. Cunha churned out this quickie to fill out a bill with *Frankenstein's Daughter.* 🦴🦴▷

1959 78m/B Gary Clarke, Cathy Downs, K.T. Stevens, Laurie Mitchell, Michael Whalen, Nina Bara, Richard Travis, Tommy Cook, Marjorie Hellen; **D:** Richard Cunha. **VHS, Beta $9.95** *RHI, SNC, CNM*

Mom & Dad

An innocent young girl's one night of passion leads to an unwanted pregnancy. Still shocking stock footage of childbirth (including cesarean—gulp!) and a lecture on the evils of syphilis concludes this campy schlock that features the national anthem. Produced by the legendary showman Kroger Babb, this is one of the most profitable movies of any kind ever made. A handful of prints were taken from town to town like a carnival and drew in the entire population with an endless supply of publicity gimmicks, playing for decades across the country. In addition, a live lecture in the middle of the picture sold millions of hygiene booklets. Although seen as camp now, and pure razzle-dazzle salesmanship at the time, there is no misinformation presented, and this was probably the most honest, straightforward sex education that the majority of people in the audience would ever get. 🦴🦴🦴

1947 97m/B Hardie Albright, Sarah Blake, George Eldridge, June Carlson, Jimmy Clark, Bob Lowell; **D:** William Beaudine. **VHS, Beta $19.95** *VDM*

Mommie Dearest

It is ironic that one of Joan Crawford's greatest films was *Mildred Pierce,* in which a long-suffering mother is betrayed by her ungrateful daughter. What would Joan have thought of this major studio, big budget adaptation of her daughter Christina's corpse-kicking bestseller? In her tour-de-force performance, Faye Dunaway seems possessed as Crawford, a shoulder-padded human pit bull who heaps verbal and physical abuse on her adopted daughter (played as an adult by underrated actress Diana Scarwid). The dialogue reaches such hysterical melodramatic heights as "Tina, bring me the axe!" (for Joan's nighttime assault on her garden after being fired from Metro-Goldwyn-Mayer), and depths as when Joan cautions the board members of Pepsi-Cola, "Don't f— with me, fellas." When critics savaged the film, Paramount went for the camp and cult crowd with a shockingly tasteless (even for Hollywood) "No more wire hangers" ad campaign that made light of the film's graphic depiction of child abuse. Rated PG, but why would you let youngsters watch it? Try something less traumatizing, like the shooting of "Bambi's" mother. 🦴🦴 ▷

1981 (PG) 129m/C Faye Dunaway, Diana Scarwid, Steve Forrest, Mara Hobel, Rutanya Alda, Harry Goz, Howard da Silva; **D:** Frank Perry; **W:** Robert Getchell; **M:** Henry Mancini. **VHS, Beta, LV $59.95** *PAR*

Mondo Balardo

Translated as *Crazy World*, this is crude sensationalism masked as a horror story. Karloff guides the viewer through a curious mixture of society's fringe elements. A loosely connected series of sketches includes portraits of a reincarnated Rudolph Valentino, practitioners of transvestism, Roman coke whores, and an Italian-Japanese rock 'n' roll midget (Drago) in director Montero's unusual vision of an anti-paradise. Includes standard lesbian club scene. Volume 11 of Frank Henenlotter's Sexy Shockers. 🦴

1964 86m/C Franz Drago; **D:** Robert Montero; **W:** Albert T. Viola. **VHS $23.00** *SMW, TPV*

Mondo Cane

With a title translating as "dog world," you'd think the Hound would've better enjoyed this popular Italian-made "shockumentary," which bred numerous imitators (and can be considered ancestor to *Faces of Death*). Showcasing eccentricities of human behavior around the world, including cannibalism, pig killing, nude modern art, pet cemeteries, puppy chow (in which the puppies are the chow!), and cults, this barely hides its voyeuristic intent behind a thesis about parallels between civilization and so-called savages. It's just "Ripley's Believe It or Not" with an English-dubbed narrator spouting pseudo-profundities like a cross between a top-40 DJ and a coffeehouse poet. Parodied badly in *Mr. Mike's Mondo Video*. Theme song "More" became an international hit. 🦴🦴

1963 (R) 105m/C *IT* **D:** Gualtiero Jacopetti. Nominations: Academy Awards '63: Best Song ("More"). **VHS, Beta $16.95** *SNC, VDC, VDM*

Mondo Cane 2

More documentary-like views of the oddities of mankind and ethnic rituals around the world. Sequel to the very successful *Mondo Cane*, the film which defined the mondo genre as separate from the pure documentary. The mondo film is more like a carnival attraction— segments are bizarre, sensational, sometimes repellent, and often staged. Features include transvestites, weird diets, Mexico's Day of the Dead and rural bug eating festivals, eccentric artists, a face-slapping concert, and a sports riot. Next stop for Jacopetti & Prospero: *Women of the World* (1964). **AKA:** Mondo Pazzo; Mondo Insanity; Crazy World; Insane World. 🦴🦴

1964 (R) 94m/C *IT* **D:** Gualtiero Jacopetti, Franco Prosperi. **VHS, Beta $19.95** *VDC, HHE, TPV*

Mondo Magic

A compilation of tribal rituals offering viewers a look on the darker side of matters magical. 🦴 ▷

1976 100m/C **D:** Melvin Ashford. **VHS, Beta** *NO*

Mondo Trasho

John Waters' first full-length feature film (preceded by such titles as *Hag in a Black Leather Jacket* and *Eat Your Makeup*), filmed in gutters, alleys, laundromats, and other scenic sights in the Prince of Puke's hometown. A completely dialogue-less film, it will be of interest to Waters afficianados, but it isn't a good representative showing of the of humor he usually employs to make bad taste an art. Story chronicles the last day in the life of a most unfortunate woman (Mary Vivian Pearce, who would go on to appear, at least in cameo, in most of Waters' films, including his later, more mainstream, work). Waters followed up *Mondo Trasho* with *Multiple Maniacs*. 🦴🦴

1969 95m/B Mary Vivian Pearce, Divine, John Leisenring, Mink Stole, David Lochary, Chris Atkinson; **D:** John Waters; **W:** John Waters. **VHS, Beta** *NO*

M

"No more wire hangers!"
—Joan (Faye Dunaway) Crawford in *Mommie Dearest*.

Monkey Business

More fun than four barrels of Marxes, which is where we find Groucho, Harpo, Chico, and Zeppo, stowaways on an ocean liner. From their hiding pace, they sing "Sweet Adeleine" and Groucho sends insulting notes to the captain ("So, I'm an old goat, am I?"). Their first film written for the screen runs out of steam, but many priceless bits keep it afloat, including Harpo hiding out in a children's puppet show, Groucho's romancing of neglected gangster's wife Thelma Todd ("What are you doing in that closet?" "Nothing. Come on in"), Groucho's confrontation with said gangster, and all four brothers attempting to leave the boat by impersonating Maurice Chevalier. 🦴🦴🦴▷

1931 77m/B Groucho Marx, Harpo Marx, Chico Marx, Zeppo Marx, Thelma Todd, Ruth Hall, Harry Woods; **D:** Norman Z. McLeod. **VHS, Beta, LV** $14.98 *MCA*

Monsieur Verdoux

A thorough Chaplin effort, as he produced, directed, wrote, scored, and starred. A prim and proper bank cashier in Paris marries and murders rich women in order to support his real wife and family. A mild scandal in its day, though second-thought pacifism and stale humor date it. A bomb upon release (leading Chaplin to shelve it for 17 years) and a cult item today, admired for both its flaws and complexity. Raye fearlessly chews scenery and croissants. Initially based upon a suggestion from Orson Welles. 🦴🦴🦴

1947 123m/B Charlie Chaplin, Martha Raye, Isobel Elsom, Mady Correll, Marilyn Nash, Irving Bacon, William Frawley, Allison Roddan, Robert Lewis; **D:** Charlie Chaplin; **W:** Charlie Chaplin. National Board of Review Awards '47: 10 Best Films of the Year; Nominations: Academy Awards '47: Best Original Screenplay. **VHS, Beta, LV** $19.98 *FOX*

Monster a Go-Go!

A astronaut crash lands his capsule, revealing him to be a ten-foot monster from outer space whose is due to a radiation mishap. Military men scramble around, drink coffee, and talk for most of the movie. Once in a while the radioactive giant will kill somebody. The cheat ending is such a groaner that it's almost worth staying for. Lewis bought (or was hired to fix) a dull unfinished picture called *Terror at Halfday* (directed by Rebane). He added a few scenes, gave it a commercial title, and cut together a rockin' trailer that brought 'em in at the drive-ins double billed with his *Moonshine Mountain.* ♪

1965 70m/B Phil Morton, June Travis, Bill Rebane, Sheldon Seymour; **D:** Herschell Gordon Lewis. **VHS, Beta** $39.95 *VCI*

Monster from the Ocean Floor

An oceanographer (Wade) in a deep-sea minisub and a pretty tourist (Kimball) are threatened by a multi-tentacled creature (not shown until the end and not worth the wait). This one has historic value, if little else. Roger Corman's first production is obviously cheap ($12,000 budget) and slow moving. It was also very profitable and Corman was off and running. *The Fast and the Furious* came next. First teaming of Corman and Haze (Seymour Krelboin in the classic *Little Shop of Horrors*), who plays a Mexican diver and lost his job pumping gas as a result. Ordung was a fellow student of Corman, who invested $2,000 in exchange for his first directing job. He also played a supporting role, and went on to direct the early Chuck Connors vehicle *Walk the Dark Street.* **AKA:** It Stalked the Ocean Floor; Monster Maker. 🦴▷

1954 66m/C Anne Kimball, Stuart Wade, Jonathan Haze; **D:** Wyott Ordung. **VHS, Beta** $29.98 *VMK*

Monster in the Closet

A fun horror spoof about a rash of San Francisco murders that all take place inside closets (San Francisco? In closets?). A news reporter and his scientist friend discover that the killings are being done by a transdimensional monster that lives in and travels through closets. A wide variety of films take a beating, including, but not limited to, *King Kong, Superman, Psycho,* and *Close Encounters of the Third Kind.* The cast treats the material with proper respect and the film succeeds on execution as well. Henry Gibson gets too little screen time, but makes the most of it in the best scene, in which he attempts to befriend

the monster. The rest of the cast, experienced B-movie vets all, deliver the goods, often in small roles. A must for fans of horror-comedy. From the makers of *The Toxic Avenger,* though not quite up to that film's level. 🦴🦴🦴

1986 (PG) 87m/C Donald Grant, Claude Akins, Denise DuBarry, Stella Stevens, Howard Duff, Henry Gibson, Jesse White, John Carradine; **D:** Bob Dahlin. **VHS, Beta $19.98** *LHV, WAR*

Monterey Pop

If you're going to San Francisco, be sure to wear some flowers in your hair. This landmark concert film is your ticket to the 1967 Monterey International Pop Festival. Captures legendary performances by Otis Redding, Janis Joplin (doing a volcanic "Ball and Chain"), the Who, Otis Redding, and Jimi Hendrix (burning down the house, if not his guitar, on "Wild Thing"). Also appearing are the Jefferson Airplane, Simon and Garfunkle, and the Mamas and the Papas. 🦴🦴🦴🦴

1968 72m/C VHS, Beta, LV, 8mm $29.95 *MVD, COL*

Monty Python and the Holy Grail

"On second thought, let's not go to Camelot. It is a silly place." In their first original film written for the screen, Monty Python's Flying Circus depicts the Middle Ages, warts and all, and lays waste to the land of happy-ever-aftering. Graham Chapman gets absolutely no respect as King Arthur, who is charged by God to find the Holy Grail. His "silly kaniggits" include Sir Lancelot the Brave (John Cleese), Sir Galahad the Chaste (Michael Palin), and Sir Robin, the no-so-brave as Sir Lancelot (Eric Idle); look quickly for "Sir Not Appearing in this Film." The classic bits are legion, from the ever-digressing credits and the Knights Who Say Ni to the killer rabbit. But limb for limb, nothing tops King Arthur's blood-spurting duel with the Black Knight, who is reduced to a taunting stump ("Alright," says the magnanimous king, "We'll call it a draw"). Once seen, you can never take any film with knights, castles, or shrubbery quite as seriously. Connie Booth, the former Mrs. Cleese and the co-writer of *Fawlty Towers,* appears as a woman accused of being a witch ("She turned me into a newt!"). 🦴🦴🦴🦴

1975 (PG) 90m/C *GB* Graham Chapman, John Cleese, Terry Gilliam, Eric Idle, Terry Jones, Michael Palin, Carol Cleveland, Connie Booth, Neil Innes, Patsy Kensit; **D:** Terry Gilliam, Terry Jones; **W:** Graham Chapman, John Cleese, Terry Gilliam, Eric Idle, Terry Jones, Michael Palin. **VHS, Beta, LV, 8mm $19.95** *COL, SIG, TVC*

Monty Python Live at the Hollywood Bowl

Fifteen years after the Beatles played the Hollywood Bowl, British comedy's Fab Six (seven if you count Carol Cleveland, and we sure do!) perform their greatest hits. Aficionados know these by heart but who can resist the rare opportunity to see their heroes live onstage (and running amuck through the audience)? Includes such classics as "The Ministry of Silly Walks," "The Lumberjack Song," "The Argument Clinic," "World Forum" and "Whizzo Chocolate Co," with a vomit-spewing policeman who anticipates the most infamous sketch in *Monty Python's The Meaning of Life.* Not as familiar is an hilarious lecture on comedy that demonstrates the art of getting konked with a wooden plank or receiving a pie in the face. Filmed bits include such Olympian contests as the 200 Meter Freestyle for Non-swimmers or the race for people with no sense of direction. For the uninitiated, this, along with the sketch film, *And Now For Something Completely Different,* is a representative entry into the world of Monty. Say no more, nudge-nudge. 🦴🦴🦴

1982 78m/C *GB* Eric Idle, Michael Palin, John Cleese, Terry Gilliam, Terry Jones, Graham Chapman; **D:** Terry Hughes; **W:** John Cleese, Terry Gilliam; **M:** John Du Prez. **VHS, Beta, LV $14.95** *PAR*

Monty Python's Life of Brian

Though considered by many to be Monty Python's best film (John Cleese has cited it as his favorite), this is probably not the best place for newcomers to start (*And Now For Something Completely Different* and *Monty Python and the Holy Grail* are more accessible). After portraying King Arthur in *Holy Grail,* Graham Chapman has his cross to bear as Brian, who was born at the same time as

"Ni."

--the Knights in *Monty Python and the Holy Grail.*

Monty Python's Life of Brian.

Jesus and who himself becomes a most reluctant Messiah. This savage and profane take on religion and all other matters not politically correct is Monty Python's most daring and controversial film, and that is saying something. You may, however, catch yourself singing along with the crucifixion victims who try to cheer up Brian with the catchy little ditty, "Always Look on the Bright Side of Life." *AKA:* Life of Brian. 🦴🦴🦴

1979 (R) 94m/C *GB* Graham Chapman, John Cleese, Terry Gilliam, Eric Idle, Terry Jones, Michael Palin, George Harrison; *D:* Terry Jones; *W:* Graham Chapman, John Cleese, Terry Gilliam, Eric Idle, Terry Jones, Michael Palin. **VHS, Beta, LV $14.95** *PAR, SIG*

Monty Python's Parrot Sketch Not Included

Steve Martin hosts a 20th anniversary retrospective of the legendary British comedy troupe Americans tend to either love or hate. If you love them, you'll find highlights here to jog your memory and tickle your funny bone, even though you have undoubtedly seen it all before. And if you don't like Python, you probably are not reading this. Though the parrot was disappointed at his exclusion, the Spam diner, lingerie-wearing lumber jacks, the unexpected Spanish Inquisition, philosopher soccer, and The Ministry of Silly Walks are all here. For Python neophytes, this is a good place to start (and if you don't laugh out loud, probably a good place to end as well). 🦴🦴🦴🦴

1990 75m/C Graham Chapman, John Cleese, Terry Gilliam, Eric Idle, Terry Jones, Michael Palin. **VHS, LV $19.95** *PAR, SIG, TVC*

Monty Python's The Meaning of Life

Funny, technically impressive film conducts various inquiries into the most profound questions confronting humanity. Notable among the sketches here are a live sex enactment performed before bored schoolboys, a student-faculty rugby game that turns quite violent, and an encounter between a physician and a reluctant, untimely organ donor. Best sketch provides a memorable portrait of a glutton prone to nausea who has that one morsel too many. And at film's end, the meaning of life is actually revealed. 🎵🎵🎵

1983 (R) 107m/C *GB* Graham Chapman, John Cleese, Terry Gilliam, Eric Idle, Terry Jones, Michael Palin, Carol Cleveland; *D:* Terry Jones; *W:* Graham Chapman, John Cleese, Terry Gilliam, Eric Idle, Terry Jones, Michael Palin; *M:* John Du Prez. Nominations: Cannes Film Festival '93: Best Film. **VHS, Beta, LV $14.95** *MCA, CCB, SIG*

Moonshine Mountain

TV folk singer Doug Martin (Scott) heads for the hills to do some research on mountain music, is immediately carjacked for his sport jacket, and runs across the local co-op moonshine business. When his ex-fiancee disappears after trying to get him to return home, it's discovered that the town sheriff and his deputy have been murdering G-men to protect the still. The titles all contain jokes. H.G. Lewis ("who ought to know better but don't") was known for his horror and nudie films, but he occasionally produced dramas, musicals, comedies, or a combination of all three, as in this hillbilly picture—although he can't resist adding an ax murder. It's odd to see Jeffrey Allen and others from *2000 Maniacs* welcoming the city slicker and spouting cornpone—one expects them to whip out butcher knives at any moment. Lewis also "decomposed" the theme song, "Love That White Lightnin'," and there are performances by the Sweetum Sisters and Brother, and Gay Land & the Thunderbirds. Shot on a plantation in Bullock Creek, South Carolina. **AKA:** White Trash on Moonshine Mountain. 🎵

1964 90m/C Chuck Scott, Adam Sorg, Jeffrey Allen, Bonnie Hinson, Carmen Sotir, Ben Moore, Pat Patterson, Mark Douglas; *D:* Herschell Gordon Lewis. **VHS, Beta $16.95** *SNC*

Mortuary Academy

To win an inheritance two brothers must attend the family mortician school, paving the way for aggressively tasteless jokes about necrophilia. An attempt to recapture the successful black humor of the earlier Bartel/Woronov teaming *Eating Raoul*, this one's dead on arrival except for an uproarious animated title sequence. 🎵

1991 (R) 86m/C Christopher Atkins, Perry Lang, Paul Bartel, Mary Woronov, Tracey Walter, Lynn Danielson, Cesar Romero, Wolfman Jack; *D:* Michael Schroeder. **VHS, LV $79.95** *COL*

Motel Hell

"Meat's meat and a man's gotta eat." So says Farmer Vincent (Calhoun), famous for his preservative-free smoked sausages. But what does he have to do with the automobile accidents that happen nightly near his motel? And what's going on in that walled garden out back? The answers are graphically (but not too graphically) provided in this blackly comic version of *The Texas Chainsaw Massacre*. Before it's over, virtually every melodramatic cliche imaginable—including the heroine on the buzz saw—has been brought into play. The filmmakers make good use of stark lighting and gurgling sound effects to create their creepy atmosphere. Recommended for horror fans. 🎵🎵🎵

1980 (R) 102m/C Rory Calhoun, Nancy Parsons, Paul Linke, Nina Axelrod, Wolfman Jack, Elaine Joyce, Dick Curtis; *D:* Kevin Connor. **VHS, Beta, LV $14.95** *MGM*

"No harm in one tiny little chocolate, is there?" Terry Jones and John Cleese in *Monty Python's The Meaning of Life*.

THE HOUND SALUTES: BORIS KARLOFF

To hear the name is to think of Horror. The first image that comes to mind is the face of the Frankenstein Monster, the hideous visage of a corpse come to full life. Though familiar, it still sends a quiet chill over your vertebrae every time you see it. The second image is perhaps of a distinguished gentleman, sometimes sporting a mustache, deviously plotting murder in the name of forbidden science. But the third image is completely different: a kind and gentle man, cordial and entertaining guest on a TV variety show, someone you look up to and trust. The jolly Uncle to the Shock Theater Generation, who tells us spooky stories when the lights go down.

To the fanatic and to the world at large, Karloff is the foremost name in horror films (or "terror" as he preferred). His death was reported on national network newscasts, to the surprise of many a youngster whose stack of monster magazines had yet to gather dust (or be thrown out by an abusive parent). Mom and Pop knew him, too. He was great in all those old monster movies they'd seen as kids, and wasn't he great on *The Man From U.N.C.L.E.* that time? He was as good as Jimmy Cagney or Clark Gable, in his own way (but not the Duke, of course).

But the fans came to claim him as one of their own. They came to know that his real name was William Henry Pratt, born November 23, 1887 (illegitimately, some say). When the acting bug bit him he ran away (or was pushed by embarrassed relatives) to Canada, worked his way back and forth across the continent, alternating acting and manual labor. He made his way to Hollywood, and kept at it until somebody took notice. One of his film roles was as a killer in *The Criminal Code.* He got good notices, more work, and was spotted in the studio commissary by director James Whale, who was looking for someone to play a monster in his new film. Unfazed by the heavy makeup, Karloff gave the role his all and created a masterpiece, all the while half expecting to be back driving a truck the following week. Within the year, the film's runaway success had him moving his family into a

continued...

Mother's Day

Three female college chums take a camping trip for their yearly reunion. They're hoping to meet guys from a Molsen's ad, but, Surprise!, they discover that the area is populated by folks whose spouses and siblings are one in the same. Not only that, but they're uncivilized and, for the most part, toothless. Notable among them are a demented duo of brothers (Holden McGuire and Billy Ray McQuade) who enjoy, not trout fishing, but torturing and killing unsuspecting victims, while their loony mother (Rose Ross) watches and approves. When the boys aren't busy murdering, they're eating cereal from aluminum buckets and watching the tube (Ah! Wilderness). "We ain't backwards," they claim. "We citified." Mysteriously, this does not impress the uppity former coeds. Before long, one is raped and tortured to death. The remaining two escape, vowing to "Get those bastards." Their revenge is sweet and satisfyingly gory: one guys gets an axe to the groin; the other gets stabbed repeatedly and is treated to a Drano cocktail. Mom gets suffocated with a pillow shaped like a woman's breast. The end, though, is a bit cheesy. Sanitized gore with black satiric intentions. 🗡🗡

1980 98m/C Tiana Pierce, Nancy Hendrickson, Deborah Luee, Holden McGuire, Billy Ray McQuade, Rose Ross; **D:** Charles Kaufman; **W:** Warren Leight, Charles Kaufman. **VHS, Beta $49.95** *MED*

Mothra

Classic Japanese monster fantasy about an enraged giant caterpillar that invades Tokyo while searching for the Alilenas, a set of very tiny, twin princesses who've been kidnapped by an evil nightclub owner in the pursuit of big profits. Presumably, the twins and Mothra, who share a telepathic bond, are the result of the nuclear testing which devastated their home island. After tiring of crushing buildings and wreaking incidental havoc, the enormous crawly thing zips up into a cocoon and emerges as Mothra, a moth distinguished by both its size and bad attitude. Mothra is unique among giant monster epics. The setting is more based in fantasy than schlocky sci-fi, and the monster (a beautifully colorful creation in adult form) is presented as a heroic creature. Features one of Akira Ifukube's most beautiful scores. Mothra and the musical twin fairies (who were played by a popular recording duo known as The Peanuts) make appearances in later Godzilla epics. 🦴🦴🦴

1962 101m/C *JP* Yumi Ito, Frankie Sakai, Lee Kresel, Emi Ito; **D:** Inoshiro Honda. **VHS, Beta $9.95** *GKK*

Motor Psycho

When a motorcycle gang rapes and kills a woman, her husband (Rocco) and another of the gang's victims (Haji) pursue them into the desert to seek brutal revenge. A change of pace for Meyer, in that the focus here is on violence and the men who perpetrate it, rather than on sexy superwomen. This was Meyer's first film with Haji; she would show up again the next in several of his other features. Rocco, the hero of the tale, was soon to become a familiar supporting actor on TV and in movies. Since the biker movie craze had yet to begin, the gang is rather clean cut, and ride Hondas instead of Harleys. Meyer liked the idea of the motorized gang in the desert, but seems less enthusiastic about the tough guy material. The next year he transformed the idea into the classic *Faster Pussycat! Kill! Kill!* 🦴🦴🦴

1965 73m/B Haji, Alex Rocco, Stephen Oliver, Holle K. Winters, Joseph Cellini, Thomas Scott, Coleman Francis, Sharon Lee; **D:** Russ Meyer. **VHS** *RMF*

Ms. 45

After debuting with the gory black comedy *Driller Killer*, Abel Ferrara made this rough, bristling cult favorite about a mute seamstress (Tamerlis) who, in response to being raped and beaten twice in one night, finds empowerment in the form of a stolen gun and goes on a man-killing murder spree. Leads to a totally wild ending. Ferrara would go on to make slightly more mainstream pictures (*Body Snatchers, Bad Lieutenant*), but without losing his cynical eye. Tamerlis is excellent, stalking the streets of New York with a gleam in her eye. **AKA:** Angel of Vengeance. 🦴🦴🦴

1981 (R) 84m/C Zoe Tamerlis, Steve Singer, Jack Thibeau, Peter Yellen, Darlene Stuto, Editta Sherman, Albert Sinkys, Jimmy Laine; **D:** Abel Ferrara. **VHS, Beta, LV $19.95** *LIV, FCT*

Multiple Maniacs

Waters' follow-up to *Mondo Trasho* was inspired by the Sharon Tate murder, at that time unsolved (Divine would take credit for the deed in the flick), reflecting Waters' self-proclaimed obsession with serial killers. Divine stars as the ring leader of a travelling freak show ("The Cavalcade of Perversion"), filled with such sideshow acts as a girl sniffing and licking a bicycle seat, a pornographer snapping the crotch of a drunken model, and the "puke eater" (which is pretty self-explanatory); the whole circus (aside from being pretty entertaining) is really just the vehicle for robbing and killing hapless spectators. Highlight of the sordid lot is Divine being raped by Lobstora, a 15-food broiled lobster, for no apparent reason (the Hound isn't sure what a viable reason might be, but it is somehow delightfully out of context). 🦴🦴🦴

1970 90m/B Divine, David Lochary, Mary Vivian Pearce, Edith Massey, Mink Stole; **D:** John Waters. **VHS** *NO*

The Mummy

Eerie chills mark this classic horror tale of an Egyptian priest, buried alive nearly 4000 years earlier, who comes back to life after a 1921 archeological dig. Eight hours of extraordinary makeup transformed Karloff into the macabre mummy, who believes the soul of the long-deceased (and probably long-decayed) lover resides in the body of a young woman. Marked the directing debut of famed German cinematographer Freund. 🦴🦴🦴🦴

1932 72m/B Boris Karloff, Zita Johann, David Manners, Edward Van Sloan; **D:** Karl Freund. **VHS, Beta, LV $14.95** *MCA, TLF*

Munchies

Gremlins rip-off about tiny aliens (who love beer and fast food) that invade a small town. Imported by accident from South America, the title beasties are soon wreaking havoc on Smalltown, USA. Regretfully, not a single joke works, the beasties aren't lovable or cute, there's no blood for the gore hounds, and not an uncovered breast in sight. Truly a film with nothing for everyone. Tough to believe it's a Roger Corman production. Strictly for viewing by masochists. 🦴

"It takes all kinds of critters to make Farmer Vincent fritters."
--Farmer Vincent (Rory Calhoun) in *Motel Hell*.

"Save me from that mummy! It's dead!"
--Zita Johann in *The Mummy*.

Story continued...

big Mexican farmhouse with plenty of dogs, a giant turtle and a rather large pet pig named Violet.

The fans learned every available detail. They knew he'd had five wives (or was it seven?), that he'd been in over 150 films, was crazy about cricket, helped to found the Screen Actors Guild, made frequent appearances on radio and television, "edited" collections of weird fiction, starred on Broadway in several productions, and even had his own comic-book. And they knew that he loved them so much that he continued to work in his final years despite his near total confinement to a wheelchair, with a tank of oxygen close at hand. And for all this and much more, they loved him right back.

Newspapers and magazines never failed to remark on the contrast between the charming gentleman and the monsters he played on the screen. How can he possibly scare anyone? But this very contrast is perhaps the key to his success. Like a loving parent who scares the kids with a Halloween maskthe mask is so perfect that it can't fail to frighten, while the face behind it can only be loved. Isn't your favorite uncle the one who would take you Trick-or-Treating, or stay up late and watch Creature Features with you? And isn't it Uncle Boris that does the same?

To many contemporary actors, Karloff's style is old fashioned. The basics of his technique, developed over many years on the stage in touring stock companies, are as follows: he learns his lines exactly as written and delivers them like he means every word. But his range of talent is not quite so deceptively simplistic. In *Frankenstein*, for example-though he has no lines whatsoever, his character is brilliantly well thought out. The monster is a newborn adult, a middle-aged infant, met with fear and violent rejection wherever he goes--and reacts with more of the same, while longing for understanding. In a much less known performance in the film *Before I Hang*, Karloff plays a Jekyll & Hyde type character. Scenes in which his personality changes from good to evil in the space of a few seconds, without any sort of makeup or camera tricks, are truly startling--you

continued...

1987 (PG) 83m/C Harvey Korman, Charles Stratton, Nadine Van Der Velde; *D:* Bettina Hirsch. **VHS, Beta $14.98** *MGM*

Murder Weapon

Low-budget horror movie that reverses all of the conventions of the slasher flick. Here, the heavy-breathing killer stalks young guys. Heroines Dawn (co-producer Linnea Quigley) and Amy (Karen Russell) are two young women who have recently been released from a psychiatric institution and have, perhaps unadvisedly, gone off their medication. They have invited several guys over to their house for an afternoon of beer and whatever. In flashback scenes, their psychiatrist (Lyle Waggoner, veteran of *The Carol Burnett Show*) tries to explain the root of their problems, while, one by one, the guys disappear. Film doesn't try to be anything more than low-budget escapism and succeeds admirably. 🦴🦴🦴

1990 (R) 90m/C Linnea Quigley, Karen Russell, Lyle Waggoner. **VHS, LV** *NO*

Muscle Beach Party

Sequel to *Beach Party* finds Frankie and Annette romping in the sand again. Trouble invades teen nirvana when a new gym opens and the hardbodies try to muscle in on surfer turf. Meanwhile, Paluzzi tries to muscle in on Funicello's turf. Good clean corny fun, with the usual lack of script and plot. Lorre appeals in a cameo, his final screen appearance. Watch for "Little" Stevie Wonder in his debut. Rickles' first appearance in the "BP" series; Lupus was credited as Rock Stevens. Followed by *Bikini Beach*. 🎵 Muscle Beach Party; Runnin' Wild; Muscle Bustle; My First Love; Surfin' Woodie; Surfer's Holiday; Happy Street; A Girl Needs a Boy; A Boy Needs a Girl. 🦴🦴

1964 94m/C Frankie Avalon, Annette Funicello, Buddy Hackett, Luciana Paluzzi, Don Rickles, John Ashley, Jody McCrea, Morey Amsterdam, Peter Lupus, Candy Johnson, Dolores Wells, Stevie Wonder, Donna Loren, Amadee Chabot; *Cameos:* Peter Lorre; *D:* William Asher; *W:* William Asher, Robert Dillon; *M:* Les Baxter. **VHS, Beta, LV $29.95** *NO*

My Darling Clementine

One of the best Hollywood westerns ever made, this one recounts the precise events leading up to and including the gunfight at the O.K. Corral. Ford claimed that he knew Wyatt Earp and used his stories to recount the details vividly, though not always accurately. In this telling of the famous tale, Mature is a fine Doc Holliday to Fonda's Earp and, once again, Ford made excellent use of Monument Valley locations. An earlier version that Ford screened for preview audiences has recently been rediscovered; less romantic than the familiar theatrical release and with a more downbeat ending, it's been shown on cable television but, to date, is not available on tape. Remake of 1939's *Frontier Marshal.* The story was also retold as *Gunfight at the O.K. Corral* (1957), *Tombstone* (1993), and *Wyatt Earp* (1994).

1946 97m/B Henry Fonda, Victor Mature, Walter Brennan, Linda Darnell, Tim Holt, Ward Bond, John Ireland; *D:* John Ford. **VHS, Beta, LV $19.98** *FOX, TLF*

My Little Chickadee

W.C. Fields goes West in this designated comedy classic that is not the side-splitter a summit meeting between these two legends would promise. Their initial meeting on a Greasewood City-bound train is a gem ("Will you take me?" he proposes and she, suspecting he is wealthy, coos, "I'll take you...and how"), as is their wedding night when she substitutes a goat in their conjugal bed. But they are much funnier apart. Sitting down with Fields to a card game, a cowboy asks, "Is this a game of chance?" "Not the way I play it," is Fields's immortal reply. Meanwhile, Mae is romanced by the town's crusading newspaper editor and the saloon owner, who moonlights as the infamous Masked Bandit.

1940 91m/B W.C. Fields, Mae West, Joseph Calleia, Dick Foran, Margaret Hamilton, Donald Meek; *D:* Eddie Cline. **VHS, Beta, LV $14.98** *MCA, MLB, BTV*

Myra Breckinridge

Tasteless adaptation of Gore Vidal novel about a film critic who, after undergoing a sex change operation, plots the destruction of the American male movie-star stereotype. Starring Rex Reed, who may have seen a little of himself in the story; Mae West, for whom this was intended as a comeback film after a 27-year absence from the screen (she tried it again in 1978 with the equally ludicrous *Sextette*); and the lesbian love team of Raquel Welch and Farrah Fawcett. This was the second major studio attempt (Russ Meyer's *Beyond the Valley of the Dolls* was the first) to cash in on the new sexual permissiveness of American films with a big budget X-rated extravaganza.

1970 (R) 94m/C Mae West, John Huston, Raquel Welch, Rex Reed, Farrah Fawcett, Jim Backus, John Carradine, Andy Devine, Tom Selleck; *D:* Michael Sarne. **VHS, Beta** *FOX*

Mysterious Island

The special effects of stop-motion master Ray Harryhausen are the star of this awesome Jules Verne adventure that continues the saga of Captain Nemo. A behemoth crab, a giant bird, and a swarm of gargantuan bees are just some of the fantastic creatures awaiting Civil War soldiers and a reporter who escape in a wayward observation balloon. They are later joined by two shipwrecked women and saved from pirates by Nemo (Herbert Lom, most fondly remembered as the put-upon victim of Inspector Clouseau in the *Pink Panther* films). Michael Callan starred in *Cat Ballou* and *Gidget Goes Hawaiian.* Another memorable soundtrack by Bernard Herrmann.

1961 101m/C *GB* Michael Craig, Joan Greenwood, Michael Callan, Gary Merrill, Herbert Lom, Beth Rogan, Percy Herbert, Dan Jackson, Nigel Green; *D:* Cy Endfield; *M:* Bernard Herrmann. **VHS, Beta, LV $19.95** *COL, MLB*

Mystery Train

The ramshackle Arcade Hotel, Elvis Presley's haunting version of "Blue Moon" on the radio, and a gunshot in the night link nine real characters and three concurrent stories in Jim Jarmusch's minimalist comedy. In the first, a Japanese couple "Far From Yokohama" have come to Memphis to visit Graceland. She likes Carl Perkins. He is devoted to the King. How she finally makes her stone-faced companion smile is a highlight. In "Ghost," an Italian widow spends the night while waiting to accompany her husband's coffin back to Rome. In a diner, she has a memorable encounter with a stranger who tries to sell her a comb that purportedly belonged to a hitch-

"During one of my trips through Afghanistan, we lost our corkscrew. Had to live on food and water for several days."

--W. C. Fields in *My Little Chickadee.*

can sense the change in his thoughts on a subliminal level.

To those that have yet to join the Karloff Kult: seek out the titles in his filmography. You will be thrilled. You may be shocked. You might even be...horrified!

But, you'll be back for more.

Naked Kiss

A brutalized prostitute escapes her pimp, and moves to a small town, where she becomes a respectable nurse in a children's hospital. She falls in love and nearly marries a man who turns out to be a child molester. This is one of Sam Fuller's most savage pictures, and is truly shocking for its in-your-face candor about forbidden subjects. The opening sequence shows off Fuller's iconoclastic style to maximum effect. **AKA:** The Iron Kiss. 🎞🎞🎞🎞

1964 92m/B Constance Towers, Anthony Eisley, Michael Dante, Virginia Grey, Patsy Kelly, Betty Bronson; **D:** Samuel Fuller. **VHS, LV $59.95** *HMV*

hiking Elvis. In "Lost in Space," the final story, "Elvis" appears in the form of sneering, sideburned Joe Strummer, who lays low with two companions after a botched liquor store robbery. Steve Buscemi, of *Reservoir Dogs*, is one of the fugitives. Cinque Lee (Spike's brother) and Screaming Jay Hawkins (the patron saint of Jarmusch's *Stranger Than Paradise*) star as the Arcade's night shift. That's the voice of Tom Waits as a radio DJ. Like the Arcade Hotel, this is off the beaten track, but it is perhaps Jarmusch's most accessible film. 🎞🎞🎞

1989 (R) 110m/C Masatoshi Nagase, Youki Kudoh, Jay Hawkins, Cinque Lee, Joe Strummer, Nicoletta Braschi, Elizabeth Bracco, Steve Buscemi, Tommy Noonan, Rockets Redglare, Rick Aviles, Rufus Thomas; **D:** Jim Jarmusch; **W:** Jim Jarmusch; **M:** John Lurie; **V:** Tom Waits. **VHS, LV $79.98** *ORI*

"Your body is your only passport."

--Anthony Eisley in *The Naked Kiss.*

The Naked Flame

O'Keefe plays an aging mining company investigator in a strange town inhabited by Nordic people whose old country traditions die hard. There's trouble brewing over some kind of weird Canuck version of racial tension. As a demonstration of protest, the womenfolk shed their clothes for some ancient traditional pagan nude torchlight chanting, meant to shame the menfolk into coming to their senses. It gets their attention anyway. There's arson, murder, then murder and arson, and it all ends up in a tedious courtroom trial. Pitiful and pathetic. 🎞

1968 (R) ?m/C Dennis O'Keefe, Linda Bennett, Kasey Rogers. **VHS $16.95** *SNC*

Naked Lunch

Whacked-out movie based on William S. Burroughs' autobiographical account of drug abuse, homosexuality, violence, and weirdness set in the drug-inspired land called Interzone. Weller plays William Lee, a recovered junkie turned exterminator. Unfortunately, his wife (Davis) gets hooked on the bug powder, and drags him down with her. Hallucinogenic images are carried to the extreme: typewriters metamorphose into beetles, bloblike creatures with sex organs scurry about, and characters mainline insecticide. Still, this world is so bleak, you don't want to live there or visit. It is as if Lee is permanently on bad acid trip to beatnik hell. Some of the characters are clearly based on writers of the Beat generation, including Jane and Paul Bowles, Allen Ginsberg, and Jack Kerouac. If you understood the book, you may understand the movie. Of course, the Hound doesn't know anyone who understood the book. 🎞🎞

1991 (R) 117m/C Peter Weller, Judy Davis, Ian Holm, Julian Sands, Roy Scheider, Monique Mercure, Nicholas Campbell, Michael Zelniker, Robert A. Silverman, Joseph Scorsiani; **D:** David Cronenberg; **W:** David Cronenberg; **M:** Howard Shore. Genie Awards '92: Best Director (Cronenberg), Best Film, Best Supporting Actress (Mercure); National Society of Film Critics Awards '91: Best Director (Cronenberg). **VHS $94.98** *TCF, INJ*

Nam Angels

The Hell's Angels actually sued producer Roger Corman over defamation for this film, in which some of their bikers happen to be in Saigon during the Vietnam War to get rich off the heroin-smuggling trade. Army brass instead tricks the outlaws into entering the battle zone and carrying out a POW rescue mission. And if you believe that, you'll believe the bad guy, an ex-Nazi who's set himself up as a god amidst the NVA. Philippines-made production falls slightly short of *Apocalypse Now*. For more in the cycle-savages-in-Nam microgenre, 1970's *The Losers* is also on video. ♫

1988 (R) 91m/C Brad Johnson, Vernon Wells, Kevin Duffis; *D:* Cirio H. Santiago. **VHS, Beta $79.95** *MED*

National Lampoon's Animal House

Classic Belushi vehicle running amuck. Set in 1962 and responsible for launching Otis Day and the Knights and defining cinematic food fights. Every college tradition from fraternity rush week to the homecoming pageant is irreverently and relentlessly mocked in this wild comedy about Delta House, a fraternity on the edge. Climaxes with the homecoming parade from hell. Boasts a host of young stars, including Kevin Bacon, who went on to more serious work. Remember: "Knowledge is good." *AKA:* Animal House. ♫ ♫ ♫ ♪

1978 (R) 109m/C John Belushi, Tim Matheson, John Vernon, Donald Sutherland, Peter Riegert, Stephen Furst, Bruce McGill, Mark Metcalf, Verna Bloom, Karen Allen, Tom Hulce, Mary Louise Weller, Kevin Bacon; *D:* John Landis; *W:* Harold Ramis; *M:* Elmer Bernstein. People's Choice Awards '79: Best Film. **VHS, Beta, LV $14.95** *MCA*

National Lampoon's Attack of the 5 Ft. 2 Women

Satirist Brown, who gave the world the novelty songs "'Cause I'm a Blonde" and "I Like 'Em Big and Stupid," and the feature-length Madonna rip "Medusa: Dare to be Truthful," parodies two of 1994's most notorious trash-tabloid queens. In "Tonya: The Battle of Wounded Knee," ambitious (but not-so-bright) Olympic figure-skating contender Tonya Hardly hires a thug to literally knock skinny, popular Nancy Cardigan out of competition. Then comes "He Never Give Me Orgasm: The Lenora Babbitt Story," the title of which sums

up the lament of the notorious Venezuelan va-sectomist who severs her drunk hunk husband's male organ due to sexual frustration. The draggy second segment could have used some judicious cutting...er, pruning...er, editing. Sorry. Made for cable TV. *AKA:* Attack of the 5 Ft. 2 Women. ♫ ♫ ♪

1994 (R) 82m/C Julie Brown, Sam McMurray, Adam Storke, Priscilla Barnes, Lauren Tewes, Dick Miller, Rick Overton, Stanley DeSantis, Anne DeSalvo, Liz Torres, Vicki Lawrence, Stella Stevens, Peter DeLuise; *D:* Julie Brown, Richard Wenk; *W:* Julie Brown, Charlie Coffey; *M:* Christopher Tyng. **VHS** *PAR*

Nature's Playmates

A beautiful private eye tours Florida nudist camps in search of a missing man with a distinctive tattoo on his posterior. One of H.G. Lewis' obscure "nudie" flicks, sexually tame by modern standards, awful by any standards. ♫

1962 56m/B Vicki Miles, Scott Osborne; *D:* Herschell Gordon Lewis. **VHS $19.95** *VDM, TPV*

Nekromantik

The sad story of Rob, a necrophile whose girlfriend leaves him when he loses his job at Joe's Streetcleaning Agency (a service that sends plastic-suited men to clean up after dead bodies). His job provided them with bed partners; there is a soft-focus slow-mo sex scene with a rotting corpse with a lead pipe stuck in his groin adorned with a condom (hey, they're sick, but they're safe), filmed to the back drop of romantic piano music ("Love Theme from *Nekromantik*"?) Now that his source of corpses is dried up, she leaves, taking their latest "friend" with her. In his rage, he puts their pet cat in a garbage bag and beats it to death against the walls of their home (the phrase "not enough room to swing a dead cat" comes to mind...), and then in his love-sick despair, well, the Hound won't ruin the ending, but it is powerful and ironic (let's just say she does love him after all). Stark underground flick with cheap yet effective f/x; if you can stomach the plot, it's fairly coherent. In German with English subtitles. ♫ ♫

1987 74m/C *GE* Daktari Lorenz, Harald Lundt, Henri Boeck, Clemens Schwenter, Holger Suhr; *Cameos:* Jorg Buttgereit; *D:* Jorg Buttgereit; *W:* Jorg Buttgereit, Franz Rodenkirchen; *M:* Herman Kopp. **VHS $29.95** *FLT*

N

"**Over?** Did you say over? Nothing is over until we say it is. Was it over when the Germans bombed Pearl Harbor? Hell no! And it ain't over now!"

—John "Bluto" Blutarsky (John Belushi) motivating the members of the Delta House Fraternity for one last assault on their school and town in *National Lampoon's Animal House.*

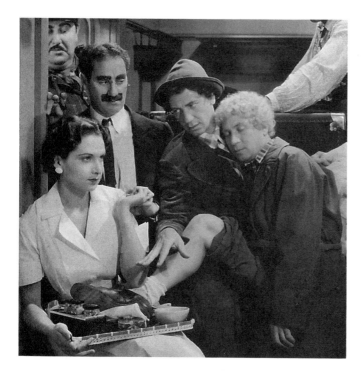

Nekromantik 2

"You'll gasp as a beautiful necrophile discovers true love, proving again that there is sex after death!" proclaim the ads. Includes highlights from the first *Nekro* (for those who haven't seen it); the sequel picks up with a new nekro-chick who obtains the head of Rob, the jilted necrophile of the previous movie. Slicker than its predecessor, with less non-stop shock and a little more plot. In German with English subtitles. If you like this, check out Buttgereit's *Der Todesking.* ♫ ♫ ▷

1991 100m/C *GE* Monika M., Mark Reeder, Simone Sporl, Wolfgang Muller; *D:* Jorg Buttgereit; *M:* Herman Kopp, Daktari Lorenz. **VHS $29.95** *FLT*

Nevada

Entertaining silent western with a great cast finds gunslinger Cooper running from the law and winding up on a ranch where he falls for Todd, the rancher's daughter. Naturally, Cooper redeems himself by going after a gang of cattle rustlers, led by Powell. Based on a novel by Zane Grey. ♫ ♫ ▷

1927 67m/B Gary Cooper, Thelma Todd, William Powell, Ernie Adams, Philip Strange; *D:* John Waters. **VHS $16.95** *GPV*

Never Give a Sucker an Even Break

Field's feckless farewell feature was reputedly based on an idea he wrote on a napkin; in any case, he took screenplay credit as Otis Criblecoblis, and stars at his most unleashed, playing himself on a "typical" day. The comic admires a billboard for his earlier hit *The Bank Dick*, then meets with his producer at Esoteric Pictures, to whom he submits an unfilmable script about himself wooing wealthy, man-hating Mrs. Hemoglobin (Dumont) and her lovely daughter, who are guarded by apes in a mountaintop fortress. Thrown out of the studio, Fields gets involved in a wild, though thoroughly unmotivated car chase that's a classic. Uneven, infamously plotless comedy hasn't aged well over the years, but remains one of the strangest things ever to emerge from the Hollywood studio system and is pure Fields. The Hound would like to see that napkin! **AKA:** What a Man. ♫ ♫ ♫

1941 71m/B W.C. Fields, Gloria Jean, Franklin Pangborn, Leon Errol, Margaret Dumont; *D:* Eddie Cline. **VHS, Beta, LV $14.95** *MCA, BAR*

A Night at the Opera

Grand opera—could there be a more fitting and deserving target of the Marx Brothers' pomposity-puncturing anarchy? No, and they do it up right in the movie that many fans consider their best and laugh-out-loud funniest. Jones, as a budding opera singer, warbles "Alone" and "Cosi Cosa," but she's got nothing on the orchestra's version of "Take Me Out to the Ball Game," which has never been put to better use. Working with an unusually big budget, the guys reach epic comic heights. Some scenes were tested on audiences, including the Groucho/Chico paper-tearing contract negotiation and the celebrated stateroom scene, in which the boys are joined in a small closet by two maids, the ship's engineer, his asistant, a manicurist, a young woman, a cleaning lady, and four food-laden waiters. Laserdisc includes letterboxing, digital sound, original trailers, production photos,

memorabilia, and soundtrack commentary by film critic Leonard Maltin. ♫♫♫♫

1935 92m/B Groucho Marx, Chico Marx, Harpo Marx, Allan Jones, Kitty Carlisle Hart, Sig Rumann, Margaret Dumont, Walter Woolf King; **D:** Sam Wood; **W:** George S. Kaufman, Morrie Ryskind, Bert Kalmar, Harry Ruby, Al Boasberg; **M:** Herbert Stothart. **VHS, Beta, LV $19.95** *MGM, CRC, CCB*

Night Call Nurses

Three gorgeous nurses find danger and intrigue on the night shift at a psychiatric hospital. Third in the "nurse" quintet is back on target, shrugging off the previous film's attempts at "serious" social commentary. Corman regular Dick Miller provides comic relief. Preceded by *The Student Nurses* and *Private Duty Nurses* and followed by *The Young Nurses* and *Candy Stripe Nurses*. **AKA:** Young L.A. Nurses 2. ♫♫

1972 (R) 85m/C Patricia T. Byrne, Alana Collins, Mittie Lawrence, Clinton Kimbrough, Felton Perry, Stack Pierce, Richard Young, Dennis Dugan, Dick Miller; **D:** Jonathan Kaplan; **W:** George Armitage. **VHS, Beta $59.98** *NLC*

Night Gallery

Submitted for your approval is Rod Serling's follow-up to *The Twilight Zone*. This feature-length trilogy launched the television series as well as the career of Steven Spielberg. His segment, "Eyes," stars Joan Crawford as a blind woman who blackmails a doctor into performing an operation that would allow her to see for 24 hours. But the first episode is even better, with Roddy McDowall as a scoundrel who can't wait to inherit the family estate. He kills his uncle...or does he? That scene-shifting painting on the wall suggests that the not-so-dear departed is coming back from the grave. In the well-intentioned but predictable concluding episode, Richard Kiley stars as a Nazi war criminal who cannot escape his past. ♫♫♫

1969 95m/C Joan Crawford, Roddy McDowall, Tom Bosley, Barry Sullivan, Ossie Davis, Sam Jaffe, Kate Greenfield; **D:** Steven Spielberg, Boris Sagal. **VHS, Beta $59.95** *MCA*

A Night in Casablanca

Groucho, Harpo, and Chico find themselves in the luxurious Hotel Casablanca, going af-

ter some leftover Nazis searching for treasure. Groucho, considered quite expendable, is hired to replace the murdered manager and wastes no time in trying to convert the place into his own private paradise. Chico and Harpo, however, garner the most laughs. Scenes of special note are Harpo's sword duel with a Nazi fencing master and an outlandish sequence in which the boys help the Nazis pack, er, unpack, no, er, pack... well, you get the idea. The film is flawed slightly by some lame, old jokes that slipped in, but is far better than many sources give it. Perhaps not the best film for a first time viewer of a Marx Brothers comedy; for those to whom the boys are old friends, it's a warm, fuzzy experience. ♫♫♫

1946 85m/B Groucho Marx, Harpo Marx, Chico Marx, Charles Drake, Dan Seymour, Sig Rumann; **D:** Archie Mayo. **VHS, Beta** *NO*

Night of the Blood Beast

An astronaut comes back from space, only to find that he's been impregnated by an alien creature, and a mass of extraterrestrial larvae is growing within him. Adding to his problem: his parental instincts are kicking in. Creepy venereal horror, decades before Cronenberg and *Alien*. The low-budget, most apparent when the rubber monster waddles out of Bronson Canyon cave, defeats a valiant attempt at a story. **AKA:** Creature From Galaxy 27. ♫♫♫

1958 65m/B Michael Emmet, Angela Greene, John Baer, Ed Nelson; **D:** Bernard L. Kowalski. **VHS $16.95** *SNC, MRV*

Night of the Bloody Apes

When a doctor transplants an ape's heart into his dying son's body (shown in actual surgical footage), the son turns into an ape man and goes berserk. Police race to end the bloody rampage. Gory Mexican-made horror is a color remake of Cardona's *Doctor of Doom* (1962, aka: *Wrestling Women Vs. the Aztec Ape*), but with a lot of added blood and nudity. **AKA:** Gomar the Human Gorilla; La Horriplante Bestia Humana. ♫♫

1968 (R) 84m/C *MX* Jose Elias Moreno, Carlos Lopez Moctezuma, Armando Silvestre, Norma Lazarendo, Augustin Martinez Solares, Gina Moret, Noelia Noel, Gerard Zepeda; **D:** Rene Cardona Jr. **VHS, Beta $59.95** *MPI*

THE HOUND SALUTES: TRACI LORDS

It's not everyday that someone goes from starring in *New Wave Hookers* to a role on *Melrose Place*, but former porn actress turned video vixen Traci Lords has managed to pull off the career switch. Born Nora Louise Kuzma in 1968 in Steubenville, Ohio, Lords first earned film notoriety when it was learned that her first 80 or so porno flicks were made while she was underage (Oops! Who knew?). After all the legal hubbub over that scandal died down, Lords did one more X-rated turn in *I Love You Traci* (allegedly on her 18th birthday) before making the move to mainstream Hollywood. Cult favorite Roger Corman gave Lords her first break in 1988's remake of *Not of This Earth*, and a B-movie queen was born. Her undeniably sultry good looks and sexy pout made her a natural for the tawdry bad girl role, which John Waters took full advantage of in both *Cry-Baby* and *Serial Mom*. Since then, Lords has had a recurring role on *Melrose* and made several appearances on the always tasteful *Married With Children*. Lords has also turned to music in her post-X years, making appearances with the Ramones and Manic Street Preachers before cutting her own techno/dance album in 1995 that was generally well-received by critics.

> "**The good news is your dates are here. The bad news is, they're dead!**"
>
> --*Night of the Creeps*.

Night of the Creeps

In 1958 alien meanies crash-land on Earth and assume the form of parasitic slugs. The man they infect is cryogenically frozen, then thawed out thirty years later on the campus of Corman University, where he staggers about as a moldering zombie, spreading the living-dead contagion throughout the town. Good-looking B-movie satire plays around with every schlock-horror cliche there is, yet manages to avoid the sleaze factor itself. Still, these B-movie homages have been multiplying themselves at the rate of parasitic alien slugs, and *Night of the Creeps* doesn't do enough fresh to stand out substantially from the pack. Director Dekker's first film. 🎬🎬◗

1986 (R) 89m/C Jason Lively, Jill Whitlow, Tom Atkins, Dick Miller, Steve Marshall; **D:** Fred Dekker; **W:** Fred Dekker. **VHS, Beta, LV $14.99** *NO*

Night of the Demon

"Bigfoot's not playing games anymore," announces an anthropologist who journeys with his students to remote wilderness where an antisocial sasquatch has been murdering folks and is worshipped by a backwoods cult. Whenever the pace slows down, which is often, there are crude flashbacks to the cave-man-like beast committing rape and gore murders. Hits the depths with scene of a biker getting his penis ripped out. Almost as painful is sitting through the start of the cassette; no fewer than eight coming attractions of releases by the same cheapjack tape distributor. WOOF!

1980 97m/C Jay Allen, Michael J. Cutt, Bob Collins, Jodi Lazarus; **D:** James C. Watson. **VHS, Beta $49.95** *VHE*

Night of the Ghouls

In this long lost marginal sequel to Wood's *Bride of the Monster* and *Plan 9 From Outer Space,* a phony spiritualist swindles the grieving by pretending to raise the dead. To his great surprise he actually does enliven some cadavers, who then go after him. Duncan makes for a seedy and ill-tempered mystic, in a role written for Bela Lugosi. Narrator Criswell seems unconcerned that he's in a film exposing fake spiritualism. Johnson reprises his role as Lobo, with a surprisingly good makeup job. Moonlighting chiropractor Tom Mason, who doubled for the deceased Lugosi in *Plan 9,* returns to the screen to play the leader of the living dead. Tony Cardoza, who looks a lot like Wood in his small role here, went on to direct and star in his own series of awful movies. Unreleased for over 20 years because Wood couldn't pay the film lab. Like *Bride of the Monster,* this one almost reaches the mundane quality typical of '40s B-movies. Not quite as classically bad as his other films, but still a laugh riot. **AKA:** Revenge of the Dead. 🎬🎬🎬

1959 69m/B Paul Marco, Tor Johnson, Duke Moore, Kenne Duncan, John Carpenter; **D:** Edward D. Wood Jr. **VHS, Beta $9.95** *RHI, SNC, MED*

The Night of the Hunter

Charles Laughton's only directorial effort is one of the best and most unusual films noir

Hollywood ever produced. Casting Robert Mitchum as the charismatic villain and Lillian Gish as a resourceful rescuer was a stroke great luck or genius. Though the roles go directly against their images, both stars are at their best. Mitchum is a psychotic preacher who marries a lonely widow (Winters) with two children in the hopes of finding the $10,000 her thieving husband had stashed. This dark, terrifying tale with almost surrealistic symbolism is completely unique in Hollywood's history. Even judged by today's standards, some moments—notably the underwater scene—are so nightmarish, startling, and unpredictable that they defy description. For those who have missed it, this one's required viewing. From the novel by Davis Grubb. 🎵🎵🎵🎵

1955 93m/B Robert Mitchum, Shelley Winters, Lillian Gish, Don Beddoe, Evelyn Varden, Peter Graves, James Gleason, Billy Chapin, Sally Jane Bruce; **D:** Charles Laughton; **W:** James Agee. **VHS, Beta, LV** $19.98 *MGM*

Night of the Living Dead

A low-budget masterpiece that is powerfully frightening. The newly dead arise as flesh-eating ghouls; a handful of holdouts find shelter in a farmhouse, but fight among themselves almost as much as they fight the marauding zombies—a siege plotline that has worked in the movies since *The Lost Patrol* (1929). Claustrophobic, terrifying, gruesome, extreme, and at times humorous. An article by critic Roger Ebert that appeared in *Reader's Digest* condemning the picture (since recanted) did much to bolster business, but the filmmakers saw little of the money. Since this was thought to be a public domain title for many years, it became one of the most commonly released titles on home video. The poor quality of the original prints, combined with this widespread and continuous cheap duplication, have lead many critics to praise its black & white documentary-style realism. A new print struck from the original negative in 1994 for a deluxe laserdisc release revealed that the photography was actually quite beautiful, equal to most Hollywood productions of the day. Followed by *Dawn of the Dead* (1979) and *Day of the Dead* (1985). Romero's feature directorial debut. Available in a horri-

ble colorized version. **AKA:** Night of the Flesh Eaters. 🎵🎵🎵🎵

1968 90m/B Judith O'Dea, Duane Jones, Russell Streiner, Karl Hardman; **D:** George A. Romero. **VHS, LV** $19.95 *REP, MRV, NOS*

Night Tide

Youthful Hopper plays a sailor, and no wonder—his acting's as wooden as a ship's figurehead. He falls for a disturbed girl (Lawson) working at a seedy dockside carnival as a freak-show mermaid and whose previous boyfriends tended to turn up drowned. Warned to stay away from her, Hopper dreams of wrestling a rubber octopus that would make Ed Wood guffaw. Seldom-seen, critically overrated psychothriller has a strong key performance from Muir, but Hopper and writer/director Harrington were just too inexperienced at this point in their careers to pull off such delicate material. 🎵🎵

1963 84m/B Dennis Hopper, Gavin Muir, Luana Anders, Marjorie Eaton, Tom Dillon; **D:** Curtis Harrington. **VHS** $16.95 *SNC, FRG, TPV*

The Nightcomers

Prequel to Henry James' *The Turn of the Screw* has an Irish gardener (Brando) carrying on an overheated, kinky S&M affair with the nanny (Beacham) under the curious eyes of two watchful children. James' fans may be horrified that the master's overwritten little ghost story could be the source of such a gleefully sordid film. The result has a strongly prurient edge but, unlike the source material, it's seldom boring, and the conclusion is a shocker. 🎵🎵🎵

1972 (R) 96m/C *GB* Marlon Brando, Stephanie Beacham, Thora Hird; **D:** Michael Winner. **VHS, Beta, LV** $14.95 *COL, NLC*

Nightmare

Boring splatterthon has a young boy hacking his father and his aggressive mistress to pieces when he discovers them in bed. He grows up to be a psycho who continues along the same lines. Humorless and dreadful, the original ads claimed Tom Savini did the special effects. He had nothing to do with it. **AKA:** Blood Splash. **WOOF!**

N

"**G**et your state troopers out to my place. I got something trapped in my barn."
--Lillian Gish in *Night of the Hunter*, referring to Robert Mitchum.

"**W**e may not enjoy living together, but dying together isn't going to help."
--Marilyn Eastman in *Night of the Living Dead*.

1982 (R) 97m/C Baird Stafford, Sharon Smith, C.J. Cooke, Mik Cribben, Kathleen Ferguson, Danny Ronan; *D:* Romano Scavolini; *W:* Romano Scavolini. **VHS, Beta** *NO*

The Nightmare Before Christmas

Back when he was an animator trainee at Disney, Burton came up with this adventurous idea but couldn't get it made; subsequent directorial success brought more clout. Relies on a painstaking stop-motion technique that took more than two years to film and is justifiably amazing. The story revolves around Jack Skellington, the Pumpkin King of the dangerously weird Halloweentown. Suffering from ennui, he accidentally discovers the wonders of Christmastown and decides to kidnap Santa and rule over this peaceable holiday. Fast pace is maintained by the equally breathless score. Not cuddly, best appreciated by those with a feel for the macabre. *AKA:* Tim Burton's The Nightmare Before Christmas. 🦴🦴🦴

1993 (PG) 75m/C D: Henry Selick; *W:* Caroline Thompson, Tim Burton; *M:* Danny Elfman; *V:* Danny Elfman, Chris Sarandon, Catherine O'Hara, William Hickey, Ken Page, Ed Ivory, Paul (Pee Wee Herman) Reubens, Glenn Shadix. Nominations: Academy Awards '93: Best Visual Effects; Golden Globe Awards '94: Best Original Score. **VHS, LV $19.99** *TOU*

A Nightmare on Elm Street

Feverish, genuinely frightening horror film about Freddy Krueger (Englund), a scarred maniac in a fedora and razor-fingered gloves who kills neighborhood teens in their dreams and, subsequently, in reality. Of the children-fight-back genre, in which the lead victim (Heather Langenkamp) ingeniously goes to great lengths to destroy Freddy. Look for a young Johnny Depp as Langenkamp's boyfriend. In the tradition of *Friday the 13th* and *Halloween*; spawned a "Freddy" phenomenon: six sequels (to date); a TV series (*Freddy's Nightmares*, a horror anthology show hosted by Englund capitalized on his character); and an army of razor-clawed trick or treaters at Halloween. Also notable because not all of it's sequels sucked; the lastest (last? is there ever a last sequel?) took a new twist and focused on the hauntings of the actors (including Langenkamp and Englund) who appeared in Freddie's movies and who are tormented by him by association. 🦴🦴🦴🦴

1984 (R) 92m/C John Saxon, Heather Langenkamp, Ronee Blakley, Robert Englund, Amanda Wyss, Nick Corri, Johnny Depp, Charles Fleischer; *D:* Wes Craven; *W:* Wes Craven; *M:* Charles Bernstein. **VHS, Beta, LV $24.95** *MED, CDV, IME*

Nine Deaths of the Ninja

Faceless ninja warrior Kosugi leads a team of commandos on a mission to rescue a group of political prisoners held captive in the Philippine jungles. Features Ozone-depleted plot, incongruous performances, and inane dialogue, not to mention two main villains—a neurotic Nazi in a wheelchair and a black lesbian amazon—who chew jungle and bring bad art to a new level of appreciation. Amazing in its total badness. Produced by Cannon. WOOF!

1985 (R) 93m/C Sho Kosugi, Brent Huff, Emelia Lesniak, Regina Richardson; *D:* Emmett Alston; *W:* Emmett Alston. **VHS, Beta $69.95** *MED*

Northville Cemetery Massacre

Amateurish biker exploitation pic with a message. A scruffy gang of hog-riders arrive in a small town and rile the residents with their freewheeling ways. But guess what? The conservative citizens prove to be the real savages when the rowdies are falsely accused of rape; grey-haired townsfolk borrow some military hardware and ambush the bikers in a bloody My Lai/Kent State/Attica-inspired gundown. Like, don't trust the squares, man! Filmed near Detroit, with real-life motorcycle clubs participating. Co-directed by William Dear, later to do family-oriented features like *Harry and the Hendersons* and *Angels in the Outfield*. Music by former Monkee Mike Nesmith. *AKA:* The Northfield Cemetery Massacre. 🦴

1976 (R) 81m/C David Hyry, Craig Collicott, Jan Sisk; *D:* William Dear, Thomas L. Dyke; *M:* Michael Nesmith. **VHS, Beta** *NO*

Not of This Earth

In a remake of the 1957 Roger Corman quickie, an alien wearing sunglasses makes an unfriendly trip to Earth. In order to save his dying planet he needs major blood donations from unsuspecting Earthlings. Not a match for the original version, some may nevertheless want to see ex-porn star Lords in her role as the nurse. 🦴🦴▷

1988 (R) 92m/C Traci Lords, Arthur Roberts, Lenny Juliano, Rebecca Perle; **D:** Jim Wynorski; **W:** Jim Wynorski, R.J. Robertson. **VHS, Beta $14.95** *MGM*

Nuke'Em High III: The Good, the Bad and the Subhumanoid

Classic good twin vs. evil subhumanoid twin wage battle against each other, aided by chicks with guns and tin undergarments, in this follow-up to Troma's *Class of Nuke 'Em High* parts one and two. Supposedly inspired by Shakespeare's *Comedy of Errors*. Tip: stick to the BBC production for your senior thesis. WOOF!

1994 (R) 95m/C Brick Bronsky, Lisa Gaye; **D:** Eric Louzil; **W:** Lloyd Samuel Weil Kaufman. **VHS** *NYR*

The Nutty Professor

Jean-Luc Godard praised it. Yves Robert paid homage in his comedy, *Pardon Mon Affaire*. But you don't have to be French to regard this Jekyll and Hyde comedy to be Jerry Lewis's masterwork. Lewis stars as the hapless buck-toothed, bespectacled Professor Kelp, who develops a formula that transforms him into swinging, slicked-down ladies' man Buddy Love. Stella Stevens is the improbable adoring co-ed torn between both men. Any resemblance between Buddy and Jerry's former partner, Dean Martin, is a coincidence...or is it? 🦴🦴🦴▷

1963 107m/C Jerry Lewis, Stella Stevens, Howard Morris, Kathleen Freeman; **D:** Jerry Lewis; **W:** Jerry Lewis. **VHS, Beta, LV $14.95** *PAR*

Oasis of the Zombies

European students set out to find buried treasure in Saharan oasis but instead find corps of Nazi zombie ghosts still protecting their caravan of gold. An intriguing premise (similar to *The Fog* and *Shock Waves*) is completely undone by sloppy editing, clumsy camera work, poor dubbing, amateurish makeup (nice to see that the long dead soldiers keep up with the latest groovy hairstyles), and a horrible synth score (possible tacked onto the video version). Logic is also faulty—since the ghouls only come out at night, why not hunt for the gold only in the daylight and camp somewhere else? Hiding behind the Eurocine pen name is none other than Jesus Franco, who found this one to be not up to even his standards. Some nice WWII battle footage is obviously lifted from another movie (Alfredo Rizzo's *I Giardini del Diavolo*). This Spanish/French production used the rare practice of filming scenes twice in different languages and with some difference in casts. Many different versions of this are in existence, adding to the shame. *AKA:* Bloodsucking Nazi Zombies. 🦴

1982 75m/C *SP FR* Manuel Gelin, France Jordan, Jeff Montgomery, Miriam Landson, Eric Saint-Just, Caroline Audret, Henry Lambert; **D:** A.M. Frank. **VHS, Beta $59.95** *NO*

Ocean's 11

The Rat Pack rules! Frank Sinatra and a band of war buddies plot to knock off five Las Vegas casinos simultaneously on New Year's Eve. Great comic support by Joey Bishop and Akim Tamiroff, and a surprise ending that will bury you. Sinatra, Dean Martin, and Sammy Davis, Jr., filmed in Vegas during the day and performed on the Strip at night. Those were the days! *High Times* magazine called Frankie and his pals "the hipster saints of the booze culture." Ring-a-ding-ding. 🦴🦴🦴

1960 148m/C Frank Sinatra, Dean Martin, Sammy Davis Jr., Angie Dickinson, Peter Lawford; **D:** Lewis Milestone. **VHS, Beta, LV $19.98** *WAR*

Octaman

Comical thriller featuring non-threatening octopus-man discovered by scientists in Mexico. It's one thing to suffer for arts sake, but the poor sap who had to waddle around in the octo-costume—zipper plainly in evidence, sweating under a hot sun, knowing that it'll all look awful anyway—should get some kind of special Oscar. Not without its curiosity factor: young makeup f/x genius Rick Baker designed the octopus man, and claims it might have worked if it hadn't been so poorly photographed. Cast is an odd mix. Mathews and Morrow look slightly embarrassed to be fighting this schlocky creature after facing the creatures in the classics *Seventh Voyage of Sinbad* and *This Island Earth* (respectively). Actress Angeli died of a drug overdose during filming. Director Essex, who co-wrote the script for *Creature from the Black Lagoon*, should have known better. David Essex went on to star in the faux-Beatles movies *That'll Be the Day* and *Stardust.* ♫ ▷

1971 79m/C Kerwin Mathews, Pier Angeli, Harry Guardino, David Essex, Jeff Morrow, Norman Fields; **D:** Harry Essex. **VHS, Beta $19.95** *GEM, CNG, PSM*

Oh! Calcutta!

Film version of the first nude musical to play on Broadway, which caused a sensation in the late 1960s. It's really a collection of skits, some of which were written by such notables as John Lennon, Sam Shepard, and Jules Feiffer. And it's really not that funny or erotic (Bill Macy—TV's long-suffering husband of Bea Arthur in *Maude*—naked?). ♫ ▷

1972 105m/C Bill Macy, Mark Dempsey, Raina Barrett, Samantha Harper, Patricia Hawkins, Mitchell McGuire; **D:** Guillaume Martin Aucion. **VHS, Beta** *NO*

Oh Dad, Poor Dad (Momma's Hung You in the Closet & I'm Feeling So Sad)

Cult fave black comedy about a bizarre family on a vacation in Jamaica. The domineering mother travels with a coffin containing the stuffed body of her late husband. Additional corpses abound. Based on the play by Arthur L. Kopit. ♫ ♫

1967 86m/C Rosalind Russell, Robert Morse, Barbara Harris, Hugh Griffith, Lionel Jeffries, Jonathan Winters; **D:** Richard Quine. **VHS, Beta $49.95** *PAR*

Omega Man

In post-holocaust Los Angeles, Heston is immune to the effects of a biologically engineered plague and battles those who aren't—an army of albino victims bent on destroying what's left of the world. Strong suspense with considerable violence, despite the PG rating. Based on the science fiction thriller "I Am Legend" by Richard Matheson, which is also the basis for the film *The Last Man on Earth.* ♫ ♫ ▷

1971 (PG) 98m/C Charlton Heston, Anthony Zerbe, Rosalind Cash, Paul Koslo; **D:** Boris Sagal. **VHS, Beta, LV $14.95** *WAR*

On the Edge: The Survival of Dana

Generation X-ers of A Certain Age have fond memories of this hand-wringing attempt by '70s prime-time TV to examine juvenile delinquency, with as much success as Ed Wood had back in 1956 in his script for *The Violent Years*. Anderson was also residing in *Little House on the Prairie* at the time she was calculatingly cast as Dana, angelic figure-skater from North Dakota who moves to L.A. and gets busted unfairly when her new high school comrade shoplifts. Our tainted heroine falls in with a bad crowd of mean teens, a "car club" called the Roadrunners, and goes from crisis to crisis. A stinker that may appeal to those with campy tastes, though on cassette the feature proves especially dreary without commercial interruptions. Retitling of *The Survival of Dana*; not to be confused with Jonathan Kaplan's *Over the Edge,* an excellent drama of troubled youth, also available on tape. ♫ ▷

1979 92m/C Melissa Sue Anderson, Robert Carradine, Marion Ross, Talia Balsam, Michael Pataki, Kevin Breslin, Judge Reinhold, Barbara Babcock; **D:** Jack Starrett. **VHS, Beta** *GEM*

One Down, Two to Go!

When the mob is discovered to be rigging a championship karate bout, two dynamic expert fighters join in a climactic battle against the hoods. Example of really bad blaxploitation that wastes talent, film, and the audience's time. **WOOF!**

1982 (R) 84m/C Jim Brown, Fred Williamson, Jim Kelly, Richard Roundtree; **D:** Fred Williamson. **VHS, Beta $59.95** *MED, RHI, HHE*

Orgy of the Dead

Classic anti-canon film scripted by Ed Wood, Jr., from his own novel. Two innocent travelers are forced to watch an even dozen spooky strip acts in a cardboard graveyard, presided over by two-bit King of Darkness Criswell and his Vampira-clone Queen. A mummy and a werewolf step in to act as comic stooges and supernatural stage hands. Director Stephen (real name Stephen Apostolof) somehow manages to reproduce Wood's inept style, right down to the mismatched day and night footage. Hilariously bad. 🎬🎬🎬▷

1965 90m/C Criswell, Fawn Silver, William Bates, Pat Barringer; **D:** A.C. Stephen; **W:** Edward D. Wood Jr. **VHS, Beta $19.95** *RHI*

Out of the Dark

The fleeting pleasures of glimpsing such cult movie icons as Divine (John Waters' leading "lady" in a rare non-drag role) and Paul Bartel, some quirky dialogue, and movie in-jokes are not enough to wash out the bad taste of this slasher film that is dressed to kill with pretentious, De-Palma-style kinetics. Karen Black, once an Oscar-nominee, stars as Ruth, the owner of a Los Angeles phone sex line, Suite Nothings, whose employees are being stalked by Bobo, a clown-masked killer. The obvious suspect is sweaty, creepy accountant Bud Cort (from midnight movie classic *Harold and Maude*). The police, however, focus on handsome photographer Cameron Dye, who, as one officer notes, "probably gets more ass than a toilet seat." Bartel, who portrays a peeping tom hotel clerk, was the executive producer. A movie theatre marquee displays *Mortuary Academy*, director Michael Shroeder's first film. Bartel executive produced that one, too. With cameos by Tab Hunter and Lainie Kazan, who with Divine, starred in Bartel's *Lust in the Dust*. 🎬

1988 (R) 98m/C Cameron Dye, Divine, Karen Black, Bud Cort, Lynn Danielson, Geoffrey Lewis, Paul Bartel, Tracey Walter, Silvania Gallardo, Starr Andreeff, Lainie Kazan, Tab Hunter; **D:** Michael Schroeder; **M:** Paul Antonelli. **VHS, Beta, LV $89.95** *COL*

Out of the Past

In one of his defining roles, Mitchum is a none-too-honest detective caught up in love, lust, murder, and money. It's a complex web spun by gangster Douglas and bad girl Greer. The plot of this film noir classic is torturous but clear thanks to Tourneur's fine directing, and the ending is right on target. Mitchum became an overnight star after this film, which was overlooked but is now considered one of the best in its genre. Geoffrey Homes wrote the script from his novel *Build My Gallows High*. Weakly remade in 1984 as *Against All Odds*. **AKA:** Build My Gallows High. 🎬🎬🎬▷

1947 97m/B Robert Mitchum, Kirk Douglas, Jane Greer, Rhonda Fleming, Steve Brodie, Dickie Moore; **D:** Jacques Tourneur; **W:** Geoffrey Homes. **VHS, Beta, LV $19.98** *MED, TTC*

The Outlaw

Hughes's variation on the saga of Billy the Kid, which spends more time on Billy's relationship with girlfriend Rio than the climactic showdown with Pat Garrett. The famous Russell vehicle isn't as steamy as it must have seemed to viewers of the day, but the brouhaha around it served to keep it on the shelf for six years. Also available colorized, but who cares? 🎬🎬

1943 123m/B Jane Russell, Jack Beutel, Walter Huston, Thomas Mitchell; **D:** Howard Hughes. **VHS, Beta, LV $8.95** *CNG, MRV, NOS*

Outrageous!

An offbeat comedy about the strange relationship between a gay female impersonator and his pregnant schizophrenic friend. This 1977 release was one of the first gay films to find a cult audience on the midnight circuit. Star Craig Russell's impersonations of female film stars earned him the best actor prize at the Berlin Film Festival, and he continued performing the routines live for several years. Audiences continue to be fascinated by this type of material, as evidenced by the recent success of the Australian hit, *Priscilla, Queen of the Desert*. 🎬🎬

1977 (R) 100m/C *CA* Craig Russell, Hollis McLaren, Richard Easley, Allan Moyle, Helen Shaver; **D:** Richard Benner. **VHS, Beta $64.95** *COL*

Over the Edge

The kids aren't alright in New Grenada, a planned suburban community that was designed to shield families and their children from the bad influences of the city, only to have violence, vandalism, and substance abuse take root in their own backyard. Michael Kramer stars as 14-year-old Carl, a good student and model son who falls in with delinquent Matt Dillon (in his first film) and

"**The kid who tells on another kid is a dead kid.**"
—Matt Dillon in *Over the Edge.*

the other bored and restless youths who congregate at the recreation center. Tensions explode one night when the parents meet at school to discuss what do about their children as the brood gathers menacingly outside. Richard Linklater, director of *Slacker* and *Dazed and Confused*, once said that "the true way to end a teenage movie is complete apocalypse." "Over the Edge" is true. Completed in 1979, but criminally mis-marketed (as a horror film!) and shelved until 1981. It received limited art house release that was buoyed by critical acclaim. Director Jonathan Kaplan apprenticed under Roger Corman on such 1970s drive-in gems as *The Student Nurses* and *Night Call Nurses*. More recently, he directed Jodie Foster to an Oscar in *The Accused*, and Bonnie Bedelia and Michelle Pfeiffer to Best Actress nominations in *Heart Like a Wheel* and *Love Field*. Screenwriter Tim Hunter later directed another disturbing look at youth, *River's Edge*. The subversive soundtrack includes Cheap Trick, the Ramones, Van Halen, and Jimi Hendrix. Worth seeking out. 🐢🐢🐢▷

1979 (PG) 91m/C Michael Kramer, Matt Dillon, Pamela Ludwig, Vincent Spano; *D:* Jonathan Kaplan. **VHS, Beta $19.98** *WAR*

Pagan Island

A sailor (Dew) is stranded on a South Pacific island with 30 beautiful girls who tie the white devil up and plan to kill him. Nani Maki (as herself), chosen to be sacrificed to the sea god, helps Dew protect the island from invading tribesmen, whereupon he's set free, providing he keeps his grubby paws off their chosen sacrifice. But he just can't keep away from Nani Maki. This fairy tale south seas adventure was sold to nudie theatres due to the fact that the women are mostly topless, but it's more charming than lascivious. The weird sea god totem was made of chicken wire and cement for $500, and looks like something from Gumby's nightmares. Casting was done by famed photographer Bunny Yeager, who also played herself in a trio of Mahon nudies (*Nude Las Vegas, Nude Camera,* and *Nudes on Tiger Reef*). Mahon, who got his start as Errol Flynn's agent and director of his final film *Cuban Rebel Girls*, went on to become a legend in exploitation, churning out films with great titles like *Run, Swinger, Run!, Fanny Hill Meets Dr. Erotico, Some Like It Violent,* and *Sex Club International.* Mahon's daughter, now a well known TV movie producer, appears as one of the island girls, billed as *Yanka Mann.* ♪♪

1960 67m/B Eddie Dew, Nani Maka; **D:** Barry Mahon; **W:** Clelle Mahon. **VHS $23.00** *SMW, TPV*

Panic in the Year Zero!

Cold-War miniclassic about Milland and family leaving Los Angeles for a fishing trip just as global nuclear war breaks out and the city vanishes in a mushroom cloud. Continuing out into the wilderness for safety, Milland adopts a ruthless survivalist code as civilization crumbles, fellow refugees clog the highways, and stereotypical juvenile delinquents run wild. The somewhat stodgy uncle of *Mad Max* and other post-apocalyptic action sagas, this stark and unsentimental drama made the point plain to *American Graffiti*-era audiences that when the bomb drops their fellow citizens, not bug-eyed mutants, will be the real monsters. The best of actor Milland's directorial efforts. Nice bonus: cassette includes original coming-attraction trailers to a motley assortment of vintage sci-fi flicks on tape from the same distributor. **AKA:** End of the World. ♪♪♪

1962 92m/B Ray Milland, Jean Hagen, Frankie Avalon, Mary Mitchell, Joan Freeman, Richard Garland, Rex Holman; **D:** Ray Milland; **M:** Les Baxter. **VHS $18.00** *FRG*

Paradise, Hawaiian Style

Out-of-work pilot returns to Hawaii, where he and a buddy start a helicopter charter service. Four years after *Blue Hawaii,* Elvis returns to the Islands for another glamourous advertisement for life in our 50th state. Countless exservicemen were suckered by these movies into relocating to the Pacific where life promised to be abundant with opportunities for small business and big-time romance. Elvis himself seems a little tired this time around, perhaps due to the mediocrity of the songs he is given to sing. ♪ Paradise, Hawaiian Style; Scratch My Back (Then I'll Scratch Yours); Stop Where You Are; This Is My Heaven; House of Sand; Queenie Wahine's Papaya; Datin'; Drums of the Islands; A Dog's Life. ♪♪

1966 91m/C Elvis Presley, Suzanna Leigh, James Shigeta, Donna Butterworth, Irene Tsu, Julie Parrish, Philip Ahn, Mary Treen, Marianna Hill, John Doucette, Grady Sutton; **D:** Michael Moore. **VHS, Beta $14.98** *FOX, MVD*

Parasite

A small town is beset by giant parasites, in 3-D no less, during that technique's brief return in the early '80s. Notable only for a young Demi Moore in one of her first big screen appearances (her little screen appearances included TV's *General Hospital,* where she played reporter Jackie Templeton). While the Hound is at it, *General Hospital* represents another soap/trash film connection: early episodes of GH have shown up on *Mystery Science Theater 3000.* ♪♪

1982 (R) 90m/C Demi Moore, Gale Robbins, Luca Bercovici, James Davidson, Al Fann, Cherie Currie, Cheryl "Rainbeaux" Smith, Vivian Blaine; **D:** Charles Band; **W:** Alan J. Adler; **M:** Richard Band. **VHS, Beta, LV $89.95** *PAR*

Parents

Actor-turned-director Bob Balaban goes to work in *Blue Velvet* territory and comes up with a film that's much more effective and unsettling. Young Michael (Madorsky) moves to a new town with Dad (Quaid) and Mom (Hurt). They set up housekeeping in a split-level filled with coral and turquoise furniture and appliances. The shy, silent, and basically unlikable boy is troubled by dreams and visions of his parents with bloodstained mouths. When they give evasive answers about the main course at dinner, he comes to believe that they are cannibals. Is that the truth, or is he a very disturbed child? The script presents no easy answers or escapes. For the most part, Balaban succeeds in making this a disturbing, unnerving piece of work. All of the colors, for example, are slightly off, slightly too intense. Food, notably meat, has seldom been so revoltingly photographed. The characters are just a notch or two off dead center and a soundtrack of syrupy '50s big band hits like "Cherry Pink and Apple Blossom White" has been poured over these disquieting visual im-

CULT FILMS: THE CAMPUS CONNECTION

Lower Learning

The VCR has not been around forever. Strange as it may seem, there was a time when the only way you could catch a cult flick was at an honest-to-goodness cinema, commonly a revival house. And the wildest, woolliest revival houses ever were (and still are) located on college campuses.

Student film societies and indie cinemas catering to the campus crowd were the spawning ground for many of today's cult classics and established midnight movies. Nothing relieves the pressure-cooker atmosphere of exams like a diverting, big screen movie, and it was in university auditoriums across the nation that the Three Stooges, the Marx Brothers, and W.C. Fields went from old-timey comedy stars to perennial cult faves. Young scholars of the '60s adopted the late Humphrey Bogart as their idol, one writer dubbing him "the living essence of cool."

Because student film groups have more freedom to experiment (and go overboard) than their civilian counterparts, colleges were able to exhibit and popularize non-mainstream movies nobody else would touch. Some of the more outrageous titles became so identified with the college experience that it became a rite of passage; you knew you'd arrived in the halls of higher learning once you'd endured a squalid dorm screening of *Pink Flamingos*, *A Clockwork Orange*, or *Night of the Living Dead*.

Some films, notably David Lynch's *Eraserhead*, are said to owe all their popularity to the college circuit. One upstate New York campus claims to have "discovered" *The King of Hearts* before anyone else; only after they played the whimsical European comedy did it become a staple of '70s art houses.

And the specialized college appeal of movies like *Reefer Madness*, *The Trip*, *Sex Madness*, and *Marihuana: The Weed with Roots in Hell* needs no explanation.

continued...

ages. Though there is a grimly humorous angle to the story, this is not a comedy. It's made of the stuff of nightmares. ♫♫♫
1989 (R) 81m/C Randy Quaid, Mary Beth Hurt, Sandy Dennis, Kathryn Grody, Deborah Rush, Graham Jarvis, Bryan Madorsky, Juno Mills-Cockell; **D:** Bob Balaban; **W:** Christopher Hawthorne; **M:** Angelo Badalamenti, Jonathan Elias. **VHS, Beta, LV $14.98** *LIV, VES, HHE*

The Pee Wee Herman Show

The original HBO special which introduced Pee Wee to the world, taped live at the Roxy Theatre in LA. It's got all the simplicity of his Saturday morning show, but with the adult humor you knew Pee had in him. When Jambi the Genie grants Pee Wee a wish, he reluctantly uses it to help out Miss Yvonne, who has the hots for Kap'n Karl (Phil Hartmann). Jambi, in the meantime, receives a pair of hands he ordered through mail order, with this comment: "I've had something I've wanted to do for a long time...." Pee Wee is amazed when he is able to hypnotize a woman from the audience with a Captain Picard puppet, convincing her to strip to her slip on stage (he then peeks up her slip, via the puppet). Great stuff, and a must for fans of Pee. ♫♫♫♫
1982 60m/C Paul (Pee Wee Herman) Reubens, Phil Hartman, John Paragon, Edie McClurg; **D:** Marty Callner. **VHS** *NO*

Pee Wee's Big Adventure

Before the darkened Florida porno theatre, before the reclusiveness and occasional cameos in movies and on TV, there was this—a sweet, zany, and endearing comedy about an adult nerd's many adventures while attempting to recover his stolen bicycle. By creating alter-ego Pee Wee Herman, Paul Reubens developed one of the most memorable characters of the 1980s. Host of his own Saturday morning children's show and frequent guest on *Late Night with David Letterman,* Herman/Reubens was loved by children and had a die-hard following of adult fans also (although he was hated by just as many adults, most of whom had little tolerance for his child-like shtick and annoying collection of voices). Pee-wee was at the top of his game in this film—he moved easily between the worlds of children and adults, equally at home in a name-calling con-

test ("I know you are, but what am I?") or his first love scene. Followed up by the less successful *Big Top Pee Wee*, this film best captures the true essence of being Pee Wee and is chock full of classic sequences—his encounter with Large Marge, big-shoe dancing to The Champs "Tequila," looking for the basement of the Alamo (look for Jan Hooks as the southern belle tour guide), and rescuing all the pets from a burning pet store. The movie also served as the first exposure that many film goers had to director Tim Burton, whose trademark strong visual style and simple storytelling are readily apparent. A colorful, exhilarating experience. 🎵🎵🎵▷

1985 (PG) 92m/C Paul (Pee Wee Herman) Reubens, Elizabeth Daily, Mark Holton, Diane Salinger, Judd Omen, Cassandra Peterson, James Brolin, Morgan Fairchild, Tony Bill, Jan Hooks; **D:** Tim Burton; **W:** Paul (Pee Wee Herman) Reubens, Phil Hartman, Michael Varhol; **M:** Danny Elfman. **VHS, Beta, LV** **$19.98** *WAR*

Peeping Tom

Controversial, unsettling thriller in which a psychopath lures women before his film camera, then records their deaths at his hand. Unnerving subject matter is rendered impressively by British master Powell. A milestone in serial killer cinema history, made the same year as *Psycho*. As much an examination of the nature of cinema as it is a cracking good terror thriller, it was so reviled by critics and public alike that it all but ruined Powell's career. Boehm is excellent as the nervous and shy murderer, who realizes that he's insane but can't help himself. Powell himself appears in home movie footage as Boehm's father, who abuses the boy with experiments in fear. This is the original uncut version of the film, released in the U.S. in 1979 with the assistance of Martin Scorsese. 🎵🎵🎵🎵

1963 88m/C Karl-Heinz Boehm, Moira Shearer, Anna Massey, Maxine Audley, Esmond Knight, Shirley Anne Field, Brenda Bruce, Pamela Green, Jack Watson, Nigel Davenport, Susan Travers, Veronica Hurst; **D:** Michael Powell. **VHS, Beta, LV $39.95** *HMV, AOV*

Performance

"I know a thing or two about performing," landlord Mick Jagger tells new tenant James Fox, and indeed he does. In his first film, Jagger stars as a reclusive former rock star who has "lost his demons." Enter Fox, an "out of date" mob enforcer who likes his work too much. He hides out in Jagger's unorthodox household that includes two women and some mind-melding psychedelic mushrooms. States Jagger: "The only performance that really makes it, the one that goes all the way, is the one that achieves madness." Ahead of its time, this hallucinatory mind-trip benefits from repeated viewings. The soundtrack includes Jagger's awesome rendition of "Memo From Turner." Anita Pallenberg, who was Keith Richards' girlfriend at the time, relishes her role as Jagger's house (and bed) mate. Erotic, violent, unsettling, and ultimately exhilarating. 🎵🎵🎵▷

1970 (R) 104m/C *GB* James Fox, Mick Jagger, Anita Pallenberg; **D:** Donald Cammell, Nicolas Roeg; **W:** Donald Cammell; **M:** Jack Nitzsche. **VHS, Beta, LV** **$19.98** *WAR*

Persona

A certified masterpiece of world cinema, but don't worry if some aspects leave you scratching your head. Ingmar Bergman himself is quoted as saying, "On many points I am unsure, and in one instance, at least, I know nothing." Thanks, Ingmar. Traumatized actress Liv Ullmann has mysteriously become mute and is sent to recuperate at a seaside cottage in the company of nurse Bibi Andersson. "I'm a good listener," Bibi states, but she is a better talker. Gradually, her confidences become more intimate and personal (particularly memorable is her reminiscence of a day at the beach during which she and a friend seduced two strangers), and a love-hate relationship develops between the two, with the balance of power shifting back and forth. Much is made of the physical similarity between Ullmann and Andersson and in one of Bergman's most famous images (courtesy of his legendary cinematographer Sven Nykvist), the faces of the two women are juxtaposed and become one. An absolutely mesmerizing, dreamlike film with an undeniable erotic charge. This was Bergman's first film with leading lady Ullmann. Look for the *Persona* reference in Bergman-fan Woody Allen's *Love and Death*. 🎵🎵🎵🎵

Story continued...

Possibly the last major film baptized as a cult hit by students was *The Adventures of Buckaroo Banzai*. Mishandled upon its initial theatrical release, dumped onto a still-maturing home-video market with little fanfare, the sci-fi satire had to wait for the student viewers to gain any sort of broad cult status. Now Team Banzai T-shirts and Yoyodyne bumper stickers mark BB fans as members of the elect.

Student film societies still thrive, but the video revolution has made many of them more followers than leaders, picking up "safer" movies that have proven reputations. But every once in a while something weird still comes along, something unknown...but better than studying for exams.

"It keeps me reminded of the other dreamless sleep that cures all ills-- forever."

--Erik/The Phantom (Lon Chaney) to Christine Daae (Mary Philbin) explaining the bed/coffin in *Phantom of the Opera* (1925).

206

Cult Flicks and Trash Pics

1966 100m/C *SW* Bibi Andersson, Liv Ullmann, Gunnar Bjornstrand, Margareta Krook; **D:** Ingmar Bergman; **W:** Ingmar Bergman. National Board of Review Awards '67: 5 Best Foreign Films of the Year; National Society of Film Critics Awards '67: Best Actress (Andersson), Best Director (Bergman), Best Film. **VHS, Beta, 8mm $19.98** *MGM, VYY, VDM*

The Perverse Countess

Romay is a bored tourist who spends a free weekend on a fling with Woods, who procures human flesh for the cannibalistic Count and Countess Zaroff (Vernon and Arno). Romay accompanies her lover to the haunted castle on a delivery, not realizing she is the package. When the Countess sees what a succulent bon-bon Romay is, she faces difficult choices. Subtitled in English. **AKA:** La Comtesse Perverse. 🦴

1973 86m/C *FR* Lina Romay, Robert Woods, Howard Vernon, Alice Arno, Caroline Riviere; **D:** Jess (Jesus) Franco. **VHS $27.90** *VSM*

Petulia

Overlooked, offbeat drama about a flighty woman who spites her husband by dallying with a sensitive, recently divorced surgeon. Classic '60s document and cult favorite offers great performance from the appealing Christie, with Scott fine as the vulnerable surgeon. On-screen performances by the Grateful Dead and Big Brother. Among idiosyncratic director Lester's best. Photographed by Nicholas Roeg. From the novel *Me and the Arch Kook Petulia* by John Haase. 🦴🦴🦴

1968 (R) 105m/C George C. Scott, Richard Chamberlain, Julie Christie, Shirley Knight, Arthur Hill, Joseph Cotten, Pippa Scott, Richard Dysart, Kathleen Widdoes, Austin Pendleton, Rene Auberjonois; **D:** Richard Lester; **W:** Lawrence B. Marcus; **M:** John Barry. **VHS, Beta $19.98** *WAR*

Phantasm

The ads call this one "a truly bizarre science-fiction horror fantasy" and for once they aren't exaggerating. The senseless plot concerns two parentless brothers who discover weird goings-on at the local funeral parlor, including the infamous airborne, brain-chewing chrome ball; malevolent hooded midgets, and the Tall Man (Scrimm). Creepy, unpredictable nightmare fashioned on a shoestring by young independent producer-director Coscarelli. Contains enough wildly imaginative twists and inventions for a dozen horror movies. Scenes were cut out of the original film to avoid "X" rating. Followed by *Phantasm II* and *III* which don't come close to the original. 🦴🦴🦴

1979 (R) 90m/C Michael Baldwin, Bill Thornbury, Reggie Bannister, Kathy Lester, Terrie Kalbus, Ken Jones, Susan Harper, Lynn Eastman, David Arntzen, Angus Scrimm, Bill Cone; **D:** Don A. Coscarelli. **VHS, Beta, LV $14.95** *COL, SUE*

The Phantom of the Opera

Deranged, disfigured music lover haunts the sewers of a Parisian opera house and kills to further the career of an unsuspecting young soprano. First of many film versions still packs a wallop, with fine playing from Chaney, Sr., whose make-up creation was frightening enough to make many viewers faint during the famous unmasking scene. Silent with two-color Technicolor *Bal Masque* sequence. The original 114 minute version survives and is available on video, but it is the trimmed 77 minute version that was released in 1929 that is most widely available. An 88-minute version with an introduction by Christopher Lee is also available. 🦴🦴🦴🦴

1925 79m/B Lon Chaney Sr., Norman Kerry, Mary Philbin, Gibson Gowland; **D:** Rupert Julian. **VHS, Beta, LV, 8mm $9.95** *CNG, NOS, FUS*

The Phantom of the Opera

Modern-day diva gets conked by a sandbag and flashes back to Victorian London, where opera composer Eric has sold his soul to Satan in exchange for occult power but acquired a scarred face in the bargain. The lurking villain grows obsessed with the time-tripping heroine and commits splattery murders to assure her casting in his show. Blood-drenched, *Elm Street* reinvention of the Gaston Leroux classic actually has intriguing touches, but whatever new life the much-rewritten script brings to an old plot quickly submerges in mucho facile gore and supernaturally stupid characters. 🎵▷

1989 (R) 93m/C Robert Englund, Jill Schoelen, Alex Hyde-White, Bill Nighy, Terence Harvey, Stephanie Lawrence; **D:** Dwight Little. **VHS, Beta, LV $14.95** *COL*

Phantom of the Paradise

A rock 'n roll parody of *Phantom of the Opera.* Splashy, only occasionally horrific spoof in which cruel music executive Williams, much to his everlasting regret, swindles a songwriter. Violence ensues. Not for most, or even many, tastes. Graham steals the film as rocker Beef. A failure at the box office, and now a cult item (small enthusiastic cult with few outside interests) for its oddball humor and outrageous rock star parodies. Williams also wrote the turgid score. 🎵 Goodbye, Eddie, Goodbye; Faust; Upholstery; Special to Me; Old Souls; Somebody Super Like You; Life At Last; The Hell of It; The Phantom's Theme (Beauty and the Beast). 🎵🎵

1974 (PG) 92m/C Paul Williams, William Finley, Jessica Harper, Gerrit Graham; **D:** Brian DePalma; **W:** Brian DePalma; **M:** Paul Williams. Nominations: Academy Awards '74: Best Original Score. **VHS, Beta, LV $14.98** *FOX*

Picasso Trigger

Gonzo action movie sets a modern Olympic record with seven—count 'em, seven—ex-Playmates in the cast. The gadget-filled story is about a group of villainous drug-selling international assassins and white slavers who report to their superiors in rhymed couplets. ("The ones with the flower have been scattered this hour.") They're trying to kill off true-blue American secret agents because their boss (the title character!) has just been rubbed out. Or something. None of it tries to make much sense. Imagine a *Mission Impossible* plot outline told with an MTV sensibility, lots of explosions, and several hottub scenes. Cast members display a certain lack of acting skills, but their suntans and overdeveloped physiques are terrific; the screen is filled with bulging biceps and breasts. Sequel to *Hard Ticket to Hawaii* and *Malibu Express,* followed by several others. 🎵🎵🎵

1989 (R) 99m/C Steve Bond, Dona Speir, John Aprea, Hope Marie Carlton, Guich Koock, Roberta Vasquez, Bruce Penhall; **D:** Andy Sidaris. **VHS $19.98** *WAR*

Pink Flamingos

The film that defined bad taste. . .that celebrated bad taste. . .and that allowed self-proclaimed "Prince of Puke" John Waters to make his mark (albeit a brown smudged mark). Babs Johnson (Divine) battles Connie and Raymond Marvel for the title of "Filthiest Person Alive." All are strong contenders; the Marvels run a baby ring, in which they keep two women hostage at all times, and impregnate them with the help of their "rather fertile" servant. Then they sell the babies to lesbian couples and invest the money in porno theatres and a heroin ring in inner-city elementary schools. Divine lives in a baby-blue trailer with her son, Crackers (who's into chicken sex), her mother (the equally divine Edith Massey, here portraying "the egg lady"), and her travelling companion, Cotton (who likes to watch the aforementioned chicken sex). They stage parties featuring entertainment by a singing rectum (literally; it just can't be described). The battle cry is sung when the Marvels send Babs a birthday gift ("Oh my God almighty, someone has sent me a bowel movement!"). Babs and her son retaliate by breaking into the Marvels home and licking all their belongings; this excites them so much that she performs oral sex on her son ("Prepare to receive the most divine gift a mother can give!"). Don't worry— the Hound hasn't given away all the good parts. Definitely not for all tastes, as it is truly

> **"Kill everyone now! Condone first-degree murder! Advocate cannibalism! Eat shit! Filth are my politics; filth is my life!"**
>
> --Babs Johnson (Divine) outlines her political beliefs for the press in *Pink Flamingos.*

THE HOUND SALUTES: BELA LUGOSI

While a generation of young moviegoers may have gotten their first exposure to film legend Lugosi in Tim Burton's *Ed Wood*, true film fans know that Lugosi has a body of work that is matched only by Boris Karloff and Lon Chaney in the horror genre. Born in Hungary in 1882 as Bela Blasko, Lugosi gained lasting fame when he played Dracula on stage in 1927 and then brought the role to the silver screen in 1931 in Tod Browning's definitive film version. With his rich accent and aristocratic good looks, Lugosi was a natural screen star and sex symbol (in fact, more than 90 percent of his fan mail was from women).

While Lugosi went on to star in many more classic horror films in the 30s and '40s, he turned out to be his own worst enemy. Eager to work, he took almost any role, no matter how small or ridiculous, even reprising his Dracula role in *Abbott and Costello Meet Frankenstein*. Lugosi's money and marital problems led him into drug abuse, and in 1955 he checked himself into a drug treatment center. Alas, it was too little, too late, and in 1956, the greatest Dracula of them all passed away at age 73. Lugosi's later years and demise were documented in *Ed Wood*, Burton's affectionate tribute to the legendary cult director. Wood and Lugosi were working together on all-time stinker *Plan 9 from Outer Space* when Lugosi passed away. Some of his scenes were kept, in others he was replaced by an obviously different actor, with no explanation offered to the viewer. In the end, just another odd chapter in the very odd life of Bela Lugosi.

1972 95m/C Divine, David Lochary, Mary Vivian Pearce, Mink Stole, Danny Mills, Edith Massey, Cookie Mueller, Susan Walsh, Pat Moran, Steve Yeager, Ed Peranio; **D:** John Waters; **W:** John Waters. **VHS, Beta, LV** *NO*

Pink Floyd: The Wall

Film version of Pink Floyd's 1979 LP, *The Wall*; a surreal, impressionistic tour-de-force about a boy who grows up numb from society's pressures. The concept is bombastic and overwrought, but Geldof manages to remain somewhat likeable as the cynical rock star and the Gerald Scarfe animation perfectly complements the film. Visually rather stunning and at times unnerving. Laserdisc edition includes the original theatrical trailer and the letterboxed format of the film. 🦴🦴🦴

1982 (R) 95m/C *GB* Bob Geldof, Christine Hargreaves, Bob Hoskins; **D:** Alan Parker; **M:** Michael Kamen. **VHS, Beta, LV** $19.95 *MVD, MGM*

Piranha

A rural Texas resort area is plagued by attacks from tiny but ferocious man-eating fish created by a scientist to be used as a secret weapon in the Vietnam War. Spoofy horror film—the title monsters are little more than bubbles and red dye in the water—features the now-obligatory Dante film in-jokes in the background. One tiny stop-motion critter appears in an all-too-brief cameo. Script by novelist/filmmaker John Sayles was his first to be produced. He also appears as the Army sentry. 🦴🦴🦴

1978 (R) 90m/C Bradford Dillman, Heather Menzies, Kevin McCarthy, Keenan Wynn, Barbara Steele, Dick Miller, Paul Bartel; **Cameos:** John Sayles; **D:** Joe Dante; **W:** John Sayles; **M:** Pino Donaggio. **VHS, Beta** $39.98 *WAR, OM*

The Pit and the Pendulum

In a grand castle in Spain, a woman and her lover plan to drive her brother (Price) mad. Oops! It works—and he responds by locking them in his torture chamber, which was built by his loony dad, whom he now thinks he is. Second of Corman's productions only remotely derived from the classic Poe tale, with the cast chewing on a loopy script. Price is a hoot, raving and cackling at Kerr, bound

tasteless and crude, in a most unabashed fashion, all the way to the end where Divine chews real dog excrement while wearing a you-know-what eating grin. In 1988 Waters published an unproduced followup script, "Flamingos Forever," in a collection of his screenplays entitled *Trash Trio*. Without the talents of the dearly departed Divine and Edith Massey, however, the work may remain unproduced. 🦴🦴🦴

within the title torture device. A landmark in Gothic horror. Corman's Poe films were more expensive than his previous films, but not half as expensive as they look due to a great deal of talent and craft supplied them. ♫♫♫
1961 80m/C Vincent Price, John Kerr, Barbara Steele, Luana Anders; **D:** Roger Corman; **W:** Richard Matheson; **M:** Les Baxter. **VHS, Beta $19.98** *WAR, OM*

Plan 9 from Outer Space

Two or three aliens in silk pajamas conspire to resurrect several slow-moving zombies from a cardboard graveyard and conquer the Earth before the warlike earthlings destroy the rest of the universe with "solarite bombs." Spaceships that look suspiciously like paper plates blaze across the sky. Lugosi's actual screen time is under two minutes, since he died before the film was complete. Note the taller and younger replacement (the chiropractor of Wood's wife) they found for Lugosi, who remains hooded to protect his identity. Many of the stories surrounding this alternative classic were dramatized in Tim Burton's *Ed Wood*. In fact, the film has become so famous for its own badness that it's now beyond criticism. Today's audiences still laugh at Wood's wonderfully naive excesses, and appreciate the his goofy exuberance more than his contemporaries did. What goes around comes around, indeed. **AKA:** Grave Robbers from Outer Space. ♫♫♫♫
1956 78m/B Bela Lugosi, Tor Johnson, Lyle Talbot, Vampira, Gregory Walcott; **D:** Edward D. Wood Jr. **VHS, Beta, LV $19.95** *NOS, SNC, MED*

Planet of Blood

Space opera about an female alien vampire (Marly) discovered in a derelict spaceship on Mars by a rescue team. If you've ever seen the Soviet film *Niebo Zowiet*, don't be surprised if some scenes look familiar; the script was written around f/x segments cut from that film. Surprisingly effective nonetheless; Harrington wrings suspense within the limited confines of the low-budget sets, and Marly (*Sealed Verdict*) makes for a sexy/creepy monster. Yet another inspiration for *Alien*. Rathbone is mainly seen standing around mission control barking orders via radio. Hopper and Harrington had collaborated previously on

the atmospheric *Night Tide* (1963). **AKA:** Queen of Blood. ♫♫♫
1966 81m/C John Saxon, Basil Rathbone, Judi Meredith, Dennis Hopper, Florence Marly, Forrest J. Ackerman; **D:** Curtis Harrington. **VHS $16.95** *SNC, NOS, MRV*

Planet of the Apes

Astronaut Charleton Heston crash lands on a planet in the future (3978 A.D.) where apes are masters and humans are merely brute animals. Superior science fiction with sociological implications. Heston delivers one of his more plausible performances, and superb ape makeup creates realistic pseudo-simians of Roddy McDowall, Kim Hunter, Maurice Evans, James Whitmore, and James Daly. The story is slightly reminiscent of the *Twilight Zone* episode in which astronauts end up inhabitants in an alien zoo; in fact, Rod Serling co-wrote the screenplay for *Planet of the Apes*, adapted from Pierre Boulle's novel *Monkey Planet*. Followed by four sequels (some of which are pretty good), including : *Beneath ...*, *Escape from...*, *Conquest of...*, and *Battle for...*, and two television series. ♫♫♫▷
1968 (G) 112m/C Charlton Heston, Roddy McDowall, Kim Hunter, Maurice Evans, Linda Harrison, James Whitmore, James Daly; **D:** Franklin J. Schaffner; **W:** Rod Serling, Michael G. Wilson; **M:** Jerry Goldsmith. National Board of Review Awards '68: 10 Best Films of the Year; Nominations: Academy Awards '68: Best Costume Design, Best Original Score. **VHS, Beta, LV $19.98** *FOX, FUS*

Planet of the Vampires

Astronauts search for missing comrades on a planet dominated by mind-bending forces. When members of the crew go insane and kill each other, aliens possess and reanimate the corpses for use in an invasion of Earth. Acceptable atmospheric filmmaking from genre master Bava, but it's not among his more compelling ventures, although better than most Italian science fiction. One of the many inspirations for *Alien*. Dubbing is poorly done— who know what other tampering AIP did to it. **AKA:** Terror in Space; Terreur dans l'Espace; Space Mutants; The Demon Planet. ♫♫▷
1965 86m/C *IT* Barry Sullivan, Norman Bengell, Angel Aranda, Evi Marandi; **D:** Mario Bava. **VHS, Beta $9.98** *ORI*

P

> **"Unspeakable horrors from outer space paralyze the living and resurrect the dead!"**
> *--Plan 9 From Outer Space.*

> **"Take your stinking paws off me, you damn dirty ape."**
> *--George Taylor (Charlton Heston) in Planet of the Apes.*

vinced him he had a buried treasure on his hands, and Roemer entered it on the film festival circuit where it received rapturous critical acclaim and at last found a distributor. Martin Priest stars as Harry, a low-level Jewish racketeer just out of prison who finds that the blacks and Latinos who once worked for him have now taken over the New York inner-city neighborhood he once controlled. Will he find salvation and respectability with his estranged family? Roemer's only previous film was the landmark racial drama *Nothing But a Man*. Most of his excellent ensemble cast never acted again. Ben Lang, a standout as Harry's ingratiating, always-smiling brother-in-law, returned to his job as a state auditor. 🦴🦴🦴▷

1969 81m/B Martin Priest, Ben Lang, Maxine Woods, Henry Nemo; *D:* Michael Roemer; *W:* Michael Roemer. **VHS $79.95** *NYF, FCT*

Polyester

Waters' first rather mainstream movie (but don't let that deter you), a witty satire on middle-class life, described by producer, director, and writer Waters as "'Father Knows Best' gone berserk." Forlorn housewife Francine Fishpaw (Divine), who is obsessed with the way things smell, pines away in her baby blue house in the suburbs for the man of her dreams while the rest of her life, well, stinks. Her husband, the owner of a porno theatre, is sleeping with his secretary; her son is the infamous "Foot Fetishist"; and her daughter is running around with a bad boy (punk rocker Stiv Bators). Her only solace is her can of air freshener, her best friend (Edith Massey, in her cutest role yet as an aging debutante), and her fantasies of Todd Tomorrow (Tab Hunter). Filmed in "Odorama," a hilarious gimmick in which theatre goers were provided with scratch-n-sniff cards that contained specific scents corresponding to key scenes, so you can smell Francine's husband's intestinal gas right along with her. Soundtrack features music performed by Deborah Harry, Tab Hunter, and Bill Murray. 🎵 Polyester; Be My Daddy Baby; The Best Thing (Love Theme from Polyester). 🦴🦴🦴🦴

1981 (R) 86m/C Divine, Tab Hunter, Edith Massey, Mink Stole, Stiv Bators, David Samson, Mary Garlington, Kenneth King, Joni-Ruth White, Jean Hill,

---

Who can resist a pretty pout? Divine in *Polyester.*

"Oooh, smell...oh, oh, everything smells so much better now!"
--Francine Fishpaw (Divine) at the happy ending in *Polyester.*

Please Don't Eat My Mother

An unauthorized softcore remake of *Little Shop of Horrors* in which lonely voyeur Henry Fudd (Kartalian) plays host to a human-eating plant. This time, our horticulturally inclined nebbish hides the plant in his pin-up adorned bedroom and tries to hide it from his nosy mom. Humor is actually not bad, but the sex scenes are mostly dull and slow things down. The amusing plant monster is a bit more vicious than the original. Features a pre-enhanced Renee Bond in a hilarious scene as the better half of a bickering couple. Monson also directed the old house thriller *Blood Legacy* (1971). *AKA:* Hungry Pets; Glump. 🦴🦴

1972 95m/C Buck Kartalian, Renee Bond; *D:* Carl Monson. **VHS $19.98** *MOV, VDM, TPV*

The Plot Against Harry

One of the great cinematic Cinderella stories in recent years. Deemed commercially unreleasable, this quirky and darkly comic character study languished on a shelf for 20 years until director Martin Roemer decided to transfer it to video for his family. A technician con-

Hans Kramm, Mary Vivian Pearce, Cookie Mueller, Susan Lowe; **D:** John Waters; **W:** John Waters; **M:** Deborah Harry, Michael Kamen. **VHS, Beta, LV $19.95** *COL*

Porky's

Investigation of teen horniness set in South Florida during the fab '50s. Irreverent comedy follows the misadventures of six youths imprisoned in Angel Beach High School who share a common interest: girls. Their main barrier to sexual success: the no-touch babes they lust after and the incredibly stupid adults who run the world. Fairly dumb and tasteless with occasional big laughs that earned mega bucks at the drive-in and created perceived popular outcry for more porky: *Porky's II: The Next Day* (1983) and *Porky's Revenge* (1985). 🦴🦴🦴▷

1982 (R) 94m/C *CA* Dan Monahan, Wyatt Knight, Scott Colomby, Tony Ganios, Mark Herrier, Cyril O'Reilly, Roger Wilson, Bob (Benjamin) Clark, Kim Cattrall, Kaki Hunter; **D:** Bob (Benjamin) Clark; **W:** Bob (Benjamin) Clark. **VHS, Beta, LV $14.98** *FXV, FOX*

Porky's 2: The Next Day

More tame tomfoolery about teenage sex drives, Shakespeare, fat high school teachers, the Ku Klux Klan, and streaking in the Florida high school where it all began. Like most sequels, lacks any wit (however adolescent it might have been) that the original might have had, and begins to feel more like a perverse episode of *Happy Days*. 🦴

1983 (R) 100m/C *CA* Bill Wiley, Dan Monahan, Wyatt Knight, Cyril O'Reilly, Roger Wilson, Tony Ganios, Mark Herrier, Scott Colomby; **D:** Bob (Benjamin) Clark; **W:** Alan Ormsby, Bob (Benjamin) Clark. **VHS, Beta, LV $29.98** *FOX*

Porky's Revenge

The same characters from Bob Clark's first two films are played by the same overaged, overweight teen-age impersonators and they go through the motions again. But the wild, ribald sense of humor from the original is thoroughly watered down here. Angel Beach High School students are out to get revenge against Porky who orders the school basketball coach to throw the championship game in some of the most inept athletic scenes ever put on film.

The second, last, and least of the *Porky's* sequels. 🦴

1985 (R) 95m/C *CA* Dan Monahan, Wyatt Knight, Tony Ganios, Nancy Parsons, Chuck "Porky" Mitchell, Kaki Hunter, Kimberly Evenson, Scott Colomby; **D:** James Komack. **VHS, Beta, LV $29.98** *FOX*

DO-IT-YOURSELF "ODORAMA" INSTRUCTIONS FOR VIEWING *POLYESTER*

For those John Waters die-hards who just can't seem to truly enjoy viewing *Polyester* again without the "Odorama" card, we've outlined the scents contained on those collector's items so that you can assemble the products and have your own "Odorama" party while playing the video on your VCR. It's great fun for the whole family!

1. A rose (just to start you out gently)

2. Elmer Fishpaw's flatulence

3. Airplane glue (be careful with this one; the Hound will not be responsible)

4. Pizza (and your movie-watching snack to boot!)

5. Gasoline (exercise caution here as well)

6. A skunk

7. Natural gas (like from a gas oven, not as in number 2 above)

8. New car

9. Moldy tennis shoe

10. Air freshener (the happy ending)

Pot, Parents, and Police

A 13-year-old boy (Mantell) gets upset when his dog dies and soon befriends a hippie couple who get him stoned and desert him when he's picked up by a cop (Battanides), all of which confounds his parents (Pine and Keen). The script is so true to life that it's actually fairly mundane. Auteur Pine, a veteran actor whose face should be familiar from a hundred movies and TV episodes, went into hock to fi-

THE HOUND SALUTES: DAVID LYNCH

David Lynch's career defies easy categorization. From his debut with the nightmarish experimental student film *Eraserhead* to his work on prime time network television, *Twin Peaks*, he has managed to keep his particular artistic vision intact. His work has been praised and damned by critics, and often ignored by audiences. Not surprisingly, even among those who are fans of off-beat cult films, Lynch has as many detractors as admirers.

His most accessible mainstream work may be his second film, *The Elephant Man*, for which he received several Academy Award nominations in 1980. But where another filmmaker might have used that prestigious picture as a springboard to Hollywood's "A-list," Lynch turned his attention to a huge and seemingly unsuitable project for him--producer Dino de Laurentiis' adaptation of Frank Herbert's popular novel, *Dune*. The result is a long, impossible-to-follow tale that's peppered with striking visual images. (Having been re-edited for multi-part broadcast on television, and then re-edited again into a longer feature, the film now exists in several lengths and versions.)

Lynch followed that box office disaster with the surrealistically violent and sexually charged *Blue Velvet*, which solidified his reputation as one of the business's truly eccentric visionaries. That film takes many of the devices and conventions of the traditional crime story and twists them into a dark parody of themselves. Lynch ventured even farther into that territory with *Wild at Heart*, which won the Palme d'Or at Cannes but ran into trouble with the MPAA ratings board and was tidied up for domestic consumption. Again, it was embraced by the Lynch faithful, but proved to be too bleak and disturbing to attract a wider audience.

The same could be said of *Twin Peaks*, both the TV series and the "prequel" feature film, *Fire Walk With Me*, that followed it. In both of them, Lynch presents contemporary middle-class America as a sea of twisted sexuality and madness roiling beneath a thin, easily broken

continued...

nance this realistic family drama, and lost everything when its release fell through. In a stretch performance, the lead pot smoking hippie is played by Margulies, who is now known worldwide as actor, producer, rockabilly singer, and agent Johnny Legend. Also with Honeycomb as herself. Included on the tape is a reminiscence between Pine and Legend, which should be interesting to fans, but no one else. *AKA:* The Cat Ate the Parakeet. 🐾🐾

1971 m/C Phillip Pine, Robert Mantell, Madelyn Keen, Arthur Battanides, Martin Margulies; *D:* Phillip Pine; *W:* Phillip Pine. **VHS $23.00** *SMW, MOV, TPV*

The Power

Forgettable low-budgeter about an ancient Aztec clay idol that possesses incredible destructive power. The perilous, pop-eyed paperweight is brought to a college campus and tempts or terrorizes the actors unlucky enough to get cast in this. Closing credits acknowledge special thanks to the L.A. Lakers. Huh? **WOOF!**

1980 (R) 87m/C Warren Lincoln, Susan Stokey, Lisa Erickson, Jeffrey Obrow; *D:* Stephen Carpenter; *W:* Stephen Carpenter, John Penney. **VHS $69.98** *LIV, VES*

Premature Burial

An Englishman (Milland), who believes his cataleptic father was buried prematurely, is obsessed with the fear that he's inherited the condition and that he'll be buried alive as well. He even goes so far as to move into a tomb equipped with multiple devises designed to insure his escape. His wife and doctor, fearing for his mental health, convince him to destroy the tomb and open his father's crypt to assure himself that dad wasn't buried alive. It backfires—the sight of the corpse brings on real catalepsy and his worst fears come true when he helplessly watches his own funeral. The third of Corman's adaptations from stories by Edgar Allan Poe—slightly more talky than the others, but also more faithful. Corman wanted Vincent Price for the lead, but since he was producing the film independently, he couldn't get Price out of his contract with AIP. Later, AIP bought out Corman's partner and got the film anyway. 🐾🐾🐾

1962 81m/C Ray Milland, Richard Ney, Hazel Court, Heather Angel; **D:** Roger Corman. **VHS, Beta, LV** **$69.98** *LIV, VES, MLB*

The President's Analyst

A superbly written, brilliantly executed satire from the mind of Theodore J. Flicker, who wrote as well as directed. Coburn has the role of his life as a hip psychiatrist who has the dubious honor of being appointed "secret shrink" to the President of the U.S. Pressures of the job steadily increase his paranoia until he suspects he is being pursued by agents and counter agents alike. Cambridge and Darden stand out as the U.S. and Soviet agents, who take spying and assassination with a blue collar attitude. Their dismissal of politics in the face of their friendship—despite the fact that they may be ordered to kill each other at any moment—is touching, funny, and often chilling. Coburn flees to the hippie counterculture including a free-love fling with *Spider Baby* Jill Banner, but can't escape the attentions of every espionage agency on Earth, not to mention T.P.C.! Vastly entertaining. 🦴🦴🦴🦴

1967 104m/C James Coburn, Godfrey Cambridge, Severn Darden, Joan Delaney, Pat Harrington, Will Geer, William Daniels, Arte Johnson, Barry McGuire; **D:** Theodore J. Flicker; **W:** Theodore J. Flicker; **M:** Lalo Schifrin. **VHS $14.95** *PAR*

Pretty Baby

Shield's launching pad and Malle's first American film is a masterpiece of "post-Impressionist" cinematography (from Sven Nykvist) and style, nearly undone by a deliberate pace. Carradine is effective as the New Orleans photographer obsessed with, and finally married to, an 11-year old prostitute (Shields) in New Orleans, 1917. Antonio Fargas' Professor provides the film's conscience. He's loosely based on "Jellyroll" Morton whose music is used, too. The low-key and disturbing story is never exploitative. Malle fills the screen with Felliniesque faces and refuses to pass judgment on the characters. 🦴🦴🦴🦴

1978 (R) 109m/C Brooke Shields, Keith Carradine, Susan Sarandon, Barbara Steele, Diana Scarwid, Antonio Fargas; **D:** Louis Malle. National Board of Review Awards '78: 10 Best Films of the Year; Nominations: Academy Awards '78: Best Original Score; Cannes Film Festival '78: Best Film. **VHS, Beta, LV** **$14.95** *PAR*

Pretty in Pink

More teen angst from the pen of Hughes. Poor girl falls for a rich guy. Their families fret, their friends are distressed, and fate conspires against them. If you can suspend your disbelief that a teenager with her own car and answering machine is financially inferior, then you may very well be able to accept the entire premise. Slickly done and adequately, if not enthusiastically, acted. In 1987, Hughes essentially remade this film with *Some Kind of Wonderful,* the same story with the rich/pauper characters reversed by gender. 🦴🦴🦴

1986 (PG-13) 96m/C Molly Ringwald, Andrew McCarthy, Jon Cryer, Harry Dean Stanton, James Spader, Annie Potts, Andrew Dice Clay, Margaret Colin, Alexa Kenin, Gina Gershon, Dweezil Zappa; **D:** Howard Deutch; **W:** John Hughes; **M:** Michael Gore. **VHS, Beta, LV, 8mm $14.95** *PAR*

Prick Up Your Ears

Film biography of popular subversive playwright Joe Orton depicts his rise to fame and his eventual murder at the hands of his homosexual lover in 1967. Acclaimed for its realistic and sometimes humorous portrayal of the relationship between two men in a society that regarded homosexuality as a crime, the film unfortunately pays scant attention to Orton's theatrical success. The occasional sluggishness of the script detracts a bit from the three leads' outstanding performances. 🦴🦴🦴

1987 (R) 110m/C *GB* Gary Oldman, Alfred Molina, Vanessa Redgrave, Julie Walters, Lindsay Duncan, Wallace Shawn, James Grant, Frances Barber, Janet Dale, David Atkins; **D:** Stephen Frears; **W:** Alan Bennett; **M:** Stanley Myers. New York Film Critics Awards '87: Best Supporting Actress (Redgrave). **VHS, Beta, LV** *NO*

The Princess Bride

Director Reiner scores again with this take on the basic fairy tale formula that masterfully works as both a spoof and the real thing. Crammed wittily with all the cliches, this adventurously irreverent love story centers around a beautiful maiden and her young swain as they battle the evils of the mythical

P

"Hello. My name is Inigo Montoya. You kill' my father. Prepare to die."

—Mandy Pantinkin in *Princess Bride.*

surface of respectability. That's often been said before in fiction and film. David Lynch puts his own particular spin--either completely serious nor completely comic--on the idea.

> **"Well, Gilbert, I think sexual intercourse is in order."**
> --Maggie Smith to Michael Palin in *A Private Function.*

kingdom of Florin. Great dueling scenes, scary beasts (especially the "Rodents of Unusual Size"), and offbeat satire of the genre make this perhaps even more fun for adults than for children. Inspired cast, including Andre the Giant as, well, a giant; Mandy Patinkin as a Spanish swordsman; Christopher Guest as a five-fingered villain; and cameos by Billy Crystal and Carol Kane as too-cute wizards. You don't have to even like fairy tales to love this film; like the reluctant little boy (*Wonder Year*'s Fred Savage) who's being read this tale by his Grandfather (Peter Falk), you will be drawn to the story and it's humor—we promise. Based on William Goldman's cult novel. 🦴🦴🦴🦴

1987 (PG) 98m/C Cary Elwes, Mandy Patinkin, Robin Wright, Wallace Shawn, Peter Falk, Andre the Giant, Chris Sarandon, Christopher Guest, Billy Crystal, Carol Kane, Fred Savage, Peter Cook, Mel Smith; **D:** Rob Reiner; **W:** William Goldman; **M:** Mark Knopfler. Nominations: Academy Awards '87: Best Song ("Storybook Love"). **VHS, Beta, LV, 8mm $14.95** *COL, SUE, HMV*

Private Duty Nurses

Three nurses take on racism, war wounds, and a menage-a-trois (between one nurse, a doctor, and a drug addict). Second in Roger Corman's "nurse" quintet takes itself too seriously to be entertaining, but the gals make good use of those exciting new inventions, waterbeds. Preceded by *The Student Nurses* and followed by *Night Call Nurses, The Young Nurses,* and *Candy Stripe Nurses.* **AKA:** Young L.A. Nurses. 🦴🦴

1971 (R) 80m/C Kathy Cannon, Joyce Williams, Pegi Boucher, Joseph Kaufmann, Dennis Redfield, Herbert Jefferson Jr., Paul Hampton, Paul Gleason; **D:** George Armitage; **W:** George Armitage. **VHS, Beta $59.98** *NLC, SUE*

A Private Function

Ribald tale set in Yorkshire against the backdrop of post-WWII food rationing. Urged on by his icily ambitious wife, milquetoast Palin steals and fattens a contraband pig against all regulations, unhappily preparing the animal for the main course at a banquet celebrating the crowning of Queen Elizabeth. It's not very Pythonesque, but rather a stagy social satire that ranges from biting to downright nasty. Question is, will American viewers identify with the highly British era and attitudes? Palin remains likeable in the center of it all. 🦴🦴🦴

1984 (PG) 96m/C *GB* Michael Palin, Dame Maggie Smith, Denholm Elliott, Bill Paterson, Liz Smith; **D:** Malcolm Mowbray; **W:** Alan Bennett; **M:** John Du Prez. British Academy Awards '84: Best Actress (Smith), Best Supporting Actor (Elliott), Best Supporting Actress (Smith). **VHS, Beta $19.95** *PAR, TVC, FCT*

Private Parts

Nothing to do with Howard Stern, this bizarre first feature from *Eating Raoul*'s Bartel is a *Psycho* takeoff with black comedy ingredients, yet it avoids being mere camp. A runaway nymphet moves into a seedy L.A. hotel full of weirdos and perverts, including a voyeuristic photographer, bondage freaks, and a gross landlady with a grosser secret. Murders ensue. Edgy and compelling, but definitely not for all tastes. Scene with the water-filled inflatable sex doll is not soon forgotten. 🦴🦴🦴

1972 (R) 87m/C Ayn Ruymen, Lucille Benson, John Ventantonio, Laurie Main, Stanley Livingston, Charles Woolf; **D:** Paul Bartel. **VHS $18.00** *FRG, MGM*

The Producers

Mel Brooks's first—and arguably his funniest—film earned him an Academy Award for Best Screenplay. Zero Mostel stars as Max Bialystock, a down-and-out theatrical producer whose only investors are lovelorn elderly ladies "looking to catch one last thrill on their way to the graveyard." Enter Gene Wilder as meek, naive accountant Leo Bloom, who postulates that by overselling shares of a play, a producer could make more money with a flop than with a hit. Thus begins the search for the worst play (a musical called "Springtime for

Hitler"), the worst playwright (Kenneth Mars as Nazi Fran Liebkind), the worst actor (Dick Shawn as hippie Lorenzo St. Du Bois; L.S.D. to his friends) and the worst director (a cross-dresser whose plays are so bad they close during rehearsal). The scheme backfires when the play is a smash. In dubious taste, but sheer joy from beginning to end. They don't make 'em like this anymore. Unfortunately, neither does Mel. 🦴🦴🦴🦴▷

1968 90m/C Zero Mostel, Gene Wilder, Dick Shawn, Kenneth Mars, Estelle Winwood; **D:** Mel Brooks; **W:** Mel Brooks. Academy Awards '68: Best Story & Screenplay; Nominations: Academy Awards '68: Best Supporting Actor (Wilder). **VHS, Beta, LV, 8mm $14.95** *COL, CRC*

The Projectionist

This independently produced, low-budget oddity has been described as the forerunner of Woody Allen's *The Purple Rose of Cairo* and HBO's *Dream On* series, but it's really quite unique, a disjointed and thoughtful whimsy about a lonely misfit working as a projectionist in a NYC revival-house. In silent-movie daydreams, however, he's Captain Flash, portly costumed hero who bumbles through an amazing—sometimes disturbing—collection of archival clips in combat against master villain "The Bat" (comic Rodney Dangerfield, in his film debut), who is the typrannical theatre manager back in reality. But just what is reality? Amindst the footage in the projectionist's mind are scenes of Chuck McCann attending the gala premiere of a new flick called...*The Projectionist.* McCann is best known for his work on TV kiddie shows, but the movie is more than simply a childish, slapticky spoof, and film buffs in particular should try to puzzle it out. 🦴🦴🦴

1971 (PG) 84m/C Rodney Dangerfield, Chuck McCann, Ina Balin; **D:** Harry Hurwitz; **W:** Harry Hurwitz. **VHS, Beta $69.98** *LIV, VES*

The Psychic

An ad executive gains psychic powers after he falls off a ladder. He goes into show business, ditches his family, and burns everyone that gets involved with him. Then his powers start to wane. Repeat of Lewis' *Something Weird* psychic plotline with a more serious tone and without the witchcraft angle. Not a

bad story, and the acting is adequate, but it's ruined by the cheapness of the production, Lewis' static direction, and damaged even further by voiced-over sex scenes that were sloppily edited in for an adults-only rerelease. The inserts have little to do with the plot and even feature characters who aren't really in the movie. **AKA:** Copenhagen's Psychic Loves. 🦴▷

1968 90m/C Dick Genola, Robin Guest, Bobbi Spencer; **D:** Herschell Gordon Lewis. **VHS, Beta** *NO*

Psycho

Twelve cabins, twelve vacancies, and one infamous shower. Alfred Hitchcock's wickedly funny classic begins with illicit lover Janet Leigh's heist of $10,000 and takes a shocking detour after she checks in to the Bates Motel. In the role that would define his career, Anthony Perkins stars as Norman Bates, the mother of psycho killers. The genius is in the details, from the creepy stuffed birds that hover over Norman to composer Bernard Herrmann's stabbing violins that pierce the still-shocking "shower" scene. With Vera Miles as the inquiring sister and Martin Balsam as the ill-fated private detective. Look for Ted Knight (Ted Baxter on *The Mary Tyler Moore Show*) as one of Norman's police guards. Hitchcock's most notorious film, and Robert Bloch's novel on which it was based, were inspired by the exploits of Ed Gein, Wisconsin's most infamous serial killer before Jeffrey Dahmer. Gein also inspired *The Texas Chainsaw Massacre.* Of the three *Psycho* sequels, number three, which Perkins directed, is best. 🦴🦴🦴🦴

1960 109m/B Anthony Perkins, Janet Leigh, Vera Miles, John Gavin, John McIntire, Martin Balsam, Simon Oakland, Ted Knight, John Anderson, Frank Albertson, Patricia Hitchcock; **D:** Alfred Hitchcock; **W:** Joseph Stefano; **M:** Bernard Herrmann. Edgar Allan Poe Awards '60: Best Screenplay; Golden Globe Awards '61: Best Supporting Actress (Leigh); Nominations: Academy Awards '60: Best Art Direction/Set Decoration (B & W), Best Black and White Cinematography, Best Director (Hitchcock), Best Supporting Actress (Leigh). **VHS, Beta, LV $19.95** *MCA, TLF*

Psychomania

A drama of the supernatural, the occult, and the violence which lies just beyond the con-

P

"Not many people know it, but the Fuhrer was a terrific dancer."
--Kenneth Mars defending his new musical, *Springtime for Hitler,* in *The Producers.*

"Mother... what's the phrase? Isn't quite herself today."
--Norman Bates (Anthony Perkins) *Psycho.*

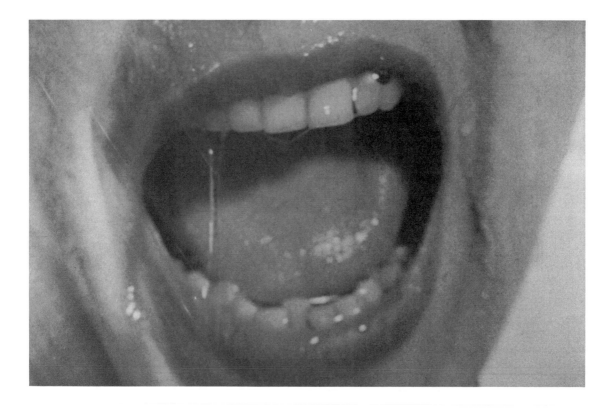

ventions of society for a group of dead mo-
torcyclists, the Living Dead, who all came
back to life after committing suicide with the
help of the devil. Sanders looks like he's about
to die of boredom. Not to be confused with
Psycho-Mania. **AKA:** The Death Wheelers.
🦴🦴

1973 (R) 89m/C *GB* George Sanders, Beryl Reid,
Nicky Henson, Mary Laroche, Patrick Holt; **D:** Don
Sharp. **VHS, Beta $29.95** *MED, MRV*

Pulp Fiction

Tarantino moves into the cinematic mainstream with his trademark violence and '70s
pop culture mindset intact in this stylish crime
trilogy. A day in the life of a criminal community unexpectedly shifts from outrageous,
esoteric dialogue to violent mayhem with
solid scripting that takes familiar stories to un-
explored territory. Offbeat cast offers superb
performances, led by Travolta, who ditches
the baby talk for his best role to date as a hit
man whose adventures with partner Jackson
tie the seemingly unrelated stories together.

Clever, almost gleeful look at everday life on
the fringes of mainstream society. Inspired by
Black Mask magazine. 🦴🦴🦴🦴

1994 (R) 153m/C John Travolta, Samuel L. Jackson,
Uma Thurman, Harvey Keitel, Tim Roth, Amanda
Plummer, Maria De Medeiros, Ving Rhames, Eric
Stoltz, Rosanna Arquette, Christopher Walken, Bruce
Willis, Quentin Tarantino; **D:** Quentin Tarantino; **W:**
Quentin Tarantino, Roger Roberts Avary. Academy
Awards '94: Best Original Screenplay; Cannes Film
Festival '94: Best Film; Golden Globe Awards '95:
Best Screenplay; Independent Spirit Awards '95: Best
Actor (Jackson), Best Director (Tarantino), Best Film,
Best Screenplay; Los Angeles Film Critics Association
Awards '94: Best Actor (Travolta), Best Director
(Tarantino), Best Film, Best Screenplay; National
Board of Review Awards '94: Best Director (Taran-
tino), Best Film; New York Film Critics Awards '94:
Best Director (Tarantino), Best Screenplay; National
Society of Film Critics Awards '94: Best Director
(Tarantino), Best Film, Best Screenplay; Nominations:
Academy Awards '94: Best Actor (Travolta), Best Di-
rector (Tarantino), Best Film Editing, Best Original
Screenplay, Best Picture, Best Supporting Actor (Jack-
son), Best Supporting Actress (Thurman); Golden
Globe Awards '95: Best Actor—Drama (Travolta),
Best Director (Tarantino), Best Film—Drama, Best
Supporting Actor (Jackson), Best Supporting Actress
(Thurman); Screen Actors Guild Award '94: Best Ac-
tor (Travolta). **VHS** *MAX*

Q: The Winged Serpent

A cult of admirers surrounds this goony monster flick about dragonlike Aztec god Quetzlcoatl, summoned to modern Manhattan by gory human sacrifices, and hungry for rooftop sunbathers and construction teams. Direction and special effects are pretty ragged, but witty script helps the cast shine, especially Moriarty as a lowlife crook who's found the beast's hidden nest. ♪♪♪

1982 (R) 92m/C Michael Moriarty, Candy Clark, David Carradine, Richard Roundtree; **D:** Larry Cohen; **W:** Larry Cohen. **VHS, Beta $14.98** *MCA*

Quackser Fortune Has a Cousin in the Bronx

An Irish fertilizer salesman (that is, Gene Wilder pushing a cart through the streets picking up horse doo-doo) meets an exchange student from the U.S., who finds herself inexplicably attracted to this unlearned, but not unknowing, man. A unique little Wilder vehicle that offers an original love story with drama and appeal. *AKA:* Fun Loving. ♪♪♪

1970 (R) 88m/C *IR* Gene Wilder, Margot Kidder; **D:** Waris Hussein. **VHS, Beta, LV $19.95** *VCI*

Quadrophenia

It's the Mods versus the Rockers in '60s England. Gangs of disaffected youth fight over everything, particularly the kind of music they listen to. An allegory for all the social clashes of the 1960s, including rock vs. punk, rebellion vs. authority, and really bad clothes vs. even worse clothes. Everything about this film is drab, from the blacks and grays of the palette to the dull performances. The only highlight is a great score by The Who, from their album of the same name, which adds punch to this otherwise bleak drama. Look for then-emerging punk star Sting as the Bellboy. ♪♪

1979 (R) 115m/C *GB* Phil Daniels, Mark Wingett, Philip Davis, Leslie Ash, Sting; **D:** Franc Roddam. **VHS, Beta, LV $19.95** *MVD, COL, RHI*

Queen of Outer Space

Notorious male-chauvinist sci-fi cheapie starts out slow, but then the laughs keep coming as the cast plays the hyperdumb material straight. Space cadets crash on Venus, find it ruled by women—and the dolls have wicked plans in store for mankind. Don't be surprised if you've seen the sets before since they were borrowed from *Forbidden Planet, World Without End,* and *Flight to Mars.* ♪♪ ▷

1958 80m/C Zsa Zsa Gabor, Eric Fleming, Laurie Mitchell, Paul Birch, Barbara Darrow, Dave Willcock, Lisa Davis, Patrick Waltz, Marilyn Buferd, Marjorie Durant, Lynn Cartwright, Gerry Gaylor; **D:** Edward L. Bernds. **VHS, Beta $14.98** *FXV*

LE BIG MAC

"In Paris, you can buy beer in MacDonald's. You know what they call a Quarter Pounder with cheese?"

"They don't call it a Quarter Pounder with cheese?"

"No, they got the metric system there...they call it a Royale with cheese."

"Royale with cheese...what do they call a Big Mac?"

"A Big Mac's a Big Mac, but they call it 'Le Big Mac.'"

"'Le Big Mac'...huh...what do they call a Whopper?"

"I don't know, I didn't go to Burger King."

--John Travolta and Samuel L. Jackson in *Pulp Fiction.*

The Quiet Earth

Serious science-fiction film about a scientist who awakens to find himself seemingly the only human left on earth as the result of a misfired time/space government experiment. He later finds two other people, a girl and a Maori tribesman, and must try to repair the damage in order to save what's left of the humankind. The more interesting segments of the film occur early on as our Everyman begins to explore the world around him. Believing himself alone in a world of empty buildings, he

A gang of British mods (including Sting) exude the joys of youth in *Quadrophenia*.

"**S**on, you know you got a pair of panties on your head?"

--a robbery victim in *Raising Arizona*.

begins to approach the edge of madness. Then he meets up with other survivors, a beautiful and not unfriendly woman, and another man, and, having discovered that the deterioration of their reality will worsen, they set out to restore the space/time continuum. A slickly produced Aussie flick, it does suffer from slow pacing through the middle and characters that fail to evoke sympathy. It's more of an intellectual excursion rather than an emotional one. The final shot, however, is not to be missed. 𝄞 𝄞 𝄞

1985 (R) 91m/C *NZ* Bruno Lawrence, Alison Routledge, Peter Smith; *D:* Geoff Murphy; *W:* Bruno Lawrence, Sam Pillsbury, Bill Baer; *M:* John Charles. **VHS, Beta, LV $19.98** *FOX*

Rabid

It's the Armpit That Devoured Montreal! Really. This early David Cronenberg horror film stars former porn legend Marilyn Chambers as a motorcycle accident victim whose experimental plastic surgery goes tragically awry. She grows a hideous, toothy little "mouth" in her armpit, and it's hungry. The rest is a fairly blatant variation on *Night of the Living Dead*. Everyone involved plays it straight—no deodorant jokes. *AKA:* Rage. 𝄞 𝄞 𝄞

1977 (R) 90m/C *CA* Marilyn Chambers, Frank Moore, Joe Silver; *D:* David Cronenberg; *W:* David Cronenberg. **VHS, Beta $29.98** *WAR*

Rabid Grannies

Imported schlock from France! Yes, the folks at Troma who brought you *The Toxic Avenger* and so many other deliberately bad movies decided to add this one to their list. It's a wicked (and sometimes too talky) satire about two aging sisters who receive a surprise birthday gift from their devil-worshipping nephew. The gift turns their party into a gorefest as they rip into various family members—literally. The bloody effects are laughably amateurish, but that's somehow appropriate. Dubbed. Recommended for fans of bad movies only. 𝄞 𝄞 𝄟

1989 (R) 89m/C *BE* Catherine Aymerie, Caroline Brackman, Danielle Daven, Raymond Lescot, Anne

Marie Fox, Richard Cotica, Patricia Davie; **D:** Emmanuel Kervyn; **W:** Emmanuel Kervyn. **VHS, Beta, LV $79.95** *MED, VTR*

Raiders of the Sun

After the Earth has been ruined in a biological disaster, a futuristic warrior arrives to help restore world peace and order. Aussie kickboxer Norton plays the lead, shooting, punching, and kicking his way to a wooden-faced victory. Directed by Corman regular Santiago, this has all the usual staples of his films: sneering bad guys, a good looking babe or two, and lots of low-budget action with a wisp of a plot to hang it all on. Despite how it all sounds this is actually one of Cirio's better efforts, though not in the same league as *Angelfist* or *Angel of Destruction*. Worth seeking for fans of either the star or the director, though Norton's best work to date remains the films he's done with Cynthia Rothrock in both the U.S. and Hong Kong. 🦴🦴🦴▷

1992 (R) 80m/C Richard Norton, Rick Dean, William Steis, Blake Boyd, Brigitta Stenberg; **D:** Cirio H. Santiago. **VHS $89.98** *NHO*

The Rain People

Pregnant housewife (Shirley Knight) takes to the road in desperation and boredom. Along the way, she meets mentally impaired ex-football player Caan. Pretentious and dull, this is a prime example of a big director making a little film. Reputedly a personal project of director Coppola, it is an aimless, self-indulgent road movie that ends where it began: nowhere. Knight is perhaps the most colorless actress of her generation, and Caan looks and sounds just like Adam Sandler. 🦴

1969 (R) 102m/C Shirley Knight, James Caan, Robert Duvall; **D:** Francis Ford Coppola; **W:** Francis Ford Coppola. **VHS, Beta $19.98** *WAR*

Raising Arizona

Hi's an ex-con and the world's worst hold-up man. Ed's a policewoman. They meet, fall in love, marry, and kidnap a baby (one of a family of quints). Why not? Ed's infertile and the family they took the baby from has "more than enough," so who will notice? But unfinished furniture tycoon Nathan Arizona wants his baby back, even if he has to hire an axe-murderer on a motorcycle to do it. A brilliant, original comedy narrated in notorious loopy deadpan style by Cage. Innovative camerawork by Barry Sonnenfeld. Wild, surreal, and hilarious. Another hit for the Coen brothers. 🦴🦴🦴▷

1987 (PG-13) 94m/C Nicolas Cage, Holly Hunter, John Goodman, William Forsythe, Randall "Tex" Cobb, Trey Wilson, M. Emmet Walsh, Frances McDormand; **D:** Joel Coen; **W:** Ethan Coen, Joel Coen; **M:** Carter Burwell. **VHS, Beta, LV $19.98** *FOX*

Rat Pfink a Boo-Boo

Saxon plays rock and roll star "Lonnie Lord," whose girlfriend (Brandt) is being terrorized, and eventually kidnapped, by a gang of lowlifes. Tiring of this straightforward thriller plot, director Steckler decided to suddenly shift gears. From then on, the film becomes an outrageous parody—a zero-budget version of the *Batman* TV show— in which a bumbling superhero and his sidekick (Moede) race to save Brandt on their Pfinkcycle, shouting slogans like "Fight crime!" Features a special guest appearance by Kogar the gorilla. Story of the ti-

Did we catch the Golden Girls without their makeup? Nah-- it's just the *Rabid Grannies*.

219

Cult Flicks and Trash Pics

Holly Hunter and Nicholas Cage bask in the sun and dream of little nippers in *Raising Arizona*.

"Maybe if a man looks ugly he does ugly things."

--Boris Karloff to Bela Lugosi in *The Raven*.

1972 (R) 92m/C Hope Stansbury, Jackie Skarvellis, Noel Collins, Joan Ogden, Douglas Phair, Bernard Kaler; **D:** Andy Milligan; **W:** Andy Milligan. **VHS, Beta** *NO*

The Raven

Roger Corman filmed this very loose adaptation of Edgar Allen Poe's poem in just three weeks utilizing sets from his previous Poe films. The cast makes this a must-see for horror buffs. Vincent Price stars as a reclusive sixteenth century sorcerer. Boris Karloff is his sinister rival. Peter Lorre is a magician that Karloff transformed into a raven, and who has come to Price to break the spell. Jack Nicholson also stars as Lorre's despised, idiot son ("Don't do that, Rexford!"). More comedy than horror, and a lot of fun. The climactic duel between Price and Karloff literally brings down the house. ♫♫♫

1963 86m/C Vincent Price, Boris Karloff, Peter Lorre, Jack Nicholson, Hazel Court; **D:** Roger Corman; **W:** Richard Matheson; **M:** Les Baxter. **VHS, Beta, LV** *MLB*

The Re-Animator

Based on an H.P. Lovecraft story (although Lovecraft probably wouldn't find it funny), this grisly film deals with a medical student who re-animates the dead. When they come back, they're not happy about it, and heads roll. It has quickly turned into a black humor cult classic. Gordon was a Chicago theatre director before directing this entertaining gorefest, followed up with *From Beyond,* and continues to deliver fun shockers and sci-fi adventures. Combs has become a familiar character actor specializing in psychosis. Crampton, who's become a scream-queen favorite, has done several more sci-fi and horror features, and also joined the cast of a daytime soap opera. Also available in an "R" rated version, and followed by Brian Yuzna's *Bride of Re-Animator.* ♫♫♫♪

1985 86m/C Jeffrey Combs, Bruce Abbott, Barbara Crampton, David Gale, Robert Sampson; **D:** Stuart Gordon; **W:** Stuart Gordon, Dennis Paoli, William J. Norris; **M:** Richard Band. **VHS, Beta, LV** $19.98 *LIV, VES*

Really Weird Tales

Three comic tales featuring SCTV alumni. The first story, "All's Well That Ends Strange," stars

tle is legendary—it was misspelled accidentally and Steckler didn't have the cash to fix it. Dated, but still fun. Ron Haydock & the Boppers perform several boppy tunes. ♫♫ You Is a Rat Pfink; Big Boss A-Go-Go Party; Running Wild. ♫♫

1966 72m/B Vin Saxon, Carolyn Brandt, Titus Moede, Mike Kannon; **D:** Ray Dennis Steckler. **VHS, Beta** *NO*

The Rats Are Coming! The Werewolves Are Here!

Revolves around a family of werewolves and the daughter who decides to put an end to the curse. As with all Milligan films, imaginative title promises much more than the film delivers; the result is interminably photographed and paced, which makes gore effect near-impossible to see. Originally titled *Curse of the Full Moon,* it was shot in England back-to-back with *The Body Beneath* and *Bloodthirsty Butchers.* To pad its short running time, producer Mishkin filmed subplot of man-eating rats (after the success of *Willard*) in Milligan's hometown of Staten Island. Ads offered: "Win a live rat for your mother-in-law!" ♫♪

Martin Short as a lounge singer seduced by the strange world of a Hugh Hefner-like magazine publisher. "Cursed With Charisma" stars John Candy as shady real estate schemer who entices a small town with his no-money-down plans. Finally, Catherine O'Hara stars as a girl with the strange power of causing anything she loves to explode in "I'll Die Loving." None of the tales were weird enough nor funny enough to make this effort worthwhile. Although each of the stars delivers an amusing performance (especially Candy), all have been better used elsewhere, especially on SCTV. ♫

1986 85m/C John Candy, Martin Short, Joe Flaherty, Catherine O'Hara. **VHS, Beta $7.00** *VTR*

Rebel Without a Cause

James Dean's most memorable screen appearance has become the stuff of legend. In the second of his three films, he plays a troubled, alienated teenager from the right side of the tracks. He befriends outcasts Wood and Mineo, and together the screen's three most misunderstood-ever teens form a new "family" to replace their absent or ineffective parents. Superb young stars carry this in-the-gut story of adolescence. Key scenes and images—the "chickie run," the planetarium, the swimming pool—define '50s movies as well. All three leads met with real-life tragic ends. Dean's death in a car crash immediately before the film's release doubtless has a lot to do with its mythic stature. And his own. ♫♫♫♫

1955 111m/C James Dean, Natalie Wood, Sal Mineo, Jim Backus, Nick Adams, Dennis Hopper, Ann Doran, William Hopper, Rochelle Hudson, Corey Allen, Edward Platt; **D:** Nicholas Ray; **W:** Stewart Stern; **M:** Leonard Rosenman. Nominations: Academy Awards '54: Best Supporting Actor (Mineo); Academy Awards '55: Best Story, Best Supporting Actress (Wood). **VHS, Beta, LV $19.98** *WAR*

Red

Lawrence Tierney stars in this dramatization of the "Red Tapes." For those of you who don't know, the Red Tapes were a series of taped phone pranks in which a witty young man phones a bar and asks to speak to "Mike Hunt," "Al Koholic," "Stu, last name, Pid," "Ben Dover," "Pepe, last name, Roney," etc., the prank made most commercially famous by

Bart Simpson. Tierney plays Red, the bartender who receives these calls; he responds to the prankster with mounting incoherent expletives and unfavorable references to the caller's mother. It becomes a bit tiring through the middle (some of the dialogue is hard to follow), but picks up with Red's fantasy sequences of both revenge and scantily clad women ("Come on, honey, bounce over here, you cutie pie."), the latter of which may have been Tierney's impetus for doing the part. Features Scott Spiegel as "the Caller," who wrote and produced *Thou Shalt Not Kill...Except,* among other acting and directing credits. Written and directed by *Film Threat* magazine founder Chris Gore. ♫♫♫

1991 35m/B Lawrence Tierney, Scott Spiegel, Carmen Von Daacke, Ron Zwang, J. J. Hommel; **D:** Christian Gore; **W:** Christian Gore. **VHS $19.95** *FLT*

"I'm not falling for that old 'look out behind you' gag!" The re-animated seeks out the re-animator in *The Re-Animator.*

Red Rock West

Nothing is what it seems in this stylish and entertaining film noir set in a desolate Wyoming town. Perennial loser and nice guy Michael (Cage) is headed to a job at oil rig,

TELL YOUR CHILDREN!

"The motion picture you are about to witness may startle you. It would not have been possible, otherwise, to sufficiently emphasize the frightful toll of the new drug menace which is destroying the youth of America in alarmingly increasing numbers. *Marihuana* is that drug--a violent narcotic--an unspeakable scourge--*The Real Public Enemy Number One!* Its first effect is sudden violent, uncontrollable laughter; then come dangerous hallucinations--space expands--time slows down, almost stands still...fixed ideas come next, conjuring up monstrous extravagances--followed by emotional disturbances, the total inability to direct thoughts, the loss of power to resist physical emotions...leading finally to acts of shocking violence...ending often in incurable insanity. In picturing its soul-destroying effects, no attempt was made to equivocate. The scenes and incidents, while fictionized for the purposes of this story, are based upon actual research into the results of Marihuana addiction. If their stark reality will make you *think*, will make you aware that something *must be done* to wipe out this ghastly menace, then the picture will not have failed in its purpose...Because the dread *Marihuana* may be reaching forth next for your son or daughter...or *yours*...or *YOURS!*"

--Foreword to *Reefer Madness.*

"**T**obacco chewin', gut chompin', cannibal kinfolk from hell!"

--*Redneck Zombies.*

but blows his chance by admitting he has a bad leg. Landing in the tiny burg of Red Rock, he's mistaken for the hit man hired by local barkeep Walsh to kill his pretty wife (Boyle). Then Boyle doubles Walsh's offer— what's a film noir boy to do? And Hopper, the real killer, strides into town. Full of twists, turns, and shades of *El Mariachi*, this enjoyable, well-acted thriller is a real gem that escaped directly to cable before being rescued by a San Francisco exhibitor. 🦴🦴🦴🦴

1993 (R) 98m/C Nicolas Cage, Dennis Hopper, Lara Flynn Boyle, J.T. Walsh, Timothy Carhart, Dan Shor, Dwight Yoakam, Bobby Joe McFadden; **D:** John Dahl; **W:** John Dahl. Nominations: Independent Spirit Awards '95: Best Director (Dahl), Best Screenplay. **VHS, LV $19.95** *COL*

Redneck Zombies

A bunch of backwoods rednecks become zombies after chug-a-lugging some radioactive beer. Eating local tourists becomes a hard habit to break. Betcha can't have just one! 🦴

1988 (R) 83m/C Floyd Piranha, Lisa DeHaven, W.E. Benson, William W. Decker, James Housely, Zoofoot, Tyrone Taylor, Perieles Lewnes. **VHS, Beta $79.95** *TWE*

Reefer Madness

Propaganda piece that was actually intended as a serious attempt to deter pot smoking and is now an underground comedy favorite. Movie opens with a PTA meeting on the topic: "Tell Your Children." The speaker warns the audience about various dangerous drugs, including opium, morphine, and heroin, but "more vicious, more deadly than even these soul-destroying drugs is the meance of marijuana!" After the speaker has educated the parents on drugs (and offered many handy methods for hiding and transporting weed), he tells the story of "something that happened in our own city. You probably read about it in the papers...." See naive school boys turn into homicidal maniacs on the first puff; see chaste ingenues smoke their virtues away. Overwrought acting and a lurid script only enhance the effects of the low-budget depiction of the horrors of the demon weed. *AKA:* Tell Your Children. 🦴🦴🦴🦴

1938 (PG) 67m/B Dave O'Brien, Dorothy Short, Warren McCollum, Lillian Miles, Thelma White, Carleton Young, Josef Forte, Harry Harvey Jr.; **D:** Louis Gasnier. **VHS, Beta $16.95** *SNC, NOS, HHT*

The Reflecting Skin

In a 1950s prairie town a small boy sees insanity, child-murder, and radiation sickness, leading him to fantasize that the tormented young widow next door is a vampire. Surreal story of our little hero's loss of innocence. Horror for the arts crowd, a grotesque menagerie that dares you to watch. The exploding-frog opener is already notorious. Beautiful photography, with vistas inspired by the painting of Andrew Wyeth. 🦴🦴🦴

1991 116m/C Viggo Mortensen, Lindsay Duncan, Jeremy Cooper, Duncan Fraser, Shiela Moore, David

Longworth; **D:** Philip Ridley; **W:** Philip Ridley; **M:** Nick Bicat. **VHS, LV** *NO*

Reform School Girl

A young girl (Castillo) ends up behind bars when her boyfriend (Byrnes) steals a car to go joy-riding and is involved in a hit-and-run murder. The only witness is Byrnes' ex-girl Anders, so he has her sent up on a car stripping charge. A cheap production and the incredulous story are the highlights of this early teen "chicks in chains" epic. Castillo was the young girl seduced by evil Robert Mitchum in *Night of the Hunter,* then had to face the *Invasion of the Saucermen.* Jailhouse hellcats Anders and Vickers both became AIP regulars. Look for Kellerman (*M*A*S*H*) in a bit part in her first screen appearance. Due to Byrnes celebrity on *77 Sunset Strip,* this was released to TV just two years later. Double billed with *Rock Around the World.* Bernds' directing career contains an odd mix of teen pix like this one, wacky comedy series (Blondie, Bowery Boys, Three Stooges), and schlock sci-fi (*Queen of Outer Space, Valley of the Dragons, Return of the Fly*). 🦴🦴🦴

1957 71m/B Gloria Castillo, Ross Ford, Edward Byrnes, Ralph Reed, Jack Kruschen, Sally Kellerman, Luana Anders, Yvette Vickers, Diana Darr; **D:** Edward L. Bernds; **W:** Edward L. Bernds. **VHS $9.95** *NLC*

Remo Williams: The Adventure Begins

The adventure also seems to have stopped for the long-time paperback hero with this one-shot series. In some ways, it's hard to understand why. How could you not like a superhero who gets his name from a bedpan manufacturer? The film is deliberately paced but that leaves room for considerable dry humor and some well-staged action sequences. The best of those take place on a huge ferris wheel and atop the Statue of Liberty. Also, don't miss the scene involving the world's smartest Doberman. Joel Grey steals the show as Chiun, the serene Korean martial arts master who teaches the titular hero (Ward) how to dodge bullets, walk on water, etc. All that's really missing here is the big pyrotechnic finish. Look for Reginald Veljohnson and William Hickey in small roles. 🦴🦴🦴

1985 (PG-13) 121m/C Fred Ward, Joel Grey, Wilford Brimley, Kate Mulgrew, Reginald Veljohnson, William Hickey; **D:** Guy Hamilton. Nominations: Academy Awards '85: Best Makeup. **VHS, Beta, LV $14.99** *NO*

Rentadick

A precursor to the Monty Python masterpieces, written by future members Chapman and Cleese. Private eye spoof isn't as funny as later Python efforts; but it is an indication of what was yet to come and fans should enjoy it. 🦴🦴

1972 94m/C *GB* James Booth, Julie Ege, Ronald Fraser, Donald Sinden, Michael Bentine, Richard Briers, Spike Milligan; **D:** Jim Clark; **W:** Graham Chapman, John Cleese; **M:** Carl Davis. **VHS** *NO*

Repo Man

Following a limited theatrical release, this buzzed-out s-f satire became one of the first true cult hits on video. It's an inventive, witty portrait of sun-blasted Southern California, a place that appears to be crumbling before the camera. The story follows the adventures of a punk rocker (Estevez) turned car repossessor, his deadpan mentor (Stanton) and a '64 Malibu with something in the trunk. The landscape is filled with pointless violence, no-frills packaging, media hypnosis, and aliens. Beneath the pessimistic mood there's a happy Marx Brothers anarchy. Executive producer: none other than ex-Monkee Michael Nesmith. 🦴🦴🦴🦴

1983 (R) 93m/C Emilio Estevez, Harry Dean Stanton, Sy Richardson, Tracey Walter, Olivia Barash, Fox Harris, Jennifer Balgobin, Vonetta McGee, Angelique Pettyjohn; **D:** Alex Cox. **VHS, Beta, LV $14.98** *MCA*

Reservoir Dogs

Violent tale of honor among thieves. Six professional criminals known by code names to protect their identities (Misters Pink, White, Orange, Blonde, Blue, and Brown) are assembled by Tierney to pull off a diamond heist. But two of the gang are killed in a police ambush. The survivors regroup in an empty warehouse and try to discover the informer in their midst. In probably the most stomach-churning scene (there is some competition here), a policeman is tortured just for

"Herbert West has a very good head on his shoulders-- and another one in a dish on his desk."
--Re-Animator.

"Everybody's into weirdness right now."
--Tracey Walter *in* Repo Man.

Emilio Estevez
rides shotgun in
Repo Man.

cape and flying without a license. Now a U.S. president decides the country needs its hero again, and puts the now-derelict Legend in Leotards through alcohol rehab and super-power retraining. Australian spoof has great premise, let down too often by slipshod storytelling and weak F/X. Gains altitude with its outlandish musical numbers, some of them written by the Rocky Horror team of Richard Hartley and Richard O'Brien. A singing Christopher Lee plays archvillain Mr. Midnight with lordly gusto. *AKA:* Legend in Leotards. 🦴🦴

1983 (PG) 90m/C *AU* Alan Arkin, Christopher Lee, Kate Fitzpatrick, Bill Hunter, Graham Kennedy, Michael Pate, Hayes Gordon, Max Phipps, Noel Ferrier; *D:* Philippe Mora; *W:* Steven E. de Souza. **VHS, Beta, LV** *NO*

The Return of Spinal Tap

Cult-fave mock rock group Spinal Tap is back with a feature-length video of performance and backstage footage from its recent reunion concert tour promoting their album "Break Like the Wind." Sequel to *This is Spinal Tap* features lots of head-banging hits; not as great as the original satire, but will appeal to Tap fans. 🎵 Break Like the Wind; Majesty of Rock; Bitch School; Diva Fever; Clam Caravan; Stinkin' Up the Great Outdoors. 🦴🦴▷

1992 110m/C Christopher Guest, Michael McKean, Harry Shearer, Rick Parnell, C.J. Vanston; *Cameos:* Paul Anka, Jeff Beck, Jamie Lee Curtis, Richard Lewis, Martha Quinn, Kenny Rogers, Martin Short, Mel Torme; *W:* Christopher Guest, Michael McKean, Harry Shearer. **VHS, LV $19.98** *MPI, MVD*

Return of the Jedi

Third film in George Lucas' popular space saga. Against seemingly fearsome odds, Luke Skywalker battles such worthies as Jabba the Hut and heavy-breathing Darth Vader to save his comrades and triumph over the evil Galactic Empire. Han and Leia reaffirm their love and team with C3PO, R2D2, Chewbacca, Calrissian, and a bunch of furry Ewoks to aid in the annihilation of the Dark Side. The special effects are still spectacular, even the third time around. Sequel to *Star Wars* (1977) and *The Empire Strikes Back* (1980). 🦴🦴🦴▷

1983 (PG) 132m/C Mark Hamill, Carrie Fisher, Harrison Ford, Billy Dee Williams, David Prowse, James

the heck of it to the tune of the Stealers Wheel "Stuck in the Middle with You." Unrelenting; auspicious debut for Tarantino with strong ensemble cast anchored by Keitel (who invested cash as well as talent) as the very professional Mr. White. Well-founded charges have been made that Tarantino lifted much of his plot situations from other sources (mainly Ringo Lam's *City on Fire,* not that there's so much completely original there either), but there's no denying his originality when it comes to characters and dialogue. He keeps the audience constantly interested in his storyline, springing thoughtful surprises at every turn. 🦴🦴🦴🦴

1992 (R) 100m/C Harvey Keitel, Tim Roth, Michael Madsen, Steve Buscemi, Christopher Penn, Lawrence Tierney, Kirk Baltz, Quentin Tarantino; *D:* Quentin Tarantino; *W:* Quentin Tarantino. Independent Spirit Awards '93: Best Supporting Actor (Buscemi). **VHS, LV $19.98** *LIV, BTV*

Return of Captain Invincible

Beloved wartime superguy Captain Invincible was subpoenaed before a McCarthyite panel and blacklisted for wearing a red-colored

Earl Jones, Kenny Baker, Denis Lawson, Anthony Daniels, Peter Mayhew; **D:** Richard Marquand; **W:** George Lucas, Lawrence Kasdan; **M:** John Williams; **V:** Alec Guinness, Frank Oz. Academy Awards '83: Best Visual Effects; People's Choice Awards '84: Best Film; Nominations: Academy Awards '83: Best Art Direction/Set Decoration, Best Sound, Best Original Score. **VHS, Beta, LV $19.98** *FOX, RDG, HMV*

Return of the Killer Tomatoes

The man-eating plant-life from 1977's *Attack of the Killer Tomatoes* are back, able to turn into people due to the slightly larger budget. Astin is mad as the scientist. Produced on a wacky, yet more mainstream level than it's predecessor, it's been far too ignored by the general public. In fact, it's quite humorous on a relatively immature, juvenile level. In this sequel, the evil Professor Gangrene is revealed as the true mastermind behind the tomato hordes. This time he invents a machine that can convert his little tomatoes into Rambos, babes, etc. The populace at large, meanwhile, has developed tomato paranoia. Tomatoes have been outlawed and even your pizzas are available only with fruit toppings (blueberry and anchovies, anyone?). One of the tomato babes escapes into the world and falls mutually in love with a human. When the Rambo dudes steal her back he must foil Gangrene and rescue the hamburger garnish of his dreams. Stupid jokes and bad puns come rapid fire. Most effective are the string of product placement jokes, as these guys relentlessly bite the hand that feeds them. This film introduces the lovable little mutant, Fuzzy Tomato. ♪

1988 (PG) 98m/C Anthony Starke, George Clooney, Karen Mistal, Steve Lundquist, John Astin, Charlie Jones, Rock Peace, Frank Davis, C.J. Dillon, Teri Weigel; **D:** John DeBello. **VHS, Beta, LV $19.95** *STE, NWV*

Revenge of the Creature

In this follow up to *The Creature From the Black Lagoon*, the Gill-man is captured in the Amazon and taken to a Florida marine park. There he is put on display for visitors and subjected to heartless experiments. Growing restless in his captive surroundings, the creature breaks free and makes for the ocean. Includes screen debut of Clint Eastwood as a lab technician. Originally shot in 3-D. Based on a story by William

Alland. Available on laserdisc as part of a special Encore Edition Double Feature with *The Creature Walks Among Us.* ♪ ♪

1955 82m/B John Agar, Lori Nelson, John Bromfield, Robert Williams, Nestor Paiva, Clint Eastwood; **D:** Jack Arnold; **W:** Martin Berkeley. **VHS, LV $14.98** *MCA, FCT*

Revenge of the Virgins

A tribe of topless "Indian" women protect their sacred land from the white men. Like many nudies of the period, the whole point was to get some nudity on the screen with the minimum of plot necessary to get things going. Interesting variation on the popular Amazon tribe theme, but that's about it. Exhumed exploitation for bad-film junkies, narrated by Kenne Duncan, an Ed Wood cohort. Amazingly, this one turned up on local PBS stations in 1994. ♪ ▷

1962 53m/B Jewell Morgan, Charles Veltman, Jodean Russo, Stanton Pritchard; **D:** Paul Perri. **VHS $19.95** *NOS, SMW, VDM*

Ride the High Country

The cult classic western about two old friends who have had careers on both sides of the law. One, Joel McCrea, is entrusted with a shipment of gold, and the other, Randolph Scott, rides along with him to steal the precious cargo. Although barely promoted by MGM, became a critics' favorite. Grimacing and long in the tooth, McCrea and Scott enact a fitting tribute and farewell to the myth of the grand ol' West. Wonderfully photographed by Lucien Ballard. The laserdisc edition carries the film in widescreen format along with the original movie trailer. *AKA:* Guns in the Afternoon. ♪ ♪ ♪ ♪

1962 93m/C Randolph Scott, Joel McCrea, Mariette Hartley, Edgar Buchanan, R.G. Armstrong, Ronald Starr, John Anderson, James Drury, L.Q. Jones, Warren Oates; **D:** Sam Peckinpah. **VHS, Beta, LV $19.98** *MGM*

Risky Business

Sexy comedy about an uncertain high school student (Cruise), a savvy hooker (DeMornay), her pimp, and assorted others has aged well. Many elements—the cold mother, the sports car that dad loves, pressures of upper middle-class adolescence, Chicago locations—have been used in many other recent movies. But director Brickman handles things with a strong visual style most notable in the vivid dream-like quality he gives to some sequences. The love scene on the El is a real showstopper. Cruise is likeable, especially when dancing in his underwear. Funny, well-paced, stylish prototypical '80s teen flick reintroduced Ray-Bans as the sunglasses for the wannabe hip. What a party! ♫♫♫

1983 (R) 99m/C Tom Cruise, Rebecca DeMornay, Curtis Armstrong, Bronson Pinchot, Joe Pantoliano, Kevin Anderson, Richard Masur, Raphael Sbarge, Nicholas Pryor, Janet Carroll; **D:** Paul Brickman; **W:** Paul Brickman; **M:** Tangerine Dream. VHS, Beta, LV, 8mm $19.98 *WAR*

The Road to Utopia

The fourth and arguably the best of the "Road" films, with Bob and Bing posing as two feared Klondike killers. Humorist Robert Benchley contributes wry commentary and there's even a talking fish and bear, who complains that his finned co-star gets all the good lines while all he gets to do is growl. A gold mine of in-jokes, as when Bing makes his entrance and Bob remarks in disgust, "I thought this was going to be an A picture." Later, riding across the tundra, they gaze upon a majestic mountain, which Bob calls his bread and butter. Bing protests that it is a mountain, to which Bob replies, "It may be a mountain to you, but it's bread and butter to me," after which we see the Paramount logo above it. The defining Hope moment: Bob, posing as the dreaded outlaw, saunters up to the bar and orders a lemonade. Realizing his mistake, he quickly asserts, "...in a dirty glass." ♫♫ Put It There, Pal; Welcome to My Dreams; Would You?; Personality; Sunday, Monday, or Always?; Goodtime Charlie; It's Anybody's Spring. ♫♫♫

1946 90m/B Bing Crosby, Bob Hope, Dorothy Lamour, Jack LaRue, Robert Benchley, Douglass Dumbrille, Hillary Brooke; **D:** Hal Walker; **W:** Norman Panama. Nominations: Academy Awards '46: Best Original Screenplay. VHS, Beta, LV $29.95 *MCA*

The Road Warrior

Incredible photography, terrific stunts, and full-tilt pace make this futuristic s-f western one of the most influential movies of the early '80s. It's a rare sequel (to *Mad Max*) that surpasses the original on sheer intensity. The action takes place after nuclear war has destroyed Australia. Max (Gibson) helps a colony of oil-drilling survivors defend themselves from the roving murderous outback gangs and escape to the coast. Well-drawn characters and a climactic chase scene that's among the most exciting ever filmed. Worth another look any time; worth owning. ♫♫♫♫

1982 (R) 95m/C Mel Gibson, Bruce Spence, Emil Minty, Vernon Wells; **D:** George Miller; **W:** George Miller. VHS, Beta, LV $19.98 *WAR*

Robin and the Seven Hoods

The Rat Pack is back in business in this musical take on the Robin Hood legend set in Prohibition-era Chicago. Frank Sinatra stars as suave mobster Robbo, who vies with Peter Falk's Guy Gisbourne for control of the city. Robbo's merry men include Dean Martin as Little John, Sammy Davis, Jr., as Will, and new recruit Bing Crosby as Allen A. Dale, who transforms Robbo into a charitable folk hero. Luscious Barbara Rush co-stars as—who else—Marian, but she's no maiden. She wants revenge for the hit on her father Big Jim (Edward G. Robinson in an all-too-brief nostalgic cameo). Great fun, with songs that became Sinatra's signatures. ♫ Bang! Bang!; Style; Mister Booze; Don't Be a Do-Badder; My Kind of Town. ♫♫♫

1964 124m/C Frank Sinatra, Bing Crosby, Dean Martin, Sammy Davis Jr., Peter Falk, Barbara Rush, Allen Jenkins; **Cameos:** Edward G. Robinson; **D:** Gordon Douglas. Nominations: Academy Awards '64: Best Song ("My Kind of Town"), Best Original Score. VHS, Beta, LV $19.98 *WAR*

Robot Monster

Ludicrous cheapie is widely considered one of the worst films of all time. A handful of surviving hu-mans struggle against the assault of Ro-man, apparently a super-intelligent gorilla in a space helmet (the producers being unable to afford a full alien costume), who conspires to take over the Earth from his station in a small, bubble-filled cave in Bronson Canyon. However, Ro-man turns out to be a peculiarly inept conqueror, angering his

"When I was a kid, he caught me stealing hubcaps off his car, and he said 'Kid, don't steal the hubcaps, steal the car.'"

--Peter Falk in
Robin and the Seven Hoods.

boss on several occasions by failing to follow *The Great Plan*—he even falls for Earth chick Barrett. Contains many bizarre stock footage montages. Although a hilariously threadbare and preposterous production all around, since it's presented as a dream of little Johnny (knocked unconscious while playing in the cave), who is your typical sci-fi-crazed 1950s boy, the whole thing can be viewed as oddly accurate, right down to fantasy of his kid sister's murder! Available in original 3-D format, but the tape is so poorly produced that it's impossible to watch—stick with the flat version. **AKA:** Monsters From the Moon. 🎵🎵🎵🎵

1953 62m/B George Nader, Claudia Barrett, Gregory Moffett, Selena Royle; **D:** Phil Tucker; **M:** Elmer Bernstein. **VHS, Beta, LV $12.95** *RHI, FCT, COL*

Rock All Night

Typically trashy Corman quickie (filmed in five days on one set) about some wild fifties teens and, in this case, a couple of murderers. Seems Cloud Nine, the local teen hangout, is invaded by a couple of murderers who hold the kids hostage. It's up to the hipster bartender, known as Shorty because he's five-foot-one, to save the day. Unrelated concert footage of The Platters and The Blockbusters opens the film. 🎵🎵

1957 62m/B Dick Miller, Abby Dalton, Russell Johnson, Jonathan Haze, Robin Morse; **D:** Roger Corman. **VHS $9.95** *COL, MOV, MVD*

Rock Hudson's Home Movies

Artistic documentary in which Farr re-creates the character of the late actor to take a look back at Hudson's films, specifically those scenes that seemingly support the fact that Hudson was gay (lines taken out of context, repetitive bachelor themes, and even a shot of him in drag), showing the "real" Rock Hudson behind the screen idol. A sensitive look at the actor's works that avoids exploitation of his personal choices, while presenting a truly witty, clever, and sadly, foreboding selection of "telling" clips. Highly recommended. 🎵🎵🎵🎵

1992 63m/C Eric Farr; **D:** Mark Rappaport; **W:** Mark Rappaport. **VHS $39.95** *WBF*

Rock 'n' Roll High School

Roger Corman-produced, high-energy cult classic about the kids at Vince Lombardi High, out to thwart the new rock 'n' roll- hating principal Miss Togar at every turn. When the coolest band in the world—the Ramones—comes to town the fuse is lit, figuratively and literally. Director Arkush burlesques classroom cliches with snide exaggeration, and lively performances include Ron Howard's brother Clint as the hyperactive student entrepreneur (reigning over his empire from a bathroom-stall office). If the slouching Ramones aren't exactly charismatic, they make up for it in frenzied musical numbers like "Teenage Lobotomy" (with subtitles), "Blitzkrieg Bop," "I Wanna Be Sedated," and the title track. Ignore sequel *Rock 'n' Roll High School Forever*; check out instead Arkush's equally anarchic rock farce *Get Crazy*. 🎵 Teenage Lobotomy; Blitzkrieg Bop; I Wanna Be Sedated; Rock and Rock Hill School. 🎵🎵🎵

1979 (PG) 94m/C The Ramones, P.J. Soles, Vincent Van Patten, Clint Howard, Dey Young, Mary Woronov, Alix Elias, Dick Miller, Paul Bartel; **D:** Allan Arkush. **VHS, Beta $64.95** *MVD*

Rock 'n' Roll High School Forever

Corey and his metalheads just want to rock 'n' roll, but the new principal doesn't share their enthusiasm. Way late, way lame sequel to *Rock 'n' Roll High School* accomplishes what Miss Togar in the original couldn't: makes homework seem a preferable alternative to listening (or watching). Stupid gags aren't even redeemed by return of Woronov—with a hook hand—as an all-new villainess. Mojo Nixon portrays the "Spirit of Rock 'n' Roll," to no avail. Other soundtrack guests: The Divinyls, Dee Dee Ramone, Will and the Bushmen, The Pursuit of Happiness, and Feldman's own real-life combo. **WOOF!**

1991 (PG-13) 94m/C Corey Feldman, Mary Woronov, Mojo Nixon, Evan Richards, Michael Ceveris, Patrick Malone, Larry Linville, Sarah Buxton; **D:** Deborah Brock; **W:** Deborah Brock. **VHS, Beta, LV $89.95** *LIV, IME*

R

Rock 'n' Roll Nightmare

A rock band and their bimbo groupies move into an empty house of the *Amityville Horror* variety to cut their next album. One by one the musical morons are murdered by demons (some of whom are clearly sock puppets a la *Beany & Cecil*). Sex, slash, and rock-video scenes proliferate without mercy, and just when you're about to write the whole mess off as utterly useless garbage, there's a lunatic twist ending that's almost worth the pain. Almost. Good Sunday-school discussion material. *AKA:* The Edge of Hell. 🎵🎵

1985 (R) 89m/C *CA* Jon Mikl Thor, Paula Francescatto, Rusty Hamilton; *D:* John Fasano. **VHS, Beta $29.95** *ACA*

The Rocky Horror Picture Show

Anyone out there who purchased this book NOT see this movie? Campy, vampy, and anything but subtle, the mother of all cult hits arrived on home video after 15 years of mid-night screenings. On tape, of course, the audience participation element is lost. (Or at least lessened; what you and your friends want to do and wear in the privacy of your own place is none of the Hound's business.) So, what about the movie itself? It's not bad. The story isn't too important in this kinky musical send-up of old horror movies. The rock score is loud and energetic; the lyrics surprisingly witty. Sarandon and Bostwick are fine as the innocent heroine and hero, but the film belongs to Tim Curry's Dr. Frank-N-Furter. He redefines outrageous excess as the mad scientist who favors mascara, high heels, and fishnet hose. Curry wrings every drop of mad humor from the role—and there's a lot to wring. In the process, he shows how a talented stage actor can overpower a screen production, either film or video. Followed by the disappointing *Shock Treatment.* 🎵🎵 The Time Warp; Science Fiction Double Feature; Wedding Song; Sweet Transvestite; The Sword of Damocles; Charles Atlas Song; Whatever Happened to Saturday Night; Touch-a Touch-a Touch-a Touch Me; Eddie's Teddy. 🎵🎵🎵🎵

1975 **(R)** 105m/C Tim Curry, Susan Sarandon, Barry Bostwick, Meat Loaf, Little Nell, Richard O'Brien; **D:** Jim Sharman; **M:** John Barry. **VHS, LV $19.98** *FOX, FCT, PMS*

Roger & Me

Mordant, partisan docu-diary about reporter Moore's protracted efforts to personally meet General Motors CEO Roger Smith and confront him with the poverty and despair afflicting Flint, Michigan, after GM closed its plants there. Includes emotionally grabbing scenes: a sympathetic sheriff evicts folks just before Christmas; a woman makes a living raising rabbits as "pets or meat" (killing one onscreen for supper); and Flint's rich folks amidst living statues at a garden party. All interspersed with David Letterman-type segments in which the rumpled, mischievous Moore trudges corridors of GM or invades a shareholder's meeting in quest for the unreachable Smith. Some scenes are just cheap ambushes, like Moore seeking economic analyses from an unprepared Miss Michigan,

or gleefully catching Flint celebrity and game-show host Bob Eubanks telling racist jokes. Others, like the pathetic failure of Flint's auto-themed amusement park, add a properly acid bite to this skeptical look at corporate responsibility. During theatrical showings an empty chair was reserved for Roger Smith, while a humiliated GM's public-relations department huffily challenged Moore's credibility. This became one of the most commercially successful nonfiction features ever, and Moore later shot a short-subject epilogue *Pets or Meat.* ♫♫♫♪

1989 **(R)** 91m/C Michael Moore, Bob Eubanks, Pat Boone, Anita Bryant; **D:** Michael Moore; **W:** Michael Moore. **VHS, Beta, LV $19.95** *WAR*

Roller Blade

Are you sitting down for this? In a post-holocaust world where the slogan "skate or die" is taken quite literally, a sexy sect of Amazonian nuns on in-line rollerskates worship a "have a nice day" happy face and battle forces of evil (a masked-wrestler type with a gnome-

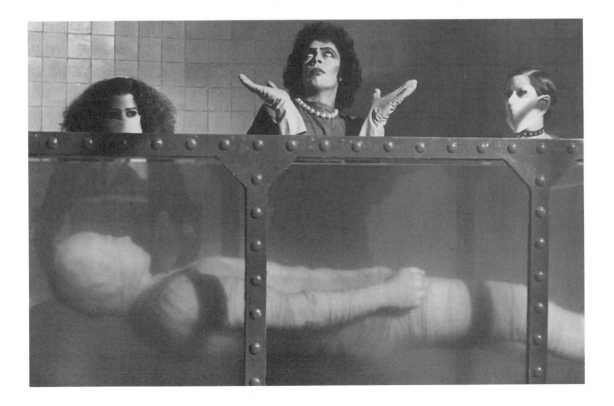

Tim Curry admires his handiwork in *The Rocky Horror Picture Show.*

THE HOUND SALUTES: RUSS MEYER

Russ Meyer is unique in the entertainment industry. Screenwriter William Goldman put it this way in his book *Adventures in the Screen Trade*: "Is there then no American auteur director? Perhaps there is one. One man who thinks up his own stories and produces his pictures and directs them too. And also serves as his own cinematographer. Not to mention he also does his own editing. All of this connected with an intensely personal and unique vision of the world. That man is Russ Meyer."

His films are exaggerated live-action cartoons, overstated satires on sex and violence unlike any others. His characters are overblown archetypes and stereotypes: women with huge breasts, men with granite jaws, supernatural deities, goose-stepping Nazis, lust-crazed homosexuals.

Meyer has maintained control over most of his films on videocassette, and distributes almost all of them through his own company, RM Films International. In the late '50s when Meyer made the first "nudie" movie, *The Immoral Mr. Teas*, he and a partner set up their own distribution system. Since then, with the exception of two films he made for Hollywood studios, he has kept full creative and business control over his work.

"I own the films outright," he said in an interview. "There's no point in giving them to anybody else who'd sacrifice them, like books are sacrificed after they've reached their peak in bookstores. I made a mistake in 1975. I didn't have any real confidence that it [home video] really would amount to anything so I licensed a man to distribute some of my films. He had no concern for quality. He would make video masters from used, scratchy 16mm prints. He didn't care what he gave the customer. With the proper legal eagle, I was able to wrestle them away from him."

Meyer's concern for the quality of the image is justified. His films are often criticized for their wild plots and characterizations of women (some feminists are especially outraged), but no

continued...

like puppet pal fixed to his hand) using martial arts, mysticism, communal bathing, and hockey sticks. Cheapjack filmed-on-video mutation must truly be seen to be believed. It's good for a few laughs, but once you realize the no-brainer dialogue and schlock production values aren't going to improve the bizarre novelty turns into an irritant very quickly. Sequellized in *Roller Blade Warriors*; not surprisingly, filmmaker Jackson also wrought *Hell Comes to Frogtown.* ♫ ▷

1985 88m/C Suzanne Solari, Jeff Hutchinson, Shaun Mitchelle; **D:** Donald G. Jackson. **VHS, Beta $19.95** *NWV*

Room Service

The Marx Brothers provide less mayhem than usual here. Groucho is a penniless theatrical producer who can't pay his hotel bill, among other things. During the agonizing wait for funds for his next show, Groucho, Harpo, and Chico pull scam after desperate scam (including a fake measles outbreak) to keep the whole cast secure in their crowded, high-rise suite. Not as anarchic as previous Marx Brothers comedies, mainly because it's based on a hit Broadway play by Allen Boretz and John Murray (later remade as the musical *Step Lively*), with the Marxists following the script straight and imposing a minimum of their own personalities. Harpo comes off best; he and Lucille Ball would later reteam for an unforgettable pantomime routine on her classic TV show. ♫ ♫ ▷

1938 78m/B Groucho Marx, Harpo Marx, Chico Marx, Lucille Ball, Ann Miller, Frank Albertson, Donald MacBride, Charles Halton; **D:** William A. Seiter. **VHS, Beta, LV $19.95** *CCB, MED, TTC*

Rosemary's Baby

A young innocent wife (Farrow) and her ambitious actor husband (Cassavetes) move into a new apartment. Soon the woman is pregnant, but she begins to suspect that something evil is happening to her. Is she overreacting to hormonal changes, or are her apparently normal neighbors actually servants of Satan? Gripping and powerful, subtle yet utterly horrifying, with luminous performances by a flawless supporting cast of some of the best character actors ever to work together. Pace is the other key, with seemingly unconnected everyday events inexorably becoming more eerie and ominous. Produced by William Castle—and he also appears in the cast. Polanski's first American film; from Levin's bestseller, itself a classic of horror literature. Many other films—notably the *Omen* series—have attempted to repeat the successful combination of the commonplace and the supernatural, but none have come close. This is simply one of Hollywood's best horror films. ♫♫♫♫

1968 (R) 134m/C Mia Farrow, John Cassavetes, Ruth Gordon, Maurice Evans, Patsy Kelly, Elisha Cook Jr., Charles Grodin, Sidney Blackmer, William Castle, Ralph Bellamy; **D:** Roman Polanski; **W:** Roman Polanski; **M:** Krzysztof Komeda. Academy Awards '68: Best Supporting Actress (Gordon); Golden Globe Awards '69: Best Supporting Actress (Gordon); Nominations: Academy Awards '68: Best Adapted Screenplay. **VHS, Beta, LV $14.95** *PAR, MLB, BTV*

Rosencrantz & Guildenstern Are Dead

Playwright Stoppard adapted his own absurdist 1967 play to film—which at first viewing makes as much sense as a *Swan Lake* ballet on radio. Two tragicomic minor characters in *Hamlet* squabble rhetorically and misperceive Shakespeare's plot tightening fatally around them. As they try to figure out who everyone is (they can't even decide which one is Rosencrantz and which is Guildenstern) and what they're doing, they are aided (?) by the leader of the players (Dreyfuss), who seems to be the only one who knows the whole story. Oldman and Roth, freed from playing their usual array of psychopaths and killers, get to drop the American accents, while Dreyfuss goes over the top as the slightly sinister lead actor. Keep the rewind button handy for the game of "Questions." ♫♫♫♪

1990 (PG) 118m/C Gary Oldman, Tim Roth, Richard Dreyfuss, Iain Glen; **D:** Tom Stoppard; **W:** Tom Stoppard. Venice Film Festival '91: Best Picture. **VHS, Beta, LV $92.95** *TOU, FCT*

The Ruling Class

Outrageous cult satire featuring O'Toole in an Oscar-nominated role as the unbalanced 14th Earl of Gurney, latest in a lordly but mentally degenerate clan of English aristocrats. Emerging from the asylum to assume the title after his father dies, the Earl believes he is Jesus Christ—and later a few other, less benevolent historical figures. O'Toole saying grace: "For what I am about to receive, may I be truly thankful," and then he breaks into an utterly inexplicable rendition of "The Varsity Drag," one of several musical numbers that pop up seemingly at random. Uneven, chaotic, surreal, and bitter slam against the decaying (literally, in a notable zombie sequence) British class system, with plenty of slow spots and windy speeches that betray its origins as a stage play (by Peter Barnes, who wrote the script). A must-see, nonetheless, worth sitting through to the nightmarish finale. ♫♫♫

1972 (PG) 154m/C *GB* Peter O'Toole, Alastair Sim, Arthur Lowe, Harry Andrews, Coral Browne, Nigel Green; **D:** Peter Medak. National Board of Review Awards '72: 10 Best Films of the Year, Best Actor (O'Toole); Nominations: Academy Awards '72: Best Actor (O'Toole); Cannes Film Festival '72: Best Film. **VHS, Beta, LV $19.98** *SUE, NLC*

Rush

Phony attempt at portraying '70s drug culture via the degeneration of two undercover cops who are drawn deeper into the drug-addicted world they are supposed to destroy. The overly sincere thespian efforts of leads Jennifer Jason-Leigh and Jason Patric make the autobiographical material provided by ex-narcotics cop Kim Wozencraft ring false. They give the kind of performances that win Emmys. Eric Clapton's turgid blues score is so unrelentingly moody that it seems to predestine their doom. The big surprise here is Gregg Allman's frighteningly natural performance as a drug dealer. Perhaps, like a good method actor, he is drawing upon life experiences. ♫♫

1991 120/m C Jason Patric, Jennifer Jason Leigh, Gregg Allman, Max Perlich, Sam Elliott; **D:** Lili Fini Zanuck; **W:** Pete Dexter; **M:** Eric Clapton. **VHS** *MGM*

The Sadist

Three teachers on their way to Dodger Stadium find themselves stranded at a roadside garage and terrorized by a sniveling lunatic (Hall). Tense and plausible, inspired by the late-'50s multistate murder spree of teenager Charles Starkweather and his girlfriend Caril Fugate, who claimed the lives of at least ten people, including Fugate's family. Although a

"It's really pretty popular; a lot of people come down here...they're only open on Mondays and Tuesdays and Wednesdays and Thursdays and Fridays."
--A professional blood bank donor in *Roger & Me.*

"This isn't a dream, this is really happening!"
--Rosemary (Mia Farrow) during an interlude with the devil in *Rosemary's Baby.*

Story continued...

one can question the look of a Russ Meyer film. His work has an unusual texture that reveals detail in fairly hard focus while softening colors, even in outdoor shots. It translates well from the large screen to video. He creates it by diffusing and reflecting natural light, rather than using direct sunlight or artificial light.

Meyer's assessment of his own work combines objectivity and a certain nostalgia. Even though it was made for one of the major studios, 20th Century-Fox, and co-written with critic Roger Ebert, *Beyond the Valley of the Dolls* is his favorite. It was out of print for years and his other major-studio film, *The Seven Minutes*, has never appeared on tape.

When he talks about his work for the studios, he sounds almost wistful, as if he's fondly remembering a marriage that ended badly: "My life would not have been complete without it. I was asked to come to the mountain and I agreed and I made two damn good pictures. One was very, very successful."

Today, all of his films, particularly those distributed under his own "Bosomania" imprimatur are enduring cult favorites. One of them (*Faster Pussycat! Kill! Kill!*) even enjoyed a recent theatrical re-release.

bit too manic, Hall's performance is surprisingly good (much better than his atrocities in *Wild Guitar* and *Eegah!*), probably due to the sure handling of Landis (*Stakeout*). Another trash film with cinematography by future Oscar winner Vilmos Zsigmond. *AKA:* The Profile of Terror. 🎵🎵▷

1963 95m/B Arch Hall Jr., Helen Hovey, Richard Alden, Marilyn Manning, Don Russell; *D:* James Landis; *W:* James Landis. **Beta $16.95** *SNC, RHI*

St. Elmo's Fire

Socially significant as perhaps the peak of the Brat Pack's grip on Hollywood—after this it was downhill into the straight-to-video section for some (Judd Nelson, perhaps?) or uphill into true superstardom for others—Demi Moore comes to mind (and you can bet Demi doesn't have any names from this movie still on her speed-dial). The movie itself documents the trials and tribulations of seven Georgetown graduates confronting adult problems during their first post-graduate year. The movie tries to operate as a twenty-something *Big Chill,* but a weak story wastes lots of talent and time. Mare Winningham turns in a "winning" performance as the good girl attracted to the bad boy (Rob Lowe), while Moore is very believable in her vapid portrayal of the drug-addled party girl. Viewed from the distance that ten years provides, its hard to believe that anyone liked any of these people enough to sit through this movie, but at the time, it captured a certain slice of post-college trauma in the '80s. Notable for a shower sex scene between Andrew McCarthy and Ally Sheedy that isn't as awful as that sounds, and for the success found by lesser cast member Andie MacDowell, who went on to the wildly successful *Sex, Lies, and Videotape* and *Four Weddings and a Funeral.* Writer and director Joel Schumacher landed the plum film job of 1995 when he inherited the Batman franchise from Tim Burton and directed the cash-cow *Batman Forever.* 🎵🎵▷

1985 (R) 110m/C Rob Lowe, Demi Moore, Andrew McCarthy, Judd Nelson, Ally Sheedy, Emilio Estevez, Mare Winningham, Martin Balsam, Joyce Van Patten, Andie MacDowell, Anna Maria Horsford, Jenny Wright; *D:* Joel Schumacher; *W:* Joel Schumacher; *M:* David Foster. **VHS, Beta, LV $12.95** *COL*

The St. Valentine's Day Massacre

"I'm gonna deliver a valentine to Bugs he will never forget." Jason Robards may not be the ideal casting choice for Al Capone (director Roger Corman wanted Orson Welles), but this authentic, violent, and blood-soaked recreation of the gangland war between Capone and Bugs Moran (Ralph Meeker) is a gangster movie you can't refuse. The ensemble cast is character actor's heaven with George Segal as Moran's chief enforcer and Harold J. Stone as Frank Nitti. This was Corman's first for a major studio (20th Century-Fox), and he made the most out of his unprecedented (for him) million-dollar budget and 35-day shooting schedule. But old habits die hard. He enlisted the manor in *The Sound of Music* for Al Capone's house, the bar in *The Sand Pebbles* as a brothel, and the *Hello, Dolly!* exteriors into downtown Chicago. And he took some of his stock company with him, including Jonathan Haze (*Little Shop of Horrors*), Dick Miller (*Bucket of Blood*), Bruce Dern (*The Wild Angels*), Barboura Morris (*The Wasp Woman*), and Jack Nicholson, who cameos as a chauffeur. 🦴🦴🦴

1967 100m/C Jason Robards Jr., Ralph Meeker, Jean Hale, Joseph Campanella, Bruce Dern, Clint Ritchie, Richard Bakalayan, George Segal, Harold J. Stone, Jonathan Haze, Dick Miller, Barboura Morris; *Cameos:* Jack Nicholson; *D:* Roger Corman. **VHS, Beta $14.98** *FOX, FCT*

Santa Claus Conquers the Martians

The green-faced Martian children are feeling blue, so to speak, and their parents decide it's because Earth has a Santa Claus and the Red Planet does not. Consequently the aliens decide to invade the North Pole and abduct Kris Kringle from his workshop (which looks like a tacky department store display). Fortunately human kids tag along for a rescue and some awful songs. Yes, Virginia, this one's just terrible, though with the proper sense of humor, a la *Mystery Science Theater 3000,*—you can have fun with this. Come to think of it, you can have fun without it too. Features then-child actress Pia Zadora. *AKA:* Santa Claus Defeats the Aliens. 🦴🌙

1964 80m/C John Call, Pia Zadora, Leonard Hicks, Vincent Beck, Victor Stiles, Donna Conforti; *D:* Nicholas Webster. **VHS, Beta $19.95** *COL, SNC, SUE*

Santa Sangre

A circus in Mexico City, a temple devoted to a saint without arms, and a son who faithfully dotes upon his armless mother are just a few of the bizarre things in this wildly fantastic film. Fenix acts as his mother's arms, plays the piano for her, and carries out any wish she

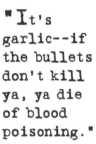

"It's garlic--if the bullets don't kill ya, ya die of blood poisoning."

--Jack Nicholson in *The St. Valentine's Day Massacre.*

Ho, ho, holy aliens! *Santa Claus Conquers the Martians.*

THE HOUND SALUTES: MYSTERY SCIENCE THEATER 3000

Now entering its seventh season as of this writing, *Mystery Science Theater 3000* (or "MST3K" to the show's fans, known as Misties) celebrates bad movies, reveling in the hackneyed writing and excruciating performances that elevate a simply bad movie into true cult status. Without going into too much detail (true Misties, a cult of their own, would be happy to fill you in), the show features a wisecracking human and two robot pals who watch truly cheesy movies and provide their own twisted running commentary throughout. What makes this goofy premise work brilliantly is two things: first, EVERYONE can relate to talking back to the screen when watching TV, and second and most importantly, the writing that goes into each episode is simply outstanding. Every show features a couple hundred jokes and put-downs, and the pop culture references are too numerous for all but the most socially aware to follow.

Created by a crew called Best Brains, Inc., the show first aired on November 24, 1988, on station KTMA in Minneapolis, MN, before switching over to cable's Comedy Central, where it currently resides. To its credit, the show has undergone numerous changes (founder Joel Hodgeson left the show after the fifth season to pursue other options) and continued to thrive. In 1995, the first big screen version of MST3K will hit theatres when Hodgeson's replacement Mike Nelson and his 'bot friends Tom Servo and Crow T. Robot rip into the nuclear disaster flick *This Island Earth.*

desires—including murder. Visually intoxicating but strange outing may prove too graphic for some viewers. Not as rigorous as other Jodorowsky outings. Also available in an NC-17 version. ♫ ♫ ♫

1990 (R) 123m/C *IT MX* Axel Jodorowsky, Sabrina Dennison, Guy Stockwell, Blanca Guerra, Thelma Tixou, Adan Jodorowsky, Faviola Tapia, Jesus Juarez; **D:** Alejandro Jodorowsky; **W:** Robert Leoni, Claudio Argento, Alejandro Jodorowsky; **M:** Simon Boswell. **VHS, LV $19.98** *REP, FCT, INJ*

Satan in High Heels

Sordid show-biz tale of a carnival dancer (Myles) who dreams of making it big on Broadway. First she finagles her way into a position as a nightclub singer and the mistress of a convenient millionaire. But she plays with fire when she falls for the millionaire's misbehaving son. Before long her past, in the form of the drunkard husband she ran out on, catches up to her. Myles' song numbers sizzle with hard-boiled sensuality, especially the B&D-tinged *More Deadly Than the Male.* Flamboyant performance by Hall (who fans will recognize from the spooky soap *Dark Shadows*) as the lesbian nightclub owner. Whole show is nearly stolen by the atomic sex-bomb Sabrina. Del Tenney would go on to direct *Horror of Party Beach* and other classics. ♫ ♫ ♪

1962 90m/C Meg Myles, Grayson Hall, Del Tenney; **D:** Jerald Intrator; **W:** John T. Chapman. **VHS $23.00** *SMW, TPV*

Satan's Cheerleaders

A fun and harmless horror spoof that fans of such should include as must viewing. The high school cheerleading squad is under the watchful eye of a local Satanist (the janitor). While on the way to a game at a rival high school, he abducts the girls and their coach. Seems his coven, headed by the local sheriff and his fat wife (DeCarlo, in a most unworthy role) need a virgin sacrifice to gain Satan's complete favor. What they don't know is that one of the girls is descended from witches also and is less than happy with their plans. The girls are properly sassy and certainly look good in their shower scene; the pacing is adequate, ensuring no long, boring stretches, and the twist ending, while not totally unexpected, is satisfying. Although there are no out and out guffaws, the light treatment does make for many smiles. Gimme an S! Gimme an A! Gimme a T!... ♫ ♫ ♫

1977 (R) 92m/C John Carradine, John Ireland, Yvonne De Carlo, Kerry Sherman, Jacqulin Cole, Hilary Horan, Alisa Powell, Sherry Marks, Jack Kruschen, Sydney Chaplin; **D:** Greydon Clark. **VHS, Beta $24.95** *VCI*

Satan's Sadists

Sleazy rider Tamblyn and his biker gang terrorize folks in the southern California desert, including a retired cop, Vietnam vet, and a trio of vacationing coeds. Adamson completists will appreciate this gleefully rotten biker flick which wallows in murder, rape, and childish brutality, with a hefty, numb-skulled Tamblyn in granny glasses cornering the market in psycho cyclists (see also *Free Grass* and Adamson's *Dracula vs. Franken-stein*). Cast of regulars include tough guy Brady (*Five Bloody Graves*), Clark Gable stand-in Kent Taylor (*Brain of Blood, Angels' Wild Women*), wife Regina Carroll as "the Freak-Out Girl," and future exploitation di-rectors John "Bud" Cardos and Gredon (*Black Shampoo*) Clark, who sports a droopy mo-hawk. Adamson takes pride in this being al-legedly the first film to show someone drown-ing in a toilet. 🦴🦴🦴

1969 (R) 88m/C Russ Tamblyn, Regina Carrol, Gary Kent, Jackie Taylor, John Cardos, Kent Taylor, Robert Dix, Scott Brady, Evelyn Frank, Greydon Clark, Bill Bonner, Bobby Clark, Yvonne Stewart, Cheryl Anne, Randee Lynn, Bambi Allen, Breck Warwick; **D:** Al Adamson. **VHS** *NO*

Satan's School for Girls

When a young woman investigates the cir-cumstances that caused her sister's suicide, it leads her to a satanic girl's academy. Dumb and puerile made for TV "horror" that, iron-ically, features a couple of "angels" (Charlie's, that is). 🦴▷

1973 74m/C Pamela Franklin, Roy Thinnes, Kate Jackson, Lloyd Bochner, Jamie Smith-Jackson, Jo Van Fleet, Cheryl Ladd; **D:** David Lowell Rich. **VHS, Beta** **$19.99** *PSM*

Saturday Night Fever

This musical became a landmark of the 1970s despite some glaring flaws. It's too long; the ending doesn't ring true and for anyone but the diehard disco fan, the music quickly be-comes unbearable. So what? The film has en-ergy to burn and a real chemistry between leads John Travolta, who took off on the rocky road of stardom, and Karen Gorney, who did-n't. The story of a Brooklyn kid's using a dance hall as a way out of his dead-end world has been told often before because it's such a crowd pleaser. Based on a story published in *New York Magazine* by Nik Cohn. Followed by the sequel *Staying Alive*. Also available in

a 112-minute "PG" rated version that cuts most of the raw language. 🎵 Staying Alive; Night Fever; More Than a Woman; How Deep Is Your Love?. 🦴🦴🦴

1977 (R) 118m/C John Travolta, Karen Gorney, Barry Miller, Donna Pescow; **D:** John Badham; **M:** David Shire. National Board of Review Awards '77: 10 Best Films of the Year, Best Actor (Travolta); Nominations: Academy Awards '77: Best Actor (Travolta). **VHS, Beta, LV $29.95** *PAR*

Saturday Night Sleazies, Vol. 1

Two sleazy films: *College Girl Confidential* (1968) presents us with a typical frat house toga party, complete with lots of drugs, sex, initiations, folk singing, and accidental death. Marsha Jordan, a regular presence in '60s sex films, plays one of the frat little sisters. Be-cause of the decency laws in effect at that par-ticular moment, the men all keep their boxer shorts on during intercourse. And in the an-thology *Suburban Confidential* (1966, aka: *Suburban Roulette*, not to be confused with the Herschell Gordon Lewis movie of the same title), a doctor disregards professional ethics and gives us a peek into his private files for anecdotes from the sex lives of his house-wife patients. Both films are directed by the Bulgarian born Stephen (aka: Stephen Apos-tolof) who helmed *Orgy of the Dead*. Also in-cludes sleazy short subjects. 🦴🦴

1966 150m/B Marsha Jordan, Harvey Shane; **D:** A.C. Stephen; **W:** A.C. Stephen. **VHS, Beta $49.95** *RHI*

Saturday Night Sleazies, Vol. 2

Another sleazy '60s double feature from di-rector Stephen. In *Lady Godiva Meets Tom Jones* (1969, aka: *Lady Godiva Rides*), Jordan plays the very American-sounding Lady in a wild plot which has her escape the hangman's noose after being convicted of murder aboard the phoniest looking sailing ship in cinema history, and becoming a wrasslin' dancehall girl in Tombstone, Arizona. For Stephen's first color feature since the classic *Orgy of the Dead*, he saved money on period costumes by not giving any to some of the women. *Bachelor's Dream* (1967, aka: *Naked Dream*

S

"**Funnier than** *The Omen....* **scarier than** *Silent Movie.*"
--*Satan's Cheerleaders.*

"**You make it with some of these chicks, they think you gotta dance with them.**"
--John Travolta in *Saturday Night Fever.*

SKELETONS IN THEIR CLOSETS...

stars who have their roots in trash.

Kevin Bacon (*Friday the 13th*)

Kevin Costner (*Sizzle Beach U.S.A.*)

Robert DeNiro (*Bloody Mama*)

Johnny Depp (*A Nightmare on Elm Street*)

Clint Eastwood (*Revenge of the Creature*)

Jane Fonda (*Barbarella*)

Melanie Griffith (*Smile*)

Tom Hanks (*He Knows You're Alone*)

Ron Howard (*Village of the Giants*)

Don Johnson (*A Boy and His Dog*)

Michael Landon (*I Was a Teenage Werewolf*)

Demi Moore (*Parasite*)

Jack Nicholson (*Little Shop of Horrors*)

Susan Sarandon (*Rocky Horror Picture Show*)

Arnold Schwarzenegger (*Hercules in New York*)

John Travolta (*The Devil's Rain*)

of the Naughty Nerd) is a throwback to the nudie-cutie days of *The Immoral Mr. Teas.* Nebbishy comic Bidle can only daydream that he's a voyeur watching old burlesque stripper footage, plus some new color scenes of girls undressing. Also includes sleazy shorts and trailers. For adults only, provided they're not too mature. 🦴🦴▷

1967 150m/C Marsha Jordan, Harvey Shane, Abner Bidle, Liz Renay; **D:** A.C. Stephen. **VHS $49.95** *RHI*

Saturday Night Sleazies, Vol. 3

The sleazebag productions this time around start out with *Motel Confidential* (1967), Stephen's follow-up to *Suburban Confidential,* which presents sexual escapades that transpire within the $8/night rooms of a chintzy motel, run by a comic Italian and his son. *Office Love-In* (1968, aka: *White Collar Style, Swinging Secretary*) is actually a predecessor to the light-hearted sex comedies of the '70s. Williams stars as the secretary at a computer dating company who has affairs with her boss, her boss' wife (Jordan), and both their sons, while various other employees and customers have adventures of their own. The beautiful Williams can also be seen in *Love Camp 7, The Ramrodder,* and many other sleazy movies. The tape also has a selection of adults-only trailers and shorts. 🦴🦴▷

1967 150m/C Marsha Jordan, Kathy Williams; **D:** A.C. Stephen. **VHS $49.95** *RHI*

Saturday the 14th

Despite the title, this Roger Corman production is no parody of the axe-wielding-maniac dramas like *Friday the 13th,* but a scattershot spoof of classic horror cliches. Husband-and-wife team of Benjamin and Prentiss lead a typical American family who inherit a spooky mansion the all-powerful book of evil (yeah, another one of those) resides. There's a mummy in the kitchen, ghouls in the hall, an alien in the den, a gill-man in the bathtub, etc. Some funny moments before the whole mess goes to pieces. Followed by even worse sequel: *Saturday the 14th Strikes Back.* 🦴▷

1981 (PG) 91m/C Richard Benjamin, Paula Prentiss, Severn Darden; **D:** Howard R. Cohen. **VHS, Beta $19.98** *SUE*

Saturday the 14th Strikes Back

Pathetic followup (not really a sequel; not really much of anything) to 1981's Richard Benjamin horror spoof has a teenage boy defending his oblivious, idiot family when evil demons, sexy spirits, and film clips from earlier Roger Corman movies invade their suburban home. Just when you think it can't possibly get worse, it turns into a musical. Videocassette is notable for having box art by fantasy gag cartoonist Gahan Wilson—just about his only contribution so far to the silver screen. **WOOF!**

1988 91m/C Ray Walston, Avery Schreiber, Patty McCormack, Julianne McNamara, Jason Presson; **D:** Howard R. Cohen. **VHS, Beta $79.95** *MGM*

Scenes from the Class Struggle in Beverly Hills

The goodwill Paul Bartel has generated as a B-movie actor (*Rock 'n' Roll High School, Hollywood Boulevard*) and director (*Death Race 2000, Eating Raoul*) is not enough to sustain this rude farce that manages to maintain interest with its escalating perversities and expert B-movie cast. The late, great Ray Sharkey and Robert Beltran star as two servants in neighboring Beverly Hills mansions, who wager to see who can be first to seduce each other's employer. In oddball casting not to be rivalled until Kathleen Turner starred in John Waters' *Serial Mom,* Jacqueline Bisset stars as a recently widowed former sitcom actress who opens her doors to next-door neighbor Mary Woronov, who is having her house fumigated. They are soon joined by Woronov's brother Ed Begley, Jr., whose African-American bride (scene-stealer Arnetia Walker) is revealed to be a former porn actress, and Woronov's unfaithful ex-husband Wallace Shawn. Bartel also appears as defensive "thinologist" Dr. Mo Van de Kamp ("When you get a bunch of rich fat people who are determined to thin at any cost, some of them are going to die. It's a rule of thumb.") Bartel, Woronov, Beltran, and Begley all starred in *Eating Raoul*. Director Paul Mazursky appears throughout as the rather horny ghost of Bisset's huband. Shortly after this film was completed, costar Rebecca Schaeffer was murdered by an obsessed fan. Remake of Renoir's *The Rules of the Game.* 🐕🐕▷

1989 (R) 103m/C Jacqueline Bisset, Ray Sharkey, Mary Woronov, Robert Beltran, Ed Begley Jr., Wallace Shawn, Paul Bartel, Paul Mazursky, Arnetia Walker, Rebecca Schaeffer; *Cameos:* Little Richard; **D:** Paul Bartel; **W:** Bruce Wagner; **M:** Stanley Myers. **VHS, Beta, LV** *NO*

Schlock

B-movie monkey business directed by John Landis when he was a mere 22. Landis also stars as the title character, a missing link that runs amuck in a small town. Loaded with in-jokes that ape such films as *2001: A Space Odyssey* and *King Kong,* with an affectionate nod to Oliver Hardy. Eliza Garrett, who costars as the blind beauty that captivates the beast, made a memorable appearance in Landis's phenomenally successful *National Lampoon's Animal House* as one of the co-eds in the roadhouse scene ("Do you mind if we dance wif your dates?"). The ape costume was designed by Rick Baker, who won the first Academy Award for Best Makeup for Landis' *An American Werewolf in London.* This film also marks the first appearance of the fictitious film *See You Next Wednesday,* a line of dialogue Landis lifted from *2001* and proceeded to work into all of his films. *AKA:* The Banana Monster. 🐕🐕

1973 (PG) 78m/C John Landis, Saul Kahan, Joseph Piantadosi, Eliza Garrett; *Cameos:* Forrest J. Ackerman; **D:** John Landis; **W:** John Landis. **VHS** *NO*

Screen Test

The '60s' and '70s' trash movie worlds were dominated by an endless assortment of horror, comedy, and action fare laced with cheesy sex and violence. The 80s and 90s have been dominated by made-for-video and limited (or no) theatrical release product. *Screen Test* is one of the more likable comedies of the later period. Two bozos (the male equivalent of a bimbo) decide to meet girls by casting a nonexistent film. Soon they run afoul of the mob and end up on the run accompanied, naturally, by several of the bountiful babes. Lightweight, harmless fun with some nice-looking babes and some silly laughs. The best bits are the goofy auditions that take place early on. If this is your cup of tea, also check out the similarly themed *Glitz* and *Nudity Required.* Look for scream queen Monique Gabrielle in an early role. 🐕🐕🐕

1985 (R) 84m/C Michael Allan Bloom, Robert Bundy, Paul Lueken, David Simpatico; **D:** Sam Auster; **W:** Sam Auster. **VHS, Beta, LV** $79.95 *COL*

Sebastiane

The legend of St. Sebastiane is a pretext for a soft-core gay sex romp in this early effort by Derek Jarman, who went on to become a leading figure in avant garde cinema before succumbing to AIDS in 1994. As in his later, more skillful *Edward II,* Jarman draws parallels with modern homophobia as he details the conflicts between the saint and Roman authorities. Jarman enthusiasts will enjoy the visuals,

THE HOUND SALUTES: SAM RAIMI

I'll Be Stupidly Happy

Sam Raimi has taken his time on the rough road from low-budget horror movies to mainstream Hollywood. His career began with the effects-driven *Evil Dead* horror comedies. Those are ultra-low-budget shockers that depended on fast pace and inventive effects for their thrills. The first one cost only $385,000 in 1983. To make it, Raimi and his roommate Rob Tappert, who became his producer, dropped out of Michigan State University and borrowed the money they needed. The film developed a strong cult following in limited theatrical release and then attracted more fans when it appeared on home video. Its success led Dino DeLaurentiis to finance a sequel that was even more graphically violent and silly.

Between the two, Raimi made the less-successful comedy *Crimewave* with the Coen brothers (*Blood Simple*). His association with them also includes other joint production and writing efforts, as well as occasional cameos. (Raimi is gunned down in *Miller's Crossing*.)

In 1990, Raimi went legit, so to speak, with *Darkman*. It's a deliberate throwback to the great horror characters from Universal studios in the 1930s, Frankenstein's Monster and the Wolfman, "the man trapped inside the beast," as Raimi put it in an interview. The character has reappeared in a sequel that debuted on home video and will probably continue there, with Raimi acting as producer of the series.

He has also been working in television and he directed Sharon Stone in *The Quick and the Dead*, a wickedly funny parody of spaghetti Westerns. In any medium, the best of Raimi's work is characterized by sharp humor, dazzling camera work, and simple stories. His aim, he admits, is to entertain:

"The bottom line is that I'm as happy as the audience is. I read about filmmakers and they always say, 'I make the movie for myself and then if the audience likes it, great; if not, that's how it is.' But I can't be that confident

continued...

while others may feel they are walking that thin line between pornography and art. Music by Brian Eno. 🦴🦴▷

1979 90m/C Leonardo Treviglio, Barney James, Richard James, Neil Kennedy; **D:** Derek Jarman; **M:** Brian Eno. **VHS, Beta $29.95** *FCT, INJ*

The Secret Cinema/ Naughty Nurse

Bartel's audition piece, filmed while he was making TV commercials, was written in a weekend and filmed over a year while he begged, borrowed, and stole resources. The film was shot silently, with dialog added after the fact (Bartel comments, "But I think the film compensates on a dramatic level for whatever technical proficiences it may lack."). This self-described "paranoid fantasy" tells the story of Jane, whose pathetic life (she is dumped by her boyfriend, who explains, "It's not that you bore me, I just don't like girls.") is being secretly taped and is a smash hit as a serial at a very exclusive theatre. This piece launched his film career when Roger Corman's brother Gene saw it and let him direct his first feature piece, *Private Parts*. The story was rewrote by Bartel in 1985 as an episode of Steven Spielberg's *Amazing Stories* TV show (Bartel also directed and starred). The tape also includes the wry very-short "Naughty Nurse," in which the title character cleans up for the day and heads out for some S&M. 🦴🦴▷

1978 37m/C Amy Vane, Gordon Felio, Connie Ellison, Phillip Carlson, Estelle Omens, Barry Dennen; **D:** Paul Bartel. **VHS $19.95** *RHI*

Secret Policeman's Private Parts

Various sketches and performances from the various Secret Policeman occasions, featuring classic Python sketches including "I'm a Lumberjack and I'm OK." Also featured are performances by Phil Collins, Pete Townshend, Donovan, and Bob Geldof. Thank you very much. Followed by *The Secret Policeman's Other Ball* (1982) and *The Secret Policeman's Third Ball* (1987). 🦴🦴▷

1981 77m/C *GB* John Cleese, Michael Palin, Terry Jones, Pete Townshend, Julien Temple; **D:** Roger Graef. **VHS, Beta, LV $59.95** *MED*

Sgt. Kabukiman N.Y.P.D.

When a New York cop investigates the death of a famous Japanese Kabuki actor, he suddenly finds himself in a kimono, having really bad hair-days, and vested with the powers of "Kabukiman." With the help of his beautiful teacher Lotus, he learns to channel his commmand of such amazing weapons as suffocating sushi rolls and lethal chopsticks into crime fighting. Stupid and insulting (deliberately so), all at the same time. 🦴 ▷

1994 (PG-13) 95m/C Rick Gianasi, Susan Byun, Brick Bronsky; **D:** Lloyd Samuel Weil Kaufman, Michael Herz; **W:** Andrew Osborn, Lloyd Samuel Weil Kaufman. **VHS** *NYR*

Serial Mom

June Cleaver-like housewife Turner is nearly perfect, except when someone disrupts her orderly life. Didn't rewind your videotape? Chose the white shoes after Labor Day? Uh oh. Stardom reigns after she's caught and the murderer-as-celebrity phenomenon is exploited to the fullest. Darkly funny Waters satire tends toward the mainstream and isn't as perverse as earlier efforts, but still maintains a shocking edge (vital organs are good for an appearance or two). Turner's chameleonic performance as the perfect mom/crazed killer is right on target, recalling *The War of the Roses.* Waterston, Lake, and Lillard are terrific as her generic suburban family. The scenes of vendors hawking t-shirts outside the courtroom during Turner's trial seemed funny, yet implausible, when the movie came out, but now they just seem kind of creepy in light of the O.J. debacle. 🦴🦴🦴

1994 (R) 93m/C Kathleen Turner, Ricki Lake, Sam Waterston, Matthew Lillard, Mink Stole, Traci Lords; **Cameos:** Suzanne Somers, Joan Rivers, Patty Hearst; **D:** John Waters; **W:** John Waters; **M:** Basil Poledouris. **VHS, LV** *HBO*

Seven Faces of Dr. Lao

Step right up for George Pal's wonderful fantasy that boasts a tour-de-force performance by Tony Randall. As the ancient Dr. Lao, who brings his mysterious traveling circus to the western town of Abalone, he portrays seven characters, including Merlin the Magician, the Abominable Snowman, Pan, and a very fetching snake-maned Medea. Slow-going at first, but kids will love it once the circus opens for business and the special effects conjure up some memorable creatures. Villain Arthur O'Connell, who wants to buy the town, mends his ways after seeing himself as a snake. His henchmen are not so lucky. When they try to stomp Lao's pet fish, it grows into a seven-headed beast. William Tuttle won a special Oscar for make-up. Check out Barbara Eden (*I Dream of Jeannie*) as the town librarian. Puppeteer Pal produced or directed some of the classics of sci-fi and fantasy cinema, including *The Time Machine, War of the Worlds,* and *The Wonderful World of the Brothers Grimm.* Also worth seeking out on video is *The Fantasy Film Worlds of George Pal,* an affectionate career retrospective. 🦴🦴🦴

1963 101m/C Tony Randall, Barbara Eden, Arthur O'Connell, Lee Patrick, Noah Beery Jr., John Qualen; **D:** George Pal. **VHS, Beta, LV $59.95** *MGM*

The Seventh Voyage of Sinbad

Sinbad seeks to restore his fiancee from the midget size she's been reduced to by an evil magician (Thatcher). Ray Harryhausen works his animation magic around a well-developed plot and engaging performances by the real actors. Bernard Herrmann's score is one of his best, but nothing outshines Harryhausen's wonderful stop-motion creations. Note the nictitating membrane over the eyes of the baby Roc and the way it stumbles and teeters just like any newly hatched chick. Despite all the advances in special effects, this one is still a real crowd-pleaser for audiences of all ages. 🦴🦴🦴 ▷

1958 (G) 94m/C Kerwin Mathews, Kathryn Grant, Torin Thatcher, Richard Eyer; **D:** Nathan Hertz Juran; **W:** Kenneth Kolb; **M:** Bernard Herrmann. **VHS, Beta, LV $14.95** *COL, MLB, CCB*

Sex Madness

Deadly serious in 1937, this campy educational melodrama about the "madness" of sex and the peril of syphilis is quaint, to say the least, in view of all the current onscreen sex scenes. Tom Moran, son of a crusading reformer, runs wild with his pals and attends a burlesque show. At a house party afterwards,

S

"You're bigger than Freddie and Jason now...only you're real!"

--*Serial Mom*'s son Chip (Matthew Lillard) is in awe of his mother.

with my own feelings. I live and die for the audience, like a child that needs attention and approval. If they like it, I'll be stupidly happy."

showgirl Sheila invites him upstairs to "look at a darling Pomeranian," and gives him a dose. The tap dancing girls in shorts also inspire lesbianism and the sex murder of a little girl. Showgirl Millisent catches the clap as well. After her doctor shows her some gruesome evidence, she heads back to her small town. But when a quack M.D. talks her into a quickie cure, she nearly brings tragedy to her entire family. This is one of the very cheapest of the '30s roadshow features, with crude direction, and hilarious histrionics. In one scene, a window falls shut in the background, but nobody bothered with a retake. Despite these faults, and their generally exploitative nature, the roadshow pictures message of enlightenment probably did a lot of good wherever they played. *AKA:* They Must Be Told. 🦴🦴

1937 50m/B Duncey Taylor. **VHS, Beta $19.95** *NOS, HHT, DVT*

"**The Citizen Kane of alcoholic clown movies.**"
--*Shakes the Clown.*

Shakes the Clown

The decline and fall of Shakes, an alcoholic birthday-party clown wandering the lowdown town of Palukaville. After debauching *Brady Bunch* mom Florence Henderson, Shakes is framed for the juggling-pin murder of his boss by drug-crazed rival Binky. The fugitive Shakes is aided by bowler/waitress lover Judy in trying to clear his name. Meant as a satire of stand-up comics and the supposed tragedies of a artist's life, this is sometimes zany but more often merely unpleasant and forced. Auteur Goldthwait ended up having to defend his directorial debut against real clowns, who felt insulted. Quoth the Bobcat: "Clowns have no sense of humor." Robin Williams, under the pseudonym Marty Fromage, cameos as a mime instructor. 🦴🐾

1992 (R) 83m/C Bob(cat) Goldthwait, Julie Brown, Blake Clark, Adam Sandler, Tom Kenny, Sydney Lassick, Paul Dooley, Tim Kazurinsky, Florence Henderson, LaWanda Page; *Cameos:* Robin Williams; *D:* Bob(cat) Goldthwait; *W:* Bob(cat) Goldthwait. **VHS, LV** *COL*

Shame

Strangely unsuccessful low-budget Corman effort, starring pre-*Star Trek* Shatner as Cramer, a freelance bigot who travels around Missouri stirring up opposition to desegregation, while pausing for a little adultery and extortion on the side. Moralistic and topical but still powerful. Adapted from the equally excellent novel by Charles Beaumont (who also plays the school principal), based on an actual incident. Uses Sikeston, Mississippi, location filming superbly to render a sense of everydayness and authenticity. Reportedly Corman told the locals that they were making a pro-Klan picture to head off trouble. Won prizes at the Venice Film Festival for Corman and Shatner. Not to be confused with the *Shame* made by Ingmar Bergman. Or the Australian feminist revenge movie, or its TV movie remake. *AKA:* The Intruder; I Hate Your Guts; The Stranger. 🦴🦴🦴

1961 84m/B William Shatner, Frank Maxwell, Jeanne Cooper, Robert Emhardt, Leo Gordon, Charles Beaumont; *D:* Roger Corman; *W:* Charles Beaumont. **VHS, Beta, LV $19.95** *NOS, DVT, FCT*

She Demons

Pleasure craft loaded with three men (including *From Hell It Came* Andrews and "Number 2 Son" Sen Yung) and babe-a-licious McCalla (TV's Sheena, Queen of the Jungle) crashes into a remote island controlled by a gang of Nazi bad guys led by mad scientist who transforms pretty girls into rubber-faced Frankensteins. Incomprehensible, to say the least. Gets points for the respectful handling given Sen Yung's sidekick character, and for the knockout presence of McCalla. A perfect example of the type of story published in men's adventure pulps of the day. Cunha went on to the equally goofy *Missile to the Moon.* 🦴🦴🐾

1958 68m/B Irish McCalla, Tod Griffin, Victor Sen Yung, Rudolph Anders, Tod Andrews; *D:* Richard Cunha. **VHS, Beta $9.95** *RHI, SNC, MWP*

She-Devils on Wheels

Havoc erupts as an outlaw female motorcycle gang, known as *Maneaters on Motorbikes*, terrorizes a town—especially the men. Girl who wins the bike race has first pick of the "stud line." Heads roll when the Maneaters are on the road. Contains scenes of assault, kidnapping, torture, robbery, murder, and disturbing the peace. Really, really bad biker flick finely honed by Lewis, which made tons of money at the drive-ins. Theme song "Get Off the Road" became very popular with riot grrrls. ♫ Get Off the Road. 🦴🦴🦴◁

1968 83m/C Betty Connell, Christie Wagner, Pat Poston, Nancy Lee Noble, Ruby Tuesday; **D:** Herschell Gordon Lewis. **VHS, Beta $19.95** *VTR*

She Done Him Wrong

"Why don't you come up sometime, and see me?" Mae West utters these immortal words to Cary Grant in her best film, a Gay Nineties romp based on her Broadway hit. The censors dictated that true love must triumph, but until then, West lives it up as a saloon singer with a yen for diamonds until she meets Grant, the captain at the local mission. It's a bit creaky now, but West's suggestive roll of the eyes, voluptuous hourglass figure, and racy repartee liven things up. "You bad girl," Grant scolds. "You'll find out," she replies. ♫ Silver Threads Among the Gold; Masie, My Pretty Daisy; Easy Rider; I Like a Guy What Takes His Time; Frankie and Johnny. 🦴🦴🦴◁

1933 65m/B Mae West, Cary Grant, Owen Moore, Noah Beery Sr., Gilbert Roland, Louise Beavers; **D:** Lowell Sherman. National Board of Review Awards '33: 10 Best Films of the Year; Nominations: Academy Awards '33: Best Picture. **VHS, Beta, LV $14.98** *MCA, MLB, BTV*

She-Freak

Remake of Tod Browning's *Freaks* (1932). A cynical waitress (Brennan) runs away from her dead-end job in a Texas diner and joins a carnival, where she marries the freak show owner (McKinney). She has an affair with a sleazy roustabout, who's killed by McKinney. After he's locked up for murder, she takes over the show and burns everyone. The resident freaks (mostly fakes) get their revenge, and Brennan ends up as an exhibit. Lots of great carnival footage. Pales beside its unacknowledged, classic original. Of his own films, this is producer Dave Friedman's favorite, probably due to the fact that it gave him a chance to relive his early career with the carnival, and because *Freaks* had always been one of his childhood favorites. Mabe can be seen in Lee Frost's *The Defilers*, and also in *The Doberman Gang* in a supporting role (to the dogs). Sideshow owner McKinney later raped Ned Beatty in *Deliverance*. **AKA:** Alley of Nightmares. 🦴🦴🦴◁

1967 87m/C Claire Brennan, Lynn Courtney, Bill McKinney, Lee Raymond, Madame Lee; **D:** Byron Mabe. **VHS, Beta** *NO*

Shock Corridor

A reporter, dreaming of a Pulitzer Prize, fakes mental illness and gets admitted to an asylum, where he hopes to write an expose of murder among the inmates. "Their sickness is bound to rub off on you!" warns his stripper girlfriend, who subsequently haunts him in superimposed visions like Tinkerbell in a feather boa. Our hero's lurid ordeal runs the gamut from shock therapy to being ravished in the all-female "nympho ward," and he loses more and more of his sanity the closer he gets to the murderer. Sometimes goofy, more often genuinely disturbing suspense drama with a bizarre yet sympathetic cuckoo's-nestful of lunatics (including a black man who insists he's a Klan Wizard). Maverick touches from cult filmmaker Fuller include sudden intervals of distorted color stock footage and a hallucinatory indoor rainstorm. 🦴🦴🦴

1963 101m/B Peter Breck, Constance Towers, Gene Evans, Hari Rhodes, James Best, Philip Ahn; **D:** Samuel Fuller; **W:** Samuel Fuller. **VHS, LV $59.95** *HMV, CRC*

Shock Treatment

The less popular semi-sequel to the cult classic, *The Rocky Horror Picture Show,* by the creators of the original, gets half a bone just for not being a carbon copy of its predecessor. Still, that film hung its outrageous premise on a comfortably familiar structure of Gothic horror cliches. *Shock Treatment* is like an incomprehensible Fire Sign Theatre media satire that goes on and on... Brad and Janet, now

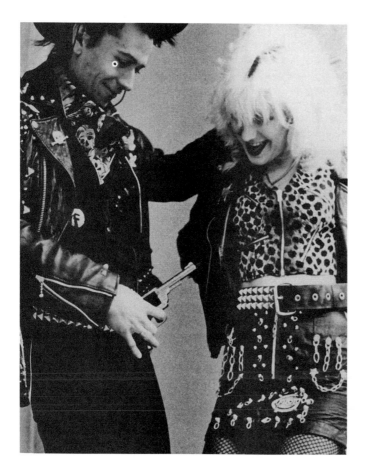

Just a couple of kids in love: Gary Oldman and Chloe Webb are *Sid & Nancy*.

a deserted motel on a small island. Cushing is the mad scientist intent on recreating the Nazi glory days with the seaweed-attired zombies. Odd B-grade, more or less standard horror flick somehow rises (slightly) above badness. Halpin's name was erroneously listed as Halprin—even on the original movie poster! *AKA:* Death Corps; Almost Human. ♫♫

1977 (PG) 90m/C Peter Cushing, Brooke Adams, John Carradine, Luke Halpin; *D:* Ken Wiederhorn; *M:* Richard Einhorn. **VHS, Beta $9.99** *PSM*

Shocking Asia

For the eye-covering delight of Eastern and Western audiences alike, Mr. Fox compiles gruesome Asian oddities. This Germany/HK production features the usual mix of bizarre happenings such as snake eating, faith healers, piercing, etc. A tour of the world of Japanese sex weirdness provides some entertainment, but the total show stopper is the graphic documentation of how desperate young hopefuls sell their altered wares on the streets in the hopes of raising enough cash for their final crude sex change operations. All phases of the process are shown. NOT for the squeamish. Though not the best of the mondo pictures, this one at least delivers what the title promises. ♫♫

1975 94m/C *GE D:* Emerson Fox. **VHS, Beta** *HHE*

Shocking Asia 2

Second *Mondo Cane*-style documentary about various unpleasant Asian oddities, including voodoo, cannibalism, and other strange practices seems largely made up of leftover footage from the previous film. Features a disturbing visit to a Thai leper colony, an expose of psychic surgery, a crippled artist who paints with her feet, etc. Again, much of the show is devoted to a parade of weird Japanese sex shows and prostitution. The *Shocking Asia* duo was a big hit in Asia itself, as well as jolting hardened American grindhouse audiences. Both became early video rental releases that did very well. ♫♫

1976 90m/C *D:* Emerson Fox. **VHS, Beta $49.98** *VCD*

portrayed by different leads, try to patch up their marriage on an elaborate TV game show/interactive soap opera. The mysterious sponsor, obsessed by Janet, seduces her with a superstar makeover while Brad remains confined to a cage in a psychiatric clinic. There may be an ironic comment on *Rocky Horror* fans in this movie's onscreen studio audience, a mindless rabble who spend days happily encamped in their seats. Songs by Richard Hartley and Richard O'Brien remain the highlight, especially "Little Black Dress" and the title number. ♫♫

1981 (PG) 94m/C Richard O'Brien, Jessica Harper, Cliff DeYoung, Patricia Quinn, Charles Gray, Ruby Wax; *D:* Jim Sharman. **VHS, Beta $14.98** *FOX*

Shock Waves

Group of mutant-underwater-zombie-Nazi-soldiers terrorizes stranded tourists staying at

Shogun Assassin

Story of a proud samurai named Lone Wolf who served his Shogun master well as the Official Decapitator, until the fateful day when the aging Shogun turned against him. Extremely violent, with record-breaking body counts. Edited from two other movies in a Japanese series called *Sword of Vengeance*; a tour de force of the cutting room. 🦴🦴🌀

1980 (R) 89m/C *JP* Tomisaburo Wakayama; **D:** Kenji Misumi, Robert Houston. **VHS, Beta, LV** *MCA, OM*

Shriek of the Mutilated

An anthropological expedition made up of swinging collegiate hipsters journey to on a deserted island on the Pacific coast in search of bigfoot. It turns into an expedition into horror as a savage beast kills the members of the group one by one. Are the bloody murders the work of the legendary beast? A plodding monster version of *Ten Little Indians* with chunks of sex and gore frequently thrown in for spice, some of which goes way over the top. Findlay, with his wife Roberta, were also responsible for a series of extremely twisted roughies in the mid-to-late '60s, including *Touch of Her Flesh, Curse of Her Flesh,* and *A Thousand Pleasures.* 🦴🦴

1974 (R) 85m/C Alan Brock, Jennifer Stock, Michael Harris; **D:** Michael Findlay. **VHS, Beta $59.98** *LIV, SNC*

Sid & Nancy

The tragic, brutal, true love story of The Sex Pistols' Sid Vicious and American groupie Nancy Spungen, from the director of *Repo Man.* Remarkable lead performances in a very dark story that manages to be funny at times. Depressing but engrossing; no appreciation of punk music or sympathy for the self-destructive way of life is required. Oldman and Webb are superb. Music by Joe Strummer, the Pogues, and Pray for Rain. 🦴🦴🦴🌀

1986 (R) 111m/C Gary Oldman, Chloe Webb, Debbie Bishop, David Hayman; **D:** Alex Cox. National Society of Film Critics Awards '86: Best Actress (Webb). **VHS, Beta, LV $14.95** *MVD, SUE, NLC*

The Sinister Invasion

A turn-of-the-century scientist (Karloff) discovers a death ray. Aliens, who would like a closer peek at what makes it work, use a sex-fiend's body to do so. One of Karloff's last four films, made simultaneously in Mexico. Excruciating. **AKA:** Alien Terror; The Incredible Invasion. 🦴

1968 95m/C *MX* Boris Karloff, Enrique Guzman, Jack Hill; **D:** Juan Ibanez. **VHS, Beta $49.95** *SNC*

The Sinister Urge

Vice cops Duncan and Moore search for the murderer of three women and the porno racket connected to the murders. Seems the disturbed slayer (Dino Fantini, who looks like Frankie Avalon gone psycho) is unbalanced because he's been looking at pictures of ladies in their underwear. As one cop says: "Show me a crime, and I'll show you the dirty picture that caused it." Was this meant to be taken seriously at the time? Fontaine is hilarious as the bitchy vicelord. Carl Anthony plays a nudie film director who wistfully remembers when he "used to make good movies." Wood himself appears in a fight scene with Conrad Brooks filmed in 1956 (for the unfinished *Hellborn*). A must-see for Wood fans. **AKA:** The Young and the Immortal; Hellborn. 🦴🦴🌀

1960 82m/B Kenne Duncan, Duke Moore, Jean Fontaine; **D:** Edward D. Wood Jr. **VHS, Beta $59.98** *AOV, SNC*

Sixteen Candles

Over a decade after hitting the theatres, *Sixteen Candles* is still popular—reaching near cult status among generation X-ers. Hilarious comedy of errors features the pouty Ringwald as an awkward teen who's been dreaming of her sixteenth birthday and getting a date with the high school hunk in the red Porsche. However, the rush of her sister's wedding causes everyone to forget her birthday and throws her life into chaos. Hughes may not be critically acclaimed, but his movies are so popular they nearly take on a life of their own. Ringwald and Hall are especially charming as the angst ridden teens, encountering one trauma after another. Hall, before he became a buffed bodybuilder (take a look at him in *Edward Scissorhands),* plays one of the best geeks ever seen on film. Together with his two computer nerd buds (one played by a very young John Cusack), he has a number of hysterical scenes

THE HOUND SALUTES: FRED OLEN RAY

Tight Said Fred

Hollywood is no place to brag that mine is smaller than yours. Yet when it comes to budgets, nobody can beat writer/director/producer Fred Olen Ray's largesse for chintziness.

Ray boasts that he made his first black-and-white 16mm feature *The Brain Leeches* for all of $298 (adding that it's the worst thing ever on celluloid and will never be formally released). Ray's official debut, shot in Florida in 1978, was a zombiethon known as *The Alien Dead*. It cost $12,000--$2,000 of which went to the guest-star, an elderly Buster Crabbe.

Ray subsequently moved from his native Florida to Los Angeles to realize his dream; not to be the next Spielberg but inherit Roger Corman's crown for tight-fisted penny-pinching combined with commercial success in exploitation quickies. Ray named his own little company American Independent Productions--or A.I.P., in tribute to the famous American International Productions that released many a Corman title.

While his budgets have "skyrocketed" to as much as $150,000 per movie, Ray still manages to deliver his audience (usually a direct-to-video one) a saleable mix of recognizable actors, established scream queens, iffy but generous F/X scenes, gore and/or sex, and a gonzo sense of humor likely to surface at any time, in productions like *Bad Girls From Mars*, *Beverly Hills Vamp*, *Armed Response*, and *Hollywood Chainsaw Hookers*. This last title was a return to form for Ray, having been shot in 35mm in five days for a mere $23,000.

Not surprisingly, a young Ray contacted Edward D. Wood, Jr., not long before the infamous cult filmmaker died. Ray wanted Wood to author a script called *Beach Blanket Bloodbath*.

Ray has also cameoed onscreen for other filmmakers, especially in Roger Corman productions. Recently Fred Olen Ray invaded the

continued...

as he tries to get Ringwald to notice him and tries to hang out with the cool crowd. Gedde Watanabe is also pretty damn funny as exchange student Long Duk Dong (yes it's semiblatant ethnic stereotyping, but the Donger is a sympathetic character and has some of the best lines of the movie). 🐾🐾🐾

1984 (PG) 93m/C Molly Ringwald, Justin Henry, Michael Schoeffling, Haviland Morris, Gedde Watanabe, Anthony Michael Hall, Paul Dooley, Carlin Glynn, Blanche Baker, Edward Andrews, Carole Cook, Max Showalter, Liane Curtis, John Cusack, Joan Cusack, Brian Doyle-Murray, Jami Gertz, Cinnamon Idles, Zelda Rubinstein; **D:** John Hughes; **W:** John Hughes; **M:** Ira Newborn. **VHS, Beta, LV $19.95** *MCA*

Sizzle Beach U.S.A.

Three young women who want a shot at becoming famous travel to Los Angeles and play on the beach with little budget and no particular purpose. Also available in an unrated version. Although released in 1986, this was made in 1974. Kevin Costner's film debut. 🐾

1986 (R) 90m/C Terry Congie, Leslie Brander, Roselyn Royce, Kevin Costner; **D:** Richard Brander. **VHS, Beta, LV $19.95** *VMK*

Slap Shot

"A freewheeling mixture of slapstick humor and grisly physical violence," cheerfully brags the cassette box, without irony. The deadpan satire body-checks the world of professional hockey with the story of the Chiefs, a failing rust-belt team ready to go under. Aging coach Newman pragmatically initiates his players in the art of provoking gratuitous brawls on the ice to win the hearts and minds of bloodthirsty fans. Considered shocking for its unprecedented profanity (which is almost average by today's standards) and raunch, the comedy makes a serious point about how honest, if rowdy, athletes turn into thugs to appease the lowest common denominator. Question is, did this film's audience get the message? The goonish Hanson Brothers must be seen to be believed. A celluloid fave of hockey fans—naturally. 🐾🐾🐾

1977 (R) 123m/C Paul Newman, Michael Ontkean, Jennifer Warren, Lindsay Crouse, Jerry Houser, Melinda Dillon, Strother Martin; **D:** George Roy Hill; **M:** Elmer Bernstein. **VHS, Beta, LV $14.98** *MCA*

Slave Girls from Beyond Infinity

Bikini-clad space babes escape prison ship only to crash on maniac's planet in s-f remake of *The Most Dangerous Game*. This version is pure exploitation, with the women's wardrobe consisting entirely of slinky dresses, lingerie, and underwear. Special effects range from fair to good, and the pace is brisk. Fun spoof of '50s movies takes nothing, including itself, seriously. Star Cayton also works as Elizabeth Kaitan. 🦴🦴🦴

1987 80m/C Elizabeth Cayton, Cindy Beal, Brinke Stevens; **D:** Ken Dixon. **VHS, Beta, LV** *NO*

Slaves in Bondage

Young, country girls are lured into the big city and initiated into a life of ill repute in this exploitation classic produced by J.D. Kendis. After her fiancee is framed for a crime, pretty young Dona Lee (Andre) learns the hard way that the manicure shop where she works is actually a front for a vice racket. Villain Oakman (who does everything but twirl his mustache) lends money to the girls in the shop, then extorts them into prostitution. Spends a lot more time on mainstream gangster material than most roadshow pictures, but it makes up for it with a wild tour of the brothel, complete with a catfight, spankings, and other 'racy' shenanigans. A must for camp fans of the 1930s. Oakman was a former silent star (*Peck's Bad Boy*, *The Spoilers*), apparently down on his luck. Director Elmer Clifton (*Assassin of Youth*) got his start acting in silent pictures, notably with D. W. Griffith. He fell ill while working on *Not Wanted*, giving Ida Lupino her change to direct. 🦴🦴▷

1937 ?m/C Lona Andre, Wheeler Oakman; **D:** Elmer Clifton. **VHS $16.95** *SNC*

Sleazemania: The Special Edition

A tantalizing array of smutty, exploitative and just plain bad film clips, from directors like auteur provocateur Edward D. Wood, Jr., and including *Orgy of the Dead*, *The Flesh Merchants*, *The Smut Peddler*, and the like. 🦴🦴

1972 18m/B VHS, Beta $9.95 *RHI*

Sleazemania Strikes Back

Another crapulous collection of trashy trailers from the sultan of cinema du scum, Johnny Legend. Plenty of blood, broads, and bad manners on display from the likes of Ed Wood (*The Violent Years*, *The Sinister Urge*, and "lost" bondage footage added to *Glen or Glenda?*) and Herschell Gordon Lewis (*Suburban Roulette*, *This Stuff'll Kill Ya!* with a young Larry Drake). The usual taboos are addressed as well: drugs (*Assassin of Youth*), sex (*Mr. Mari's Girls*, *The Girl From S.I.N.*), and gore (*Invasion of the Blood Farmers*), plus stripper loops, intermission promos, and a clip from a non-existent Fred Olen Ray movies, *Beach Blanket Bloodbath* with Forrest J. Ackerman, all hyped with breathlessly hysterical ballyhoo ("SEE: THE SMUT RACKET LAID BARE!"). Indispensable artifacts for serious students of sleaze. 🦴🦴🦴

1985 60m/C VHS, Beta $39.95 *RHI*

Sleazemania III: The Good, the Bad & the Sleazy

Yet another compilation of the cheapest, funniest, and scurviest moments from grade-Z horror and nudie films. Not as outrageous as the previous two, but you can still get heapin' helpings of '40s sex madness like *Child Bride* and *Test Tube Babies*; '50s trash madness like *Dance Hall Racket* with Lenny Bruce, or *Pin-Down Girls*; and '60s sexploitationers *Office Love-In* and *Motel Confidential*. The drawback, however, is Rhino's Elvira-like attempts at humor by renaming trailers with already hilarious titles (*Blaze Starr Goes Nudist* becomes *This Little Girl Had Knockers!*), as well as a misleading bogus trailer (*Mondo Psycho*) with scenes culled from the entire series. Fine for Sleazemania completists; a fourth volume is also available. 🦴🦴▷

1986 90m/B VHS, Beta $39.95 *RHI*

Slithis

Slithis, a seagoing creature spawned from nuclear waste, terrorizes the canals and marinas of Venice, California. Cheap, thinly scripted throwback to atomic-mutant flicks of the '50s, with token social commentary (nobody minds

literary world, with a book on tacky, low-budget cinema called *The New Poverty Row*. In 1994 he delivered a cheesy-looking anthology of pulp horror/sci-fi tales called *Fred Olen Ray's Weird Menace*. The initials of Ray's publishing company once again spelled out A-I-P.

In *The New Poverty Row* Ray writes that he plans to "branch out into bigger-budgeted productions and leave the shaky, ramshackle structure we have built behind." A shaky, ramshackle structure without Fred Olen Ray around it just wouldn't be the same.

ol' Slithis as long as he just kills homeless people), toxic performances, and a dumb twist ending. Fancy monster suit, though. *AKA:* Spawn of the Slithis. ♪

1978 (PG) 86m/C Alan Blanchard, Judy Motulsky; *D:* Stephen Traxler; *W:* Stephen Traxler. **VHS, Beta $19.95** *MED*

The Slumber Party Massacre

Influential but unredeemed sex 'n' slash exploitation about a psycho with a power drill terrorizing some of the ripest-looking high school girls you'll ever see. Some effective satiric touches (mainly in the editing), but this gained its cult rep through political correctness; presence of a female director and a female scriptwriter (author Rita Mae Brown, of all people) won interpretations as some kind of feminist statement. If so, statement is "You've sunk a long way, baby." Sequels, *Slumber Party Massacre 2, Slumber Party Massacre 3*, and *Hard to Die* are, respectively, comic, serious, and who cares? ♪♪

1982 (R) 84m/C Michele Michaels, Robin Stille, Andre Honore, Michael Villela, Debra Deliso, Gina Mari, Brinke Stevens; *D:* Amy Holden Jones, Aaron Lipstadt; *W:* Rita Mae Brown. **VHS, Beta $14.98** *SUE*

Small Change

Pudgy, timid Desmouceaux and scruffy, neglected Goldman lead a whole pack of heart-warming tykes. A realistically and tenderly portrayed testament to the great director's belief in childhood as a "state of grace." Criticized for sentimentality, *Small Change* followed Truffaut's gloomy *The Story of Adele H.* Steven Spielberg suggested the English translation of "L'Argent de Poche." In French with English subtitles. ♪♪♪♪

1976 (PG) 104m/C *FR* Geory Desmouceaux, Philippe Goldman, Jean-Francois Stevenin, Chantal Mercier, Claudio Deluca, Frank Deluca, Richard Golfier, Laurent Devlaeminck, Francis Devlaeminck; *D:* Francois Truffaut; *W:* Suzanne Schiffman. National Board of Review Awards '76: 5 Best Foreign Films of the Year. **VHS, Beta, LV $19.99** *MGM, FCT, INJ*

Smile

The Candidate meets *Invasion of the Body Snatchers*. While his Stepford robo-wife and the Santa Rosa, California, townspeople prepare for the Young American Miss beauty pageant, neglected husband Nicholas Pryor becomes increasingly disillusioned by it all. Naturally, everyone thinks something is wrong with him. Michael Ritchie's unjustly neglected satire is a small-town echo of Robert Altman's *Nashville,* which was released the same year. In one of his best roles, Bruce Dern stars as true believer Big Bob Freelander, a mobile home salesperson and pageant judge. In a dramatic departure, Barbara Feldon breaks out of her Agent 99 persona as Pryor's wife, who puts the pageant and her "girls" above her marriage. Geoffrey Lewis (Juliette's dad) is the cost-cutting pageant organizer. The contestants (who engage in some dirty tricks that would be the envy of any political campaign) include Annette O'Toole and Melanie Griffith. Michael Kidd is smug perfection as a once-celebrated choreographer in a career slump. Titos Vandis, the drink-sneaking custodian, was the owner of Daisy, the sheep that stole Gene Wilder's heart in Woody Allen's *Everything You Always Wanted to Know About Sex....* May not win any points for congeniality, but a real winner. ♪♪♪♪

1975 (PG) 113m/C Bruce Dern, Barbara Feldon, Michael Kidd, Nicholas Pryor, Geoffrey Lewis, Colleen Camp, Joan Prather, Annette O'Toole, Melanie Griffith, Denise Nickerson, Michael Kidd, Titos Vandis; *D:* Michael Ritchie; *W:* Jerry Belson. **VHS, Beta, LV $19.95** *MGM*

Smokey Bites the Dust

Car-smashing gag-fest about a sheriff's daughter kidnapped by her smitten beau. Near-plotless and literally unoriginal: lifted footage from several other Corman-produced flicks, a technique that can aptly be called garbage picking. 🦴

1981 (PG) 87m/C Janet Julian, Jimmy McNichol, Patrick Campbell, Kari Lizer, John Blythe Barrymore Jr.; **D:** Charles B. Griffith; **W:** Max Apple. **VHS, Beta** **$19.98** *NLC*

Snow White and the Three Stooges

Explain this if you can. The aging Stooges, late in their careers, sub for the Seven Dwarfs as the peasant miners who discover and protect Snow White. She's played by champion figure-skater Carol Heiss, and much of her screen time is devoted to elaborate ice ballets that re-enact the fairy tale on a mirrorlike surface, photographed in glorious color—and grinding the plot to a halt. Alas, see any Stooge feature but this one. For all the slapstick comics' efforts to fill in, the names "Dopey" and "Sleepy" still come to mind. *AKA:* Snow White and the Three Clowns. 🦴

1961 107m/C Moe Howard, Curly Howard, Larry Fine, Carol Heiss, Patricia Medina; **D:** Walter Lang. **VHS, Beta $14.98** *FOX, FCT*

Solaris

With this the USSR tried to eclipse *2001: A Space Odyssey* in terms of cerebral science-fiction. Some critics thought they succeeded. You may disagree now that the lumbering effort is available on tape. Adapted from a Stanislaw Lem novel, it depicts a dilapidated space lab orbiting the planet Solaris, whose ocean, a vast fluid "brain," materializes the stir-crazy cosmonauts' obsessions—usually morose ex-girlfriends. Talk, talk, talk, minimal special effects. In Russian with English subtitles. In a two-cassette package, with a letterbox format preserving Tarkovsky's widescreen compositions. 🦴🦴

1972 167m/C *RU* Donatas Banionis, Natalya Bondarchuk; **D:** Andrei Tarkovsky; **M:** Eduard Artemyev. Nominations: Cannes Film Festival '72: Best Film. **VHS, LV $79.95** *FXL, FCT, INJ*

Something Weird

This flick opens with a murder, sex, and an accidental death and mutilation right off the bat...and the lover of camp is hooked. Wonderfully cheap story of Mitch, who is accidentally electrocuted in the face—which, if you've ever wondered, makes you look like you have Silly Putty stuck to your face and somehow gives you mind-reading abilities. Mitch, who was quite the stud muffin before the accident, is propositioned by a wicked witch of the west wannabe to become her lover in exchange for the return of his pretty face. He is at first hesitant ("Become your lover? Why, that's a laugh...you're even uglier than I am!") but his vanity wins out, and a bizarre love rectangle ensues. Overacted (and oddly underacted at the same time); the acting and costumes remind the Hound of his high-school play. The cheesiest fx (flashing colored lights and other pseudo-psychedelic tricks) and great background music, reminiscent of *Lost in Space* and *Mission: Impossible* (on a budget). Some versions of the tape include an intro by Joe Bob Briggs. 🦴🦴▷

1968 80m/C Tony McCabe, Elizabeth Lee, William Brooker, Mudite Arums, Taed Heil, Lawrence Wood, Larry Wellington, Roy Colodi, Jeffrey Allen, Stan Dale, Richard Nilsson, Carolyn Smith, Norm Lenet, Louis Newman, Dick Gaffield, Janet Charlton, Lee Ahsmann, Roger Papsch, Daniel Carrington; **D:** Herschell Gordon Lewis; **W:** James F. Hurley. **VHS, Beta** **$29.95** *VMK, VDM, TWE*

Something Wild

One minute you're living your every-day, suburban life, the next you're on some twisted ride with a beautiful woman and a psychotic criminal. Such is the predicament Charlie Driggs (Daniels) finds himself in when he accepts a ride from Lulu (Griffith) in this slightly twisted comedy from Jonathan Demme. Figuring it's time he had a walk on the wild side, mild-mannered Charlie lets Lulu have her way, accompanying her to her hometown and posing as her husband at her high school reunion. Hey, the sex is good and nobody is getting hurt, right? In fact, button-downed Charlie is having the time of his life—until Ray shows up. Lulu's ex-boyfriend and recent parolee, Ray (played by Liotta, with all the gusto he usually brings to his nutso charac-

Melanie
Griffiths and
Jeff Daniels
look fairly tame
in *Something
Wild*.

ters) most definitely wants his little woman back. Will Charlie give her up? Will Lulu dump Charlie? Will Ray hurt everyone? The plot keeps you guessing until the very end, as layers of personality and lies are peeled back from each character. Sharp-edged comedy turns to explosive violence, with lots of changes of pace in-between. Look for cameos from filmmakers John Waters and John Sayles. 🦴🦴🦴

1986 (R) 113m/C Jeff Daniels, Melanie Griffith, Ray Liotta, Margaret Colin, Tracey Walter, Dana Peru, Jack Gilpin, Su Tissue, Kenneth Utt, Sister Carol East; *Cameos:* John Sayles, John Waters; *D:* Jonathan Demme; *W:* E. Max Frye; *M:* Laurie Anderson, Rosemary Paul, John Cale. Edgar Allan Poe Awards '86: Best Screenplay. **VHS, Beta, LV $19.99** *HBO*

Son of Godzilla

The second of Godzilla's "south seas" pictures (after *Godzilla Vs. the Sea Monster*), this one concerns the adventures of a group of scientists trying to control weather conditions on a tropical island. Their lives are threatened when their experiments hatch the title infant,

drawing the unwelcome attention of the adult monster and some gigantic insects as well. It's refreshing to see Godzilla marching among the waving palms instead of smashing cities, and no doubt less expensive for the producers. While Godzilla and his young ward (dubbed "Minya" in Japan) look awful in this entry, and the juvenile aspect of the baby's antics are slightly annoying, this is nevertheless a solidly paced and plotted sci-fi adventure, with good performances, memorable music, and some genuinely touching moments. Minya would return to tug at our heartstrings in *Destroy All Monsters* and *Godzilla's Revenge* before retiring from the screen forever. *AKA:* Gojira no Musuko. 🦴🦴🦴

1966 86m/C JP Akira Kubo, Beverly Maeda, Tadao Takashima, Akihiko Hirata, Kenji Sahara; *D:* Jun Fukuda; *W:* Shinichi Sekizawa, Kazue Shiba; *M:* Masaru Sato. **VHS, Beta $19.95** *PSM, HHT, DVT*

Son of Ingagi

A lonely ape-man Ingreena (Zack Williams), supposedly created by the experiments of a female mad scientist, breaks loose and kidnaps a newlywed bride. Early all-black horror film from the story "House of Horror" by star Spencer Williams, later in TV's *Amos 'n' Andy*. Williams was one of the leading actors of "race pictures" of the '30s and '40s, writing, directing, and producing several of them, including the hits *The Blood of Jesus* (1941) and *Go Down Death* (1944). He can also be seen in a trio of westerns starring blues singer turned musical cowboy Herbert Jeffries. The title is a take off from the successful early mondo movie *Ingagi*, which had phony scenes of apes abducting topless starlets. Although race movies were made in every genre, strangely, this is one of very few black-cast horror films. 🦴🦴

1940 70m/B Zack Williams, Laura Bowman, Alfred Grant, Spencer Williams Jr.; **D:** Richard C. Kahn; **W:** Spencer Williams Jr. **VHS $19.98** *NOS, SNC, MLB*

Sonny Boy

A psychopathic couple (Smith and Carradine!) adopt a young boy whose parents they've killed. The lock him away like a beast and train him to do their bidding, which includes murder. This white-trash version of Tarzan, with the family of degenerates (which resembles the Sawyers of *Texas Chainsaw Massacre* fame) replacing the tribe of Great Apes, fails to satisfy. When our savage "hero," raised like a fighting pitbull to an almost superhuman physical level, makes his escape for adventures in the nearby community, it seems as if all the action had been cut out of the movie. We see him under attack, hunted by local rednecks, but we cut away just as the expected mayhem is about to start. After showing no hesitation in showing earlier scenes of violence and torture, this failure on the part of Carroll to include the level of excitement that he's built up to is all that stands in the way of the creation of a boldly original new film hero. Psycho specialists Smith and Dourif deliver their usual high-grade wretchedness, while Carradine has the weirdest role of his career, playing what is either a woman or a transvestite. 🦴🦴

1987 (R) 96m/C *IT* David Carradine, Paul Smith, Brad Dourif, Conrad Janis, Sydney Lassick, Savina Gersak, Alexandra Powers, Steve Carlisle, Michael Griffin; **D:** Robert Martin Carroll; **W:** Graeme Whifler. **VHS, Beta, LV $89.98** *TWE, MED*

Sorority Babes in the Slimeball Bowl-A-Rama

Nerds and bountiful sorority babes invade a bowling alley as part of a typical initiation stunt. There they meet up with a street-smart kid (scream queen Linnea Quigley, who actually makes it to the final reel) and a grumpy little imp who's been trapped in a trophy for decades. Naturally the imp, like a demented genie, backfires on all his promises all great rewards. Half the kids get possessed by the little demon, who then sets them against their comrades. Plenty of sex, violence, and twisted humor highlight this trashy gem. Lensed in only a few days, this DeCoteau quickie is worthy of inclusion in the library of anybody who would by this book. Regretfully, the director also handled distribution and wasn't all that quality conscious when selecting a firm for the video transfer. If you can find it uncut on cable, tape it. 🦴🦴🦴🦴

1987 (R) 80m/C Linnea Quigley, Brinke Stevens, Andras Jones, John Wildman; **D:** David DeCoteau; **M:** Guy Moon. **Beta, LV** *NO*

Sorority Girl

Camp classic in which beautiful college co-ed Cabot is presented as a malicious rich kid involved in everything from petty fights to blackmail to arson, supposedly striking back at her self-centered mother. Her poor meek roommate is treated like a slave and even spanked. Eventually, her devious manipulations catch up with her. Cheap melodrama production from the Corman factory; regular Dick Miller gets the rare chance to play the romantic lead. However, Cabot is excellent. She would go on to star in Corman's classic *The Wasp Woman*. Remade for cable TV in 1994. 🦴🦴

1957 60m/B Susan Cabot, Dick Miller, Barbara Crane, June Kennedy, Fay Baker, Jeane Wood; **D:** Roger Corman. **VHS $9.95** *NLC*

Soul Vengeance

Black man is jailed and brutalized for crime he didn't commit and wants revenge. In prison, a voodoo priest teaches him many secrets of black magic. When released, he uses his magic abilities for revenge—forcing his enemies

wives to have sex with him under hypnosis, and even strangling a man with his extended penis! Many afros and platform shoes. Vintage blaxploitation weirdness from Fanaka, who would move on to the *Penitentiary* series. *AKA:* Welcome Home Brother Charles. 🦴🦴

1975 91m/C Marlo Monte, Reatha Grey, Stan Kamber, Tiffany Peters, Ven Bigelow, Jake Carter; ***D:*** Jamaa Fanaka; ***W:*** Jamaa Fanaka. **VHS $39.95** *XVC*

Soylent Green

In the 21st Century, hard-boiled police detective Heston investigates a murder and discovers a deep secret. Its view of the future and of human nature is relentlessly dark. Unlike the source novel *Make Room! Make Room!* by Harry Harrison, it concentrates more on the detective story and less on the horribly overcrowded future society, where everyone has to fight for space, water, and the government-distributed "soylent" wafers of the title. Robinson's final film ironically gives him an awesome send-off. During the early '70s, Biblical epic star Heston's hit *Planet of the Apes*

gave him a new career in sci-fi pictures such as this one, *Omega Man, Earthquake,* and *Solar Crisis.* Fleischer, the son of animation legend Max Fleischer, also gave us *20,000 Leagues Under the Sea, Fantastic Voyage,* and *The Boston Strangler.* 🦴🦴🦴

1973 (PG) 95m/C Charlton Heston, Leigh Taylor-Young, Chuck Connors, Joseph Cotten, Edward G. Robinson, Brock Peters; ***D:*** Richard Fleischer. **VHS, Beta, LV $19.98** *MGM*

Space Monster

Really bad, low-budget flick with a rubber monster and a climactic crash into a "sea of monsters" which is really a fish tank full of crabs. Ultra cheap production with handed down cast and props. *AKA:* First Woman Into Space; Voyage Beyond the Sun. 🦴🦴

1964 ?m/B VHS $20 *SMW*

Spider Baby

A tasteless horror-comedy about a chauffeur who takes care of the psychotic Merrie family, who all inherit the trait of madness. Much like the Addams family, but with a much wickeder edge to the humor, as the Merries actually practice murder and cannibalism (which probably wouldn't go over too well on network television). Jill Banner is the spider of the title, who playfully seduces her victims into her web, and then stings them. An underappreciated little gem from Hill, who went on to direct a string of great exploitation films. Theme song sung by Lon Chaney. *AKA:* The Liver Eaters; Spider Baby, or the Maddest Story Ever Told; Cannibal Orgy, or the Maddest Story Ever Told. 🎵🎵🎵◻

1964 86m/B Lon Chaney Jr., Mantan Moreland, Carol Ohmart, Sid Haig; *D:* Jack Hill. **VHS, Beta $19.98** *SNC, AOV, MLB*

Spirit of '76

A '70s spoof that sports David Cassidy AND Leif Garrett, with such tunes as "Kung Fu Fighting" and "A Fifth of Beethoven," and helped along by both Carl and Rob Reiner, should just keep on truckin' but this one bought the stairway to hell. It's Bill & Ted's not-so-excellent adventure meets *Spaceballs* as a 22nd-century David Cassidy trips back in time with uptight Olivia D'Abo to reclaim the original constitution; they miss the mark by 200 years, landing in the height of the disco era. The flick has all the right elements: halter tops, eight tracks, platforms, and a proliferation of bicentennial bunk, but the movie misses the mark as well. Worth a look anyway just the hear the music, a discriminating selection of disco, along with a theme song by The Dickies, who did for off-beat movie theme songs what the Bee Gees did for every other type of movie theme song. 🎵◻

1991 (PG-13) 82m/C David Cassidy, Olivia D'Abo, Leif Garrett, Geoff Hoyle, Jeff McDonald, Steve McDonald, Liam O'Brien, Barbara Bain, Julie Brown, Thomas Chong, Iron Eyes Cody, Don Novello, Carl Reiner, Rob Reiner, Moon Zappa; *D:* Lucas Reiner; *W:* Lucas Reiner. **VHS, LV** *NO*

Splatter University

Grade-F Troma release about a deranged killer who slaughters and mutilates comely coeds at a local college. Abysmally motiveless killing

and rock-bottom acting; flunks even as camp. Also available in a 78-minute "R" rated version. **WOOF!**

1984 79m/C Francine Forbes, Dick Biel, Cathy Lacommaro, Ric Randing, Dan Eaton; *D:* Richard W. Haines. **VHS, Beta $69.98** *LIV, VES*

Squeeze Play

New Jersey's Troma Studio has proudly made its name synonymous with bad movies, and it certainly lives down to that reputation with this one. The age-old battle of the sexes is replayed on the softball diamond as the Beaverettes challenge the Beavers, the Serta mattress factory team, to see who's best. It's all about as subtle as a wet T-shirt contest with lots of rude and obnoxious bathroom humor. Not exactly *Masterpiece Theatre* material. 🎵🎵

1979 92m/C Al Corley, Jenni Hetrick, Jim Metzler; *D:* Lloyd Samuel Weil Kaufman. **VHS, Beta, LV** *NO*

Star Trek: The Motion Picture

After numerous false starts, TV's most famous cancelled show lumbered onto the screen, reuniting the original cast and piling on visual whammies Desilu Productions could never had imagined, pushing the budget to a then-stratospheric $47 million. For all the effort there's only meagre payoff as the Enterprise intercepts a vast alien special effect on a collision course with Earth. Trekkers will notice a certain resemblance to the much cheaper (and more satisfying) program episode "The Changeling." Not a happy experience for Gene Roddenberry, who was mostly frozen out of the production. The ponderous spectacle loses its widescreen impact on video, but gains 12 additional minutes of previously unseen footage that help flesh out the characters. Laserdisc edition offers the film in letterbox format. 🎵🎵◻

1980 (G) 143m/C William Shatner, Leonard Nimoy, DeForest Kelley, James Doohan, Stephen Collins, Persis Khambatta, Nichelle Nichols, Walter Koenig, George Takei; *D:* Robert Wise; *M:* Jerry Goldsmith. Nominations: Academy Awards '79: Best Art Direction/Set Decoration, Best Original Score. **VHS, Beta, LV $14.95** *PAR*

"It's life, Captain, but not life as we know it."
--Mr. Spock (Leonard Nimoy) in *Star Trek: The Motion Picture.*

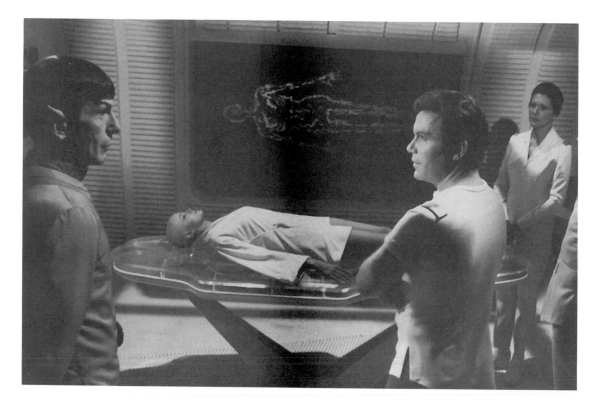

Star Trek 2: The Wrath of Khan

After mixed audience response and Klingon-like critical reaction to *Star Trek: The Motion Picture,* this streamlined, modestly budgeted follow up put the franchise back on track. Taking up a narrative thread from the 1967 TV episode "Space Seed" (also on video from Paramount) an aging Admiral James T. Kirk and the Enterprise crew are lured into a trap by Khan Noonian Singh, genetically engineered super-foe out for revenge. Script warmly evokes the comradely "classic Trek" feeling that brought the show its legions of fans. To cover all bets, the filmmakers concocted Mr. Spock's alleged death, which would have either made a heroic finale to the whole Star Trek mythos, or led straight into the next sequel. Guess which happened. Originally subtitled "The Vengeance of Khan," with a name change was forced by the competing *Star Wars* sequel *Revenge of the Jedi*—which subsequently became *Return of the Jedi* anyway.

Under any name, *Star Trek 2* can be seen in widescreen format on laserdisc. ♫ ♫ ♫

1982 (PG) 113m/C William Shatner, Leonard Nimoy, Ricardo Montalban, DeForest Kelley, Nichelle Nichols, James Doohan, George Takei, Walter Koenig, Kirstie Alley, Merritt Butrick, Paul Winfield; **D:** Nicholas Meyer; **M:** James Horner. **VHS, Beta, LV, 8mm $14.95** *PAR*

Star Trek 3: The Search for Spock

Captain Kirk hijacks his old starship and takes the faithful bridge crew on an unauthorized mission to the Genesis Planet spawned in *Star Trek II,* to discover whether Mr. Spock still lives. Klingons threaten, as usual. Nimoy's impressive feature directorial debut suffers from being a middle chapter in the Star Trek saga, but pulls off the considerable feat of making Spock's fate truly moving, not just a cliffhanger gimmick. Noteworthy also as the final voyage of the original USS Enterprise. Curtis took over Kirstie Alley's role from the previous film.

Laserdisc edition carries the film in wide-screen format. 🐾🐾🐾

1984 (PG) 105m/C William Shatner, Leonard Nimoy, DeForest Kelley, James Doohan, George Takei, Walter Koenig, Mark Lenard, Robin Curtis, Merritt Butrick, Christopher Lloyd, Judith Anderson, John Larroquette, James B. Sikking, Nichelle Nichols, Cathie Shirriff, Miguel Ferrer, Grace Lee Whitney; **D:** Leonard Nimoy; **M:** James Horner. **VHS, Beta, LV, 8mm $14.95** *PAR*

Star Trek 4:
The Voyage Home

With an alien probe threatening Earth unless a signal is received from vanished humpback whales, Kirk and the gang use the captured Klingon vessel from *Star Trek III* to go back in time (to the 1980s, conveniently) and save the great mammals from future extinction. More comedic than other Trek features, with hilarious moments of culture shock mixed with soft-edged action; the already disoriented Spock is particularly funny as he impersonates a hippie acid casualty and tries to learn '80s lingo via gratuitous swearing. The Hound officially protests the watery climax, however—if you look closely, you can see the emotionless Vulcan laughing himself silly! Can be seen in widescreen format on laserdisc. Also available as part of Paramount's "director's series," in which actor-turned-filmmaker Nimoy discusses various special effects aspects in the making of the film. 🐾🐾🐾

1986 (PG) 119m/C William Shatner, DeForest Kelley, Catherine Hicks, James Doohan, Nichelle Nichols, George Takei, Walter Koenig, Mark Lenard, Leonard Nimoy; **D:** Leonard Nimoy; **W:** Nicholas Meyer. Nominations: Academy Awards '86: Best Cinematography, Best Sound, Best Original Score. **VHS, Beta, LV, 8mm $14.95** *PAR*

Star Trek 5:
The Final Frontier

A renegade Vulcan religious fanatic seizes control of the Enterprise and takes it on a dangerous journey to the mythic center of the universe. Shatner's big-action directorial debut (he also co-wrote the script) is a slipshod and unsatisfying entry bearing a resemblance to *The Way to Eden,* one of the weakest episodes in the classic series—remember, the one with the space hippies? Pretentiously pseudo-theo-logical, with melodramatic revelations about the characters (and, for that matter, the structure of the universe) that previous installments and the TV show never even hinted at. Even the Klingons are wimps! Available in widescreen format on laserdisc. 🐾▷

1989 (PG) 107m/C William Shatner, Leonard Nimoy, DeForest Kelley, James Doohan, Laurence Luckinbill, Walter Koenig, George Takei, Nichelle Nichols, David Warner; **D:** William Shatner; **W:** William Shatner; **M:** Jerry Goldsmith. **VHS, Beta, LV, 8mm $14.95** *PAR*

Star Trek 6:
The Undiscovered Country

Rousing chapter in the Star Trek movie series, released just after Gene Roddenberry's death, was—as always—supposed to be the last one, no kidding, honest. The Federation and the Klingon Empire are finally preparing a peace summit but Captain (demoted from Admiral) Kirk has doubts about the true intentions of his longtime enemies. When a Klingon ambassador is murdered, Kirk stands accused of the misdeed. Spock and the crew must uncover the real perpetrator, while Kirk and McCoy face the Klingon criminal justice system. Breathless plotting, great F/X and an ironic sense of humor are never far off (Spock's latest Old Vulcan Proverb: "Only Nixon could go to China"). Autograph hounds take note: the classic Trek cast literally sign their own credits at the close. 🐾🐾🐾

1991 (PG) 110m/C William Shatner, Leonard Nimoy, DeForest Kelley, James Doohan, George Takei, Walter Koenig, Nichelle Nichols, Christopher Plummer, Kim Cattrall, Iman, David Warner, Mark Lenard, Grace Lee Whitney, Brock Peters, Kurtwood Smith, Rosana De Soto, John Schuck, Michael Dorn; **D:** Nicholas Meyer; **W:** Nicholas Meyer, Denny Martin; **M:** Cliff Eidelman. Nominations: Academy Awards '91: Best Makeup. **VHS, Beta, CD-I $14.95** *PAR*

Star Trek: Generations

The sci-fi phenomena continues with the first film spun off from the dearly departed *Star Trek: The Next Generation* TV series. Captain Kirk is propelled into the future thanks to an explosion and manages to hook up with current Enterprise captain, Picard. Of course, just in time to save the galaxy from the latest

S

253

VIDEO SLEEPERS

The incredible growth of the home video market has created a demand for mid- to low-budget entertainment--new titles to fill the shelves of video stores.

Many of those films follow the established patterns of theatrical releases: teen comedies, horror, science-fiction, adventure, serious drama. But the home market has also proven itself to be a particularly fertile field for other genres: action-adventure, erotic thrillers, martial-arts, and even star vehicles. (See "What You See and What You Get," page 60).

The rental side of the business has been most successful in providing a medium for off-beat independent films; those curious "little" movies that are more difficult to categorize. They're the kinds of films that tend to do well at festivals, where the patrons are more open-minded. These movies almost never attract large enough audiences to make wide theatrical distribution financially feasible. On video, the best of them become sleeper hits or cult favorites when word gets around.

In the early days of home video, films like *Repo Man* and *Basket Case* became rental favorites in video stores with virtually no advertising or publicity. More recently, *Apartment Zero*, *The Banker*, and *Hold Me, Thrill Me, Kiss Me* have done the same.

There are no easy ways to separate the wheat from the chaff in the world of low-budget movies. Because there's so little money in the budget for advertising, they show up in video stores every week as unknown quantities. How to tell which new title is going to be the next *Hard-Boiled* and which is another *Hudson Hawk*?

The adventurous videophile simply has to work at it, to search diligently through dozens of unknown movies, to fast forward across dull stretches and then to rewind and replay those wonderful moments of outrageous invention.

After all, isn't that the fun of it?

space loon, the villainous Dr. Soren (McDowell), renegade Klingons, and your basic mysterious space entity. For comic relief, android Data gets an emotion chip. Terrific special effects and yes, Kirk gets a grandiose death scene. The only other original characters to make a (brief) appearance are Scotty and Chekov. ♫♫♫

1994 (PG) 110m/C William Shatner, Patrick Stewart, Malcolm McDowell, Whoopi Goldberg, Jonathon Frakes, Brent Spiner, LeVar Burton, Michael Dorn, Gates McFadden, Marina Sirtis, James Doohan, Walter Koenig, Alan Ruck; *D:* David Carson; *W:* Ronald D. Moore, Brannon Braga; *M:* Dennis McCarthy. **VHS**

Star Wars

First entry Lucas's *Star Wars* trilogy proved to be one of the biggest box-office hits of all time. A young hero, a captured princess, a hot-shot pilot, cute robots, a vile villain, and a heroic and mysterious Jedi knight blend together with marvelous special effects in a fantasy tale about rebel forces engaged in a life or death struggle with the tyrant leaders of the Galactic Empire. Set a new cinematic standard for realistic special effects, making many pre-*Star Wars* effects seem almost laughable in retrospect. Followed by *The Empire Strikes Back* (1980) and *Return of the Jedi* (1983). ♫♫♫♫

1977 (PG) 121m/C Mark Hamill, Carrie Fisher, Harrison Ford, Alec Guinness, Peter Cushing, Kenny Baker, James Earl Jones, David Prowse, Anthony Daniels; *D:* George Lucas; *W:* George Lucas; *M:* John Williams. Academy Awards '77: Best Art Direction/Set Decoration, Best Costume Design, Best Film Editing, Best Sound, Best Visual Effects, Best Original Score; Golden Globe Awards '78: Best Score; Los Angeles Film Critics Association Awards '77: Best Film; National Board of Review Awards '77: 10 Best Films of the Year; People's Choice Awards '78: Best Film; Nominations: Academy Awards '77: Best Director (Lucas), Best Original Screenplay, Best Picture, Best Supporting Actor (Guinness). **VHS, Beta, LV $19.98** *FOX, RDG, HMV*

Start the Revolution Without Me

This switched-at-birth farce focuses on a string of events that nearly averted the French Revolution. It's *Les Miserables* a la Monty Python. Gene Wilder and Donald Sutherland play two sets of twins inadvertently mismatched by a country doctor. (Not an entirely uncommon premise, but done here with the basic imagination and humor lacking in more recent twin movies.) Two of the babies are raised as royalty and become the renowned de Sisi brothers. The other two, raised as peasants, wind up reluctant members of the revolutionary forces. When the two sets cross paths 30 years later, the result is some good old-fashioned silliness set to manic clavier music. Wilder is hilarious as both the sensible-but-cowardly Claude Coupe and the bizarre Philippe de Sisi (who goes horseback riding with a stuffed falcon attached to his arm and acts out elaborate nursey rhyme fantasies with his wife.) Sutherland is particularly funny as Phillipe's more sensitive brother, Pierre, who exclaims "I will be queen!" as they plot to rule France. An equally quirky assortment of characters surrounds the brothers, including Orson Welles as the stoic narrator, the Duke d'Escargot, a doddering, clock-fixated King Louis, and a scheming Queen Marie. The man in the iron mask and a roaming band of monks also make cameo appearances. Worth watching for the abundant puns and clever banter alone. 🦴🦴🦴🦴

1970 (PG) 91m/C Gene Wilder, Donald Sutherland, Orson Welles, Hugh Griffith, Jack MacGowran, Billie Whitelaw, Victor Spinetti, Ewa Aulin; **D:** Bud Yorkin; **M:** John Addison. **VHS, Beta $19.98** *WAR*

Stone Cold

Former overrated pro football "star" Brian Bosworth made his first and (to date) only screen appearance in this ultra-violent guilty-pleasure biker flick. He's an Alabama cop who infiltrates a white supremacist cycle gang led by B-movie vets Henriksen and Forsythe. The last reel—an excessive courtroom shootout—is a real corker. Oodles of graphic violence, paint-peeling profanity, and gratuitous violence make this one high-cholesterol macho cinematic popcorn. 🦴🦴🦴

1991 (R) 91m/C Brian Bosworth, Lance Henriksen, William Forsythe, Arabella Holzbog, Sam McMurray; **D:** Craig R. Baxley. **VHS, Beta, LV, 8mm $64.99** *COL*

Stoogemania

A nerd becomes so obsessed with the Three Stooges that they begin to take over his life

and ruin it. Harmless except as a waste of time. Includes actual Stooge footage including some colorized—but see an old Stooges movie instead. 🦴

1985 95m/C Josh Mostel, Melanie Chartoff, Sid Caesar; **D:** Chuck Workman; **M:** Hummie Mann. **VHS, Beta $19.95** *PAR*

Straight to Hell

This punk spaghetti oat-opera is the piece of unwatchable garbage that destroyed the credibility of director Alex Cox, who had previously scored big with *Repo Man* and *Sid and Nancy*. Upon release, its big drawing card was the appearance of cult figures Grace Jones, Elvis Costello, Joe Strummer, and Jim Jarmusch in cameos. Today the reason for seeing the film is Courtney Love. Sadly, the outing is such an inert piece of failed parody that the temporal celebrity of that rock n' roll widow is not likely to captivate a new audience. 🦴

1987 (R) 86m/C Dennis Hopper, Joe Strummer, Elvis Costello, Grace Jones, Jim Jarmusch, Dick Rude, Courtney Love, Sy Richardson; **D:** Alex Cox. **VHS, Beta** *FOX, OM*

Strait-Jacket

After Crawford is released from an insane asylum where she was sent 20 years for axing her husband and his mistress, mysterious axe murders begin to occur in the neighborhood. Coincidence? Aging axist Crawford is the prime suspect, and even she cannot say for sure who's doing it. Daughter Baker is there to help her adjust. Moderately creepy grade B+ slasher is lifted somewhat by Crawford. Written by Robert Bloch (*Psycho*). Never one to miss a gimmick, director Castle arranged for the distribution of cardboard "bloody axes" to all theatre patrons attending the movie. 🦴🦴🦴

1964 89m/B Joan Crawford, Leif Erickson, Diane Baker, George Kennedy; **D:** William Castle; **W:** Robert Bloch; **M:** Van Alexander. **VHS, Beta $59.95** *COL*

Strange Brew

The screen debut of the SCTV characters Doug & Bob MacKenzie (Thomas and Moranis), the Great White North duo. Using the old "rat-in-the-bottle" scam, the brothers go to extreme lengths to get a free case of beer. Their jour-

"If I didn't have puke breath, I'd kiss you."
--Bob (Rick Moranis) McKenzie in *Strange Brew.*

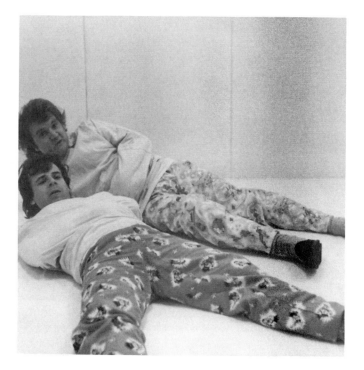

Streetfight

Ralph Bakshi owes more than a little to the Uncle Remus stories in this live action animated look at Black life in America. The film, released under the title *Coonskin,* was attacked as a racist and virtually pulled from theatres after its first week. Bakshi, who works in the tradition of underground cartoonist R. Crumb (his first film was an adaptation of *Fritz the Cat* which creator Crumb disowned), doesn't respect any sacred cows, and African Americans are subject to the same derision he expressed toward Italians in the earlier *Heavy Traffic* (one of the first modern commercial films to be screened at New York's Museum of Modern Art). Although not among his best work, *Streetfight* is worth of look for those interested in pioneering work in the combination of live action and animation that became so popular in the '80s with *Who Framed Roger Rabbit. AKA:* Coonskin. 🎵🎵

1975 (R) 89m/C Philip Michael Thomas, Scatman Crothers; *D:* Ralph Bakshi. **VHS, Beta $29.95** *ACA, WTA*

Rick Moranis and Dave Thomas prove that getting dressed is a lot harder than it sounds in Strange Brew.

ney takes them to mysterious brewery/insane asylum Elsinore Castle, where they meet the megalomaniacal brewmeister (Von Sydow) who has plans to take over the world. He must have a great marketing department. The boys' move to the big screen works thanks to the good-natured beer and hockey humor, sharp set pieces, and quirky dialogue. 🎵🎵🎵

1983 (PG) 91m/C Rick Moranis, Dave Thomas, Max von Sydow, Paul Dooley; *D:* Rick Moranis, Dave Thomas; *W:* Rick Moranis, Dave Thomas, Steve DeJarnatt; *M:* Charles Fox. **VHS, Beta, LV $19.98** *MGM*

Strange Cargo

Convicts escaping from Devil's Island are mystically entranced by a Christ-like fugitive en route to freedom. An odd, pretentious Hollywood fable waiting for a cult following. Gable and Crawford's eighth and final pairing. Adapted by Anita Loos from the book *Not Too Narrow...Not Too Deep* by Richard Sale. 🎵🎵▷

1940 105m/B Clark Gable, Joan Crawford, Ian Hunter, Peter Lorre, Paul Lukas, Albert Dekker, J. Edward Bromberg, Eduardo Ciannelli, Frederick Worlock; *D:* Frank Borzage. **VHS, Beta $19.98** *MGM*

Strictly Ballroom

Offbeat, cheerfully tacky dance/romance amusingly turns every movie cliche slightly askew. Scott (Mercurio) has been in training for the Pan-Pacific ballroom championships since the age of six. While talented, he also refuses to follow convention and scandalizes the stuffy dance establishment with his new steps. When his longtime partner leaves him, Scott takes up with a love-struck beginner (Morice), with some surprises of her own. Ballet dancer Mercurio (in his film debut) is appropriately arrogant yet vulnerable, with Morice as the plain Jane turned steel butterfly. Wonderful supporting cast; great debut for director Luhrmann. 🎵🎵🎵▷

1992 (PG) 94m/C *AU* Paul Mercurio, Tara Morice, Bill Hunter, Pat Thomsen, Barry Otto, Gia Carides, Peter Whitford, John Hannan, Sonia Kruger-Tayler, Kris McQuade, Pip Mushin, Leonie Page, Antonio Vargas, Armonia Benedito; *D:* Baz Luhrmann; *W:* Craig Pearce, Baz Luhrmann; *M:* David Hirshfelder. Australian Film Institute '92: Best Costume Design, Best Director (Luhrmann), Best Film, Best Supporting Actor (Otto), Best Supporting Actress (Thomsen), Best Writing; Nominations: Golden Globe Awards '94: Best Film—Musical/Comedy. **VHS, LV $19.99** *MAX, TOU, BTV*

Stripped to Kill

A female cop goes undercover (figuratively speaking) as a stripper to catch a psycho killing her co-workers. Not-bad entry from Corman and cohorts. The cast is good; the story's fair and the ending is bizarre. The strip scenes are lively and imaginative enough to satisfy fans of that odd little sub-genre, and director Ruben gives the rest of the action has a properly gritty atmosphere. Followed by—you guessed it—*Stripped to Kill II*. Ruben also made the underrated *Streets* and *Poison Ivy*. 🦴🦴▷

1987 (R) 88m/C Kay Lenz, Greg Evigan, Norman Fell; *D:* Katt Shea Ruben; *W:* Katt Shea Ruben, Andy Ruben. **VHS, Beta $79.95** *MGM*

Student Confidential

A Troma-produced spoof of seedy high school youth movies, new and old, involving four students who are led into the world of adult vices by a mysterious millionaire. Badly made and dull. Douglas and Jackson both have brothers named Michael. 🦴

1987 (R) 99m/C Eric Douglas, Marlon Jackson, Susan Scott, Ronee Blakley, Elizabeth Singer; *D:* Richard Horian. **VHS, Beta $79.95** *MED*

The Student Nurses

For the first film produced for his fledgling New World Pictures studio, Roger Corman took a turn for the nurse with this trend-setting exploitation film. As per formula, it's got liberal doses of sex, nudity, and violence, but also a sense of humor and feminist sympathies for its four heroines. One falls in love with a terminally ill patient, another becomes involved with radicals, and so on. Directed by Stephanie Rothman in three weeks for $150,000, this flick grossed more than a million dollars, which led to the inevitable *Private Duty Nurses*, *Night Call Nurses* (directed by Jonathan Kaplan), *Candy Stripe Nurses,* and even *Student Teachers* and *Summer School Teachers*. Rothman also directed a young Tom Selleck in *Terminal Island* ("...where we dump our human garbage." the ads proclaimed) and *The Velvet Vampire*. 🦴🦴

1970 (R) 89m/C Elaine Giftos, Karen Carlson, Brioni Farrell, Barbara Leigh, Reni Santoni, Richard Rust, Lawrence Casey, Darrell Larson, Paul Camen, Richard Stahl, Scottie MacGregor, Pepe Serna; *D:* Stephanie Rothman. **VHS, Beta $59.98** *NLC*

The Stuff

A strange discovery in the Arctic gives rise to this comic horror flick about a marshmallow-like substance marketed as a desert. Folks become addicted to The Stuff, which takes control of their minds and bodies. An industrial spy (Michael Moriarty) teams up with militant right wingers (led by Paul Sorvino) to put a stop to the evil white fluff. This strange combination of *The Blob* and *Invasion of the Body Snatchers* is surprisingly fun. Some neat effects and a hilarious performance by Garrett Morris (of the original Prime Time Players on TV's *Saturday Night Live*) as a Famous Amos-like cookie mogul whose hands are lethal weapons, highlight this offbeat film. Also look for a cameo by Danny Aiello. Amusing social satire from prolific producer/director/writer Larry Cohen. 🦴🦴🦴

1985 (R) 93m/C Michael Moriarty, Andrea Marcovicci, Garrett Morris, Paul Sorvino, Danny Aiello, Brooke Adams; *D:* Larry Cohen; *W:* Larry Cohen. **VHS, Beta $9.95** *NWV, STE*

Suburban Roulette

"Adults only" feature from splattermaster Lewis caters to the prurient. Groovy themes like wife swapping and other very daring subjects. Totally '60s. Presented as part of Joe Bob Brigg's "Sleaziest Movies in the History of the World" series. 🦴

1967 91m/C *D:* Herschell Gordon Lewis. **VHS $19.98** *VTR*

Suddenly

Crazed gunman Sinatra holds a family hostage in the hick town of Suddenly, California, as part of a plot to kill the president, who's passing through town. Tense thriller is a good display for Sinatra's acting talent; unfortunately, it is also hard to find because Sinatra forced United Artists to take it out of distribution after hearing that Kennedy assassin Lee Harvey Oswald had watched *Suddenly* only days before November 22, 1963. Really, Ol' Blue Eyes should have stuck with

onds—while his plots became much more light-hearted and cartoonish. ♫♫♫♪
1975 105m/C Shari Eubank, Charles Napier; **D:** Russ Meyer; **W:** Russ Meyer. **VHS $59.99** *RMF*

The Sure Thing

Calling a movie "sweet and funny" usually conjures up visions of syrupy romance and cloying performances, but damn it, sweet and funny is the best way to describe this flick. This was director Rob Reiner's follow-up to *This Is Spinal Tap,* and his second straight box office winner. Frustrated by his failure to lose his virginity at his own school, John Cusack decides it's time to visit his buddy in California, where, he is assured, a Sure Thing awaits him in a bikini. He ends up travelling across country with Alison, the Queen of the Anal Retentive Prisses. You can probably guess the rest—boy and girl bicker, suffer various trials and tribulations, and then fall madly in love— but great performances overcome the predictability. Cusack is great as Gib, your basic nice guy trying to get lucky, while Daphne Zuniga is absolutely perfect as the high-strung Alison. Tim Robbins and Lisa Jane Persky have hilarious cameos as a happy couple from hell, while Anthony Edwards is a long way from the operating rooms of *ER* as Cusack's California connection. Nice companion piece to *Say Anything,* which Cusack later starred in. ♫♫♫
1985 (PG-13) 94m/C John Cusack, Daphne Zuniga, Anthony Edwards, Boyd Gaines, Lisa Jane Persky, Viveca Lindfors, Nicolette Sheridan, Tim Robbins; **D:** Rob Reiner; **W:** Jonathan Roberts. **VHS, Beta, LV, 8mm $14.95** *COL, SUE*

Not having access to their boards, the girls make the best of it in *Surf Nazis Must Die.*

making top-notch thrillers like this one, instead of degenerating into the world's greatest lounge singer. ♫♫♫♪
1954 75m/B Frank Sinatra, Sterling Hayden, James Gleason, Nancy Gates, Paul Frees; **D:** Lewis Allen. **VHS, Beta $16.95** *SNC, NOS, VEC*

Supervixens

True to Meyer's low-budget exploitation film canon, this wild tale is filled with characteristic Amazons, sex, and violence. A gas station attendant is framed for the grisly murder of his girlfriend and hustles out of town, meeting a succession of well-endowed women during his travels. A tasteless storyline and incoherent writing add to the fun. Recommended (for adults). Meyer cranked the cutting speed of his editing up a notch here, and he only got faster from this point on, rarely holding on a shot for more than a few sec-

Surf Nazis Must Die

A piece of deliberate camp from the Troma team, about a group of psychotic neo-Nazi surfers taking over the beaches of California in the wake of a devastating earthquake (not shown). Who will stand up to Adolf, the lead bully in leather, and his sexy moll Eva? When they kill a nice young black man, the victim's motorcycle-ridin' mama scours the sand with revenge on her mind. Tongue-in-cheek, tasteless, and deliberately stupid, but put together with a little panache on a meagre budget. ♫♫

1987 83m/C Barry Brenner, Gail Neely, Michael Sonye, Dawn Wildsmith, Tom Shell, Bobbie Bresee; **D:** Peter George; **W:** John Ayre. **VHS, Beta $19.98** *MED, VTR*

Suspiria

An American dancer (Harper) enters a weird Berlin ballet academy and finds they teach more than movement as bodies begin piling up. She discovers that the school is a front for an ancient coven of black witches, and hides one of the Three Mothers of evil legend. Once again, Argento uses the device of a hidden detail in the opening providing a vital clue. Sometimes weak plot is aided by great, gory special effects, fine photography, terrific (and loud) music, and a nightmarish opening sequence that you won't soon forget. Bennet, unable to escape the *Dark Shadows* of her past, plays the vicious headmistress, and Kier is a blind music teacher who becomes a target for demonic forces. One of Argento's best, and a rare journey into the blatantly supernatural. Also available in unrated version. 🦴🦴🦴

1977 (R) 92m/C *IT* Jessica Harper, Joan Bennett, Alida Valli, Udo Kier; **D:** Dario Argento; **W:** Dario Argento. **VHS, Beta, LV** *HHE, QVD*

Swamp Women

Ads shrieking "Flaming Passions! Weird Adventures!" as four escaped women convicts known as the "Nardo Gang" chase after a stash of stolen diamonds in the Louisiana bayou. Complications arise when the gang encounters "Touch" Connors (from Corman's *Five Guns West*) and his fiancee, who is later eaten by a stock footage alligator; hard-bitten B-queens Windsor (Kubrick's *The Killing*) and Garland (*It Conquered the World*, TV's *My Three Sons*) duke it out to win the captive he-man's charms. High camp swamp romp shot on location in Louisiana by Roger Corman for New Orleans drive-in moguls the Woolner Brothers (who later distributed numerous sword-and-sandal epics). Filmed in Wide Vision. *AKA:* Swamp Diamonds; Cruel Swamp. 🦴🦴🦴

1955 73m/C Mike Connors, Marie Windsor, Beverly Garland, Carole Mathews, Susan Cummings; **D:** Roger Corman. **VHS $16.95** *SNC*

Sweet Movie

South African tycoon purchases a virgin bride whom he sexually exploits. More soft core sex masquerading as Marxist dialectic from exploitation king Dusan Makavejev, who has spent his entire professional life trying to break into Capitalist cinema, all the while feigning superiority to it. In the '80s, his dream came true with the mediocre comedies *Montenegro* (which sexually exploited poor Susan Anspach) and *The Coca Cola Kid* (which launched the career of talentless sexpot Greta Scacchi). Makavejev is a case study in the hypocrisy of so many perverts who conceal their misanthropy under the banner of radical politics. 🦴

1975 120m/C *YU* Carole Laure, Pierre Clementi, Sami Frey; **D:** Dusan Makavejev; **W:** Dusan Makavejev; **M:** Manos Hadjidakis. **VHS, Beta $79.95** *FCT, MOV*

Tales from the Gimli Hospital

"It all happened in the Gimli we no longer know...." Calling all "Eraserheads." Winnipeg hyphenate (writer-director-editor-photographer) Guy Maddin's first feature is positively Lynchian in its dreamlike and grotesque black and white imagery. Like *Eraserhead*, it defies description, but here goes: As their mother lies dissipated in her hospital bed, a nurse relates to her children some Gimlian folk history, mostly about Einar the Lonely and his friend, Gunnar, who are among the epidemic victims taxing the makeshift turn-of-the-century facility and its staff. An instant midnight movie classic. There are no doubt many out there who "get" this. Watch them closely. Very closely. 🦴🦴🦴

1988 72m/B Kyle McCulloch, Michael Gottli; **D:** Guy Maddin. **VHS $79.95** *KIV, FCT*

Tales of Terror

Three tales of terror based on stories by Edgar Allan Poe. Price stars in all three segments and is excellent as the bitter and resentful husband in *Morella*. Although similar to several roles which found a haunted Price staring at his dead wife's portrait, here he found more depth and subtlety than in the others, often making

John Cusack, Tim
Robbins, Junior
Walker, and Sam
Moore discuss
eveningwear in
Tapeheads.

**"You
talkin'
to me?"**

--Robert DeNiro in
Taxi Driver.

the most of his angular form and features. This film also provides an ample demonstration of his acting range, when compared to his camp clowning in the *Black Cat* segment. Lorre, who is the real star of this segment, has a fine time ad libbing his way through his role, as he usually did at this stage of his career. In *The Case of M. Valdemar,* Rathbone and Price have a fine chemistry in their scenes together. It's a pity they came together so rarely. Art direction by Daniel Haller works miracles with the small budget. The letdown here is with Corman's direction, which too often relies on lame camera tricks, and sometimes seems to be stretching the material, despite the short story format. *AKA:* Poe's Tales of Terror. 🎵🎵♭

1962 90m/C Vincent Price, Peter Lorre, Basil Rathbone, Debra Paget, Joyce Jameson; *D:* Roger Corman; *W:* Richard Matheson; *M:* Les Baxter. **VHS, Beta** *MLB, ORI*

Tapeheads

Security guards Josh (Robbins) and Ivan (Cusack) try to break into the rock video business,

with bizarre results. The boys start out doing funerals, living wills, and local commercials before getting their break doing videos on spec for Mo Fuzz (Cornelius) and becoming involved, accidently, in a presidential candidate's sex scandal. Sam Moore and Junior Walker add great music and more than a little class to the proceedings as The Swanky Modes, the boyhood idols of Josh and Ivan. Hilarious videos, numerous music industry cameos and in-jokes, and a great soundtrack make repeated viewings a necessity. Watch for former *Dallas* vixen Crosby as a femme fatale. 🎵🎵♭

1989 (R) 93m/C John Cusack, Tim Robbins, Mary Crosby, Connie Stevens, Susan Tyrrell, Lyle Alzado, Don Cornelius, Katy Boyer, Doug McClure, Clu Gulager, Jessica Walter, Sam Moore, Junior Walker; *Cameos:* Stiv Bators, Martha Quinn, Ted Nugent, Weird Al Yankovic; *D:* Bill Fishman. **VHS, Beta, LV** *NO*

Targets

Bogdanovich's suspenseful directorial debut is still his best film, in some ways. An aging horror film star (Karloff) plans his retirement, convinced that real life is too scary for his films to have an audience. A mad sniper—loosely based on Charles Whitman, the Texas tower killer—murders his family and several other randomly chosen victims, ending his senseless attack a drive-in movie where "fiction" and "reality" collide. Bogdanovich also plays the ambitious young director hoping to persuade the older star to be in his film. His script, a trenchant and prescient comment on gun violence, was essentially "re-created" by veteran film maker Sam Fuller. Some prints still have anti-gun prologue, which was added after Robert Kennedy's assassination. 🦴🦴🦴

1969 (PG) 90m/C Boris Karloff, James Brown, Tim O'Kelly; **D:** Peter Bogdanovich. **VHS, Beta $44.95** PAR

Tarzan, the Ape Man

This remake is enough to make Cheetah roll over in his grave. Director Derek tries to cash in on his wife's bod in a slow moving, actionless retelling of the classic Burroughs' tale.

Most of what we get are people traipsing through the jungle interspersed with Bo looking for the occasional excuse to disrobe. The thrill-packed(?) conclusion has Bo kidnapped by natives and rescued by the ape man in predictable fashion. With no script, no laughs, no action, and only Bo's skin shots to carry it, this baby sinks faster than a torpedoed rowboat. Give it half a point for the closing credits which are far more entertaining than the film. Don't rent this; borrow it from some crazed Bo fan and fast forward directly to this part. You'll save yourself a couple of hours of boredom. 🦴

1981 (R) 112m/C Bo Derek, Richard Harris, John Phillip Law, Miles O'Keeffe; **D:** John Derek. **VHS, Beta, LV $79.95** MGM

Taxi Driver

Some see this tale of urban alienation as glorification of vigilante violence; others see it as a brilliant portrait of madness. In either case, De Niro's Travis Bickle has become an archetypal figure of the 1970s; "God's lonely

We'd tell Mr. DeNiro what a fine job he did in *Taxi Driver,* but we're NOT talking to him.

THE HOUND SALUTES: GENE RODDENBERRY

Star Trek Sick? Try Undiscovered Roddenberry

Gene Roddenberry, a WWII fighter pilot and LAPD patrolman-turned writer/producer, will always remain identified with the prime-time TV series he unveiled in 1966, *Star Trek*. It opened to generally scornful reviews and never amounted to much in the ratings. Yet even before its cancellation, the five-year mission of the USS Enterprise had a tractor-beam lock onto a loyal cult of fans. Viewer rallies and write-in campaigns kept the original show on the air for a third season, until the final episode aired in June 1969.

Roddenberry died in 1991, having lived to see *Star Trek* revived, first in paperback novels, then as a Saturday-morning animated series, then as a series of blockbuster motion pictures, and finally as *Star Trek: The Next Generation*, the most successful syndicated TV program of its day. All 79 classic Trek episodes, plus a recreation of the unbroadcast, original pilot "The Cage," are now available on home video-- joined, of course, by the movies, the cartoons, and both new series *Next Generation* and *Deep Space Nine*.

Roddenberry completists might want to check out a few other projects associated--or sometimes disassociated--with the man. Commentators dispute how much overall influence Gene Roddenberry exerted over the western series he helped script, *Have Gun, Will Travel*, but two episodes are preserved on tape to set fans arguing whether quirky saddle hero Paladin (Richard Boone) is a run-up to Kirk, Spock, or McCoy.

The cassettes *Planet Earth* and *Strange New World* are two consecutive remakes of the proposed '70s TV-series pilot *Genesis II*. Essential storyline in all is a scientist awakening after two centuries in suspended animation, to an Earth drastically changed after a nuclear holocaust. The hero wanders from one scrambled society to another trying to get post-apocalyptic civilization back on track.

continued...

man," as he calls himself. Key scenes—"Are you talking to me?"—have become touchstones. Bernard Herrmann's haunted score (alto sax solos by Tom Scott) is one of his best. The film is dedicated to him. The laserdisc version is slightly longer, with commentary by Scorsese and screenwriter Paul Schrader, storyboards, complete screenplay, and Scorsese's production photos. The film's central point— that in a complex world there's a fine line between hero and villain—is often overlooked. 𝄞𝄞𝄞𝄞

1976 (R) 112m/C Robert De Niro, Jodie Foster, Harvey Keitel, Cybill Shepherd, Peter Boyle, Albert Brooks; **D:** Martin Scorsese; **W:** Paul Schrader. British Academy Awards '76: Best Supporting Actress (Foster); Cannes Film Festival '76: Best Film; Los Angeles Film Critics Association Awards '76: Best Actor (De Niro); New York Film Critics Awards '76: Best Actor (De Niro); National Society of Film Critics Awards '76: Best Actor (De Niro), Best Director (Scorsese), Best Supporting Actress (Foster); Nominations: Academy Awards '76: Best Actor (De Niro), Best Picture, Best Supporting Actress (Foster), Best Original Score. **VHS, Beta, LV, 8mm $14.95** *COL*

Teenage Caveman

After *I Was a Teenage Werewolf* and *I Was a Teenage Frankenstein*, intrepid American International Pictures further mined the youth market with—what else—*Teenage Caveman*. Robert Vaughn stars as "The Boy," (he would later become "The Man"...from U.N.C.L.E., that is), who defies his elders by venturing from his clan's desolate terrain into the forbidden land beyond, where he encounters the dreaded God That Gives Death With Its Touches. If you have seen *Planet of the Apes*, you can anticipate the surprise ending. Villain Frank deKova is more fondly remembered as Chief Wild Eagle of the Hekawi tribe on TV's *FTroop*. Look for Jonathan Haze (*Little Shop of Horrors*) as one of the tribespeople. Roger Corman directed in ten days on a $70,000 budget. He certainly got his money's worth out of Beach Dickerson, who was utilized for four roles, including that of a bear. Corman even recruited him to play the drum in the funeral scene for one of his characters. Dinosaur footage courtesy of the film, *One Million B.C.* **AKA:** Out of the Darkness; Prehistoric World. 𝄞𝄞

1958 66m/B Robert Vaughn, Darrah Marshall, Leslie Bradley, Frank De Kova; **D:** Roger Corman. **VHS $9.95** *COL*

Teenage Gang Debs

Straight out of Brooklyn comes this story of the guys who run with gangs and the girls who love them. Conti stars as Terry, the new chick from Manhattan that moves into Rebel territory and quickly becomes top girl in the gang. Like a Lady Macbeth in leather, she pulls the strings of the top man, inciting plenty of fights, murder, torture, and just plain trouble, until the gang debs get wise. From the days when gang leaders were not afraid to wear cardigan sweaters. Lots of authentic scenery and atmosphere, much of it due to the cooperation of the Queensboro Motorcycle Club. Not exactly *West Side Story*, although one scene tries to promote a new dance craze. ♫♫

1966 77m/B Diana Conti, Linda Gale, Eileen Scott, Sandra Kane, Robin Nolan, Linda Cambi, Sue McManus, Geri Tyler, Joey Naudic, John Batis, Tom Yourk, Thomas Andrisano, George Winship, Doug Mitchell, Tom Eldred, Frank Spinella, Alec Primrose, Gene Marrin, Lyn Kennedy, Janet Banzet; **D:** Sande Johnsen; **W:** Hy Cahl. **VHS $23.00** *SMW, TPV*

Teenage Mother

A Swedish sex education teacher comes to Claremont High to teach "anatomical biology," and poisons the minds of the local high school kids. Naturally one becomes pregnant and has to try to trick her boyfriend Tony into marrying her. Basically an update of roadshow features like *Mom and Dad* and *Because of Eve,* and one of the last pictures sold via its birth-of-a-baby footage. Maintains the movie tradition of hiring 30 year olds to play high school students; as it is, most of them would be unconvincing trying to play anything. There's some misleading racing footage during the titles—there is no racing during the rest of the film. More wonderfully awful stuff from the director of the repellent *Girl on a Chain Gang,* which appears during the drive-in scene. Gross later produced the outrageous *I Drink Your Blood.* ♫♫▷

1967 78m/C Arlene Sue Farber, Frederick Riccio, Julie Ange, Howard Le May, George Peters; **D:** Jerry Gross. **VHS, Beta $16.95** *SNC, TPV*

Teenage Strangler

"Budding young teenie-boppers were this Bluebeard's prey!" A homicidal "lipstick killer" terrorizes a high school in this incredible home-made obscurity filmed in Huntington, WV. The murders are pinned on Jimmy, a good kid who runs with the Fastbacks gang, but of course, there's a ridiculous surprise ending. *Teen-Age Strangler,* how do I love thee? Let me count the ways: for your vain attempts at suspense; the wildly overwrought performances of your cast; your 20 m.p.h. car chases and drag races (filmed in day-for-night Ed Wood-Vision!); for "Yipes Stripes," your Hootenanny in Hell musical number; but most of all, for Jimmy's weepy little brother Mikey, certainly the most gender-confused individual in the history of American film. Played on a double bill with producer Herschell Gordon Lewis's *A Taste of Blood* in 1967. That's exploitation legend Ron Ormond (*Mesa of the Lost Women, Untamed Mistress*) as the creepy school janitor. Cool, twangy soundtrack by Danny Dean and the Daredevils. ♫♫♫

1964 61m/C Bill A. Bloom, Jo Canterbury, John Ensign; **D:** Bill Posner. **VHS, Beta $16.95** *SNC, SMW*

Teenagers from Outer Space

Low-budget sci-fi effort finds extraterrestrials visiting earth to conquer it and find humans to feed their monstrous livestock, the Gargons (they're really big lobster shadows.) Graeff is the rebellious teenage soldier who doesn't dig the master plan, and runs off to avoid execution for his unbecoming behavior. Naturally he's taken in as a boarder by the first old man (Ed Wood player Dunn) with a teenage granddaughter (Anderson) that he meets. One of his nasty ex-comrades goes after him, pausing only to kill innocent bystanders with his skeleton-making zap gun. So cheaply made and melodramatic that it's good for a laugh. Auteur Graeff actually managed to sell this to Warner Brothers. *AKA:* The Gargon Terror. ♫♫▷

1959 86m/B Tom Graeff, Dawn Anderson, Harvey B. Dunn, Bryant Grant, Tom Lockyear; **D:** Tom Graeff. **VHS $16.95** *SNC*

"**The world belongs to the young. Make way for them. Let them have it. I am an anachronism.**"
--Boris Karloff in *Targets.*

Story continued...

That no *Genesis II* conventions now visit Holiday Inns indicates the poor reception this material had; still, it would be nice to see the original version and compare. But *Genesis II* (1973) remains commercially unavailable on tape, as do a few other, more intriguing Roddenberry projects:

The Questor Tapes--A 1974 TV pilot about a manlike robot with superhuman abilities but no memories of his origin, who sets out to search for his creator. Reportedly Roddenberry had concocted it with Leonard Nimoy in mind, but the feature pilot aired with Robert Foxworth in the role of Questor.

Spectre--A 1977 TV movie with Robert Culp as an occult investigator and Gig Young a skeptical sideckick who discover that an English aristocrat (John Hurt) harbors a demonic secret. Majel Barret, *Star Trek*'s Nurse Chapel and Mrs. Roddenberry in real life, cameos as a spellcasting housekeeper.

Pretty Maids All in a Row--Roddenberry was unhappy with the way this 1971 dark sex comedy (directed by Roger Vadim) turned out, though among critics it has a cult reputation. High-school guidance counselor Rock Hudson regularly seduces teenage girls, then casually kills them if they threaten to tell all. James Doohan, *Star Trek*'s engineer Scotty, has a supporting part.

Tentacles

Cheesy Italian version of *Jaws* lacking only the suspense and cogent storytelling. Huston slums as the investigator charged with finding the octopus gone mad, while Fonda collects check and makes a quick exit. Hopkins is in charge of the killer whales that save the day. You'll cheer when Winters is devoured by sea pest. From the director of an *Exorcist* rip-off, *Beyond the Door* (that's not a recommendation). ♫

1977 (PG) 90m/C *IT* John Huston, Shelley Winters, Bo Hopkins, Henry Fonda, Cesare Danova; **D:** Oliver Hellman. **VHS, Beta $59.98** *LIV, VES*

10th Victim

Sci-fi cult film set in the 21st century has Mastroianni and Andress pursuing one another in a futuristic society where legalized murder is used as the means of population control. Intriguing movie where Andress kills with a double-barreled bra, the characters hang out at the Club Masoch, and comic books are considered literature. Based on "The Seventh Victim" by Robert Sheckley. *AKA:* La Decima Vittima; La Dixieme Victime. ♫♫♫

1965 92m/C *IT* Ursula Andress, Marcello Mastroianni, Elsa Martinelli, Salvo Randone, Massimo Serato; **D:** Elio Petri; **W:** Tonino Guerra. **VHS, Beta $14.95** *SUE, NLC*

The Terror

A lieutenant in Napoleon's army (Nicholson) chases a lovely maiden (Knight, then Mrs. Nicholson) and finds himself trapped in a creepy castle by a mad baron (Karloff). Movie legend has it that Corman was finishing principal photography on his previous movie *The Raven* a few days early, and the Ernie Banks of film of course decided "Let's make two!" Karloff was quickly convinced to stay on for an extra fee, and the movie was shot in two days while the sets were being torn down around them, improvising plot and dialogue as they went along. Francis Coppola, Dennis Jakob, Monte Hellman, Jack Hill, and even Nicholson shot enough extra footage over the next several months for Corman to piece together a semi-coherent movie. Public domain video prints and transfers vary greatly in quality—beware. *The Terror* was featured as a drive-in attraction showing during Bogdonavich's *Targets*. *AKA:* Lady of the Shadows. ♫♫♪

1963 81m/C Boris Karloff, Jack Nicholson, Sandra Knight; **D:** Roger Corman. **VHS, Beta $19.95** *NOS, SNC, PSM*

Terror in the Haunted House

Filmed in "Psycho-Rama—The Fourth Dimension!", a technique (which was subsequently banned for years) whereby subliminal images and messages were flashed on the screen at crucial points in the movie. The insidious messages that the Rhino people integrated include such plugs as "Rent Rhino Videos every day!" Story centers on a neurotic and annoying Olivia-DeHavilland-wannabe who is plagued by dreams of a "hideous form waiting for her at the top of the stairs" of an old house. When she and her husband leave Switzerland (where she'd been recovering in a sanitarium) to a home they've rented in Florida, to her horror she finds that, you guessed it, the house of her dreams is real. The movie contains a wonderfully '50s scene where she makes a sandwich by placing a slice of olive loaf between two pieces of Wonderbread...which just about sums up this flick. Worth watching—the plot actually isn't too bad if you can get past the melodramatic style of acting. 🦴🦴▷

1958 90m/C Gerald Mohr, Cathy O'Donnell, William Ching; **D:** Harold Daniels. **VHS, Beta $9.95** *RHI, MLB, CCB*

Terror of Tiny Town

Four words: all midget musical western. So what if the plot is fairly average—a bad guy and the good guy who finally teaches him a lesson, with a little music and romance on the side. This was based on a stage show performed by Jed Buell's Midgets. Watchable mainly due to the fact that Newfield plays up the cast's short stature—they walk under saloon doors, ride Shetland ponies, and the six-guns are excessively large. At 63 minutes, considered a little short for a feature. Johnnie Fern sings "Hey, Look Out! (I Want to Make Love to You)," while Curtis and Moray duet on "The Marriage of Jack and Jill," and an ensemble performs "Laugh Your Troubles Away." Curtis later popped up (from the Earth's core) in *Superman and the Mole Men.* The prolific Newfield also directed hundreds of B-movies for poverty row studios, including *Dead Men Walk, I Accuse My Parents, The Monster Maker,* and 93 action-packed westerns. 🦴🦴

1938 65m/B Bill Curtis, Yvonne Moray; **D:** Sam Newfield. **VHS, Beta $16.95** *SNC, NOS, DVT*

Test Tube Babies

A married couple's morals begin to deteriorate as they mourn the fact they can't have a child, and not even a sheer nighty seems to help. The tensions spill over into the rest of their lives, and erupt at a wild party the wife throws while hubby works late. The day is saved, however, when they learn from their kindly doctor (Farrell, who always seemed to be playing either kindly doctors or vicious criminals) about the new artificial insemination process. Amusing, campy propaganda in the vein of *Reefer Madness*—most of the laughs come from the wretched dialogue clumsily delivered by Dube and Thomason as the troubled couple. Rereleased in 1967 as *The Pill* with extra scenes featuring Monica Davis and John Maitland. From the director of *The Flesh Merchants.* **AKA:** Sins of Love. 🦴🦴▷

1948 83m/B Dorothy Dube, Timothy Farrell, William Thomason; **D:** W. Merle Connell. **VHS, Beta $19.95** *GVV, SNC, DVT*

Test Tube Teens from the Year 2000

This is a throwback to the mid-'60s. The opening titles, presented over the silhouette of a naked dancing woman, could have come straight from that era. The fast-forwardable plot concerns the title characters' efforts to go back in time and stop Camella Swales (Fairchild) from banning conventional reproduction. Production designers took their cue from the deliberately cheesy sets and props used on television's *Mystery Science Theater 3000.* Don't miss the apple corer that's glued to the front of the time machine and the white "boots" made of cardboard sleeves over tennis shoes. This, folks, is what low-budget video is all about. **AKA:** Virgin Hunters. 🦴🦴

1993 (R) 74m/C Morgan Fairchild, Ian Abercrombie, Brian Bremer, Christopher Wolf, Michelle Matheson, Sara Suzanne Brown, Don Dowe; **D:** Ellen Cabot; **W:** Kenneth J. Hall; **M:** Reg Powell. **VHS, Beta, LV** *PAR*

The Texas Chainsaw Massacre

The movie that put the "power" in power tools. An idyllic summer afternoon drive becomes a nightmare for a group of young people when they take a wrong turn in the Texas badlands. They end up being terrorized by a family of inbred cannibals, the most menacing of which is a huge, chainsaw-wielding ma-

"I can't take no pleasure in killin'. There's some things you gotta do. Don't mean you gotta like it."
—Jim Siedow in *The Texas Chainsaw Massacre.*

THE HOUND SALUTES: ANDY SIDARIS

Andy and Arlene Sidaris make tongue-in-cheek action/exploitation movies that are the video equivalent of take-out pizza.

They feature flashy locations and sets; silly plots filled with gadgets, explosions, and shoot-outs; flagrant bad acting from stem to stern; attractive young actors and actresses with large, well-tanned chests; and oodles of gratuitous nudity.

Andy Sidaris' career started in television. He worked with series, specials, and live sports, where he won several Emmys. After some film work (the football sequences in Robert Altman's original *M*A*S*H*), Sidaris began creating his own kind of screwball adventures in the '80s and '90s. Recently, he retired from the director's chair, but he continues to produce films with his wife Arlene, and they have turned the creative duties over to sons Christian, who writes, and Drew, who directs. A combination of unpredictability and fast-paced tongue-in-cheek comedy is what makes these films so much fun. Here's a short self-scoring quiz on Cinema Sidaris.

1. When the heroines of *Savage Beach* crash land on a remote Pacific island, they:
(a) Radio for help.
(b) Pay no attention to that man with the samurai sword.
(c) Go skinny-dipping.

2. At the end of *Hard Ticket to Hawaii* the meanest of the villains is:
(a) Shot and speared.
(b) Stabbed and snakebitten.
(c) All of the above.

3. When the fiery Filipino Communist in *Savage Beach* learns that her companion has found a hidden treasure, she:
(a) Sings a rousing chorus of the *Internationale*.
(b) Rededicates herself to the principles of Karl Marx and Vanessa Redgrave.
(c) Says, "My ideology means far more to me than fame and adulation. The good of the party is my reward," and slips off her negligee.

continued...

niac wearing a human-skin mask. Like *Psycho* and *Deranged,* this was inspired by the exploits of real-life killer cannibal Edward Gein. Made with tongue firmly in cheek, this is nevertheless a disturbing and mesmerizing saga of gore, flesh, mayhem, and violence whose reputation has only grown over the years. Future TV star Larroquette (a radio disc jockey at the time) is narrator. Followed by two sequels. ♫♫♫♪
1974 (R) 86m/C Marilyn Burns, Allen Danzinger, Paul A. Partain, William Vail, Teri McMinn, Edwin Neal, Jim Siedow, Gunnar Hansen, John Dugan, Jerry Lorenz; **D:** Tobe Hooper; **W:** Tobe Hooper, Kim Henkel. **VHS, LV $19.98** *MPI*

The Texas Chainsaw Massacre, Part 2

A tasteless, magnified sequel to the notorious 1974 low-budget horror sleeper. The cannibal Sawyer family has somehow survived, and now find themselves on the verge of financial success due to the marketing of their "special recipe" Texas chili. By night, they prowl the back roads in search of fresh meat. When they interrupt one of their victims on the phone with a radio deejay (Williams), she enlists the aid of wacko Ranger Hopper, who tracks them to their bizarre landfill hideout and fights fire with fire. With severed tongue stuffed in cheek, Hooper delivers a gloriously excessive splatter comedy, wallowing in all the buckets of gore that the critics thought they saw in the original. A spine-shaking performance by Hopper, raving and bellowing in a frenzy of holy vengeance. A must for gorehounds and fans of dueling chainsaws. Followed by the uninspired *Leatherface: Texas Chainsaw Massacre III.* ♫♫♫♪
1986 (R) 90m/C Dennis Hopper, Caroline Williams, Bill Johnson, Jim Siedow; **D:** Tobe Hooper. **VHS, Beta, LV $19.95** *MED, VTR*

Theatre of Blood

Critics are unkind to Shakespearian ham Price, and he eliminates them by various Bard-inspired methods with the assistance of his lovely daughter. This top-drawer comedy noire features outstanding performances by both Price and Rigg, who plays his beautiful, but evil, daughter. This is a must film for fans of either star. Contains some deliciously creative murders as Price, bamboozling Scotland Yard at every turn, does in his critics one by one. Perhaps the best of the lot is the pet murder; chef extraordinaire Price cooks up one of the critic's pets, then force feeds it to him. Really, it's too much to swallow. An outstanding horror/comedy classic. 🦴🦴🦴🦴

1973 (R) 104m/C *GB* Vincent Price, Diana Rigg, Ian Hendry, Robert Morley, Dennis Price, Diana Dors, Milo O'Shea; *D:* Douglas Hickox. **VHS, LV $14.95** *MGM*

Them!

A group of mutated giant ants wreak havoc on a New Mexico town. The first of the big-bug movies, far surpassing the rest, this is a classic fun flick. Many effective human touches in the script and lots of neat WWII hardware (flame throwers, Tommy guns, B-24s). Throughout, the focus is more on the characters' reactions to the situation than on the critters themselves. That's fine because these are not particularly convincing and the real point is audiences' fears of the then-new "atomic age." See how many names you can spot among the supporting cast, including Leonard Nimoy. 🦴🦴🦴◁

1954 93m/B James Whitmore, Edmund Gwenn, Fess Parker, James Arness, Onslow Stevens, Jack Perrin; *D:* Gordon Douglas. **VHS, Beta, LV $19.98** *WAR*

There's Nothing Out There

Seven teenagers spend Spring Break at a secluded mountain cabin, anticipating sex and wild times. But one boy, who claims to have seen every horror movie on video, knows the signs of a horror plot just waiting to happen. He's the only one prepared when an idiotic-looked alien frog monster attacks and kills. There's one already-famous scene in which a potential victim swings out of the danger by grabbing the dangling microphone boom at the top of the frame. That's amusing, but in general this no-budget parody of screen schlock is barely better than the dreck it imitates. 🦴

1990 91m/C Craig Peck, Wendy Bednarz, Mark Colver, Bonnie Bowers, John Carhart III, Claudia Flores, Jeff Dachis; *D:* Rolfe Kanefsky; *W:* Rolfe Kanefsky. **VHS, Beta, LV $49.95** *PSM*

They Came from Within

The occupants of a high-rise building go on a sex and violence spree when an aphrodisiac parasite gets loose. The first major film from Canadian horrormeister David Cronenberg is queasy, sleazy, and weird, one of the scariest movies of the 70s. The director's deadpan style eyeballs the mounting hysteria with a biological realism that gives the picture a documentary-like feel. It stands with Don Siegal's *Invasion of the Body Snatchers* as a classic of the "alien invasion of the human body" genre. The picture has a strong anti-smut undertone which Cronenberg developed in his subsequent films like *Rabid,* which featured porn star Marilyn Chambers as a disease-spreading sex vampire, and *Videodrome,* a vision of erotic snuff television that creates brain tumors in the viewer. In the '80s, Cronenberg watered down his biological nightmares for a shot at big time commercial filmmaking. *AKA:* Shivers; The Parasite Murders. 🦴🦴🦴🦴

1975 (R) 87m/C *CA* Paul Hampton, Joe Silver, Lynn Lowry, Barbara Steele; *D:* David Cronenberg; *W:* David Cronenberg. **VHS, Beta $69.98** *LIV, VES*

They Live

A semi-serious science-fiction spoof about a drifter who discovers an alien conspiracy. When the drifter (played quite well by Piper) discovers a pair of glasses used by the aliens, he finds that he can really "see." Turns out that there are not only aliens amongst us but that virtually all media messages are disguised alien propaganda designed to destroy the will of humanity. Soon he joins up with the human underground and becomes the key figure in the fight for freedom. Successfully blends both action and humor, with the advertising business being a prime target. Only in the last fifteen minutes does it break down into a more routine shoot-'em-up, though the final conclusion is appropriate. The tongue-in-cheek screenplay was written by Carpenter under a pseudonym. J.C. also scored the music, which blends in perfectly and sets the tone for most of the film. 🦴🦴🦴

1988 (R) 88m/C Roddy Piper, Keith David, Meg Foster, George Flower, Peter Jason, Raymond St. Jacques, John Lawrence, Sy Richardson, Jason Robards III, Larry Franco; *D:* John Carpenter; *W:* John Carpenter;

"We may be witnessing a Biblical prophecy come true-- the beasts will reign over the earth."
--Edmund Gwenn respects the ants in *Them!*

As video fare, Sidaris flicks are not completely wholesome or nutritious, and they're probably low in fiber. No one would want to make a steady diet of them. But when it's 9:00 Friday night and you're in the mood for something quick and zesty, an Andy Sidaris epic might just fill the bill.

> **"An intelligent carrot--the mind boggles."**
> --Reporter Douglas Spencer in *The Thing*.

> **"This one goes to eleven."**
> --Nigel Tufnel (Christopher Guest) bragging about his amp in *This Is Spinal Tap*.

M: Alan Howarth, John Carpenter. **VHS, Beta, LV** $19.95 *MCA*

They Saved Hitler's Brain

Fanatical Nazi survivors of World War II give eternal life to the brain of their leader in the last hours of the war. Now it's on a Caribbean island of Mandoras giving orders again. The fuhrer looks mighty cranky to be stuck in a pickle jar for all those years. Shot in pieces in the U.S., the Philippines, and elsewhere, with chunks of other footage (shot many years apart) sloppily stuck in to hold the "story" together. Much of it seems to be an unfinished, but nicely shot B-grade adventure film from the early 1950s, while early scenes make no effort to look anything like the rest. Was it an attempt to lure in audiences by fooling them into thinking this was brand new, or was it just plain incompetence? Paiva was also in *Mighty Joe Young, Creature From the Black Lagoon, Revenge of the Creature, The Mole People, Tarantula,* and *Jesse James Meets Frankenstein's Daughter.* Bradley, whose 16mm college features debuted Charleton Heston, also gave us *Dragstrip Riot* and the goofy *12 to the Moon.* *AKA:* Madmen of Mandoras; The Return of Mr. H. 🦴🦴🦴

1964 91m/B Walter Stocker, Audrey Caire, Nestor Paiva, Carlos Rivas, Dani Lynn; *D:* David Bradley. **VHS, Beta, 8mm** $24.95 *VYY*

Thief of Baghdad

Jaffar and away, this dazzling Oscar-winning Technicolor spectacle is one of the best fantasy films ever made. Sabu stars as Abu, the resourceful street thief. Towering Rex Ingram (who played "De Lawd" in the musical *Green Pastures*) is the djinni who reluctantly grants Abu three wishes ("To hear is to obey, little master of the universe"). Conrad Veidt is the evil Jaffar, who covets enchanting princess June Deprez. Truly magical. The magnificent mechanical winged horse, the flying magic carpet, and Sabu's djinni-powered transcontinental flight are the stuff dreams are made of. Even more amazing is how exquisitely seamless this is, despite the participation of six directors and the fact that World War II forced suspension of the production and its relocation from England to Hollywood. 🦴🦴🦴🦴

1940 106m/C Sabu, Conrad Veidt, June Duprez, Rex Ingram; *D:* Tim Whelan, Michael Powell, Ludwig Berger; *M:* Miklos Rozsa. Nominations: Academy Awards '40: Best Color Cinematography, Best Original Score. **VHS, Beta, LV** $14.98 *SUE, MLB, FUS*

The Thing

One of the best of the Cold War allegories and a potent lesson to those who won't eat their vegetables. Sci-fi classic begins with an alien spacecraft embedded in the Artic ice and the creature (Arness as the killer carrot), discovered by a research team. The critter is accidentally thawed and then wreaks havoc, sucking the life from sled dog and scientist alike. It's a giant seed-dispersing vegetable run amuck, unaffected by missing body parts, bullets, or cold. In other words, Big Trouble. Excellent direction—assisted substantially by producer Hawks—and supported by strong performances, sparkling dialogue, and a machine-gun pace. Even more important is the film's atmosphere of frozen claustrophobia and isolation. Available colorized (don't do it). Remade in 1982 and often copied. Loosely based on *Who Goes There?* by John Campbell. *AKA:* The Thing From Another World. 🦴🦴🦴🦴

1951 87m/B James Arness, Kenneth Tobey, Margaret Sheridan, Dewey Martin; *D:* Christian Nyby, Howard Hawks; *W:* Charles Lederer; *M:* Dimitri Tiomkin. **VHS, Beta, LV** $14.98 *MED, TTC, MLB*

Things to Come

Using technology, scientists aim to rebuild the world after a lengthy war, followed by a plague and other unfortunate events. Massey and Scott each play two roles, in different gen-

erations. Startling picture of the world to come, with fine sets and good acting. Easily the biggest science fiction production since *Metropolis.* Menzies' art direction, well represented here, was his real claim to fame, in such films as *Gone With the Wind* and *Thief of Bagdad,* but he is also highly regarded as a director (*Drums in the Deep South, Invaders from Mars*) and producer (*Around the World in 80 Days, Reign of Terror*). Based on an H.G. Wells prophetic story, "The Shape of Things to Come." Many cheap video releases are from very bad prints. 𝄞𝄞𝄞◁

1936 92m/B *GB* Raymond Massey, Ralph Richardson, Cedric Hardwicke, Derrick DeMarney; **D:** William Cameron Menzies. **VHS, Beta $19.95** *NOS, PSM, SNC*

13 Ghosts

A dozen ghosts need another member to round out their ranks. They find four likely candidates to choose from when all-American Zorba family inherits the house inhabited by the ghoulish group. Slight horror-comedy by showman supreme Castle; it's no *Tingler,* but it manages to scare up a few chills. Fun spooks are hard to see but watch close for Emilio the homicidal Italian chef and Shadrach the Great, a headless lion tamer. Most TV prints are missing the three-minute prologue of Castle explaining film's gimmick, "Illusion-O," a technology much like 3-D which allowed the viewing of ghosts only through a special pair of glasses (with a red lens to see the ghosts and a blue to "remove" them). With Margaret Hamilton as a "witchy" housekeeper. 𝄞𝄞𝄞

1960 88m/C Charles Herbert, Jo Morrow, Martin Milner, Rosemary DeCamp, Donald Woods, Margaret Hamilton; **D:** William Castle. **VHS, Beta $9.95** *GKK*

This Is Spinal Tap

Pseudo-rockumentary about heavy-metal band Spinal Tap, profiling their career from "England's loudest band" to an entry in the "where are they now file." Hilarious satire; watch it three or four times to pick up on the more subtle humor. The music (including the Hound's favorite Tap ditty, "Big Bottom") is even really performed by Guest, McKean, and Shearer (with help from R. J. Parnell and David Kaff). Features great cameos, particularly David Letterman's Paul Schaefer as a record promoter, and Billy Crystal and Dana Carvey as mime waiters ("C'mon, don't talk back, huh? Mime is money."). First feature for Reiner, and it's a winner; on a scale of one to ten, this flick rates an "eleven." Included on the tape, after the credits, are Spinal Tap's music video, "Hell Hole," and an ad for their greatest hits album, "Heavy Metal Memories." Followed by *The Return of Spinal Tap* and a follow-up album (*Break Like the Wind*) to the original soundtrack. *AKA:* Spinal Tap. 𝄞𝄞𝄞𝄞

1984 (R) 82m/C Michael McKean, Christopher Guest, Harry Shearer, Tony Hendra, Bruno Kirby, Rob Reiner, June Chadwick, Howard Hesseman, Fran Drescher; *Cameos:* Billy Crystal, Dana Carvey, Ed Begley Jr., Patrick Macnee, Paul Shaffer, Anjelica Huston, Fred Willard; **D:** Rob Reiner; **W:** Michael McKean, Christopher Guest, Harry Shearer. **VHS, Beta, LV, 8mm $14.95** *MVD, SUE, NLC*

Christopher Guest expresses his appreciation for big bottoms in *This Is Spinal Tap.*

This Stuff'll Kill Ya!

A backwoods preacher who believes in free love and moonshining runs into trouble with the locals when a series of gruesome religious

THE HOUND SALUTES: ALAN SMITHEE

Under no spreading chestnut tree/ Alan Smithee stands...

Writer/director Alan Smithee seems to have no trouble finding steady employment in Hollywood--though absolutely nobody wants to hire him, and he's never shown up for work.

"Alan Smithee" is actually a traditional pseudonym, variously spelled Alan/Allen Smithee/Smythee, adopted by numerous members of the Directors Guild and the Screenwriters Guild of America in the case of contractual disputes. Or, simply put, when a scenario or movie sucks so much that the real filmmakers don't want to be associated with it.

The Smithee name applied to film can be taken as a warning--you wouldn't want to wish Smithee's retro-racist spook comedy *Ghost Fever* (actual perpetrator: Lee Madden) on your worst enemy. Smithee's Down Under comedy *The Shrimp on the Barbie* (perp: Michael Gottlieb) hardly enhanced the career of its star Cheech Marin.

But not every Smithee title is as obscure as, for example, 1990's Herschell Gordon Lewis parody *Bloodsucking Pharoahs of Pittsburgh* (perp: Dean Tschetter). When David Lynch's *Dune* broadcast on network TV in a two-part expanded version, with added scenes and a prologue composed of sloppy paintings, outraged auteur Lynch took his trendy name off the special edition. It was replaced by Smithee--and was one of Smithee's better efforts, being easier to comprehend than Lynch's initial theatrical release.

More recently Smithee had the hubris to helm *The Birds II: Land's End*, a lousy made-for-cable-TV sequel that tarred the good name of Alfred Hitchcock's suspense classic about nature on the rampage. Actual perpetrator here was Rick Rosenthal.

At least one movie has intentional fun with Smithee. The otherwise-negligible horror anthology *Terrorgram* (1990) casts character actor Jerry Anderson as Alan Smythee, Hollywood's worst director. Smythee is

continued...

murders are committed. Best known for the famous triple crucifixion scene, but you'll have to suffer a long time through Allen's sermons to get to it. Allen was also in Lewis' *Two Thousand Maniacs* and *Moonshine Mountain*; Sager was also a Lewis' repeat offender. Southern drive-in material from one of the genre's masters. Last film for Holt, who'd been a young cowboy star in the '30s, had a standout role in *Treasure of the Sierra Madre* (with his silent star father Jack in a bit part), and was the complex hero in *The Monster That Challenged the World*. 🦴

1971 (PG) 100m/C Jeffrey Allen, Tim Holt, Gloria King, Ray Sager, Eric Bradly, Terence McCarthy; **D:** Herschell Gordon Lewis; **W:** Herschell Gordon Lewis. **VHS $29.95** *TWE, FRG, TPV*

Thou Shalt Not Kill. . . Except

Sam Raimi hams it up in front of the cameras this time. The *Evil Dead* filmmaker portrays a Manson-style hippie cult leader in '69, whose gory rampage (including "jarting" to death the father of a vacationing family) finally becomes too much for some take-charge vets, led by fellow Detroiter Brian Schulz, just back from Vietnam. The heroes form their own private militia, and send those psycho peacenik freaks (Sam's brother Ted among them) straight to hell with maximum carnage. It would be nice to report that this ugly-looking, reactionary cheapie is a spoof. . .except. Filmmaker Becker went on to do the kinder, gentler *Lunatics: A Love Story*. 🦴🦴 ▷

1987 84m/C Brian Schulz, Robert Rickman, John Manfredi, Tim Quill, Sam Raimi, Cheryl Hansen, Perry Mallette, Theodore (Ted) Raimi, Glenn Barr; **D:** Josh Becker; **W:** Josh Becker, Glenn Barr; **M:** Joseph Loduca. **VHS, Beta $9.99** *PSM*

Three on a Meathook

A young man and his father dwell on an isolated farm. Whenever the boy brings home a female guest, bloodshed quickly follows. It takes forever for junior to realize dad's an ax-murderer. Despite brief bouts of gore, this is neither as graphic or as campy as the title promises. Dull cheapie has gained an unwarranted amount of attention from claims that it's based on the crimes of Ed Gein, the cannibal necrophiliac/counterculture hero whose sickening career inspired screen serial killers in *Psycho, The Texas Chainsaw Massacre,* and *Silence of the Lambs.* Without that link (Mr Gein's genes?) *Three on a Meathook* would barely have make it out of Louisville, Kentucky, where it was filmed. WOOF!

1972 85m/C Charles Kissinger, James Pickett, Sherry Steiner, Carolyn Thompson; *D:* William Girdler; *W:* William Girdler. **VHS, Beta** *NO*

The Three Stooges Meet Hercules

In probably the best of their few feature films from late in their careers, the Three Stooges accidentally activate a time machine and go from Ithaca, New York, to Ithica, ancient Greece, joined by a Clark-Kentish scientist and his girlfriend. There the maiden is kidnapped by Hercules (a bad guy!), and our heroes must use brain and brawn to battle the muscleman. Occasionally inventive spoofing, best appreciated if you remember this came out when the Steve Reeves *Hercules* spectacles were in vogue. 🦴🦴🦴▷

1961 80m/B Moe Howard, Larry Fine, Joe DeRita, Vicki Trickett, Quinn Redeker; *D:* Edward L. Bernds. **VHS, Beta $9.95** *GKK*

The Thrill Killers

Mort "Mad Dog" Click (Flagg) is a thrill killer on his way to meet up with his brother Herbie and two fellow psychos who have just escaped from the insane asylum. Meanwhile, when would-be actor Joe Saxon (Bardo) can't get a job, pampered wife Liz (played by stripper Renay) runs away and ends up at her sister Linda's diner in the hills. They're held up and terrorized by psycho Herbie (T.V. Mikels associate Herb Robins, who would go on to make *The Worm Eaters*) and his two crazy buddies, who've just come from killing a nice young couple (Brandt and Ron Burr). Linda poisons Herb's coffee, a fight breaks out, and Liz runs free—right into the clutches of Mad Dog Click. It all leads to a thrilling climax featuring gunplay, fisticuffs, and a chase between a horse and a motorcycle (30 years before *True Lies*). Another typical straightforward Steckler plotline. Does *Psycho* one better by killing off the protagonist (King) before the opening ti-tles! Hero "Brick Bardo" (who also played one of the policemen) also acted, wrote scripts and porn novels, and recorded rock music under the various names Vin Saxon, Lonnie Lord and his own Ron Haydock. Producers George Morgan and Arch Hall play themselves. Sometimes shown with Hallucinogenic Hypo-Vision—a color prologue announcing the special effect would be shown before the film, and on cue, hooded ushers (and sometimes Flagg himself) would run through the theatre with cardboard axes. One of Steckler's best. *AKA:* The Monsters Are Loose; The Maniacs Are Loose. 🦴🦴🦴▷

1965 82m/C Cash Flagg, Liz Renay, Brick Bardo, Carolyn Brandt, Atlas King; *D:* Ray Dennis Steckler. **VHS, Beta** *NO*

Thunder Road

Mitchum comes home to Tennessee from Korea and takes over the family moonshine business, fighting both mobsters and federal agents. An exciting chase between Mitchum and the feds ends the movie with the appropriate bang. Robert Mitchum not only produced, wrote, and starred in this best of the moonshine-running films, but also wrote the theme song "Whippoorwill" (which later became a radio hit). Mitchum's son, James, made his film debut, and later starred in a similar movie *Moonrunners.* A cult favorite, still shown in many drive-ins around the country. 🦴🦴🦴

1958 (PG) 92m/B Robert Mitchum, Jacques Aubuchon, Gene Barry, Keely Smith, Trevor Bardette, Sandra Knight, Jim Mitchum, Betsy Holt, Frances Koon; *D:* Arthur Ripley; *W:* Robert Mitchum. **VHS, Beta $19.98** *MGM*

Time Bandits

When a knight in armor bursts out of the closet one night, young Kevin (Craig Warnock) knows something is up. The following night, mad dwarves lead him on an adventure through time and across dimensions. The middle part of the film is comparatively weak but the pace picks up in last section when Evil Incarnate (David Warner) shows up. Then the action takes on the logic of a good cartoon. Absolutely anything can happen: Giants rise up out of the sea and

Story continued...

visualized as a diminutive pill-popping tyrant who gets a supernatural punishment for offenses against cinema; he must live out his own sleazoid scripts.

As for the "real" Alan Smithee, his offscreen life may not be colorful enough to warrant a cult following a la Ed Wood, but you can be assured of one thing: anytime the movie business needs his special brand of services, Alan Smithee will be available.

> "**About ten minutes ago I tried to kill a cat with a cabbage.**"
> —Vincent Price in *The Tomb of Ligeia*.

what appears to be real may, without warning, shatter like glass. Monty Python veteran Terry Gilliam went on to direct *Brazil* and *The Fisher King*. 🦴🦴🦴🦴

1981 (PG) 110m/C *GB* John Cleese, Sean Connery, Shelley Duvall, Katherine Helmond, Ian Holm, Michael Palin, Ralph Richardson, Kenny Baker, Peter Vaughan, David Warner; ***D:*** Terry Gilliam; ***W:*** Michael Palin, Terry Gilliam. **VHS, Beta, LV $14.95** *PAR*

The Time Machine

Turn-of-the-century inventor Rod Taylor has "all the time in the world" in George Pal's fantastic science fiction classic based on the novel by H. G. Wells. Testing out his time machine, he zips through two world wars and atomic devastation before coming to rest in the year 802,701. To his horror, he discovers that the human race has been reduced to edible chattel for the green, whip-wielding Morlocks, mutant cannibals who live below ground. Kids will love the fast-forward photography as Taylor tentatively tests out his machine, but the Morlocks can be pretty gross (they decompose when you punch them). Oscar-winning special effects. Before Taylor heads back to the future, he tells his incredible tale to friends Sebastian Cabot (Mr. French on TV's *Family Affair*) and Alan Young (who portrayed Wilbur, owner of the talking horse *Mr. Ed*, of course, of course). 🦴🦴🦴🦴

1960 103m/C Rod Taylor, Yvette Mimieux, Whit Bissell, Sebastian Cabot, Alan Young; ***D:*** George Pal.

Time Trackers

A Roger Corman cheapie about a race through time, from present-day New York to medieval England, to recover a time machine before it alters the course of history. 🦴🦴

1988 (PG) 87m/C Kathleen Beller, Ned Beatty, Will Shriner; ***D:*** Howard R. Cohen. **VHS, Beta $14.95** *MGM*

Tomb of Ligeia

The ghost of a reclusive Verdon Fell's first wife expresses her displeasure when the groom and his new little missus return to the manor from their honeymoon. A Gothic psychological horror story with echoes of *Vertigo*. The fine script by Towne (*Chinatown*), as well as wonderful UK locations, make this last Corman Poe adaptation one of the better ones. Also one of Price's most complex and subtle performances. Shepherd plays both wives. Some scenes were shot on leftover sets from *Becket*. Strangely, Corman's autobiography makes almost no mention of this film. Also available with *The Conqueror Worm* on laserdisc. **AKA:** Tomb of the Cat. 🦴🦴🦴

1964 82m/C *GB* Vincent Price, Elizabeth Shepherd, John Westbrook, Oliver Johnston, Richard Johnson; ***D:*** Roger Corman; ***W:*** Robert Towne. **VHS, Beta, LV $59.99** *MLB*

Tommy

Pete Townshend's enduring rock opera, as visualized in the usual hyper Ken Russell style, about a boy driven into his own world after witnessing his mother and her lover kill his father. The deaf, dumb, and blind boy becomes a messiah to millions of adoring fans due to his amazing skill at pinball. The film holds up well as a comment on mislaid hero worship, hypocrisy, child abuse, and organized religion even in the '90s. Roger Daltery as Tommy sings heartfelt pleas of "See me, feel me/Touch me, heal me" as he begs for release from his psychological prison. Look for cameos by Jack Nicholson as the Doctor, Elton John as the Pinball Wizard, Tina Turner as the Acid Queen, and Eric Clapton as the Hawker. Pete Townshend won an Oscar for adapting the score,

after winning a Grammy for the album. Recently, he won a Tony award for the stage play, completing the award trifecta. ♫ Underture; Captain Walker Didn't Come Home; It's A Boy; '51 Is Going to Be a Good Year; What About the Boy?; The Amazing Journey; Christmas; See Me, Feel Me; Eyesight to the Blind. 🎵🎵🎵◁

1975 (PG) 108m/C Ann-Margret, Elton John, Oliver Reed, Tina Turner, Roger Daltrey, Eric Clapton, Keith Moon, Pete Townshend, Jack Nicholson, Robert Powell; *D:* Ken Russell; *W:* Ken Russell. Golden Globe Awards '76: Best Actress—Musical/Comedy (Ann-Margret); Nominations: Academy Awards '75: Best Actress (Ann-Margret), Best Original Score. **VHS, Beta, LV $14.95** *COL, MVD, WME*

Too Hot to Handle

Voluptuous hitwoman fights against the mob and the cops with all the weapons at her disposal. More action and (marginally) less sex than found in Caffaro and Shain's *Ginger* trilogy, but it's still got everything a fan of guilty pleasures could ask for. Filmed on location in Manila with lots of local color. 🎵🎵◁

1976 88m/C Cheri Caffaro, Aharon Ipale, Vic Diaz, Corinne Calvet; *D:* Don Schain. **VHS, Beta $39.98** *WAR*

The Toolbox Murders

Unknown psychotic murderer brutally claims victims one at a time using various pieces of home repair equipment, leaving police mystified and townsfolk terrified. Too sick and exploitative for general audiences, but nothing new for fans, with predictably poor production values, watchable mainly for Mitchell's typically unrestrained performance as the psychotic handyman. An answer for those seeking to find out what became of Aneta Corseaut after starring in *The Blob*. Mitchell's prolific career ranges from starring in *Death of a Salesman* to European features (notably with Mario Bava) to TV's *High Chapparall* to appearances in trash like *Screamers* and *Frankenstein Island*. 🎵🎵

1978 (R) 93m/C Cameron Mitchell, Pamelyn Ferdin, Wesley Eure, Nicholas Beauvy, Aneta Corseaut, Tim Donnelly, Evelyn Guerrero; *D:* Dennis Donnelly. **VHS, Beta $19.95** *VCI, VTR*

That's not a pinball! Oliver Reed, Roger Daltrey, and Ann-Margret in *Tommy*.

The *Toxic Avenger* starts his day.

Touch of Evil

Beginning with the famous long opening shot (3 minutes and 20 seconds from the moment that the bomb is armed and put in the trunk of the convertible until it blows up), Orson Welles' other masterpiece is a fast-paced, innovative roller-coaster ride that was years ahead of its time. It's a stark, perverse story of murder, kidnaping, and police corruption in Mexican border town. Welles portrays a police chief who invents evidence to convict the guilty; Heston is the younger cop and Leigh is his wife caught in the middle. Top-notch photography by Russell Metty and jazzy score by Henry Mancini. Because his direction is so striking, Welles' sweat-stained performance is often overlooked. ♫♫♫♫

1958 108m/B Charlton Heston, Orson Welles, Janet Leigh, Joseph Calleia, Akim Tamiroff, Marlene Dietrich, Valentin de Vargas, Dennis Weaver, Zsa Zsa Gabor, Mort Mills, Victor Milian, Joanna Moore, Joi Lansing; *Cameos:* Ray Collins, Mercedes McCambridge, Joseph Cotten; *D:* Orson Welles; *W:* Orson Welles; *M:* Henry Mancini. **VHS, Beta, LV $29.95** *MCA*

The Tower of London

Tells the story of Richard III (Rathbone), the English monarch who fiendishly assassinated the people who stood between him and his ascension to the throne. This historical drama with horror overtones was considered extremely graphic for its time (though much tamer than real history), and some of the torture scenes had to be cut before it was released. Classic scene has first meeting of Karloff (who plays the royal executioner loyal to Richard), Rathbone, and Price as the foppish cousin who duels Richard at wine drinking. Excellent cast and direction hides the fact that Universal saved money by limiting most of the action to the same interior sets. Lee and Rathbone (and Karloff) made *Son of Frankenstein* the same year, but first teamed on the great, little known British thriller *Love from a Stranger.* ♫♫♫

1939 93m/B Basil Rathbone, Boris Karloff, Barbara O'Neil, Ian Hunter, Vincent Price, Nan Grey, John Sutton, Leo G. Carroll, Miles Mander; *D:* Rowland V. Lee. **VHS $14.98** *MCA*

Top Secret!

The *Airplane!* team of Zucker, Abrams, and Zucker concocted this lesser-known but still sidesplitting musical spoof of spy movies and Elvis Presley films. American rock star Nick Rivers goes to East Germany on a goodwill tour and tangles with Nazis, the French Resistance, a captured scientist, and more. The *Blue Lagoon* parody is worth the price of rental alone, and Peter Cushing cameos in a bizarre, all-backwards role. Wuz robbed at the box-office by opening the same day as Sylvester Stallone's *Rhinestone*; well worth rediscovering. ♫♫♫

1984 (PG) 90m/C Val Kilmer, Lucy Gutteridge, Christopher Villiers, Omar Sharif, Peter Cushing, Jeremy Kemp, Michael Gough; *D:* Jim Abrahams, Jerry Zucker, David Zucker; *W:* Jim Abrahams, Jerry Zucker, David Zucker, Martyn Burke; *M:* Maurice Jarre. **VHS, Beta, LV $14.95** *PAR*

Tower of London

The deranged Richard the Ruthless (Price), furthering his ambitions by murdering his way to the throne of England, is eventually crowned Richard III. But he can't escape his victims' ghosts. Sophisticated and well-made Poe-like thriller. More interesting as historic melodrama than as horror film. A remake of the 1939 version starring Basil Rathbone, in which Price played a supporting role. Pate takes the Karloff role as the royal executioner that helps out with the killing. Much ignored by fans, perhaps partially because Corman made this for United Artists rather than AIP, but more likely due to the fact that it's so obviously inferior to the original. Pate was also in two early '50s Karloff thrillers (*The Strange Door, The Black Castle*) as well as the vampire western *Curse of the Undead* (1959). 🎞🎞

1962 79m/B Vincent Price, Michael Pate, Joan Freeman, Robert Brown; **D:** Roger Corman. **VHS, Beta $14.95** *MGM, FCT*

The Toxic Avenger

Tongue-in-cheek, cult fave has 98-pound weakling fall into barrel of toxic waste to emerge as a lumbering, bloodthirsty hulk of sludge and mire. His murderous rages are set off, however, only by the presence of evil. Soon he is fighting bad guys, falling in love with a blind babe (whom he rescues while foiling a fast food joint robbery), and gaining fame as "The Monster Hero." None of this sets well with the mayor of Tromaville, who is the mastermind of criminal activities in the town. An unmatched parody of both super-hero and horror flicks, much of the fun comes from watching the comic book gore taken to an absurd excess. Combined with clever one liners, visual jokes, and loopy situations, *The Toxic Avenger* is not to be missed. Four edits of the film exist: U.S. "R" rated, U.S. unrated, European unrated, and Japanese unrated; of the four, the European cut seems the most complete. "The first Super-Hero from New Jersey" also stars in two sequels: *Toxic Avenger Part II* and *Toxic Avenger Part III: The Last Temptation of Toxie.* 🎞🎞🎞🎞

1986 (R) 90m/C Mitchell Cohen, Andree Maranda, Jennifer Baptist, Robert Prichard, Cindy Manion; **D:** Michael Herz, Lloyd Samuel Weil Kaufman; **W:** Joe Ritter. **VHS, Beta, LV $29.98** *VES, LIV*

The Toxic Avenger, Part 2

In the sequel to *Toxic Avenger,* we discover the secret of Toxic's power: tromatons. These little sub-atomic particles react violently to evil and cause our hero to fall into an unrelenting rage whenever he's confronted with wickedness. We also learn of an evil corporation with designs on Tromaville, the toxic waste capital of the world. But first they must eliminate the beloved "Monster Hero." When an absurd frontal assault filled with funny, gory violence, fails the corporation resorts to trickery. They enlist a shrink to convince Toxic he is going psycho and must find his father to solve his problems. Off we go with Toxic to Japan for more zany, brutal, comedy while the corporation takes over Tromaville. Funny and bloody, this entry into the series is worth a watch, but lacks the originality of the first film. At least two cuts exist: U.S. "R" rated version, and a Japanese unrated version. The latter is worth pursuing, if you can find it, and contains more gore than the domestic video release. 🎞🎞🎞📼

1989 (R) 90m/C Ron Fazio, Phoebe Legere, Rick Collins, John Altamura; **D:** Michael Herz, Lloyd Samuel Weil Kaufman; **W:** Lloyd Samuel Weil Kaufman, Gay Partington Terry. **VHS, Beta, LV $14.95** *WAR*

The Toxic Avenger, Part 3: The Last Temptation of Toxie

The third installment in the adventures of Toxic is both forced and pretty lame. This time round the head of the evil corporation is revealed to be a demonic being. When Toxic's blind girlfriend, Claire, needs an eye operation, he waves big bucks and success on the corporate ladder in our hero's face. Never having been overly bright, our hero accepts the offer, unwittingly selling out the good folk of Tromaville in the process. The slightly sadistic will get a few yucks watching the townsfolk get kicked around by the minions of the corporation. The rest hits the viewer like a breath of stale air. Available in both "R" and unrated versions, this one is strictly for Troma addicts. 🎞

"I look at it this way: I'll never have to see the ugliness of poverty or war or the Chevrolet Nova."
--Toxie's girlfriend, the "beautiful blind buxom bimbo" (Phoebe Legere) in *The Toxic Avenger Part III: The Last Temptation of Toxie.*

THE HOUND SALUTES: TROMA

While many studios and video distributors have begun with low-budget exploitation flicks and then slowly climbed the ladder to more respectable forms of entertainment, one company has courageously clung to the low road.

Troma, Inc., makes bad movies that revel in their own badness, alternative epics that proudly trumpet their lack of polish, and thumb their celluloid noses at the Hollywood establishment. In fact, the organization has been so successful in its niche that it has been recognized and honored by both the British and American Film Institutes. It's astonishing what can be accomplished with low budgets and an irreverent attitude, and Troma's got both of those in spades.

The company was founded in the early 1970s by Lloyd Kaufman and Michael Herz who co-write, -produce, and -direct many Troma films and buy the rest from other independent producers. They got their start with B-movies to fill smaller theatres in the new multi-screen complexes that were popping up across the country in those days. From that humble beginning, the filmmakers have created a growing library of more than 100 titles. And though the studio has branched out into other genres, the basic make-'em-cheap philosophy hasn't changed. Today, most Troma films cost around a million dollars while even a "little" Hollywood movie can cost ten to 20 times as much.

It would, of course, be wrong to dismiss Kaufman and Herz as pure schlockmeisters. Their films address such pressing contemporary issues as nuclear power (*Class of Nuke 'Em High*), the environment (*The Toxic Avenger*), race relations (*Def by Temptation*), unemployment (*Waitress*), and health care (*Rabid Grannies*). Fans can be assured that each of these subjects is given the penetratingly shallow and superficial treatment that they expect from the Tromarians. And that's what makes Troma different from all other studios: It delivers exactly what it promises-- cheesy special effects, rude humor, rough production values, attitude.

continued...

1989 (R) 102m/C Ron Fazio, Phoebe Legere, John Altamura, Rick Collins, Lisa Gaye, Jessica Dublin; **D:** Michael Herz, Lloyd Samuel Weil Kaufman; **W:** Lloyd Samuel Weil Kaufman, Gay Partington Terry. **VHS** $14.98 *VES, LIV*

Trash

Joe Dallesandro and female impersonator Holly Woodlawn share a basement on the lower East side, where they scrounge out a depraved living. This is the apex of Warhol's commercial period, with his "Superstars" in rare form. It is a delightfully obnoxious foray into the world of male prostitution, drugs, and melodramatic desire. In one of the most hilarious episodes, Woodlawn feigns pregnancy in an attempt to swindle the Welfare Department. When the claim investigator turns out to have a shoe fetish, the "couple" realize he is completely in their power. For anyone wondering if they may have a taste for underground films, this is the place to start. 🦴🦴🦴🦴

1970 110m/C Joe Dallesandro, Holly Woodlawn, Jane Forth, Micael Sklar, Geri Miller, Bruce Pecheur; **D:** Paul Morrissey. **VHS, Beta** *PAR*

The Trial of Billy Jack

Half-Native American ex-Green Beret ass-kicking machine Billy Jack takes on the feds and beats the hell out of a lot of people to prove that the world can live in peace. Laughlin directs, produces, and co-writes this successful third entry in "Peace Through Violence" series begun in 1967 with *The Born Losers*. Laughlin acts well and his hapkido is impressive, but the film is overlong and stumbles with silly psychedelic "spirit" encounters before lengthy kung-fu finale. Followed by underrated *The Master Gunfighter* and *Billy Jack Goes to Washington,* both of which helped sink Billy Jack Enterprises. With Laughlin's wife, Delores Taylor, and Sacheen Littlefeather (she accepted Brando's *Godfather* Oscar). 🦴🦴🦴

1974 (PG) 175m/C Tom Laughlin, Delores Taylor, Victor Izay, Terasa Laughlin, William Wellman Jr.; **D:** Frank Laughlin; **M:** Elmer Bernstein. **VHS** *NO*

Trilogy of Terror

Karen Black shows her versatility as she plays a tempting seductress, a mousy schoolteacher, and the terrified victim of an African Zuni fetish doll in three horror shorts in this made-for-television anthology. Although the first two episodes are okay, it's the wild grand finale that everyone remembers. A sequel is said to be in the works. One of our nation's most courageous actors, Chicago-native Black made her film debut in Herschell Gordon Lewis' *The Prime Time,* and went on to roles in films by Coppola (*You're a Big Boy Now*), Hopper (*Easy Rider*), Nicholson (*Drive, He Said*), Altman (*Nashville, The Player*), Hitchcock (*Family Plot*), Margheriti (*Killer Fish, The Squeeze*), Deodato (*Cut and Run*), Hooper (*Invaders From Mars '86*), Cohen (*It's Alive 3*), Graver (*Evil Spirits*), and Fred Olen Ray (*Haunting Fear*). At 50 plus, the cross-eyed beauty still looks great. Curtis hit big with his gothic soap opera *Dark Shadows,* and spent most of the '70s making TV horror films, often written by Matheson. 🎞️🎞️▷

1975 78m/C Karen Black, Robert Burton, John Karlen, Gregory Harrison; **D:** Dan Curtis; **W:** Richard Matheson. **VHS, Beta $59.95** *NO*

The Trip

Just "say yes" to this flick. Peter Fonda plays a television director, unsure where his life is going, who decides to try a "trip" to expand his understanding. A very young-looking Dennis Hopper is the drug salesman, and Bruce Dern, the tour guide for Fonda's LSD trip through sex, witches, torture chambers, midgets, men in black cloaks on horses, and a beach scene that looks a lot like the conclusion to *Planet of the Apes*. Groovy period piece, complete with pink pantsuits, love beads, op art, psychedelic murals, strobe lights, painted bodies, God's Eyes (remember those?), kaleidoscope images set to music, and a world where every sentence ends in "...man." Hopper appears in Fonda's trip as the caretaker of a torture chamber, perhaps foreshadowing many of his future sadistic roles. Dern has some great hep lines, like "I don't want to bring you down, but, like, let's sort out the real from the trip." Scripted by Jack Nicholson (who would write the screenplay for *Head* the next year), the movie begins with a sober foreword ending with "...The picture represents a shocking commentary on a prevalent trend of our time and one that must be of great concern to all." 🎞️🎞️🎞️

1967 85m/C Peter Fonda, Susan Strasberg, Bruce Dern, Dennis Hopper, Salli Sachse, Barboura Morris, Judith Lang, Luana Anders, Beach Dickerson, Dick Miller, Michael Nader, Michael Blodgett, Caren Bernsen, Katherine Walsh; **D:** Roger Corman; **W:** Jack Nicholson; **M:** Barry Goldberg. **VHS, Beta $29.98** *LIV, VES*

Troll

Mischievous troll haunts an urban apartment building, tries to make a little girl his princess, and turn all humans into mythical flora and fauna. Mild fantasy from producer Charles Band, with charming creature F/X by director John Buechler matched against awful performances by the grownups (exception: *Lassie's* June Lockhart and her daughter Anne, as different incarnations of the same sassy witch). Undeniable highlight is a scene in which future senator Sonny Bono metamorphs into an entire forest. Watch the gorier, basically unrelated *Troll 2* only if you want learn how to be a cannibal and a vegetarian at the same time! Watch *Troll 3* (on video in the U.S. as *The Crawlers*) only if you're a masochist. 🎞️🎞️▷

1985 (PG-13) 86m/C Noah Hathaway, Gary Sandy, Anne Lockhart, Sonny Bono, Shelley Hack, June Lockhart, Michael Moriarty; **D:** John Carl Buechler; **M:** Richard Band. **VHS, Beta, LV $79.98** *LIV, VES*

Troma's War

The survivors of an air crash find themselves beached on a not-so-deserted tropical island. Seems they're sharing their space with a horde of terrorists training for an assault on the good ol' U.S. of A. Hunted by villains, can our band of urban heroes survive and save the day? Perhaps the best movie from Troma to date, this film boasts an impressive array of quirky characters, twisted humor (including, according to the hype, the first AIDS jokes), and unlikely scenarios. Almost as many rounds get fired as in *The Longest Day*. Despite the absurdity of it all, our heros manage to win the viewers' heart and loyalty and you may well find yourself cheering for your favorites as the tale unfolds. The final battle is utterly preposterous, but fun. Keep watching through the end credits for the final joke. Available in both "R" and unrated versions, with the latter 105-minute version being far superior. Devotees of trash films shouldn't miss this one. 🎞️🎞️🎞️🎞️

"**You look like two decent, respectable hippies.**"
--Welfare examiner Michael Sklar to Joe Dallesandro and Holly Woodlawn in *Trash*.

"**You can't expect me to let you go trippin' in a messed up place, do ya?**"
--Bruce Dern in *The Trip*, just before he introduced Peter Fonda to LSD.

"**Not a true story but who cares!**"
-- *Troma's War*.

277

Cult Flicks and Trash Pics

Story continued...

But the winds of change are blowing in Tromaville, New Jersey, the "little postage stamp of soil" where many of the films take place. As of this writing, Troma stands on the brink of respectability! After an investment by a Swiss holding company, as reported in the *Wall Street Journal*, Kaufman and Herz are about to go global with TV productions and other new enterprises. They've even got "legit," or at least semi-legit productions in mind--an adaptation of Nathaniel Hawthorne's "Young Goodman Brown" and their first attempt at Shakespeare, *Tromeo and Juliet*.

However, with such titles as *Blondes Have More Guns*, *Maniac Nurses Find Ecstasy* ("filmed in Hungary...the birthplace of Franz Liszt!"), and *Femme Fontaine: Killer Babe for the CIA* on the most recent production schedule, it looks like Troma will maintain its cherished position on the video foodchain.

1988 (R) 90m/C Ara Romanoff, Michael Ryder, Carolyn Beauchamp, Sean Bowen; **D:** Michael Herz, Lloyd Samuel Weil Kaufman. **VHS, Beta $19.98** *MED*

> "Blessed are those who expect nothing, for they shall not be disappointed."
>
> --Edmund Gwenn in *The Trouble With Harry*.

Tron

A video game designer enters into his computer, where he battles the MCP (Master Control Program) he created and seeks revenge on other designers who have stolen his creations. Sounds better than it plays. Terrific special effects, with lots of computer-created graphics which still hold up fairly well by today's standards. The graphics are the true star of this somewhat experimental Disney piece. The real action begins when the designer is sucked into his computer and there does battle with the megalomaniacal MCP in a series of video games. From there we get caught in a series of roller coaster rides and chases, pausing only occasionally for brief plot development scenes. It is, after all, Disney, so the conclusion is foregone, eliminating any true suspense. Just sit back and enjoy the ride. 🦴🦴

1982 (PG) 96m/C Jeff Bridges, Bruce Boxleitner, David Warner, Cindy Morgan, Barnard Hughes, Dan Shor; **D:** Steven Lisberger. Nominations: Academy Awards '82: Best Costume Design, Best Sound. **VHS, Beta, LV $19.99** *DIS*

Trouble in Mind

Stylized romance features Kris Kristofferson as an ex-cop who gets involved in the lives of a young couple looking for a better life. Director Alan Rudolph was Robert Altman's protege, and made a series of films that shared the master's loose improvisational style but were grounded by the lackluster vision of a sentimentalist. The picture is helped by odd character bits from actors like Keith Carridine, Genevieve Bujold, Joe Morton, and John Waters' regular Divine; but the rainy-day moodiness of the picture will fatigue all but the most passionate follower of the director's work. Filmed in Seattle, the climactic siege of gangster Divine's compound is set in the local art museum (a fitting habitat for one such as s/he). 🦴🦴▷

1986 (R) 111m/C Kris Kristofferson, Keith Carradine, Genevieve Bujold, Lori Singer, Divine, Joe Morton, George Kirby, John Considine; **D:** Alan Rudolph; **W:** Alan Rudolph. Independent Spirit Awards '86: Best Cinematography. **VHS, Beta, LV, 8mm $14.95** *COL, NLC*

The Trouble with Harry

When a little boy (Mathers, of TV's immortal *Leave It to Beaver*) finds a dead body in a Vermont town, it causes all kinds of problems for the community. No one is sure who killed Harry and what to do with the body. A rare Hitchcock black comedy, which also touches on our attitudes toward ethics and death in general. The community's attitude is that no one is particularly upset that Harry's dead—he was a shnook after all—but they're terribly bothered to have a corpse around, and wish that Harry'd taken it with him. Forsythe plays an artist who wants to do the "right thing," but can't seem to figure out what that is. MacLaine's film debut and Herrmann's first musical score for Hitchcock. Inspired the low comedy *Weekend at Bernie's*. 🦴🦴🦴

1955 (PG) 90m/C John Forsythe, Shirley MacLaine, Edmund Gwenn, Jerry Mathers, Mildred Dunnock, Mildred Natwick, Royal Dano; **D:** Alfred Hitchcock; **W:** John Michael Hayes; **M:** Bernard Herrmann. **VHS, Beta, LV $19.98** *MCA, HMV*

True Romance

The hero (Slater) is a young comic store clerk turned knight errant; his beloved (Arquette) is a neophyte working girl. They leave Detroit for La-la Land in a purple Caddy convertible with a suitcase full of cocaine to sell and a gaggle of gangsters on their trail. On hand for scenery-shredding cameos are Walken as a mob lawyer, Oldman as a grotesque pimp, Kilmer as the spirit of Elvis, and Pitt as the terminally stoned roommate. Tarantino's script contains all the elements that have become his trademarks. Director Scott gives the action the jittery pace and vivid colors of a rock video. But is there anything beneath that highly polished surface? Not really. This is unapologetically mindless, violent entertainment; a self-satisfied B-movie filled with sleazy charm. An even more violent unrated version is also available. 🦴🦴🦴

1993 (R) 116m/C Christian Slater, Patricia Arquette, Gary Oldman, Brad Pitt, Val Kilmer, Dennis Hopper, Christopher Walken, Samuel L. Jackson, Christopher Penn, Bronson Pinchot, Michael Rapaport, Saul Rubinek, Conchata Ferrell, James Gandolfini; *D:* Tony Scott; *W:* Quentin Tarantino; *M:* Hans Zimmer. Nominations: MTV Movie Awards '94: Best Kiss (Christian Slater/Patricia Arquette). **VHS, Beta, LV** *WAR, BTV*

True Stories

Wry bemusement, ironic detachment, and smug condescension only takes you so far, and David Byrne wears out his welcome long before his tour of the Texas town of Virgil runs its post-modern course. The former Talking Heads frontman trades in the Big Suit from "Stop Making Sense" for a big Stetson and bolo tie as he introduces Virgil's eccentric citizens in preparation for their town's "Celebration of Specialness." What gives this film its amiable heart is the brilliant ensemble cast, whose characters were inspired by supermarket tabloids. John Goodman is Louis, who has erected a billboard advertising for a wife. Spalding Grey, best known for his performance pieces *Swimming to Cambodia* and *Monster in a Box,* is a married man who hasn't spoken directly to his wife in years. Swoosie Kurtz is the Laziest Woman in America. Also memorable is Jo Harvey Allen as the Lying Woman who claims to have dated,

among others, Burt Reynolds. The musical highlight is a lip-synced rendition of the Talking Heads' "Wild Wild Life," during which Goodman moonwalks and Byrne's bandmates cameo incognito. Had this perhaps been directed by Jonathan Demme, whose *Handle With Care* and *Melvin and Howard* this most resembles, these "Stories" might have been special indeed. 🎵 Love for Sale; Puzzlin' Evidence; Hey Now; Papa Legba; Wild Wild Life; Radio Head; Dream Operator; People Like Us; City of Dreams. 🦴🦴▷

1986 (PG) 89m/C David Byrne, John Goodman, Swoosie Kurtz, Spalding Gray, Annie McEnroe, Pops Staples, Tito Larriva; *D:* David Byrne; *W:* David Byrne, Beth Henley; *M:* David Byrne. **VHS, Beta, LV** **$19.98** *MVD, WAR*

The Tune

30,000 ink and watercolor drawings make up this animated gem which tells the story of Del (Neiden), a failed songwriter who gets a fresh start when he makes a wrong turn on the freeway and winds up in Flooby Nooby. The strange inhabitants of this town teach Del to

```
Looks like the
Beav won't be
getting his bath
after all: Jerry
Mathers and
Shirley MacLaine
in The Trouble
with Harry.
```

279

Cult Flicks and Trash Pics

THE HOUND SALUTES:
MAMIE VAN DOREN

In the early 1950s, the American scene was rocked by what may be called "The Blonde Explosion." The sudden stardom of a young actress named Marilyn Monroe resulted in a flood of cinematic blonde sirens, both real and manufactured. Second in rank to Monroe was Jayne Mansfield, who created an incredible public persona that exaggerated and parodied the ideal of Hollywood sex symbol glamour, and the concept of celebrity itself. The "third blonde" to rise to movie stardom was a teenage model/actress named Joan Lucille Olander from Rowena, South Dakota, who would come to carve out a special niche all her own.

As a teenager, she'd already left behind a secretarial job as offers for photo modeling were piling up. Taking the name Mamie Van Doren (a combination taken from the current first lady and a quiz show champion), she began her acting career, and made her movie debut in the 1951 Jack Paar vehicle *Footlight Varieties* at age 20. Two years later, she became a contract player at Universal, showing up in gradually larger roles in pictures, including *Forbidden*, *Ain't Misbehavin'*, and *Running Wild*.

Running Wild was the film that provided Mamie with her own defining place amidst The Blonde Explosion. One of the first teen-oriented pictures, it told the story of juvenile delinquents raising hell in their stolen hot rods, all set to the beat of Bill Haley & the Comets. Paramount took notice of *Running Wild*'s success, and after Mamie finished up her Universal contract, they hired her for their own sock hop opera, 1957's *Untamed Youth*. This picture, in which Mamie is top billed as a kid who gets railroaded into juvie prison for hitch-hiking, solidified her image as the drive-in's Marilyn Monroe. What's more, she got to sing some hot numbers written by Eddie Cochran. Meanwhile, her image as a singing sex symbol was aided by her marriage to band leader Ray Anthony, her appearances on his television show, and the attendant publicity generated. Mamie's public image was given a name in the 1958 A-picture *Teacher's Pet*. Stars Doris Day and

continued...

throw out his rhyming dictionary and write about his experiences. Plympton's first full-length animated feature. Also includes "The Making of The Tune" and the animated short "Draw." ♫♫♪

1992 80m/C D: Bill Plympton; **W:** Maureen McElheron, Bill Plympton; **V:** Daniel Neiden, Maureen McElheron, Marty Nelson, Emily Bindiger, Chris Hoffman. **VHS $59.95** *TRI, WTA*

20 Million Miles to Earth

A spaceship returning from an expedition to Venus crashes on Earth, releasing a fast-growing reptilian beast that rampages throughout Athens. Another entertaining example of stop-motion animation master Ray Harryhausen's work, offering a classic battle between the monster and an elephant. ♫♫♪

1957 82m/B William Hopper, Joan Taylor, Frank Puglia, Joan Zaremba; **D:** Nathan Hertz Juran. **LV $19.95** *COL*

Twilight Zone: The Movie

Four original TZ tales and one new story comprise this tribute to Rod Serling and the 'Zone legend. Stories from the original series include "Kick the Can," "Nightmare at 20,000 Feet," and "It's a Good Life." The latter story was treated with most originality; you remember it—Billy Mumy as a terrifying tot declaring "You be dead!" and wishing people into the cornfield. The new version becomes colorful and surreal as the new little Anthony "wishes" people into garish and macabre cartoon-like characters. And, for humor, Billy Mumy himself cameos at the beginning of the story. Vic Morrow's last work, as he was killed in a helicopter crash during the filming of this movie. ♫♫♫

1983 (PG) 101m/C Dan Aykroyd, Albert Brooks, Vic Morrow, Kathleen Quinlan, John Lithgow, Scatman Crothers, Kevin McCarthy, Bill Quinn, Selma Diamond, Abbe Lane, John Larroquette, Jeremy Licht, Patricia Barry, William Schallert, Burgess Meredith, Cherie Currie; **Cameos:** Billy Mumy; **D:** John Landis, Steven Spielberg, George Miller, Joe Dante; **W:** John Landis; **M:** Jerry Goldsmith. **VHS, Beta, LV $19.98** *WAR*

Twin Peaks

The Hound's giving two bones to this sketchy home video distillation of the eccentric TV series, but for the record, rates that ground-breaking series itself at four bones. The video preserves much of the setup episode (the murder of teen-queen Laura Palmer and nest of small-town weirdness it reveals), then rushes piecemeal through the rest of the season. There's also an altered quasi-solution to the enigma and a bizarre backward sequence not broadcast in the U.S. In this compressed form it's best for initiates of the TP cult; others won't be converted. 🎵🎵

1990 113m/C Kyle MacLachlan, Michael Ontkean, Sherilyn Fenn, Lara Flynn Boyle, Joan Chen, Peggy Lipton, Piper Laurie, Michael Horse, Russ Tamblyn, Richard Beymer, Madchen Amick, Catherine Coulson, Warren Frost, Everett McGill, Jack Nance, Ray Wise, Eric Da Re, Harry Goaz, Sheryl Lee; **D:** David Lynch; **M:** Angelo Badalamenti. **VHS, LV $79.99** *WAR, FCT*

Twin Peaks: Fire Walk with Me

Prequel to the cult TV series is weird and frustrating, chronicling the week before Laura Palmer's death. Suspense is lacking since we know the outcome, but Lynch manages to intrigue with dream-like sequences and interestingly offbeat characters. On the other hand, it's exploitative and violent enough to alienate series fans. Includes extremely brief and baffling cameos by Bowie as an FBI agent and Stanton as the manager of a trailer park. Several of the show's regulars are missing, and others appear and disappear very quickly. On the plus side are the strains of Badalamenti's famous theme music and Isaak as an FBI agent with amazingly acute powers of observation. 🎵🎵

1992 (R) 135m/C Kyle MacLachlan, Sheryl Lee, Moira Kelly, Chris Isaak, Ray Wise, Kiefer Sutherland, Peggy Lipton, Dana Ashbrook, James Marshall, David Lynch; *Cameos:* David Bowie, Harry Dean Stanton; **D:** David Lynch; **W:** David Lynch; **M:** Angelo Badalamenti. Independent Spirit Awards '93: Best Score; Nominations: Cannes Film Festival '92: Best Film. **VHS, LV $19.95** *NLC, COL*

Twister

Cockeyed, low-key independent feature about the Clevelands, an eccentric modern prairie family with too much time and money for their own good. Son Glover follows a fruit-less anticareer as a new-wave rocker, while alcoholic daughter Amis sweats out unwed motherhood and refuses to reconcile with her boyfriend. Father Stanton barely reacts to any of his useless brood, as he pursues romance with a Christian-TV kidshow hostess. Title refers to a tornado alert that prefigures the fall of the House of Cleveland. Based on the novel *Oh!* by Mary Robison, this strange little film barely won a release due to the financial collapse of its distributor, but has a small cult following. Watch for a great cameo appearance by the man, the legend, William S. Burroughs. 🎵🎵▷

1989 (PG-13) 93m/C Dylan McDermott, Crispin Glover, Harry Dean Stanton, Suzy Amis, Jenny Wright, Lindsay Christman, Lois Chiles, William S. Burroughs; **D:** Michael Almereyda; **W:** Michael Almereyda; **M:** Hans Zimmer. **VHS, Beta, LV $89.98** *LIV, VES*

2000 Maniacs

One of cult director Lewis' most enjoyably watchable films is this follow-up to his landmark *Blood Feast* (also with Wood and Mason). A literal Civil War "ghost town," like a splatter film version of Brigadoon, takes its revenge 100 years after being slaughtered by renegade Union soldiers by luring unwitting "Yankee" tourists to their centennial festival. The hapless Notherners are then chopped with an ax, crushed by a huge boulder, ripped apart in a barrel of nails, etc., while the ghostly rebels party. Quite fun in a cartoonishly gruesome sort of way. Filmed in St. Cloud, FL. Lewis wrote and performed the theme song. 🎵🎵🎵▷

1964 75m/C Thomas Wood, Connie Mason, Jeffrey Allen, Ben Moore, Gary Bakeman, Jerome Eden, Shelby Livingston, Michael Korb, Yvonne Gilbert, Mark Douglas, Linda Cochran, Vincent Santo, Andy Wilson; **D:** Herschell Gordon Lewis; **W:** Herschell Gordon Lewis. **VHS, Beta $29.95** *NO*

2001: A Space Odyssey

Space voyage to Jupiter turns chaotic when a computer, HAL 9000, takes over. Seen by some as a mirror of man's historical use of machinery and by others as a grim vision of the future, the special effects and music are still stunning. Critically acclaimed and well accepted by the some, simply confusing to oth-

"There is a sixth dimension beyond that which is known to man. It is a dimension as vast as space and timeless as infinity. It is an area that we call the Twilight Zone."
--Burgess Meredith, a la Rod Serling, in *Twilight Zone: The Movie*.

"There's a fish...in the percolator!"
--Pete (Jack Nance) in *Twin Peaks*.

Story continued...

Clarke Gable do a scene where they end up in a night club, in which Mamie belts out what may as well be her theme song, *The Girl Who Invented Rock 'n' Roll*.

Producer Albert Zugsmith (*The Incredible Shrinking Man*) recognized Mamie's special appeal, and signed her up for a series of pictures aimed at the youth market. In films like *High School Confidential*, *Beat Generation*, *Born Reckless*, and *Girls Town*, Mamie played her trademark tough-and-sexy characters, and occasionally got to sing a few rockin' tunes. When the public's tastes turned to comedy in the early '60s, Mamie followed by appearing in lighter fare, such as *Sex Kittens Go to College*, *The Private Lives of Adam and Eve*, and *Las Vegas Hillbillies*. In 1964's *Three Nuts in Search of a Bolt*, she caused a mild sensation with her famous nude beer bath scene. But by this time, though she still looked great, she was finding roles demanding an over-30 blonde bombshell to be few and far between. She wound up the '60s playing in the schlocky sci-fi flicks *Navy vs. the Night Monsters* and *Journey to the Planet of Prehistoric Women*.

Mamie moved on to a Las Vegas act, singing tours, and theatrical work. In 1976, she was on TV's *General Hospital*, and in the '80s she hosted a series of films (including some of her own) for Rhino Video under the "Teenage Theater" banner. Of all the '50s blondes, she's the one that's survived to look back with genuine affection on her cult film favorites, which may be the reason why the Girl Who Invented Rock 'n' Roll is the cult film fan's favorite blonde.

ers. Martin Balsam originally recorded the voice of HAL, but was replaced by Rain. From Arthur C. Clarke's novel *The Sentinel*. Followed by a sequel, *2010: The Year We Make Contact*. Laserdisc edition is presented in letterbox format and features a special supplementary section on the making of *2001*, a montage of images from the film, production documents, memos, and photos. Also in-

cluded on the disc is a NASA film entitled *Art and Reality*, which offers footage from the Voyager I and II flybys of Jupiter. 🦴🦴🦴🦴

1968 139m/C *GB* Keir Dullea, Gary Lockwood, William Sylvester, Dan Richter; **D:** Stanley Kubrick; **W:** Arthur C. Clarke, Stanley Kubrick; **V:** Douglas Raines. Academy Awards '68: Best Visual Effects; National Board of Review Awards '68: 10 Best Films of the Year; Nominations: Academy Awards '68: Best Art Direction/Set Decoration, Best Director (Kubrick), Best Story & Screenplay. **VHS, Beta, LV** $19.98 *MGM, CRC, FCT*

2010: The Year We Make Contact

This sequel to Stanley Kubrick's trippy 1968 masterpiece *2001: A Space Odyssey,* is also based on a novel by prolific science fiction author Arthur C. Clarke. The story picks up with Dr. Heywood Floyd (Scheider) leading a joint expedition of American and Russian astronauts. Their mission is to investigate the mysteriously abandoned starship Discovery's decaying orbit around Jupiter, and try to determine why the HAL 9000 computer sabotaged its mission years before. At the same time, signs of cosmic change are detected on and around the giant planet, perhaps related to the strange events of the first film. Though not nearly as mind-blowing as the original, this is worthwhile attempt, and actually answers some of the questions raised by the first film. Look for Keir Dullea as Dave and listen for Douglas Raines as HAL. 🦴🦴🦴▷

1984 (PG) 116m/C Roy Scheider, John Lithgow, Helen Mirren, Bob Balaban, Keir Dullea, Madolyn Smith, Mary Jo Deschanel; **D:** Peter Hyams; **W:** Peter Hyams; **M:** David Shire; **V:** Douglas Raines. Nominations: Academy Awards '84: Best Art Direction/Set Decoration, Best Makeup, Best Sound. **VHS, Beta, LV** $19.95 *MGM*

Uforia

There is a special place in movie heaven for sweet little movies like this. Fred Ward stars as a charismatic drifter who hitches up with unscrupulous tent evangelist Harry Dean Stanton, whose philosophy is, "Everybody ought to believe in something, I believe I'll have another drink." They both meet their match in born-again supermarket checker Cindy Williams, who believes in flying saucers and is convinced they are on their way. John Binder's first and only film recalls such early Jonathan Demme gems as *Citizen's Band* and *Melvin and Howard.* For all their eccentricities, Binder clearly loves his characters and refuses to condescend and put them down. Look for John Ford regular Hank Worden (Mose in *The Searchers*) as the Colonel. Filmed in 1981, *UFOria* was grounded by studio politics and indifference that caused it to be shelved until 1986 when it was granted a limited, but critically acclaimed, art house release. Despite what the credits say, the incredible country music soundtrack was, criminally, never released. 𝄞 𝄞 𝄞 ▷

1981 92m/C Cindy Williams, Harry Dean Stanton, Fred Ward, Hank Worden; *D:* John Binder; *M:* Richard Baskin. **VHS, Beta $59.95** *MCA*

UHF

In the finest movie ever made in an abandoned Tulsa, Oklahoma, shopping center, "Weird Al" Yankovic treats such sacred subjects as TV, capitalism, movies, poodles, and rock music with the disrespect they so richly deserve. Forget the throwaway plot and concentrate on the star's spoofy humor as he plays a daydreamer who stumbles into a job managing a struggling TV station. He inadvertently turns it into a ratings smash with programs like "Wheel of Fish," where contestants can win their weight in red snapper, and a talk show featuring "Lesbian Nazi Hookers Abducted by UFOs and Forced Into Weight-Loss Programs." The best parts are "Weird Al"'s famous parodies. He takes on Indiana Jones, Rambo, and, in one inspired moment, a rock video of *The Beverly Hillbillies* theme redone as Dire Straits' "Money for Nothing," complete with computer animation. 𝄞 𝄞 𝄞

1989 (PG-13) 97m/C Weird Al Yankovic, Kevin McCarthy, Victoria Jackson, Michael Richards, David Bowie, Anthony Geary; *D:* Jay Levey; *M:* John Du Prez. **VHS, Beta, LV $19.98** *ORI*

The Undead

A prostitute (Duncan) is accidentally sent back to the Middle Ages as the result of a hypnotism experiment and finds herself condemned to die for witchcraft. Hayes (*Attack of the 50*

Foot Woman) plays a real witch who consorts with the Devil (Devon). Early Corman picture is filled with violence and heaving bosoms, as well as some nice in-studio atmosphere. Script by Charles Griffith (with Mark Hanna) lacks cohesion, giving it a dreamlike quality. If this seems rushed together it may be because Corman directed nine pictures in 1957. Duncan was busy that year as well, acting in *My Gun is Quick, Gun Battle at Monterey,* and Corman's *Attack of the Crab Monsters,* before disappearing from movies. Twin billed with *Voodoo Woman.* 𝄞 𝄞 ▷

1957 75m/B Pamela Duncan, Richard Garland, Allison Hayes, Mel Welles, Richard Devon, Billy Barty, Dick Miller; *D:* Roger Corman; *W:* Charles B. Griffith. **VHS $19.95** *NOS, AIP, MLB*

Maybe if you adjust the vertical hold...Fran Drescher, "Weird Al" Yankovic, and David Bowe in *UHF*.

Unsane

Peter Neal, an American mystery novelist visiting Rome (played by a reportedly drunk and uncooperative Franciosa) is embroiled in the investigation of a series of bizarre murders that strangely resemble those in his latest book *Tenebrae.* Victims are found with pages from

We're sure he's not inhaling... Frederic Forrest in *Valley Girl*.

the book stuffed in their mouths. Bloody fun from Argento and one of his most interesting giallo thrillers. Includes some of Argento's most shocking and suspenseful scenes. U.S. video version is cropped and heavily edited. *AKA:* Tenebrae. 🦴🦴🦴▷

1982 91m/C *IT* Anthony (Tony) Franciosa, John Saxon, Daria Nicolodi, Giuliano Gemma, Christian Borromeo, Mirella D'Angelo, Veronica Lario; *D:* Dario Argento; *W:* Dario Argento. **VHS $9.95** *MED*

Until the End of the World

Convoluted road movie set in 1999 follows the travails of Sam Farber (Hurt) through 15 cities in 8 countries on 4 continents as he is chased by Dommartin, her lover (Neill), a bounty hunter, a private detective, and bank robbers, until all wind up in the Australian outback. And this is only the first half of the movie. For true cinematic satisfaction, don't expect logic—just go with the flow. Visually stunning, unexpectedly humorous, with excellent performances from an international cast. Footage created with high definition (HDTV) video technology is a technological first. The soundtrack features Lou Reed, David Byrne, U2, and others. 🦴🦴🦴▷

1991 (R) 158m/C William Hurt, Solveig Dommartin, Sam Neill, Max von Sydow, Ruediger Vogler, Ernie Dingo, Jeanne Moreau; *D:* Wim Wenders; *W:* Wim Wenders, Peter Carey; *M:* Graeme Revell. **VHS, Beta, LV $92.99** *WAR*

Used Cars

"You've got to get their friendship. Get their confidence. Get their trust. Get their money.": the credo of Rudy Russo (Russell), ruthless used-car salesman and aspiring politician, fighting off schemes by a powerful competitor to put him out of business. Russo and his gang use scams, strippers, a dead dog, TV commercials jamming a presidential address, and anything they can think of to sucker customers onto their lot and purchase disintegrating gas-guzzlers. Those same critics who wrote hymns to Robert Zemeckis for embodying the American spirit in *Forrest Gump* virtually lynched him over this rude, raunchy comedy; fortunately, fans who know a good comedy deal when they see one made this a cult item. Concludes with a chase worthy of *The Road Warrior*. Watch for Al "Grampa" Lewis in the supporting cast. 🦴🦴🦴

1980 (R) 113m/C Kurt Russell, Jack Warden, Deborah Harmon, Gerrit Graham, Joe Flaherty, Michael McKean; *D:* Robert Zemeckis; *W:* Robert Zemeckis. **VHS, Beta, LV, 8mm $12.95** *COL*

Valley Girl

Slight but surprisingly likeable teen romantic-comedy inspired by Frank Zappa novelty tune. Title stereotype (Foreman) falls for a leather-jacketed rebel (Cage). Really. It may look like a music video, but the story is straight from *Romeo and Juliet* via Southern California. Some of the observations about adolescent behavior are absolutely accurate, and despite a sometimes cliched script, the characters are convincing. Helped launch Cage's career. Music by Men at Work, Culture Club, and others makes for a terrific soundtrack. 🦴🦴🦴

1983 (R) 95m/C Nicolas Cage, Deborah Foreman, Colleen Camp, Frederic Forrest; *D:* Martha Coolidge. **VHS, Beta, LV $29.98** *VES*

The Valley of Gwangi

One of the best prehistoric-monster-westerns out there, much better than the tedious *Beast of Hollow Mountain*. Cowboys discover a lost valley of dinosaurs down in Mexico and capture a vicious, carnivorous allosaurus. Bad move, kemosabe! The set-up scenes involving con man Franciscus and carnival performer Golan are quite good. The creatures move via the stop-motion model animation by f/x maestro Ray Harryhausen (*Jason & the Argonauts*), here at his finest. Topped off with a fine score by Jerome Moross. From one of the projects developed by f/x pioneer Willis O'Brien (*King Kong*). 🦴🦴🦴

1969 (G) 95m/C James Franciscus, Gila Golan, Richard Carlson, Laurence Naismith, Freda Jackson; *D:* James O'Connolly; *W:* William Bast. **VHS, Beta, LV $19.98** *WAR*

Valley of the Dolls

Camp/trash adaptation of Jacqueline Susann's phenomenal best-seller was rated as a bomb by many critics but is really of the so-bad-it's-good variety. Three beauties, Tate, Duke, and Parkins, dream of Hollywood stardom but fall victim to Hollywood excess, including drug dependency (the "dolls" of the title). There are unhappy love affairs, porno parts, health risks, and hysterics of various kinds—all designed to have you dropping your jaw in disbelief. Hard as it may be to believe, mid-'60s America was shocked to learn that outwardly respectable women took too many pills, drank too much booze, had impure thoughts, and acted on them. The glossy slickness of the expensive production has worn well. It really captures the look and feel of the times much better than many more openly nostalgic works. Don't miss the terrific hyperventilating theatrical trailer that begins the tape, the bathroom scene between Duke and Hayward involving a wig, and, yes, toward the end, that is a young Richard Dreyfuss. Susann herself has a small cameo as a reporter. Remade for television as *Jacqueline Susann's Valley of the Dolls* in 1981. 🦴🦴🦴

1967 (PG) 123m/C Barbara Parkins, Patty Duke, Sharon Tate, Paul Burke, Tony Scotti, Martin Milner, Susan Hayward, Charles Drake, Lee Grant, Alex Davion, Robert Harris, Robert Viharo, Joey Bishop, George Jessel, Richard Dreyfuss; *Cameos:* Jacqueline

Susann; *D:* Mark Robson; *W:* Dorothy Kingsley; *M:* John Williams. Nominations: Academy Awards '67: Best Original Score. **VHS $19.98** *FXV, BTV*

Vampire's Kiss

Cage makes this one worthwhile; his twisted transformation from pretentious post-val dude to psychotic yuppie from hell is inspired. If his demented torment of his secretary (Alonso) doesn't give you the creeps, his scene with the cockroach will. Cage fans will enjoy his facial aerobics; Beals fans will appreciate her extensive sucking scenes (she's the vamp of his dreams). More for psych majors than horror buffs. 🦴🦴🦴

1988 (R) 103m/C Nicolas Cage, Elizabeth Ashley, Jennifer Beals, Maria Conchita Alonso, Kasi Lemmons, Bob Lujan, Jennifer Lundy; *D:* Robert Bierman; *M:* Colin Towns. **VHS, Beta, LV $89.99** *HBO*

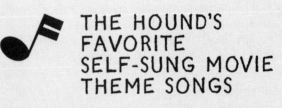

THE HOUND'S FAVORITE SELF-SUNG MOVIE THEME SONGS

Bedazzled (Peter Cook)

Female Trouble (Divine)

Ishtar (Dustin Hoffman and Warren Beatty)

Paradise Alley (Sylvester Stallone)

Polyester (Tab Hunter)

Spider Baby (Lon Chaney)

Vampyres

Alluring female vampires coerce unsuspecting motorists to their castle for a good time, which ends in bloody death. One victim thinks it's worth it. Anulka was the centerfold girl in *Playboy*'s May 1973 issue and this was named the "most erotic vampire movie of all time." One of the last appearances of longtime star Bessie Love, who had been in everything from *Intolerance* to *Battle Beneath the Earth*. Spanish director Larraz also gave us *Whirlpool*,

THE HOUND SALUTES: ANDY WARHOL
Fifteen Minutes of VideoHound Fame

Andrew Warhola, a native of Pittsburgh, was one of the founders of pop art, a stylistic movement that representationally portrays the collective subconscious psyche of society through the common images of popular culture. Whatever. All the Hound cares about is that in addition to forming and producing the too-cool band the Velvet Underground (featuring Lou Reed and John Cale) and founding *Interview* magazine, he was responsible for some very classic mongrel video, including *Andy Warhol's Dracula* and *Andy Warhol's Frankenstein* (both filmed in the same year and you can tell...), *Trash*, *Cocaine Cowboys*, *Flesh*, *Heat*, and *Andy Warhol's Bad*, all of which can be found within these pages. He also gave the world *Haircut*, a thirty-three-minute long chronicle of someone getting a haircut, *Eat*, *Poor Little Rich Girl*, *Empire*, and *Chelsea Girls*. The Campbell Soup can man survived a critical gunshot wound at the hand of a mentally unbalanced young feminist in 1968, but succumbed to heart failure hours after undergoing gall bladder surgery in 1987. For an ironic statement on Warhol's death, check *Andy Warhol's Frankenstein* for Udo Kier's philosophical statement on life, death, sex, and gall bladders (all contained in one sentence).

> **"They drummed you right out of Hollywood, so you came crawling back to Broadway. Well, Broadway doesn't go for booze and dope!"**
>
> --Susan Hayward in *Valley of the Dolls*.

286

Symptoms, Scream and Die, Stigma, and *The National Mummy.* **AKA:** Vampyres, Daughters of Dracula; Blood Hunger; Satan's Daughters; Vampire Orgy. 🦴🦴◁

1974 (R) 90m/C *GB* Marianne Morris, Anulka, Murray Brown, Brian Deacon, Sally Faulkner; *D:* Joseph Larraz. **VHS, Beta** *NO*

Vanishing Point

Drive-in hit combines a few existential pretensions with a straightforward chase structure to tell the story of Kowalski (Barry Newman) and his attempts to drive a white Dodge Challenger from Denver to San Francisco in 15 hours. Whenever the action moves away from the cars and the asphalt, it tends to run into trouble. One key flashback is unintentionally hilarious. Two gay characters are crude stereotypes. The rural characters don't fare much better, and the naked blonde on the motorcycle is still ridiculous, at best. As an accurate reflection of the times in which it was made, the film proudly wears its counterculture politics on its sleeve. Newman's performance is still effective, and veteran Jagger steals his scenes as a cagy desert rat. Director Sarafian and cinematographer John Alonzo give the proceedings a good, gritty look that fits this overachieving cult favorite. 🦴🦴🦴◁

1971 (PG) 98m/C Barry Newman, Cleavon Little, Gilda Texler, Dean Jagger, Paul Koslo, Robert Donner, Severn Darden, Victoria Medlin; *D:* Richard Sarafian. **VHS, Beta, LV $59.98** *FOX*

Vegas in Space

Four male astronauts take a secret mission to the planet Clitoris, the all-female pleasure plant where men are forbidden to trod. To capture a heinous villainous, they swallow gender-reversal pills in order to infiltrate the resort as show-girls. Typical Troma, but we give it an extra bone because it boasts an all-transvestite cast. 🦴🦴◁

1994 85m/C *D:* Phillip R. Ford; *W:* Phillip R. Ford. **VHS** *NYR*

Village of the Damned

Linda Blair in *The Exorcist.* Harvey "Damien" Stevens in *The Omen.* Mary-Kate and Ashley Olsen. These spawns from Hell are kid stuff compared to the blonde, cherubic aliens bent on world domination in this classic thriller based on John Wyndham's novel, *The Midwich Cuckoos.* Following a mysterious blackout, a dozen Midwich women are shocked to discover that they are pregnant (their husbands, parents, and church leaders are none too thrilled either). The women unwittingly raise the offspring as if they were their own. Though the children have superior intelligence and deadly telekinetic powers, they run into a brick wall in the person of George Sanders, the "father" of the group's leader, and their teacher who discovers their plan. The unjustly neglected sequel, *Children of the Damned,* is every bit its equal. Remade by John Carpenter in 1995 starring Christopher Reeves and Kirstie Alley. 🦴🦴🦴◁

1960 78m/B *GB* George Sanders, Barbara Shelley, Martin Stephens, Laurence Naismith, Michael C. Goetz; **D:** Wolf Rilla; **W:** Stirling Silliphant. **VHS, Beta, LV $14.95** *MGM, MLB*

Village of the Giants

Based on a classic H.G. Wells story, but there is nothing classic about this slice of psyche-delia gone bad. Meant to capitalize on the burgeoning youth movement and all the sex, drugs, and rock-and-roll that went with it, this movie tells the tale of a group of beer-guzzling teenagers who become giants after eating a mysterious substance invented by a twelve-year-old genius. Once they are ten-feet-tall (and no white rabbit in sight, although there are some giant geese), the rebellious teens take over a deserted theatre and terrorize a town. Fun to pick out all the soon-to-be stars—little Ronnie Howard is a long way from Mayberry in his role as the boy wonder, while Beau Bridges is a less-than-fabulous biker boy as the leader of the teenage losers. Totally silly premise with bad special effects and minimal plot follow-through. 🦴

1965 82m/C Ron Howard, Johnny Crawford, Tommy Kirk, Beau Bridges, Freddy Cannon, Beau Brummel; **D:** Bert I. Gordon; **M:** Jack Nitzsche. **VHS, Beta $19.95** *NLC, MLB, SUE*

The Violent Years

Spoiled high-school debutantes form a vicious all-girl gang and embark on a spree that includes murder, robbery, and the sexual assault of clean-cut young man. They kill a cop that corners them, and end up under siege at the high school, leading to the symbolic shot of the lead hellcat tossing a globe through a window. Justice wins out in the end. As the young hellcats are fond of saying: "So what!" Exploitative trash written by Wood, who directed the infamous *Plan 9 from Outer Space*, is modeled on roadshow pictures that exploited various vices, but were recommended by church groups because of the moral presented at the end. Moorehead was a 1950s Playboy centerfold. *AKA:* Female. 🦴🦴🦴

1956 60m/B Jean Moorehead, Barbara Weeks, Glenn Corbett; **D:** Edward D. Wood Jr., Franz Eichorn; **W:** Edward D. Wood Jr. **VHS, Beta $16.95** *SNC, RHI, AOV*

Voyage of the Rock Aliens

One of Pia Zadora's better celluloid moments. A quintet of aliens (the band Rhema, who look and sound like a Devo tribute group) land on the polluted shores of "Speelburgh, USA" in search of rock 'n' roll. There the lead space cadet falls for teen queen Pia, rousing the jealously of her boyfriend and his rockabilly posse. Energetic satire in spirit of innocent dumbness that characterized the vintage *Beach Party* movies, and who can resist seeing frequent psycho-geek Michael Berryman (*The Hills Have Eyes*) play the romantic hero for a change? One caveat: the whole opening of the film is just a pretext to unreel a lengthy music-video for the Pia Zadora/Jermaine Jackson duet "When the Rain Begins to Fall." 🦴🦴🦴

1987 97m/C Pia Zadora, Tom Nolan, Craig Sheffer, Rhema, Ruth Gordon, Michael Berryman, Jermaine Jackson; **D:** James Fargo. **VHS, Beta $79.95** *PSM*

"He followed me home, Mommy, can I keep him?" *The Village of the Giants.*

VIDEOHOUND SALUTES: JOHN WATERS

Watersworld

And where were you on February 7, 1985? In Baltimore, the date was officially proclaimed John Waters Day, in honor of the city' favorite-son filmmaker, who has set all his notorious celluloid efforts in that locale, from his grainy 1970 feature *Mondo Trasho* to the high-gloss dark comedy *Serial Mom*.

Bridging all the troublesome Waters' work are satires of middle-class American values flavored with a peculiar sense of humor that has gained the filmmaker the title King of Bad Taste. Whether it's a rape by giant lobster, the 'filthiest person alive' eating a dog dropping, or a supporting role by Sonny Bono, the Waters touch makes itself known. He's an original, with no overt imitators.

Throughout the 1970s, Waters wrote and directed a legendary series of 16mm features like *Multiple Maniacs* and *Pink Flamingos* that nauseated mainstream critics (and many moviegoers) who chanced to see them, while becoming prime attractions on the college campus and underground midnite-movie circuit. Waters' regular assembly of Baltimore screen talent, including Edith "Egg Lady" Massey, Mink Stole, and the 300- pound Harris Glenn Milstead--better known as the transvestite Divine--became stars in their own right. But a funny thing happened in the 1980s; John Waters, the sicko outsider, went Hollywood. He parlayed his cult popularity to get bigger budgets and semi-respectable actors to appear in crowd-pleasing pics like *Hairspray* and *Cry-Baby*.

The new Waters may be sparkling, but he's hardly purified. His latter efforts continue to display the demented wit and calculated offensiveness, but in more subtle, sneakier, and subversive ways than *Pink Flamingos* ever did. And while Divine, alas, passed away some years ago, Waters' West Coast-infused stock company now encompasses the thespian talents of Ricki Lake, Traci Lords, and Patricia Hearst.

continued...

Voyage to the Planet of Prehistoric Women

Communism met a most ignominious humiliation at the hands of Yankee capitalist pig Roger Corman when the latter purchased the 1962 Soviet feature *Planeta Burg* (Planet of Storms), a serious-minded feature (with ground-breaking and costly special effects) about a collective of brave, bland cosmonauts exploring a hostile planet. Corman Americanized the picture by having newcomer Bogdanovich splice in fresh footage of Yankee actors, first in *Voyage to the Prehistoric Planet* (1965), then more elaborately here, wherein astronauts journey to Venus where they get psychic vibes from a beachful of gorgeous, sea-shell clad alien women led by Van Doren, plus meet a few monsters. Dull, but with an ironic ending. Directed and narrated by Bogdanovich under the pseudonym Derek Thomas. What, you could have done better? No relation to the 1966 cheapie *Women of the Prehistoric Planet*. *AKA:* Gill Woman; Gill Women of Venus. 🎬▷

1968 78m/C Mamie Van Doren, Mary Mark, Paige Lee; *D:* Peter Bogdanovich. **VHS $16.95** *SNC*

Wanderers

Well-made adaptation of Richard Price's acclaimed novel about coming of age in the Bronx in 1963. The *Wanderers,* named after the Dion song, are a gang of Italian-American guys about to graduate high school, who prowl the Bronx with the feeling that something is slipping away from them. Fascinating, funny, perceptive, and touching. Manz is unforgettable as a scrappy gal, and the strip poker scene is a comic delight. Wonderful soundtrack (Dion, the Four Seasons) and crisp direction. This romanticized view of '60s teens may not be the popular classic that *American Graffiti* is, but it's still one of the best of its kind, well worth another look. Novelist Price is the hustling bowler with the mustache. 🎬🎬🎬▷

1979 (R) 113m/C Ken Wahl, John Friedrich, Karen Allen, Linda Manz; *Cameos:* Richard Price; *D:* Philip Kaufman; *W:* Philip Kaufman. **VHS, Beta $19.98** *WAR*

War of the Gargantuas

In this direct (though disguised as such) sequel to Toho's *Frankenstein Conquers the World,* pieces of the monster regenerate into mammoth hairy giants, one a brown forest beast, the other an aquatic green man-eater. Military and scientific heroes seek a way to stop the threat of the titanic Cain and Abel, without spawning an army of the creatures. The more human-looking monsters are an interesting change from the usual rubber "suitamation" critters, while the script hangs together well and sustains interest throughout. Another fun monster mash from sensei Honda, with the warring beasts tearing through farmlands and cities alike. Nightclub singer Kipp Hamilton belts out "Feel in My Heart" with the chorus, "The words get stuck in my throat," but is interrupted by the green Gargantua, who wants to stick her in his! Former child actor and musical star Tamblyn (*West Side Story*) returned from Japan to act in many Al Adamson pictures (*Satan's Sadists, Dracula vs. Frankenstein*). Unfortunately, a planned sequel feturing Godzilla was never made. Tinkering by the U.S. distributor was apparently limited to the soundtrack this time, and it was released on a twin bill with *Godzilla vs. Monster Zero* in 1970. *AKA:* Furankenshutain No Kaijusanda Tai Gailah; Sanda Tai Gailah; Duel of the Gargantuas; Frankenstein Monsters: Sanda vs. Gairath. 🦝🦝🦝▷

1970 (G) 92m/C *JP* Russ Tamblyn, Kimi Mizuno, Kenji Sahara, Jun Tazaki; *D:* Inoshiro Honda; *W:* Inoshiro Honda; *M:* Akira Ifukube. **VHS, LV** *PAR*

The War of the Worlds

H.G. Wells's classic novel of the invasion of Earth by Martians, updated to 1950s California, with spectacular destruction caused by the Martian war machines. It's a scary, tense, well-acted story based more on Orson Welles' radio broadcast than on the book. Despite technical advances, the visual and sound effects are still frightening. Film hit the top 20 in sales when released on video. Classic thriller later made into a TV series. Produced by George Pal, who brought the world much sci-fi, including *The Time Machine, Destination Moon,* and *When Worlds Collide,* and who appears here as a street person. 🦝🦝🦝▷

1953 85m/C Gene Barry, Ann Robinson, Les Tremayne, Lewis Martin, Robert Cornthwaite, Sandro Giglio; *D:* Byron Haskin. Academy Awards '53: Best Special Effects; Nominations: Academy Awards '53: Best Film Editing, Best Sound. **VHS, Beta, LV $14.95** *PAR*

The Warriors

Quite possibly the coolest gang movie ever made. The plot is simple—the Warriors must fight their way back to their home turf of Coney Island after being falsely accused of killing a gang messiah—but the style, the nonstop action, and the surreal fight scenes raise the stakes. These aren't the Crips and the Bloods with assault weapons we're talking about here. All the gangs are comic-book style caricatures with catchy names—the Warriors, the Gramercy Riffs, the Baseball Furies, the Lizzies (an all-girl gang)—and even when they are fighting, the action seems very choreographed and essentially nonlethal. Nonetheless, director Hill and cinematographer Andrew Laszlo make terrific use of light and color to heighten the mood of desperation as the Warriors make their way across New York. The most notable performances are turned in by Michael Beck and James Remar as the leaders of the Warriors, and by David Patrick Kelly as Luther, the truly weasel-like leader of the rival gang who is the real killer. Look for former Oscar winner Mercedes Ruehl (*The Fisher King*) as a policewoman in a park scene. 🦝🦝🦝

1979 (R) 94m/C Michael Beck, James Remar, Deborah Van Valkenburgh, Thomas G. Waites, Mercedes Ruehl, David Patrick Kelly; *D:* Walter Hill; *W:* Walter Hill. **VHS, Beta, LV $14.95** *PAR*

The Wasp Woman

Roger Corman had already brought us female westerns (*Gunslinger*), female Vikings (*Saga of the Viking Women and the Sea Serpent*), and female crooks (*Swamp Women*), not to mention *The Last Woman on Earth.* This time he gives us a distaff version of *The Fly.* In her quest for eternal beauty, the famous and glamorous president of a cosmetics company (Cabot) uses a potion made from wasp enzymes which actually makes her look many years younger. Naturally, she turns into a bloodthirsty wasp monster at night. Thankfully, the stuff never made it past the FDA. Eisley is her prospective boyfriend, who unfor-

> **"After all that man could do had failed, the Martians were destroyed and humanity was saved by the littlest things which God in his wisdom had put upon Earth."**
> --Cedric Hardwicke in *War of the Worlds.*

289

Cult Flicks and Trash Pics

Story continued...

As further proof that still Waters run deep:
while on hiatus from filmmaking, John Waters has
taught film appreciation, such as it is, to
prison inmates, and has authored various books,
including *Shock Value* and *Crackpot: The
Obsessions of John Waters.*

> **"Meet me in
> the bedroom
> in five
> minutes, and
> bring a
> cattle
> prod."**
>
> --Detective Phil
> Moscowitz (Tatsuya
> Mihashi) to Suki
> Yaki (Akike
> Wakabayashi) in
> What's Up Tiger
> Lily?

> **"Experience
> --that's what
> separates
> the girls
> from the girl
> scouts."**
>
> --George Hamilton in
> Where the Boys Are.

290

Cult Flicks and Trash Pics

tunately seems to prefer her assistant Morris (*A Bucket of Blood, Machine Gun Kelly*). Good fun, courtesy of Corman. Extant prints have added footage shot to fill television time slots. Released on a double bill with *The Beast From Haunted Cave. Evil Spawn* (1987) was an unofficial remake. 🦴🦴🦴

1959 84m/B Susan Cabot, Anthony Eisley, Barboura Morris, Michael Marks, William Roerick, Frank Gerstle, Bruno Ve Sota, Frank Wolff; **D:** Roger Corman. **VHS $9.95** *NOS, RHI, SNC*

Watermelon Man

A loud-mouthed Ralph Kramden-type (the late stand-up comedian Cambridge, in unconvincing Caucasian body paint) falls asleep in front of the TV during news footage of a race riot, and wakes up to find he's turned black. Co-workers, neighbors, and his liberal wife are sympathetic about the "accident"—until it's obvious the change is permanent. Starts off as buffoonish, minstrel-show comedy, but the tone gets darker (pun intended) as it goes along, and the closing image of impending racial apocalypse is truly disturbing. The subversive satire of bigotry was first in a three-picture deal between Columbia Pictures and hot filmmaker Van Peebles. Once this was released, the deal was off! 🦴🦴🦴

1970 (R) 97m/C Godfrey Cambridge, Erin Moran, Estelle Parsons, Howard Caine; **D:** Melvin Van Peebles. **VHS, Beta, LV $59.95** *COL, FCT*

The Weasel that Dripped Blood

Newlyweds move into their first apartment together, only to discover that the ground it sits on it ruled by the evil spirit that manifests itself as a demonic weasel. When a visiting sister becomes possessed by the weasel and goes on a bloody rampage, all seems lost until the maintenance guy (and part-time weasel hunter) arrives. Witty no-budget (they didn't even bother with the ketchup) horror spoof. 🦴🦴🦴

1989 19m/C Larc Levy, Lisa Giordano, Steve Bogdan, Marty Smith; **Cameos:** Al Bogdan; **D:** Al Bogdan; **W:** Al Bogdan. **VHS** *NO*

We're No Angels

Three escapees from Devil's Island hide out with the family of a kindly French storekeeper. While there, they become involved in the lives of his family, saving them from a rich but vicious uncle and his scheming son. Ustinov and Ray play Larry and Curly to Bogart's deadpan Moe in one of Bogie's few comedies. Their conversation about a wayward snake is not to be missed. Dialogue and personalities provide the laughs in the understated and ultimately warm-hearted film. 🦴🦴🦴

1955 103m/C Humphrey Bogart, Aldo Ray, Joan Bennett, Peter Ustinov, Basil Rathbone, Leo G. Carroll; **D:** Michael Curtiz. **VHS, Beta $14.95** *PAR*

Werewolf of Washington

Stockwell is a White House press secretary with a problem—he turns into a werewolf. And bites the President, among others. Subplot involves a short mad scientist who operates a secret monster-making lab in a White House bathroom. Occasionally engaging horror spoof and political satire made during Watergate era. 🦴🦴

1973 (PG) 90m/C Dean Stockwell, Biff Maguire, Clifton James; **D:** Milton Moses Ginseberg. **VHS, Beta** *NO*

The Werewolf Vs. the Vampire Woman

Hirsute Polish wolfman (Naschy, aka: Jocinta Molina) teams with two female students in search of witch's tomb. One is possessed by the undead witch, and eponymous title results. Fifth in a loosely related series of nine films in which former weightlifter Naschy stars as lycanthrope Waldemar Daninsky. Though not half the actor Lon Chaney was, Naschy's wolf man is refreshingly dynamic, springing out of shadows to bite out his victims' throats in gory close-ups. Shepard, who was also in the second of the series *Assignment Terror* (1969, aka: *Dracula vs. Frankenstein*), is elegantly spooky as the undead Countess Wandessa Darvula de Nadasdy. The success of this film insured that more horror films would be produced in Spain. A lifelong horror fan, the young Naschy was thrilled to act in scenes with Boris Karloff in the 1966 *I Spy* episode "Mainly on the Plains." **AKA:** Blood Moon. 🦴🦴🦴

1970 (R) 82m/C *SP GE* Paul Naschy, Gaby Fuchs, Barbara Capell, Patty Shepard, Valerie Samarine, Julio Pena, Andres Resino; **D:** Leon Klimovsky. **VHS $19.98** *SNC, HEG*

What's Up, Tiger Lily?

This legitimate Japanese spy movie—*Kagi No Kag* (Key of Keys), a 1964 Bond imitation—was re-edited by Woody Allen, who added a new dialogue track, with hysterical results. Characters Terri and Suki Yaki are involved in an international plot to secure egg salad recipe; Allen's brand of Hollywood parody and clever wit sustain the joke. Music by the Lovin' Spoonful, who make a brief appearance. 🦴🦴🦴

1966 90m/C *JP* Woody Allen, Tatsuya Mihashi, Mie Hama, Akiko Wakabayashi; **D:** Woody Allen, Senkichi Taniguhi; **M:** Jack Lewis. **VHS, Beta, LV $29.98** *VES*

Where the Boys Are

Four college girls head south for the winter joining thousands of students in Fort Lauderdale for spring break. At one end of the spectrum is sensible Dolores Hart, who holds off the advances of Ivy Leaguer George Hamilton. At the other is Yvette Mimieux, who looks for love in all the wrong places with tragic results. Paula Prentiss hooks up with Jim Hutton, who, too, has sex on the brain ("Are you a good girl?"). Comic relief Connie Francis makes beautiful music with jazz musician Frank Gorshin (who calls her "short one" and scolds her for speaking "jive" in his presence). Lots of fun and sun but also a sincere discussion of sexual attitudes. Prentiss and Hutton were so appealing together they were paired

in such films as *Bachelor in Paradise, The Honeymoon Machine, The Horizontal Lieutenant,* and the immortal turkey *Looking for Love,* notable as Johnny Carson's only film appearance. Make sure you don't rent the putrid 1984 remake by mistake. 🦴🦴🦴

1960 99m/C George Hamilton, Jim Hutton, Yvette Mimieux, Connie Francis, Paula Prentiss, Dolores Hart, Frank Gorshin; **D:** Henry Levin. **VHS, Beta, LV $19.98** *MGM*

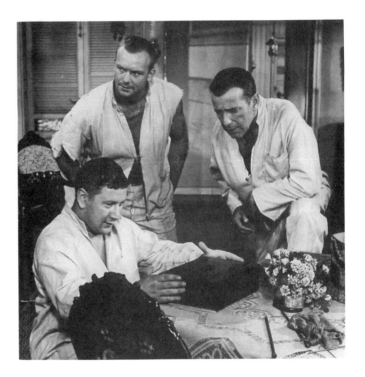

Where the Buffalo Roam

Early starring role for Murray as the legendary "gonzo" journalist Hunter S. Thompson in this meandering satire based on Thompson's books *Fear and Loathing in Las Vegas* and *Fear and Loathing on the Campaign Trail '72.* Either confusing or offensively sloppy, depending on whether you've read Thompson. Music by Neil Young, thank goodness, or this might be a woof. 🦴

1980 (R) 98m/C Bill Murray, Peter Boyle, Susan Kellerman; **D:** Art Linson; **M:** Neil Young. **VHS, Beta $19.95** *MCA*

"Wait a minute...THAT'S not the silver pattern we registered for!" Peter Ustinov, Aldo Ray, and Humphrey Bogart in *We're No Angels.*

Where's Poppa?

There is something to offend everybody in Carl Reiner's profane and scatological black comedy. George Segal stars as a New York lawyer at his wits end trying to care for Ruth Gordon, his impossible senile mother. She keeps asking for "Poppa" and does everything possible to sabotage his promising romance with winsome nurse Trish Van Devere. Contains the famous "tush" scene, in which Gordon pulls down her son's pants during a dinner with Van Devere. In these politically correct times, some of its more tasteless aspects do not play as rudely funny as they did two decades ago. Ron Leibman stars as Segal's brother who is mugged as he rushes through Central Park to stop a deranged Segal from killing Gordon. He is later mugged by the same gang and forced to rape who turns out to be a male cop in drag, who sends Leibman flowers the next day. A pre-*Saturday Night Live* Garrett Morris is one of the muggers. Carl's son Rob makes a brief courtroom cameo as an antiwar protester. The original

ending was too much even for Reiner: Segal leaves Van Devere for Gordon, climbs into her bed and announces, "Poppa's home." As should be glaringly obvious, more sensitive viewers should approach with caution. ***AKA:*** Going Ape. 🎵 🎵 ♪

1970 84m/C George Segal, Ruth Gordon, Ron Leibman, Vincent Gardenia, Rob Reiner, Trish Van Devere; ***D:*** Carl Reiner. **VHS, Beta, LV $19.95** *FOX*

White Heat

The highlight of this classic gangster film is one of Cagney's best performances as Cody Jarrett, the maniacal outlaw with a mother fixation. (The character is allegedly based on Arthur "Doc" Barker and his "Ma.") The finale—perhaps Cagney's most famous scene—is set on top of a burning oil tank, but his explosive breakdown in a prison cafeteria is just as memorable. It's almost impossible for an actor to portray that kind of insanity convincingly but Cagney doesn't make a single misstep. If his work weren't enough, there's also a terrific Max Steiner score, lots of great cars, the gritty action of a Warner Brothers crime film, and a script that's still fresh and entertaining. "Top 'o the world!" 🦴🦴🦴🦴

1949 114m/B James Cagney, Virginia Mayo, Edmond O'Brien, Margaret Wycherly, Steve Cochran; **D:** Raoul Walsh; **M:** Max Steiner. Nominations: Academy Awards '49: Best Story. **VHS, Beta, LV $19.95** *MGM, FOX*

White Pongo

A policeman goes undercover with a group of British biologists to capture a mythic white gorilla believed to be the missing link. A camp jungle classic with silly, cheap special effects, but too much talk. Surprisingly, this is not the only albino ape extravaganza—the even sillier (and cheaper) *White Gorilla* came out two years later, perhaps only to make use of Ray Corrigan's dyed-white monkey suit again. Double feature anyone? Fraser was also in *Bedlam, Blonde for a Day,* and *Gorilla Man*(?). Wrixon enlivens *Face of Marble* and *The Ape*(?!). We may just have discovered the makings of a Karloff-Fraser-Wrixon-Corrigan marathon here! 🦴🦴

1945 73m/B Richard Fraser, Maris Wrixon, Lionel Royce; **D:** Sam Newfield. **VHS, Beta $16.95** *SNC, NOS, HHT*

Whoops Apocalypse

Satiric account of events leading up to WWIII. Based on the British hit television series and scripted by series writers Marshall and Renwick. The U.S. tries to covertly bring the Shah of Iran's brother back to power, inadvertently setting the stage for World War Three. As things develop, we are treated to behind-the-scenes views of the major powers interspersed with absurdist newscasts. Unevenly executed, as might be expected in a tape edited from T.V., there's still plenty to laugh at. Best bits revolve around the British Prime Minister (he thinks he's Superman) and the hapless misadventures of the would-be Shah and his perpetually blindfolded manservant. Much duller are any and all bits staged in the U.S.S.R. Best sight gag involves the P.M. taking his pet dog, Krypto, out flying. A touch lengthy for one sitting, the viewer may wish to watch this over two evenings; the uniform style of humor displayed throughout will probably wear less thin. 🦴🦴🦴

1983 137m/C *GB* John Cleese, John Barron, Richard Griffiths, Peter Jones, Bruce Montague, Barry Morse, Rik Mayall, Ian Richardson, Alexei Sayle, Herbert Lom, Joanne Pearce; **D:** Tom Bussmann; **W:** Andrew Marshall, David Renwick. **VHS, Beta** *NO*

Wicked Stepmother

The only really redeeming quality about this flick is Bette Davis, in her final role—and she walked off shortly before her death. A family discovers that their aged stepmother (Davis) is actually a witch. Starting off old and testy, she transforms herself into her cat and is replaced (in a fast rewrite due to said walk off) by the sexy Barbara Carrera. Carrera then tries to work her evil magic on the family with the expected results transpiring in the final reel. There are a couple of chuckles, but they are few and far between. Suitable only for die hard Davis or Carrera fans; others should keep away. Davis' move was wise; the result is dismal, and would have been even if she'd stayed. As it is, the viewer wonders: How come the stepmother isn't Davis anymore? 🦴

1989 (PG-13) 90m/C Bette Davis, Barbara Carrera, Colleen Camp, Lionel Stander, David Rasche, Tom Bosley, Seymour Cassel, Evelyn Keyes, Richard Moll, Laurene Landon; **D:** Larry Cohen; **W:** Larry Cohen; **M:** Robert Folk. **VHS, Beta $14.95** *MGM*

The Wicker Man

Butchered by 15 minutes, criminally mis-marketed, and unjustly neglected upon its original release, *The Wicker Man* lives on video in this 103-minute restored director's cut. Edward Woodward stars as a devout policeman who is lured to the island community of Summerisle to investigate the disappearance of a young girl. Frustrated at every turn by citizens who claim not to know the child, he begins to suspect that the locals have conspired to kidnap her for a pagan ritual sacrifice. Little does he know that they have a much more diabolical plan in mind. This was the first screenplay by Anthony Shaffer, who later wrote the wickedly clever *Sleuth* and Alfred Hitchcock's *Frenzy.* Christopher Lee, who portrays Summerisle's leader, cited this as one of his favorite films. 🦴🦴🦴🦴

1975 103m/C Edward Woodward, Christopher Lee, Britt Ekland, Diane Cilento, Ingrid Pitt; **D:** Robin Hardy; **W:** Anthony Shaffer. **VHS, Beta $9.98** *REP*

W

THE HOUND'S FAVORITE TRASH MOVIE TITLES

(Remember, an inspired title doesn't necessarily mean an inspired movie...)

Assault of the Killer Bimbos

Attack of the Killer Refrigerator

Attack of the Mushroom People

Avenging Disco Godfather

The Beautiful, the Bloody and the Bare

Beneath the Valley of the Ultra-Vixens

Cannibal Women in the Avocado Jungle of Death

Children Shouldn't Play with Dead Things

Chopper Chicks in Zombietown

Doctor Duck's Super Secret All-Purpose Sauce

Faster Pussycat! Kill! Kill!

Ferocious Female Freedom Fighters

Gore-met Zombie Chef from Hell

I Dismember Momma

Mars Needs Women

Picasso Trigger

Rabid Grannies

Santa Claus Conquers the Martians

Satan's Cheerleaders

Sorority Babes in the Slimeball Bowl-A-Rama

Test Tube Teens from the Year 2000

Three on a Meathook

Wild Women of Wongo

The Worm Eaters

Zoltan...Hound of Dracula

The Wild Angels

Producer/director Roger Corman has written that he was trying to make a sympathetic film about California motorcycle gangs, and he had the cooperation of Hell's Angels on this one. The result, however, is anything but flattering. As Heavenly Blues, the leader of the pack, Peter Fonda comes across as petulant, shallow, and none-too-bright. Most viewers today will probably think that the gang members deserve all the rotten things that happen to them. Despite the characters' unattractiveness, the film is still quickly paced and involving (and co-star Diane Ladd's resemblance to her daughter Laura Dern is just astonishing). Corman's shot-on-the-run, cinema verite style makes for an accurate snapshot of mid-'60s America, when gasoline cost 28.9 cents a gallon. The script, written by Corman and rewritten by Bogdanovich, is based on a real incident. Remarkably violent for its PG rating. One of AIP's most successful productions. 🦴🦴🦴

1966 (PG) 124m/C Peter Fonda, Nancy Sinatra, Bruce Dern, Diane Ladd, Michael J. Pollard, Gayle Hunnicutt; **D:** Roger Corman; **W:** Charles B. Griffith, Peter Bogdanovich. **VHS $14.98** *ORI*

Wild at Heart

Dern and Cage are on the lam, going across country to escape her mother, his parole officer, and life. Humorous and frightening, sensual and evocative as only Lynch can be. Sweet love story of Sailor and Lula is juxtaposed with the violent and bizarre, obsessive brand of love of the people they encounter. Unmistakable Wizard of Oz imagery sprinkled throughout, as are some scenes of graphic violence. Ladd is unnerving as Dern's on-screen mother (she also has the role off-screen). 🦴🦴🦴🦴

1990 (R) 125m/C Nicolas Cage, Laura Dern, Diane Ladd, Willem Dafoe, Isabella Rossellini, Harry Dean Stanton, Crispin Glover, Grace Zabriskie, J.E. Freeman, Freddie Jones, Sherilyn Fenn, Sheryl Lee; **D:** David Lynch; **W:** David Lynch; **M:** Angelo Badalamenti. Cannes Film Festival '90: Best Film; Independent Spirit Awards '91: Best Cinematography; Nominations: Academy Awards '90: Best Supporting Actress (Ladd). **VHS, Beta, LV $19.98** *CCB, MED, IME*

The Wild Bunch

One of the great Westerns, and one of the great American films. Sam Peckinpah's story of a gang of outlaws on the Texas-Mexico border going out for one last job in 1913 has a lot to say about violence—its horror and its power to fascinate. Filmed at the height of social upheaval in 1968, it's also about Vietnam, authority, friendship, and betrayal. Highly influential in dialogue, editing style, and lyrical slow motion photography of gunplay. The three key scenes—the opening bank robbery, stealing the guns from the train, and the final shootout—are masterpieces of cinematic action. Holden, Borgnine, and Ryan create especially memorable characters with superb support from Johnson, Oates, and O'Brien. On video, the film exists in three versions: the "short" theatrical edition (cut by about 10 minutes at the studio's demand following the premiere) that played in theatres in 1969; the longer (145 minute) version edited by Peckinpah; and the "restored" letterboxed version of the same length with startlingly clear images and remixed stereo soundtrack released theatrically in 1995. The third is by far the best, though the "missing" footage doesn't substantially alter the film. 🦴🦴🦴🦴

1969 (R) 145m/C William Holden, Ernest Borgnine, Robert Ryan, Warren Oates, Strother Martin, L.Q. Jones, Albert Dekker, Bo Hopkins, Edmond O'Brien, Ben Johnson, Jaime Sanchez, Emilio Fernandez, Dub Taylor; *D:* Sam Peckinpah; *W:* Walon Green, Sam Peckinpah. Nominations: Academy Awards '69: Best Story & Screenplay, Best Original Score. **VHS, Beta, LV $19.98** *WAR*

Wild Guitar

A swinging youth cycles into Hollywood and, improbably, becomes an instant teen idol. Said swinging youth is the son of producer Arch Hall and, not so improbably, becomes the instant star of his own movie. This one is played so wide-eyed and stupid, that you almost have to go along for the ride. Hall, Sr., who was the subject of Jack Webb's service comedy *The Last Time I Saw Archie,* also plays the crooked agent, and Cash Flagg makes his screen debut as a henchman. Steckler got his first director's credit, after not getting credit/blame for *Secret File: Hollywood,* and shows off with an entertaining variety of camera angles and a distinctive sense of pace. Hall, Jr.'s second picture (after *The Choppers);* he warbles "Yes, I Will," "Wild Guitar," "Twist Fever," and other non-hits. Their next crime

would be *Eegah!* 🎵 Yes, I Will; Twist Fever; Wild Guitar. 🎵🎵

1962 92m/B Arch Hall Jr., Cash Flagg; *D:* Ray Dennis Steckler. **VHS, Beta $24.95** *RHI*

Wild in the Streets

Don't trust anyone over 30! This chilling black comedy stars Christopher Jones as rock idol Max Frost, who uses his influence (not to mention L.S.D. dumped in Washington, D.C.'s water supply) to get the voting age lowered to 14 and himself elected president. His first act is to incarcerate all citizens over 30 in "retirement homes." Richard Pryor co-stars as bandmember Stanley X. Shelley Winters goes over the top as Max's mother who desperately tries to prove she's groovy. The soundtrack scored a hit, "Shape of Things to Come." The last line is a knockout: "Everybody over 10 ought to be put out of business." 🦴🦴🦴▷

1968 97m/C Shelley Winters, Christopher Jones, Hal Holbrook, Richard Pryor, Diane Varsi, Millie Perkins, Ed Begley Sr.; *D:* Barry Shear; *M:* Les Baxter. Nominations: Academy Awards '68: Best Film Editing. **VHS, Beta, LV $19.99** *HBO*

The Wild One

The original biker flick: two motorcycle gangs descend upon a quiet midwestern town and each other. Brando is the leader of one, struggling against social prejudices and his own gang's lawlessness to find love and a normal life. The classic tribute to 1950s rebelliousness. Based vaguely on a real incident in California. Quaint after nearly 40 years, but still the touchstone for much that has come since, and still a central role in Brando's now-long career. Brando himself believes it failed to explore motivations for youth gangs and violence, only depicting them. Banned in Britain until 1967. 🦴🦴🦴▷

1954 79m/B Marlon Brando, Lee Marvin, Mary Murphy, Robert Keith, Jerry Paris, Alvy Moore, Jay C. Flippen; *D:* Laslo Benedek. **VHS, Beta, LV $19.95** *COL*

Wild Palms

In 2007 Los Angeles, Harry (Belushi) takes a job at a TV station that offers virtual reality programming to viewers, only this isn't benign technology. Delany is stuck in a thankless role as his wife, Cattrall is his former lover, but

W

"America's greatest contribution has been to teach the world that getting old is such a drag."
--Diane Varsi in *Wild in the Streets.*

"Man! I had a boner with a capital O'!"
--Sailor Ripley (Nicolas Cage) in *Wild at Heart.*

THERE'S NO EARTHLY
WAY OF KNOWING...

"There's no earthly way of knowing...which
direction we are going...there's no knowing
where we're rowing...or which way the river's
flowing...Is it raining, is it snowing...is a
hurricane a-blowing?...Not a speck of light is
showing, so the danger must be growing. Are the
fires of hell a-glowing? Is the grizzly reaper
mowing? Yes, the danger must be growing, for the
rowers keep on rowing, and they're certainly not
showing any signs that they are slowing!"

--Willy Wonka (Gene Wilder) in a particularly
psychedelic sequence in *Willy Wonka and the
Chocolate Factory*.

**"What is
this, a freak
out?!"**
--Violet
Beauregarde (Denise
Nickerson) in *Willy
Wonka and the
Chocolate Factory*.

Dickinson has the most fun as Harry's power-mad mother-in-law who's also a sadistic co-conspirator of a nasty senator (Loggia). Lesson in weird style over substance really doesn't make much sense, but unlike *Twin Peaks* (to which this TV miniseries was heavily compared) it at least has an ending. Executive producer Stone has a cameo which concerns the JFK conspiracy. Based on the comic strip by Wagner. In two parts. ♪♪

1993 300m/C James Belushi, Robert Loggia, Dana Delany, Kim Cattrall, Angie Dickinson, Ernie Hudson, Bebe Neuwirth, Nick Mancuso, Charles Hallahan, Robert Morse, David Warner, Ben Savage, Bob Gunton, Brad Dourif, Charles Rocket; *Cameos:* Oliver Stone; *D:* Phil Joanou, Kathryn Bigelow, Keith Gordon, Pete Hewitt; *W:* Bruce Wagner; *M:* Ryuichi Sakamoto. **VHS $99.98** *ABC, FCT*

Wild Rapture

See—the hunting and dissecting of an elephant and gorilla! See—the Ubangi tribe that is the last to practice lip-splitting! See—bug eating natives! See—pygmy children shooting poisoned arrows! See—the savage leopard hunt! These and other gruesome events abound in this shock-fest. Shot as serious documentary footage, it was edited into this feature and given smarmy narration by white devils, then given the full roadshow treatment. Another step taken in the evolution of mondo

movies, an exploitative step beyond the girls & gorillas documentaries of the '30s (*Ingagi, Forbidden Adventure, Bowanga Bowanga*), pointing the way for Kroger Babb's release of *Karamoja*. Banned for 18 years in some localities. ♪♪

1950 68m/B D: Jaques Dupont. **VHS, Beta $24.95** *NOS, HEG*

The Wild Ride

Nicholson, in an early starring role, portrays a rebellious punk of the Beat generation who hotrods his way into trouble and tragedy. He kidnaps now-straight ex-buddy Bean's squeeze (Carter); kills a few cops; then is killed. Interesting only if you're interested in Nicholson. ♪♪

1960 59m/B Jack Nicholson, Georgianna Carter, Robert Bean; *D:* Harvey Berman. **VHS, Beta $16.95** *SNC, NOS, VYY*

Wild, Wild World of
Jayne Mansfield

Mondo-madness! From Italy to France, Jayne Mansfield shares with us her "silly, wicked little daydreams" among the statues of Rome, goes native at a nudist colony, and visits some of Paris' most notorious bars. "Shocking," she coos, "but awfully French, n'est ce pas?" Oui-oui, Jayne. Footage of Mansfield's fatal car crash catapults this to the head of its class for tabloid trashiness. ♪♪▷

1968 89m/C Jayne Mansfield. **VHS, Beta $19.99** *VDM, DVT, TPV*

Wild Women of Wongo

A prehistoric fable, in bright color. The denizens of the primitive island Wongo, essentially beautiful women and ugly men, meet the natives of neighboring island Gooma, handsome men and ugly women. After some preliminary skirmishes, dancing, and sacrifices to the crocodile god, the inevitable mate-swapping gets under way. Not quite bad enough to be true camp fun, but stupidly silly in a low-budget way. Fury would go to Italy in the '60s to star in Machiste/Hercules/Ursus/Samson peplums. He returned to his roots and revealed a late-blooming gift for comedy in the recent *Dinosaur Valley Girls*. ♪♪▷

1959 73m/C Pat Crowley, Ed Fury, Adrienne Bourbeau, Jean Hawkshaw, Johnny Walsh; *D:* James L. Wolcott. **VHS, Beta $19.98** *DVT, MED, HEG*

The Wild World of Batwoman

The ultra-cheap campy cult film was made to capitalize on the original *Batman* television craze. Batwoman (who sports a mask, low-cut Merry Widow outfit, and a picture of a bat on her chest) and a bevy of Bat Girls are pitted against an evil doctor in order to find the prototype of an atomic hearing aid/nuclear bomb. The overall level of silliness is a notch or two below the old *Monkees* TV series. Kids who like to watch adults making idiots out of themselves will be hugely entertained. *AKA:* She Was a Hippy Vampire. 🦴🦴▷

1966 70m/C Katherine Victor, George Andre, Steve Brodie, Lloyd Nelson; *D:* Jerry Warren. **VHS, Beta $9.95** *RHI, SNC, DVT*

Willard

Willard (Davison) is a lonely, psychotic youngster who trains a group of rats, his only friends, to attack his enemies. Not as disgusting as it might have been (rated PG), but pretty weird and not redeemed by any sense of style or humor. *Bride of Frankenstein* Lanchester plays Willard's mom, Locke is the girl he likes more than rats, and Borgnine is his evil boss. Popular at the box office, it led to a wave of similar "animals attack" films. Followed by the inferior *Ben,* most noted for it's title tune by pre-superstar Michael Jackson. Based on by Stephen Gilbert's novel *Ratman's Notebooks.* Mann was famous for his Broadway-to-Hollywood projects (*Come Back, Little Sheba*), and made the kooky *Our Man Flint,* but had little talent for horror. Coincidentally, Locke went on to direct a picture called *Ratman.* 🦴🦴

1971 (PG) 95m/C Bruce Davison, Ernest Borgnine, Elsa Lanchester, Sondra Locke; *D:* Daniel Mann; *M:* Alex North. **VHS, Beta, LV $59.95** *PSM, PAR*

Willy Wonka & the Chocolate Factory

It's not just for rugrats, this slyly subversive musicalization of Roald Dahl's classic chil-

Gene Wilder does his Margaret Hamilton impression in *Willy Wonka and the Chocolate Factory.*

THE HOUND SALUTES: ED WOOD

Coming Out of the Wood Work

Imagine how aspiring moviemakers must feel. They pay big bucks to attend a prestigious film school, sacrifice to scrape together paltry budgets for first features and short subjects, and spend lifetimes sweating over an editing table or word processor to get their masterworks just right. And all the while it's staring them in the face; the fact that most of them will never be as celebrated and adored as Edward D. Wood, Jr. Wood was the eccentric writer and/or director of the some the most fascinatingly terrible schlock ever--from the autobiographical transvestite semi-documentary *Glen or Glenda?* to the Bela Lugosi vehicle *Bride of the Monster* to a string of obscure porno features and sex novels in the '60s and '70s. Wood died of a heart attack in 1978, a penniless alcoholic bottomed-out in Los Angeles. Who would have guessed that his best days were ahead of him?

With the rise of home video, and popularity of guidebooks and TV shows devoted to celluloid turkeys and oddities, Ed Wood's stranger-than-pulp-fiction life and work rose from near-oblivion to cult legend, bordering on folklore. Thanks to his inimitable screen "style" and colorful obsessions (sex, ghosts, angora sweaters, and Bela Lugosi, not necessarily in that order), Wood posthumously inspired film fests, underground comics, and 'zines. While many viewers saw Wood as something akin to a sideshow freak, they also admired his resolve and dogged nerve in getting his weird little movies produced on a shoestring. And a few fans detected a form of greatness in Wood's twisted oeuvre. One commentator defined Wood as "Genius without talent."

Inevitably, a multi-million-dollar Hollywood biopic, *Ed Wood*, starring Johnny Depp, premiered in 1994. In true Ed Wood tradition, it was the first Tim Burton-directed movie ever to lose money, but naturally became an instant cult sensation and gained Martin Landau an Oscar for portraying a Bela Lugosi on the skids. All the publicity represented a peak in popularity for Wood.

continued...

dren's book about poor lad Charlie winning a tour of the most wonderfully strange candy factory in the world, run by mysterious recluse Willy Wonka. He leads Charlie, four other youngsters, and their guardians on a thrilling tour of the factory, but pitiless tricks and sadistic treats await each child who misbehaves. In theatres for just about a week despite the hit song "Candy Man," this box-office dud was rescued by TV rebroadcasts and has earned a cult rep as a top-quality, brainy, and bizarre family film. Some viewers claim to find hidden meanings in the material: Wonka's psychedelic boat ride on the chocolate river looks like an LSD trip (with flashes of nightmare imagery, including a chicken's head chopped off). And what does floating Charlie say while imbibing the Fizzy Lifting Drink? "I'm so hiii-iigh!" Wilder is a delight as the demented Wonka, but listen carefully for his slightly off-color mutterings. Incidentally, Roald Dahl hated this movie. And Sammy Davis, Jr., hated recording "Candy Man," convinced it would ruin his career. ♪ Willy Wonka, the Candy Man; Cheer Up, Charlie; I've Got a Golden Ticket; Oompa-Loompa-Doompa-Dee-Doo; Pure Imagination. 🎞🎞🎞🎞

1971 (G) 100m/C Gene Wilder, Jack Albertson, Denise Nickerson, Peter Ostrum, Roy Kinnear, Aubrey Woods, Michael Bollner, Ursula Reit, Leonard Stone, Dodo Denney; **D:** Mel Stuart; **W:** Roald Dahl; **M:** Leslie Bricusse, Anthony Newley. Nominations: Academy Awards '71: Best Original Score. **VHS, Beta, LV $14.95** *WAR, APD, HMV*

Witchcraft

A young mother meets a couple killed three centuries ago for performing witchcraft. They want her baby, of course, to be the son of the devil. *Rosemary's Baby/Exorcist/Amityville* rip-off is thoroughly predictable, but has its moments. The weird opening juxtaposes the Lamaze method with burning at the stake. Somehow, the title touched a chord with horror fans and generated enough interest for six—yes, six!—sequels, to date. 🎞🎞

1988 (R) 90m/C Anat "Topol" Barzilai, Gary Sloan, Lee Kisman, Deborah Scott; **D:** Robert Spera. **VHS, Beta, LV $29.95** *ACA*

Witchcraft through the Ages

The demonic Swedish masterpiece in which witches and victims suffer against various his-

torical backgrounds. Nightmarish and profane, especially the appearance of the Devil as played under much make-up by Christiansen himself. Here, the imagery is the thing as we are treated to one horrific episode after another. Best of the vignettes involves a monk who turns from the path of righteousness and embraces the path of darkness. This groundbreaking silent film isn't just for lovers of early cinema. The kaleidoscopic nature of the film makes it excellent viewing for anyone with a penchant for the unusual. Definitely not for the kiddies and far more interesting than more modern exposes (a la *Witchcraft 70*), those who dabble in psychedelic substances may be the most entertained of all. *AKA:* Haxan. 🦴🦴🦴

1922 74m/B *SW* Maren Pedersen, Clara Pontoppidan; *D:* Benjamin Christiansen. **VHS, Beta $29.98** *GPV, MPI, WFV*

The Wizard of Gore

The prototypical Lewis splatter party, about a magician (Sager) who performs on-stage mutilations upon hypnotized subjects. After the show is over, the mutilations turn out to be messily real. Confusing surreal sequences show Sager carrying the dead bodies off to some kind of alter or incinerator. Inspired by Lewis' Grand Guignol Chicago theatre, The Blood Shed, in which this kind of act was a regular feature. High camp and barrels of bright movie blood, but Sager's speeches go on for too long, and the heroic young couple isn't as much fun as they could be. Similar in theme to *They Hypnotic Eye* (1960) and *Blood Sucking Freaks* (1975). 🦴🦴🦴

1970 (R) 96m/C Ray Sager, Judy Cler, Wayne Ratay, Phil Lauenson, Jim Rau, John Elliott, Don Alexander, Monika Blackwell, Corinne Kirkin; *D:* Herschell Gordon Lewis. **VHS, Beta** *NO*

The Wizard of Speed and Time

Ambitious, self-taught young movie F/X master is hired by a greedy producer to jazz up a TV show with his gags and gadgets. But he doesn't know the same exec has vowed to stop him at all costs to win a backstage bet. Jittlov, a true special-effects expert, plays himself in this personally financed all-ages comedy that brims with inside jokes, soapbox satire, self-indulgence, and the sunniest portrayal of Hollywood fringies this side of *Ed Wood*. Its zippy, joyous style evokes a Pee Wee Herman-esque vision of life and a sincere plea for dreamers everywhere to persevere despite the odds (and unions). Constant visual trickery incorporates footage from Jittlov's many stop-motion and collage short subjects; be quick with the "freeze" and "rewind" buttons to catch it all, right down to subliminals. Plot is reportedly based on Jittlov's own fraught experience working on a prime-time special in 1979. As for the long-gestated "WoSaT," its aborted theatrical release and videocassette debut on a B-movie label set Jittlov and his estranged producer to trading accusations over what went wrong. The filmmaker subsequently took his case to cyberspace, presiding over computer bulletin boards patronized by a growing cult of WoSaT fans. 🦴🦴🦴🦴

1988 (PG) 95m/C Mike Jittlov, Richard Kaye, Page Moore, David Conrad, Steve Brodie, John Massari, Frank Laloggia, Philip Michael Thomas, Angelique Pettyjohn, Arnetia Walker, Paulette Breen; *D:* Mike Jittlov; *W:* Mike Jittlov, Richard Kaye, Deven Chierighino; *M:* John Massari. **VHS, LV** *WTA*

The Wolf Man

Fun, absorbing classic horror with Chaney in fine form as a man bitten by werewolf Lugosi. His dad (Rains) thinks he's gone nuts, and the script hints that he may have good reason—just why was he sent away to school in America after his mother's death? A nervous breakdown? Werewolf makeup is a classic creation of Jack Pierce—never a wolf man to equal it, with transformation scenes to match. Ouspenskaya's finest hour as the prophetic gypsy woman. Chilling and thrilling. Followed by *Frankenstein Meets the Wolf Man.* 🦴🦴🦴🦴

1941 70m/B Lon Chaney Jr., Claude Rains, Maria Ouspenskaya, Ralph Bellamy, Bela Lugosi, Warren William, Patric Knowles, Evelyn Ankers; *D:* George Waggner. **VHS, Beta, LV $14.95** *MCA*

Working Girls

An acclaimed, controversial look by independent filmmaker Borden into lives of modern brothel prostitutes over the period of one day. The sex is realistically candid and perfunctory; the docudrama centers on a prostitute who is a Yale graduate and aspiring photographer living with a female lover.

Story continued...

VideoHound recommends the following sources for followers of Woodcraft:

Nightmare of Ecstasy: Rudolph Grey's exhaustively researched book is the basis for Tim Burton's film, but--unlike Burton--Grey chronicles Wood's entire life to the bitter end, mainly through alternating quotations from the filmmaker's friends and associates.

Ed Wood: Look Back in Angora: Video documentary on Wood featuring clips from his notorious productions, including *Jail Bait* and *Glen or Glenda?*, mixed with interviews with Wood's former cohorts.

Flying Saucers Over Hollywood: The Plan 9 Companion: Recently retitled *The Ed Wood Story*, this feature-length tribute to Wood's anti-masterpiece *Plan 9 From Outer Space* also delves into the writer/director's background and the fans who worship him.

Compelling, touching, and lasting, with sexually candid language and scenery. 🦴🦴🦴
1987 93m/C Amanda Goodwin, Louise Smith, Ellen McElduff, Maurisia Zach, Janne Peters, Helen Nicholas; **D:** Lizzie Borden; **W:** Sandra Kay; **M:** David Van Tiegham. **VHS, Beta $14.95** *COL, NLC, HHE*

World of the Depraved

Tango (Storm) runs an exercise club for young lovelies that are systematically being stalked by the mysterious full moon sex killer. Enter police detectives Riley and Hamilton (Decker, Reed), joking types who peep on their charges through keyholes, etc. When the plot finally gets around to the issue of the killer, the point of the movie has already been made clear. Silly, trivial, sophomoric humor lacking a trace of sincerity. Volume 6 of Frank Henenlotter's Sexy Shockers series. 🦴
1967 73m/C Tempest Storm, Johnnie Decker, Larry Reed; **D:** Herbert Jeffries; **W:** Herbert Jeffries. **VHS** **$23.00** *SMW*

The Worm Eaters

Greedy developers want to take over reclusive worm breeder Hermann Umgar's land. He unleashes his livestock on them, turning them into "worm people" (actors in brown sleeping bags). If seeing a mouthful of chewed-up food is your idea of a good time, this film is for you; title promise is met by countless closeups of folks gnawing on nightcrawlers. Extremely stupid film loses its childish appeal early on and becomes annoying, as does writer/director Herb Robin's Mel Brooksian Yiddish accent. Saving grace—Umgar is run over by a truck, which, in the words of the pressbook, is "one of the most horrifying messes ever seen on film"—comes nearly thirty minutes too late to save the viewer. Produced by Ted V. Mikels (*The Astro-Zombies*). Robins appeared in R. D. Steckler's *The Thrill Killers*. 🦴🦴🦴
1977 (PG) 75m/C Herb Robins, Barry Hostetler, Lindsay Armstrong Black; **D:** Herb Robins; **W:** Herb Robins. **VHS, Beta** *NO*

Wrestling Women Vs. the Aztec Mummy

Female wrestlers Loretta and the Golden Rubi grapple with the fiendish Black Dragon and his broad-shouldered sisters over the treasure of an Aztec princess's tomb guarded by mighty Tezomoc, the fearsome title dead guy. Muy loco frightflick unites two of south-of-the-border's most popular heroes for an action-packed bout, with plenty of big sweaty gals in tights if that's your bag. The long-haired Aztec Mummy, who can change into a snake or bat, started back in 1957 in a series of adventures including *Curse of the Aztec Mummy* and *The Robot vs. the Aztec Mummy,* while "La Luchadoras" debuted in *Doctor of Doom* and wrassled, among others, the infamous Aztec Ape! Rhino Video's print is the "Rock 'n' Roll" version and replaces the original creepy orchestral soundtrack with pseudo-rockabilly tunes. Director Rene Cardona Sr. is "el jefe" of Mexican low-budget cinema; his credits include several of masked wrestler Santo's films as well as the mind-altering holiday horrorshow *Santa Claus*. Son Rene Jr. followed in papa's footsteps with *Night of the*

Bloody Apes, the notorious cannibalism/plane crash movie *Survive!,* and *Guyana, Cult of the Damned.* 🎵🎵🎵

1959 88m/C *MX* Lorena Velasquez, Armando Silvestre; **D:** Rene Cardona Sr. **VHS, Beta $54.95** *SNC, RHI, HHT*

X: The Man with X-Ray Eyes

Medical researcher Milland gains the power to see through solid materials. After he's the cause of an accidental death, he runs away, eventually becoming a sideshow seer, then a storefront miracle worker. As his vision becomes ever more powerful, it begins to drive him mad. An excellent sci-fi psychological drama from Corman, with touches of philosophy and well done special effects. Milland is great playing a stuffier version of his suffering *Lost Weekend* persona. As the former A-list star and Oscar winner got older, he proved his durability by taking on roles in lower budget genre productions, even lending his directing talents to *Panic in the Year Zero.* Supporting cast is a step above as well, including regular Corman players Miller and Haze as two goofs in the carnival audience. Although famous for his potent brand of comedy, Rickles, who plays a seedy carnival man turned extortionist, has proven himself as a dramatic actor as well, beginning with *Run Silent Run Deep* (1958). Possibly inspired by a magician named Kuda Bux who had a television show in the early '60s, and who was billed as "the man with the x-ray eyes." **AKA:** The Man With the X-Ray Eyes; X. 🎵🎵🎵

1963 79m/C Ray Milland, Diana Van Der Vlis, Harold J. Stone, John Hoyt, Don Rickles, Dick Miller, Jonathan Haze; **D:** Roger Corman; **W:** Ray Russell, Robert Dillon; **M:** Les Baxter. **VHS, Beta, LV $59.95** *WAR*

Yellow Submarine

The acclaimed animated fantasy based on a plethora of mid-career Beatles songs, sees the Fab Four battle the Blue Meanies for the sake of Sgt. Pepper, the Nowhere Man, Strawberry Fields, and Pepperland. The first full-length British animated feature in 14 years features a host of talented cartoonists. Fascinating LSD-esque animation and imagery. Speaking voices provided by John Clive (John), Geoff Hughes (Paul), Peter Batten (George), and Paul Angelis (Ringo). The Beatles themselves do appear in a short scene at the end of the film. Martin fills in as music director, and Segal of *Love Story* fame co-scripts. 🎵 Yellow Submarine; All You Need is Love; Hey, Bulldog; When I'm Sixty Four; Nowhere Man; Lucy in the Sky With Diamonds; Sgt. Pepper's Lonely Hearts Club Band; A Day in the Life; All Together Now. 🎵🎵🎵▷

1968 (G) 87m/C *GB* **D:** George Duning, Dick Emery; **W:** Erich Segal; **M:** George Martin. **VHS, Beta, LV $19.95** *MVD, MGM, WTA*

Yellowbeard

Who would have thought nonstop gags about rape, torture, malice, avarice and debauchery would be so dull? Melange of pirate cliches follows the efforts of famously ferocious buccaneer Yellowbeard (Chapman) to locate a buried treasure using the map tattooed on his son's head. Lavish production design and incredible aggregation of mostly British comedic talent—including three Monty Python alumni—yields something very close to nothing at all. Final role for Feldman, who died during production. Bowie makes a very short cameo. **WOOF!**

1983 (PG) 97m/C Graham Chapman, Peter Boyle, Richard "Cheech" Marin, Thomas Chong, Peter Cook, Marty Feldman, Martin Hewitt, Michael Hordern, Eric Idle, Madeline Kahn, James Mason, John Cleese, Susannah York, David Bowie; **D:** Mel Damski; **W:** Graham Chapman, Peter Cook, Bernard McKenna. **VHS, Beta, LV $14.95** *VES*

Yog, Monster from Space

When a spaceship crashes on an island somewhere near Japan, the alien spores in it create giant monsters out of ordinary critters in order to destroy the population. A promoter gets a gleam in his eye and sees the potential for a vacation spot featuring the vicious creatures, while his companions try to help the natives battle the monsters. Plot is lacking in logic, and Tsubaraya's f/x are cheaply done. Below-average monster flick for Honda. Dubbing is also poor. **AKA:** The Space Amoeba. 🎵▷

1971 (G) 105m/C *JP* Akira Kubo, Yoshio Tsuchiya; **D:** Inoshiro Honda. **VHS, Beta $49.95** *SNC*

"It's amazing, isn't it? You can handle any man as long as you know what his sexual trip is."

--Marsia Zach gives advice on tricks of the trade in *Working Girls.*

DON'T HOLD YOUR BREATH...

Movie audiences are suckers for sequels (which explains why most movie sequels seem to be made for suckers). Even the most hardened, cynical, anti-mainstream alternative cineaste will reluctantly fork over his or her dollars to get a look at a followup to a cult fave.

Studios know this commercial fact well, and now barely a Hollywood extravaganza is made that doesn't leave the storyline open for a potential part II, II, IV, or more, until the franchise is well and truly beaten to death. As Danny DeVito once said of sequels, "Hollywood will keep on trying until they get it wrong."

Of course, if the first movie bombs worse than a B-52, there's not much chance of an encore. You can forget about that to-be-continued final scene in *Super Mario Brothers* ever leading anywhere. But there have been some movies so confident in their own sequelability that they've even predicted the titles of their successors--and cause much confusion for devoted viewers when the vaunted followups never came to pass:

Airplane 3: "That's just what they'd expect us to do!" says guest star William Shatner after this teaser appears at the end of *Airplane 2: The Sequel* (1982). Expect the unexpected, since a part 3 never got off the ground.

Remo Williams: Here's hubris for you. The makers of *Remo Williams: The Adventure Begins* (1985) used the title to announce they'd be cranking out a whole series of Bond-style actioners featuring the character of Williams, drawn from the ever-popular "Destroyer" series of pulp novels. *The Adventure Begins* didn't begin to captivate audiences, and Remo has yet to resume.

Buckaroo Bonzai Vs. The World Crime League: This teaser appears at the end of *The Adventures of Buckaroo Bonzai Across the Eighth Dimension* (1984), predicting a followup before that phantasmagorical superhero spoof stumbled at the box office. Now cult fans who discover BB for the first time are left browsing video racks

continued...

Young Einstein

This cheerful slapstick comedy deliberately recalls silent movies with its simple plot, innocent hero, and sight gags. Star-writer-producer-editor-director Yahoo Serious is an inspired Outback Einstein who figures out relativity and carbonates beer before he goes to college. The film is visually rich and fascinating all the way through; sometimes baffling too, but never boring. Serious claims that the his main influences are *Lawrence of Arabia* and Chuck Jones' cartoons (Road Runner, Bugs Bunny, etc.), and that's easy to believe. This one was followed by the sadly neglected *Reckless Kelly* in 1995. 🦴🦴🦴🦴

1989 (PG) 91m/C *AU* Yahoo Serious, Odile Le Clezio, John Howard, Pee Wee Wilson, Su Cruickshank; *D:* Yahoo Serious; *W:* Yahoo Serious; *M:* Martin Armiger. **VHS, Beta, LV $19.95** *WAR*

Young Frankenstein

Gene Wilder plays Dr. Frankenstein ("It's pronounced 'Frahnkenschteen'," he corrects), a brain surgeon who inherits the family castle back in Transylvania. He's skittish about the family business, but when he learns his grandfather's secrets, he becomes obsessed with making his own monster, aided by Marty Feldman as Igor ("It's pronounced 'Eyegor'," he returns). Wilder and monster Boyle make a memorable song-and-dance team to Irving Berlin's "Puttin' on the Ritz," and Hackman's cameo as a blind man is inspired. Garr ("What knockers!" "Oh, sank you!") is adorable as a fraulein, and Leachman ("He's vass my—boyfriend!") is wonderfully scary. Wilder saves the creature with a switcheroo, in which the doctor ends up with a certain monster-sized body part. Hilarious parody (written by Mel Brooks and Wilder himself) that pays an accurate and witty homage to the original. 🦴🦴🦴🦴

1974 (PG) 108m/B Peter Boyle, Gene Wilder, Marty Feldman, Madeline Kahn, Cloris Leachman, Teri Garr, Kenneth Mars, Richard Haydn; *Cameos:* Gene Hackman; *D:* Mel Brooks; *W:* Gene Wilder, Mel Brooks; *M:* John Morris. Nominations: Academy Awards '74: Best Adapted Screenplay, Best Sound. **VHS, Beta, LV $14.98** *FOX, HMV*

The Young Nurses

The fourth entry in the Roger Corman produced "Nurses" series. Three sexy nurses uncover a drug ring run from their hospital, headed by none other than director Fuller. Also present is Moreland, in his last role. Preceded by *The Student Nurses, Private Duty Nurses, Night Call Nurses,* and followed by *Candy Stripe Nurses.* Also on video as *Young L.A. Nurses 3.* **AKA:** Nightingale. 🦴🦴

1973 (R) 77m/C Jean Manson, Ashley Porter, Angela Gibbs, Zack Taylor, Dick Miller, Jack LaRue, William Joyce, Sally Kirkland, Allan Arbus, Mary Doyle, Don Keefer, Nan Martin, Mantan Moreland, Samuel Fuller; **D:** Clinton Kimbrough. **VHS, Beta $59.98** *NLC*

You've Ruined Me, Eddie

A dramatization of the social outrage expressed toward teenage pregnancy in the '50s. A spoiled rich girl gets knocked up by her boyfriend and is willing to go along with anything her father proposes in order to avoid her share of the blame. No worse, no better than several others of its kind. 🦴🦴

1958 m/B VHS $23.00 *SMW, TPV*

Zachariah

Billed as "The first electric western," this semi-spoof with '60s touches concerns two childhood pals in the old west who turn outlaw, then pursue different destinies. Matthew (future star Don Johnson) intends to become the most feared gunfighter of all, while Zachariah learns music, peace, love, and all that stuff. After quixotic journeys through the cliched landscape, the pair reunite and face off in a test of flower power. Badly dated material was scripted by members of The Firesign Theater (who cameo), but their trademark stream-of-consciousness media satire rarely surfaces. Nostalgia buffs may hearken to appearances by Country Joe and The Fish, The New York Rock Ensemble, and The James Gang. 🦴🦴

1970 (PG) 93m/C Don Johnson, John Rubinstein, Pat Quinn, Dick Van Patten; **D:** George Englund. **VHS, Beta $19.98** *FOX*

Zardoz

Sean Connery in a loin cloth, covorting to a soundtrack by Beethoven; what more do you need to know? The Hound will add that it's also a surreal parable of the far future, when Earth society has been divided into a stagnant, civilized bunch and a group of up-and-coming intellectuals. Offers a quirky sense of humor and wonderful images, particularly the post-apocalyptic hordes battling the "thinkers," and cinematography so lush you could watch it with the sound turned down and still enjoy it (the Hound does have a few friends that claim they couldn't possibly understand it less without the dialogue). It is a bit slow at times, but if you like the post-apocalyptic thing (or Sean Connery), *Zardoz* is well worth watching. 🦴🦴

1973 105m/C Sean Connery, Charlotte Rampling, John Alderton, Sara Kestelman; **D:** John Boorman. **VHS, Beta, LV $19.98** *FOX*

Zipperface

A Palm Beach serial murderer in leather bondage gear is cutting up local prostitutes. What luck that the new police detective is a beautiful girl. Shoehorned into a barely-there outfit, she goes undercover as sexy bait for the kinky killer. Sleazy cheese with feminist themes kicked around—literally. Director Pourmand's previous major showbiz credit was a staged audience-participation bar mitzvah. **WOOF!**

1992 90m/C Dona Adams, David Clover, John Dagnen; **D:** Mansour Pourmand. **VHS, LV $89.95** *AIP*

Zoltan. . .Hound of Dracula

In this canine version of the Dracula story, the resurrected undead Doberman Zoltan and creepy vampire dog wrangler Nalder (*The Man Who Knew Too Much, Salem's Lot*) have a mission: go to Los Angeles to find the last of Count Dracula's living descendants (Pataki). They track him to a vacation camp and Zoltan gets busy recruiting furry vampire brides of his own, attracting the attention of vampire hunter Ferrer (*The Cain Mutiny, Dune*). It's fun to see the dogs tearing up cabins and campers in search of prey. Campy and just original enough to make it worth watching, but it could use more plot and less endless footage of growling dogs. Director Band, who made the excellent *I Bury the Living* (1958) early in his career, survived this film, and went on to form the Full Moon company, which specializes in low budget, straight-to-video horror movies. **AKA:** Dracula's Dog. 🦴🐾

Story continued...

in vain for any reference to the World Crime League.

That New Columbus: The Brazzo Brothers, villains in the spoof *I Was a Zombie for the FBI* (1982) were supposed to return in this promised followup to the feature made by Memphis State University students. Clearly a case of homework not turned in.

History of the World: Part Two: Scenes from this are shown as a gag trailer at the end of Mel Brooks' *History of the World: Part One* (1982). If it was ever meant seriously it never came to pass, though the "Jews in Space" sequence could be viewed as a dry run for *Spaceballs*.

Cyborg: Well, yes, okay, this film actually was made--but not as intended. The ultraviolent Jean-Claude Van Damme spectacle was originally devised as part two of the He-Man movie *Masters of the Universe* (1987). Remember Skeletor reappearing at the end and promising "I'll be back!" No? Neither did anybody else, which was why the sequel mutated from a toy-chest spinoff into kickboxer carnage with no Mattel connection. It must have worked; *Cyborg* has so far begat two sequels of its own.

1977 85m/C Michael Pataki, Reggie Nalder, Jose Ferrer; *D:* Albert Band; *W:* Frank Ray Perilli. **VHS, Beta** **$9.98** *REP, VCI, FCT*

Zombie High

Freshman at Ettinger Academy Prep School stumble onto plot by the evil Dean and board of directors. They produce a serum made from blood and brains that keeps them forever young, a la Dorian Grey, while the students are turned into zombies. They replace the lost brain matter with crystals, allowing them to control the students by radio waves. Funny thing is, the zombies have done very well for themselves, making Ettinger a very prestigious school. Nevertheless, they must be stopped, and it is up to our young heroes to do just that. Fun rock

sound track and sense of humor make this tongue-in-cheek zombie flick watchable. Look for a pre-Twin Peaks Sherilyn Fenn. Reminded the Hound of his own obedience school days. *AKA:* The School That Ate My Brain. 🦴🦴🦴

1987 **(R)** 91m/C Virginia Madsen, Richard Cox, Kay E. Kuter, James Wilder, Sherilyn Fenn, Paul Williams, Scott Coffey; *D:* Ron Link. **VHS, Beta** **$9.95** *VTR*

Zombies on Broadway

Ever hear of the comedy team of Wally Brown and Alan Carney, RKO's answer to Abbott and Costello? Thought not, and while this zombie comedy is neither very funny nor very scary, it does manage to get under your skin. Press agents Brown and Carney are dispatched to the Caribbean to bring back real zombies, the promised attraction at gangster Sheldon Leonard's New York nightclub. A post-Dracula, pre-Ed Wood Bela Lugosi stars as Dr. Renault, whose injections create the living dead. Things get really creepy when Carney is transformed into a bug-eyed zombie. Leonard was the original voice of Post Cereal's Sugar Bear ("Can't get enough of that Sugar Crisp"). He was also a producer of classic TV (*The Dick Van Dyke Show, I Spy*). Onscreen, he is perhaps best known as bartender Martini ("Out you pixies go, through the door or out the window") in *It's a Wonderful Life*. The imposing Darby Jones and calypso singer Sir Lancelot recreate their roles from RKO's classic, *I Walked With a Zombie*. *AKA:* Loonies On Broadway. 🦴🦴🦴

1944 68m/B Wally Brown, Alan Carney, Bela Lugosi, Anne Jeffreys, Sheldon Leonard, Frank Jenks, Russell Hopton, Joseph Vitale, Ian Wolfe, Louis Jean Heydt, Darby Jones, Sir Lancelot; *D:* Gordon Douglas. **VHS, LV $29.95** *TTC, FCT, IME*

Zontar, the Thing from Venus

Scientist Huston contacts an alien intelligence from Venus by radio, and helps it come to Earth, believing it will end all of mankind's problems. The alien batlike thing soon begins taking over by taking control of key citizens and shutting off power sources, and only veteran sci-fi hero Agar can stop it. Are YOUR appliances working? Incredibly, this is a remake of *It Conquered the World* (1956), Roger Corman's 1956 classic that swiped from both *Invasion of the Body Snatchers* and *Day the Earth Stood Still*. One of eight features that American International Pictures hired Buchanan to make for TV release, with an average budget of $22,000. This is not the worst. 🦴🦴

1966 68m/C John Agar, Anthony Huston; **D:** Larry Buchanan. **VHS $19.98** *SNC, VDM*

Zotz!

The holder of a magic coin can will people dead by uttering "zotz"; spies pursue the mild-mannered professor who possesses the talisman. Adapted from a Walter Karig novel. Typical William Castle fare; his gimic in the theatrical release of the movie was to distribute plastic "zotz" coins to the theatre patrons. 🦴🦴

1962 87m/B Tom Poston, Julia Meade, Jim Backus, Fred Clark, Cecil Kellaway; **D:** Ray Russell; **W:** Ray Russell. **VHS, Beta $59.95** *COL*

"It's true what they say about big feet!" Gene Wilder extolls Peter Boyle's proportions in *Young Frankenstein.*

Cult Connections

VideoHound's *Cult Flicks and Trash Pics'* "Cult Connections" is our added bonus effort at enabling your cult film habit. Listed below (and for endless pages) are World Wide Web home pages, online newsgroups, 'zines and newsletters, fan clubs, and selected books, if you just can't get enough. Don't forget to check out VideoHound's own home page (www.videohound.com) to communicate with the Hound himself via cyberspace (okay, so forgive us that little plug, but he's pretty excited about it).

WEB PAGES

Allen, Woody
www.idt.unit.no/~torp/woody/

Asian Movies
www.seas.upenn.edu/~luwang/homepage.html

Brazil
poppy.kaist.ac.kr/cinema/brazil/

Cult Movies
lasarto.cnde.iastate.edu/Movies/CultShop

Fast Times at Ridgemont High
turtle.ncsa.uiuc.edu/spicoli

Godzilla and Friends
tswww.cc.emory.edu/~kgowen/gamera.html
www.ama.caltech.edu/~mrm/godzilla.html

Heathers
www.best.com/~sirlou/heathers.shtml
www.duc.auburn.edu/~harshec/WWW/
 heathers.html

Hong Kong Movies
www.mdstud.chalmers.se/hkmovie

Horror Movies
www.cat.pdx.edu/~caseyh/horror/index.html

James Bond
www.dur.ac.uk/~dcs3pjb/jb/jb/home.html
www.mcs.net/~klast/www/bond.html

Kubrick, Stanley
www.lehigh.edu/~pj12/kubrick.html
www.lehigh.edu/~pjl2/2001.html

Lynch, David
web.city.ac.uk/~cb157/Dave.html
www.iac.net/~brian/bluevelvet.html
www.ksu.ksu.edu/~kxb/dune.html
www.princeton.edu/~cgilmore/dune/
dune.html

Monty Python
sashimi.wwa.com/hammers/comedy/python/
 python.html
www.iia.org/~rosenr1/python/
www.prairienet.org/rec/britcom/afmp.home.
 html

MST3K
ai.eecs.umich.edu/people/kennyp/sounds.html
bert.ils.nwu.edu/chaput/cath.html
comcentral.com
comp.uark.edu/~jwiggins/mst3k
das.ucls.uchicago.edu/students/MaryJo_
 Wood.f/broomcloset.html
ftp.netcom.com/pub/isis/www/torgo.html
grove.ufl.edu/~cirop02/mst_html/mst3k.html
grove.ufl.edu/~servo/pan_html/pan.html
info.pit.edu/~rwdst56/mst3k.html
kelvin.seas.virginia.edu/~cac2g/mst3k.html
linex.com/~la/mst3k.html

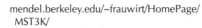

mendel.berkeley.edu/~frauwirt/HomePage/
  MST3K/
portnoy.tiac.net/mst3k
pubpages.unh.edu/~kennethd
sunsite.unc.edu/lunar/mst3k/mst3k.html
ubvms.buffalo.edu/~v131mx78/mst3k/mst3k.
  html
world.std.com/~fRiNgE/MST3K.html
www.c3.lanl.gov/~adelson/funlinks/mst.html
www.cais.com/jdfalk/html/mst3kadv.html
www.contrib.andrew.cmu.edu/usr/ar2w/mega
  weapon/megaweapon.html
www.ee.pdx.edu/~alf/html/mst3k.html
www.engin.umich.edu/~jgotts/mst3k.html
www.engin.umich.edu/~mneylon/mst3k/
www.itec.sfsu.edu/jeff/mst3k.html
www.marshall.edu/~floyd3/mst3k.html
www.mcs.net/~sftoday/sftwaste.htm
www.mindspring.com/~torgo/mst3k.html
www.mvp.com/~pravn
www.physics.duq.edu/~sensor/mst3k.html
www.primenet.com/~lathrop/mst3k.html
www.public.iastate.edu/~hunter/mst3k.html
www.rain.org/~roryh/mst3k
www.smartpages.com/faqs/top.html
www.ssc.com/~roland/mst3k/mst3k.html
www.teleport.com/~lynsared/mst.html
www.together.net/~croooow/mst3k.html
www.usgcc.odu.edu/~ty/mst3k/MST3K.html
www.webcom.com/~cgould/mstcrit.html
www.well.com/user/jennya/
www.wpi.edu/~patrickd/tomservo.html
www2.msstate.edu/~gec2/mst3k.html

Princess Bride

cactus.cedarville.edu/~brian/pb.html
www.engin.umich.edu/~cstrick/PrincessBride/
  sounds.html

Raimi, Sam

b62528.student.cwru.edu/home.html

Rocky Horror

chs-web.umdl.umich.edu/odd/RHPS/index.html
heinlein.k2nesoft.com/~smw/rhps.html
radon.gas.uug.arizona.edu/~jnorman/rhps/
www.cs.wvu.edu/~paulr/rhps/rhps.html
www.uta.fi/~cstivi/rocky.html

Rosencrantz and Guildenstern Are Dead

earthvision.asu.edu/~jason/rg_dead/

Scott, Ridley

anubis.science.unitn.it/services/blob/
  bladerunner/index.html
dutial.twi.tudelft.nl/~alien/alien.html
kzsu.stanford.edu/uwi/br/off-world.html
www.uq.oz.au/~csmchapm/bladerunner/

SF Movies

www.maths.tcd.ie/mmm/ReviewsFrom
  TheForbiddenPlanet.html

Star Trek/Gene Roddenberry

cruciform.cid.com/~werdna/sttng/gene.html
www.ama.caltech.edu/~mrm/kirk.html
www.astro.lsa.umich.edu:80/users/sewin/
  Continuum/

Star Wars

bantha.pc.cc.cmu.edu:1138/SW_HOME.html
cactus.cedarville.edu/~tyler/bobafett.html
hubcap.demson.edu/~pranks/sw.html
stwing.resnet.upenn.edu:8001/~jruspini/star
  wars.html
underground.net/~koganuts/Galleries/sw.html
www.broken.org/~starwars/
www.cc.utah.edu/~tjp3154/starwars
www.interaccess.com/users/csphil/hamm.html
www.mgt.purdue.edu/~vkoser/starwars/star.
  html
www.unisuper.com.au/starwars
www.wpi.edu:8080/ftp/starwars

Tarantino, Quentin

colargol.edb.tih.no/~kennetha/dogs.html
colargol.edb.tih.no/~kennetha/pulp.html
crow.acns.nwu.edu:8082/pulp/
iris.asij.ac.jp/techskills/abjornho/SHRINE.html
metro.turnpike.net/ravven/
rmd-www.mr.ic.ac.uk/~dan/tarantino/
  tarantino.html
underground.net/~koganuts/Galleries/qt.main.
  html
wolf.cso.uiuc.edu/pulpfict.html
www.foresight.co.uk/ents/dogs/
www.iac.net/~brian/reservoir.html
www.kean.edu/~lisajoy/PulpFiction/
www.nvg.unit.no/~eddie/tarantino.html
www.paranoia.com/~kevintx/rd.html
www.phantom.com/~jbonne/tarantinoworld/
www._usacs.rutgers.edu/~zonker.pulp.html
www2.ncsu.edu/eos/users/s/smlane/WWW/qt.
  html

Woo, John

trill.pc.cc.cmu.edu:80/~jkoga/jw_gallery.html
underground.net/~koganuts/Galleries/jw.main.
  html

Wood, Ed

www.futurenet.co.uk/edwood/CONTENTS.
  html

Zinescope

www.uta.fi/~tlakja/index.html

NEWSGROUPS

alt.asian.movies
alt.cult-movies
alt.cult-movies.evil-deads
alt.cult-movies.rocky-horror
alt.fan.bruce-campbell
alt.fan.dune
alt.fan.james-bond
alt.fan.mike-jittlov
alt.fan.monty-python
alt.fan.mst3k
alt.fan.spinal-tap
alt.fan.tarantino
alt.fan.woody-allen
alt.horror
alt.horror.cthulhu
alt.horror.shub-internet
alt.horror.werewolves
alt.movies.branagh-thmpsn
alt.movies.independent
alt.movies.indian
alt.movies.kubrick
alt.movies.monster
alt.movies.scorsese
alt.movies.spielberg
alt.movies.tim-burton
alt.movies.visual-effects
alt.sex.startrek.fetish
alt.startrek.klingon
alt.tv.startrek.creative
bit.listserv.cinema-1
bit.listserv.screen-1
rec.arts.animation
rec.arts.anime
rec.arts.disney
rec.arts.movie-going
rec.arts.movies
rec.arts.movies.announce
rec.arts.movies.current-films
rec.arts.movies.lists+surveys
rec.arts.movies.misc
rec.arts.movies.past-films
rec.arts.movies.people
rec.arts.movies.production
rec.arts.movies.reveiws
rec.arts.movies.tech
rec.arts.sf.movies
rec.arts.sf.starwars.misc
rec.arts.sf.starwars
rec.arts.startrek.current
rec.arts.startrek.info
rec.arts.startrek.misc
rec.arts.startrek.tech
rec.arts.startreknew
rec.arts.tv.mst3k
rec.arts.tv.mst3k.misc
rec.music.movies

'ZINES/NEWSLETTERS

Alternative Cinema

Attn: Orders
PO Box 6573
Akron OH 44312

$18/4 issues; $28 outside the U.S. Covers newer Poverty Row video, and Hollywood product from its own perspective.

Animerica

Viz Communications, Inc.
PO Box 77010
San Francisco CA 94107

$58/12 issues; $70 in Canada and Mexico; $158 elsewhere.

Anti-Hollywood Reporter

Frank Wallis
PO Box 654
Monroe CT 06468-0654

Monthly. $10/6 issues.

Asian Trash Cinema

Vital Sounds Inc.
PO Box 16-1917
Miami FL 33116

$30/6 issues; $60 outside the U.S. and Canada.

Bits and Pieces

John Clayton
10354 Windstream Dr.
Columbia MD 21044

$3.50/issue. Print organ of the Horror and Fantasy Film Society of Baltimore.

Blood Times

Louis Paul
44 E. 5th St.
Brooklyn NY 11218

$15/5 issues; $25 outside the U.S.

Cashiers du Cinemart

Mike White
PO Box 2401
Riverview MI 48192-7417

$5/5 issues.

Chiller Theatre

PO Box 23
Rutherford NJ 07070

$19/4 issues. "The magazine filled with horrible stuff."

Cinefantastique

Box 270
Oak Park IL 60303
(708)366-5566
(708)366-1441 (fax)
1-800-798-6515
Bimonthly. $27/year; $32 outside the U.S.

Cineraider

Richard Akiyama
PO Box 240226
Honolulu HI 96824-0226
$7/3 issues. Mainly HK coverage.

Cult Movies

6201 Sunset Blvd. Ste. 152
Hollywood CA 90028
$18/4 issues; $21.77 in Mexico and Canada;
$23.77 elsewhere. Exotic esoterica about exploitation films.

Draculina

PO Box 969
Centralia IL 62801
$24/4 issues. Covers low-budget horror video.

Dreadful Pleasures

Mike Accomando
650 Prospect Ave.
Fairview NJ 07022
$3/issue.

The Drive-In Theatre Newsletter

Nathan Miner
225 W. 1st St.
Frostburg MD 21532
$1.50/issue.

Ecco

Kill-Gore Productions
PO Box 65742
Washington DC 20035
$15/4 issues; $20 outside the U.S.

Ejecto-Pod

Jan Johnson
29 Darling St. No. 2
Boston MA 02120

El Loco

Miriam Linna
Box 646, Cooper Sta.
New York NY 10003
$3/issue. Covers Mexican cinema; is also a catalog of available posters and lobby cards.

European Trash Cinema

c/o Craig Ledbetter
PO Box 5367
Kingwood TX 77325
(713)251-0637
74563.1756@compuserve.com
$20/4 issues.

The Exploitation Journal

Keith J. Crocker
40 S. Brush Dr.
Valley Stream NY 11554
$22/5 issues. "The connoisseur's guide to horror and exploitation in the cinema."

Exploitation Retrospect

Dan Taylor
PO Box 1155
Haddonfield NJ 08033-0708
$10/6 issues.

Famous Monsters of Filmland

Dynacomm
Subscription Dept.
PO Box 9669
North Hollywood CA 91609
$24.95/5 issues; $40 in Canada and Mexico;
$50 elsewhere.

Fangoria

PO Box 142
Mount Morris IL 61054
10/year. $34.47/year; $43.47 outside the U.S.

Fatal Visions

Box 133
Northcote Victoria 3070 Australia
$6/issue.

Femme Fatales

Cinefantastique
PO Box 270
Oak Park IL 60303
(708)366-5566
(708)366-1441 (fax)
1-800-798-6515
$18/4 issues; $21 outside the U.S.

Film Canon

Dave Filipi
2825 Neil Ave. No. 714
Columbus OH 43202
$10/4 issues.

Film Threat

PO Box 341
Mount Morris IL 61054-9840
1-800-201-4442

Bimonthly. $11.85/year. "The Other Movie Magazine."

Filmfax

PO Box 1900
Evanston IL 60204

$30/6 issues; $40 in Canada; $65 elsewhere. Specializes in vintage TV and movies.

Filmmaker

5550 Wilshire Blvd. Ste. 204
Los Angeles CA 90036-3888

$14/4 issues. Professional 'zine on the independent movie business.

Forbidden Zone

Jeff Smith
1817 Oates Dr. Apt. 529
Mesquite TX 75150

$10/5 issues.

G-Fan

Daikaiju Enterprises
Box 3468
Steinbach MB Canada R0A 2A0

$20/6 issues; $20 outside the U.S. and Canada. Official fanzine of G-Force, the Godzilla Society of North America.

Ghoulpardi

Box 505
Barberton OH 44203

Newsletter for fans of Ohio TV horror hosts.

Gore Gazette

c/o Rick Sullivan
643 Bloomfield Ave.
Nutley NJ 07110

$13/12 issues. "Guide to horror, exploitation, and sleaze in the NY area."

Hong Kong Film Magazine

601 Van Ness Ave. Ste. E3728
San Francisco CA 94102

Quarterly. $23/6 issues.

The Hong Kong Film Connection

PO Box 867225
Plano TX 75086-7225

$15/6 issues; $16 in Canada. "The best news & reviews this side of the Pacific."

Imagi-Movies

Cinefantastique
PO Box 270
Oak Park IL 60303
(708)366-5566
(708)366-1441 (fax)
1-800-798-6515

$18/4 issues; $21 outside the U.S.

Independent Video Magazine

PO Box 219
West Islip NY 11795-0219

$12/6 issues; $16 in Canada; $27 elsewhere. Covers low-budget moviemakers.

It's Only a Movie!

Michael Flores
PO Box 14683
Chicago IL 60614-0683

$12/12 issues. Print organ of the Chicago Psychotronic Film Society.

The Joe Bob Report

PO Box 2002
Dallas TX 75221
(214)985-7448 (fax)

Biweekly. $65/26 issues; $100 outside the U.S.

Kung Fu Girl

Keith Allison
1215 SW 4th Ave., Down
Gainesville FL 32601

$3/issue.

Let It Bleed

Dan Cziraky
100 Sunset Ave.
Newark NJ 07106

$12/12 issues. Exploitation news, gossip, and interviews.

M.A.M.A.

William Connolly
6635 Delongpre No. 4
Hollywood CA 90028

$10/4 issues. Photocopy fanzine of chopsocky cinema history by the Martial Arts Movie Association.

The Michelle Mystique

Michael Shutter
PO Box 8936
Cincinnati OH 45208

$2/issue. For fans of Michelle Bauer, star of trash and sex films.

Cult
Connections

Monster! International

Kronos Productions
MPO Box 67
Oberlin OH 44074-0067

Movie Club

Don Dohler
12 Moray Ct.
Baltimore MD 21236

$15.80/6 issues. Covers B movies, classic horror, and sci fi.

Nippon Rando No Yumei Kaiju

Montag Enterprises
1151 Raymond Ave. No. 205
Glendale CA 91201-1850

$12/6 issues. "Famous Monsters of Japanland."

Oriental Cinema

Draculina
PO Box 969
Centralia IL 62801

$20/4 issues. Covers Japanese giants to Hong Kong Fu and more.

Outre

Filmfax
PO Box 1900
Evanston IL 60204

$20/4 issues; $30 in Canada; $50 elsewhere. "Entertainment from the world of Ultramedia."

Pagoda

Garo Nigoghossian
2 Holworthy Terr.
Cambridge MA 02138

$4/issue. Provides Hong Kong movie news, reviews, and fanzine gossip.

Parts

Friday Jones
451 Moody St. No. 134
Waltham MA 02154-0442

$3/issue; $5 outside the U.S. Fanzine of all things connected with *Re-Animator*.

Phantom of the Movies' Videoscope

PhanMedia
PO Box 216
Ocean Grove NJ 07756

$19.97/6 issues; $26 in Canada; $36 elsewhere.

Pitt of Horror

Chiller Theatre
PO Box 23, Dept. IP
Rutherford NJ 07070

Newsletter of the Ingrid Pitt International Fan Club (included in $19.95 membership).

Planet B

Basement Productions
728 James St. Apt 4
Pittsburgh PA 15212

SASE. Two-page B-movie newsletter.

Planet X

Scott Moon
PO Box 161221
Sacramento CA 95816

$3.95/issue. "An SF/pop culture escape from world gone mad!"

Psychotronic

Michael J. Weldon
3309 Rt. 97
Narrowsburg NY 12764-6126
(914)252-6803
(914)252-3905 (fax)

$22/6 issues; $24 in Canada.

Pychoholics Unanimous

709 Ottilia SE
Grand Rapids MI 49507

$10/12 issues; $1 sample issue. Devoted to drive-in movies and experiences.

Samhain

77 Exeter Rd.
Topsham, Exeter
Devon EX3 OLX, England

$20/5 issues. Britain's oldest horror film magazine.

Santo Street

PO Box 561307
Orlando FL 32856

Quarterly. $10/year. Meximovie newsletter.

Satellite News

Mystery Science Theater 3000 Information Club
Best Brains, Inc.
PO Box 5325
Hopkins MN 55343

Included in membership.

Scary Monsters

Dennis Druktenis Publishing & Mail Order, Inc.
348 Jocelyn Pl.
Highwood IL 60040

$20/4 issues; $28 in Canada; $40 elsewhere.

Schlock

John Chilson
3841 4th Ave.
San Diego CA 92103

$1/issue.

Schock Cinema

Steve Puchalski
PO Box 518, Peter Stuyvesant Sta.
New York NY 10009

$4/issue; $5 outside the U.S. "Your guide to cult movies, arthouse oddities, drive-in swill, and underground obscurities."

Sci Fi Universe

PO Box 358
Mount Morris IL 61054
1-800-217-9306

$29.95/yr (9 issues). "The magazine for science fiction fans with a life!"

Scream Factory

Deadline Press
4884 Pepperwood Way
San Jose CA 95124

$21/4 issues.

Screem Magazine

490 S. Franklin St.
Wilkes-Barre PA 18702-3765

$15/4 issues; $20 in Canada; $40 elsewhere. Covers horror, sci-fi, and exploitation film from all eras.

She

24 Wellesly St. W. Ste. 408
Toronto ON Canada M4Y 161

$4/issue. "Guide for strolling the back alleys of bad girl cinema."

Shocking Images

Mark Jason Murray
PO Box 7853
Citrus Heights CA 95621

$14/4 issues; $16 in Mexico and Canada; $18 elsewhere. Contains exploitation film reviews, interviews, and articles.

The Stark Fist of Removal

The SubGenius Foundation
PO Box 140306
Dallas TX 75214

$30. Periodical outlet of the Church of the Sub-Genius; contains discussion of "badfilm" aesthetics.

Sticky Carpet Digest

Tom Deja
55-35 Myrtle Ave., Top Floor
Ridgewood NY 11385

$1/issue.

Sub-Terranea

Jason Gray
47 Thorncliffe Park Dr. No. 609
Toronto ON Canada M4H 1J5

$4/issue. Covers international exploitation film.

Terminal Brain Rot

Michael Heugen
7312 Reynard Ln.
Charlotte NC 28215

$4/4 issues. Pop culture review 'zine.

They Won't Stay Dead

Brian Johnson
11 Werner Rd.
Greenville PA 16125

$2.50/issue.

Trash Compactor

253 College St. Ste. 108
Toronto ON Canada M5T 1R5

$3.75/issue. Covers grindhouse favorites.

Ultramontane

Mike Benson
1644 N. Hill Ave.
Pasadena CA 91104

$4/4 issues.

Vamos

Pat Drummond
PO Box 5871
Kansas City MO 64171

$5/6 issues. Pop culture review 'zine.

Video Eyeball

122 Montclair Ave.
Boston MA 02131-1344

Bimonthly. $15/6 issues. "The video suggestion rag with optic nerve."

Cult
Connections

Video WatchDog

PO Box 5283
Cincinnati OH 45205-0283

$24/6 issues; $33 outside the U.S. "The per-
fectionist's guide to fantastic video." Contains
very cool illustrations.

Videooze

PO Box 9911
Alexandria VA 22304

$15/4 issues; $20 outside the U.S. "Your guide
to European horror and exploitation on videotape."

Weird City

Dave Szurek
1206 Wheeler Ave. Apt 2
Hoquiam WA 98550-1901

$2.50/issue.

Wrapped in Plastic

Win-Mill Productions
1912 E Timberview Ln.
Arlington TX 76014

Bimonthly. $29/year. Wrap-up of everything
connected with Mark Frost & David Lynch's
Twin Peaks.

Xeromorphic

Terrance Jennings Wharton
PO Box 481
Lancaster OH 43130

$7/volume. Contains tons of vintage drive-in
ad mats, with articles and interviews.

The Zombie Chronicles

John Milford
1722 Dulong Ave.
Madison Heights MI 48071-2668

$21/6 issues. All about George Romero's (and
other) zombies.

Zon-Tower

Jan Johnson
29 Darling St. No. 2
Boston MA 02120

Zontar, the Magazine from Venus

Jan Johnson
29 Darling St. No. 2
Boston MA 02120

FAN CLUBS

Abbott and Costello Fan Club

PO Box 2084
Toluca Lake CA 91610
(818)558-3799
(818)566-4062 (hotline)
Chris Costello, Contact

Annette Funicello Fan Club

RR2
1618 Park Ridge Way
Pontypool ON canada 10A 1K0

Elvira Fan Club

14755 Ventura Blvd., 1-710
Sherman Oaks CA 91403
(818)995-3461

Elvis Forever TCB Fan Club

PO Box 1066
Pinellas Park FL 34665
Susan and Robert Still, Co-Pres.

Elvis Lives on Fan Club

10631 N. 190th Ave.
Bennington NE 68007
(402)238-2868
Connie Quinn, Exec. Officer

Elvis Now Fan Club

PO Box 6581
San Jose CA 95150
(408)923-0978
Sue McCasland, Pres.

Elvis Teddy Bears

744 Caliente Dr.
Bradenton FL 33511
(813)684-6522
Mary Ann Paris, Pres.

Elvis Worldwide Fan Club

c/o Will McDaniel
3081 Sunrise
Memphis TN 38127
(901)357-9910
Will McDaniel, Pres.

Eternally Elvis TCB

2251 NW 93rd Ave.
Pembroke Pines FL 33024
(305)431-6297
June Poalillo, Pres.

Fans of Leonard Nimoy and DeForest Kelley

7959 W. Portland Ave.
Littleton CO 80123
(303)972-8966
Laura Guyer, Exec. Officer

For the Heart Elvis Presley Fan Club

5004 Lyngail Dr. NW
Huntsville AL 35810
Stella Camp, Pres.

G-Force, the Godzilla Society of North America

Daikaiju Enterprises
Box 3468
Steinbach MB Canada R0A 2A0

The Hamill Exchange

PO Box 526177
Salt Lake City UT 84152
Nacolle Parsons, Exec. Officer

Ingrid Pitt International Fan Club

Chiller Theatre
PO Box 23, Dept. IP
Rutherford NJ 07070

King of Our Hearts Elvis Presley Fan Club

2445 Fernwood Dr.
San Jose CA 95128
(408)248-8641
Irene Maleti, Pres.

Leonard Nimoy Fan Club

17 Gateway Dr.
Batavia NY 14020
(716)343-6605
Barbara Walker, Pres.

Mamie Van Doren Fan Club

8340 E. Rush St.
Rosemead CA 91770
(818)280-1440
Joe Doyle, Pres.

Martial Arts Movie Association

6635 Delongpre No. 4
Hollywood CA 90028
William Connolly, Contact

Mystery Science Theater 3000 Information Club

Best Brains, Inc.
PO Box 5325
Hopkins MN 55343

National Association of Fan Clubs

PO Box 7487
Burbank CA 91510
(818)763-3280
Linda Kay, Pres.

Presley-ites Fan Club International

6010 18th St.
Zephyrhills FL 33540
(813)788-9133
Kathy Ferguson, Pres.

The Rocky Horror Picture Show Fan Club

220 W. 19th Ste. 2-A
New York NY 10011

Starfleet

PO Box 980008
West Sacramento CA 95798
(916)348-0726
(916)334-5641 (electronic bulletin board)
Rob Lerman, Pres.

Starfleet Command

PO Box 180637
Casselberry FL 32718
(904)724-3651
Rita Cawthon-Clark, Chief of Staff

TCB for Elvis Fan Club

PO Box 2655
Gastonia NC 28053
(704)864-3187
Joanne R.Young, Exec. Officer

Three Stooges Fan Club

PO Box 747
Gwynedd Valley PA 19437
(215)654-9466
Gary Lassin, Pres.

Trekville U.S.A.

c/o Jay S. Hastings
1021 S. 9th Ave.
Scranton PA 18504
(717)343-7806
Jay S. Hastings, Pres.

Cult
Connections

Walter Koenig International

PO Box 10731
Burbank CA 91510
Carolyn Atkinson, Chm.

We Remember Elvis Fan Club

1215 Tennessee Ave.
Pittsburgh PA 15216
(412)561-7522
Priscilla A. Parker, Pres.

Welcome to Our Elvis World

PO Box 501
Lutherville MD 21093
(410)296-2958
Ed Allan, Pres.

William Shatner Connection

7059 Atoll Ave.
North Hollywood CA 91605
(818)764-5499
Joyce Mason, Pres.

Zacherley Fans at Large

c/o Lynda Bramberger
PO Box 434
Vails Gate NY 12584
Lynda Bramberger, Pres.

BOOKS

Akira Kurosawa: Something Like an Autobiography

Akira Kurosawa. 1983. Random House. $12 (paper).

The Amazing Herschell Gordon Lewis

Daniel Krogh & John McCarty. 1983. FantaCo.

Bogdanovich's Picture Shows

Thomas J. Harris. 1990. Scarecrow. $42.50.

Brian de Palma

Michael Bliss. 1983. Scarecrow. $20.

Burton on Burton

Tim Burton. 1995. Faber & Faber. $22.95.

The "B" Directors: A Biographical Directory

Wheeler W. Dixon. 1985. Scarecrow. $52.50.

A Clean Breast: The Lives and Loves of Russ Meyer

Adolph A. Schwartz (aka Russ Meyer). 2nd ed., 1993. Hauck. $79.50.

Broken Mirrors, Broken Minds: The Dark Dreams of Dario Argento

Maitland McDonaugh. 1994. Carol Publishing. $18.95.

Crackpot: The Obsessions of John Waters

John Waters. 1987. Vintage Books. $10 (paper).

Cronenberg on Cronenberg

David Cronenberg. 1994. Faber & Faber. $19.95.

David Lynch

Kenneth Kaleta. 1992. Macmillan. $22.95; $13.95 (paper).

David Cronenberg: A Delicate Balance

Peter Morris. 1994. InBook. $9.95 (paper).

The Fearmakers: The Screen's Directorial Masters of Suspense and Terror

John McCarty. 1994. St. Martin's. $14.95 (paper).

Filmmaking on the Fringe: The Good, the Bad, and the Deviant Directors

Maitland McDonagh. 1994. Carol Publishing. $18.95 (paper).

The Films of Win Wenders

Robert P. Kolker. 1993. Cambridge Univ. $44.95; $13.95 (paper).

The Films of Paul Morrissey

Maurice Yacowar. 1993. Cambridge Univ. $47.95; $13.95 (paper).

George Lucas: The Creative Impulse

Charles Champlin. 1992. Abrams. $39.95.

How I Made a Hundred Movies in Hollywood and Never Lost a Dime

Roger Corman with Jim Jerome. 1990. Delta. $12 (paper).

Interviews with B Science Fiction and Horror Movie Makers

Tom Weaver. 1988. McFarland. $38.50.

John Waters

John G. Ives. 1992. Thunder's Mouth. $11.95 (paper).

Martin Scorsese and Michael Cimino

Michael Bliss. 1985. Scarecrow. $27.50.

Midnight Movies

J. Hoberman and Jonathan Rosenbaum. 1983. Harper & Row.

The Monster Show: A Cultural History of Horror

David J. Skal. 1993. Norton. $25.

The New Poverty Row: Independent Filmmakers As Distributors

Fred O. Ray. 1991. McFarland. $29.95.

Nightmare of Ecstasy: The Life and Art of Edward D. Wood, Jr.

Rudolph Grey. 1992. Feral House. $14.95 (paper).

Not Simply Divine

Bernard Jay. 1993. Fireside. $12 (paper).

Pandemonium: Freaks, Magicians, and Movie-Stars Special

John Waters. 1989. Living Color. $15 (paper).

Psychos: Ninety Years of Mad Movies, Maniacs, and Murderous Deeds

John McCarty. 1993. Carol Publishing. $14.95 (paper).

Roger Corman: The Best of the Cheap Acts

Mark McGee. 1988. McFarland. $32.50.

Russ Meyer: The Life and Films

David K. Frasier. 1990. McFarland. $49.95.

Shock Value: A Tasteful Book about Bad Taste

John Waters. 1981. Dell.

Sleaze Merchants: Adventures in Exploitation Filmmaking

John McCarty. 1995. St. Martin's. $16.95 (paper).

Step Right Up! I'm Gonna Scare the Pants Off America: Memoirs of a B-Movie Mogul

William Castle; intro by John Waters. 2nd ed., 1992. Pharos. $12.95 (paper).

Steven Spielberg

Donald R. Mott. 1988. Macmillan. $14.95 (paper).

Trash Trio: Three Screenplays by John Waters

John Waters. 1988. Vintage Books. $10.95 (paper). Includes *Pink Flamingos*, *Desperate Living,* and *Flamingos Forever.*

The Video Watchdog Book

Tim Lucas; Brian Thomas, illus. 1992. Video Watchdog. $19.95 (paper).

Woody Allen

Nancy Pogel. 1987. Macmillan. $23.95; $13.95 (paper).

A Youth in Babylon: Confessions of a Trash-Film King

David Friedman. 1990. Prometheus. $21.95.

Cult Connections

Alternate Titles Index

Ever have trouble finding your favorite obscure gem because the video people have released it under a new name? And even worse, don't you just hate it when you rent the same dog (er, "woof," let's say) two and even three times because it's appearing on the shelves with new and different titles? Just for you people, our friends, we've provided an index cross-referencing all those titles. Don't fall victim to the retitled ploy again.

The Gargon Terror *See* Teenagers from Outer Space (1959)

Gas-s-s-s. . . or, It May Become Necessary to Destroy the World in Order to Save It *See* Gas-s-s-s! (1970)

Ghidora, The Three-Headed Monster *See* Ghidrah the Three Headed Monster (1965)

Ghidorah Sandai Kaiju Chikyu Saidai No Kessan *See* Ghidrah the Three Headed Monster (1965)

Ghidrah *See* Ghidrah the Three Headed Monster (1965)

The Giant Leeches *See* Attack of the Giant Leeches (1959)

Gill Woman *See* Voyage to the Planet of Prehistoric Women (1968)

Gill Women of Venus *See* Voyage to the Planet of Prehistoric Women (1968)

Glump *See* Please Don't Eat My Mother (1972)

Godzilla Fights the Giant Moth *See* Godzilla Vs. Mothra (1964)

Godzilla vs. the Giant Moth *See* Godzilla Vs. Mothra (1964)

Godzilla vs. the Thing *See* Godzilla Vs. Mothra (1964)

Going Ape *See* Where's Poppa? (1970)

Gojira *See* Godzilla, King of the Monsters (1956)

Gojira no Musuko *See* Son of Godzilla (1966)

Gojira Tai Megaro *See* Godzilla Vs. Megalon (1976)

Gomar the Human Gorilla *See* Night of the Bloody Apes (1968)

Grave Robbers from Outer Space *See* Plan 9 from Outer Space (1956)

Graveyard Tramps *See* Invasion of the Bee Girls (1973)

The Greatest Battle on Earth *See* Ghidrah the Three Headed Monster (1965)

Guns in the Afternoon *See* Ride the High Country (1962)

Guns, Sin and Bathtub Gin *See* Lady in Red (1979)

The Hands of Orlac *See* Mad Love (1935)

The Hangover *See* The Female Jungle (1956)

The Hatchet Murders *See* Deep Red: Hatchet Murders (1975)

The Haunted and the Hunted *See* Dementia 13 (1963)

Haxan *See* Witchcraft through the Ages (1922)

He or She *See* Glen or Glenda? (1953)

The Head That Wouldn't Die *See* The Brain That Wouldn't Die (1963)

Hellborn *See* The Sinister Urge (1960)

Hercules and the Hydra *See* The Loves of Hercules (1960)

Hercules Goes Bananas *See* Hercules in New York (1970)

Hercules: The Movie *See* Hercules in New York (1970)

Hidden Face *See* Jail Bait (1954)

Hide and Shriek *See* American Gothic (1988)

Holy Terror *See* Alice Sweet Alice (1976)

The Horrible Mill Women *See* Mill of the Stone Women (1960)

Horror Hotel Massacre *See* Eaten Alive (1976)

Horror of the Stone Women *See* Mill of the Stone Women (1960)

House of Doom *See* The Black Cat (1934)

House of Usher *See* The Fall of the House of Usher (1960)

The Human Tornado *See* Dolemite 2: Human Tornado (1976)

Hungry Pets *See* Please Don't Eat My Mother (1972)

Hustler Squad *See* The Doll Squad (1973)

Hydra *See* Attack of the Swamp Creature (1975)

I Changed My Sex *See* Glen or Glenda? (1953)

I Hate Your Guts *See* Shame (1961)

I Led Two Lives *See* Glen or Glenda? (1953)

I Love to Kill *See* Impulse (1974)

I Married Too Young *See* Married Too Young (1962)

I Tre Volti della Paura *See* Black Sabbath (1964)

Identikit *See* Driver's Seat (1973)

Il Disprezzo *See* Contempt (1964)

Il Mulino Delle Donne di Pietra *See* Mill of the Stone Women (1960)

The Incredible Invasion *See* The Sinister Invasion (1968)

The Incredible Torture Show *See* Bloodsucking Freaks (1975)

The Incredibly Strange Creatures *See* Incredibly Strange Creatures Who Stopped Living and Became Mixed-Up Zombies (1963)

The Infra Superman *See* Infra-Man (1976)

Insane World *See* Mondo Cane 2 (1964)

The Intruder *See* Shame (1961)

Invasion of Planet X *See* Godzilla Vs. Monster Zero (1968)

Invasion of the Astro-Monsters *See* Godzilla Vs. Monster Zero (1968)

Invasion of the Astros *See* Godzilla Vs. Monster Zero (1968)

Invasion of the Zombies *See* Horror of Party Beach (1964)

The Iron Kiss *See* Naked Kiss (1964)

The Island of the Last Zombies *See* Doctor Butcher M.D. (1980)

It Fell From the Sky *See* Alien Dead (1985)

It Happened at Lakewood Manor *See* Ants (1977)

It Stalked the Ocean Floor *See* Monster from the Ocean Floor (1954)

Jesus de Montreal *See* Jesus of Montreal (1989)

Alternative
Titles
Index

Mysterious Invader *See* The Astounding She-Monster (1958)

Nature's Mistakes *See* Freaks (1932)

Night of the Flesh Eaters *See* Night of the Living Dead (1968)

Nightingale *See* The Young Nurses (1973)

Nightmare Circus *See* Barn of the Naked Dead (1973)

The Northfield Cemetery Massacre *See* Northville Cemetery Massacre (1976)

Occhi Senza Volto *See* The Horror Chamber of Dr. Faustus (1959)

Oh, Charlie *See* Hold That Ghost (1941)

Out of the Darkness *See* Teenage Caveman (1958)

The Pace That Kills *See* Cocaine Fiends (1936)

Panic at Lakewood Manor *See* Ants (1977)

The Parasite Murders *See* They Came from Within (1975)

Pardon Me, Your Teeth are in My Neck *See* The Fearless Vampire Killers (1967)

Paura Nella Citta Dei Morti Viventi *See* Gates of Hell (1983)

Percy's Progress *See* It's Not the Size That Counts (1974)

The Phantom of Terror *See* The Bird with the Crystal Plumage (1970)

Planet of Horrors *See* Galaxy of Terror (1981)

The Playgirls and the Bellboy *See* The Bellboy and the Playgirls (1962)

Poe's Tales of Terror *See* Tales of Terror (1962)

Poor Albert and Little Annie *See* I Dismember Mama (1974)

Porklips Now *See* Hardware Wars and Other Film Farces (1978)

Prehistoric World *See* Teenage Caveman (1958)

The Profile of Terror *See* The Sadist (1963)

Profundo Rosso *See* Deep Red: Hatchet Murders (1975)

Psycho a Go Go! *See* Blood of Ghastly Horror (1972)

Psychotic *See* Driver's Seat (1973)

Queen of Blood *See* Planet of Blood (1966)

Queen of the Cannibals *See* Doctor Butcher M.D. (1980)

Queen of the Gorillas *See* The Bride & the Beast (1958)

Quemimada! *See* Burn! (1970)

Rage *See* Rabid (1977)

Red Nightmare *See* The Commies Are Coming, the Commies Are Coming (1957)

Renegade Girls *See* Caged Heat (1974)

Return from the Past *See* Alien Massacre (1967)

The Return of Mr. H. *See* They Saved Hitler's Brain (1964)

The Revenge of Dracula *See* Dracula Vs. Frankenstein (1971)

Revenge of the Dead *See* Night of the Ghouls (1959)

Revenge of the Living Dead *See* Children Shouldn't Play with Dead Things (1972)

Rocket to the Moon *See* Cat Women of the Moon (1953)

Roger Corman's Frankenstein Unbound *See* Frankenstein Unbound (1990)

The Rutles *See* All You Need Is Cash (1978)

Sanda Tai Gailah *See* War of the Gargantuas (1970)

Santa Claus Defeats the Aliens *See* Santa Claus Conquers the Martians (1964)

Satan's Daughters *See* Vampyres (1974)

Satyricon *See* Fellini Satyricon (1969)

The School That Ate My Brain *See* Zombie High (1987)

She Was a Hippy Vampire *See* The Wild World of Batwoman (1966)

She-Wolf *See* The Legend of the Wolf Woman (1977)

Shivers *See* They Came from Within (1975)

Sins of Love *See* Test Tube Babies (1948)

Snow White and the Three Clowns *See* Snow White and the Three Stooges (1961)

The Space Amoeba *See* Yog, Monster from Space (1971)

Space Mutants *See* Planet of the Vampires (1965)

Spawn of the Slithis *See* Slithis (1978)

Spider Baby, or the Maddest Story Ever Told *See* Spider Baby (1964)

Spinal Tap *See* This Is Spinal Tap (1984)

Spirit of the Dead *See* The Asphyx (1972)

The Split *See* The Manster (1959)

The Spooky Movie Show *See* The Mask (1961)

Starlight Slaughter *See* Eaten Alive (1976)

Strange Journey *See* Fantastic Voyage (1966)

The Stranger *See* Shame (1961)

The Sun Demon *See* Hideous Sun Demon (1959)

The Super Inframan *See* Infra-Man (1976)

Swamp Diamonds *See* Swamp Women (1955)

Sweet Candy *See* Candy Stripe Nurses (1974)

Sweet Kill *See* The Arousers (1970)

Tales of the City *See* Armistead Maupin's Tales of the City (1993)

The Teenage Psycho Meets Bloody Mary *See* Incredibly Strange Creatures Who Stopped Living and Became Mixed-Up Zombies (1963)

Tell Your Children *See* Reefer Madness (1938)

Tenebrae *See* Unsane (1982)

Terreur dans l'Espace *See* Planet of the Vampires (1965)

Terror Circus *See* Barn of the Naked Dead (1973)

Alternative Titles Index

Alternative Titles Index

Cast Index

What's to explain? The following index lists all actor-types credited in the main review section, alphabetically by their last names (although they are presented here in first name/last name format—the Hound thinks it looks friendlier, and he'd like to think he's on a close personal basis with every person listed). Know the actor but not the movie? Try this index. Still not sure of the title? Cross-reference it by any one of an outrageous number of subject categories listed in the aptly named "Category Index."

Bruce Abbott
Bride of Re-Animator '89
The Re-Animator '85

Bud Abbott
Abbott & Costello Go to Mars '53
Abbott & Costello Meet Dr. Jekyll and Mr. Hyde '52
Abbott & Costello Meet Frankenstein '48
Abbott & Costello Meet the Invisible Man '51
Abbott & Costello Meet the Killer, Boris Karloff '49
Abbott & Costello Meet the Mummy '55
Hold That Ghost '41

Kareem Abdul-Jabbar
Airplane! '80

Alfred Abel
Metropolis '26

Ian Abercrombie
Army of Darkness '92
Test Tube Teens from the Year 2000 '93

Jim Abrahams
Kentucky Fried Movie '77

Michele Abrams
Cool World '92

Frankie Acciario
Bad Lieutenant '92

Sharon Acker
Happy Birthday to Me '81

Forrest J. Ackerman
Dracula Vs. Frankenstein '71
Planet of Blood '66
Schlock '73

Noelle Adam
Beat Girl '60

Brooke Adams
Shock Waves '77
The Stuff '85

Don Adams
Back to the Beach '87

Dona Adams
Zipperface '92

Dorothy Adams
Laura '44

Edie Adams
Armistead Maupin's Tales of the City '93
Cheech and Chong's Up in Smoke '79
It's a Mad, Mad, Mad, Mad World '63

Ernie Adams
Nevada '27

Julie Adams
Creature from the Black Lagoon '54

Nick Adams
Godzilla Vs. Monster Zero '68

Rebel Without a Cause '55

Wesley Addy
Kiss Me Deadly '55

Danny Ades
Aguirre, the Wrath of God '72

Isabelle Adjani
Ishtar '87

Luther Adler
D.O.A. '49

Iris Adrian
Carnival Rock '57

Max Adrian
The Devils '71

John Agar
The Brain from Planet Arous '57
Revenge of the Creature '55
Zontar, the Thing from Venus '66

Pierre Agostino
The Hollywood Strangler Meets the Skid Row Slasher '79

Janet Agren
Gates of Hell '83

Kris Aguilar
Bloodfist '89

Jenny Agutter
An American Werewolf in London '81

Philip Ahn
Paradise, Hawaiian Style '66
Shock Corridor '63

Lee Ahsmann
Something Weird '68

Kyoko Ai
Destroy All Monsters '68

Danny Aiello
The Stuff '85

Maria Aitken
A Fish Called Wanda '88

Claude Akins
Battle for the Planet of the Apes '73
The Killers '64
Monster in the Closet '86

Captain Lou Albano
Complex World '92

Sherry Alberoni
Barn of the Naked Dead '73

Eddie Albert
Devil's Rain '75

Edward Albert
Galaxy of Terror '81

Frank Albertson
It's a Wonderful Life '46
Psycho '60
Room Service '38

325

Cult Flicks and Trash Pics

Cast
Index

Cast Index

Cast
Index

Cast
Index

Cast
Index

Robert Bundy
Screen Test '85

Victor Buono
Arnold '73
Beneath the Planet of
the Apes '70

Kathleen Burke
Island of Lost Souls '32

Michelle Burke
Dazed and Confused
'93

Paul Burke
Valley of the Dolls '67

Laura Burkett
Daddy's Boys '87

Rick Burks
Blood Diner '87

Marilyn Burns
Eaten Alive '76
Helter Skelter '76
The Texas Chainsaw
Massacre '74

Tim Burns
Mad Max '80

Raymond Burr
Airplane 2: The Sequel
'82
Godzilla, King of the
Monsters '56
Godzilla 1985 '85
Love Happy '50

Jackie Burroughs
Careful '94

**William S.
Burroughs**
Twister '89

Darren E. Burrows
Cry-Baby '90

Ellen Burstyn
The Exorcist '73

Julian Burton
A Bucket of Blood '59

LeVar Burton
Star Trek: Generations
'94

Richard Burton
Absolution '81

Robert Burton
Trilogy of Terror '75

Tony Burton
Assault on Precinct 13
'76

Steve Buscemi
Mystery Train '89
Reservoir Dogs '92

Dennis Busch
Faster Pussycat! Kill!
Kill! '66

Gary Busey
Angels Hard as They
Come '71

Billy Green Bush
Five Easy Pieces '70

Kent Butler
Curse of the Queerwolf
'87

William Butler
Leatherface: The Texas
Chainsaw Massacre 3
'89

Yancy Butler
Hard Target '93

Merritt Butrick
Star Trek 2: The Wrath
of Khan '82
Star Trek 3: The Search
for Spock '84

**Charles
Butterworth**
Hollywood Party '34

Donna Butterworth
Paradise, Hawaiian
Style '66

Tyler Butterworth
Consuming Passions '88

Jorg Buttgereit
Nekromantik '87

Red Buttons
The Ambulance '90

Sarah Buxton
Rock 'n' Roll High
School Forever '91

David Byrne
True Stories '86

Gabriel Byrne
Cool World '92

Patricia T. Byrne
Night Call Nurses '72

Edd Byrnes
Back to the Beach '87

Edward Byrnes
Reform School Girl '57

Bruce Byron
Kenneth Anger, Vol. 3:
Lucifer Rising '65

Susan Byun
Sgt. Kabukiman
N.Y.P.D. '94

James Caan
The Rain People '69

Bruce Cabot
King Kong '33

Sebastian Cabot
The Time Machine '60

Susan Cabot
Carnival Rock '57
Machine Gun Kelly '58
Sorority Girl '57
The Wasp Woman '59

Sid Caesar
The Fiendish Plot of Dr.
Fu Manchu '80
Grease '78
History of the World:
Part 1 '81
It's a Mad, Mad, Mad,
Mad World '63
Stoogemania '85

Cheri Caffaro
The Abductors '72
Ginger '72
Girls Are for Loving '73
Too Hot to Handle '76

Nicolas Cage
Raising Arizona '87
Red Rock West '93
Valley Girl '83
Vampire's Kiss '88
Wild at Heart '90

James Cagney
White Heat '49

Barry Cahill
Grand Theft Auto '77

Howard Caine
Watermelon Man '70

Audrey Caire
They Saved Hitler's
Brain '64

Paul Calderone
Bad Lieutenant '92

Don Calfa
Chopper Chicks in
Zombietown '91

Louis Calhern
Blackboard Jungle '55
Duck Soup '33

Rory Calhoun
Motel Hell '80

Joseph Cali
The Lonely Lady '83

John Call
Santa Claus Conquers
the Martians '64

Michael Callan
Mysterious Island '61

Joseph Calleia
My Little Chickadee '40
Touch of Evil '58

Cab Calloway
The Blues Brothers '80

Corinne Calvet
Too Hot to Handle '76

Linda Cambi
Teenage Gang Debs '66

Godfrey Cambridge
The President's Analyst
'67
Watermelon Man '70

Paul Camen
The Student Nurses '70

Marjorie Cameron
Kenneth Anger, Vol. 2:
Inauguration of the
Pleasure Dome '54

Colleen Camp
Apocalypse Now '79
Clue '85
Smile '75
Valley Girl '83
Wicked Stepmother '89

Joseph Campanella
The St. Valentine's Day
Massacre '67

Bruce Campbell
Army of Darkness '92
Crimewave '85
Evil Dead '83
Evil Dead 2: Dead by
Dawn '87
Lunatics: A Love Story
'92

Nicholas Campbell
Naked Lunch '91

Patrick Campbell
Smokey Bites the Dust
'81

William Campbell
Armistead Maupin's
Tales of the City '93
Dementia 13 '63

Wally Campo
Little Shop of Horrors
'60
Machine Gun Kelly '58

Rafael Campos
The Astro-Zombies '67

Cast
Index

Rosanne Cash
Doctor Duck's Super
  Secret All-Purpose
  Sauce '85

Barbara Cason
Honeymoon Killers '70

John Cassavetes
The Killers '64
Rosemary's Baby '68

Sandra Cassel
Last House on the Left
  '72

Seymour Cassel
Wicked Stepmother '89

David Cassidy
Spirit of '76 '91

Joanna Cassidy
Blade Runner '82

Stefania Cassini
Andy Warhol's Bad '77

Willy Castello
Cocaine Fiends '36

Gloria Castillo
Reform School Girl '57

Peggy Castle
Beginning of the End
  '57

William Castle
Bug '75
Rosemary's Baby '68

Phoebe Cates
Fast Times at Ridgemont
  High '82

Juliette Caton
The Last Temptation of
  Christ '88

Kim Cattrall
Porky's '82
Star Trek 6: The Undis-
  covered Country '91
Wild Palms '93

Paul Cavanagh
House of Wax '53

Dick Cavett
The Marx Brothers in a
  Nutshell '90

Elizabeth Cayton
Slave Girls from Beyond
  Infinity '87

Adolfo Celi
The King of Hearts '66

Joseph Cellini
Motor Psycho '65

Michael Ceveris
Rock 'n' Roll High
  School Forever '91

Amadee Chabot
Muscle Beach Party '64

June Chadwick
Forbidden World '82
This Is Spinal Tap '84

Richard
  Chamberlain
The Last Wave '77
Petulia '68

Marilyn Chambers
Rabid '77

Eric Champnella
The Invisible Maniac
  '90

Philip Chan
Hard-Boiled '92

Betty Chandler
Don't Look in the Base-
  ment '73

Helen Chandler
Dracula '31

Lane Chandler
Laura '44

Lon Chaney, Jr.
Abbott & Costello Meet
  Frankenstein '48
Alien Massacre '67
Cobra Woman '44
Dracula Vs. Franken-
  stein '71
Film House Fever '86
The Haunted Palace '63
Hillbillies in a Haunted
  House '67
Spider Baby '64
The Wolf Man '41

Lon Chaney, Sr.
The Phantom of the
  Opera '25

Stockard Channing
The Applegates '89
The Big Bus '76
Grease '78
The Hospital '71

Billy Chapin
The Night of the Hunter
  '55

Charles Chaplin,
  Jr.
High School Confiden-
  tial '58

Charlie Chaplin
Monsieur Verdoux '47

Sydney Chaplin
Satan's Cheerleaders '77

Graham Chapman
And Now for Something
  Completely Different
  '72
The Magic Christian '69
Monty Python and the
  Holy Grail '75
Monty Python Live at the
  Hollywood Bowl '82
Monty Python's Life of
  Brian '79
Monty Python's Parrot
  Sketch Not Included
  '90
Monty Python's The
  Meaning of Life '83
Yellowbeard '83

Marguerite
  Chapman
The Amazing Transpar-
  ent Man '60

Jay Charbonneau
Complex World '92

Patricia
  Charbonneau
Brain Dead '89

Ray Charles
The Blues Brothers '80

Janet Charlton
Something Weird '68

Melanie Chartoff
Stoogemania '85

Chevy Chase
Caddyshack '80
The Groove Tube '72

Lilyan Chauvin
Bloodlust '59
Lost, Lonely, and Vi-
  cious '59

Andrea Checchi
Black Sunday '60

Joan Chen
Twin Peaks '90

Leslie Cheung
A Better Tomorrow '86

Huang Chien-lung
Infra-Man '76

Linden Chiles
Forbidden World '82

Lois Chiles
Twister '89

Tsai Chin
The Castle of Fu
  Manchu '68

William Ching
Terror in the Haunted
  House '58

Nicholas Chinlund
The Ambulance '90

Paris Chong
Far Out Man '89

Rae Dawn Chong
Far Out Man '89

Shelby Chong
Far Out Man '89

Thomas Chong
After Hours '85
Cheech and Chong's Up
  in Smoke '79
Far Out Man '89
Spirit of '76 '91
Yellowbeard '83

Marilyn Chris
Honeymoon Killers '70

Claudia Christian
The Hidden '87

Paul Christian
The Beast from 20,000
  Fathoms '53

Julie Christie
Don't Look Now '73
Fahrenheit 451 '66
Petulia '68

Virginia Christine
Billy the Kid Vs. Drac-
  ula '66

Lindsay Christman
Twister '89

Eric Christmas
Harold and Maude '71

Francoise
  Christophe
The King of Hearts '66

Robin Christopher
Equinox '71

Eduardo Ciannelli
Strange Cargo '40

Diane Cilento
The Wicker Man '75

Jany Clair
Hercules Against the
  Moon Men '64

Eric Clapton
Tommy '75

Betsy Clark
Boxing Helena '93

335

Cult Flicks and Trash Pics

Cast Index

Cast Index

Cast Index

Cast Index

<label>Cast
Index</label>

Cast Index

Cast
Index

Cast Index

Shelley Hack
Annie Hall '77
Troll '85

Buddy Hackett
It's a Mad, Mad, Mad,
Mad World '63
Muscle Beach Party '64

Gene Hackman
Bonnie & Clyde '67
Young Frankenstein '74

Dayle Haddon
Cyborg '89

Sara Haden
Mad Love '35

Reed Hadley
Brain of Blood '71

Jean Hagen
Panic in the Year Zero!
'62

Ross Hagen
Dinosaur Island '93

Julie Hagerty
Airplane! '80
Airplane 2: The Sequel
'82

Dan Haggerty
Bury Me an Angel '71

Larry Hagman
The Big Bus '76

Eliska Hahn
Invasion of the Space
Preachers '90

Lisa Hahn
Alien Contamination
'81

Charles Haid
Altered States '80

Sid Haig
The Big Bird Cage '72
The Big Doll House '71
Spider Baby '64

Jester Hairston
I'm Gonna Git You
Sucka '88

Alan Hale, Jr.
The Giant Spider Inva-
sion '75

Barbara Hale
The Giant Spider Inva-
sion '75

Jean Hale
The St. Valentine's Day
Massacre '67

Albert Hall
Apocalypse Now '79

Anthony Michael
Hall
The Breakfast Club '85
Sixteen Candles '84

Arch Hall, Jr.
Eegah! '62
The Sadist '63
Wild Guitar '62

Arsenio Hall
Amazon Women on the
Moon '87

Grayson Hall
Satan in High Heels '62

Huntz Hall
Auntie Lee's Meat Pies
'92

Jon Hall
The Beach Girls and the
Monster '65
Cobra Woman '44

Lois Hall
Kalifornia '93

Ruth Hall
Monkey Business '31

Zooey Hall
I Dismember Mama '74

Charles Hallahan
Body of Evidence '92
Wild Palms '93

Luke Halpin
Matinee '92
Shock Waves '77

John Halsey
All You Need Is Cash
'78

Charles Halton
Dr. Cyclops '40
It's a Wonderful Life '46
Room Service '38

Mie Hama
King Kong Vs. Godzilla
'63
What's Up, Tiger Lily?
'66

Veronica Hamel
Cannonball '76

Mark Hamill
The Empire Strikes Back
'80
Return of the Jedi '83
Star Wars '77

Carrie Hamilton
Cool World '92

George Hamilton
Where the Boys Are '60

Margaret
Hamilton
My Little Chickadee '40
13 Ghosts '60

Murray Hamilton
The Amityville Horror
'79

Rusty Hamilton
Rock 'n' Roll Nightmare
'85

Ben Hammer
Invasion of the Bee
Girls '73

Olivia Hamnett
The Last Wave '77

Paul Hampton
Private Duty Nurses '71
They Came from Within
'75

Daryl Haney
Daddy's Boys '87
Lords of the Deep '89

Tom Hanks
He Knows You're Alone
'80

Jenny Hanley
Flesh and Blood Show
'73

Julie Hanlon
I Was a Teenage TV Ter-
rorist '87

Daryl Hannah
Blade Runner '82

John Hannan
Strictly Ballroom '92

Marilyn Hanold
Frankenstein Meets the
Space Monster '65

Cheryl Hansen
Thou Shalt Not Kill. . .
Except '87

Gunnar Hansen
Hollywood Chainsaw
Hookers '88
The Texas Chainsaw
Massacre '74

Ty Hardin
I Married a Monster
from Outer Space '58

Kadeem Hardison
I'm Gonna Git You
Sucka '88

Karl Hardman
Night of the Living
Dead '68

Cedric Hardwicke
Things to Come '36

Oliver Hardy
Hollywood Party '34

Sam Hardy
King Kong '33

Mickey Hargitay
The Loves of Hercules
'60

Christine
Hargreaves
Pink Floyd: The Wall '82

John Hargreaves
Malcolm '86

John Harkins
Amityville 3: The De-
mon '83

Deborah Harmon
Used Cars '80

Ralf Harolde
I'm No Angel '33

Jessica Harper
Phantom of the Paradise
'74
Shock Treatment '81
Suspiria '77

Samantha Harper
Oh! Calcutta! '72

Susan Harper
Phantasm '79

Tess Harper
Amityville 3: The De-
mon '83

Curtis Harrington
Cult People '89

Pat Harrington
The President's Analyst
'67

Ann Harris
Honeymoon Killers '70

Barbara Harris
Family Plot '76
Oh Dad, Poor Dad
(Momma's Hung You
in the Closet & I'm
Feeling So Sad) '67

Brad Harris
The Freakmaker '73

Ed Harris
Creepshow '82

349

351

Cult Flicks and Trash Pics

Cast
Index

Cast Index

Cast
Index

Cast Index

Norma Lazarendo
Night of the Bloody
    Apes '68

Jodi Lazarus
Night of the Demon '80

George Lazenby
Kentucky Fried Movie
    '77

Odile Le Clezio
Young Einstein '89

Howard Le May
Teenage Mother '67

John Le Mesurier
Jabberwocky '77

Cloris Leachman
Crazy Mama '75
History of the World:
    Part 1 '81
Kiss Me Deadly '55
Young Frankenstein '74

Timothy Leary
Hold Me, Thrill Me,
    Kiss Me '93

Jean-Pierre Leaud
Last Tango in Paris '73

Anna Lee
Bedlam '45

Bernard Lee
Dr. No '62
From Russia with Love
    '63
Goldfinger '64

Bruce Lee
Enter the Dragon '73

Christopher Lee
Beat Girl '60
The Castle of Fu
    Manchu '68
The Curse of Franken-
    stein '57
Dr. Terror's House of
    Horrors '65
The Magic Christian '69
Return of Captain Invin-
    cible '83
The Wicker Man '75

Cinque Lee
Mystery Train '89

Cosette Lee
Deranged '74

Danny Lee
The Killer '90

Elizabeth Lee
Something Weird '68

Guy Lee
Girls! Girls! Girls! '62

Jesse Lee
The Brady Bunch Movie
    '95
Matinee '92

Madame Lee
She-Freak '67

Paige Lee
Voyage to the Planet of
    Prehistoric Women
    '68

Robbie Lee
Big Bad Mama '74

Sharon Lee
Motor Psycho '65

Sheryl Lee
Twin Peaks '90
Twin Peaks: Fire Walk
    with Me '92
Wild at Heart '90

Phoebe Legere
The Toxic Avenger, Part
    2 '89
The Toxic Avenger, Part
    3: The Last Tempta-
    tion of Toxie '89

Bela Lehoczky
Hold Me, Thrill Me,
    Kiss Me '93

Fritz Leiber
Equinox '71

Ron Leibman
Where's Poppa? '70

Don Leifert
The Alien Factor '78

Barbara Leigh
The Student Nurses '70

Janet Leigh
The Manchurian Candi-
    date '62
Psycho '60
Touch of Evil '58

**Jennifer Jason
    Leigh**
Fast Times at Ridgemont
    High '82

Suzanna Leigh
Paradise, Hawaiian
    Style '66

Margaret Leighton
The Loved One '65

Leila
From Russia with Love
    '63

John Leisenring
Mondo Trasho '69

Virginia Leith
The Brain That Would-
    n't Die '63

Harvey Lembeck
Beach Blanket Bingo
    '65
Beach Party '63

Kasi Lemmons
Hard Target '93
Vampire's Kiss '88

Mark Lenard
Star Trek 3: The Search
    for Spock '84
Star Trek 4: The Voyage
    Home '86
Star Trek 6: The Undis-
    covered Country '91

Norm Lenet
Something Weird '68

John Lennon
A Hard Day's Night '64
Help! '65
The Magic Christian '69
Magical Mystery Tour
    '67

Jay Leno
Doctor Duck's Super
    Secret All-Purpose
    Sauce '85

Lotte Lenya
From Russia with Love
    '63

Kay Lenz
Stripped to Kill '87

Sheldon Leonard
Abbott & Costello Meet
    the Invisible Man '51
It's a Wonderful Life '46
Zombies on Broadway
    '44

Robert Lepage
Jesus of Montreal '89

Baby LeRoy
It's a Gift '34

Raymond Lescot
Rabid Grannies '89

Emelia Lesniak
Nine Deaths of the
    Ninja '85

Jeff Lester
In the Cold of the Night
    '89

Kathy Lester
Phantasm '79

David Letterman
Cabin Boy '94

Tony Leung
Hard-Boiled '92

Barry Levinson
History of the World:
    Part 1 '81

Stan Levitt
Carnival of Souls '62

Steve Levitt
Blue Movies '88

Larc Levy
It's Dead—Let's Touch
    It! '92
The Weasel that
    Dripped Blood '89

Margaret LeWars
Dr. No '62

Jose Lewgoy
Fitzcarraldo '82
Kiss of the Spider
    Woman '85

Dawnn Lewis
I'm Gonna Git You
    Sucka '88

Diana Lewis
Go West '40

Geoffrey Lewis
Lust in the Dust '85
Out of the Dark '88
Smile '75

Jerry Lewis
The Bellboy '60
It's a Mad, Mad, Mad,
    Mad World '63
The Nutty Professor '63

Jerry Lee Lewis
High School Confiden-
    tial '58

Juliette Lewis
Kalifornia '93

Linda Lewis
Alien Dead '85

Louise Lewis
Blood of Dracula '57
I Was a Teenage Were-
    wolf '57

Richard Lewis
The Return of Spinal
    Tap '92

Robert Lewis
Monsieur Verdoux '47

Pericles Lewnes
Redneck Zombies '88

Liberace
The Loved One '65

Cast
Index

359

Cult Flicks and Trash Pics

Cast Index

Cast Index

Cast
Index

Cast
Index

Cast
Index

367

Cult Flicks and Trash Pics

Cast
Index

Cast Index

Randy Quaid
Freaked '93
Parents '89

John Qualen
Casablanca '42
Seven Faces of Dr. Lao
'63

Iain Quarrier
The Fearless Vampire
Killers '67

Anthony Quayle
It Takes a Thief '59

Clint Quigley
Lost, Lonely, and Vi-
cious '59

Linnea Quigley
Hollywood Chainsaw
Hookers '88
Linnea Quigley's Horror
Workout '89
Murder Weapon '90
Sorority Babes in the
Slimeball Bowl-A-
Rama '87

Tim Quill
Army of Darkness '92
Thou Shalt Not Kill. . .
Except '87

Kathleen Quinlan
Twilight Zone: The
Movie '83

Bill Quinn
Twilight Zone: The
Movie '83

Martha Quinn
Bad Channels '92
Chopper Chicks in
Zombietown '91
The Return of Spinal
Tap '92
Tapeheads '89

Pat Quinn
Alice's Restaurant '69
Zachariah '70

Patricia Quinn
Shock Treatment '81

Tandra Quinn
Mesa of Lost Women
'52

Beulah Quo
Girls! Girls! Girls! '62

Catherine Rabett
Frankenstein Unbound
'90

Lisa Rack
The Flesh Merchant '55

Toby Radloff
Killer Nerd '91

Gilda Radner
All You Need Is Cash
'78

Deborah Raffin
God Told Me To '76

Steve Railsback
Helter Skelter '76

Ivan Raimi
Army of Darkness '92

Sam Raimi
Evil Dead 2: Dead by
Dawn '87
Thou Shalt Not Kill. . .
Except '87

**Theodore (Ted)
Raimi**
Army of Darkness '92
Evil Dead 2: Dead by
Dawn '87
Lunatics: A Love Story
'92
Thou Shalt Not Kill. . .
Except '87

Claude Rains
Casablanca '42
The Wolf Man '41

Charlotte Rampling
Angel Heart '87
Zardoz '73

Anne Ramsey
The Boy in the Plastic
Bubble '76

Thea Ramsey
Maniac '34

Tony Randall
Seven Faces of Dr. Lao
'63

Ric Randing
Splatter University '84

Jane Randolph
Abbott & Costello Meet
Frankenstein '48
Cat People '42

Salvo Randone
Fellini Satyricon '69
10th Victim '65

Michael Rapaport
True Romance '93

Anthony Rapp
Dazed and Confused
'93

David Rappaport
The Bride '85

David Rasche
Wicked Stepmother '89

Fritz Rasp
Metropolis '26

Thalmus Rasulala
Blacula '72

Wayne Ratay
The Wizard of Gore '70

Basil Rathbone
The Comedy of Terrors
'64
Hillbillies in a Haunted
House '67
Planet of Blood '66
Tales of Terror '62
The Tower of London '39
We're No Angels '55

Gregory Ratoff
I'm No Angel '33

Heather Rattray
Basket Case 2 '90

John Ratzenberger
The Empire Strikes Back
'80

Jim Rau
The Wizard of Gore '70

Samuel Rauch
Alien Contamination
'81

Herbert Rawlinson
Jail Bait '54

Aldo Ray
We're No Angels '55

Nicholas Ray
The American Friend
'77

Martha Raye
Monsieur Verdoux '47

Gary Raymond
Jason and the Argonauts
'63

Lee Raymond
She-Freak '67

Paula Raymond
The Beast from 20,000
Fathoms '53
Blood of Dracula's Cas-
tle '69

Robin Raymond
High School Confiden-
tial '58

Ronald Reagan
Bedtime for Bonzo '51
The Killers '64

Rex Reason
The Creature Walks
Among Us '56

Bill Rebane
Monster a Go-Go! '65

Richard Rebrere
Happy Birthday to Me
'81

Veronica Redburn
The Ghastly Ones '68

Quinn Redeker
The Three Stooges Meet
Hercules '61

Dennis Redfield
Private Duty Nurses '71

William Redfield
Fantastic Voyage '66

Rockets Redglare
Mystery Train '89

Lynn Redgrave
The Bad Seed '85
The Big Bus '76

Vanessa Redgrave
Blow-Up '66
Consuming Passions '88
The Devils '71
Prick Up Your Ears '87

Emiliano Redondo
Black Venus '83

Dolly Reed
Beyond the Valley of
the Dolls '70

Donna Reed
It's a Wonderful Life '46

Lady Reed
Avenging Disco Godfa-
ther '76
Dolemite 2: Human
Tornado '76

Larry Reed
World of the Depraved
'67

Lou Reed
Get Crazy '83

Oliver Reed
The Adventures of
Baron Munchausen
'89
Beat Girl '60
The Brood '79
The Devils '71
The House of Usher '88
Tommy '75

Ralph Reed
Reform School Girl '57

Cast
Index

Cast
Index

Cast Index

Cast
Index

Cast Index

Cast Index

Bill Thornbury
Phantasm '79

Dyanne Thorne
Hellhole '85
Ilsa, Harem Keeper of
the Oil Sheiks '76
Ilsa, She-Wolf of the SS
'74
Ilsa, the Tigress of
Siberia '79

Rex Thorson
The Female Jungle '56

William Thourlby
Creeping Terror '64

Beverly Thurman
The Giant Gila Monster
'59

Bill Thurman
It's Alive! '68

Theodora Thurman
Jail Bait '54

Uma Thurman
The Adventures of Baron
Munchausen '89
Pulp Fiction '94

Michael Thys
The Gods Must Be
Crazy '84

Gene Tierney
Laura '44

Lawrence Tierney
Casualties of Love: The
"Long Island Lolita"
Story '93
The Female Jungle '56
Red '91
Reservoir Dogs '92

Charles Tingwell
Malcolm '86

Su Tissue
Something Wild '86

Ginny Tiu
Girls! Girls! Girls! '62

Thelma Tixou
Santa Sangre '90

Kenneth Tobey
The Beast from 20,000
Fathoms '53
The Thing '51

George Todd
Creature of the Walking
Dead '60

James Todd
High School Confiden-
tial '58

Thelma Todd
Horse Feathers '32
Monkey Business '31
Nevada '27

Ugo Tognazzi
La Cage aux Folles '78

Fabiola Toledo
Demons '86

David Tomlinson
The Fiendish Plot of Dr.
Fu Manchu '80

Franchot Tone
Dancing Lady '33

Jacqueline Tong
How to Get Ahead in
Advertising '89

Regis Toomey
Change of Habit '69

Sarah Torgov
American Gothic '88

Peter Tork
The Brady Bunch Movie
'95
Head '68

Mel Torme
The Return of Spinal
Tap '92

Rip Torn
Airplane 2: The Sequel
'82
Beastmaster '82
Canadian Bacon '94
The Man Who Fell to
Earth '76

Liz Torres
National Lampoon's At-
tack of the 5 Ft. 2
Women '94

Raquel Torres
Duck Soup '33

Audrey Totter
The Carpetbaggers '64

Constance Towers
Naked Kiss '64
Shock Corridor '63

Tom Towles
Henry: Portrait of a Ser-
ial Killer '90

Robert Townsend
I'm Gonna Git You
Sucka '88

Pete Townshend
Secret Policeman's Pri-
vate Parts '81
Tommy '75

Marlene Tracy
I Dismember Mama '74

Spencer Tracy
It's a Mad, Mad, Mad,
Mad World '63

Henry Travers
It's a Wonderful Life '46

Marisa Travers
Frankenstein '80 '79

Susan Travers
The Abominable Dr.
Phibes '71
Peeping Tom '63

Henry Travis
The Brain from Planet
Arous '57

June Travis
Monster a Go-Go! '65

Richard Travis
Mesa of Lost Women '52
Missile to the Moon '59

Tony Travis
Flesh Gordon 2: Flesh
Gordon Meets the
Cosmic Cheerleaders
'90

John Travolta
The Boy in the Plastic
Bubble '76
Carrie '76
Devil's Rain '75
Grease '78
Pulp Fiction '94
Saturday Night Fever
'77

Mary Treen
I Married a Monster
from Outer Space '58
It's a Wonderful Life '46
Paradise, Hawaiian
Style '66

Les Tremayne
The Angry Red Planet '59
Creature of Destruction
'67
The War of the Worlds
'53

**Johanne-Marie
Tremblay**
Jesus of Montreal '89

Cheryl Trepton
Mantis in Lace '68

Leonardo Treviglio
Sebastiane '79

Vicki Trickett
The Three Stooges Meet
Hercules '61

Ivan Triesault
The Amazing Transpar-
ent Man '60

Paul Trinka
Faster Pussycat! Kill!
Kill! '66

Laura Trotter
Rush '84

Al Troupe
Microwave Massacre
'83

Natalie Trundy
Battle for the Planet of
the Apes '73
Beneath the Planet of
the Apes '70
Conquest of the Planet
of the Apes '72
Escape from the Planet
of the Apes '71

Tom Tryon
I Married a Monster
from Outer Space '58

Kenneth Tsang
The Killer '90

Irene Tsu
Paradise, Hawaiian
Style '66

Yoshio Tsuchiya
Attack of the Mushroom
People '63
Destroy All Monsters
'68
Yog, Monster from
Space '71

Michael Tucker
Diner '82

Ray Tudor
The Flesh Eaters '64

Ruby Tuesday
She-Devils on Wheels
'68

Sonny Tufts
Cat Women of the
Moon '53

Ann Turkel
Humanoids from the
Deep '80

Joe Turkel
Blade Runner '82

Janine Turner
The Ambulance '90

Kathleen Turner
Body Heat '81
Serial Mom '94

Cast
Index

Bonnie & Clyde '67
The Producers '68
Quackser Fortune Has a
Cousin in the Bronx
'70
Start the Revolution
Without Me '70
Willy Wonka & the
Chocolate Factory '71
Young Frankenstein '74

James Wilder
Zombie High '87

John Wildman
Sorority Babes in the
Slimeball Bowl-A-
Rama '87

Dawn Wildsmith
Surf Nazis Must Die '87

Bill Wiley
Porky's 2: The Next
Day '83

Kathleen Wilhoite
Angel Heart '87

**Catherine
Wilkening**
Jesus of Montreal '89

Donna Wilkes
Grotesque '87

Elaine Wilkes
Killer Party '86

Barbara Wilkin
The Flesh Eaters '64

June Wilkinson
The Bellboy and the
Playgirls '62

Fred Willard
This Is Spinal Tap '84

Dave Willcock
Queen of Outer Space
'58

Warren William
The Wolf Man '41

Barry Williams
The Brady Bunch Movie
'95

Bill Williams
The Giant Spider Inva-
sion '75

Billy Dee Williams
The Empire Strikes Back
'80
Return of the Jedi '83

Caroline Williams
The Texas Chainsaw
Massacre, Part 2 '86

Cindy Williams
The First Nudie Musical
'75
Gas-s-s-s! '70
Uforia '81

**Clarence Williams,
III**
I'm Gonna Git You
Sucka '88

Don Williams
The Ghastly Ones '68

Edy Williams
Bad Girls from Mars '90
Beyond the Valley of
the Dolls '70
Hellhole '85

Grant Williams
Brain of Blood '71

Guy Williams
I Was a Teenage Were-
wolf '57

Ian Patrick Williams
Bad Channels '92

Jason Williams
Flesh Gordon '72

Joyce Williams
Private Duty Nurses '71

Kathy Williams
Saturday Night Sleazies,
Vol. 3 '67

Lori Williams
Faster Pussycat! Kill!
Kill! '66

Paul Williams
Battle for the Planet of
the Apes '73
The Loved One '65
Phantom of the Paradise
'74
Zombie High '87

Robert Williams
Revenge of the Creature
'55

Robin Williams
The Adventures of
Baron Munchausen
'89
Shakes the Clown '92

**Spencer Williams,
Jr.**
Son of Ingagi '40

Zack Williams
Son of Ingagi '40

Fred Williamson
One Down, Two to Go!
'82

Noble Willingham
Big Bad Mama '74

Bruce Willis
Pulp Fiction '94

Sherry Willis-Burch
Killer Party '86

Maury Wills
The Black Six '74

Shannon Wilsey
The Invisible Maniac '90

Alex Wilson
Gas-s-s-s! '70

Andy Wilson
2000 Maniacs '64

Barbara Wilson
Lost, Lonely, and Vi-
cious '59

Brian Wilson
Beach Party '63

**Don "The Dragon"
Wilson**
Bloodfist '89
Bloodfist 2 '90
Futurekick '91

Dooley Wilson
Casablanca '42

Earl Wilson
Beach Blanket Bingo
'65

George Wilson
Attack of the Killer
Tomatoes '77

Pee Wee Wilson
Young Einstein '89

Richard Wilson
How to Get Ahead in
Advertising '89

Roger Wilson
Porky's '82
Porky's 2: The Next
Day '83

Sheree J. Wilson
Crimewave '85

Thomas F. Wilson
April Fool's Day '86

Trey Wilson
Raising Arizona '87

Walter Winchell
The Bellboy '60

William Windom
Escape from the Planet
of the Apes '71

Marie Windsor
Abbott & Costello Meet
the Mummy '55
Cat Women of the
Moon '53
Swamp Women '55

Romy Windsor
The House of Usher '88

Tammy Windsor
Little Shop of Horrors
'60

Janu Wine
Mantis in Lace '68

Paul Winfield
Star Trek 2: The Wrath
of Khan '82

Mark Wingett
Quadrophenia '79

Kitty Winn
The Exorcist '73

Mare Winningham
St. Elmo's Fire '85

George Winship
Teenage Gang Debs '66

Michael Winslow
Far Out Man '89

Dennis Winston
The Adventures of Baron
Munchausen '89

Alex Winter
Freaked '93

Deborah Winters
Blue Sunshine '78

Holle K. Winters
Motor Psycho '65

Jonathan Winters
It's a Mad, Mad, Mad,
Mad World '63
The Loved One '65
Oh Dad, Poor Dad
(Momma's Hung You
in the Closet & I'm
Feeling So Sad) '67

Roland Winters
Abbott & Costello Meet
the Killer, Boris
Karloff '49

Shelley Winters
Bloody Mama '70
The Night of the Hunter
'55
Tentacles '77
Wild in the Streets '68

Estelle Winwood
The Producers '68

Cast
Index

387

Cult Flicks and Trash Pics

Maurisia Zach
Working Girls '87

John Zacherle
Geek Maggot Bingo '83

Pia Zadora
Hairspray '88
The Lonely Lady '83
Santa Claus Conquers
  the Martians '64
Voyage of the Rock
  Aliens '87

Elliot Zamuto
The Legend of the Wolf
  Woman '77

Lenore Zann
Happy Birthday to Me '81

Dweezil Zappa
Pretty in Pink '86

Frank Zappa
Head '68

Moon Zappa
Spirit of '76 '91

Joan Zaremba
20 Million Miles to
  Earth '57

Michael Zelniker
Naked Lunch '91

Suzanne Zenor
The Baby '72

Gerard Zepeda
Night of the Bloody
  Apes '68

Anthony Zerbe
KISS Meets the Phantom
  of the Park '78
Omega Man '71

Howard Zieff
Flesh Gordon '72

Terri Zimmern
The Manster '59

Karl Zinny
Demons '86

Zoofoot
Redneck Zombies '88

David Zucker
Kentucky Fried Movie
  '77

Jerry Zucker
Kentucky Fried Movie
  '77

Alex Zuckerman
Freaked '93

Daphne Zuniga
The Sure Thing '85

Ron Zwang
Red '91

Cast
Index

389

Cult Flicks and Trash Pics

Director Index

If you understood the "Cast Index" (and who wouldn't?), this one is a cinch. This index lists all the director-types credited in the main review section, alphabetically by their last names (although they are presented here in first name/last name format). Just for fun, you might also take a peek at the "Cast Index" to see if your favorite director has ever had a gratuitous cameo or foot-in-the-door debut in any of the mongrel videos listed in the main review section.

Jim Abrahams
Airplane! '80
Top Secret! '84

Al Adamson
Blazing Stewardesses '75
Blood of Dracula's Castle '69
Blood of Ghastly Horror '72
Brain of Blood '71
Dracula Vs. Frankenstein '71
Satan's Sadists '69

Lou Adler
Cheech and Chong's Up in Smoke '79

Carlton J. Albright
Luther the Geek '90

Robert Aldrich
Kiss Me Deadly '55

Lewis Allen
Suddenly '54

Woody Allen
Annie Hall '77
What's Up, Tiger Lily? '66

Michael Almereyda
Twister '89

Emmett Alston
Nine Deaths of the Ninja '85

James Amonte
The Alchemist '81

Kenneth Anger
Kenneth Anger, Vol. 1: Fireworks '47
Kenneth Anger, Vol. 2: Inauguration of the Pleasure Dome '54
Kenneth Anger, Vol. 3: Lucifer Rising '65
Kenneth Anger, Vol. 4: Invocation of My Demon Brother '80

Michelangelo Antonioni
Blow-Up '66

Denys Arcand
Jesus of Montreal '89

Dario Argento
The Bird with the Crystal Plumage '70
Deep Red: Hatchet Murders '75
Suspiria '77
Unsane '82

Allan Arkush
Death Sport '78
Get Crazy '83
Hollywood Boulevard '76
Rock 'n' Roll High School '79

George Armitage
Private Duty Nurses '71

Jack Arnold
Creature from the Black Lagoon '54
High School Confidential '58
It Came from Outer Space '53
Revenge of the Creature '55

Dorothy Arzner
Dance, Girl, Dance '40

Hal Ashby
Harold and Maude '71

Ronnie Ashcroft
The Astounding She-Monster '58

William Asher
Beach Blanket Bingo '65
Beach Party '63
Muscle Beach Party '64

Melvin Ashford
Mondo Magic '76

Guillaume Martin Aucion
Oh! Calcutta! '72

Carlos Aured
Curse of the Devil '73

Sam Auster
Screen Test '85

Hector Babenco
Kiss of the Spider Woman '85

John Badham
Saturday Night Fever '77

Ralph Bakshi
Cool World '92
Fritz the Cat '72
Streetfight '75

Bob Balaban
Parents '89

Albert Band
Zoltan. . .Hound of Dracula '77

Charles Band
Parasite '82

Paul Bartel
Cannonball '76
Death Race 2000 '75
Eating Raoul '82
Lust in the Dust '85
Private Parts '72
Scenes from the Class Struggle in Beverly Hills '89
The Secret Cinema/Naughty Nurse '78

Charles T. Barton
Abbott & Costello Meet Frankenstein '48
Abbott & Costello Meet the Killer, Boris Karloff '49

Lamberto Bava
Demons '86

Mario Bava
Black Sabbath '64
Black Sunday '60
Blood and Black Lace '64
Planet of the Vampires '65

Craig R. Baxley
Stone Cold '91

William Beaudine
Bela Lugosi Meets a Brooklyn Gorilla '52
Billy the Kid Vs. Dracula '66

**Director
Index**

Director Index

393

Cult Flicks and Trash Pics

**Director
Index**

John Golden
Fat Guy Goes Nutzoid
'86

Bob(cat)
Goldthwait
Shakes the Clown '92

Bert I. Gordon
The Amazing Colossal
Man '57
Beginning of the End
'57
Village of the Giants '65

Keith Gordon
Wild Palms '93

Stuart Gordon
The Re-Animator '85

Christian Gore
Red '91

Carl Gottlieb
Amazon Women on the
Moon '87

Roger Graef
Secret Policeman's Private Parts '81

Tom Graeff
Teenagers from Outer
Space '59

William A.
Graham
Change of Habit '69

Joseph Green
The Brain That Wouldn't Die '63

William Grefe
The Death Curse of
Tartu '66
Impulse '74

Edmond T.
Greville
Beat Girl '60

Tom Gries
Helter Skelter '76

Giuseppe Patroni
Griffi
Driver's Seat '73

Charles B. Griffith
Eat My Dust '76
Smokey Bites the Dust
'81

Brad Grinter
Blood Freak '72

Jerry Gross
Teenage Mother '67

Mark Haggard
The First Nudie Musical
'75

Piers Haggard
The Fiendish Plot of Dr.
Fu Manchu '80

Richard W. Haines
Class of Nuke 'Em High
'86
Splatter University '84

Jon Hall
The Beach Girls and the
Monster '65

Daniel Haller
The Dunwich Horror
'70

Guy Hamilton
Goldfinger '64
Remo Williams: The
Adventure Begins '85

Curtis Hanson
The Arousers '70

Robin Hardy
The Wicker Man '75

Wayne A. Harold
Killer Nerd '91

Curtis Harrington
Night Tide '63
Planet of Blood '66

Herk Harvey
Carnival of Souls '62

Kohji Hashimoto
Godzilla 1985 '85

Byron Haskin
The War of the Worlds
'53

Steve Hawkes
Blood Freak '72

Howard Hawks
The Thing '51

John Hayes
All the Lovin' Kinfolk
'89

John Patrick Hayes
Hollywood After Dark
'65

Amy Heckerling
Fast Times at Ridgemont
High '82

Victor Heerman
Animal Crackers '30

Monte Hellman
Cockfighter '74

Creature from the
Haunted Sea '60

Oliver Hellman
Tentacles '77

Frank Henenlotter
Basket Case '82
Basket Case 2 '90
Basket Case 3: The
Progeny '92
Brain Damage '88
Frankenhooker '90

Perry Henzell
The Harder They Come
'72

Joel Hershman
Hold Me, Thrill Me,
Kiss Me '93

Nathan Hertz
Attack of the 50 Foot
Woman '58

Michael Herz
Sgt. Kabukiman
N.Y.P.D. '94
The Toxic Avenger '86
The Toxic Avenger, Part
2 '89
The Toxic Avenger, Part
3: The Last Temptation of Toxie '89
Troma's War '88

John Herzfeld
Casualties of Love: The
"Long Island Lolita"
Story '93

Werner Herzog
Aguirre, the Wrath of
God '72
Fitzcarraldo '82

Gordon Hessler
KISS Meets the Phantom
of the Park '78

David L. Hewitt
Alien Massacre '67

Jean Hewitt
Blood of Dracula's Castle '69

Pete Hewitt
Wild Palms '93

Douglas Hickox
Theatre of Blood '73

George Roy Hill
Slap Shot '77

Jack Hill
The Big Bird Cage '72
The Big Doll House '71
Spider Baby '64

Walter Hill
The Warriors '79

Arthur Hiller
The Hospital '71

Arthur Hilton
Cat Women of the
Moon '53

Bettina Hirsch
Munchies '87

Alfred Hitchcock
The Birds '63
Family Plot '76
Marnie '64
Psycho '60
The Trouble with Harry
'55

Lyndall Hobbs
Back to the Beach '87

Allan Holleb
Candy Stripe Nurses '74

Allan Holzman
Forbidden World '82

Inoshiro Honda
Attack of the Mushroom
People '63
Destroy All Monsters
'68
Ghidrah the Three
Headed Monster '65
Godzilla, King of the
Monsters '56
Godzilla Vs. Monster
Zero '68
Godzilla Vs. Mothra '64
King Kong Vs. Godzilla
'63
Mothra '62
War of the Gargantuas
'70
Yog, Monster from
Space '71

Tobe Hooper
Eaten Alive '76
The Texas Chainsaw
Massacre '74
The Texas Chainsaw
Massacre, Part 2 '86

Dennis Hopper
Easy Rider '69

Richard Horian
Student Confidential '87

Peter Horton
Amazon Women on the
Moon '87

Dan Hoskins
Chopper Chicks in
Zombietown '91

Director Index

**Director
Index**

Director
Index

Director Index

Director Index

Category List

This is one of the Hound's favorite parts. Listed below are countless arduously researched and frantically brainstormed subjects by which the main reviews are categorized. No one list is inclusive...you wouldn't believe how hard this is. We've tried to be very specific in some areas (note the progression from "Zombies" to "Nazi Zombies" and "Underwater Zombies"...we considered slipping in "Underwater Nazi Zombies," but you have to draw the line somewhere). Feel very welcome to join in the fun by sending in new titles for existing categories, as well as brand spankin' new categories (which should be accompanied by titles that fit the category). Following the "Category List" is, miraculously, the "Category Index" itself, making the "Category List" a practical item and not just an amusing use of paper.

Abbott & Costello Those social butterflies A&C meet just about everyone.

Action Adventure Adrenaline busters for those weary of the conventions of plot.

Adapted from a Book Movies that borrowed their plots from real writers and actually gave them credit for it. You might be surprised at some on the list—run right out to the library.

Adapted from a Play or Musical Same thing, originally live.

Adapted from a Story Same thing but usually shorter.

Adventure Drama Action with more attention to dramatic content.

Advertising A business where two heads are often better than one.

Alcoholism see On the Rocks

Alien Beings—Benign Friendly well-meaning space visitors, including Kathy Ireland.

Alien Beings—Vicious Not-so-friendly, and, well, *mean* space visitors, often bent on world domination (but not including Microsoft).

Amy Fisher Tri-network vixen who remarkably merits her own category.

Animals see Cats; Killer Birds; King of Beasts (Dogs)

Animation see 'Toons

Anthologies When the plot isn't long enough to allow the film to last even an hour and a half.

Anti-Heroes Bad role models (or relatively good ones, depending upon your criminal record).

Archaeology see Big Digs

Artists Usually unemployed people seeking alternate means of income.

At the Movies Movie makers making movies from their movie-making experiences.

Australia see Down Under

Automobiles see Fast Cars; Motor Vehicle Dept.

Babies see That's a Baby?

Bang! You're Dead Someone's a target for an assasination.

Banned! Movies that we weren't allowed to see at some point, making us want to see them all the more.

Barney's Scarier Cousins Dinosaurs and other prehistoric creatures running amok.

Beach Blanket Bingo Virginal babes in bikinis you feel bad about fantasizing over.

Behind Bars see Great Escapes; Men in Prison; Women in Prison

Behind the Scenes A peek behind the show biz curtain.

Big Battles Big-budget (or least the illusion of it) clash of large, opposing military forces on Earth and other locales.

Big Budget/Bad Movie Pathetic wastes of money; think *Ishtar*, or *Waterworld* (which isn't in this book but we wanted to make that connection anyway).

Big Business Invariably concerning corruption, soul-selling, or revenge by the corporate cogs—*Roger & Me*, or *Freaked*.

Big Digs Archaeological disasters, often involving someone wrapped in bandages.

Bigfoot What is a bigfoot anyway? Is it an ape? Is it a bear? Will someone please tell us?

morality tales, rigged to take advantage of the viewer.

Eyeballs! Unnerving scenes involving eyeballs.

Family Ties Blood runs deep—*American Gothic* or *Wicked Stepmother.*

Fantasy Tales of the (sometimes twisted) imagination.

Fast Cars Racing in the street or on the track.

Feminism *see Women; Wonder Women*

Femme Fatale She done him and him and him wrong.

The '50s *see Nifty '50s*

Film History America at the movies.

Film Noir Dark and moody or tributes to dark and moody.

Film Stars Bios of cinema celebs, real and make-believe.

Filmmaking The making of a film within a film.

Flower Children Long-haired freaky pinko peace-luvin' mello-headed hippie types.

Flying Saucers *see Alien Beings—Benign; Alien Beings—Vicious; Space Operas*

Folklore Age-old tales handed down through the generations.

Food *see Edibles*

Four Bones Yep! Here it is! Our picks!

France Not the nicest selection of scenes from the land of romance...

Frankenstein Well known guy with bolts in his neck.

Friendship *see Buddies*

Front Page Stop the presses!

Funerals The final goodbye, usually over and over again.

Gambling Sometimes it happens in states other than Nevada.

Gangs Criminally enterprising teens and adults running in packs.

Gender Bending Men who want to be women and, less often, vice-versa.

Genetics Fooling with the double helix.

Genies It won't be Robin Williams who pops out of these bottles.

Genre Spoofs Serious looks at film genres—not!

Ghosts, Ghouls & Goblins Haunting spirits of the dead.

Giants *The Amazing Colossal Man* visits *The Village of the Giants.*

Gimmickola! 3-D, William Castle capers, and other ingenuous ways to cover up the inherent lack in a movie.

Godzilla & Friends Big battling reptiles and insects, usually poorly dubbed.

Golf Believe it or not, there were a few cool movies made about golf.

Grand Hotel Check-out time might be noon, then again, it might be never.

Great Death Scenes If you gotta go, you might as well make the most of it.

Great Depression The era, not the state of mind.

Great Escapes Men and women break out.

Growin' Old What happens just seconds after growin' up.

Growin' Up What happens just seconds before growin' old.

Happy Hookers Actually, some not-so-happy ones too.

Heists The big lift.

Hell High School Isn't that redundant?

Hillbillies The Clampetts weren't the only ones to capitalize on their southern "charm."

Historical Drama Usually at least loosely based on a real person or incident.

Hit Men Hired men and women armed with silencers.

Hockey Puckin' around on the ice.

Holidays From Hell *April Fool's Day* to *Santa Claus Conquers the Martians.*

Horror Just plain scary stuff that isn't classic or overtly funny or relying heavily on a proliferation of blood.

Horror Comedy Laughing all the way to the grave.

Hospitals Institutions with lots of sick people—and patients, too.

Hostage! People held against their will for bargaining purposes.

I Can't See Movies containing blindness.

I Can't See You Movies containing invisibility.

I Spy Trench coats, fedoras, dark glasses, and often martinis (shaken, not stirred).

Identity Who am I? Who are you? Who are we? Why do you ask so many questions?

Jail *see Great Escapes; Men in Prison; Women in Prison*

Journalism *see Front Page*

Jungles Tarzan, tribes, trees, treasure, temperature, temptresses, and tigers.

Kidnapped! Held for ransom or just for the heck of it.

Killer Apes They think they're King Kong on the Planet of the Apes.

Killer Appliances Goes way beyond trying to program your VCR.

Killer Birds *Beaks: The Movie, The Birds,* and other instances of death swooping down from the trees.

Killer Brains Literally, they have a mind of their own.

Killer Bugs & Slugs Ants to *The Worm Eaters.*

Killer Cars It's what happens when you don't change their oil.

Killer Dreams On and off Elm Street.

Killer Kats Kitties with a killer instinct.

Killer Plants Including foliage, fruits, and fungi.

Killer Reptiles Alligators, frogs, gila monsters, and whatever the hell Godzilla is.

Killer Rodents Mickey's evil twins.

Killer Sea Critters Wet and squishy things from the deep.

King of Beasts (Dogs) Need we say more?

Kings *see Royalty*

Kung Fu *see Ever'body Was Kung Fu Fighting*

Law & Lawyers First, kill all the...

Category Index

The Legend of Ed Gein Movies based on the exploits of the infamous serial killer/cannibal.

Loneliness *see Only the Lonely*

Loner Cops You'd be lonely too if you had a body like Harvey Keitel.

Lovers on the Lam Boy meets girl and they leave.

The Loving Dead Necrophilia, not including zombie love, for zombies are technically the "undead."

Macho Men Testosterone overload.

Mad Scientists Sin in the name of science.

Made for Television *see TV Movies; TV Series*

Mafia *see Organized Crime*

Magic Hocus pocus, often with an evil intent.

Magic Carpet Rides A rug with a mind of its own, not to be confused with killer hairpieces.

Marriage *I Married a Vampire,* for example.

Martial Arts *see Ever'body Was Kung Fu Fighting*

The Marx Brothers Zany siblings with a knack for making people laugh.

Medieval Romps Dirty peasants, deodorized kings and queens, and knights in shining armor.

Meltdown Or, how I learned to stop worrying and love the bomb.

Men in Prison Macho guys behind bars.

Metamorphosis Ch-ch-ch-ch-changes.

Missing Persons People who disappear for a variety of reasons, sometimes because other people have taken them away.

Mondo Movies Collections of trashy, gratuitous, and shocking scenes without even the pretense of plot for the viewer's amusement.

Monkee Business Here they come, walking down the street and right into a few movies, if you still haven't gotten over your crush on Davey

Category Index

Jones.

Monkey Business Here they come, walking down...oops, wrong monkeys.

Monster Moms Joan Crawford, Kathleen Turner, and the ilk.

Monsters, General Killer beasts not elsewhere classified.

Monty Python British comedy troupe whose talents are often not appreciated by the uptight.

Motor Vehicle Dept. Fords, Chevys, and other cars, vans, and light trucks.

Mummies Withered folks wrapped in toilet paper.

Music All You Need Is Cash, This Is Spinal Tap, and other movies with good soundtracks.

Musicals High-energy dancing and singing, often for no apparent reason.

Mystery & Suspense Edge-of-the-couch thrillers and whodunits.

Nasty Diseases *The Boy in the Plastic Bubble* to *Rabid.*

Nazi Zombies The undead, sometimes underwater but always fascist.

Nazis & Other Paramilitary Slugs The real jack-booted government thugs.

Negative Utopia Things seemed so perfect until...

New Zealand *see Down Under*

Newspapers *see Front Page*

Nifty '50s Movies that feature, for better or for worse, the *Happy Days* decade.

Nightclubs Birds of a feather often flock to these smoky, dark hot spots.

Ninjitsu *see Ever'body Was Kung Fu Fighting*

No-Exit Motel Where "check out time" has a new meaning.

Nuclear Disaster *see Disaster Strikes; Meltdown*

Nuns & Priests Real and imposters.

Nurses *see Women in (and out of) Uniform*

Occult Witches, warlocks, devil worshippers, spell makers, spell breakers, haunted houses, and so on.

Oceans *see Killer Sea Critters*

Oedipal Allegories Really, *really* close family ties.

On the Rocks Alcoholism, alcohol, barflies, moonshining, prohibition....

Only the Lonely Fifty ways to play solitaire.

Organized Crime Gangsters with Franklin planners.

Painting *see Artists*

Parenthood Moms, Dads, substitutes...

Party Hell There are worse things than running out of Chex Mix.

Patriotism & Paranoia Excessive flag-waving and over-allegiance to countries or leaders.

Period Piece Costume epics or evocative of a certain time and place.

Phone Terror Usually worse than a wrong number.

Photography *see Shutterbugs*

Pill Poppin' Consumption of drugs, mostly illegal or in extra-large doses.

The Planet of the Apes Because the Hound himself keeps forgetting that there wasn't one titled *Revenge of the Planet of the Apes...* or *Return to the Planet of the Apes...* or *Bride of the....*

Pleased to Meet You Some most outrageous pairings.

Politics Sort of like organized crime.

Post Apocalypse No more convenience stores.

Presidents Movies involving presidents (either as characters or actors).

Price of Fame What goes up...

Princes/Princesses *see Royalty*

Prison *see Great Escapes; Men in Prison; Women in Prison*

Producers: William Castle For those Castle completists.

Producers: Roger Corman/New World It might be easier to list what wasn't produced by Mr. Corman.

Producers: Hammer It's Hammer time!

Producers: Val Lewton High falutin' Val Lewton creepers.

Producers: Troma Did you ever wonder why Troma doesn't have a funnier name for it's production company?

Producers: Andy Warhol And usually directed by Paul Morrissey.

Producers: Zucker/Abrahams/Zucker ZAZ yucks like *Airplane!* and *Kentucky Fried Movie.*

Propaganda *see Patriotism & Paranoia; Politics*

Prostitutes *see Happy Hookers*

Psychiatry *see Shrinks*

Psycho-Thriller It's all in your mind...

Psychotics/Sociopaths Social deviants without a conscience.

Queens *see Royalty*

Rape Victims and often their revenge.

Rebel With a Cause Bucking the establishment for a reason.

Rebel Without a Cause Bucking the establishment just because it's the establishment.

Red Scare Cold war and communism (not the cancer-causing M n' Ms).

Religion Organized or otherwise.

Renegade Body Parts Hands, fingers, eyes, brains, and other appendages with a life of their own.

Revenge Generally of the bloody variety.

Road Trip Escapism courtesy two- and four-wheeled vehicles.

Roadshow Movies Exploitation/morality tales that were peddled on the road from town to town; people were often hired to "protest" the films, and when attendance slowed down, the movies were simply renamed (a practice that unfortunately carried over to video distribution).

Robots & Androids Danger, Will Robinson!

Rock Stars on Film But can they act?

Role Reversal Walkin' in another man's shoes for a few reels.

Romance *see Lovers on the Lam; Romantic Comedy; Romantic Drama*

Romantic Comedy Love thing leads to laughs.

Romantic Drama Love thing leads to tension and anxiety.

Royalty Emperors, kings, queens, princes, princesses, crowns, and scepters.

Sail Away Adventure on the high seas.

Sanity Check Inmates running the asylum; also deviant states of mind.

Satanism Speak of the devil...

Satire & Parody Biting social comment or genre spoofs.

Scams, Stings & Cons *A Fish Called Wanda* to *We're No Angels.*

School *see Hell High School; Teacher, Teacher*

Sci Fi Imagination fueled by science and a vision of the future.

Scientists If they could have only left well enough alone...

Screwball Comedy Stupid is a stupid does.

Serial Killers Includes doctors, exterminators, newlyweds, and moms, among other monotonous murderers.

The '70s Mood rings, eight tracks (okay, the Hound will admit to still having one), and macrame, and often with a disco soundtrack.

Sex & Sexuality Focus is on lust, for better or worse.

Sexploitation Softcore epics usually lacking in plot but not skin.

Ships *see Sail Away*

Showbiz Behind the scenes in Hollywood or on Broadway.

Shower & Bath Scenes The ultimate in wet, porcelain-tainted sequences.

Shrinks As in head shrinkers (psychiatrists, not witch doctors).

Shutterbugs Snapshot specialists.

Silent Films *see The Sound of Silence*

The '60s *see Flower Children*

Slapstick Comedy Humor of the physical sort, including A&C, The Marx Brothers, The Three Stooges...

The Sound of Silence Silent films, often employing a very rudimentary means of subtitling.

Space Operas Going where no spam has gone before.

Special F/X Extravaganzas The spaceships is these films don't have strings attached.

Special F/X Extravaganzas: Make-Up Faces only a mother could love.

Special F/X Wizards: Rick Baker He went from *Octaman* to *Star Wars.*

Special F/X Wizards: Anton Furst Responsible for the slimey creature in *Alien.*

Special F/X Wizards: Ray Harryhausen Heart-stopping stop-motion animation at its best.

Special F/X Wizards: Herschell Gordon Lewis This jack o'lantern of all trades did more than just direct.

Special F/X Wizards: Tom Savini How does he do it?

Special F/X Wizards: Dick Smith Amazing vomit meister.

Special F/X Wizards: Douglas Trumball Futuristic, sci fi specialist.

Sports *see Golf; Hockey; Sports Comedies; Surfing*

Sports Comedies Maybe it's the sound of all those high-paid pros laughing their way to the bank.

Star Wars Just in case anyone can't remember all three titles.

Stewardesses *see Women in (and out of) Uniform*

Strained Suburbia Pleasant Valley Sundays in hell.

Struggling Musicians Johnny Bravo, Nigel & David, etc.

Suicide Premature ends, either attempted, threatened, faked, or successful.

Category Index

407

Cult Flicks and Trash Pics

Super Heroes Men and women of extraordinary strength and/ or abilities wearing silly-looking costumes.

Supernatural Comedies Funny forces from beyond.

Supernatural Horror Forces from beyond terrorize those who are here.

Supernatural Martial Arts Forces from beyond terrorize via head kicking and rib crunching.

Supernatural Westerns Forces from beyond terrorize those in the west.

Surfing Balancing acts on boards.

Survival Nobody said it was going to be easy.

Swashbucklers Crossed swords and rope swinging.

Teacher, Teacher Dedicated educators.

Technology—Rampant Machines that wreak havoc.

Teen Angst Adolescent anxieties.

Television see *TV Movies; TV Series; TV Tales*

Tell Us About Yourself Movies with ego-centric titles.

Terror in the Woods Summer camp isn't what it used to be.

The Terror of Ted Turner Make sure you don't accidently acquire the colorized versions of these titles.

That's a Baby? Faces even a mother can't love.

This Is Your Life Biography and autobiography

3-D Flicks Movies requiring special glasses that often cause headaches (watching the movies without the glasses can cause headaches as well).

Time Travel Fast forward or reverse.

Toilets see *Shower & Bath Scenes*

'Toons Animated features.

Torrid Love Scenes Steamy and/or sticky.

Trains Rhythm of the clackity-clack.

Transvestites & Transsexuals see *Gender Bending*

Treasure Hunt Looking for hidden riches, often with a weathered map (especially in *Lust in the Dust*).

Trees & Forests Can't see one through the other.

True Stories Approximations of real-life events, often significantly fictionalized for the screen.

TV Movies First shown on broadcast, cable, or foreign television before hitting your VCR.

TV Series Collections, anthologies, and individual episodes of memorable TV shows.

TV Tales Movies about TV (not to be confused with TV movies)—*Amazon Women on the Moon* to *UHF*.

20-Something Cult Items Those movies that the younger 20-somethings watch obsessively.

Twins Seeing double.

UFOs see *Alien Beings—Benign; Alien Beings—Vicious; Space Operas*

Uncharted Desert Isle Land masses surrounded by water.

Underwater Zombies Sometimes Nazis but always wet at some point.

Unexplained Phenomena Ummm, it's hard to define....

Universal Studios' Classic Horror All the biggies (and some not-so-biggies).

Vacations Nice places to visit, but...

Vampire Babes Bloodsucking dames.

Vampire Spoof Bloodsucking buffoons.

Vampires More serious vein of bloodsucking varmint, including Dracula in his many manifestations.

Veterans They often have trouble re-assimilating.

Vietnam War Actually, a police action.

Vincent Price Pines Away at His Dead Wife's Portrait Need we be more specific?

Vomit see *Chunky Delight*

Voodoo Sport involving sticking pins in dolls.

War Between the Sexes Women vs. men and men vs. women.

War Is Hell Actually, more like "War is insane."

Wedding Hell Marriages that don't start off on the right foot.

Werewolves Full moon wonders.

Western Comedy Bumbling cowpeople.

Westerns *El Topo* to *Zachariah*.

Westrogens Wonder women of the West.

Where's My Johnson? Movies that may have inspired Lorena Bobbit.

Witchcraft That old black magic.

Women Impressive women, less than impressive women, and issues concerning women.

Women in (and out of) Uniform Cheerleaders, nurses, and stewardesses.

Women in Prison Even includes some flicks not starring Linda Blair.

Wonder Women *Alien, Attack of the 50 Foot Woman, Attack of the 60 Foot Centerfold*, etc.

World War I The first big one.

World War II The last big one.

Worst Ape Costumes Our candidates for movies most likely to have been snubbed by Roddy McDowall.

Wrestling Choreographed sport taking place on a mat.

Wrong Side of the Tracks Often involves relationship with someone on the right side.

You Lose, You Die Sports taken to the extreme, where only the winner survives.

Zombies The undead, of any political persuasion, in and out of water.

Category Index

Category Index

Sigh...the Hound doesn't want to repeat himself, so if you desire an explanation, flip back to page 403 to see the "Category List," which makes some surreal sense of the subject categories and corresponding movie titles on the following pages. Thanks for your cooperation.

Abbott & Costello
Abbott & Costello Go to Mars
Abbott & Costello Meet Dr. Jekyll and Mr. Hyde
Abbott & Costello Meet Frankenstein
Abbott & Costello Meet the Invisible Man
Abbott & Costello Meet the Killer, Boris Karloff
Abbott & Costello Meet the Mummy
Hold That Ghost

Action Adventure
See also Adventure Drama; Disaster Strikes; Ever'body Was Kung Fu Fighting; Macho Men; Swashbucklers
The Abductors
Alien from L.A.
All the Lovin' Kinfolk
The Amazing Transparent Man
Android
Angels Hard as They Come
Avenging Disco Godfather
The Banker
Batman
A Better Tomorrow
The Big Doll House
The Black Six
Bloodfist
Bloodfist 2
Caged Heat
Cannibal Women in the Avocado Jungle of Death
Cannonball
Chained Heat
City on Fire
Cobra Woman
Combat Shock
The Conqueror
Deadly Weapons
Death Race 2000

Dr. No
Dolemite 2: Human Tornado
The Doll Squad
Enter the Dragon
Escape from New York
Exterminator
Faster Pussycat! Kill! Kill!
From Russia with Love
Fugitive Girls
Futurekick
Ginger
Girls Are for Loving
Goldfinger
Grand Theft Auto
Hard-Boiled
Hard Target
Hell's Angels Forever
Hercules Against the Moon Men
Hercules in New York
Highlander
Jail Bait
King Kong
King Kong Versus Godzilla
The Loves of Hercules
Lust in the Dust
Mad Max
Master Blaster
Motor Psycho
Northville Cemetery Massacre
One Down, Two to Go!
Picasso Trigger
Raiders of the Sun
The Road Warrior
Rush
Satan's Sadists
Saturday Night Sleazies, Vol. 1
Saturday Night Sleazies, Vol. 2
Saturday Night Sleazies, Vol. 3
Sgt. Kabukiman N.Y.P.D.
The Seventh Voyage of Sinbad
Smokey Bites the Dust

Stone Cold
Supervixens
Surf Nazis Must Die
Swamp Women
Tarzan, the Ape Man
Thunder Road
Troma's War
The Warriors
White Pongo
The Wild Angels
The Wild World of Batwoman
Zipperface

Adapted from a Book
Altered States
The American Friend
The Amityville Horror
Angel Heart
Apocalypse Now
Armistead Maupin's Tales of the City
Battle Beyond the Stars
The Beast Within
Blackboard Jungle
Blade Runner
Blood and Roses
Boxcar Bertha
The Bride of Frankenstein
The Carpetbaggers
Catch-22
A Clockwork Orange
Contempt
The Curse of Frankenstein
Day of the Triffids
Death Race 2000
The Devils
Dr. No
Dr. Strangelove, or: How I Learned to Stop Worrying and Love the Bomb
Don't Look Now
Dracula
Driver's Seat
Dune
The Dunwich Horror
Fahrenheit 451

The Fall of the House of Usher
Fellini Satyricon
Fitzcarraldo
Frankenstein
Frankenstein Unbound
The Haunted Palace
The Haunting
Helter Skelter
Invasion of the Body Snatchers
Island of Lost Souls
It Came From Outer Space
King Creole
Kiss of the Spider Woman
The Last Temptation of Christ
Laura
The Lonely Lady
The Man Who Fell to Earth
The Manchurian Candidate
Mandingo
Myra Breckinridge
Mysterious Island
Naked Lunch
The Night of the Hunter
Omega Man
Out of the Past
Petulia
The Phantom of the Opera
The Phantom of the Opera
Planet of the Apes
The Princess Bride
Psycho
Remo Williams: The Adventure Begins
Room Service
Rosemary's Baby
Seven Faces of Dr. Lao
Solaris
Tarzan, the Ape Man
10th Victim
The Thing
Things to Come
The Time Machine

Category Index

Category Index

Category
Index

Category
Index

413

Cult Flicks and Trash Pics

Frigid Wife
Glen or Glenda?
Heat
Hell's Angels on Wheels
Helter Skelter
Henry: Portrait of a Ser-
ial Killer
High School Confiden-
tial
Hollywood After Dark
Honeymoon Killers
I Accuse My Parents
I Am Curious (Yellow)
Ilsa, She-Wolf of the SS
Ilsa, the Tigress of
Siberia
Impulse
Jackson County Jail
Jesus of Montreal
Just for the Hell of It
Kalifornia
Kenneth Anger, Vol. 1:
Fireworks
Kenneth Anger, Vol. 2:
Inauguration of the
Pleasure Dome
Kenneth Anger, Vol. 3:
Lucifer Rising
Kenneth Anger, Vol. 4:
Invocation of My De-
mon Brother
Kiss of the Spider
Woman
Lady in Red
Last Tango in Paris
The Last Temptation of
Christ
The Last Wave
The Lonely Lady
Machine Gun Kelly
Mandingo
Marihuana
Married Too Young
Massacre at Central
High
Mommie Dearest
Moonshine Mountain
The Naked Flame
Naked Kiss
Naked Lunch
Night Call Nurses
Night Gallery
On the Edge: The Sur-
vival of Dana
Over the Edge
Panic in the Year Zero!
Persona
Petulia
Pot, Parents, and Police
Pretty Baby
Prick Up Your Ears
Private Duty Nurses
The Rain People
Rebel Without a Cause
Reefer Madness
The Reflecting Skin
Reform School Girl
Reservoir Dogs
Rock All Night
St. Elmo's Fire
Santa Sangre
Sex Madness

Shame
She-Devils on Wheels
Shock Corridor
Sid & Nancy
Sorority Girl
Strange Cargo
The Student Nurses
Suburban Roulette
Targets
Taxi Driver
Teenage Mother
Thou Shalt Not Kill. . .
Except
Too Hot to Handle
The Trial of Billy Jack
The Trip
Twin Peaks
Twin Peaks: Fire Walk
with Me
Valley of the Dolls
Vanishing Point
The Violent Years
Wanderers
White Heat
Wild Guitar
The Wild One
The Wild Ride
The Young Nurses
You've Ruined Me, Eddie

Dream Girls
Cheerleader Camp
Deadly Weapons
Dr. No
The Doll Squad
Forbidden Planet
It Takes a Thief
The Loves of Hercules
Missile to the Moon
Queen of Outer Space
Sizzle Beach U.S.A.
The Slumber Party Mas-
sacre
The Sure Thing
Tarzan, the Ape Man
Vampire's Kiss
Voyage to the Planet of
Prehistoric Women

Drugs
See Pill Poppin'

Eating
See Cannibalism; Edibles

Eco-Vengeance!
See also Killer Bugs &
Slugs
Alligator
Ants
The Applegates
The Birds
Frogs
Piranha
The Toxic Avenger
Willard

Edibles
See also Cannibalism
Blood Diner
Consuming Passions
Eating Raoul
Gore-Met Zombie Chef
From Hell

Elvisfilm
Change of Habit
Clambake
Flaming Star
Girls! Girls! Girls!
Jailhouse Rock
King Creole
Love Me Tender
Paradise, Hawaiian
Style
Top Secret!

**Ever'body Was
Kung Fu Fighting**
Bloodfist
Bloodfist 2
Born Losers
Dolemite
Enter the Dragon
Ferocious Female Free-
dom Fighters
Futurekick
Goldfinger
Nine Deaths of the
Ninja
One Down, Two to Go!
Remo Williams: The
Adventure Begins
Roller Blade

Evil Doctors
See also Mad Scientists
The Abominable Dr.
Phibes
The Awful Dr. Orlof
Doctor Butcher M.D.
Dr. Cyclops
Dr. No
Dr. Terror's House of
Horrors
Mad Doctor of Blood
Island
Night of the Bloody
Apes

Exploitation
See also Sexploitation
Assassin of Youth
Bad Girls from Mars
Barn of the Naked Dead
Battle of the Bombs
Beyond the Valley of
the Dolls
Blackenstein
Blue Movies
Chained for Life
Child Bride
Faces of Death, Part 1
Film House Fever
Frigid Wife
Hollywood After Dark
The Hollywood Stran-
gler Meets the Skid
Row Slasher
House of Whipcord
I Accuse My Parents
The Naked Flame
One Down, Two to Go!
Reefer Madness
Satan's Cheerleaders
Saturday Night Sleazies,
Vol. 1

Slaves in Bondage
Sleazemania: The Spe-
cial Edition
Sleazemania Strikes
Back
Sleazemania III: The
Good, the Bad & the
Sleazy
Smile
Something Weird
Student Confidential
Swamp Women
Test Tube Babies
Wild Rapture
Wild, Wild World of
Jayne Mansfield

Eyeballs!
The Birds
A Clockwork Orange
Evil Dead 2: Dead by
Dawn
Maniac
Peeping Tom
Manaic
X: The Man with X-Ray
Eyes

Family Ties
See also Parenthood
American Gothic
The Baby
Back to the Beach
The Bad Seed
Based on an Untrue
Story
Basket Case
Basket Case 2
Basket Case 3: The
Progeny
The Beast Within
Beat Girl
Bloody Mama
The Brady Bunch Movie
Cat People
Complex World
Daddy's Boys
Desperate Living
The Empire Strikes Back
The Fall of the House of
Usher
Five Easy Pieces
Hard Target
The Horror Chamber of
Dr. Faustus
I Accuse My Parents
It's a Wonderful Life
Love Me Tender
Mad Max
Mom & Dad
Monsieur Verdoux
The Night of the Hunter
Oh Dad, Poor Dad
(Momma's Hung You
in the Closet & I'm
Feeling So Sad)
Panic in the Year Zero!
Parents
Peeping Tom
The Pit and the Pendulum
Raising Arizona
Santa Sangre
Satan in High Heels

Category
Index

415

Cult Flicks and Trash Pics

Category
Index

Category
Index

Category Index

Nightmare
A Nightmare on Elm Street
Oasis of the Zombies
Pagan Island
The Perverse Countess
The Power
Premature Burial
Rabid
The Rats are Coming! The Werewolves are Here!
The Raven
Rock 'n' Roll Nightmare
Rosemary's Baby
The Sadist
Satan in High Heels
Satan's Cheerleaders
Satan's School for Girls
The Secret Cinema/Naughty Nurse
She Demons
She-Freak
Shock Waves
Shriek of the Mutilated
The Sinister Invasion
Sleazemania III: The Good, the Bad & the Sleazy
Slithis
The Slumber Party Massacre
Something Weird
Splatter University
Strait-Jacket
Suspiria
Tales from the Gimli Hospital
Tales of Terror
Teenage Gang Debs
Teenage Strangler
Tentacles
The Terror
Terror in the Haunted House
The Texas Chainsaw Massacre
Texas Chainsaw Massacre, Part 2
They Came from Within
They Saved Hitler's Brain
Three on a Meathook
Tomb of Ligeia
The Toolbox Murders
Trilogy of Terror
Troll
Twilight Zone: The Movie
2000 Maniacs
The Undead
Vampyres
The Wasp Woman
Werewolf of Washington
The Wicker Man
Willard
Witchcraft
The Wizard of Gore
The Worm Eaters

Wrestling Women vs. the Aztec Mummy
Zoltan. . .Hound of Dracula
Zombie High

Horror Comedy
See also Horror

Andy Warhol's Dracula
Andy Warhol's Frankenstein
April Fool's Day
Army of Darkness
Attack of the Killer Refrigerator
Attack of the Killer Tomatoes
Auntie Lee's Meat Pies
Bad Channels
Bad Taste
Bela Lugosi Meets a Brooklyn Gorilla
Beverly Hills Bodysnatchers
Big Meat Eater
Billy the Kid Versus Dracula
Blood Beach
Bloodbath at the House of Death
The Bone Yard
Brain Damage
Bride of Re-Animator
A Bucket of Blood
C.H.U.D.
The Comedy of Terrors
Creature from the Haunted Sea
Curse of the Queerwolf
Elvira, Mistress of the Dark
The Fearless Vampire Killers
Frankenhooker
Geek Maggot Bingo
Hillbillies in a Haunted House
I Married a Vampire
Incredibly Strange Creatures Who Stopped Living and Became Mixed-Up Zombies
The Invisible Maniac
It Came from Hollywood
Killer Klowns from Outer Space
Killer Tomatoes Eat France
Killer Tomatoes Strike Back
Little Shop of Horrors
Microwave Massacre
Monster in the Closet
Motel Hell
Munchies
Night of the Creeps
Out of the Dark
Piranha
Q: The Winged Serpent
Rabid Grannies
The Re-Animator
Redneck Zombies

Return of the Killer Tomatoes
Saturday the 14th
Saturday the 14th Strikes Back
Schlock
Son of Ingagi
Sorority Babes in the Slimeball Bowl-A-Rama
Spider Baby
The Stuff
Theatre of Blood
There's Nothing Out There
The Thrill Killers
The Toxic Avenger
The Toxic Avenger, Part 2
The Toxic Avenger, Part 3: The Last Temptation of Toxie
The Weasel That Dripped Blood
Zombies on Broadway

Hospitals
See also Nasty Diseases; Sanity Check; Shrinks

Frankenstein General Hospital
The Hospital
Tales from the Gimli Hospital

Hostage!
See also Kidnapped!; Missing Persons

Escape from New York
Rock All Night
Suddenly

I Can't See
See also I Can't See You

Don't Look Now
The Killer
Night Gallery
Schlock
The Toxic Avenger
Until The End of The World

I Can't See You

Abbott & Costello Meet the Invisible Man
The Amazing Transparent Man
The Invisible Maniac

I Spy

Casablanca
Dr. No
The Doll Squad
Duck Soup
From Russia with Love
Girls Are for Loving
Goldfinger
Hillbillies in a Haunted House
Ishtar
A Night in Casablanca
Picasso Trigger
Top Secret!
What's Up, Tiger Lily?
Zotz!

Identity
See also Role Reversal

Far Out Man
Marnie
The Nutty Professor
Rebel Without a Cause

Jail
See Great Escapes; Men in Prison; Women in Prison

Journalism
See Front Page

Jungles
See also Monkey Business; Treasure Hunt

Aguirre, the Wrath of God
Bela Lugosi Meets a Brooklyn Gorilla
Cannibal Women in the Avocado Jungle of Death
Cobra Woman
Dr. Cyclops
Fitzcarraldo
Tarzan, the Ape Man
Troma's War
White Pongo

Kidnapped!
See also Hostage!; Missing Persons

Beach Blanket Bingo
The Nightmare Before Christmas
Raising Arizona
Thou Shalt Not Kill. . . Except

Killer Apes
See also Monkey Business

A*P*E*
Battle for the Planet of the Apes
The Beast that Killed Women
Beneath the Planet of the Apes
Conquest of the Planet of the Apes
King Kong
King Kong Versus Godzilla
Planet of the Apes
Rat Pfink a Boo-Boo
Son of Ingagi

Killer Appliances
See also Technology-Rampant

Attack of the Killer Refrigerator
Hardware Wars
Microwave Massacre

Killer Birds

Beaks: The Movie
The Birds
Cockfighter
Ghidrah the Three Headed Monster

Category Index

The Horrible Dr. Hich-
cock
I Married a Vampire
Married Too Young
Microwave Massacre
My Little Chickadee
Petulia
Red Rock West
Sweet Movie

Martial Arts
See Ever'body Was Kung
Fu Fighting

The Marx Brothers
Animal Crackers
At the Circus
Big Store
The Cocoanuts
A Day at the Races
Duck Soup
Go West
Horse Feathers
Love Happy
The Marx Brothers in a
Nutshell
Monkey Business
A Night at the Opera
A Night in Casablanca
Room Service

Medieval Romps
See also Historical
Drama; Period Piece;
Swashbucklers
Army of Darkness
Jabberwocky
Monty Python and the
Holy Grail
The Princess Bride
Time Bandits
Time Trackers
The Undead

Meltdown
See also Disaster Strikes
The Atomic Cafe
Dr. Strangelove, or:
How I Learned to
Stop Worrying and
Love the Bomb
Panic in the Year Zero!

Men in Prison
See also Great Escapes;
Women in Prison
Escape from New York
Jailhouse Rock
Kiss of the Spider
Woman
Soul Vengeance
We're No Angels

Metamorphosis
See also Genetics;
Werewolves
An American Werewolf
in London
Cat People
The Fly
The Howling
I Was a Teenage Were-
wolf
Naked Lunch

Missing Persons
See also Hostage!;
Kidnapped!
Equinox
Raising Arizona
The Wicker Man

Mondo Movies
Africa, Blood & Guts
The Atomic Cafe
Ecco
Faces of Death, Part 1
Mondo Balardo
Mondo Cane
Mondo Cane 2
Mondo Magic
Shocking Asia
Shocking Asia 2
Wild Rapture
Wild, Wild World of
Jayne Mansfield
Witchcraft Through the
Ages

Monkee Business
See also Rock Stars on
Film
The Brady Bunch Movie
Doctor Duck's Super
Secret All-Purpose
Sauce
Elephant Parts
Head
Northville Cemetery
Massacre
Repo Man

Monkey Business
See also Jungles; Killer
Apes; Worst Ape
Costumes
A*P*E*
Battle for the Planet of
the Apes
The Beast that Killed
Women
Bedtime for Bonzo
Bela Lugosi Meets a
Brooklyn Gorilla
Beneath the Planet of
the Apes
Conquest of the Planet
of the Apes
Escape from the Planet
of the Apes
King Kong
King Kong Versus
Godzilla
Planet of the Apes
Rat Pfink a Boo-Boo
Schlock
Son of Ingagi
White Pongo

Monster Moms
See also Parenthood
The Baby
Big Bad Mama
Big Bad Mama 2
Carrie
Invaders from Mars
Mommie Dearest
Mother's Day

Parents
Psycho
Serial Mom

Monsters, General
See also Ghosts, Ghouls &
Goblins; Giants; Killer
Bugs & Slugs; Killer
Plants; Killer Sea
Critters; Mad Scientists;
Robots & Androids;
Vampires; Werewolves;
Zombies
The Astounding She-
Monster
Barn of the Naked
Dead
Basket Case
Basket Case 2
Basket Case 3: The
Progeny
The Beast of Yucca Flats
The Beast Within
Blackenstein
The Blob
Brain of Blood
The Brainiac
The Bride
Bride of the Monster
C.H.U.D.
Creature of Destruction
Creeping Terror
Creepshow
Deepstar Six
Demons
Destroy All Monsters
Equinox
Evil Dead
Forbidden Planet
Frankenstein
Frankenstein '80
Frankenstein General
Hospital
Frankenstein Unbound
Gamera, the Invincible
Geek Maggot Bingo
Ghidrah the Three
Headed Monster
Godzilla, King of the
Monsters
Godzilla 1985
Godzilla vs. Biollante
Godzilla vs. Megalon
Godzilla vs. Monster
Zero
Godzilla vs. Mothra
Hideous Sun Demon
Horror of Party Beach
The Incredible Two-
Headed Transplant
Infra-Man
It's Alive!
Jason and the Argonauts
The Killer Shrews
Mad Doctor of Blood
Island
The Manster
Saturday the 14th
Strikes Back
Space Monster
20 Million Years to
Earth

Voyage to the Planet of
Prehistoric Women
War of the Gargantuas
Yog, Monster from
Space

Monty Python
The Adventures of
Baron Munchausen
All You Need Is Cash
And Now for Something
Completely Different
Brazil
Consuming Passions
Erik the Viking
A Fish Called Wanda
Jabberwocky
Monty Python and the
Holy Grail
Monty Python Live at
the Hollywood Bowl
Monty Python's Life of
Brian
Monty Python's Parrot
Sketch Not Included
Monty Python's The
Meaning of Life
A Private Function
Rentadick
Secret Policeman's Pri-
vate Parts
Time Bandits
Whoops Apocalypse
Yellowbeard

Motor Vehicle
Dept.
See also Bikers; Fast Cars;
Killer Cars
The Blues Brothers
Duel
Ferris Bueller's Day Off
Repo Man
Roger & Me
Used Cars
Vanishing Point

Mummies
See also Horror; Zombies
Abbott & Costello Meet
the Mummy
The Mummy
Wrestling Women vs.
the Aztec Mummy

Music
See also Rock Stars on
Film; Struggling
Musicians
All You Need Is Cash
Allegro Non Troppo
Diner
Doctor Duck's Super
Secret All-Purpose
Sauce
Fantasia
Five Easy Pieces
Get Crazy
A Hard Day's Night
Johnny Guitar
Leningrad Cowboys Go
America
Monterey Pop

Category
Index

Category Index

Category
Index

Category
Index

Category Index

I Eat Your Skin
I Walked with a Zombie

War Between the Sexes
See also Marriage
Annie Hall
Cannibal Women in the
   Avocado Jungle of
   Death
Casablanca
Queen of Outer Space
The Thing

War Is Hell
Catch-22
Dr. Strangelove, or: How
   I Learned to Stop
   Worrying and Love
   the Bomb
The King of Hearts

Wedding Hell
See also Marriage
The Bride
The Bride & the Beast
The Bride of Frankenstein
Bride of Re-Animator
Bride of the Monster
Child Bride
Frigid Wife
He Knows You're Alone
Honeymoon Killers
I Married a Monster
   from Outer Space
I Married a Vampire
Married Too Young
Mom & Dad

Werewolves
See also Metamorphosis
An American Werewolf
   in London
Blood of Dracula's Castle
Curse of the Devil
Curse of the Queerwolf
Dr. Terror's House of
   Horrors
The Howling
I Was a Teenage Were-
   wolf
The Legend of the Wolf
   Woman
Orgy of the Dead
The Rats are Coming!
   The Werewolves are
   Here!
Werewolf of Washington
The Werewolf vs. the
   Vampire Woman
The Wolf Man

Western Comedy
See also Comedy; Westerns
Blazing Saddles
Go West
Lust in the Dust
Terror of Tiny Town

Westerns
See also Western Comedy;
   Westrogens

El Topo
Flaming Star
The Gunslinger
Jesse James Meets
   Frankenstein's Daugh-
   ter
Johnny Guitar
My Darling Clementine
Nevada
The Outlaw
Revenge of the Virgins
Ride the High Country
Straight to Hell
Terror of Tiny Town
The Wild Bunch
Zachariah

Westrogens
See also Westerns; Wonder
   Women
The Gunslinger
Lust in the Dust
She Done Him Wrong

Where's My Johnson?
See also Renegade Body
   Parts
The Amazing Trans-
   plant
Blood Beach
Bloodsucking Freaks
Caged Heat
Desperate Living
Frankenhooker
I Spit on Your Grave
Ilsa, She-Wolf of the SS
Invasion of the Bee Girls
National Lampoon's At-
   tack of the 5 Ft. 2
   Women
Night of the Demon
Shocking Asia

Witchcraft
See also Demons &
   Wizards; Occult
Black Sunday
The Conqueror Worm
Curse of the Devil
The Devils
The Haunted Palace
The Hospital
Something Weird
The Undead
The Werewolf vs. the
   Vampire Woman
Wicked Stepmother
Witchcraft

Women
See also Dream Girls;
   Femme Fatale;
   Westrogens; Women in
   Prison; Wonder Women
The Astounding She-
   Monster
Crazy Mama
House of Whipcord
Mars Needs Women
Murder Weapon
Working Girls

Women in (and out of) Uniform
Blazing Stewardesses
Candy Stripe Nurses
Cheerleader Camp
National Lampoon's Ani-
   mal House
Night Call Nurses
Private Duty Nurses
Satan's Cheerleaders
The Student Nurses
The Young Nurses

Women in Prison
See also Exploitation; Men
   in Prison; Sexploitation
The Big Bird Cage
The Big Doll House
Born Innocent
Caged Heat
Chained Heat
Fugitive Girls
Jailbird Rock
Reform School Girl

Wonder Women
See also Dream Girls
The Abductors
Alien
Aliens
Attack of the 50 Foot
   Woman
Attack of the 60-Foot
   Centerfold
Big Bad Mama 2
Bury Me an Angel
Chopper Chicks in Zom-
   bietown
Deadly Weapons
I Spit on Your Grave
Roller Blade
The Wild World of Bat-
   woman
Wrestling Women vs. the
   Aztec Mummy

World War I
The King of Hearts

World War II
Casablanca
Catch-22
December 7th: The Movie

Worst Ape Costumes
See also Killer Apes;
   Monkey Business
A*P*E*
The Beast that Killed
   Women
King Kong Versus
   Godzilla
Schlock

Wrestling
Wrestling Women vs. the
   Aztec Mummy

Wrong Side of the Tracks
Cry-Baby
Eegah!

Grease
The Phantom of the
   Opera
Pretty in Pink
Reform School Girl
Valley Girl

You Lose, You Die
See also Post Apocalypse
Death Race 2000
Roller Blade
Tron

Zombies
See also Death & the
   Afterlife; Ghosts, Ghouls
   & Goblins; Nazi
   Zombies; Underwater
   Zombies
The Alchemist
Alien Massacre
The Astro-Zombies
Bride of Re-Animator
Carnival of Souls
Children Shouldn't Play
   with Dead Things
Chopper Chicks in
   Zombietown
Creature of the Walking
   Dead
Dawn of the Dead
The Death Curse of
   Tartu
I Eat Your Skin
I Walked with a Zombie
Isle of the Dead
The Legend of the 7
   Golden Vampires
The Mummy
Night of the Creeps
Night of the Ghouls
Night of the Living Dead
Oasis of the Zombies
Orgy of the Dead
Plan 9 from Outer
   Space
The Re-Animator
Redneck Zombies
She Demons
Shock Waves
The Stuff
Zombie High
Zombies on Broadway

Category
Index

Distributor List

The "Distributor List" explains what those cryptic codes mean that appear at the end of each movie review; cracking that code will afford you super-secret ability to obtain those classics that the vid stores in your neighborhood for some unfathomable reason do not carry. And we're not done yet! You can find the addresses, phone numbers, and yes, even fax numbers for those distributors in the "Distributor Guide" following this list. What more could you want?

ABC—ABC Video

ACA—Academy Entertainment

AHV—Active Home Video

AIP—A.I.P. Home Video, Inc.

AOV—Admit One Video

APD—Applause Productions, Inc.

AUD—Audio-Forum

BAR—Barr Films

BBF—Bonnie Business Forms

BFA—Phoenix/BFA Films

BMG—BMG

BTV—Baker & Taylor Video

CAB—Cable Films & Video

CCB—Critics' Choice Video, Inc.

CDV—Condor Video

CIC—Cinema International Canada

CNG—Congress Entertainment, Ltd.

CNM—Cinemacabre Video

COL—Columbia Tristar Home Video

CPM—Central Park Media/U.S. Manga Corps

CRC—Criterion Collection

CVC—Connoisseur Video Collection

DIS—Walt Disney Home Video

DVT—Discount Video Tapes, Inc.

EPC—Epic Records

FCT—Facets Multimedia, Inc.

FLT—Film Threat Video

FOX—CBS/Fox Video

FRG—Fright Video

FST—Festival Films

FUS—Fusion Video

FXL—Fox/Lorber Home Video

FXV—FoxVideo

GEM—Video Gems

GHV—Genesis Home Video

GKK—Goodtimes Entertainment

GLV—German Language Video Center

GPV—Grapevine Video

GVV—Glenn Video Vistas, Ltd.

HBO—HBO Home Video

HEG—Horizon Entertainment

HHE—Hollywood Home Entertainment

HHT—Hollywood Home Theatre

HMV—Home Vision Cinema

HTV—Hen's Tooth Video

HVL—Home Video Library

IGP—Ignatius Press

IHF—International Historic Films, Inc. (IHF)

IME—Image Entertainment

ING—Ingram Entertainment

INJ—Ingram International Films

JEF—JEF Films, Inc.

JFK—Just for Kids Home Video

KAR—Karol Video

KIT—Kit Parker Video

KIV—Kino on Video

LHV—Lorimar Home Video

LIV—Live Home Video

LOO—Loonic Video

LSV—LSVideo, Inc.

LUM—Lumivision Corporation

MAX—Miramax Pictures Home Video

MCA—MCA/Universal Home Video

MED—Media Home Entertainment

MFV—Mystic Fire Video

MGM—MGM/UA Home Entertainment

MLB—Mike LeBell's Video

MLT—Music for Little People

MON—Monterey Home Video

MOV—Movies Unlimited

MPI—MPI Home Video

MRV—Moore Video

MVD—Music Video Distributors

MWF—Monday/Wednesday/Friday Video

MWP—Wade Williams Productions, Inc.

NHO—New Horizons Home Video

NLC—New Line Home Video

NOS—Nostalgia Family Video

NWV—New World Entertainment

NYF—New Yorker Video

NYR—*Not Yet Released*

OM—*On Moratorium*

ORI—Orion Home Video
PAP—Pacific Arts Publishing
PAR—Paramount Home Video
PBS—PBS Video
PGV—Polygram Video (PV)
PMS—Professional Media Service Corp.
PSM—Prism Entertainment
PYR—Pyramid Film & Video
QVD—Quality Video
RDG—Reader's Digest Home Video
REP—Republic Pictures Home Video
RHI—Rhino Home Video
RMF—RM Films International, Inc.
RXM—Rex Miller
SGE—SGE Entertainment Corp.
SIG—Signals
SIM—Simitar Entertainment
SMW—Something Weird Video
SNC—Sinister Cinema
STE—Starmaker Entertainment

SUE—Sultan Entertainment
TCF—20th Century Fox Film Corporation
TIM—Timeless Video Inc.
TLF—Time-Life Video and Television
TOU—Buena Vista Home Video
TPV—Tapeworm Video Distributors
TRI—Triboro Entertainment Group
TTC—Turner Home Entertainment Company
TVC—The Video Catalog
TWE—Trans-World Entertainment
UND—Uni Distribution
UNI—Unicorn Video, Inc.
VCD—Video City Productions
VCI—Video Communications, Inc. (VCI)
VCN—Video Connection
VDC—Vidcrest

VDM—Video Dimensions
VEC—Valencia Entertainment Corp.
VES—Vestron Video
VHE—VCII Home Entertainment, Inc.
VIP—VIP Video
VMK—Vidmark Entertainment
VSM—Video Search of Miami
VTR—Video Treasures
VYY—Video Yesteryear
WAR—Warner Home Video, Inc.
WAX—Waxworks/Videoworks, Inc.
WBF—Water Bearer Films
WFV—Western Film & Video, Inc.
WME—Warren Miller Entertainment
WOV—Worldvision Home Video, Inc.
WTA—Whole Toon Catalogue
XVC—Xenon

Distributor Guide

Submitted for your approval are the addresses and phone numbers of the benevolent distributors that offer the superlative videos listed in this unparalled book. Those listings with the code **OM** are on moratorium (distributed at one time, though not, unfortunately, currently—go figure). Since a title relegated to such status was once distributed to the masses, it may still be nestled on the shelves of the really cool video store in your Anytown, USA. When the distributor is not known, the code **NO** appears in the review. For new releases to the theatre that have not yet made it to video (but likely will in the next year), the code **NYR** (not yet released) appears.

ABC Video *(ABC)*
Capital Cities/ABC Video Enterprises
1200 High Ridge Rd.
Stamford, CT 06905
203-968-9100
Fax: 203-329-6464

Academy Entertainment *(ACA)*
9250 Wilshire Blvd., Ste. 400
Beverly Hills, CA 90212
Fax: 310-275-2195

Aactive Home Video *(AHV)*
12121 Wilshire Blvd., No. 401
Los Angeles, CA 90025
310-447-6131
800-824-6109
Fax: 310-207-0411

Admit One Video *(AOV)*
PO Box 66, Sta. O
Toronto, ON, Canada M4A 2M8
416-463-5714
Fax: 416-463-5714

A.I.P. Home Video, Inc. *(AIP)*
10726 McCune Ave.
Los Angeles, CA 90034
800-456-2471
Fax: 213-559-8849

Applause Productions, Inc. *(APD)*
85 Longview Rd.
Port Washington, NY 11050
516-883-2825
800-277-5287
Fax: 516-883-7460

Audio-Forum *(AUD)*
96 Broad St.
Guilford, CT 06437
203-453-9794

800-243-1234
Fax: 203-453-9774

Baker & Taylor Video *(BTV)*
501 S. Gladiolus
Momence, IL 60954
800-775-2300
Fax: 800-775-3500

Barr Films *(BAR)*
12801 Schabarum
Irwindale, CA 91706
818-338-7878
800-234-7878
Fax: 818-814-2672

BMG *(BMG)*
6363 Sunset Blvd., 6th Fl.
Hollywood, CA 90028-7318
213-468-4067

Bonnie Business Forms *(BBF)*
2691 Freewood
Dallas, TX 75220
214-357-3956
Fax: 214-357-4512

Buena Vista Home Video *(TOU)*
350 S. Buena Vista St.
Burbank, CA 91521-7145
818-562-3568

Cable Films & Video *(CAB)*
Country Club Sta.
PO Box 7171
Kansas City, MO 64113
913-362-2804
800-514-2804
Fax: 913-341-7365

CBS/FOX Video *(FOX)*
1330 Avenue of the Americas, 5th Fl.
New York, NY 10019
212-373-4800

800-800-2369
Fax: 212-373-4803

Central Park Media/U.S. Manga Corps *(CPM)*
250 W. 57th St., Ste. 317
New York, NY 10107
212-977-7456
800-833-7456
Fax: 212-977-8709

Cinema International Canada *(CIC)*
8275 Mayrand
Montreal, PQ, Canada H4P 2C8
514-342-2340
Fax: 514-342-1922

Cinemacabre Video *(CNM)*
PO Box 10005-D
Baltimore, MD 21285-0005

Columbia Tristar Home Video *(COL)*
Sony Pictures Plaza
10202 W. Washington Blvd.
Culver City, CA 90232
310-280-7799
Fax: 310-280-2485

Condor Video *(CDV)*
c/o Jason Films
2825 Wilcrest, Ste. 670
Houston, TX 77042
713-266-3097

Congress Entertainment, Ltd. *(CNG)*
Learn Plaza, Ste. 6
PO Box 845
Tannersville, PA 18372-0845
717-620-9001
800-847-8273
Fax: 717-620-9278

Connoisseur Video Collection (CVC)
1575 Westwood Blvd., Ste. 305
Los Angeles, CA 90024
310-231-1350

Criterion Collection (CRC)
c/o The Voyager Company
1 Bridge St.
Irvington, NY 10533-1543

Critics' Choice Video, Inc. (CCB)
PO Box 749
Itasca, IL 60143-0749
800-367-7765
Fax: 708-775-3355

Discount Video Tapes, Inc. (DVT)
PO Box 7122
Burbank, CA 91510
818-843-3366
Fax: 818-843-3821

Epic Records (EPC)
550 Madison Ave.
New York, NY 10022-3297
212-833-7442
Fax: 212-833-5719

Facets Multimedia, Inc. (FCT)
1517 W. Fullerton Ave.
Chicago, IL 60614
312-281-9075

Festival Films (FST)
6115 Chestnut Terr.
Excelsior, MN 55331-8107
612-470-2172
800-798-6083
Fax: 612-470-2172

Film Threat Video (FLT)
PO Box 3170
Los Angeles, CA 90078-3170
800-795-0969

FOX/Lorber Home Video (FXL)
419 Park Ave., S., 20th Fl.
New York, NY 10016
212-532-3392
Fax: 212-685-2625

Foxvideo (FXV)
2121 Avenue of the Stars, 25th Fl.
Los Angeles, CA 90067
310-369-3900
800-800-2FOX
Fax: 310-369-5811

Fright Video (FRG)
16 Ken Mar Dr., Unit 141
Billerica, MA 01821-4788

Fusion Video (FUS)
100 Fusion Way
Country Club Hills, IL 60478
708-799-2073
Fax: 708-799-2350

Genesis Home Video (GHV)
15820 Arminta St.
Van Nuys, CA 91406

German Language Video Center (GLV)
7625 Pendleton Pike
Indianapolis, IN 46226-5298
317-547-1257

800-252-1957
Fax: 317-547-1263

Glenn Videos Vistas, Ltd. (GVV)
6924 Canby Ave., Ste. 103
Reseda, CA 91335
818-881-8110
Fax: 818-981-5506

Goodtimes Entertainment (GKK)
16 E. 40th St., 8th Fl.
New York, NY 10016-0113
212-951-3000
Fax: 212-481-9067

Grapevine Video (GPV)
PO Box 46161
Phoenix, AZ 85063
602-973-3661
Fax: 602-973-0060

HBO Home Video (HBO)
1100 6th Ave.
New York, NY 10036
212-512-7400
Fax: 212-512-7498

Hen's Tooth Video (HTV)
2805 E. State Blvd.
Fort Wayne, IN 46805
219-471-4332
Fax: 219-471-4449

Hollywood Home Entertainment (HHE)
6165 Crooked Creek Rd., Ste. B
Norcross, GA 30092-3105

Hollywood Home Theatre (HHT)
1540 N. Highland Ave., Ste. 110
Hollywood, CA 90028
213-466-0127

Home Video Library (HVL)
Better Homes & Gardens Books
PO Box 10670
Des Moines, IA 50336
800-678-2665
Fax: 515-237-4765

Home Vision Cinema (HMV)
5547 N. Ravenswood Ave.
Chicago, IL 60640-1199
312-878-2600
800-826-3456
Fax: 312-878-8648

Horizon Entertainment (HEG)
45030 Trevor Ave.
Lancaster, CA 93534
805-940-1040
800-323-2061
Fax: 805-940-8511

Ignatius Press (IGP)
33 Oakland Ave.
Harrison, NY 10528-9974
914-835-4216
Fax: 914-835-8406

Image Entertainment (IME)
9333 Oso Ave.
Chatsworth, CA 91311
818-407-9100
800-473-3475
Fax: 818-407-9111

Ingram Entertainment (ING)
2 Ingram Blvd.
La Vergne, TN 37086-7006
615-287-4000
800-759-5000
Fax: 615-287-4992

Ingram International Films (INJ)
7900 Hickman Rd.
Des Moines, IA 50322
515-254-7000
800-621-1333
Fax: 515-254-7021

Iinternational Historic Films, Inc. (IHF) (IHF)
PO Box 29035
Chicago, IL 60629
312-927-2900
Fax: 312-927-9211

JEF Films, Inc. (JEF)
Film House
143 Hickory Hill Circle
Osterville, MA 02655-1322
508-428-7198
Fax: 508-428-7198

Just for Kids Home Video (JFK)
6320 Canoga Ave., Penthouse Ste.
PO Box 4112
Woodland Hills, CA 91365-4112
818-715-1980
800-445-8210
Fax: 818-716-0168

Karol Video (KAR)
PO Box 7600
Wilkes Barre, PA 18773
717-822-8899
Fax: 717-822-8226

Kino on Video (KIV)
333 W. 39th St., Ste. 503
New York, NY 10018
212-629-0871
800-562-3330
Fax: 212-714-0871

Kit Parker Video (KIT)
c/o Central Park Media
250 W. 57th St., Ste. 317
New York, NY 10107
212-977-7456
Fax: 212-977-8709

Live Home Video (LIV)
15400 Sherman Way
PO Box 10124
Van Nuys, CA 91410-0124
818-988-5060

Loonic Video (LOO)
2022 Taraval St., Ste. 6427
San Francisco, CA 94116
510-526-5681

Lorimar Home Video (LHV)
15838 N. 62nd St., Ste. 100
Scottsdale, AZ 85254
602-596-9970
Fax: 602-596-9973

Lsvideo, Inc. (LSV)
PO Box 415
Carmel, IN 46032

Lumivision Corporation *(LUM)*
877 Federal Blvd.
Denver, CO 80204-3212
303-446-0400
Fax: 303-446-0101

**MCA/Universal Home
Video** *(MCA)*
70 Universal City Plaza
Universal City, CA 91608-9955
818-777-1000
Fax: 818-733-1483

**Media Home
Entertainment** *(MED)*
510 W. 6th St., Ste. 1032
Los Angeles, CA 90014
213-236-1336
Fax: 213-236-1346

**MGM/UA Home
Entertainment** *(MGM)*
2500 Broadway
Santa Monica, CA 90404-6061
310-449-3000

Mike Lebell's Video *(MLB)*
75 Freemont Pl.
Los Angeles, CA 90005
213-938-3333
Fax: 213-938-3334

Rex Miller *(RXM)*
Rte. 1, Box 457-D
East Prairie, MO 63845
314-649-5048

**Miramax Pictures Home
Video** *(MAX)*
500 S. Buena Vista St.
Burbank, CA 91521

**Monday/Wednesday/Friday
Video** *(MWF)*
123 Scribner Ave.
Staten Island, NY 10301
718-447-1347

Monterey Home Video *(MON)*
28038 Dorothy Dr., Ste. 1
Agoura Hills, CA 91301
818-597-0047
800-424-2593
Fax: 818-597-0105

Moore Video *(MRV)*
PO Box 5703
Richmond, VA 23220
804-745-9785
Fax: 804-745-9785

Movies Unlimited *(MOV)*
6736 Castor Ave.
Philadelphia, PA 19149
215-722-8298
800-523-0823
Fax: 215-725-3683

MPI Home Video *(MPI)*
16101 S. 108th Ave.
Orland Park, IL 60462
708-460-0555
Fax: 708-873-3177

Music for Little people *(MLT)*
Box 1460
Redway, CA 95560
707-923-3991

800-727-2233
Fax: 707-923-3241

**Music Video
Distributors** *(MVD)*
O'Neill Industrial Center
1210 Standbridge St.
Norristown, PA 19403
215-272-7771
800-888-0486
Fax: 215-272-6074

Mystic Fire Video *(MFV)*
524 Broadway, Ste. 604
New York, NY 10012
212-941-0999
800-292-9001
Fax: 212-941-1443

**New Horizons Home
Video** *(NHO)*
2951 Flowers Rd., S., Ste. 237
Atlanta, GA 30341
404-458-3488
800-854-3323
Fax: 404-458-2679

New Line Home Video *(NLC)*
116 N. Robertson Blvd.
Los Angeles, CA 90048
310-967-6670
Fax: 310-854-0602

**New World
Entertainment** *(NWV)*
1440 S. Sepulveda Blvd.
Los Angeles, CA 90025
310-444-8100
Fax: 310-444-8101

New Yorker Video *(NYF)*
16 W. 61st St., 11th Fl.
New York, NY 10023
212-247-6110
800-447-0196
Fax: 212-307-7855

Nostalgia Family Video *(NOS)*
PO Box 606
Baker City, OR 97814
503-523-9034

Orion Home Video *(ORI)*
1888 Century Park E.
Los Angeles, CA 90067
310-282-0550
Fax: 310-282-9902

Pacific Arts Publishing *(PAP)*
11858 La Grange Ave.
Los Angeles, CA 90025
800-538-5856
Fax: 310-826-9351

Paramount Home Video *(PAR)*
Bluhdorn Bldg.
5555 Melrose Ave.
Los Angeles, CA 90038
213-956-8090
Fax: 213-956-1100

PBS Video *(PBS)*
1320 Braddock Pl.
Alexandria, VA 22314
703-739-5380
800-344-3337
Fax: 703-739-5269

Phoenix/BFA Films *(BFA)*
2349 Chaffee Dr.
St. Louis, MO 63146
314-569-0211
800-221-1274
Fax: 314-569-2834

Polygram Video (PV) *(PGV)*
825 8th Ave.
New York, NY 10019
212-333-8000
800-825-7781
Fax: 212-603-7960

Prism Entertainment *(PSM)*
1888 Century Park, E., Ste. 1000
Los Angeles, CA 90067
310-277-3270
Fax: 310-203-8036

**Professional Media Service
Corp.** *(PMS)*
19122 S. Vermont Ave.
Gardena, CA 90248
310-532-9024
800-223-7672
Fax: 800-253-8853

Pyramid Film & Video *(PYR)*
Box 1048
2801 Colorado Ave.
Santa Monica, CA 90406
310-828-7577
800-421-2304
Fax: 310-453-9083

Quality Video *(QVD)*
7399 Bush Lake Rd.
Minneapolis, MN 55439-2027
612-893-0903
Fax: 612-893-1585

**Reader's Digest Home
Video** *(RDG)*
Reader's Digest Rd.
Pleasantville, NY 10570
800-776-6868

**Republic Pictures Home
Video** *(REP)*
5700 Wilshire Blvd., Ste. 525
Los Angeles, CA 90036
213-965-6900
Fax: 213-965-6963

Rhino Home Video *(RHI)*
10635 Santa Monica Blvd., 2nd Fl.
Los Angeles, CA 90025-4900
310-828-1980
800-843-3670
Fax: 310-453-5529

**RM Films International,
Inc.** *(RMF)*
PO Box 3748
Los Angeles, CA 90078
213-466-7791
Fax: 213-461-4152

SGE Entertainment Corp. *(SGE)*
12001 Ventura Pl., 4th Fl.
Studio City, CA 91604
818-766-8500
Fax: 818-766-7873

Signals *(SIG)*
PO Box 64428

Distributor
Guide

Cult Flicks and Trash Pics

St. Paul, MN 55164-0428
612-659-4738
800-669-5225
Fax: 612-659-4320

Simitar Entertainment (SIM)
3850 Annapolis Ln., Ste. 140
Plymouth, MN 55447
612-559-6660
800-486-TAPE
Fax: 612-559-0210

Sinister Cinema (SNC)
PO Box 4369
Medford, OR 97501-0168
503-773-6860
Fax: 503-779-8650

Something Weird Video (SMW)
c/o Mike Vraney
PO Box 33664
Seattle, WA 98133
206-361-3759
Fax: 206-364-7526

Starmaker Entertainment (STE)
500 Kirts Blvd.
Troy, MI 48084
810-362-9660
800-786-8777
Fax: 810-362-6451

Sultan Entertainment (SUE)
116 N. Robertson Blvd.
Los Angeles, CA 90048
310-976-6700

Tapeworm Video Distributors (TPV)
27833 Ave. Hopkins, Unit 6
Valencia, CA 91355
805-257-4904
Fax: 805-257-4820

Time-Life Video and Television (TLF)
1450 E. Parham Rd.
Richmond, VA 23280
804-266-6330
800-621-7026

Timeless Video Inc. (TIM)
10010 Canoga Ave., Ste. B2
Chatsworth, CA 91311
818-773-0284
800-478-6734
Fax: 818-773-0176

Trans-World Entertainment (TWE)
8899 Beverly Blvd., 8th Fl.
Los Angeles, CA 90048-2412
213-969-2800

Triboro Entertainment Group (TRI)
12 W. 27th St., 15th Fl.
New York, NY 10001
212-686-6116
Fax: 212-686-6178

Turner Home Entertainment Company (TTC)
Box 105366
Atlanta, GA 35366
404-827-3066
800-523-0823
Fax: 404-827-3266

20TH Century Fox Film Corporation (TCF)
PO Box 900
Beverly Hills, CA 90213
310-277-2211
Fax: 310-369-3318

UNI Distribution (UND)
60 Universal City Plaza
Universal City, CA 91608
818-777-4400
Fax: 818-766-5740

Unicorn Video, Inc. (UNI)
9811 Independence Ave.
Chatsworth, CA 91311
818-407-1333
800-528-4336
Fax: 818-407-8246

Valencia Entertainment Corp. (VEC)
45030 Trevor Ave.
Lancaster, CA 93534-2648
805-940-1040
800-323-2061
Fax: 805-940-8511

VCII Home Entertainment, Inc. (VHE)
13418 Wyandotte St.
North Hollywood, CA 91605
818-764-1777
800-350-1931
Fax: 818-764-0231

Vestron Video (VES)
c/o Live Home Video
15400 Sherman Way
PO Box 10124
Van Nuys, CA 91410-0124
818-988-5060
800-367-7765
Fax: 818-778-3125

Vidcrest (VDC)
PO Box 69642
Los Angeles, CA 90069
213-650-7310
Fax: 213-654-4810

The Video Catalog (TVC)
PO Box 64267
Saint Paul, MN 55164-0267
612-659-4312
800-733-6656
Fax: 612-659-4320

Video City Productions (VCD)
4266 Broadway
Oakland, CA 94611
510-428-0202
Fax: 510-654-7802

Video Communications, Inc. (VCI) (VCI)
6535 E. Skelley Dr.
Tulsa, OK 74145
918-622-6460
800-331-4077
Fax: 918-665-6256

Video Connection (VCN)
3123 W. Sylvania Ave.
Toledo, OH 43613
419-472-7727
800-365-0449
Fax: 419-472-2655

Video Dimensions (VDM)
322 8th Ave., 4th Fl.
New York, NY 10001
212-929-6135
Fax: 212-929-6135

Video Gems (GEM)
12228 Venice Blvd., No. 504
Los Angeles, CA 90066

Video Search of Miami (VSM)
PO Box 161917
Miami, FL 33116
305-279-9773
Fax: 305-598-2665

Video Treasures (VTR)
500 Kirts Blvd.
Troy, MI 48084
810-362-9660
800-786-8777
Fax: 810-362-4454

Video Yesteryear (VYY)
Box C
Sandy Hook, CT 06482
203-426-2574
800-243-0987
Fax: 203-797-0819

Vidmark Entertainment (VMK)
2644 30th St.
Santa Monica, CA 90405-3009
310-314-2000
Fax: 310-392-0252

VIP Video (VIP)
c/o JEF Films
Film House
143 Hickory Hill Circle
Osterville, MA 02655-1322
508-428-7198

Wade Williams Productions, Inc. (MWP)
13001 Wornall Rd.
Kansas City, MO 64145-1211
816-241-6684
Fax: 816-941-7055

Walt Disney Home Video (DIS)
500 S. Buena Vista St.
Burbank, CA 91521
818-562-3560

Warner Home Video, Inc. (WAR)
4000 Warner Blvd.
Burbank, CA 91522
818-954-6000

Warren Miller Entertainment (WME)
2540 Frontier Ave., Ste. 104
Bouldeer, CO 80301
303-442-3430
800-523-7117
Fax: 303-442-3402

Water Bearer Films (WBF)
205 West End Ave., Ste. 24H
New York, NY 10023
212-580-8185
800-551-8304
Fax: 212-787-5455

Waxworks/Videoworks, Inc. (WAX)
325 E. 3rd St.
Owensboro, KY 42303
502-926-0008
800-825-8558
Fax: 502-685-0563

Western Film & Video, Inc. (WFV)
30941 Agoura Rd., Ste. 302
Westlake Village, CA 91361
818-889-7350
Fax: 818-889-7350

Whole Toon Catalogue (WTA)
PO Box 369
Issaquah, WA 98027-0369
206-391-8747
Fax: 206-391-9064

Worldvision Home Video, Inc. (WOV)
1700 Broadwaay
New York, NY 10019-5905
212-261-2700

Xenon (XVC)
211 Arizona Ave.
Santa Monica, CA 90401
800-468-1913

Distributor
Guide